The Rough Guide to

Puerto Rico

written and researched by

Stephen Keeling

NEW YORK • LONDON • DELHI

www.roughguides.com

Contents

Festivals of Puerto Rico color section following p.144

Puerto Rican food and drink color section following p.272

◀◀ Playa Crash Boat ◀ El Yunque National Forest

Introduction to

Puerto Rico

Long familiar to North Americans fleeing the winter chill, Puerto Rico is graced by fabulous beaches, year-round sun and numerous opportunities for deep-sea fishing, diving and surfing, though there's far more to the island than suntans and snorkeling. Beyond the glitzy veneer of San Juan the coast remains incredibly raw and unspoiled, lined with miles of glittering white sands. Dig deeper and you'll see the influence of the island's rich stew of cultures – African, European and Taíno – in an exuberant array of festivals, tantalizing criollo food, gracious colonial towns, the finest rum in the world and a dynamic musical tradition that gave birth to salsa.

The island's mountainous interior is just as enticing as the beaches, a land of torpid Spanish hill towns and gourmet **coffee** plantations. Ranches still raise **Paso Fino horses**, the finest in the Americas, and state forests preserve lush, jungle-covered peaks, fish-filled lakes and gurgling waterfalls. Puerto Rico boasts an astounding diversity of **landscapes**, from the misty rainforests of El Yunque and the crumbling outcrops of karst country, to reef-encrusted desert islands and the withering dry forests of the southwest. And in several places, impenetrable mangrove swamps cradle one of nature's most mind-boggling spectacles, the glowing waters of **bioluminescent bays**.

The old Puerto Rico of sun-tanned *jíbaros* and horse-drawn carts has largely disappeared, and rather than a nostalgic throw-back frozen in time, you'll find a constantly evolving juxtaposition of old and new, a place where bare-back horse riders use mobile phones, and beautifully preserved colonial architecture co-exists with modern shopping malls and speeding SUVs.

Beaches understandably remain one of the biggest draws. Thanks in part to a small but vigorous coalition of environmental groups, property development has been confined to small clusters, with low-key resorts such as Rincón successfully holding back the tide of condo and hotel building, at least for now. Occupied by the United States Navy until relatively recently, Vieques and Culebra in particular offer some of the most idyllic coastlines in the Caribbean, the military having ensured that both islands were spared the excesses of tourism.

Despite all this, the perception of Puerto Rico is inextricably shaped by its sometimes bewildering relationship with the US. Not a state, nor independent, Puerto Rico has been a "commonwealth" since 1952, making it especially attractive to Americans looking for a passport- and hassle-free holiday in the sun, but creating the misconception elsewhere that the island is simply an extension of the US in the Caribbean – quite untrue. Whilst it lacks the revolutionary chic of other Latin American nations, Puerto

Fact file

• Puerto Rico is the fourth largest island in the Caribbean with an area of around 3435 square miles, a little smaller than the US state of Connecticut or the island of Cyprus.

• The island has a population of around four million, but there are more people of Puerto Rican descent in the New York area than in the capital, San Juan.

• The Puerto Rican flag and the Cuban flag are identical but with inverted colors.

• Puerto Rico has more pharmaceutical plants per square mile than any other country (sixty in total).

▲ Boquerón waterfront

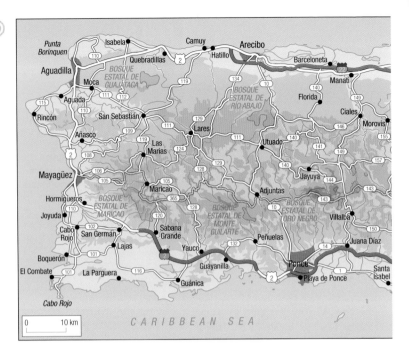

Ricans have created one of the region's most vibrant cultural identities. Puerto Ricans may be divided over their political future, but their sense of cultural pride in **Boricua**, the indigenous name for the island and its people, unites them.

Rent a car and it's easy to escape the tourist areas, and you can zip between cool mountain forests and sun-bleached beaches in minutes. The island is remarkably safe, and though it can be tough for budget travelers, Puerto Rico compares favorably with other islands in the region.

Where to go

Most trips to Puerto Rico start in the capital, **San Juan**, one of the largest and most dynamic cities in the Caribbean. Old San Juan is a Spanish colonial gem, while the resort zones of Condado and Isla Verde have surprisingly handsome stretches of beach. Wickedly tempting *kiosco* food is one of the main reasons to visit **Luquillo**, the gateway to the **east coast**, while **Fajardo** is the departure point for **La Cordillera**, a haven for snorkeling and swimming. Looming

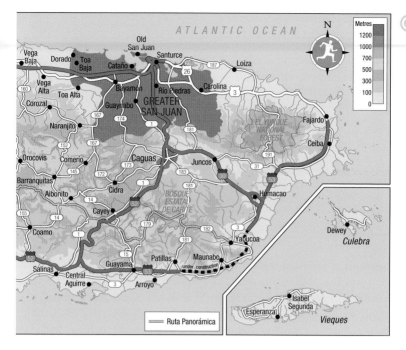

over the whole region, **El Yunque National Forest** is a rainforest of lofty, jungle-covered peaks crisscrossed with hiking trails.

To the east, the offshore island of **Vieques** is blessed with vast stretches of sugary sand backed with nothing but scrub, palm trees and sea grape. Swimming in the **bioluminescent bay** here is a bewitching experience, boats leaving ghostly clouds of fluorescence in their wake. **Culebra** is much smaller and even more languid, a rocky island ringed with turquoise waters, empty beaches and dazzling cays.

Inland from the **north coast** lies the bizarre, crumbling limestone peaks of **karst country**, containing the **Observatorio de Arecibo**, the **Cavernas del Río Camuy** and the ruined Taíno ball-courts at the **Centro Ceremonial Indígena de Caguana**.

The **Porta del Sol**, "gateway to the sun," starts at the **northwest coast**, justly regarded as a surfing paradise that peaks at **Rincón**. Divers should check out **Isla Desecheo**, a protected island reserve encircled by brilliant sapphire waters. Back on land, **Mayagüez** is the "sultan of the west," a once-depressed industrial city gradually regaining its former colonial glory. Beyond the city lies a chain of low-key resorts: **Playa Buyé** and **Boquerón** boast gorgeous white-sand beaches, before the west coast ends at the weathered cliffs of **Cabo Rojo**. On the south coast, **La Parguera** faces a tangled labyrinth of channels and mangrove cays while inland, **San**

US colony or 51st state?

Puerto Rico's political status is a highly emotive issue, and though it looks set to remain a Commonwealth of the US for the immediate future, there's a lot of truth in the old adage, "after two or three drinks every Puerto Rican is pro-independence." Most Puerto Ricans fear that becoming a US state would mean a dilution of their Hispanic identity, but that full independence would lead to economic and political chaos – even a cursory look at the modern history of Cuba, Haiti and the Dominican Republic looks pretty bleak. Although the island has a lot more freedom than the stereotypical colony, liberals and artists generally despair at the US association. Esmeralda Santiago in *Island of Lost Causes* says, "the truth is, we do have a history of struggle for independence, but the opposition has always won. The failure of our best hopes…has caused many Puerto Ricans to simply give up." That may be true: many Puerto Ricans now believe US statehood is inevitable.

Germán is crammed with flamboyant mansions and charming Spanish churches. East of here, the southern coastal plain is known as the **Porta Caribe**, "gateway to the Caribbean." Don't miss **Guilligan's Island**, a mangrove cay spliced by a lagoon of crystal-clear water, and **Ponce**, still proud of its fine mansions, museums and extensive **art gallery**. Just to the north, the **Centro Ceremonial Indígena de Tibes** is another rare reminder of Puerto Rico's pre-Columbian past, while the best of the once booming sugar towns are **Guayama** and **Coamo**.

▶ Raíces statue, Old San Juan

While the coast attracts the most tourists, the spiritual heart of Puerto Rico lies in the mountains, accessed by the winding **Ruta Panorámica** and famous for its **lechoneras**, roadside diners roasting suckling pig over wood or charcoal fires. Other highlights include the massive flower festival at **Aibonito**, the jaw-dropping **Cañón de San Cristóbal**, and the rural town of **Jayuya**, which offers poignant reminders of Puerto Rico's Taíno heritage. At the far end of the route, **Maricao** is the producer of some of the world's finest coffee.

When to go

▲ Pelican on the fort walls in Old San Juan

Puerto Rico has a hot and sunny tropical climate with an average yearly temperature of 80°F (26–27°C), but this can drop well into the 50s at higher elevations in January and February. The driest period of year runs roughly between January and April, but the island doesn't really have distinct dry and wet seasons – showers are possible year-round, though the southwest corner is extremely dry and the north coast gets twice as much rain as the south. Rainfall usually picks up between May and October, and hurricanes are possible anytime between June and November. Major hurricanes are mercifully rare, but can be devastating if they score a direct hit.

The **peak tourist seasons** run roughly from December to April and all of July and August. The winter sees North Americans flock to the island to escape cold weather, with San Juan inundated by cruise-ship visitors, while high summer is the holiday season for Puerto Ricans. Prices are highest and crowds thickest at these times, especially on the coast, and if you

▼ Coquí frog

Beach life

The **beach** holds a special place in Puerto Rican life. On weekends families all over the island make for the coast with piles of food, music and deck chairs to enjoy a day of sun-drenched fun, barbecue, beer and salsa reminiscent of a fully-blown fiesta. It doesn't even have to be proper sand: the "beach" at Playa Salinas is little more than a muddy break in the mangroves, but the party goes on nevertheless. The most popular type of beach tends to be the *balneario*, literally "bathing place" or spa, but usually translated, rather misleadingly, as "public beach." In Puerto Rico a *balneario* is just a beach with facilities such as toilets, showers, barbecue grills, lifeguards, shelters and picnic tables. In fact, every beach in Puerto Rico is public by law, but resorts and private landowners can technically stop you from reaching them, making beach access a contentious issue in some places.

intend to visit at Christmas, New Year or Easter, book well in advance. The island has also been a popular **Spring Break** destination in recent years, with thousands of US college students invading the main resorts between February and March – bear this in mind when booking accommodation, especially if you want a tranquil experience.

Average daily temperatures and monthly rainfall

	Jan	Feb	Mar	Apr	May	Jun	Jul	Aug	Sep	Oct	Nov	Dec
San Juan												
max (°F)	82	83	83	85	86	88	87	88	88	88	85	83
max (°C)	28	28	28	29	30	31	31	31	31	31	29	28
min (°F)	71	71	72	73	75	77	77	77	77	76	74	72
min (°C)	22	22	22	23	24	25	25	25	25	24	23	22
rainfall (inch)	3	2	2	4	5	4	4	5	6	5	6	5
rainfall (mm)	76	51	51	102	127	102	102	127	152	127	152	127
Mayagüez												
max (°F)	86	86	87	88	89	91	91	91	91	90	89	87
max (°C)	30	30	31	31	32	33	33	33	33	32	32	31
min (°F)	64	64	65	67	69	70	70	70	70	70	68	66
min (°C)	18	18	18	19	21	21	21	21	21	21	20	19
rainfall (inch)	1	3	3	4	7	6	9	9	11	9	5	2
rainfall (mm)	25	76	76	102	178	152	229	229	279	229	127	51

things not to miss

It's not possible to see everything Puerto Rico has to offer in a single trip – and we don't suggest you try. What follows is a selective taste of the island's highlights: spectacular beaches, historic towns, and a host of natural wonders. They're arranged in five color-coded categories with a page reference to take you straight into the guide, where you can find out more.

01 **Old San Juan** Page **67** • Explore one the best-preserved colonial centers in the Americas, where the narrow streets are lined with elegant townhouses and a rich choice of enticing restaurants.

02 **Paso Fino horses** Page **140** • Ride these endearingly friendly horses along the beach or through the jungle and experience their exceptionally smooth gait.

04 **Playa Flamenco, Culebra** Page **184** • Nothing beats waking up on this unspoiled expanse of silky white sand, one of the most dazzling beaches in the world.

05 **Coffee** Page **349** • Yauco coffee once supplied the Vatican, and today the island's fertile soils and ideal climate are fueling a resurgence in potent, gourmet brands.

03 **Piña colada** Page **92** • This sumptuous blend of rum and coconut is served everywhere, from ritzy hotel bars to shacks on the beach.

06 Observatorio de Arecibo
Page **211** • The world's largest radio telescope is an awe-inspiring sight, with plenty of thought-provoking exhibits on hand to satisfy budding scientists and aspiring astronauts.

07 Centro Ceremonial Indígena de Tibes
Page **295** • These ancient ball courts offer a unique insight in Pre-Taíno culture.

08 Surfing
Page **226** • Puerto Rico is hammered by the full force of the Atlantic swells in the winter, its north coast lined with dizzying breaks.

09 Diving
Page **240** • The crystalline waters off Puerto Rico contain some of the best kept secrets in the Caribbean, making it an underwater paradise ideal for diving and snorkeling.

11 El Morro Page **71** • Even Sir Francis Drake couldn't take this spectacular Spanish fortress, a whopping sledgehammer of stone and cannon that has guarded San Juan Bay for over four hundred years.

10 Salsa Page **94** • Learn to dance, check out a salsa club or just sit back and enjoy the pros on the island that was home to *El Cantante*, Gran Combo and Ricky Martin.

12 Beach hopping in Vieques Page **166** • The US Navy is long gone, so freely tour the mesmerizing beaches of Vieques, precious slices of untouched Caribbean wilderness.

13 San Germán Page **266** • Soak up the colonial history in this charming old town, with ornate mansions and delicate churches harking back to the boom days of sugar and coffee.

15 Turtle patrol on Culebra Page **183** • For a truly magical experience, volunteer for a night of scouring Culebra's beaches for giant, egg-laying leatherback turtles.

14 Bioluminescent bay, Vieques Page **167** • This mind-blowing phenomenon is best experienced during a nocturnal swim, with water glowing in the dark and dripping from your fingers like tiny sparkling gems.

16 El Yunque National Forest Page **112** • Puerto Rico's most enchanting reserve of pristine rainforest, jungle-covered peaks and bubbling cascades is laced with panoramic trails.

15

17 **Ponce** Page **280** • Puerto Rico's second city is a showcase of ebullient architecture, impressive art and poignant museums, including the lavish home of the Don Q rum empire, Castillo Serallés.

18 **Casa Bacardi** Page **102** • Learn everything there is to know about the Caribbean's favorite tipple at the "Cathedral of Rum."

19 **Guilligan's Island** Page **308** • Wallow in the clear, azure waters inside this tiny islet of knotted mangroves and bleached coral sand.

20 **La Ruta Panorámica** Page **323** • Take a ride on this winding route along the island's mountainous spine, a world of misty peaks and forests, coffee farms and roadside stalls selling roast chicken and pork.

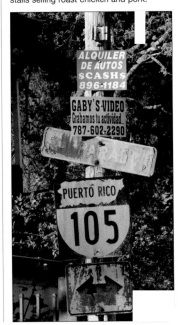

Basics

Basics

Getting there

The fastest way to get to Puerto Rico is to fly. The island is also connected to the Dominican Republic by ferry, but otherwise, unless you have your own boat, getting here by sea usually involves a leisurely and more expensive cruise.

The island's international gateway is the **Aeropuerto Internacional Luis Muñoz Marín** in San Juan, with numerous connections to the US and all over the Caribbean, while regional airports at **Aguadilla** and **Ponce** are increasingly accepting direct flights from the US mainland and nearby islands.

Visitors from outside North America usually have to fly via the US. To a certain extent, the vast number of Puerto Ricans traveling between the island and the US throughout the year, in addition to a steady stream of business traffic, means that **airfares** remain fairly consistent, though weekend flights always carry a premium. Fares do tend to rise slightly during the **peak vacation season** between November and April, and soar during **Easter** (see p.9) – the biggest holiday of the year for most Puerto Ricans – Christmas and New Year. For US flights it's especially important to book well ahead if you want to benefit from lower prices.

From the US and Canada

Numerous daily non-stop **flights** connect Puerto Rico with cities all over the US, but the cheapest and most frequent depart from "gateway" cities in the south and east, most commonly **Miami** and **New York** (JFK and Newark). San Juan is the Caribbean hub for American Airlines, so it's no surprise that this airline operates the most flights to the island and usually has the most competitively priced **fares**, though all the major US carriers offer services. For the lowest priced round-trip tickets to San Juan in high season (excluding holidays), airlines typically charge $300 from New York and Miami, $340 from Houston/Dallas and $350 from Chicago. If you're prepared to change planes a couple of times, flights from Los Angeles can be as low as $350, but American Airlines flies direct for around $430. Flights to Aguadilla and Ponce

are similarly priced. If you're flying off-peak, it's also worth checking out budget airline JetBlue, which flies non-stop from Orlando and New York's JFK to San Juan, Aguadilla, and Ponce – book online and flights can go for as little as $160 round-trip. **Flying times** are relatively short: around 3hr 45min from New York, 2hr 30min from Miami, 4hr 30min from Chicago, and just over 4hr from Dallas and Houston.

There are few direct flights from **Canada**, with Air Canada flying the only non-stop service from Toronto (4hr 35min; Can$1350). Your options increase (and prices fall) greatly if you fly through the US: fares from Montréal and Toronto via US carriers start at around Can$580.

By boat

Sailing to Puerto Rico from the US mainland or the nearby Virgin Islands is relatively straightforward if you have your own boat, with large marinas dotted all around the coast. Note, however, that even though Puerto Rico is US territory, boats from the mainland must still gain clearance from customs 24 hours before arrival (San Juan: Mon–Sat, ☏787/729-6850), and non-US citizens must clear immigration if sailing from a non-US territory (you'll usually have to travel to the nearest immigration office on arrival).

San Juan is one of the world's busiest **cruise ports**, and although arriving by ship is certainly the most romantic way to enter San Juan harbor, if you start in the US (typically Fort Lauderdale or Miami), you'll only get a few hours onshore before moving on. Many cruises start and finish in San Juan, however, and in that case it's well worth extending your holiday to explore the island. Prices start at $470 for a week-long cruise of the eastern Caribbean, excluding airfare to San Juan. Remember that if you're flying from outside

Fly less – stay longer! Travel and Climate Change

Climate change is perhaps the single biggest issue facing our planet. It is caused by a build-up in the atmosphere of carbon dioxide and other greenhouse gases, which are emitted by many sources – including planes. Already, **flights** account for three to four percent of human-induced global warming: that figure may sound small, but it is rising year on year and threatens to counteract the progress made by reducing greenhouse emissions in other areas.

Rough Guides regard travel as a **global benefit**, and feel strongly that the advantages to developing economies are important, as are the opportunities for greater contact and awareness among peoples. But we also believe in travelling responsibly, which includes giving thought to how often we fly and what we can do to redress any harm that our trips may create.

We can travel less or simply reduce the amount we travel by air (taking fewer trips and staying longer, or taking the train if there is one); we can avoid night flights (which are more damaging); and we can make the trips we do take "climate neutral" via a carbon offset scheme. **Offset schemes** run by climatecare.org, carbonneutral .com and others allow you to "neutralize" the greenhouse gases that you are responsible for releasing. Their websites have simple calculators that let you work out the impact of any flight – as does our own. Once that's done, you can pay to fund projects that will reduce future emissions by an equivalent amount. Please take the time to visit our website and make your trip climate neutral, or get a copy of the *Rough Guide to Climate Change* for more detail on the subject.

www.roughguides.com/climatechange

---

the US to pick up a ship here, you'll have to clear US immigration: if you're not eligible for a visa waiver (see p.44) you must apply for a **US visa** in advance. The same goes for port excursions to Puerto Rico, however brief.

Cruise contacts

Carnival Cruise Lines ☎1-888/227-64825, ⓦwww.carnival.com.
Celebrity Cruises US & Canada ☎1-800/ 760-0654, elsewhere ☎316/554-5961; ⓦwww .celebritycruises.com.
Cunard Line US & Canada ☎1-800/728-6273, ⓦwww.cunard.com, UK ☎0845/071 0300, ⓦwww.cunard.co.uk.
Holland America Line ☎1-877/724-5425, ⓦwww.hollandamerica.com.
Norwegian Cruise Line ☎1-866/625-1166, ⓦwww.ncl.com.
Princess Cruises ☎1-800/774-62377, ⓦwww .princess.com.
Regent Seven Seas Cruises ☎1-877/505-5370, ⓦwww.rssc.com.
Royal Caribbean Cruises US & Canada ☎1-866/562-7625, UK ☎0800/018 2020; ⓦwww .royalcaribbean.com.
Silver Sea Cruises US & Canada ☎1-800/ 722-9955, UK ☎870/333 7030; ⓦwww .silversea.com.

Sea Dream Yacht Club US & Canada ☎1-800/707-4911, UK ☎0800/783 1373, ⓦwww .seadreamyachtclub.com.

From the UK and Ireland

One of the principal reasons that Puerto Rico attracts just one to two percent of European tourists to the Caribbean is the dearth of charter and direct **flights** between Europe and the island – coming from the UK or Ireland you'll need to change planes at least once, usually in the US. From **London** the cheapest option is usually to fly with American Airlines via New York, but travel websites will also come up with various combinations of British Airways and American carriers via New York, Miami, and Washington, DC. Prices for round-trip flights in peak season usually start at £400–450, depending on the strength of the pound. Iberia offers the only non-stop flight to San Juan from Europe, a thrice-weekly service from **Madrid**: from London you can get round-trips on this route from around £600 in peak season.

From **Dublin**, you might save a few pounds flying the same routes via London; otherwise it's faster to fly with Continental or Aer Lingus and American Airlines via New York – flights cost around €630.

From Australia, New Zealand, and South Africa

Getting from **Australia**, **New Zealand** or **South Africa** to Puerto Rico means changing planes at least once somewhere in the US. From **Sydney** the cheapest option is to fly United or Qantas to Los Angeles, and connect with the American Airlines flight to San Juan – flights in high season will set you back Aus$3300. The cheapest flights from other Australian cities route through Sydney. From **Auckland**, Air New Zealand, Qantas, and United fly to Los Angeles to connect with the same American Airlines flight for around NZ$3300. Note that all these flights can entail long layovers at LAX.

From **South Africa**, Delta flies from **Johannesburg** to San Juan via Atlanta for around R9900, while South African Airways operates flights between Johannesburg and Washington, DC, where you can connect with United flights to Puerto Rico.

From the Caribbean

San Juan is one of the largest regional hubs in the **Caribbean**, making it an easy fit into a larger tour of the Antilles, or an excellent base for further exploration. The most frequent flights link San Juan with the **US** and **British Virgin Islands** (typically for $200–300 round-trip), but there are also services from Antigua, St Vincent, and Dominica on LIAT, plus several charter airlines fly from the Dominican Republic. American Eagle uses San Juan as a hub and flies all over the Caribbean, while Copa Airlines flies from Panama City.

By boat

Ferries del Caribe (℡787/832-4800, Ⓦwww.ferriesdelcaribe.com) operates a thrice-weekly ferry service between **Santo Domingo** in the Dominican Republic and Mayagüez on the west coast of Puerto Rico, a journey that usually takes around twelve hours. The M/S *Caribbean Express* is decked out like a small cruise ship, with restaurants, spa, and casino. Peak season prices (July & Aug) range from $219 round-trip for an armchair seat, to $238 round-trip for a berth in a four-bed cabin, and $325 round-trip for a single cabin with sea view (plus tax). At other times prices are $30–40 cheaper.

At the time of writing, there were no scheduled ferries between Puerto Rico and the **Virgin Islands**, and the only way to travel between the two was to use a private operator from Fajardo (see p.133).

Airlines, agents, and operators

Online booking

Ⓦ**www.ebookers.com** (in UK)
Ⓦ**www.expedia.com** (in US) Ⓦ**www.expedia.co.uk** (in UK) Ⓦ**www.expedia.ca** (in Canada)
Ⓦ**www.lastminute.com** (in UK)
Ⓦ**www.opodo.co.uk** (in UK)
Ⓦ**www.orbitz.com** (in US)
Ⓦ**www.travelocity.com** (in US) Ⓦ**www.travelocity.co.uk** (in UK) Ⓦ**www.travelocity.ca** (in Canada)
Ⓦ**www.zuji.com.au** (in Australia) Ⓦ**www.zuji.co.nz** (in New Zealand)

Airlines

Aer Lingus Republic of Ireland ℡0818/365-000, Northern Ireland ℡0870/876-5000, Ⓦwww.aerlingus.com.
Air Canada Canada ℡1-888/247-2262, Ⓦwww.aircanada.com.
Air New Zealand Australia ℡13/2476, New Zealand ℡0800/247764; Ⓦwww.airnewzealand.com.
American Airlines US & Canada ℡1-800/433-7300, UK ℡0845/7789 789, Ireland ℡01/602-0550, Australia ℡1300/650-747, New Zealand ℡0800/887-997; Ⓦwww.aa.com.
British Airways UK ℡0870/850 9850, Ireland ℡1890/626-747, South Africa ℡011/441-8600; Ⓦwww.ba.com.
Cape Air Puerto Rico ℡1-800/352-0714, Ⓦwww.flycapeair.com.
Continental Airlines US & Canada ℡1-800/231-0856, UK ℡0845/607 6760, Ireland ℡1890/925-252, Australia ℡02/9244-2242, New Zealand ℡09/308-3350; Ⓦwww.continental.com.
Copa Airlines ℡507/217-2672, Ⓦwww.copaair.com.
Delta US & Canada ℡1-800/221-1212, UK ℡0845/600 0950, Ireland ℡1850/882-031,

Australia ☎ 1300/302-849, New Zealand ☎ 09/379-3370, South Africa ☎ 011/482-4582; ⊛ www.delta.com.

Iberia UK ☎ 0870/609 0500, Ireland ☎ 0818/462-000; ⊛ www.iberia.com.

JetBlue US ☎ 1-800/538-2583, international ☎ 001/801-365-2525; ⊛ www.jetblue.com.

LIAT ☎ 1-888/844-5428, ⊛ www.liatairline.com.

Northwest ☎ 1-800/225-2525, ⊛ www.nwa.com.

Qantas Airways Australia ☎ 13/1313, New Zealand ☎ 0800/808-767; ⊛ www.qantas.com.

South African Airways ☎ 11/978-1111, ⊛ www.flysaa.com.

Spirit Airlines US ☎ 1-800/772-7117, ⊛ www.spiritair.com.

United Airlines US ☎ 1-800/538-2929, UK ☎ 0845/844 4777, Australia ☎ 13/1777; ⊛ www.united.com.

US Airways US & Canada ☎ 1-800/428-4322, UK ☎ 0845/600 3300, Ireland ☎ 1890/925-065; ⊛ www.usair.com.

Agents and operators

ebookers UK ☎ 0800/082 3000, Republic of Ireland ☎ 01/488-3507; ⊛ www.ebookers.com. Low fares on an extensive selection of scheduled flights and package deals.

North South Travel UK ☎ 01245/608 291, ⊛ www.northsouthtravel.co.uk. Friendly, competitive travel agency, offering discounted fares worldwide. Profits are used to support projects in the developing world, especially the promotion of sustainable tourism.

STA Travel US ☎ 1-800/781-4040, Canada ☎ 1-888/427-5639, UK ☎ 0870/1630 026,

Australia ☎ 1300/733-035, New Zealand ☎ 0508/782-872; ⊛ www.statravel.com. Worldwide specialists in independent travel; also student IDs, travel insurance, car rental, rail passes, and more. Good discounts for students and under-26s.

Trailfinders UK ☎ 0845/058 5858, Republic of Ireland ☎ 01/677-7888, Australia ☎ 1300/780-212, ⊛ www.trailfinders.com. One of the best-informed and most efficient agents for independent travelers.

Specialist tour operators

Acampa ☎ 787/706-0695, ⊛ www.acampapr.com. San Juan-based adventure tour outfit.

AdventTours ☎ 787/530-8311, ⊛ www.adventourspr.com. Features customized private tours that include bird-watching, hiking, camping, visits to coffee plantations and kayaking.

Amazilia Tours ☎ 506/273-6500, ⊛ www.amaziliatours.com. Bird-watching tours of Puerto Rico.

Caribtours ☎ 020/7751-0660, ⊛ www.caribtours.co.uk. Small UK-based operator, specializing in Caribbean travel – will tailor itineraries to Puerto Rico.

Classic Golf Tours ☎ 303/751-7200, ⊛ www.classicgolftours.com. Plans and arranges vacations of Puerto Rico with golf as the focus.

Golden Heron Ecotours ☎ 787/426-0979, ⊛ www.golden-heron.com. Variety of guided tours including snorkeling trips to La Cordillera and Vieques and hikes to El Yunque, all emphasizing the culture, history, and ecology of the island.

Legends of Puerto Rico ☎ 787/605-9060, ⊛ www.legendsofpr.com. Offers fascinating guided walks and bus tours of Old San Juan and beyond.

Getting around

Puerto Rico is a relatively small island and therefore easy to get around, with one important catch: formal public transport is virtually nonexistent, which means unless you rent a car or motorbike you'll be reliant on the highly localized network of públicos (despite having one of the largest railway networks in the Caribbean in the early twentieth century, the last passenger services ended in 1953). Internal flights connect Ponce and Mayagüez with San Juan, but flying is a pricey option and not really worthwhile unless you're heading for Vieques or Culebra – both islands are also connected to the main island by ferry.

By bus (*público*)

No subject seems to elicit more confusion in Puerto Rico than **públicos** (bus services), mostly because the vast majority of Puerto Ricans never take them. One of the negative impacts of American culture has been the local obsession with automobiles – big ones – and the idea of any foreigner taking a *público* between cities in Puerto Rico simply bemuses most locals. It's really not that complicated: *públicos* operate on set routes, but at the whim of the driver, waiting until the vehicle is full before departing and usually dropping people off along the way. Rates are very cheap – San Juan to Ponce is $15 and you can travel the length of the island for under $50 – and it's often a great way to meet some of the locals (the system tends to be used predominantly by students and the elderly).

If you intend to travel extensively in Puerto Rico, though, *públicos* are not recommended. Though San Juan is well connected with most of the towns on the island, services between other places are patchy at best, and these days *públicos* tend to operate more like local bus services, serving the immediate area. Long-distance trips across the country can mean changing several times, and once you get to your destination, you'll find your options extremely limited without wheels.

If you do end up taking a *público*, speaking Spanish definitely helps (drivers rarely speak English), and you must **plan ahead**. For busy routes, you can simply turn up at the local bus station (usually known as the **Terminal de Carros Públicos**, or just *la terminal*) early in the morning (7am or earlier, Mon–Sat) and

pick one up, but at other times and locations you'll need to call ahead, reserve a space, and arrange a pick-up time. Some locals differentiate between *lineas* and *públicos*: *lineas* are minibuses that follow fixed routes and timetables (like a normal bus service), while true *públicos* (which can also be taxi-like cars) go only when full, stop a lot, and vary departure times. In practice it doesn't make a lot of difference, and there are very few true *lineas* in any case.

By car

Renting a car in Puerto Rico is by far the most efficient and convenient way to get around. Rates tend to be competitive with most US cities, and gas in recent years has been cheaper than in the mainland US. You'll find all the major agencies and several local companies (usually cheaper) in San Juan, with a handful of offices scattered around the island. Culebra and Vieques have their own local companies – it's expensive and compli-cated to take rental cars across by ferry.

Rates for economy-sized cars with unlimited mileage start at $40–50 per day or $250 for seven days, but can escalate dramatically during holidays and the busy July–August period – the longer you rent, the cheaper it gets per day. Basic **insurance** (loss damage waiver, no deductible) can add another $20 per day, but is highly recommended as scrapes and knocks are common (especially in parking lots). Most **US insurance policies** should be valid in Puerto Rico, but check before you go.

Renting in Puerto Rico is much like the US and fairly straightforward for most visitors.

You must have a valid credit card and can drive for up to 120 days with a valid **driver's license** (all major countries are accepted). You must be at least 25, although some companies (Budget and most of the local outfits) allow drivers over 21 for an additional charge of $10 per day.

Car-rental agencies

Alamo US ☎1-800/462-5266, ⊛www.alamo.com.
Avis US ☎1-800/230-4898, Canada ☎1-800/272-5871, UK ☎0870/606 0100, Ireland ☎021/428-1111, Australia ☎13/6333, New Zealand ☎09/526-2847, South Africa ☎27/11-923-3660; ⊛www.avis.com.
Budget US ☎1-800/527-0700, Canada ☎1-800/268-8900, UK ☎0870/156 5656, Australia ☎1300/362-848, New Zealand ☎0800/283-438, South Africa ☎086/101-6622; ⊛www.budget.com.
Charlie Car Rental Puerto Rico ☎787/728-2418, ⊛www.charliecars.com.
Hertz US & Canada ☎1-800/654-3131, UK ☎020/7026 0077, Ireland ☎01/870-5777, Australia ☎800/654-3001, New Zealand ☎0800/654-321; ⊛www.hertz.com.
National US ☎1-800/227-7368, UK ☎0870/400 4581, Australia ☎0870/600-6666, New Zealand ☎03/366-5574; ⊛www.nationalcar.com.
Thrifty US & Canada ☎1-800/847-4389, UK ☎014/9475 1540, Ireland ☎01/844-1950, Australia ☎1300/367-227, New Zealand ☎09/256-1405; ⊛www.thrifty.com.

Driving in Puerto Rico

Driving conditions vary wildly, and how you cope is largely a matter of experience. Your biggest headache is likely to be the sheer **volume of traffic**: this is where Puerto Rico is most similar to the metropolitan US, and least like a languid Caribbean island. The main highways in San Juan and around much of the densely populated coastline are the most congested – it's best to travel at off-peak times to avoid the worst of it. In contrast, driving in more remote areas and especially in the mountains can be a real delight, and while often winding and narrow, unless it's been raining heavily, these roads are rarely dangerous.

Those used to driving in London, LA, or New York shouldn't be too fazed by the mildly frenzied driving displayed on San Juan's crammed highways, and even when driving aggressively, Puerto Ricans rarely lose their cool on the road. Nevertheless, locals do tend to drive far more recklessly than most of their compatriots on the US mainland: speeding, jumping lanes, pulling out without warning, and thrashing along the shoulder are all normal practice. Puerto Ricans are also compulsive tailgaters and accidents are common, despite a fairly heavy police presence on the roads and a system of severe fines.

Carjacking was a big problem in Puerto Rico in the early 1990s, but incidents have dropped off dramatically and tourists are rarely affected. The vast majority of crimes occur outside the tourist zones in Greater San Juan (in areas like Río Piedras), late at night, so to be safe, avoid driving in urban areas after midnight and ignore anyone trying to wave you down. It's also a bad idea to pick up hitchers. **Car theft** is a problem in some areas, which is why insurance is crucial, and you should never leave valuables in your vehicle. If you **break down**, call the rental company.

Should you have a minor **accident**, exchange names, addresses, and driver's license details with the other parties if you can, before contacting the rental company. Officially, you are supposed to notify the state police within four hours if the accident has caused damage in excess of $100, but your rental company should be able to advise you.

Roads

The Puerto Rican **road system** is the best in the Caribbean, with freeways known as *autopistas* fanning out from San Juan and four-lane highways covering all the major routes. *Autopistas* carry frequent tolls of $0.50–1.25, so bring coins if you can: lanes on the right marked "C" or *cambio* provide change, but the middle lanes are reserved for *cambio exacto* (throw coins in the bucket) and are usually faster. Avoid the *autoexpreso* lanes on the left, which require an electronic pass (you'll be fined if you go through without one).

All roads are given numbers, usually written with the prefix "PR" or "Puerto Rico," as in PR-2. Distances on the island are given in kilometers (1km=0.62 miles) and therefore appear this way in the Guide; all other measurements, however, are given in imperial units. Signage is in Spanish, but in a concession to American car makers, **speed limits** are in miles per hour: the **maximum speed limit** on most roads is 55mph, though some sections of highway and *autopista* range 65–70mph, and you should stick to 30mph in residential areas. Laws against drunk driving and speeding are strictly enforced, and everyone in the car must wear a seatbelt. It is legal to turn right on a red light, after coming to a full stop (except where signs expressly forbid this), and thanks to the threat of carjacking, you are permitted to ignore red lights altogether between midnight and 5am. Road rules otherwise follow US norms and cars **drive on the right**. For a glossary of driving terms and road signs in Spanish, see p.395.

With driving such an important part of life in Puerto Rico, you are never far from a **gas station** in the cities, and many open 24 hours. **Fuel** follows US standards, with unleaded the most common option, though it's sold by the liter and is slightly cheaper than on the US mainland (around $0.70 per liter or $3.20 per gallon in early 2008).

Parking can be a real hassle, especially in midsize towns, where locals squeeze into spaces around the plaza or along narrow side streets. If available, official parking lots outside San Juan are reasonable value for short-term stays, but if you park on the street (usually free), avoid any spaces marked with yellow lines, and always check with a local if in doubt. You'll have more luck in the early morning, afternoon, or weekend – the worst time to arrive somewhere is mid-morning.

By boat

The Puerto Rico Port Authority (☎1-800/981-2005 or 787/863-0705) runs regular **passenger ferries** to Vieques and Culebra from Fajardo, as well as a less frequent vehicle and cargo ferry. Note that you can buy advance tickets in person, but **reservations are not accepted**; see p.136 for details. Reaching other offshore islands, such as Isla de Mona (see p.260), requires the services of a private boat operator.

By air

Domestic flights from San Juan's Aeropuerto Internacional Luis Muñoz Marín to Mayagüez and Ponce are used primarily by businesspeople and wealthy locals, but can save time if you're in a hurry. Cape Air charges around $75–80 one way to Mayagüez and $60–80 to Ponce, but fares vary according to what day and time you fly.

More useful for most visitors are the frequent flights from San Juan or Fajardo to the islands of **Culebra** and **Vieques**. Several airlines run these routes, though planes are tiny eight-seaters (neither island can accept jets), so tend to book up fast during holidays. Flying at least one way is recommended – it's not that expensive and you'll get a spectacular view of the islets and reefs off the coast. The planes can be very cramped and hot, and the **excess luggage charges** can be steep, though they're often waived in practice – check the official position before you get

Addresses and road names

Puerto Rican addresses can be a little confusing, with several systems employed using a combination of English and Spanish. All roads have a number: you'll often see these prefixed by "Carr" or **Carretera** (meaning "highway" or "route") when written down, though you rarely see this on actual road signs, where just the number or the "PR" prefix is more common. Note that a sign reading "INT 3" means that an intersection with PR-3 is coming up, not that you are currently driving on PR-3.

In many places street numbers are not used, and locations are either described (*esquina* means "corner") or given a kilometer reference. A location at PR-3 km 2.1 would be 2.1km from the beginning of PR-3, though in practice it's hard to know where this is or even which end of the road is considered the beginning. In some places useful markers on the roadside show the distance every tenth of a kilometer, but these are becoming rarer. It's always faster to call your destination for directions.

to the airport. The cheapest flights operate from San Juan's tiny domestic airport, Isla Grande, and cost around $100 round-trip. Note that some of the local airlines fly "on demand" which means you need to give them plenty of notice. Cape Air and a few other airlines fly direct from the international airport, which is more convenient for connections but more expensive ($160–180 round-trip).

Domestic airlines

Air Flamenco ☎787/724-1818, 🌐www .airflamenco.net.
Air Sunshine US & Canada ☎1-800/327-8900, Puerto Rico ☎1-888/879-8900; 🌐www .airsunshine.com.
Cape Air ☎1-800/352-0714, 🌐www.flycapeair .com.
Isla Nena Air Service ☎787/863-4447 or 787/863-4449, 🌐www.islanena.8m.com.
Vieques Air Link ☎1-888/901-9247 or 787/ 741-8331, 🌐www.vieques-island.com.

Accommodation

Puerto Rico offers travelers a wide range of accommodation, from small, family-run guesthouses to plush luxury resorts, though true budget options are hard to find and there are no hostels. Finding a room is rarely a problem, though even San Juan can become full during some holiday weekends. Prices vary considerably, but usually increase dramatically at weekends or public holidays. Rates also tend to be higher during the two peak seasons (early Dec to early May, and July & Aug), while rates between September and November are usually the lowest.

Hotels

Puerto Rican **hotels** run the gamut from simple guesthouses or bed and breakfasts to standard hotels and mega-resorts, though the island has yet to establish a universal system of classification or star ratings. For tax purposes, the government divides accommodation into **three classes**: hotels with casinos (mostly in San Juan); standard hotels, guesthouses and motels; and small inns or *paradores* (see opposite). English is usually spoken by someone at even the smallest hotel, and these days almost every place has **air conditioning** and **TV** (though not all have cable with English-language channels). Exceptions tend to be in the mountains, where it's cool enough to use ceiling fans at night, or at hotels where the lack of TV or modern facilities is seen as a plus – perversely, you'll usually pay extra for such designer simplicity.

As there are no hostels in Puerto Rico, **budget hotels** offer the cheapest accommodation on the island, but bargains are hard to find. You'll rarely get a room for less than $50, with only a handful of older, slightly run-down places in the mountains offering these sorts of rates. You'll find more choice above $75, but it's unusual to find good quality accommodation with all the amenities for less than $100.

Most places describing themselves as guesthouses and bed and breakfasts fall into the **mid-range** category in Puerto Rico, more akin to the smart US version of the genre than the cheaper European variety, and can cost anything from $80 to $150. Standards vary considerably depending on the location and age of the property – price isn't always a good indication of quality, so always check the room before agreeing to pay. In general, smaller family-run places offer the best value, although some business hotels in the cities can be affordable, assuming there are no extra charges (see box, p.28).

You'll find huge **resorts** and a smaller number of posh **boutique hotels** spread across the island, predominantly on the coast.

Accommodation price codes

The accommodation listed in this book has been assigned one of nine price codes representing the price of the cheapest **double room** in peak season, which for most hotels runs from late November or early December through April. Prices between May and November will often be far lower, though some places hike prices again in July to catch vacationing Puerto Ricans.

❶ Under $50
❷ $50–74
❸ $75–99
❹ $100–124
❺ $125–149
❻ $150–199
❼ $200–249
❽ $250–299
❾ $300 and over

Prices can range from $150 up to $400 and beyond, depending on room type, resort facilities, and season, but you'll always get the best deals online. Resorts are the biggest culprits when it comes to extra charges, however (see box, p.28).

Note that in certain areas of the island you'll see "**motels**" advertised behind discreetly positioned walls or hedges – these are in fact "love hotels" with rooms rented by the hour.

Paradores and hotel programs

The **Paradores Puertorriqueños** program was established in 1973 by the Puerto Rico Tourism Company, and while being dubbed a *parador* ("country inn") brings a certain amount of cachet to a hotel, the classification has nothing to do with the Spanish system of upmarket historic properties. To qualify for official *parador* status in Puerto Rico, hotels must simply maintain quality standards set by the PRTC: minimum requirements include being located outside Greater San Juan and in an area deemed of historic or cultural importance, having fewer than 75 rooms, and being managed by the owner and their family (who are supposed to live on the property). Many of the current 21 *paradores* do feature historic properties and scenic locations, but otherwise tend to operate much like any other mid-range hotel. To add to the confusion, some equally atmospheric guesthouses that are not approved use the word *parador* anyway. Prices range $80–120; for the official list see ⓦwww.gotoparadores.com.

The *paradores* program is similar to the "small hotels of Puerto Rico" scheme (ⓦwww .puertoricosmallhotels.com) established by the **Puerto Rico Hotel & Tourism Association** (☏787/758-8001, ⓦwww.prhta.org), which

promotes small guesthouses and hotels across the island (some hotels are members of both programs). If not a member of either program, hotels and guesthouses can opt to be simply **endorsed** by the PRTC: in return for passing basic requirements (like having parking, smoke detectors, security chains, and maid service for all rooms), these hotels appear in official publications and can promote their PRTC approval. Even then, it's difficult to make generalizations: while hotels that fall in any of the three categories above will usually offer decent accommodation, standards vary wildly, and hotels that for whatever reason have opted to remain unaffiliated can be just as good.

Rental apartments and villas

Increasingly popular on the island, **renting apartments** and **villas** is an appealing alternative to staying in hotels, and is becoming relatively easy via reputable broker websites. Properties tend to be in good condition, come with kitchens, living rooms and other facilities, and are often located in highly scenic settings in some of the most attractive parts of Puerto Rico, particularly Vieques and Culebra. Note, however, that you'll usually need a car to access such properties, and that they tend to be pricey unless you're willing to stay for at least a week or have a large group. Villas that can sleep six people or more are usually a far better deal than hotels. **PR West** (☏787/420-5227 or 826-6748, ⓦwww.prwest.com) is a good place to start, with listings of hundreds of properties all over the island. Prices vary considerably, but you'll get great deals at around $1000 per week in most locations – daily rates, where available, tend to be

Taxes and charges

One of the only negative aspects of staying in Puerto Rico, and particularly San Juan, is that **taxes and charges** can increase your hotel bill by 25 percent or more. To be fair, this is common practice all over the Caribbean, but it's important to know what's mandatory and what is simply being added to your bill as a disguised **service charge**: ask to speak to the manager if it is not absolutely clear. Most of the larger hotels do spell out the extra charges, such as the notorious "**resort fee**" – to pay for things like use of towels, pool, and spa – but some will simply add a combined figure to your bill. Always demand to know exactly what's being added and why.

As of December 2007, **mandatory government taxes** on hotel occupancy were as follows: hotels with casinos eleven percent; hotels without casinos, guesthouses, and motels nine percent; small inns (*paradores*) and short-term apartment or villa rentals seven percent. Anything in excess of this has been levied by the hotel – there is **no additional sales tax** on hotel occupancy.

In 2006, the San Juan municipal government followed Caguas and Carolina (Isla Verde) by introducing a "**head tax**" for hotel occupancy: $2 per person per night in hotels with up to 25 rooms, $3 for hotels with 26 to 75 rooms, and $5 per person per night for hotels with over 76 rooms. The Puerto Rico Hotel & Tourism Association is in the process of suing the municipality in order to have the tax revoked, and many hotels are opting not to pay. Nevertheless, there's little you can do if your hotel adds this tax to your bill, other than insisting the amount is itemized rather than "rounded up." One trick hotels employ is to add this tax as a percentage rather than a set dollar amount (so the larger your bill, the higher the head tax).

much more expensive ($200 per night). Ronnie's Properties (☎787/722-1352, ⓦwww.ronniesproperties.com) is another good option for San Juan (see also p.63).

Campgrounds and cabañas

Camping is possible in Puerto Rico, though with much of the island in private hands you're generally limited to official campgrounds on public beaches and forest reserves (a law was passed in 1995 forbidding camping on public beaches without facilities). The six beach campgrounds are operated by the **Compañía de Parques Nacionales** (☎787/622-5200, ⓦwww .parquesnacionalespr.com), and all come with showers, toilets, and barbecue grills. Rates start at $10 per night for a basic pitch. Locations include Playa La Monserrate (Luquillo), Playa Seven Seas (Fajardo), Punta Guilarte (Arroyo), Sun Bay (Vieques), Tres Hermanos (Añasco), and Playa Cerro Gordo on the north coast. The company also runs inland campgrounds at the Parque Nacional Cavernas del Río Camuy ($5 per person) and at the Parque Ecológico Monte del Estado in Maricao ($15). You can just turn up without a reservation at any of these places, but in peak season (especially July & Aug) spaces can fill up fast and it's best to call in advance.

Campgrounds within Puerto Rico's forest reserves are managed by the **Departamento de Recursos Naturales y Ambientales** (DRNA, ☎787/999-2200, ⓦwww.drna .gobierno.pr), but to stay at any of them you must apply for a permit in advance (15 days ahead for Isla de Mona; see p.260). You can apply in person, by mail, by fax, and online at ⓦwww.drna.gobierno.pr/agbosques – the website is in Spanish only. Once you've made a reservation online, you still need to pay at the nearest DRNA office within three working days; if all else fails, take a taxi to the office in San Juan and apply in person (PR-8838 km 6.3, Sector El Cinco, Río Piedras).

Rates are very cheap: $4 per person per night, and campgrounds usually come with basic toilets and showers. Note that many of these sites close in the low season.

You can also camp on **Playa Flamenco** on Culebra, perhaps the most stunning location of all (see p.181 for details), and within **El Yunque** (see p.116). In many places you can rent tents for an additional fee – see relevant chapters for details.

It's important to note that **theft** can be a problem in all these locations, and if you leave anything valuable unattended in your tent it's likely to be stolen, especially on the beaches. You'll rarely encounter more serious problems, but camping alone when no one else is around is not a good idea.

The Compañía de Parques Nacionales also runs a system of **cabañas** on the public beaches at Humacao, Boquerón, and Añasco, as well as Monte del Estado. Known as **Centros Vacacionales**, these are far more popular with Puerto Rican families than foreign tourists but a lot more comfortable than camping. Rates range $65–75 for basic *cabañas* to $115 for larger villas, but accommodation is still basic – modern concrete and wood cabins with one or two bedrooms, minimal furniture and facilities – and usually uninspiring compared to the rustic chalets you might find elsewhere in the Caribbean; the locations, however, steps away from the beach, are unbeatable. You can make reservations by phone or on the website; there is a **minimum stay** of two nights and a maximum of four weeks (or seven days during the peak season).

Food and drink

Puerto Rican food is an exuberant blend of Spanish, Taíno, American, and African influences, a rich Caribbean melange known as cocina criolla (Créole cooking), not unlike Cuban and Dominican cuisine. Traditional food can be exceptionally appetizing, but it can also get monotonous after a while, the repertoire of dishes being fairly similar at most restaurants. To spice things up, seek out the island's surprising number of local specialties, or at the top end, sample some of the region's most creative restaurants, innovators of Nuevo Latino and various fusion cuisines worthy of their place in the "gastronomic capital of the Caribbean." When it comes to drinks, Puerto Rico is well entrenched as the Caribbean's leading rum producer and inventor of the piña colada, while its once lauded coffee is gradually winning back international acclaim.

Eating out

Roadside **stalls**, generally known as **kioscos** (also *kioskos*) are some of the best places to try cheap Puerto Rican food: some *kioscos* are collected together in areas on highways (such as those in Luquillo), along the coast (in Piñones), or in the mountains (Guavate), but you'll find individual stalls all over the island and in many town plazas. The most common *kiosco* food (*cocina en kiosco*) is **deep-fried fritters**, especially *alcapurrias* and *bacalaítos* (see p.31 for both), but you'll find plenty of local specialties and a range of other small snacks on offer. In larger towns, the **market** (*mercado*) is the best place to seek out no-frills snack stalls, as well as sellers of fresh fruit and coconut juices, while almost every town and village has a local **café** or bar that sells similar fare along with potent cups of coffee and cold beer.

In San Juan and larger cities you'll also find atmospheric **diners** that blend 1950s American decor and menus with a more formal Latin style reminiscent of Mexico or South America. Sit-down **restaurants** serve primarily *cocina criolla* and range from cheap, simple canteens to upscale places with designer furniture and uniformed wait staff. Especially in San Juan, the choice of restaurants serving various **international cuisines** is

Mesones

Thirty of the best Puerto Rican restaurants are members of the **mesones gastronómicos** program, established in 1987 by the Puerto Rican Tourism Company to run in tandem with their *paradores* (many of the latter feature *mesones* on their premises). The idea was to make it easier for tourists traveling around the island to choose a quality place to eat: any restaurant sporting the *mesón* title must meet certain criteria to be endorsed (and must be outside Greater San Juan), but as with the hotels, overall standards vary wildly and *mesones* also tend to charge higher prices. In general, opting for a *mesón gastronómico* should guarantee hygienic, well-cooked Puerto Rican food, but while some restaurants are truly exceptional (and feature in this guide), most of them are overpriced. Sticking to *mesones* might be safer, but you'll miss out on a wealth of cheaper, more authentic local food if you do.

getting bigger and there are plenty of straight-forward **American-style diners** around to indulge cravings for burgers, fries, Tex-Mex favorites, and pizza. If you get desperate, all the major **US fast-food** chains and several home-grown varieties can be found in almost every corner of the island.

Meals

Breakfast is the meal most influenced by American culture in Puerto Rico, with fast food, toast, and packaged cereals increasingly widespread. Traditional *mallorcas* are served in San Juan's historic coffee shops, however, and in rural areas a Spanish-style light pastry and coffee from the local bakery still reign supreme; but the Spanish tradition of leisurely **lunches** and an afternoon siesta has largely disappeared from the island. Between noon and 2pm most Puerto Ricans opt for cheap, quick snacks or light meals such as *bocadillos* (sandwiches). Outside San Juan, the best restaurants are rarely busy at lunchtimes during the week. **Dinner** is the main meal of the day, served between 6pm and 10pm and usually involving large groups of friends or family, especially on weekends. This is when the locals hit restaurants in a big way, especially on Sundays, when lunch can last all afternoon.

Puerto Rican cuisine

Core components in any Puerto Rican meal are **plantains** (*plátanos*), a type of savory banana that is not eaten raw: *tostones* are fried plantains usually served as an appetizer or starchy side dish. **Mofongo**

is the best-known plantain dish (see box, p.31) and essential eating, at least once. **Rice**, invariably accompanied by **beans** (*arroz con habichuelas*) or *gandules* (pigeon peas), is often served as a meal by itself in cheap canteens, and considered stereotypically Puerto Rican. It's the dish Puerto Ricans feel most nostalgic for overseas and not as bland as it sounds: kidney beans are richly stewed with pork and spices, Spanish-style, before being poured over the rice.

Puerto Rican cuisine has inherited plenty of other **Spanish** legacies. **Adobo** was originally a Spanish marinade, spreading throughout Spain's colonies where it was adapted to local ingredients. In the Philippines *adobo* became the national dish, while in Puerto Rico the word generally refers to the seasoning of crushed peppercorns, oregano, garlic, salt, olive oil, and lime juice rubbed into meats before grilling. Equally important in many dishes, **sofrito** is a fragrant, sautéed blend of onions, garlic, cilantro, and peppers. Other Spanish traditions include mouthwatering **lechón asado**, or barbecued suckling pig, still a Castilian specialty but with an earthier quality here, inherited from the Taíno.

Another national favorite is **asopao**, a rice stew flavored with *sofrito* and served with chicken or seafood from a *caldero* (traditional kettle). Like *mofongo*, each restaurant tends to have its own unique interpretation of the dish, but while *asopao* features on almost every tourist menu, it's worth seeking out lesser-known but equally enticing **stews**, such as *carne guisada puertorriqueña* (Puerto Rican beef stew).

Puerto Ricans love **pork** and **chicken**, with *arroz con pollo* (fried chicken and rice) featuring on just about every menu along with various incarnations of *pechuga* (grilled chicken breast) and *chuletas* (pork chops). Other juicy grilled meats that appear regularly in most restaurants include *churrasco* (skirt steak) and *chuletón* (T-bone steak).

Being an island, it's no surprise that **seafood** and **shellfish** form an important part of the restaurant scene, with prawns, crab, lobster, and octopus popping up on most menus along with the ever-present *chiollo* (red snapper) and *dorado* (mahi-mahi).

Snacking is a Puerto Rican passion, and the island's *cocina en kiosco* provides a highly addictive (if coronary-inducing) plethora of deep-fried delights to savor. The most celebrated are *bacalaítos*, thin and crunchy cod fritters, battered with garlic, oregano, and sweet chili, and *alcapurrias* (mashed yautia root and green plantain, stuffed with ground meat and fried). Other favorites are *rellenos de papa* (ground meat and mashed potato balls) and *surullitos* (fried cornmeal and cheese sticks), and you'll also find plenty of *empanadillas* (turnovers filled with meat, more crispy than the Mexican version), and deep-fried *tacos*, more like Chinese spring rolls than Mexican-style filled tortillas. See the Language section on p.396 for a complete menu reader.

Desserts

Everywhere you go in Puerto Rico, meals invariably end with coffee and **flan** (a rich blend of eggs, milk, and cream cheese, a bit like a custard tart), usually vanilla-flavored but occasionally involving tropical fruits such as guava. Restaurants often engage in feverish competition to decide who has the best *flan*, and as with many modest-looking Puerto Rican dishes, the results can be spectacular and bursting with flavor.

Other traditional desserts include *guayaba* (guava) with *queso blanco* or *queso del país* (white cheese), though the guava is usually preserved in syrup and sickly sweet – best eaten in small doses. **Cakes** feature heavily, and are also available through local bakeries and supermarkets. **Coconut** is a common ingredient in many desserts, and you'll come across plenty of examples of crispy coconut squares and candied coconut rice. **Tembleque** (coconut pudding) and coconut bread pudding (*boudin de pasas con coco*) are rare in restaurants but absolutely delicious. Candied fruits such as *dulce de papaya* are also common sweet treats. Locally made **ice cream** (*helados*), in tangy fruit flavors is incredibly refreshing and can be found in even the smallest towns, sold in cones or tubs for under $2.

Mofongo

Stay in Puerto Rico long enough, and you'll come to either love or hate **mofongo**, the celebrated national dish that appears on almost every menu on the island. Made from fried plantains mashed with garlic and olive oil, the origins of *mofongo* are hazy (it's also popular in Cuba and the Dominican Republic), but most experts think it was influenced primarily by the island's African traditions. Puerto Ricans are addicted to the stuff but, because it can be time-consuming and hard to make, tend to eat it in restaurants rather than at home. After an initial taste, most foreign tourists tend to avoid *mofongo*, put off by its heavy, starchy base, but the secret is to know where to go: not all *mofongo* is made equal, and variations differ wildly from place to place. *Mofongo* can be served plain, shaped into balls as a side dish for fried meat, or stuffed (*mofongo relleno*) with pork, chicken, or seafood such as shrimp, octopus, or lobster. The mashed and fried base can vary, made with savory green plantains or sweet bananas, while cooks tend to have their own interpretation of how to present the various components: some simply stuff the meat inside while others fill the plantain base like giant bowls. Vegetarians should check before ordering plain *mofongo*, as traditionally the plantains are also mashed with pork crackling.

Nuevo Latino

Puerto Rico is at the forefront of **Nuevo Latino** cuisine, which essentially takes a modern, creative spin on traditional *criollo* dishes – meats like chicken and fish are spiced up with sauces made from tamarind, mango, and guava, or paired with ingredients from other national cuisines such as French dressings or Italian pasta. This has evolved into full-fledged **fusion cooking**, particularly in San Juan, as more restaurants blend local food with Chinese, Indian, and European dishes.

Fruit

Puerto Rico's tropical climate is perfect for growing all sorts of luscious, exotic **fruits**, though modernization (and US import practices) has taken its toll and the selection on offer can be remarkably poor compared to other countries in the tropics. Most notably, the range of local fruits stocked in supermarkets is tiny, reflecting the relatively small scale of fruit farming on the island: drive around the hills in the summer and you'll see literally thousands of juicy, ripe **mangos** simply fallen off the trees and that have been left to rot on the ground (it's usually OK to help yourself, but check first if it looks like the tree stands on private land). The best place to buy fresh fruit is at the roadside, where local vendors sell seasonal crops: in addition to mangos, you'll see huge **avocados** (Feb to April) and **pineapples** (summer). **Guava** and **papaya** are traditional Puerto Rican fruits that have lost popularity in recent decades, but are still used in numerous preserves and jellies (jams). **Bananas** are also still grown on the island.

Adventurous eaters should try Puerto Rico's more unusual fruits: kids love the *caimito* (also known as the star apple, with a vaguely grapelike flavor), *quenepa* (Spanish lime), and *zapote* (a small fruit with a complex taste, blending peach, avocado, and vanilla). Fresh juice drinks and shakes are common.

Vegetarian food

Vegetarians will not be overly excited by the options in Puerto Rico, though San Juan does have several vegetarian restaurants and diners all over the island are starting to offer vegetarian choices. Though *cocina criolla* isn't particularly vegetarian-friendly, given their links with the US, most Puerto Ricans understand

the concept and are fairly sympathetic when it comes to special requests. Remember that even plain *mofongo* or rice and beans often contain pork or pork fat.

Drinks

Tap water in Puerto Rico is technically safe to drink, though locals have mixed feelings about it: it's treated so it should be clean, but the amount of chemicals in the water means you that may prefer to use a filter. Note also that after heavy rains some of the supply can get contaminated, so tap water is best avoided at these times. If in doubt, stick to **bottled water**, which is cheap and easily available.

Soft drinks and juices

The full range of **soft drinks** and carton **juices** are available from shops, cafés, and supermarkets in Puerto Rico, but far more tempting are natural juices, such as *jugo de china* (orange juice), and *batidas* (fruit shakes), sold from stalls all over the island. **Coconut juice** (*agua de coco*) is also best experienced fresh, from small vendors at local markets or from private sellers and roadside stalls in the country. Other local drinks to watch out for are *parcha* (made from passion fruit) and *tamarindo*, the sour-sweet juice made from tamarind.

On a sweltering day, nothing provides relief like a **piragua**, shaved ice drizzled with syrup and sold for around $1 from brightly decorated carts all over the island. Flavors include strawberry, pineapple, coconut, guava, and tamarind. For a real local experience, seek out **maví**, a fermented drink made from tree bark and often described as root beer. Primarily a home-made drink sold at markets and food stalls in towns, or from private houses in the country, you'll have to ask around to find the best supplier.

Coffee

Puerto Rico has produced some of the best **coffee** in the world since the nineteenth century, and the island is beginning to win back international respect for its small gourmet brands and *alto grande* beans. The lush Central Cordillera cradles over ten thousand coffee farms, most selling beans to just two large roasters: **Grupo Jiménez** (which produces Café Rico, Café Yauco Selecto, and the most successful brand, Café Yaucono) and **Garrido & Co** (Café Crema and Café Adjuntas). Collectively they control around ninety percent of the domestic market and often dominate supermarket shelves, but a growing number of smaller cooperatives cultivate, process, and sell their own coffee. You can visit many of these mountain *fincas* and buy whole or ground beans directly from them, though drinking coffee in cafés and restaurants is another story: most of these are supplied by the mass producers, and sometimes you'll be drinking coffee that hasn't even been grown on the island. On the other hand, some of the strongest, most aromatic Puerto Rican coffee is served at the cheapest restaurants and food stalls. Long lines in the mornings usually mean the coffee is good. *Café* can be ordered *con leche* (with milk), *negrito con azúcar* (black with sugar), or just *cortao* (with a drop of milk) and *puya* (no sugar). In the cities most people will understand the terms americano, cappuccino, and latte. For decaf, ask for *sin cafeína* or just *descafeinado*. **Tea** is available in some places, usually the imported black or herbal teas you'd expect to find in the US, but Puerto Ricans are not big tea drinkers.

Alcohol

Puerto Rico's favorite drink and one of its biggest exports is **rum** (*ron*), a potent spirit often served with Coke (rum and Coke with a wedge of lemon or lime is a *Cuba libre*) and various liquors to create all sorts of mind-bending cocktails. Buying rum in supermarkets is much cheaper than in the US and Europe, with decent bottles of the main brands around $10, though drinking in bars and restaurants isn't such a good deal unless you're propping up the local dive in a rural area.

Rum is made from sugarcane molasses (all imported), fermented with yeast, distilled, then aged for at least one year – the different flavors come from tinkering with this process, particularly the type of yeast used, length of aging, and blending with other rums, with every distillery having its own "recipe." The finished product is usually dark or gold-colored, a lighter amber, or clear ("white"). White rums are the lightest and most refined, best drunk with a mixer in cocktails, while the richer-flavored dark rums make them better for drinking straight or with Coke. Connoisseurs only drink the oldest golden rums (*anejos*), straight or on the rocks.

Puerto Rico once had hundreds of small, family-owned distilleries, but only two operate today. The largest by far is **Bacardi** (see p.102), which produces its signature Superior brand as well as various fruit- and coconut-laced flavors at its plant in Cataño. The other producer and only home-grown Puerto Rican distiller is Ponce-based **Destilería Serrallés** (see p.290), which produces the **Don Q** brand of rums, with Don Q Cristal the most popular domestically. **Ron del Barrilito** (see p.67) is now the most respected independent brand on the island, though it has to buy raw product from Bacardi. You can still find **home-made rums**, known as *pitorro* (or *cañita* when mixed with fruit flavors), particularly around Christmas, but you'll need local connections to try them: *pitorro* is technically illegal, and annual crackdowns have considerably reduced production.

Puerto Rico's national cocktail is the **piña colada**, supposedly created in a San Juan hotel in the 1950s (see p.92), and you'll also see **sangría** served in bars and restaurants, particularly on the west coast: the Puerto Rican version is usually a potent rum cocktail mixed with fruit juices.

Puerto Rican **beer** is less appealing, now represented solely by the Medalla brand, produced in Mayagüez by Cervecería India, a light lager that's refreshing enough on a hot day but nothing special. Presidente beer from the Dominican Republic is almost as prevalent. Imported beers tend to follow the traditional US school of light,

Budweiser-type brews, and it's hard to find a wider selection of real ales and microbrews, even in San Juan.

Note that the **legal drinking age** in Puerto Rico is 18, but it is strictly forbidden to drink on the streets (the beach is fine).

The media

You'll need to understand Spanish to get the most out of the news and entertainment media in Puerto Rico, where plenty of feisty political debate and steamy celebrity gossip feeds the island's highly independent press. All the major US newspapers and cable TV channels are also available.

Newspapers and magazines

US **newspapers** such as the *New York Times*, *Miami Herald*, and *USA Today* are all easy to find in larger Puerto Rican towns and cities, with prices identical to the mainland, but publications from other countries are hard to come by. **Magazines** tend to be Spanish-language editions. The only local English-language **newspaper** is the *San Juan Star* (Ⓦwww .thesanjuanstar.com), while the *Puerto Rico Herald* (Ⓦwww.puertorico-herald.org) is an online journal with a pro-independence bias. The most popular paper is the Spanish tabloid *El Nuevo Día* (Ⓦwww.elnuevodia.com), which also has the best local sports coverage. The other daily Spanish newspapers are *El Vocero* and *Primera Hora*, while Mayagüez and Ponce also have their own smaller local papers.

Television and radio

Cable and **satellite TV** is becoming increasingly available in Puerto Rico, offering a vast range of Spanish and English channels (almost all from the US). Most hotels offer some form of cable, but otherwise the local **terrestrial channels** are Spanish-only: the main stations are NBC-owned Telemundo (WKAQ-TV, channel 2), WAPA Television (channel 4), PBS-affiliated TUTV (WIPR-TV, channel 6), and the most popular Spanish-language network in the US, New York-based Univision (usually channel 11).

Puerto Rico has well over a hundred AM and FM **radio stations** blaring out all over the island, La Mega 106.9 being one of the most popular (playing primarily Latin pop). Radio WOSO (1030 AM) is the only English-language station, but although the others are Spanish-only, the music is fairly universal: flick around and you'll invariably pick up salsa, classical, rock, and pop stations wherever you are, with plenty of US and international bands featured.

The **BBC World Service** (Ⓦwww.bbc.co .uk/worldservice) is available infrequently in Puerto Rico, usually 7–8am and 5–5.30pm (9750 AM short-wave), while **Radio Canada** (Ⓦwww.rcinet.ca) tends to broadcast in Spanish only (9640 AM). **Voice of America** (Ⓦwww.voa.gov) is also sporadic, usually available 5–5.30pm, 8.30–9pm, and 9.30–10pm on the 5890, 7405, 9775, and 11675 AM short-wave frequencies.

Festivals and public holidays

One of Puerto Rico's greatest attractions is its range and depth of festivals, and the passion and fervor with which the island's inhabitants celebrate them. Traditional festivals are thoroughly grounded in the island's Spanish heritage, with African and Taíno elements added over the years to create a truly criollo mix. Altogether, there are said to be an astounding five hundred held on the island each year, including the fiestas patronales or fiestas del pueblo observed by each of the 78 municipalities to honor patron saints – the main ones are listed below and in relevant chapters. Public holidays are marked with a (P) and include all US federal holidays, when government-run offices and attractions, as well as banks, will be closed. Shops and other businesses tend to close only on New Year's Day, Three Kings' Day, Good Friday and Easter Sunday, Mothers' and Fathers' Day, Thanksgiving, and Christmas Day. However, even if it's not an official holiday, any of the festivals listed here can mean closures and time changes, so plan ahead.

Major Puerto Rican holidays and festivals

January

Año Nuevo/New Year's Day January 1 (P). Usually celebrated with fireworks displays.

Festival de los Tres Reyes (Three Kings' Day) January 6 (P). This is the day children receive gifts (rather than Christmas).

Natalicio de Eugenio María de Hostos second Monday in January (P). Commemorates the famous independence advocate, born in Mayagüez on January 11, 1839.

Martin Luther King's Birthday third Monday in January (P). US federal holiday to honor the African-American civil rights leader gunned down in 1968.

February

Carnaval de Ponce week before Ash Wednesday. This traditional pre-Lenten carnival is one of the most important festivals in Puerto Rico (see p.285).

Día de los Presidentes (Presidents' Day) third Monday in February (P). Another US holiday, originally commemorating George Washington's birthday on February 22, and associated locally with the birth of Luis Muñoz Marín on February 18, 1898.

March

Día de la Abolición de la Esclavitud (Emancipation Day) March 22 (P). Commemorates the abolition of slavery in 1873.

March/April

Viernes Santo (Good Friday) and **Domingo de la Resurrección** (Easter), the first Sunday after the first full moon between March 22 and April 25. Both (P). **Holy Week** (santa semana) is the most important Catholic festival and consequently the busiest holiday in Puerto Rico.

April

Natalicio de José de Diego third Monday in April (P). Celebrates the birth of José de Diego on April 16, 1867, the beloved poet and political leader.

contd...

May

Día de las Madres (Mothers' Day) second Sunday in May (**P**). Major celebration in Puerto Rico, with restaurants and beaches swamped.

Memorial Day last Monday in May (**P**). Federal holiday to commemorate the men and women who have died serving in the US military.

June

Día de los Padres (Fathers' Day) third Sunday in June (**P**). Almost as big as Mothers' Day.

Día de San Juan Bautista June 24. John the Baptist is the patron saint of Puerto Rico and the capital, and the biggest festivities take place in San Juan (see p.98).

July

US Independence Day July 4 (**P**). Major federal holiday.

Natalicio de Luis Muñoz Rivera third Monday in July (**P**). Celebrates the birthday of Luis Muñoz Rivera on July 15, 1859, in Barranquitas.

Conmemoración del Estado Libre Asociado July 25 (**P**). Constitution Day commemorates the signing of the 1952 constitution of Puerto Rico.

Natalicio de José Celso Barbosa July 27 (**P**). Commemorates the birth of the celebrated doctor and Republican Party founder in 1857.

Fiestas Tradicionales de Santiago Apóstol last week in July. The most vigorous celebration of St James Day (July 25) takes place in Loíza (see p.107).

September

Día del Trabajo (Labor Day) first Monday in September (**P**). US tradition that started in the 1880s as a holiday for workers.

October

Día del Descubrimiento de América (Columbus Day) second Monday in October (**P**). Commemorates the arrival of Columbus in the New World on October 12, 1492, celebrated with pride in Puerto Rico, but not in other parts of Latin America, where it's known as Día de la Raza (Day of the People).

November

Día del Veterano (Veteran's Day) November 11 (**P**). Federal holiday that honors military veterans, held on the anniversary of the armistice that ended World War I.

Día del Descubrimiento de Puerto Rico (Discovery of Puerto Rico Day) November 19 (**P**). Remembers the "discovery" of the island by Columbus in 1493.

Thanksgiving fourth Thursday in November (**P**). US federal holiday to commemorate the Pilgrim Fathers' survival in 1623.

December

Encendido Navideño December 1. Marks the beginning of the Christmas season, with celebrations to light Christmas trees.

Las Mañanitas Ponce, December 12. Major religious procession to honor the patron saint of the city, Nuestra Señora de la Guadalupe (see p.285).

Navidad Christmas Day, December 25 (**P**).

Festival de las Máscaras (Mask Festival) Hatillo, December 26–28. Originally commemorating King Herod's attempt to kill baby Jesus by ordering the murder of all firstborn sons. The men of the town wear florid masks and costumes to collect money (with as many pranks as possible) for local churches or charities.

Sports and outdoor activities

BASICS | Sports and outdoor activities

Watersports rule supreme in Puerto Rico, with swimming and surfing the most popular activities. The coral-smothered coastline is home to some of the Caribbean's best diving and snorkeling, while the trade winds that pummel the north and east coast make for some magnificent windsurfing. The island's rugged interior, great for hiking, is a potential gold mine for all types of adventure sports, largely unrealized due to the apathy of Puerto Ricans themselves, who far prefer the beach. Specialist operators have started to exploit the densely forested slopes and mountains nonetheless, with kayaking, canyoning, caving, and whitewater rafting all on offer. Golf has a major presence on the island, and you should also be able to find tennis courts in most cities and larger hotels.

Diving and snorkeling

For the best **snorkeling**, aim for **Culebra** and **Vieques**, or take a charter out of **Fajardo** (see p.133) to reach the more secluded cays of **La Cordillera**. Though it's theoretically possible to snorkel almost anywhere along the coast of Puerto Rico, the power of the surf in winter, the pollution, and the large number of silt-carrying rivers flowing into the sea year-round make much of it inaccessible or unremarkable – beaches in the Porta del Sol are slightly better, but in general the cays offshore offer the brightest coral and fish life. **Divers** should also head for Culebra (p.182), with the other major diving highlights being **La Pared** (the spectacular wall off La Parguera, p.275), **Isla de Mona** (p.260), and **Isla Desecheo** (p.243) on the west coast. Mona is best appreciated by taking a multi-day excursion planned long in advance – the waters here are unbelievably clear and teeming with exotic marine life.

Surfing

Puerto Rico is the Caribbean version of Hawaii, and surfers have been coming here since the 1960s to enjoy some of the hardest and most consistent waves in the Americas. After the World Championships were hosted at **Rincón** in 1968, the island was firmly established on the international **surf** circuit. Rincón (see p.234) is still at the heart of the Puerto Rican surf world (with thousands of locals as well as foreign *surferos*), though the beaches around Aguadilla on the **northwest**

coast (see p.226) offer just as much action, while the scene in **San Juan** (p.78) is developed and easy to get into. You'll also find plenty of great beaches along the north coast (Jobos, p.225), around **Luquillo** (p.126), and off **PR-901** (see p.141) in the east; the calmer, Caribbean south coast doesn't see as many waves. The best time is during the winter (Oct–Feb), when northerly swells generated from the US east coast slam into Puerto Rico. Local surf shops are the best places to ask about current conditions, while websites such as ⓦwww.surfpr .com and ⓦwww.downislandmagazine.com are a good resource before you leave.

Windsurfing

Since the **windsurfing** World Cup was held here in 1989, the local scene has grown rapidly, centered on the San Juan beaches of Ocean Park and Isla Verde – the shops here are the best places to get oriented (see p.84). Other hot spots are northwest beaches such as Playa Crash Boat (p.230) and Jobos (see p.225), while beginners are better off at *El Conquistador* (p.128), or the calmer west coast waters around La Parguera (p.272) and Boquerón (p.262). Check out ⓦwww.windsurfingpr.com before you go.

Sailing

The east coast of Puerto Rico is a **sailing** paradise, with massive marinas such as **Puerto del Rey** (see p.134) and **Villa Marina** (see p.133) home to charter yachts that ply the waters all the way to the Virgin Islands. You'll also find operators in Culebra, Vieques, and in all the major southwestern resorts, but although the south and west coasts are also popular with yachties, unless you have your own boat it can be hard to get on the water, and it's unusual to find anywhere in Puerto Rico that rents single- or two-person boats to tourists.

Fishing

Puerto Rico has been a light tackle and deep-sea **fishing** destination for years, especially known for its **tarpon** and **blue marlin**: the north coast is known as "blue marlin alley" thanks to the hordes of migrating fish that pass near its shores, especially in the summer, and the island plays host to an **International Billfish Tournament** (⊛www .sanjuaninternational.com) each year. Fishing is excellent year-round, but winter (Oct–March) is the best time for dolphinfish (mahi-mahi or *dorado*), wahoo, white marlin, yellowfin tuna, and the occasional sawfish and sailfish. Tarpon and **snook** thrive in the shallower waters of the island's lagoons and bays, and make easier targets from smaller boats.

Charters are available from San Juan and the major resort areas: Culebra, Vieques, Fajardo, Palmas del Mar, and all the west coast towns; see relevant chapters for details. You can expect to pay around $500 for a half-day, and up to $900 for full-day excursions.

Fly fishermen can also try Lake Dos Bocas (see p.216) and Lake Guajataca (see p.209) for catfish, tilapia, and bass. The **Asociación de Pesca Deportiva de Puerto Rico** (⊕787/842-0203, ⊛www.asociaciondepescadeportiva .com), the Sports Fishing Association, is the best source for current information.

Kayaking

Kayaking is often the best way to experience the raw beauty of the Puerto Rican coastline – the island's **bioluminescent bays** are especially magical by kayak. You can also explore the tangled mangrove lagoons of La Parguera (p.272) and Guánica (p.303), while the pristine waters and cays off Culebra (p.175) are ideal for leisurely paddling.

Hiking

Contrary to the widely held images of sea and sand, much of Puerto Rico is covered by **tropical wilderness** that offers some of the Caribbean's most scintillating **hiking** possibilities, enhanced by hundreds of tropical birds, scurrying green lizards, and a chorus of chirping *coquís*. The most accessible reserve is **El Yunque National Forest** (see p.112), managed by the US Forest Service and laced with well-maintained trails: highlights include the trek up El Yunque itself and the tougher climb up El Toro. Ecoquest Adventures and Tours (⊕787/616-7543, ⊛www.ecoquestpr .com) organizes hikes through sections of the park.

Elsewhere on the island, the DRNA maintains *reservas forestales* or **forest reserves**, also latticed with trails in varying states of upkeep. **Toro Negro** (see p.335), which sits astride the Central Cordillera, is the most rewarding, close by the island's highest peak, **Cerro de Punta** (4357ft), but you'll find the best-maintained trails in the **Bosque Estatal de Guajataca** (p.209) and within the very different landscapes of the **Guánica dry forest** (p.306). One hike that you should attempt only with a guide is the spellbinding traverse of the **Cañon de San Cristóbal** (see p.330).

In all cases elevations are not high, removing the need for serious advance preparation or above-average fitness. Your biggest problems are likely to be rain and cloud cover, and **the lack of signs**: always plan your route in advance, with local maps if possible, and avoid the mountains altogether during heavy rain.

Cycling and mountain biking

Given its hilly terrain, it's surprising Puerto Rico hasn't developed more of a **mountain biking** scene, but thanks to the Comisión Mountain Bike de Puerto Rico (⊛www.cmtbpr.com) and a handful of hardcore enthusiasts, the sport is starting to take off. **Hacienda Carabalí** (⊕787/889-5820) at PR-992 km 3 is a good place to start, a six-hundred-acre ranch near El Yunque offering a choice of four trails through the rainforest, helmets and instruction provided ($40/hr, or $75 for 2hr). The trails feature exhilarating downhill courses, some technical rock gardens, and plenty of jumps and berms. Other easily accessible trails can be found in the **Guánica dry forest** (p.306), **Bosque Estatal de Cambalache** (p.205), and along the more sedate **Cabo Rojo Refuge Bike Trail** (8.5km; see p.266), though in all cases you'll need to bring bikes from elsewhere. Check out ⓦwww.dirtworld.com or ⓦwww.singletracks.com for a full listing of tracks or rental outlets, or contact Puerto Rico's **International Mountain Biking Association** (ⓦwww.imba.com) representative, Juan Escobar (☏787/504-2281, ⓔkp4zz@prtc.net).

Touring the island by bike is a bleak prospect, mainly because of the volume of traffic, though things are better in the mountains and parts of the southwest. **Vieques** and **Culebra** are far nicer and safer areas to explore by bike, with plenty of places willing to rent (see p.151).

Whitewater rafting, canyoning, and caving

The overgrown gorges and caves around **Parque de las Cavernas del Río Camuy** (p.212) are part of the haunting landscape known as karst country, prime territory for rappeling, caving, and canyoning, while scaling the vertiginous walls of the **Cañón de San Cristóbal** is one of the most exhilarating experiences on the island (p.330). More adventures await within the forests of the Central Cordillera and the **Bosque Estatal de Toro Negro** (p.335). Unless you have lots of experience, you're better off working with established companies to make the most of these sites – access is often difficult and conditions can be precarious.

Thrill-seekers should get in touch with companies such as Aventuras Tierra Adentro (☏787/766-0470, ⓦwww.adventuraspr.com), which arranges canyoning trips to **El Yunque** (p.120) – see individual chapters for more operators.

Hang gliding and skydiving

Xtreme Divers (☏787/852-5757, ⓦwww.xtremedivers.com) is a **skydiving** school based at Humacao regional airport, offering parachute jumps for beginners (with forty seconds of freefall) during the first two weeks of every month: solo jumps are just $40, while tandem jumps for up to four people are $195. The maximum body weight is 240lb (17 stone or 109kg), and jumpers must be 18 years of age; a signed parental waiver is required for anyone under 21. To try **hang gliding**, contact Team Spirit Hang Gliding (☏787/850-0508, ⓦwww.hangglidepuertorico.com), based southwest of El Yunque (see p.120).

Golf

Puerto Rico is justly regarded as the **golf capital of the Caribbean**, with 23 highly acclaimed courses designed by international stars Robert Trent Jones Jr, Jack Nicklaus, Gary Player, and Arthur Hills, as well as the most successful Puerto Rican player, **Juan "Chi-Chi" Rodríguez**, who won eight titles on the PGA Tour between 1963 and 1979. Most of the courses are concentrated in Dorado (see p.196) or along the east coast, usually as part of luxury resorts such as *Palmas del Mar* (see p.139), which offers one of the toughest courses in the world. Day rates are expensive ($100–160), but considering the standard of the courses, not a bad deal. Renting a set of clubs will set you back $60.

Horseback riding

Puerto Rico has long attracted equestrians for the chance to ride its unique Paso Fino **horses** (see p.140), lauded for their imperious, luxuriously smooth walk. Several ranches offer guided trail rides, one of the best being **Rancho Buena Vista** on the east coast (see p.140), which offers excursions from $45 for one hour. You can also try **Tropical Trail Rides** on the north coast (see p.227), **Pintos R Us** in Rincón (p.240), and **Gaby's World** near Yauco (see p.303).

It's also worth attending one of the many special Paso Fino events and competitions held throughout the year. The two-day **Feria Dulces Sueños** takes place in Guayama on the first weekend in March and is currently the largest Paso Fino fair in the world, crammed with spectacular events. The **National Open Paso Fino Championship** (ⓦwww.losabiertos.org) usually occurs in Ponce in September or October.

Marathons

Despite the heat and apparent apathy for extreme exercise, the island hosts a number of **marathons** throughout the year, attracting plenty of home-grown talent in addition to overseas runners. Even if you're not running, watching can be entertaining, as a carnival atmosphere usually prevails. The most prestigious race is the **Maratón San Blás** (ⓦwww.maratonsanblas.com), held in Coamo in February and organized by the local branch of US fraternity Delta Phi Delta since the 1960s. Other races include the 10-kilometer **Maratón Teodoro Moscoso** (also known as the "World's Best 10K Race") in San Juan every February, and the Women's Marathon in Guayanilla, the Maratón Modesto Carrión in Juncos, and the Maratón La Guadalupe in Ponce, all held in November.

Spectator sports

The most popular spectator sports in Puerto Rico are American imports: **baseball**, **basketball**, and **boxing**. **Cockfighting** and **horse racing** hark back to the island's Spanish roots, and remain important elements of island culture.

Boxing

Puerto Rico has an impressive history of championship **boxing**: **Héctor Camacho** (who hails from Bayamón) held several world championship titles in the 1980s and 1990s, while **Félix Trinidad** (from Cupey Alto) was the world welterweight and then middleweight champion between 1993 and 2001. However, it's rare to see major fights on the island, as most of the action takes place on the mainland (and screened to massive audiences via cable TV).

Baseball

Puerto Rico's national sport is **baseball**, and the island has produced some of the US mainland's greatest ever stars (see **Roberto Clemente**, p.106).

Baseball was introduced to the island with the arrival of the Americans in 1898, and though the sport is played fanatically at school and amateur levels, Puerto Rico's **professional league** has struggled in recent years, with low crowd attendance and reduced income leading to the **cancelation** of the 2007–2008 season (games are played over the winter to avoid overlap with the US Major Leagues). In 2006–2007 the league had six teams: Lobos de Arecibo, Criollos de Caguas, Gigantes de Carolina,

Indios de Mayagüez, Leones de Ponce, and Atenienses de Manatí. Champions normally take part in the **Caribbean Series** in February to face teams from Venezuela, Mexico, and the Dominican Republic; Puerto Rican teams have won fourteen times, just behind the Dominican Republic.

Assuming the league is reinstated, games can be an entertaining and cheap way to see some explosive talent close-up. **Ballparks** are generally modern, with covered seating and parking (small fee charged). The upper seats are unreserved; the lower *palcos* cost more. **Ticket prices** have varied wildly over the years, depending on the team and importance of the game (sometimes reaching as high as $85), but the cheapest should be around $10.

Basketball

Basketball is played avidly on the island, with the Puerto Rican national squad becoming only the second team in history to defeat the US "Dream Team," at the 2004 Athens Olympics. The national league (*Baloncesto Superior Nacional*; ⓦwww.bsnpr.com) comprises twelve teams, with San Juan's Cangrejeros de Santurce (the current champions) playing well-attended games in Guaynabo and at the Coliseo de Puerto Rico (ⓦwww.coliseodepuertorico.com) in Hato Rey, which can be reached via the Tren Urbano. Tickets range from $8 to $40. The Atléticos de San Germán are the all-time championship leaders, and the Ponce Leones are also worth checking out.

Soccer (football)

Soccer, or football (*fútbol*), is slowly catching on in Puerto Rico, with just one professional team, the **Puerto Rico Islanders** (⊛www .puertoricoislandersfc.com), founded in 2003. The Islanders are a member of the United Soccer Leagues First Division (in the US), and currently play between April and September at Juan Ramón Loubriel Stadium in Bayamón, near Deportivo Tren Urbano station. For tickets, check online agents ⊛www.tcpr.com or ⊛www.ticketpop.com.

Cockfighting

Introduced to Puerto Rico in around 1770, **cockfighting** (*peleas de gallos*) was legalized in 1933 and remains the island's most controversial pastime, regularly condemned by animal rights activists all over the world. If you have the stomach, cockfights offer a vivid insight into traditional Puerto Rican culture and can be atmospheric, raucous affairs – for the best introduction check out the **Club Gallístico de Puerto Rico** in Isla Verde (p.76), where tickets start at $10.

Cockfighting pits are usually circular, with a matted stage about twenty feet in diameter. Despite regulations limiting time spent in the pit, fights should be strictly avoided by animal lovers: contests are extremely vicious, with beaks used to literally peck the opponent's head into a bloody mess. Fights stop when one of the

birds is too exhausted to continue, and watching them stagger around for one last desperate attack can be disturbing. Even worse, fights sometimes end quickly when a rooster makes a strategic or "lucky" hit, cutting nerves to its opponent's brain. When this happens the hapless victim loses all control of its movements, lying frozen on the ground, running around in circles, or even cart-wheeling around the pit.

Nevertheless, supporters defend the sport as a key aspect of Puerto Rican culture; it's worth noting too, that despite being banned in the UK and the US, cockfighting remains legal in parts of France, India, and Southeast Asia. Until a law passed in 2007, it was also permitted in the US state of Louisiana.

Horse racing

The only **racecourse** in Puerto Rico is the Hipódromo Camarero (⊛www.hipodromoca-marero.com), in Canóvanas at PR-3 km 15.3, 22km east of San Juan. The atmosphere can be electric during races, which take place Monday, Wednesday, Friday, Saturday, and Sunday from 3pm, usually wrapping up by 6 or 7pm. The **Clásico del Caribe**, the Caribbean's richest race, is held here every December. **Gambling** on all races is legal and big business on the island.

Culture and etiquette

Puerto Rico is a curious blend of Spanish tradition, dynamic criollo culture, and recent Americanization, though to be fair, the last could apply to almost any developing nation feeling the effects of globalization. Most Puerto Ricans are broadly familiar with mainland US culture and behavior, and you are unlikely to face the cultural misunderstandings that sometimes occur, for example, in rural parts of Mexico or South America.

Vestiges of the island's conservative roots do remain, however, and it pays to maintain a degree of friendly formality when meeting people for the first time – being polite and courteous is always a good idea. When it comes to bars and restaurants (unless on the beach), Puerto Ricans tend to dress up, and men with shirt-tails hanging out are regarded as a bit scruffy. Many restaurants and casinos have **dress codes**, although women tend to be treated more leniently than men. The **Catholic Church** remains very important, so always be respectful when wandering around churches, especially during Mass. Locals are generally tolerant of foreign visitors and will only approach you if you are making lots of noise, but it's best to dress conservatively if you can (no shorts or bare shoulders).

Above all, Puerto Ricans are extremely sociable, family-oriented, and friendly people. As a traveler, especially if you stay within the main tourist zones, the last quality may not always be apparent, but attempting to speak a little **Spanish** will go a long way. One of the things that makes Puerto Rico such an easy place to visit is the abundance of English-speakers – in fact, the vast majority of Puerto Ricans can understand basic English, though only those in the tourist zones speak it every day. Nevertheless, language is an important element of Puerto Rican identity, so trying to communicate in Spanish will yield far better results than assuming that a person understands *inglés* – you might end up speaking English anyway, but your efforts will still be appreciated. See p.391 for more on language.

Gay and lesbian travelers

In just a few years, Puerto Rico has become something of a trailblazer for **gay rights** in Latin America, making it a burgeoning holiday destination for gay travelers, especially the Condado and Santurce areas of San Juan (see p.93).

Though homosexuality has long been tolerated in parts of the island, the real breakthrough came in 2005, when the territory **decriminalized homosexuality** and the University of Puerto Rico became the first government institution to prohibit discrimination based on sexual orientation. The island's domestic-violence law now applies to same-sex couples, and anti-gay attacks are considered hate crimes. Groups like Puerto Rico Para Todos (Ⓦwww .prparatodos.org), aided by "Neuyorquinos" (New York-based gay activists), are now pushing for **marriage rights**. San Juan's **gay pride** events run for a week in June, with parties, fashion shows, and art exhibitions culminating in a parade through

Condado attended by thousands: the annual gay pride parade in Boquerón also attracts huge crowds.

Other parts of the island, too, are refreshingly open-minded when it comes to gay travelers. In areas such as El Yunque, Vieques, Fajardo, and Boquerón, where many guesthouses are run by liberal US expats and easygoing locals, gay couples are welcome. You can even find a list of gay-friendly hotels at Ⓦwww.puertoricosmallhotels.com.

That said, traditional Catholic morality prevails in many parts of the island, so gay visitors to rural areas should keep a low profile. The conservative and Church-influenced Puerto Rican senate tried to lead a backlash in 2008, preparing a bill that would amend the Puerto Rican constitution to ban **same-sex marriage**: Resolution 99 was defeated in the House of Representatives in June 2008. And in Puerto Rico's recently liberalized social climate, it's easy to forget that the island has one of the highest percentages of **AIDS** cases in the US, with a disproportionately high impact on the gay community.

Puerto Rico Breeze was the only gay newspaper on the island, but stopped publishing in 2006 – ask around on arrival to see if it's back, or check out the **Puerto Rico Rainbow Foundation** website (Ⓦwww .orgulloboricua.net) and the directory at Ⓦwww.gaysanjuan.com to get the latest on what's going on. For info on **Vieques**, visit Ⓦwww.gayvieques.net.

Women travelers

Women traveling alone are perfectly safe in Puerto Rico, and although gender roles remain traditional, the island has a strong record of fighting sexual discrimination. In fact, Puerto Rican women often display a degree of self-confidence and independence that many overseas female visitors find liberating. In 2000, Sila María Calderón became the first female governor of the island, and abortion has been legal since 1973 (Cuba, Guyana, and Mexico City are the only other parts of the Caribbean and Latin America where this is the case).

Machismo still exists, but it's not as prevalent as in other Latin American nations, and in the cities you'll see plenty of single women out and about – the worst you'll get is the odd catcall or beep of a horn. As always, things are a little more conservative in rural areas, but if anything, locals tend to be overprotective rather than critical of single women travelers. As anywhere, the usual **precautions** apply; take extra care when out in the evening and, if solo, avoid local bars late at night; take reputable taxis to get around San Juan; and avoid empty streets and deserted beaches if you're on your own.

Smoking

In March 2007 smoking was **banned** in all restaurants, bars, and casinos in Puerto Rico. Smoking on terraces or in outdoor bars and in cars carrying children under 13 is also prohibited, making this the Caribbean's most stringent anti-smoking law by far. Smoking is on the decline in Puerto Rico, but smoking-related illnesses still cost the country an estimated $1.1 billion annually.

Tipping

Given Puerto Rico's ties with the US, it's no surprise that **tipping** is an important part of life on the island and often an important source of income, especially for wait staff in **San Juan** restaurants, where a tip of fifteen to twenty percent is expected – unless you've had unusually bad service, anything less will be received very poorly. In local *cocinas* or bars in smaller towns and villages tips are not so common – never tip in fast-food or self-serve buffet restaurants. Porters generally expect $1 per bag, and maids $1–2 per day in posh hotels (ask the reception at other places, and leave the money in the room when you check out). Taxis get ten to fifteen percent, though this isn't as rigorously adhered to.

Travel essentials

Costs

Though the Puerto Rican economy lags far behind that of the mainland US, it remains one of the Caribbean's most developed islands, and, as such, is a more expensive place to travel than places like Cuba and the Dominican Republic. While vacationing New Yorkers will find Puerto Rico cheaper than Manhattan, prices tend to be similar to the rest of the US. For other travelers (especially Europeans) much depends on the exchange rate: while the US dollar remains at historic lows, Puerto Rico will stay much more affordable than some of the glamorous resort islands in the eastern Caribbean.

Though it's hard to survive comfortably in San Juan on less than $80 a day, it is possible if you self-cater, take buses everywhere, and stay in the cheapest hotels – in theory, you'd find this sort of budget easier outside the city, but without a car (which will add at least $50 per day), your options are extremely limited. You can tour the island with careful planning for $100–150 per day, and in style for over $200. Depending on the season, comfortable two- to three-star standard **accommodation** ranges $75–150, while **eating out** can be pricey: dinners at restaurants, especially in the cities, can be very expensive, though you should be able to find something in the $20–30 range. Lunch is much cheaper (under $20) and breakfast should be under $10. You can pick up local snack food for a few dollars at any time, comparable in price (and fat quotient) to US fast food, which is likewise available everywhere. Puerto Rico does apply a **sales tax** (see p.49) and **tipping** is standard practice (see above).

Admission prices to most museums and tourist sights are usually quite reasonable; government-run venues are typically **free**, while the cost of privately operated attractions rarely tops $10. Discounts are usually given to children, seniors, and students. Activities such as **diving** will add another $80–100 per day.

Crime and personal safety

Despite worrying **crime statistics** and highly publicized carjackings, tourists rarely run into trouble in Puerto Rico. On the contrary, most of the island is extremely **safe**, with petty theft (especially off the beaches) an occasional problem and even the mean streets of San Juan posing little danger if you stick to the main tourist zones and exercise common sense. On paper, however, it doesn't look good. Puerto Rico's **homicide rate** (19.6 per 100,000 people) is much higher than any state on the US mainland outside Washington, DC, though the 739 murder victims in 2006 represented a small drop from 2005 and violent crime was down overall.

Puerto Rico's main problem is **drugs**: the island has become one of the most important transshipment points to the US mainland for the Colombian cocaine cartels, which typically smuggle the product across from the Dominican Republic. Gun crime is overwhelmingly linked to the drug trade, with police attributing 75 percent of all murders to wars between gangs (the remainder are mostly a result of domestic disputes). Visitors are rarely affected by any of this: crime is concentrated in housing projects well away from tourist zones (which are in any case heavily policed), and if you exercise caution at night you should have no problems. In other areas Puerto Rico has made good progress in stemming petty crime in recent years, and most of the scare stories you might hear relate to the 1990s. For any **emergency**, call ☎911.

Electricity

The **electrical current** in Puerto Rico is 110 volts, exactly the same as the continental US and Canada, and outlets take the same two-prong plugs.

Entry requirements

Puerto Rico is a commonwealth of the US, so **US citizens** do not need a passport to enter the country: all you need is some form of official government-issued picture ID (a current driver's license is fine).

For everyone else, the passport and visa requirements for entering Puerto Rico are the same as for **entering the US**. Note however, that there is no passport control on flights between the US mainland and Puerto Rico – non-US citizens will have cleared immigration upon arrival in the US. Citizens of 27 countries are granted **visa-free entry** (known as visa waivers) for up to ninety days, but only with the following: a **machine-readable passport** valid for at least six months from the date of entry, a round-trip or onward air ticket for your next destination, and no criminal record. Australia, Ireland, New Zealand, the UK, and most western European nations are included (see the Department of State website at ⓦwww .travel.state.gov for a full list). All you need to do is fill out form I-94W before arrival (airlines will usually hand these out). The visa waiver program covers travel only; working is not permitted and it cannot be extended under any circumstances. Canada, Mexico, and Bermuda are not participants in the program: Canadians just need to show their passports to travel to Puerto Rico. South Africans and other nationalities must apply for a tourist visa at their nearest US embassy. For information on **longer stays and working** see p.47.

US consulates and embassies abroad

The following all issue US visas. To find the address of an embassy not listed here, see ⓦusembassy.state.gov.

Australia

Moonah Place, Yarralumla, Canberra, ACT 2600, ☎1902/941-641, ⓦcanberra.usembassy.gov.

Canada

490 Sussex Drive, Ottawa, Ontario K1N 1G8 ☎613/688-5335, ⓦcanada.usembassy.gov; Suite 904, Purdy's Wharf Tower II, 1969 Upper Water St, Halifax, NS B3J 3R7 ☎902/429-2480; 1155 Saint-Alexandre St, Montréal ☎514/398-9695, ⓦmontreal.usconsulate.gov; 2 Place Terrasse Dufferin, Québec, G1R 4T9 ☎418/692-2095, ⓦquebec.usconsulate.gov; 360 University Ave, Toronto, M5G 1S4 ☎416/595-1700, ⓦtoronto .usconsulate.gov; 201 Portage Avenue, Suite 860, Winnipeg, R3B 3K6 ☎204/940-1800, ⓦwinnipeg

.usconsulate.gov; 615 Macleod Trail SE, Room 1000, Calgary, T2G 4T8 ☎ 1-900/451-2778; 1095 West Pender St, Vancouver, V6E 2M6 ☎ 604/685-4311, ⓦ vancouver.usconsulate.gov.

Dominican Republic

Avda Pedro Henríquez Ureña 133, Edif. Empresarial Reyna I, 5to. Piso, La Esperilla, Santo Domingo ☎ 809/221-2171, ⓦ www.usemb .gov.do.

Ireland

42 Elgin Road, Ballsbridge, Dublin 4 ☎ 1/668-8777, ⓦ dublin.usembassy.gov.

New Zealand

29 Fitzherbert Terrace, Thorndon, Wellington ☎ 4/462-6000, ⓦ wellington.usembassy.gov.

South Africa

1 River St, Killarney (opposite Killarney Mall), Johannesburg ☎ 11/644-8000, ⓦ pretoria .usembassy.gov.

UK

24 Grosvenor Square, London, W1A 1AE ☎ (0)20/7499-9000, ⓦ london.usembassy.gov.

Customs

Duty-free allowances into Puerto Rico also mirror those of the US: visitors over the age of 21 can import two hundred cigarettes or fifty cigars (but not from Cuba!), one quart or liter of spirits or wine, and gifts or articles up to a value of $100. Narcotics and dangerous drugs are prohibited (make sure you have your prescription with you if taking medication). If flying back to the US mainland, you cannot take fresh mango, soursop, passion fruit (other fruits are usually OK), or plants potted in soil.

Health

As one of the Caribbean's most developed destinations, Puerto Rico doesn't present any significant **health** risks for foreign travelers and residents – heath care is on a par with the mainland US, and taking the usual precautions will be more than enough to stay healthy. For **emergencies** call ☎ 911.

Medical facilities in the big cities are of a high standard, although English-language abilities vary amongst staff, so if you don't speak Spanish you may need the help of someone who does – doctors' will almost certainly speak English, however. There are **hospitals** and clinics in most towns: see relevant chapters for details, or call the Departamento de Salud (Health Department) to find the closest (☎ 787/766-1616).

Puerto Rico's health system was **privatized** in the 1990s and works in a similar way to the US system: the government-run "Health Reform" program (*la Reforma*) provides healthcare for Puerto Rico's poorer citizens through subsidized insurance. For visitors this means you must pay for health care on the spot, and claim back the costs from your insurance provider later (see p.46). Costs vary widely, ranging from $300 upwards for treatment in an emergency room, to less than $60 to see a local doctor.

There are **pharmacies** (*farmacias*) everywhere, and US chain Walgreens (ⓦ www .walgreens.com) has a major presence, many stores in the cities open 24 hours.

Health risks

Your biggest health risk in Puerto Rico is likely **sunburn** or **dehydration**, especially in the drier, hotter southwest, though minor stomach upsets are also possible, with **travelers' diarrhea** the most common ailment. Serious cases may need antibiotics, but most bouts pass within 24 hours after drinking plenty of clean water and avoiding solids. Prevention is key: avoid unpeeled fruits or uncooked vegetables, unpasteurized milk, and food that looks as if it's been left out in the sun. If you are prone to stomach upsets, avoid food from street vendors, *kioscos*, and raw seafood. Always drink bottled or purified water. It's always a good idea to keep up with **hepatitis A**, **typhoid**, and **tetanus** shots before you travel, though these diseases are not common in Puerto Rico.

Mosquitos can be a problem in parts of Puerto Rico, and though there is no malaria, **dengue fever** – a mosquito-borne viral disease whose symptoms are similar to malaria – does occasionally appear. A particularly large outbreak occurred in 2007, resulting in over six thousand cases and four deaths, though the majority were confined to locations outside the popular tourist areas. Incidence peaks from September to November in most years. Dengue fever has no cure, but the illness is rarely life-threatening to adults and the flu-like symptoms usually subside after several days of rest; seniors and young children are most at risk.

The only way to prevent dengue fever is to **avoid being bitten** by mosquitos. The *aedes aegypti* mosquitos that transmit dengue bite day and night, so you should use insect-avoidance measures at all times. Cover exposed skin with **insect repellent** containing 20–35 percent DEET, wear loose-fitting, long sleeves and trousers, and avoid dark colors. At night, make sure your room is sealed from the outside or has **mosquito nets**. For more information about dengue, visit the Center for Disease Control and Prevention website at ⓦ www.cdc.gov.

Medical resources for travelers

Besides consulting the resources and clinics listed here, you can get practical information on staying healthy during your trip from the *Rough Guide to Travel Health*.

US and Canada

Canadian Society for International Health ⓦ www.csih.org. Extensive list of travel health centers.
CDC ⓦ www.cdc.gov/travel. Official US government travel health site.
International Society for Travel Medicine ⓦ www.istm.org. Has a full list of travel health clinics.

Australia, New Zealand, and South Africa

Travelers' Medical and Vaccination Centre ☎ 1300/658-844, ⓦ www.tmvc.com.au. Lists travel clinics in Australia, New Zealand, and South Africa.

UK and Ireland

British Airways Travel Clinics ☎ 012776/685-040, ⓦ www.britishairways.com/travel for nearest clinic.
Hospital for Tropical Diseases Travel Clinic ☎ 020/7387 5000 or 0845/155 5000, ⓦ www.thehtd.org.
MASTA (Medical Advisory Service for Travelers Abroad) ☎ 0113/238 7575, ⓦ www.masta.org for the nearest clinic.
Travel Medicine Services ☎ 028/9031 5220.
Tropical Medical Bureau ☎ 1850/487-674, ⓦ www.tmb.ie.

Insurance

It's important to take out an **insurance policy** before traveling to Puerto Rico, as much to cover against theft as illness and accidental injury. However, it's worth checking whether you are already covered: some all-risks home insurance policies may cover your possessions when overseas, and many private medical schemes include cover when abroad – this is especially true for US visitors. Given the likelihood that you'll find yourself **driving** in Puerto Rico, you should make sure this is covered as well.

Rough Guides has teamed up with Columbus Direct to offer you travel insurance that can be tailored to suit your needs. Products include a low-cost backpacker option for long stays; a short break option for city getaways; and a typical holiday package option, among others. There are also annual multi-trip policies for people who travel regularly. Different sports and activities can be usually be covered if required.

See our website (ⓦ www.roughguides.com) for eligibility and purchasing options. Alternatively, UK residents can call ☎ 0870/033 9988; US citizens ☎ 1-800/749-4922; Australians ☎ 1-300/669-999. All other nationalities should call ☎ +44 870/890-2843.

Internet

Accessing the **Internet** can be frustrating in Puerto Rico, as Internet cafés are rare and only the top hotels tend to have business centers or computer rooms where you can surf the net. Rates differ considerably but are generally expensive, and you'll rarely find anywhere that charges less than $6 for half an hour. Instead, the island seems geared up for travelers who bring their own **laptop computers**, with plenty of small hotels, restaurants, and coffee shop chains such as Starbucks offering free **WiFi** connections.

The best strategy for those without a laptop is to locate the nearest **public library** (*biblioteca pública*), which increasingly offer **free Internet** access. The only downside is that most are closed in the evenings, and some impose time limits on computer usage – students are often given priority.

Laundry

Most large hotels in Puerto Rico provide a **laundry service**, but in almost every town you can find *lavanderías* (Laundromats) that are far cheaper, typically charging $2 for 18-20 pound (8–9kg). You'll also find self-service coin laundries that take quarters, typically requiring $1.50 per load.

Living and working in Puerto Rico

American citizens are free to look for **work** in Puerto Rico just as they are in any other part of the US, though with relatively high unemployment you'll need special skills to have much chance of snagging a job. Plenty of US mainlanders head south every year, many of them ending up in the **hospitality industry**: running their own hotels or B&Bs, managing a travel-related service such as a dive or surf shop, or staffing restaurants and bars. Most of these ventures are small-scale and rarely require more than one or two employees. Plenty of Americans end up at academic institutions, teach English, or work for the government, but these are almost always transfers, or at least arranged back in the US.

It's even harder for other nationalities to work in Puerto Rico, as getting a work visa requires sponsorship from a local employer. The **US visa system** is one of the world's most complex, with a bewildering range of visa types to suit every circumstance. Post 9/11, and with the domestic debate on illegal immigration on top of the agenda, it's becoming harder than ever to enter to the US to seek work, gain a "green card," or **extend your stay**. Note that if you plan to visit Puerto Rico (or the US) three times or more on a visa waiver in one year (staying the maximum three months each time), you are likely to be severely questioned at immigration, and quite possibly refused entry. It's best to apply for a real visa if you intend to stay that long. Working on a **cruise ship** (usually out of Florida) makes it far easier: contact the companies directly for more details (see p.20).

Studying Spanish in Puerto Rico is a popular way to combine a few weeks or months of language learning with sun and surf, though again it's much easier for US citizens: you'll find most companies offering programs at the same school in San Juan. Foreigners will need to arrange **student visas**, though if you are eligible for a visa waiver (see p.44), courses that last less than three months should be no problem. You can also **volunteer** for one of the programs listed here.

Study and work programs

AFS Intercultural Programs US ☎1-800/AFS-INFO, Canada ☎1-800/361-7248, UK ☎0113/242 6136, Australia ☎1300/131736, NZ ☎0800/600-300, international inquiries ☎+1-212/807-8686, ⦿www.afs.org. Global UN-recognized organization running summer programs to foster international understanding.
American Institute for Foreign Study ☎1-866/906-2437, ⦿www.aifs.com. Language study and cultural immersion, with occasional programs at the University of Puerto Rico.
Earthwatch Institute ☎1-800/776-0188 or 978/461-0081, ⦿www.earthwatch.org. International nonprofit that does research projects in over fifty countries, running some programs in Puerto Rico – Las Casas de la Selva was the focus in 2008 (see p.326).
Spanish Abroad US & Canada ☎1-888/722-7623, UK ☎0800/028 7706, international ☎1-602/778-6791, ⦿www.spanishabroad.com. Works with the SA School in Santurce, San Juan, to provide Spanish lessons from one week to several months. Prices range $640–2420 for one to four weeks (classes of up to six students), including homestay accommodation but no meals. Private lessons start at $870 per week.
Vieques Humane Society ⦿www.viequeshs.org. Accepts volunteers to work on animal-related programs on the island: plumbing and maintenance, animal care, and photography. Volunteers need to commit to a minimum of one week and work for a minimum of 20hr/week.

Mail

Mail in Puerto Rico is managed by the **US Postal Service**, with post offices, stamps, and prices identical to those in the US, and most post office workers speaking at least some English. Service to the mainland is fairly reliable, though posting letters and cards back to Europe can take considerably longer, up to two or three weeks in some cases. You can find post offices in almost every town, usually open Monday to Friday 8am to 4 or 5pm, and some on Saturday mornings.

Money

Puerto Rico's currency is the **US dollar**, usually written $ (but sometimes referred to as *peso* locally), and made up of 100 cents. Bills come in $1, $5, $10, $20, $50, and $100, while coins comprise 1¢ (penny and *chavo* or *perrita* in Spanish), 5¢ (nickel and *vellon* or *ficha*), 10¢ (dime), and 25¢ (quarter or *peseta*). You might also see $1 coins. For current exchange rates, check ⓦwww.xe.com.

Almost all cities and towns have **ATMs** (*cajeros automaticos* or *ATHs* in Spanish, for *a todas horas*, "at all hours"), from which travelers can withdraw funds using bank **debit cards** or **credit cards** – this is by far the most convenient and safe method of obtaining cash for daily expenses. Though some ATMs are only for domestic account-holders, many of them take Visa, MasterCard, Accel, Cirrus, Interlink, Plus, and Star. The most common ATMs are those of local banks **Banco Popular** and **Westernbank**, though **Citibank** also has branches in Old San Juan and several in the outlying suburbs, as well as Arecibo, Caguas, Cayey, Fajardo, Humacao, Mayagüez, and Ponce. Local banking hours are normally Monday to Friday 9am–4pm, while some branches open Saturday mornings (all Citibank branches open Mon–Fri 8.30am–5pm, Sat 8.30am–12.30pm).

Most **hotels** accept **credit card** payment, with Visa and MasterCard the most widely accepted brands. American Express and Diners Club also are fairly commonly recognized. In the cities, stores may accept debit cards, but in many rural areas they won't.

Other than at the international airports, **moneychangers** are rare in Puerto Rico, and if you need to exchange foreign currency you'll probably have to do so in a bank. **Traveler's checks** are becoming increasingly outmoded in Puerto Rico and are probably more trouble than they're worth if the island is your only destination. US dollar checks are the easiest to cash for obvious reasons.

Opening hours

Business hours are usually 8.30am or 9am to 5pm, Monday to Friday. Shops are generally open 9am–6pm, closing later on Friday and often all day on Sunday, especially in rural areas. Government offices open 8.30am–4.30pm: in most towns this means that museums and galleries also open at these times on weekdays, closing Sunday and usually Saturday. Conversely, privately owned attractions, and most of the museums and galleries in San Juan, are open weekends, closing Mondays and sometimes Tuesday. For a list of public holidays and festivals, see p.35.

Phones

If you have a **US mobile phone**, it should work as normal in Puerto Rico: in fact, most companies treat the island as part of their domestic network and you'll be charged accordingly. Until recently, GSM mobile phones (from most other countries) would not work in Puerto Rico, but Claro GSM (ⓦwww.claropr.com) should now be offering GSM roaming agreements with overseas companies – check with your provider before you go (you'll need a 3G or tri-band phone).

Otherwise you can **rent mobile phones** via Phonerental (US ☎1-800/335-3705, international ☎+1-619-446-6980, ⓦwww.phonerentalusa.com): rental is free for the first week (though you need to make a minimum $25 in calls) and $3 per day thereafter. You get charged $0.69 per minute for incoming and all local and national outgoing calls. Triptel (☎877/874-7835, ⓦwww.triptel.com) offers a similar service with GSM phones ($15/week rental).

Within Puerto Rico, dial ☎411 for **directory information** (call ☎787/555-1212 from overseas). To call Puerto Rico from **overseas**, dial your international access code, then 1 (USA country code), then the Puerto Rico area code (787 or, less commonly, 939), then the phone number. Note that you always dial the prefix, even when calling within the island (though some mobile numbers have different codes).

Shopping

The greatest choice of Puerto Rican products and **gifts** can be found in Old San Juan (see p.98). Popular items include *santos* (traditional wood carvings of Catholic saints), local cigars, and Panama hats, though ornate *vejigante* carnival **masks** (see p.107) make more memorable souvenirs. San Juan is also the best place to pick up cutting-edge contemporary art (see p.99). The island's ever-increasing gourmet **coffee** producers usually sell their products directly from the farm, while you'll find locally made **rum** a lot cheaper in Puerto Rico than at home.

Tax

Puerto Rico has a 5.5 percent **sales tax** (payable on tours and all food and drink). Municipalities have the option of imposing an additional 1.5 percent: Ponce, Río Grande (El Yunque), and Fajardo are among the cities charging the full seven percent, while San Juan levies an additional one percent on all goods sold in the city.

Price tags in shops and entry fees at museums do not include these taxes, so the actual price will be at least 5.5 percent higher. For **hotel taxes**, see p.28.

Time

Puerto Rico is four hours behind GMT throughout the year, which means that in summer (March 11 to Nov 4) it's the same as US Eastern Standard Time (New York City, Miami), as daylight savings is not observed, and five hours behind BST (in the winter it's one hour ahead of the US east coast). GMT is five hours ahead of US Eastern Standard Time and ten hours behind Australian Eastern Standard Time. For the exact time when in Puerto Rico, call ☏787/728-9595.

Tourist information, websites, and maps

The **Puerto Rico Tourist Company** (Ⓦwww .gotopuertorico.com) has made a concerted effort in recent years to promote the island internationally, but their focus (and their primary market) remains the US. See p.50 for international offices.

In Puerto Rico itself, reliable English information is a mixed bag, with tourist centers outside San Juan thin on the ground and often opening at erratic times. The PRTC operates offices at Aguadilla airport, Ponce, Vieques, and Culebra, but **local municipalities** otherwise have the responsibility to promote tourism in their own areas; as a last resort, try visiting the local city hall (*alcaldía*) on weekdays 8am–4pm. The larger tourist offices should have copies of the annual *Travel Planner*, which has accommodation

and transportation listings, and *Qué Pasa!* (Ⓦwww.qpsm.com), a glossy bimonthly magazine that contains a calendar of events, travel-related feature stories, and more listings. Other publications include the annual *Places to Go* (Ⓦwww.enjoypuertorico.com), *Bienvenidos* (the annual magazine of the Hotel & Tourism Association), and *Tables* (a restaurant magazine published by the Puerto Rico Convention Bureau twice a year), all available for free at hotels and tourist offices. If you can read Spanish you should also check out the **Instituto de Cultura Puertorriqueña** website (Ⓦwww.icp.gobierno.pr), a font of information on museums, art centers, and historic sites.

Note that tourist attractions in Puerto Rico tend to be associated directly with their **municipality**, a confusing practice that often blurs the distinction between a city and its (usually much more appealing) surrounding area: Arecibo, a fairly ordinary industrial town, is said to be the "home" of the famous observatory, though the latter is many miles south in a separate rural location. Because it lies within the boundaries of Arecibo municipality, however, it's technically "inside" the city. Similarly, you might be told that a mountain hamlet in the middle of nowhere is in fact "Ponce." This just means that the village falls within Ponce municipality – the actual city could be many miles away.

Calling home from abroad

For the US and Canada, just dial 1 followed by the area code and the number, if you're using a land line; for mobile phones you usually don't need to dial 1 (just start with the area code). For other countries, the international access code is 011. Note that the initial zero is omitted from the area code when dialing numbers in the UK, Ireland, Australia, and New Zealand from abroad.

Australia 011 + 61 + area code.

New Zealand 011 + 64 + area code.

Republic of Ireland 011 + 353 + area code.

South Africa 011 + 27 + area code.

UK 011 + 44 + area code.

Puerto Rico tourist offices overseas

Canada 41–43 Colbourne St, Suite 301, Toronto, Ontario M5E 1E3 ☎416/368-2680.
UK Second Floor, 67a High St, Walton-on-Thames, Surrey KT12 1DJ ☎01932/253-302, ⓔ puertoricouk@aol.com.
USA 666 Fifth Ave, 5/F, New York, NY 10103 ☎212/586-6262; 901 Ponce de León Blvd, Suite 101, Coral Gables, Florida 33134 ☎305/445-9112; 3575 W Cahuenga Blvd, Suite 405, Los Angeles, CA 90068 ☎323/874-5991.

Maps

This guide aside, it's hard to find decent **maps** of Puerto Rico. Metro Data (ⓦwww .metropr.com) produces *Guía Metro*; $15.95, a handy booklet of maps covering every municipality on the island, usually available in drug and book stores in San Juan, and *Todo Puerto Rico*, with a bit more detail ($26.95). Serious hikers should order topographic maps from the US Geological Survey (ⓦwww.usgs .gov), while everyone else should be satisfied with National Geographic's detailed foldout map of El Yunque ($9.95). Rand McNally and International Travel Maps produce reasonable foldout maps of the whole island (around $10).

Travelers with disabilities

Puerto Rico prides itself on being one of the most welcoming islands in the Caribbean for **disabled travelers**, and US wheelchair access laws apply here to public buildings and transportation – this means city buses, not private *públicos*. All public beaches, museums, and galleries are also subject to the **Americans with Disabilities Act**, though again, in practice smaller places tend to have limited accessibility. Larger **hotels** and resorts will have special rooms for disabled guests, but many of the smaller hotels are not yet compliant. Most parking lots have special spaces for the disabled.

Despite this, traveling around the island remains tough for many disabled travelers, with even the narrow, steep, and generally crowded streets of **Old San Juan** hard work for wheelchair-users. The easiest option for the latter is to check in to a larger hotel with spacious disabled rooms, such as the *Marriott Resort* in Condado (see p.65), and

explore the island and city with **Rico Sun Tours** (☎787/722-2080, ⓦwww.ricosuntours .com), one of the few companies to operate tour vans with wheelchair lifts at the back. **Wheelchair Getaways** (☎787/378-9192 or 1-800/642-2042) also run specially fitted vans for tours and airport pick-up.

Three noteworthy highlights are a new **wheelchair accessible trail** in El Yunque (see p.112 – El Portal information center is also wheelchair accessible, but the other trails are not), the Bacardi Distillery, which is fully accessible, and finally, the wonderful **Mar Sin Barreras** (Sea Without Barriers; daily 8.30am–5pm) at the **Balneario de Luquillo** (see p.126). This specially constructed ramp, with equipment and staff to help disabled swimmers access the crystal-clear waters off the beach, is the one attraction that thrills every wheelchair-user who visits the island. Similar facilities are available at the **Balneario de Boquerón** (see p.262). For more information, contact the Ombudsman for Persons with Disabilities (☎787/725-2333, ⓦwww .oppi.gobierno.pr).

Traveling with children

Puerto Rican culture is very family-oriented, and **traveling with children** presents few problems. Formula, diapers, and medication are all easily available and most restaurants and **hotels** welcome youngsters – exceptions are usually confined to upscale or romantic hotels and are noted in the text. Though it's extremely rare to see diaper-changing facilities, it's perfectly acceptable to do as the locals do and change diapers wherever you can; breast-feeding in public is also fine, though you should try to be as discreet as possible. Unless you're staying in one of the large resorts, finding a babysitter will be difficult, however. In general, **resorts** are the best places to find children's activities, and all of them have excellent pools. The *Caribe Hilton* (p.64) in San Juan and *Ponce Hilton* (p.284) both run summer programs for kids in June and July, while the *El Conquistador* (p.128) offers Camp Coquí for kids aged 4 to 13, with a vast range of activities, sports, and games.

Eating should present few obstacles in Puerto Rico, with plenty of choices for kids of all ages, though you'll only find children's menus in the cities and major resort areas. Puerto Rican food usually goes down pretty well with children (especially the local ice cream), but if they get bored there are plenty of American diners and fast-food chains scattered all over the island: cruise the main highways on the outskirts of towns to find them.

With a profusion of **beaches**, Puerto Rico is a fun destination for families, and older kids will enjoy the **snorkeling** and **swimming**: the ideal place to start **surfing** is Playa Jobos on the north coast (see p.225). The Río Camuy caves (see p.212), Arecibo Lighthouse (p.205), and Observatorio de Arecibo (see p.211) make popular day-trips in this part of the island.

In San Juan, the Museo del Niño (see p.75) and Parque de las Ciencias in Bayamón cater specifically to children, but El Morro (see p.71) is also lots of fun, and you can **fly kites** on the grassy *campo* just outside. Galaxy Lanes (Ⓦwww.galaxylanespr.net) at Plaza Las Américas has 32 **bowling** lanes.

In Mayagüez, the **zoo** (p.252) is worth visiting, while Aguadilla has Las Cascadas Water Park (PR-2 km 126.5; $15.95, children $13.95) and the Aguadilla Ice Skating Arena (daily; $10–13). Rancho Buena Vista provides **pony rides** for children under 8 (see p.140), while Gaby's World (see p.303) is also a popular place to ride horses. In Ponce you can try another water park, the Complejo Turístico El Tuque (Wed–Sun; $5), west of the city at PR-2 km 220, and El Castillo Amusement Park at Añasco (PR-109 km 1.7; $5) has a sham medieval castle, wave pool, and other amusements. If it's just too rainy, most malls have **cinemas** where all the Hollywood blockbusters are shown in English.

Guide

Guide

1

San Juan and around

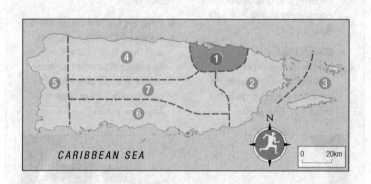

CARIBBEAN SEA

N

0   20km

CHAPTER 1 # Highlights

✻ **Old San Juan** Wander the enchanting streets of the old town, which are crammed with elegant colonial architecture, absorbing museums, and the best restaurants on the island. See p.67

✻ **El Morro** Explore one of the greatest Spanish forts in the New World, a vast bulk of stone guarding the mouth of San Juan Bay. See p.71

✻ **Cementerio Santa María Magdalena de Pazzis** This romantic nineteenth-century cemetery, is one of the most captivating sights in the city. See p.72

✻ **Beach life** Swim, surf, or simply lounge around on one of San Juan's enticing beaches – Isla Verde is the most fun. See p.80

✻ **Sipping a piña colada** Tropical, glamorous, and a symbol of the high life, this celebrated cocktail is said to have been invented in San Juan in the 1950s. See p.92

✻ **Nuyorican Café** Groove to live salsa or take Latin dance lessons at this small but vibrant club. See p.95

✻ **Casa Bacardi** The "cathedral of rum" provides an illuminating introduction to the Caribbean's favorite drink. See p.102

✻ **Piñones** Cycle through the dunes and mangroves, surf, and then stuff yourself with lip-smacking *cocina en kiosco* at this languid beachside community, just outside the city. See p.105

▲ Inside El Morro

San Juan and around

Nothing else in the Caribbean quite compares to **SAN JUAN**, the frenetic, party-loving capital of Puerto Rico. With around 1.5 million people, Greater San Juan contains over a third of the island's population. It's also one of the largest urban areas in the region, crisscrossed with highways brimming with SUVs, and the proud home of the Caribbean's biggest shopping mall, its only subway system, and all the other trappings of a modern American metropolis. Indeed, *sanjuaneros* like to compare their city with Miami, rather than more obvious regional peers like Santo Domingo and Havana. San Juan has its share of problems, however: the city has a high crime rate (much of it drug-related) and many of its neighborhoods remain economically deprived. Visitors are rarely affected though, and since the 1990s new investment has transformed the city's core districts. But while San Juan owes much to its links with the US mainland, it's the city's **criollo** roots, a rich stew of cultures and races, which provide the real allure.

Start with **Old San Juan**, a seductive blend of Spanish colonial charm, Caribbean languor, and modern chic. Protected from the Atlantic by gargantuan stone walls, its cobbled streets are laced with brightly painted houses with balconies of vivid tropical blooms, with the odd palm tree squashed in between. Get to grips with the island's turbulent history at **Casa Blanca**, the city's oldest mansion; **La Fortaleza**, the palatial governor's residence; and **El Morro**, the imposing Spanish fortress that juts into San Juan Bay like a giant stone fist. The old **cemetery** nearby offers a more poignant window into the past, the resting place of many of Puerto Rico's most illustrious citizens, while modest but engaging museums such as the **Museo de Las Américas** provide insights into the island's Taíno and African roots. Puerto Rico's rich artistic traditions are showcased at the **Galería Nacional**, while numerous private art galleries sell the latest, high-quality contemporary work. For a city of this size, San Juan's **beaches** are pretty good too, and the well-established **surf scene** has plenty to whet the appetite of serious shredders as well as beginners. The best beach is **Isla Verde**, east of the old town, where smart resorts and boutique hotels face a fine strip of sand and surprisingly clear, turquoise water.

If you have the time, it's well worth getting beyond the tourist zones and finding out what makes contemporary San Juan tick. The edgier neighborhood of **Santurce**, behind the beaches, has some of the funkiest clubs in the city, plenty of cheap *comida criolla* and a couple of excellent art galleries, the **Museo de Arte** and **Museo de Arte Contemporáneo**. Further south, **Río Piedras** is a laid-back campus district with San Juan's most vibrant market, while rural **Piñones** along the coast is where *sanjuaneros* take weekend escapes to party. When it comes to food, the city's **restaurants** are the most innovative in the

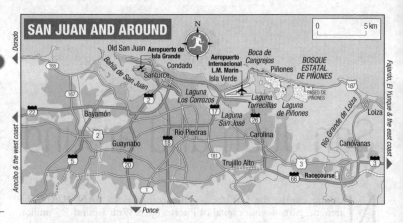

▼ Ponce

Caribbean, ranging from rustic local diners to stylish temples of fusion cuisine. San Juan is also one of the best places in the world to experience **salsa** and the distinctively Puerto Rican sound of **reggaetón** – ideally with a rum and Coke or **piña colada** in hand.

Some history

In contrast to other areas of Puerto Rico, Greater San Juan seems to have supported a relatively small number of **Taíno** settlements, and the modern history of the city begins with the arrival of **Juan Ponce de León** in 1508. The Spanish conquistador surveyed what today is San Juan Bay and named it Puerto Rico ("Rich Port") before establishing **Caparra** a few miles inland. It didn't take long to realize that laying down roots in such a swampy location was a big mistake, and the first settlement on the island never grew to more than a handful of roughly constructed houses. After a prolonged dispute between the settlers and Ponce de León (see Contexts, p.357), the colony was moved to today's **Old San Juan** and formally established in 1521. Ponce de León, who never accepted the move, sailed for Florida and died the same year – despite monuments in the city that suggest otherwise, he was not the founder of San Juan. How the name Puerto Rico was switched with "San Juan," the original name of the island, is still the source of debate: the process was probably gradual, but by the mid-eighteenth century the current conventions were firmly established.

As one of the most strategic cities in Spain's vast American empire, San Juan was the constant target of pirates and envious foreign powers. The English had a go in 1595, when **Sir Francis Drake** was rebuffed, and again in 1598, when the Earl of Cumberland captured the city for sixty days (see p.358). The Dutch sacked San Juan in 1625, while the British, under **Sir Ralph Abercromby**, were beaten off in 1797 by primarily local militia – a feat which is still the source of immense pride on the island (see p.359).

Despite its capital status, San Juan remained a small city until the twentieth century. San Germán (see p.266) was larger for much of the 1700s, and in 1899 the southern city of Ponce had 40,000 inhabitants compared to San Juan's 33,000. Nevertheless, by 1898, when the US took control of the island in the aftermath of the **Spanish–American War** (see p.361), Old San Juan was desperately overcrowded: **Puerta de Tierra** became an overspill area for the city's poor, while **Río Piedras** and **Condado** were absorbed as wealthier suburbs. Under US rule the city was rapidly modernized, with its first cinema opening in 1909 and first radio station debuting in 1922. The process was intensified under the city's immensely popular first female mayor, **Felisa Rincón de Gautier** (see p.70), who oversaw construction of new hospitals, plazas, parks, and housing projects. **Tourism** developed gradually in the 1920s after the Vanderbilts hired architects Whitney Warren and Charles Wetmore (who designed New York's Grand Central Station) to build the **Condado Vanderbilt Hotel** in 1919. Boosted by the legalization of **casinos** in 1940, the real boom came in the 1960s, when the Condado area benefited from the US embargo of Cuba.

After a period of relative decline, the city was given a much-needed face-lift in the mid-1990s, and today San Juan receives nearly 1.4 million **cruise-ship passengers** annually, making it the third busiest cruise port in the world.

Arrival, orientation, and information

The vast majority of visitors to Puerto Rico enter the country through San Juan. Many stagger off cruise ships straight into the old town, but most fly into the plush modern facilities of the international airport, further east in Isla Verde.

By air

All international flights and most domestic services arrive at **Aeropuerto Internacional Luis Muñoz Marín**, 14km east of Old San Juan, and just a few minutes' drive from the beach at Isla Verde. The airport hotel (see p.65) is located in concourse D along with a branch of Banco Popular – you'll find **ATMs** all over the airport. The **post office** (Mon–Fri 8am–4pm) is on the lower (arrival) level next to concourse D. The helpful **tourist information center** (daily 9am–7pm; ☎787/791-1014) is outside concourse C, on the lower level.

Almost every major **car rental** firm operates from the airport, most with 24hr desks at baggage claim areas. All of them run free shuttle buses from the terminal to their car locations: if the desks are unstaffed, you can use the courtesy phones to call for a pick-up. See p.24 for a list of rental firms.

Unless your hotel has a shuttle bus or has arranged to pick you up, getting a **taxi** is the most convenient way into the city. Outside the arrival halls, look for the orange booths where you can get tickets for *taxis turísticos*. Fares from the airport to the main tourist areas are fixed: Isla Verde is $10, Condado is $15, and Old San Juan is $19. You can also go direct to the ferry terminal in **Fajardo** for a flat rate of $80, though if you pre-arrange a ride with a Fajardo-based driver you can save up to $30 (see p.137). Fares to other destinations are metered (see p.62).

The only **city bus** that's any use is the C45 (Mon–Sat every 30min, Sun hourly; last bus 5.55pm; $0.75), which stops outside concourse D upper level (departures) and runs along Avenida Isla Verde: transfer here to the A5 for Old San Juan and Condado, though for the latter the bus drops you off on the corner of Calle Loíza and Avenida José de Diego (a long walk from the main hotels) and you'll have to transfer again to the B21 if you have luggage – it's easier to take a taxi.

A handful of flights from Vieques, Culebra, and St Croix in the US Virgin Islands arrive at **Aeropuerto de Isla Grande**, just across the bay from Puerta de Tierra and 3km from Old San Juan, which has a tiny terminal with a basic café and one ATM. There is no public transport here, and though taxis are supposed to meet flights you might end up having to call one – you're better off arranging a pick-up in advance (see taxis p.62). It's just a short ride into Old San Juan or Condado; fares should be around $10.

By bus and by car

Most *públicos* (minibuses and shared taxis) terminate in Río Piedras (see "Moving on" box, p.102) and you need to take a taxi or local bus to other parts of the city. **Driving** into San Juan can be confusing, though following signs to the airport is relatively straightforward. Try to avoid **rush hour** if you can (Mon–Fri 7am–10am & 4–7pm). If you're driving into Old San Juan, aim for the **major parking lots**: Paseo Portuario Estacionamiento is on Calle del Recinto Sur (24hr; $2/first hr, $1.75 thereafter) and La Puntilla is just off Paseo de La Princesa (Mon–Thurs & Sun 6am–10pm, Fri & Sat 6am–2am; $0.75/first hr, $1 thereafter). Most **hotels** have parking, but they usually charge $10-20 per day.

Orientation

Old San Juan occupies the western end of a narrow island separating San Juan Bay from the Atlantic Ocean, and is the historic heart of the city. The eastern half of this island contains **Puerta de Tierra**, connected to the main island by several bridges. From here the beach districts of **Condado**, **Ocean Park**, and **Isla Verde** follow the coast towards the east; central **Santurce** lies just inland from Condado. South of Santurce, across the Canal Martin Peña, is **Hato Rey**, the city's financial district, while **Río Piedras**, a major transport hub for *públicos*, contains the main campus of the Universidad de Puerto Rico. **Greater San Juan** encompasses several other municipalities: to the east is industrial **Carolina** (the third largest city in Puerto Rico), and suburban **Trujillo Alto**, while **Cataño**, **Bayamón** (the second largest city on the island), and **Guaynabo** lie to the west.

Information

The main **Puerto Rican Tourism Company office** sits in the historic building known as La Casita, in Plaza de la Dársena (Mon–Fri 8.30am–8pm, Sat & Sun 9am–8pm; ☎787/722-1709), close to the cruise-ship piers on the south side of Old San Juan. The office is helpful and well stocked with information, including copies of quarterly magazine *¡Qué Pasa!* (🌐www.qpsm.com), a great source of local information and listings in English. The city government also operates convenient **San Juan Tourism Information Centers** in Old San Juan, with the main office at Calle de Tetuán 250 (daily 8am–4pm) and another desk inside the city hall on Plaza de Armas (Mon–Fri 8am–4pm).

Getting around

Old San Juan and the beach districts are compact enough for strolling, but Greater San Juan is far too spread out to explore on foot. The cheapest way to get around is to use the **city buses**, which are easy to use and relatively convenient during the day. **Taxis** are expensive, but safer at night, and essential for some trips. There's not much point in **renting a car** in San Juan unless you're leaving to tour the rest of the island: traffic can be a nightmare, parking difficult, and drivers fairly aggressive (see p.24 for driving tips and p.100 for car rental companies).

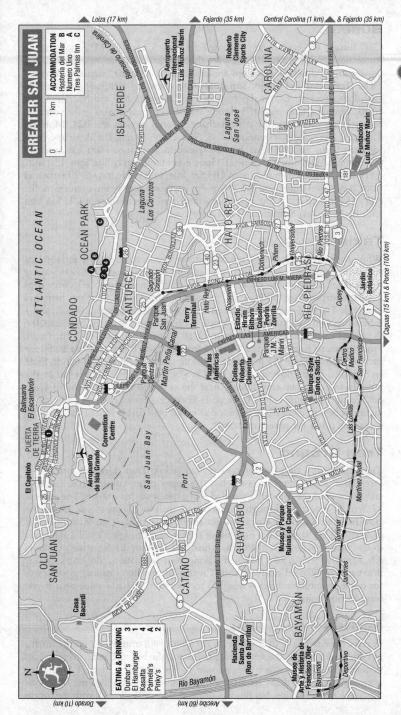

GREATER SAN JUAN

ACCOMMODATION
Hostería del Mar   B
Numero Uno   A
Tres Palmas Inn   C

EATING & DRINKING
Dunbar's   3
El Hamburger   1
Kasalta   4
Pamela's   A
Pinky's   2

0   1 km

Loiza (17 km)   Fajardo (35 km)   Central Carolina (1 km)   & Fajardo (35 km)

Dorado (10 km)

Arecibo (60 km)

Caguas (15 km) & Ponce (100 km)

ATLANTIC OCEAN

OCEAN PARK
CONDADO
PUERTA DE TIERRA
OLD SAN JUAN
SANTURCE
ISLA VERDE
HATO REY
RÍO PIEDRAS
CATAÑO
GUAYNABO
BAYAMÓN
CAROLINA

San Juan Bay
Port

Laguna Los Corozos
Laguna San José

Aeropuerto Internacional Luis Muñoz Marín
Aeropuerto de Isla Grande

El Capitolio
Balneario El Escambrón
Convention Centre
Casa Bacardi
Parque Central
Parque San Juan
Ferry Terminal
Plaza las Américas
Coliseo Roberto Clemente
Estadio Hiram Bithorn
Coliseito Pedrín Zorrilla
Parque J.M. Marín
Sagrado Corazón
Universidad
Jardín Botánico
Centro Médico
Unique Style Dance Studio
Museo y Parque Ruinas de Caparra
Hacienda Santa Ana (Ron de Barrilito)
Museo de Arte y Historia de Francisco Oller
Roberto Clemente Sports City
Fundación Luiz Muñoz Marín

Río Bayamón

SAN JUAN AND AROUND

61

1

Buses

City **buses**, or *guaguas*, are operated by the Autoridad Metropolitana de Autobuses (☎787/729-1512, ⓦwww.dtop.gov.pr) and are cheap, safe, and usually air-conditioned. Bus stops are indicated by a *"parada"* sign.

The **Terminal del Viejo San Juan** (the main bus terminal) is under the Covadonga parking lot on the edge of Old San Juan. M1 and M2 buses cost $0.50, otherwise fares are $0.75 throughout the city: pay as you get on the bus, but make sure you have the correct change. Useful services are: **B21** (Mon–Fri daytime every 20min; evenings, Sat & Sun every 30min; last departure from San Juan 9pm) from Old San Juan to Condado, and on to Plaza Las Américas (39–55min); **M1** (Mon–Fri 5am–11.15pm, every 6min; Sat & Sun 6am–11.15pm, every 12–15min), which runs from Old San Juan to Río Piedras via Santurce and Hato Rey (31–41min); and **A5** (Mon–Fri daytime every 8min; evenings & Sat every 15min; Sun every 20min; last departure 9pm), which connects Old San Juan with Isla Verde (via Santurce, not Condado).

Taxis

White *taxis turísticos* (cars and minivans) ferry between the airport and the city, and have a monopoly at the taxi ranks in Old San Juan and most hotels along the beaches. Charges are set according to tariff zones: zones 1–3 cover trips from the airport (see p.59); 4 and 5 include trips within Old San Juan and Puerta de Tierra ($7); 6 runs between Old San Juan and Condado ($12); and 7 is between Old San Juan and Isla Verde ($19). All other trips go by the meter: the initial charge is $1.75, and then it's $0.10 per 1/19 of a mile thereafter. From 10pm to 6am there is a $1 surcharge, and you'll pay an extra $0.50 for each piece of luggage ($1 per piece for more than three pieces). A trip to Plaza las Américas from Old San Juan is fixed at $14, and it's $36 to hire a taxi by the hour. In the old town taxis line up near the cruise piers or at the top of Calle del Recinto Sur, just below Calle de la Fortaleza; elsewhere, especially late at night, it's best to call cabs in advance, as it can be difficult to hail them on the street (see p.101 for phone numbers).

Tren Urbano

The Caribbean's only metro system, San Juan's **Tren Urbano** opened in December 2004 after years of delays. It's super clean, comfortable, and very safe, but – until the lines are extended – not much use for tourists. The current 17.2km system cuts through the southern half of Greater San Juan from **Bayamón** to **Sagrado Corazón** just north of Hato Rey, via Río Piedras. It makes reaching Bayamón a little more convenient, though it's still a long ride to the nearest station from Old San Juan. All fares are $1.50, which includes a bus transfer within two hours of leaving your last station. San Juan's subway ticket system is based on New York City's, with machines issuing plastic cards for single or multiple rides – hang on to your card and add value to it if you want to ride again.

Ferries

Ferries operated by Acua Expreso (☎787/788-0940) from Pier 2 on the marina in Old San Juan make the ten-minute trip across the bay to Cataño every twenty minutes ($0.50). The commuter service to the northern edge of Hato Rey normally runs every thirty minutes ($0.75), connecting with the Tren Urbano at Sagrado Corazón station, but this was suspended in 2007 – check with the tourist office. The high-speed ferry linking Old San Juan with Culebra and Vieques was cancelled in 2006.

Accommodation

You'll find clusters of hotels throughout Greater San Juan, but for visitors only two areas make sense: **Old San Juan**, which has the most historic accommodation and contains the city's best bars, restaurants, and sights; and **the beaches**, which have less character but boast a decent range of eating and drinking options in addition to the obvious attraction of surf and sand on the doorstep. **Condado** (the closest to Old San Juan) and **Isla Verde** are more developed resort areas, with **Ocean Park** in between offering a quieter experience without the choice of amenities. By 2009 the newly renovated *Condado Vanderbilt Hotel* (ⓦ www.condadovanderbilthotel .com) at Avenida Ashford 1055, a magnificent Spanish Revival villa built in 1919, should be reopened: it's likely to be one of the best hotels in the city.

For longer stays or larger groups, consider **renting apartments** or **villas** via agents such as Caleta Realty (ⓦ www.caletarealty.com), which has several smart properties in Old San Juan, or PR West (ⓦ www.prwest.com), which also rents places in Condado and Isla Verde. The Bóveda store at Calle del Cristo 209 rents a couple of comfortable apartments (ⓦ www.boveda.info) in Old San Juan.

Note that **taxes and charges** added to the price of a room are outrageously high in San Juan, sometimes increasing the bill by as much as 25 percent: check the **total price** before agreeing to pay. Depending on the size of the hotel, mandatory government taxes range 7 to 11 percent (see Basics, p.28), and anything in excess of this has been levied as a **service charge**. Some hotels also charge a **resort fee** of 10 to 15 percent to pay for things like use of towels, pool, and spa.

Old San Juan

El Boquerón c/San Sebastián 104 ⊕ 888/779-3788. This one-bedroom apartment is rented by PR West and occupies the second floor of a beautifully renovated Spanish colonial house, next to *Amadeus* restaurant. You get all the amenities – bathroom, a/c, kitchen, cable TV – with the added bonus of a small wooden balcony and the illusion of living like a real *sanjuanero*. Three nights minimum. ❺

Caleta Guesthouse Caleta de las Monjas 11 ⊕ 787/725-5347, ⓦ www.thecaleta.com. This historic apartment block contains three studios, one suite, and one apartment, ideal for long stays. Rates are considerably cheaper if you stay a month. New management gave the place a much-needed renovation in 2007, and the helpful staff and amenities – cable TV, fridge, microwave, en-suite bathroom, and compact balconies with breezy bay views – make this a good deal. ❸–❺

Chateau Cervantes c/Recinto Sur 329 ⊕ 787/724-7722, ⓦ www.cervantespr .com. Plush boutique hotel with twelve exquisite (but pricey) suites behind the marina. Local style icon Nono Maldonado designed the rooms, which feature a contemporary Puerto Rican theme using natural wood fittings and marble-tiled bathrooms,

embellished with LCD TVs, balconies, free Wi-Fi, and modern art. ❾

Da House Hotel c/San Francisco 312 ⊕ 787/977-1180 or 787/366-5074, ⓦ www.dahousehotelpr.com. This former art center above the *Nuyorican Café* (the entrance is on Callejón de la Capilla) is the best bargain in San Juan. All rooms have a/c and are smart, clean, and simply decorated with original Spanish tiled floors, wooden furnishings, and large, dazzling paintings from local artists. Bathrooms feature stylish basins and rainforest showers, while extras include free Wi-Fi, access to a local gym, and the rooftop sun deck. The streets outside can be noisy though, and there are no TVs. ❸

Gallery Inn c/Norzagaray 204–206 ⊕ 787/722-1808, ⓦ www.thegalleryinn.com. This gorgeous eighteenth-century villa overlooking the Atlantic is adorned with ornate sculptures created by host Jan D'Esopo, set around a plant-filled patio embellished with fountains and the odd parrot. The richly decorated rooms come laden with antiques and unusual trompe l'oeil walls, while thoughtful touches include complimentary breakfast served on the patio and wine and cheese offered daily from 6–7pm. ❼

Hotel El Convento c/Cristo 100
☎787/723-9020, ⓦwww.elconvento.com.
One of the most stylish hotels in the city, housed
within the tastefully restored halls of a former
seventeenth-century Carmelite convent. Mahogany
beams, antique furniture, and Spanish tile floors
add to the historic character of the rooms, which
also come with LCD TVs, and everything is
arranged around a shady interior patio with some
classy restaurants. Note that the hotel levies a 12
percent "service charge" in addition to taxes. ❾
Hotel Milano c/Fortaleza 307 ☎787/729-9050,
ⓦwww.hotelmilanopr.com. Popular, reasonably
good value mid-range hotel, though its comfortable
but bland modern rooms seem at odds with its
attractive nineteenth-century exterior. The best
feature is the rooftop restaurant, where complimentary breakfast is served. Internet is free but
only available in the restaurant, and there's a
minimum stay of two nights at the weekend. ❹
Howard Johnson Inn Plaza de Armas, c/San José
202 ☎787/722-9191, ⓦwww.hojo.com. Following
its takeover by the US chain in 2005, this 50-year-
old hotel was given a fashionable make over that
blends traditional and contemporary styles: rooms
are decked out with modern wooden furniture and
tiled floors and bathrooms. Its position right on the
plaza is excellent. Twins ❹ , doubles ❻
San Juan Guest House c/Tanca 205 ☎787/722-
5436. Basic, slightly run-down hostel on two floors,
managed by the genial Enrique Castro (he only
speaks Spanish), and the cheapest deal in town.
The best double rooms are on the upper floor,
facing the road, with brightly painted walls, fridges,
and balconies (\$50). The cheapest rooms (doubles)
are \$30 with fan (singles pay just \$15), while others
have a/c; all are clean and in the original colonial
style, but the shared toilets and showers are a bit
shabby. Ring the bell to get in. Cash only. ❶
SJ Suites Hotel c/Fortaleza 253 ☎787/725-
1351, ⓦwww.sjsuites.com. The 15 comfortable
suites here range from basic hotel rooms to
more spacious apartments with living room and
bedroom. It's close to the SoFo restaurants, but the
front rooms can be noisy (while the back rooms
look out at some grim modern blocks) – it's a bit
pricey considering, but a solid choice if you need
more space. ❺–❻
Sheraton Old San Juan c/Brumbaugh 100
☎787/721-5100, ⓦwww.sheratonoldsanjuan.com.
Luxury if standard chain hotel overlooking the
cruise-ship piers, with swish rooms equipped with
extra comfy beds, cable TV, and Internet. If you're
into casinos, the hotel has the only one in the old
town, but the best amenity here is the rooftop pool
and Jacuzzi. If you book online, it's not bad value,

though you'll pay the 9 percent "hotel service fee"
in addition to taxes regardless. ❻

Puerta de Tierra

Caribe Hilton c/Los Rosales, San Geronimo
Grounds ☎787/721-0303, ⓦwww.hiltoncaribbean
.com/sanjuan. Set on its own peninsula with 17
acres of tropical gardens, a huge pool, 9 restaurants, and a private beach, this massive resort
dates from 1949 and is the largest on the island
(it's also where the *piña colada* is said to have
been invented). Its 900 rooms are modern and
well-equipped but its vast size makes things a bit
spread out and characterless; you are a little
isolated from the rest of the city here. Note the 10
percent "service charge" in addition to taxes. ❼
Normandie Hotel Avda Muñoz Rivera 499
☎787/729-2929, ⓦwww.normandiepr.com. This Art
Deco hotel opened in 1942, but the recent restoration
has injected more character than at the sprawling
Caribe Hilton next door. The stylishly simple rooms
mix contemporary design and a beige and cream
color scheme with the original fittings and decor,
while the covered inner atrium retains its ocean liner
theme. The location isn't ideal however, and you'll
have to take a bus or taxi to get anywhere. ❻

Condado

Alelí by the Sea c/Seaview 1125 ☎787/725-
5313. One of the cheapest places to stay in
Condado, with the smallest rooms going for just
\$55. It's right on the beach but is showing its age;
the rooms are comfortable enough, however, and
come with a/c. ❷
Atlantic Beach Hotel c/Vendig 1 ☎787/721-
6900, ⓦwww.atlanticbeachhotel.net. Popular
hotel with a beachside location and a lively beach
bar, though not so gay-friendly as it once was. It
looks a little old and worn from the outside, but
the rooms are relatively new and comfortable
– you'll pay \$20 extra at weekends. The same
owners also manage the *Embassy Guest House*
nearby, which will re-open after a much-needed
renovation. ❺ , ❻ with ocean view.
El Canario by the Sea Avda Condado 4
☎787/722-8640, ⓦwww.canariohotels.com.
Small inn-type place, incongruously located amidst
the high-rises, but right next to the beach. You get
complimentary breakfast but adequate, nondescript
rooms, so this is a bit pricey – you're paying for
location, and it's only worthwhile if you intend to
spend lots of time on the beach. ❺
La Concha Renaissance Resort Avda
Ashford 1077 ☎787/721-8500, ⓦwww
.laconcharesort.com. The centerpiece of the
regeneration of Condado, the *Renaissance* opened

in 2007 and fuses the building's original "Tropical Modernist" 1958 architecture with a chic contemporary look. Its 248 rooms have been completely refurbished in bright, pastel shades with balconies overlooking the ocean. If the beach doesn't appeal, check out the huge pool. ❽

Condado Plaza Hotel Avda Ashford 999 ☎787/721-1000, ⊛www.condadoplaza.com. Smart self-contained hotel, with a 24-hour casino on site and a choice of five restaurants. Aim for the newly renovated City Vista or Ocean Vista rooms, which have been jazzed up with elegant, contemporary design, orange and ruby-red tones, LCD TVs, and balconies. Note that the sea-front terrace has no beach (it's a short walk to the main Playa Condado) and the "resort fee" of 14 percent is a bit of a rip-off. ❻

🏃 **Le Consulat** Avda Magdalena 1149, ☎787/289-9191. This cozy new hotel offers 21 comfy rooms with cable TV and Wi-Fi. Extras include a small pool and tranquil garden where complimentary breakfast is served. It's behind the *El Consulado* (same owners) at Avda Ashford 1110, the former Spanish consulate built in 1906 – this equally appealing hotel is being renovated and should be re-opened by the end of 2008 ❺

Coral Princess Avda Magdalena 1159 ☎787/977-7700, ⊛www.coralpr.com. Great little hotel in a quiet residential neighborhood, a 10min walk from the beach. Rooms are bright and still feel newish (the hotel opened in 2002), and they're relatively good value compared to the older hotels in Condado. Taxes are inexplicably high here, though: there's a 14 percent hotel tax as well as an additional $9.92 "operational fee." ❹

Holiday Inn Express c/Maringo Ramírez Bages 1 ☎787/724-4160, ⊛www.hiexpress.com /sanjuanpr. Solid chain option in spanking new premises just off the main avenue, only a short walk from the beach. Rooms are generic but very comfortable. Pluses include free Internet (in-room or in the business center), a small pool, a Jacuzzi, and a gym. Parking is $10/day. ❺

San Juan Marriott Resort & Stellaris Casino Avda Ashford 1309 ☎787/722-7000, ⊛www .marriott.com. Another monster resort-hotel and casino right on the beach, usually packed with families. Has 511 rooms with snappy, tropical decor and spray-jet tubs – the best rooms (and the best views) are in the Tower Wing, which was renovated in 2007. The restaurant is open 24hr. Watch out for the 10 percent "resort fee." Parking is $14/day. ❼

Ocean Park

At Wind Chimes Inn Avda McLeary 1750 ☎787/727-4153, ⊛www.atwindchimesinn.com.

This whitewashed 1920s Spanish villa is a refuge from the hectic San Juan streets, with bright rooms and warm, terracotta-tiled floors. It's located in a peaceful residential area, a 5- to 10min walk from the beach. With a small pool, Jacuzzi, and leafy gardens, it's a bit like staying in an exclusive club. Single rooms are a good deal here ($55). ❹

Hostería del Mar c/Tapia 1 ☎787/727-3302, ⊛www.hosteriadelmarpr.com. Little gem of a hotel, right on the beach, with a Southeast Asian feel. There's lots of dark wood, rattan, and tropical plants throughout, and the excellent *Uvva* restaurant looks like a Balinese beach café (though the food is Mediterranean). Rooms are small but cozy, with cable TV. ❸

Numero Uno c/Santa Ana 1 ☎787/726-5010, ⊛www.numero1guesthouse.com. A former private home built in the 1940s, offering compact but elegant rooms with ceiling fans and a gay-friendly atmosphere. The sleepy location on a pleasant stretch of beach is perfect for lounging, though it's not ideal for exploring the rest of the city. Note also that the 15 percent "service charge" is a bit steep, though prices almost halve in low season (Aug–Oct). ❻

Tres Palmas Inn Park Blvd 2212 ☎787/727-4617, ⊛www.trespalmasinn.com. Friendly hotel offering simple but adequate rooms with cable TV opposite the beach, and an enticing upper sun deck with two Jacuzzis. It's in a relaxed but somewhat out-of-the-way part of town – it's actually closer to Isla Verde than to the rest of the city. ❺

Isla Verde

Beach House Hotel Avda Isla Verde 4851 ☎787/268-7733. This immaculate former villa has a fabulous beach-front location and 17 very simple and tiny rooms – but it can be very noisy. The cool beach bar features four-poster beds for languid cocktail-drinkers (Mon–Fri 4pm–2am, Sat & Sun noon–4pm). Free parking for guests. ❻

Best Western San Juan Airport Hotel & Casino Aeropuerto Internacional Luis Muñoz Marín ☎787/791-1700, ⊛www.bestwestern.com. This ultra convenient but pricey airport hotel is literally inside concourse D, with spacious but standard rooms, gym, Internet access, and basic breakfast included. ❻

Coqui Inn c/Mar Mediterraneo 36, Villamar ☎787/726-4330, ⊛www.coqui-inn.com. Solid budget option, combining the *Green Isle Inn* and *Casa Mathiesen* guesthouses under single management. Both properties, a 10min walk from the beach, offer basic but clean rooms with tiled floors, cable TV, and a bathroom. Extras include a pool and free Internet access. There's a daily $5.45 "energy charge" per room, but the parking is free. ❸

Empress Oceanfront Hotel c/Amapola 2
☏ 787/791-3083. Best of two mid-range hotels
on the Punta El Media headland, which cuts the
beaches in half; magnificent views across Isla
Verde and out to sea, while the restaurant cooks up
succulent ribs and burgers. Rooms are comfortable
enough, with cable TV and balconies, but show
their age. Though cheaper than the big resorts, this
hotel is still pricey considering the overall standard
– as always, you're paying for location. **⑤**

Hotel Villa del Sol c/Rosa 4 ☏ 787/791-2600,
ⓦ www.villadelsolpr.com. Appealing Spanish-villa-
style hotel that's a far cheaper alternative to the big
resorts nearby. Rooms come with cable and have
a tropical theme, and the interior patio with pool
offers a welcome respite to the bustle outside. While
the hotel is a few minutes' walk from the beach, its
location is marred somewhat by the surrounding
high-rise condos and hotels. **④**

Ritz Carlton San Juan Hotel Avda of the
Governors 6961 ☏ 787/253-1700, ⓦ www
.ritzcarlton.com. Another self-contained luxury
resort, set on eight acres of pristine gardens and
dripping with marble and opulent fittings. The
rooms are heavenly, with pool, garden, or ocean
views (extra), and bright, tropic-inspired interiors.
The alluring pool backs onto a gorgeous stretch of

beach, and there are several posh places to eat
and drink. At least the 10 percent "resort fee" gets
you free kayaks, surfboards, and use of the spa.
Parking is $18/day. **⑨**

El San Juan Hotel & Casino Avda Isla Verde 6063
☏ 787/791-1000, ⓦ www.elsanjuanhotel.com. This
colossal former haunt of the 1950s Brat Pack
injects some glamour to the beachfront. The lobby,
with its mahogany paneling and elegant bar, sets
the tone, while the newly renovated La Vista and
Grande Vista rooms feature bright colors, LCD TVs,
and hip, contemporary design. The largest casino on
the island and a massive pool are inviting extras,
but the restaurants are overpriced and there's a
hefty 14 percent "resort fee." **⑧**

🏃 **San Juan Water & Beach Club Hotel**
c/Tartak 2 ☏ 787/728-3666, ⓦ www
.waterbeachclubhotel.com. The city's top boutique
hotel is right on the beach, with 84 funky rooms
dressed in all-white contemporary furnishings and
drapes and equipped with cable TV, CD players, and
iPod docks with speakers. There's a tiny rooftop pool
with mesmerizing sea views, a waterfall that trickles
down the elevator shaft (behind glass), and some of
the best bars and restaurants in the city (see p.93).
Parking is $20/day, while the hotel adds an additional
11 percent to the mandatory 9 percent tax. **⑦**

The City

San Juan is a large, sprawling city made up of several diverse *barrios*, but the
area of interest for visitors is relatively compact. Despite the scary statistics
(see Basics, p.44), it's a lot safer than the hype suggests, especially in the tourist
zones (where those high hotel taxes have, partially at least, been translated into
a heavier police presence). Nevertheless, there are still some rough areas, and it's
important to take care at night.

The obvious place to begin is **Old San Juan**, the city's most historic and enticing
neighborhood, noted chiefly for its dazzling ensemble of colonial architecture. This
is where the Spanish established their first permanent city on the island in 1521,
and their great fortress, known as **El Morro**, is one of its principal highlights,
along with the picturesque nineteenth-century **cemetery** nearby. The **Galería
Nacional** and **Museo de Las Américas** are the best of numerous museums and
galleries here, while a stroll along the outer walls is rewarded with magical views
over the bay especially at sunset.

Beyond the old town, San Juan is all about the **beaches** for most visitors,
with condos and hotels lining the sands for 12km between **Puerta de Tierra**,
revitalized **Condado** and upmarket **Isla Verde**. Though you'll find a vast range
of water sports and activities on offer, there's little to see here. Tourists tend to
ignore the rest of the city, but you should make time for the two excellent **art
galleries** in **Santurce**, and the smattering of attractions further south in **Río
Piedras**. Both *barrios* have been spruced up in recent years, and while remaining
a little rough around the edges, offer a more genuine and richer experience of
everyday life in the city.

Old San Juan

Thanks to extensive restoration in the 1990s, **OLD SAN JUAN** (Viejo San Juan) is a wonderfully preserved slice of eighteenth-century colonial Spain, its narrow streets lined with tempting restaurants and a range of modest but thought-provoking museums. Aimlessly wandering its quiet, cobbled back lanes can be an enchanting experience, with salsa music drifting out of half-shuttered windows, blossoms draped over wrought-iron balconies and the tempting aromas of *criollo* cooking wafting through the cracks of wooden doors.

The commercial parts of the old town tend to get overrun by day-trippers coming in on **cruise ships**, but it's easy to avoid the crowds, and their presence has a couple of beneficial side effects – this is the safest part of the city, and English is spoken everywhere. Begin your visit at the **tourist office** at La Casita (see p.60), in Plaza de la Dársena, where a small **outdoor crafts market** is held Saturday and Sunday 9.30am–10pm and Monday and Tuesday 11am–9.30pm.

Despite being fairly steep in parts, the streets of the old town are best appreciated on foot, though there are a couple of **free trolley buses** that trundle between the bus terminal and the main sights in case the heat starts to get to you (Mon–Fri 7am–7pm, Sat & Sun 9am–7pm, every 15–20min).

Paseo de La Princesa and around

From La Casita, the **Paseo de La Princesa** forms an elegant promenade along the southern edge of the old town, skirting the base of the imposing **city wall**. It runs west off two adjacent squares: shady Plaza del Inmigrante, with its simple but poignant contemporary statue commemorating Puerto Rican immigrants, and Plaza del Hostos, featuring a sculpture of Eugenio María de Hostos, the nineteenth-century independence activist (see p.257).

Rum capital

As the capital city of the world's leading producer of **rum**, San Juan is the perfect place to get more closely acquainted with the Caribbean's favorite tipple. Top of your list should be **Casa Bacardi**, the "cathedral of rum" that dominates the global market (see p.102). Enthusiastic guides and multimedia exhibits introduce every facet of the rum-making process, including special "nosing" barrels of various Bacardi blends – suitably tempted, you get two free cocktails at the end of the tour and a shop selling discounted bottles of its best products. Not to be outdone, Bacardi's main rival on the island (if not in the world), Don Q (see p.290), offers free samples at **Casa Don Q**, near the cruise-ship piers (see p.77), including the bestselling *Cristal*, the island's favorite cocktail mixer. The Rums of Puerto Rico association also maintains a small bar in **La Casita** (see p.60) where, once again, free rum and knockout *piña coladas* are on offer. Real connoisseurs should enquire here (ask for Ahmed Naveiras) about tours of the rambling **Hacienda Santa Ana** in Bayamón, where the Fernández family still makes the superlative **Ron de Barrilito**. This rich, dark spirit was created in 1880 and is aged in Spanish sherry barrels for a minimum of three years: many consider *Barrilito* to be the best rum in the world. Private tours are possible, but only through the tourist office. You'll visit the aging cellars, thick with the burnt, sweet aroma of sugar molasses, the rickety bottling plant, and graceful windmill dating from 1827, which today acts as an office adored with faded photographs and dusty, old bottles of rum. You'll also see "La Doña," or the **Freedom Barrel**, which was laid down in 1942 and will only be opened when Puerto Rico becomes an independent nation – by which time its potent contents will likely have evaporated in the tropical heat.

For more on rum see p.33 in Basics and the *Puerto Rican food and drink* color section.

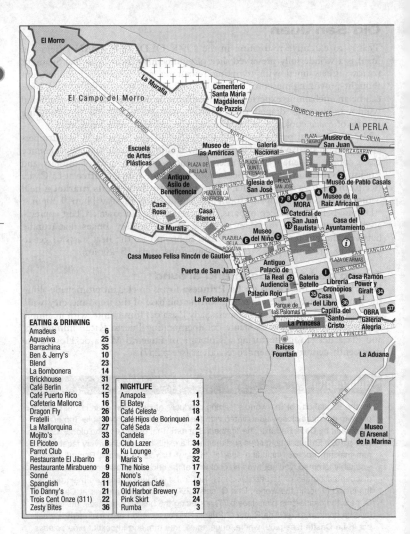

EATING & DRINKING

Amadeus	6
Aquaviva	25
Barrachina	35
Ben & Jerry's	10
Blend	23
La Bombonera	14
Brickhouse	31
Café Berlin	12
Café Puerto Rico	15
Cafeteria Mallorca	16
Dragon Fly	26
Fratelli	30
La Mallorquina	27
Mojito's	33
El Picoteo	B
Parrot Club	20
Restaurante El Jibarito	8
Restaurante Mirabueno	9
Sonné	28
Spanglish	11
Tio Danny's	21
Trois Cent Onze (311)	22
Zesty Bites	36

NIGHTLIFE

Amapola	1
El Batey	13
Café Celeste	18
Café Hijos de Borinquen	4
Café Seda	2
Candela	5
Club Lazer	34
Ku Lounge	29
Maria's	32
The Noise	17
Nono's	7
Nuyorican Café	19
Old Harbor Brewery	37
Pink Skirt	24
Rumba	3

Before you stroll along the *paseo*, take a look down Calle de La Puntilla south of the plazas. The first building on the left is the pretty pink customs house, **La Aduana**, still used by the government, and built in the early 1900s in an ornate Spanish Revival style – the main entrance is particularly elaborate, with multi-colored Spanish tiling and delicate, Mudéjar-inspired pinnacles. The old Spanish arsenal beyond it, now the **Museo El Arsenal de la Marina** (Wed–Sun 9am–5pm; free), was built in 1792, and contains a series of tranquil galleries showcasing modern Puerto Rican painters – exhibits tend to change monthly.

West of Plaza del Hostos the tree-fringed *paseo* becomes a pleasant and traffic-free place to wander, often lined with snack stalls. The thin grey building along its final section is **La Princesa**, completed in 1837. A prison until 1960, today it serves as headquarters for the Puerto Rican Tourism Company and houses a small **gallery** (Mon–Fri 8am–4.30pm; free) that features the work of

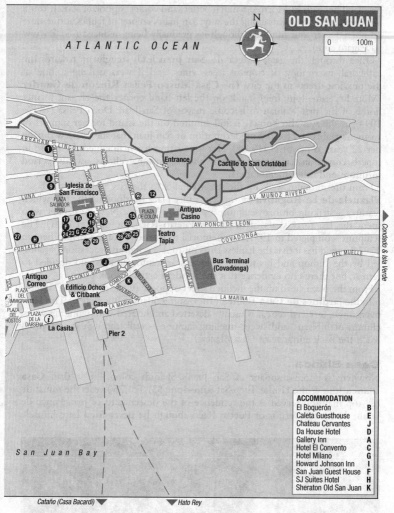

OLD SAN JUAN

ATLANTIC OCEAN

N

0   100m

Entrance

Castillo de San Cristóbal

ABRAHAM LINCOLN

Iglesia de San Francisco

PLAZA SALVADOR BRAU

SAN FRANCISCO

PLAZA DE COLÓN

Antiguo Casino

AV. MUÑOZ RIVERA

AV. PONCE DE LEÓN

Teatro Tapia

COVADONGA

DEL MUELLE

Bus Terminal (Covadonga)

RECINTO SUR

TETUAN

FORTALEZA

Antiguo Correo

Edificio Ochoa & Citibank

Casa Don Q

PLAZA DEL IMMIGRANTE

PLAZA DEL HOSTOS

PLAZA DE LA DARSENA

La Casita

Pier 2

LA MARINA

San Juan Bay

Cataño (Casa Bacardi) ▼   ▼ Hato Rey

Condado & Isla Verde ▶

SAN JUAN AND AROUND | The City

ACCOMMODATION

El Boquerón	**B**
Caleta Guesthouse	**E**
Chateau Cervantes	**J**
Da House Hotel	**D**
Gallery Inn	**A**
Hotel El Convento	**C**
Hotel Milano	**G**
Howard Johnson Inn	**I**
San Juan Guest House	**F**
SJ Suites Hotel	**H**
Sheraton Old San Juan	**K**

local artists – exhibits here are usually of a very high standard, so it's well worth a peek. At the end of the *paseo* lies a large fountain topped by *Raíces* (1992), an exuberant bronze sculpture by Spaniard Luis Sanguino symbolizing Puerto Rico's diverse cultural roots. From the fountain you can continue walking along the edge of San Juan Bay at the base of the impressively solid city wall, **La Muralla**. Constructed in phases beginning in the seventeenth century, this vast sandstone barrier – which measures 20ft thick in places – was finally completed in 1782.

Eventually the walls are breached at the **Puerta de San Juan**, a short stroll north of the fountain, the last remaining of six red-painted wooden city gates. Completed in 1635, and also known as the Water Gate, this was once the main entrance to the city for officials arriving by boat. You can re-enter the old town here, or continue along the waterside via **Paseo del Morro** as far as the

69

headland beneath El Morro – a much better (and cooler) option at sunset. You'll notice plenty of feral cats along the way: San Juan's colony of felines at one time numbered over four hundred, though it's gradually being reduced (see Ⓦ www .saveagato.com).

Once through the gate, **Caleta de San Juan** leads straight up towards the cathedral, its canopy of tropical trees, vines, and flowers making it one of the prettiest streets in the city. The **Casa Museo Felisa Rincón de Gautier** (Mon–Fri 9am–4pm; free) stands on the left-hand corner, the elegant former home of the first woman to become mayor of San Juan. Doña Felisa (1897–1994), as she was also known, is still admired on the island for her support of women's rights and for the modernization of San Juan that she oversaw during her 22 years as mayor (1946–68). Her foundation has maintained the house in superb condition, cramming it with photos, personal effects, awards, period furniture, and other memorabilia.

From the museum walk up the street parallel to the city wall and you'll see **Plazuela de La Rogativa** on the left, a tiny plaza overlooking the bay, which features a striking bronze sculpture by Lindsay Daen, a New Zealander who spent the last forty years of his life in Puerto Rico (he died in 2001). The sculpture, completed in 1971, is a memorial to the defeat of the British fleet in 1797. Legend has it that the hapless Brits mistook a religious procession (*rogativa*) led by the bishop and his female followers as reinforcements and decided to retreat, but there's no evidence that the incident actually took place.

From the plaza, head up the inclined street opposite (Calle de Rafael Cordero) into the **Jardines de Casa Blanca** (Tues–Sun 9.30am–5.30pm; free). This half-overgrown, terraced retreat is usually deserted and littered with climbing vines, clumps of hibiscus, and sweet-smelling jasmine – walk through it and you'll reach the back entrance of Casa Blanca.

Casa Blanca

Nowhere is more resonant of San Juan's Spanish colonial past than **Casa Blanca** (the White House; Tues–Sat 9am–4pm; $3). For 250 years the romantic hill-top mansion served as the residence of the descendants of Juan Ponce de León, the first governor of Puerto Rico, though he never lived here himself.

▲ Streets of Old San Juan

The first house was built in 1521 by his son-in-law Juan García Troche but was destroyed by a hurricane two years later, and what you see today dates from 1530. San Juan's nascent community of rough and ready colonizers grew up around its gleaming white walls, party to all the intrigues, plots, and brawls of the early conquistadors.

The unruly spirit of that early colony is conveyed in the stories of the site's entertaining guides, who'll provide a brief introduction to its rambling wings before allowing you to explore solo. The compact interior of old brick floors and mahogany beams is surprisingly homey, and has been carefully restored in sixteenth-century style with odd bits of period furniture, paintings, and maps. Peek through the windows to appreciate its commanding location, with a magnificent panorama of the bay through the palm-filled gardens outside.

El Morro

One of the greatest forts in the New World, the Castillo San Felipe del Morro, more commonly known as **El Morro** (June–Nov daily 9am–5pm; Dec–May daily 9am–6pm; $3 fee valid for 24hr, under-15 free; $5 with San Cristóbal, valid for 7 days), looms over the Atlantic with virtually impregnable stone walls, testimony to Spain's grim determination to defend the island over the centuries – it also proved an ideal stand-in for the terrifying slave fort in the movie *Amistad* (1997). Today El Morro is a UNESCO World Heritage Site and part of the **San Juan National Historic Site** (Ⓦ www.nps.gov/saju), managed by the US National Park service.

A short walk from Casa Blanca, the fortress occupies a dramatic spot at the top end of Old San Juan, with six levels of rock-solid defensive positions featuring the distinctive "hornwork" shape, 140ft high in places. From here it dominates the mouth of San Juan Bay, a superb strategic location that made it almost impossible to capture, especially when its fire power was combined with the small but deadly **El Cañuelo** fortress (still visible) on the other side.

Established as a small gun battery in the 1540s, El Morro was constantly expanded, and the imposing defenses you see today were completed in 1787, thanks in large part to an enterprising Irishman in the pay of Spain, **Thomas O'Daly**. The fort's defensive record is certainly impressive, and it was captured only once – by the English in 1598. Sir Francis Drake is probably the most famous flop, failing to take the fort in 1595, an event celebrated in the museum and site video, where he is repeatedly (and, more or less accurately) described as a "pirate."

You'll enter the fort at the **main plaza**, surrounded by vaulted rooms that once served as officers' quarters, magazines, and storerooms. Some of these have been converted into a small **museum** of the site and a **video room** (daily 9am–4pm; English video every 30min). From the main plaza you can clamber over the battlements above and below, taking in the stunning panoramas of the bay and cityscape to the east. The top level features the two "horns" of the Ochoa and Austria Bastions, both designed to protect the fort from landward attack, as well as the lighthouse, which dates from 1845 but was rebuilt in 1908. Lower down, the Santa Bárbara Bastion once contained the castle's largest gun battery, sticking out into the bay like the prow of a battleship.

The fort is separated from the rest of the old town by a swathe of green grass, which has no official name but is commonly known as **El Campo**, or just the "Area Verde." The US military used it as a nine-hole golf course until 1961, but now it's a popular place to **fly kites** – come here on a blustery weekend and the sky is jam-packed with them. To join in, buy one from the stalls nearby.

La Perla

La Perla is the ramshackle *barrio* just beyond the cemetery, hugging the Atlantic coast below the city walls. It's been one of San Juan's most deprived areas since the eighteenth century, when it became the refuge of city outcasts as well as the poorer families of soldiers stationed at El Morro. It won notoriety in 1966 as the subject of *La Vida*, Oscar Lewis's controversial study of poverty on the island, and in 2006 it was one of the locations for the movie *El Cantante*, the place where salsa legend Héctor Lavoe came to shoot heroin. While it's true that some of La Perla's inhabitants make a living from crime (and drugs are a problem here), they rarely pose a threat to tourists. In fact, locals observe a strict street code – harming outsiders brings unwanted police attention. Having said that, there's little reason to voyeuristically wander the area's narrow streets. You can meet some of the local characters in **La Callejón** (the alley), a cluster of bars at the northern end of c/Tanca, back in the old town above La Perla – it's best if you speak Spanish. Bars such as *El Adoquin del Patio* are usually quite safe and on Friday nights attract a boisterous, friendly crowd with live music and plenty of cheap rum.

Cementerio Santa María Magdalena de Pazzis

Wedged between the city walls and the Atlantic on the north side of the *campo*, the **Cementerio Santa María Magdalena de Pazzis** (daily 7am–3pm; free) is one of the most picturesque sights in San Juan, its ornate but tightly packed marble tombs and monuments backed by an immense span of blue stretching far into the horizon. The best views are from the walls above, but to get inside the cemetery walk through the road tunnel at the northeast corner of the *campo*. Although it's located near La Perla (see box above), there are caretakers on duty and it's usually safe to visit here during the day.

The cemetery was established in 1814, though its current form dates from 1863, when it became the resting place for some of Puerto Rico's most eminent citizens. The most famous person buried here is **Pedro Albizu Campos**, leader of the Puerto Rican Nationalist Party (see p.363). His marble tomb is marked by two national flags in a corner of the old section. Nearby is the grave of **José de Diego**, topped with a bust of the poet and independence advocate. Look out also for doctor and pro-statehood politician **José Celso Barbosa**, buried in a family tomb in the modern section of the cemetery, on the left side of the main path as you enter, and **Gilberto Concepción de Gracia** (1909–1968), founder of the Puerto Rican Independence Party (PIP). Note that the infamous pirate **Roberto Cofresí** (see p.360), who was executed outside El Morro in 1825, was buried somewhere on the *campo* – criminals could not be laid to rest inside the cemetery.

Museo de las Américas and Plaza del Quinto Centenario

One of San Juan's most absorbing museums, the **Museo de las Américas** (Tues–Sun 10am–4pm; Ⓦwww.museolasamericas.org; free to $5 per exhibit) is a thoughtful collection of art and anthropology relating to Puerto Rico and the Americas as a whole. Facing El Morro on the other side of the *campo*, the museum occupies the Cuartel de Ballajá (the old Spanish barracks), a grand, three-story imperial structure built between 1854 and 1864, and arranged around a wide central courtyard.

The museum has three permanent exhibitions. *El indio en América* is a poignant introduction to 22 indigenous American tribes, beginning with the **Taíno** and including others from South and North America. Explanations are in Spanish and English, the well-presented exhibits embellished by bronze statues created by Peru-based artist Felipe Lettersten. *La Herencia Africana* is an enlightening look at the **West African** origins of the region's black population, as well as the horrific **slave trade**; a particular emphasis is placed on Puerto Rico, naturally, and the numerous slave rebellions up to abolition in 1873. Note, however, that there are no English explanations, making this room a bit dull if you don't read Spanish. The third exhibition, *Las artes populares en Las Américas*, is an eclectic collection of traditional folk art from all over the Americas: furniture, tools, pottery, basketwork, religious artifacts, clothes, jewelry, and musical instruments. Other rooms are used for temporary exhibitions, usually paintings or artwork.

The eastern side of the Cuartel de Ballajá borders the **Plaza del Quinto Centenario**, opened in 1992 to commemorate the 500th anniversary of the "discovery" of the New World by Columbus. The centerpiece of the square is a forty-foot-high monument, designed by Jaime Suarez to look a bit like a totem pole and symbolizing the roots of American history.

Galería Nacional

Puerto Rico has produced a remarkably talented pool of artists over the centuries, and the modest but inspiring **Galería Nacional** (Tues–Sat 9.30am–4.30pm, Sun 10.30am–5.30pm; $3, free Tues) offers by far the best introduction to their work. The collection is enhanced by its romantic surroundings, the former Convento de los Dominicos, established in 1523 and now a series of beautifully presented galleries. You'll find the entrance on the eastern side of Plaza del Quinto Centenario.

Sala 1 begins with **caste painting** and the **viceregal art** of the eighteenth century, but the real highlights are in Sala 2, dedicated to icons **José Campeche** and **Francisco Oller** (see p.371). Though you won't see their most acclaimed paintings here, there are some great works on display (such as Oller's vivid still-life *Cocos*) and it's easy to appreciate the vast gulf that divides the two artistically, in part a reflection of how the art world had been transformed in the nineteenth century. Sala 3 highlights the early twentieth-century **Costumbrista** school, with its idealized view of rural Puerto Rico: **Ramón Frade**'s *El Pan Nuestro* (Our Bread) of 1905 is a memorable depiction of the *jíbaro* (Puerto Rican peasant farmer) and one of the best-known paintings in the gallery. There's also a small exhibition on *santos* carvings here. Sala 4 concludes with modern, abstract work of the 1950s and 1960s, with *La Mixta* (1960), **Fran Cervoni**'s haunting depiction of a meal in a local tavern, one of the highlights.

Plaza de San José and around

With an appropriately haughty statue of Juan Ponce de León at its center, the **Plaza de San José** seems a quiet and somewhat forlorn open space today, ringed by some of the oldest buildings in Puerto Rico. The square is just around the corner from the Galería Nacional, as the old convent adjoins the **Iglesia de San José** on the plaza's north side. The family church of Ponce de León's descendants and the oldest original church building on the island (construction began in 1523), it features fairly typical Spanish colonial architecture, though it's one of the few structures in the Western Hemisphere (along with the cathedral) that have late-Gothic elements: the stone stairs inside, not accessible to the public, and the ribbed vaults made from local stone. Painter **José Campeche** is buried inside, along with several of the early Spanish governors. Its most illustrious former inhabitant was Ponce de León himself, whose remains were returned here from Cuba in 1559. In a burst of Spanish nostalgia in the wake of the 1898 US occupation, the conquistador's remains were transferred to the Catedral de San Juan Bautista (see below) with much pomp and ceremony in 1908 – his statue had already been moved here from Plaza de Colón in 1893, to make way for the memorial to his former boss and rival (see p.77). Legend has it that the statue is made from melted down cannons captured from the British in 1797.

The eastern side of the plaza is bound by the Casa de los Contrafuertes, one of the oldest houses in San Juan, dating back to the early eighteenth century. Inside is the **Museo de Pablo Casals** (Tues–Sat 9.30am–4.30pm; $1), more of a memorial to the great Spanish cellist than a museum, displaying various awards on the first floor and an exhibition of related photography upstairs that tends to change every few months. Casals (1876–1973) moved to Puerto Rico in 1955, settling in Isla Verde, after becoming disillusioned with the Franco regime (his mother was from Mayagüez, on the west coast). He established the Puerto Rican Symphony Orchestra in 1957 and **Festival Casals** (Ⓦ www.festcasalspr.gobierno.pr; tickets $20–40) – the island's premier classical music festival – in 1956; it still runs from February through March every year.

Next door is the **Museo de La Raíz Africana** (Tues–Sat 8.30am–4.20pm; $2) which has a similar African focus as the Museo de las Américas (see p.72) and is also presented solely in Spanish, but with a slightly stronger, thought-provoking section on the slave trade. Grim displays (note the horrific *collar de hierro*, or "iron necklace") bring home the iniquity of slavery in general, and there's a detailed history of the trade in Puerto Rico. On a lighter note, it's also the best place to see the spiky, multicolored masks used in Loíza's **Fiestas Tradicionales de Santiago Apóstol** (see p.107) and to learn about the *bomba* and *plena* music and dance styles that evolved from African traditions (see Contexts, p.373).

Around the corner, housed in the former *mercado* building, the **Museo de San Juan** (Tues–Fri 9am–4pm, Sat & Sun 10am–4pm; free) offers a brief account of the city's history from its foundation in 1521 through to the present day, with a gallery of modest displays highlighting all the major political events as well as the earthquakes and hurricanes that periodically devastated the city. The building itself, constructed in 1855, is a wonderful example of colonial architecture, but the museum's small size is a little disappointing and there are no artifacts or objects, just descriptions and images. If you can't read Spanish, you might consider skipping it altogether – English leaflets are available but these are heavily abridged. The main entrance is on Calle de Norzagaray facing the ocean, but you can also use the back entrance at the end of Calle Mercado, off Calle de San Sebastián.

Plaza de Armas and the cathedral

Once the center of the city and home to a teeming market, **Plaza de Armas** is a far more languorous affair these days, a pleasant, tree-lined square where locals meet to drink *kiosco* coffee, and visitors feed the flocks of *tranquilo* pigeons that loiter at each end.

To get here from the Museo de San Juan, retrace your steps along Calle Mercado and then head downhill along Calle de San José for three blocks. The northern side of the plaza is taken up by the arcaded facade and twin towers of the **Casa del Ayuntamiento** (City Hall), which was completed in 1799 and still houses local government offices. It's off limits to the public, but you can get a taster of the historic interior by visiting the **Galería San Juan Bautista** (Tues–Sat 9am–4.30pm; free), which occupies a section of the first floor facing the plaza, and showcases local artists.

Head west one block along Calle de San Francisco and turn right along Calle del Cristo to reach shady Plazuela de la Monjas, the oldest square in the city and dominated by the **Catedral de San Juan Bautista** (daily 8am–5pm; free;

Wwww.catedralsanjuan.com). Puerto Rico's first bishop, Alonso Manso, had the original wooden structure built in 1521, but it was destroyed five years later by a hurricane. The first stone cathedral was completed in 1549, though it's been reconstructed many times since and most of what you see today was part of a major restoration in 1917. Architecturally the cathedral is rather plain, but the interior boasts a few interesting features, notably a marble monument on the left side containing the remains of **Juan Ponce de León**, interred here in 1908. Nearby is a marble tablet marking the tomb of Alonso Manso (buried here in 1539), and on the other side of the aisle are chapels dedicated to Carlos Manuel Rodríguez, the first Puerto Rican to be beatified (see p.148), La Virgen de Guadalupe (patron saint of Latin America), and San Pío (Saint Pius), an early Christian martyr who was killed in the first century – a Puerto Rican bishop was permitted to bring back his remains (revered as holy relics) from Rome in the nineteenth century, said to comprise his teeth, bits of skull, and bones from his hands and feet. These relics are supposed to be part of a wax-covered mannequin of the saint, displayed in a glass case.

Opposite the cathedral, on the other side of the plaza, the **Museo del Niño** (Tues–Thurs 9am–3.30pm, Fri 9am–5pm, Sat & Sun 12.30–5pm; kids $5, $7; Wwww.museodelninopr.org) is a must-see if you're traveling with kids. The three floors are divided into themed areas, with the emphasis on hands-on learning: displays on the culture, geography, and ecology of Puerto Rico is the focus on the first floor, while the second floor features giant models of various parts of the body (heart, lungs, eyes, and mouth). The new third floor contains the NASA Space Place, with displays on the space shuttle and solar system, as well as exhibits on caves, hurricanes, and water.

La Fortaleza

Described as "half palace, half castle" by US President Theodore Roosevelt, **La Fortaleza** (Mon–Fri 9am–5pm, tours only; suggested donation $3; Wwww .fortaleza.gobierno.pr) is the oldest governor's mansion still in use in the Americas. Since Roosevelt stayed here in 1906 the main building has changed little, its elegant Greek Revival exterior contrasting with the solid stone remnants of the original fortress.

To reach it from the cathedral, head south two blocks along Calle del Cristo and turn right along Calle de la Fortaleza. Security is tight here, and the only way to visit the grounds is as part of a **guided tour**: buy tickets in the Antiguo Palacio de la Real Audiencia, the yellow-painted former Royal Court of Appeals building, on the south side of the street near the main entrance. There are usually at least two daily tours in English, at 9am and 3pm (more in high season), but only if it's not raining. Note also that the thirty-minute tour does not get you inside the main building – to do that you'll have to arrange a visit weeks in advance, in writing.

When construction began on La Fortaleza in 1533, the idea was that the building would serve as a fortress to defend the harbor. By the time it was finished in 1540, however, the Spanish had realized that its location was not ideal, and El Morro became the focus of subsequent defensive efforts. Initially the home of military commanders, it became the permanent residence of Puerto Rican governors in 1639. Over the years the house has been expanded, notably from 1853 to 1860, when it acquired its current palatial facade, but the core remains the original sixteenth-century fortress. Today it's a powerful symbol of the subordinate political status of Puerto Rico, its thick stone walls having sheltered over one hundred Spanish governors and several US presidents: in addition to Teddy Roosevelt, Franklin D. Roosevelt, Harry Truman, and John F. Kennedy all spent the night here.

The enthusiastic guides are a mine of information: you'll be shown the charming inner patio of the original building, site of the governor's offices (second floor) and living quarters (third floor; if the white flag is flying, the governor is in residence), before having a peek in the old dungeon and Saint Catherine's chapel. One of the oldest parts of the building is the circular fortification known as the Torre del Homenaje. This is where nervous governors would swear an oath of fidelity to the ruler of Spain in times of crisis, presumably to guarantee loyalty, particularly during one of the city's many sieges. The second tower, the Torre Austral, was added later. The tour ends in the pristine half-sunken **Spanish garden** that surrounds the house, with its Mudéjar fountain, Mango Patio, and wishing well.

Parque de las Palomas and around

Perched at the southern end of Calle del Cristo, **Parque de las Palomas** (daily 7am–6pm; free), a pleasant garden overlooking the walls, is aptly named considering the great flocks of pigeons that congregate here (*palomas* means "doves"). Next to the park at the end of the street, the tiny **Capilla del Santo Cristo de la Salud** (Tues 11am–3pm; free), established in 1753, is a much venerated place of worship, with a beautiful altar of silver repoussé work, laden with silver and gold ex-votos – offerings left in gratitude for good health granted by the saints worshipped here. The chapel is said to mark the spot where a horse rider was thrown over the walls and miraculously survived. Abandoned by the early twentieth century, it was restored in 1927. Look out for the two oil paintings by José Campeche inside.

Nearby at no. 255, the **Casa del Libro** (Tues–Sat 11am–4.30pm; free; Ⓦ www .lacasadellibro.org) is a repository of over five thousand aged books, with around two hundred of them created before 1501, mostly in Spain. Walk east along Calle de Tetuán from here and just beyond Calle de San José, at no. 155, is **Casa Ramón Power y Giralt** (Tues–Sat 9am–5pm; free), named after the Puerto Rican patriot who was born here in 1775. Ramón Power represented the island at the Cádiz Cortes in Spain in 1810, and died there in 1813 (see p.359). Today his house is the headquarters of the **Conservation Trust of Puerto Rico** (Ⓦ www.fideicomiso.org), which has a shop and a mildly

Cockfights

Cockfighting is one of the most traditional, and controversial, pursuits in Puerto Rico, a blood sport which dates back to the Spanish colonial period and is vigorously defended by its chief supporters (see p.41). The main arena for cockfights in San Juan is **Club Gallistico de Puerto Rico**, at Avda Isla Verde 6600 (Tues–Fri 4–10pm, Sat 2–10pm). Ringside seats are $20–35 (plus tax), but the $10 seats higher up provide perfectly adequate views. Women are welcome, though in practice you won't see many inside.

After being weighed and given a brief "warm-up," the two combatants are released and the fight begins, accompanied by frenetic shouting around the ring as bets are placed. You'll hear cries of "azul, azul!" (blue) for one, and "blanco, blanco!" (white) for the other, followed by the amount being waged – white or blue ribbons denote which rooster is which. Fights run almost continuously throughout the day and last a maximum of fifteen minutes each, or until one of the roosters can no longer stand (you'll rarely see them die in the ring). It's certainly a unique experience, but be warned: the roosters really do peck the hell out of each other, and the arena floor can become smeared with blood – the whole thing may be too disturbing for some to watch. The main season is January to May, so check in advance at other times.

interesting exhibition room highlighting some of the island's major ecological issues, as well as traditional musical instruments and a handful of Taíno artifacts (on loan from the Smithsonian). Labels are in Spanish only, but English information sheets are available.

From here you can keep walking east to the other side of the old town, or head down Calle del Recinto Sur back to the marina and **Casa Don Q** (Mon–Fri 9am–6pm; free), just across from Pier 1. The San Juan outpost of distinguished Ponce rum-maker Destilería Serrallés (see p.290) houses a small exhibition about the company, as well as a bar where you can sample its award-winning rums for free.

Castillo de San Cristóbal and around

Guarding the eastern side of the old city, the **Castillo de San Cristóbal** (daily: June–Nov 9am–5pm, Dec–May 9am–6pm; $3, valid for 24hr; under-15 free; $5 with El Morro, valid for 7 days), built in stages between 1634 and 1790, is the largest colonial fortress in the Americas. The entrance is near the northern city walls on Avenida Boulevard del Valle, at the end of Calle del Sol.

The fort, with its panoramic views from the battlements, is worth a look even if you've been to El Morro, despite the fact that most of what you see today is also the work of engineer Thomas O'Daly. In contrast to El Morro, San Cristóbal protected the land approaches to the city, and it's a fine example of the principle of "defense-in-depth," where each section of a fort is supported by one or more other parts, making it virtually impregnable. Inside, exhibits outline the history of the fort and particularly the **Fixed Regiment**. Established in 1765, this was one of the first local battalions ever to be raised in the Spanish colonies, and they were instrumental in the defeat of the British in 1797 (see p.359).

Just south of the fort is **Plaza de Colón**, once the location of the main landward gate into the city, and renamed in 1893 to honor Christopher Columbus on the 400th anniversary of his "discovery" of Puerto Rico; his marble statue tops a column in the center of the square. The pale-pink Neoclassical building on the south side of the plaza is **Teatro Tapia**, completed in 1834 to mimic the lavish Italian opera houses of the period. Its graceful wooden interior is undergoing an ambitious renovation that should be complete by 2009 – stop by to find out what's showing. The theater is named after **Alejandro Tapia y Rivera** (1826–1882), the local playwright known as the "Father of Puerto Rican literature" (see p.377). On the eastern edge of the plaza is the **Antiguo Casino**, constructed in 1917 in opulent French Second Empire style; today it's a government reception center.

Beach districts

East of the old town, resorts and posh condominiums line the Atlantic almost as far as Piñones, well outside the city limits. Each of the coastal neighborhoods has its own distinct character, but there's little in the way of traditional sights - the main attraction is undoubtedly the **beach**.

Closest to Old San Juan is **Puerta de Tierra**, a rather dingy *barrio* that nevertheless contains some of the island's most important government buildings and the grandiose **Capitolio**, its legislature, the only sight along the coast that has nothing to do with the water. The small beaches here are surprisingly undeveloped, perfect for an easy excursion from the old town.

The amusement park atmosphere begins in earnest at **Condado**, San Juan's oldest resort neighborhood, an area gradually recovering some of its former ritz thanks to some hefty investment. You'll find a quieter scene at **Ocean Park**, a little further on, a shady residential area with a smattering of choice hotels and restaurants. Finally, **Isla Verde** is the smartest and newest of the resort zones, with the best beach and a happening scene at the weekends, fueled by some of the city's most fashionable nightlife.

Although San Juan's beaches can't compare with the pristine stretches of sand elsewhere on the island, it's hard to beat the sheer diversity of activities on offer: you can **swim** everywhere, take **diving**, **fishing**, or **kayaking** excursions, **surf** several decent breaks, **windsurf** at Ocean Park, and **jet-ski** at Isla Verde. Note however that these are still city beaches and that overcrowding and trash can be a problem, especially at the weekends. Foreign tourists are often additionally frustrated by afternoon rain showers, possible year-round – do as the locals do, and just ignore them.

Puerta de Tierra

To the east of Old San Juan lies **PUERTA DE TIERRA**, a mixture of government offices and low-rent residential neighborhoods. It also has one of the

---

Surfing San Juan

The local **surf** scene in San Juan is well established, and with the coast taking an almost constant battering from the Atlantic Ocean, there are plenty of enticing breaks to suit all levels.

Beginners should make for **Pine Grove**, a beach break in **Isla Verde** (in front of the *Ritz*), which has small waves and a sandy bottom. If you're a little more experienced, **La Ocho** should pose no problems: you have to paddle out a bit and there's a rocky bottom, but the water's deep and it's popular with long boarders – note, however, that when the swell's up La Ocho can get quite nasty. You'll find it just west of Escambrón beach in **Puerta de Tierra**.

In **Condado**, **La Punta** offers a mix of shore and reef breaks and fast waves, while **La Concha** is fast and very hollow, popular with body-boarders. For a real challenge, experienced surfers should head off the Balneario de Carolina for **Caballos**, a right reef break with some of the biggest waves on the island. It's popular with wind-surfers but a long 20 to 30 minutes paddle if you can't get a jetski to pull you out there.

The **best surfing** in the area is actually in **Piñones** (see p.105), on the eastern edge of the city. Be warned, however, that the main breaks here are normally packed at the weekends and the local surfers can get very territorial. First up is **Chatarras**, a hollow, fast reef break, not far from the last line of *kioscos* off PR-187 (see p.107), and suitable for experienced surfers only: the swell is not consistent but when it gets up you'll score some excellent tubes. Next is **Playa Aviones**, a more consistent reef break in shallower water suitable for most levels, while **Tocones** is a short beach break with fast waves popular with body-boarders, though you should watch the currents here.

La 8 Surf Shop (Mon–Sat 10am–6pm; ☎787/723-9808, ⓦwww.la8surf.com), at Avda Ponce de León 450 in Puerta de Tierra (near La Ocho), is one of the best in the city, selling, fixing, and renting boards ($25/3hr; $50/day), as well as arranging lessons with a couple of pro surfers. You can also contact the instructors yourself: William "Chino" Sue A Quan (ⓦwww.wowsurfingschool.com, ☎787/955-6059) and Fernando Alvarez (ⓦwww.prsurfingschool.com, ☎787/426-8219) are both good teachers who are used to dealing with both beginners and more experienced surfers. Lessons are around $50 per person for 1hr. **Veluano** (see p.84) also offers surf lessons from $50/hr and rents boards from $35/day.

In Condado, **Lost Surf**, at Avda Ashford 1129, stocks surf wear, while **Costazul Surf Shop**, Avda Condado 64 (Mon–Sat 10am–6.30pm, ⓦwww.costazulsurfshop.com), also offers lessons and board rental in addition to surfing gear. It has a branch in Old San Juan at c/San Francisco 264 (daily 9am–7pm). In Isla Verde make for **Surf Face**, in La Plazoleta shopping court (Mon–Sat 9am–9pm, Sun 11am–5pm ☎787/791-6800), for a good selection of surf gear and boards.

best-kept secrets in the city: the narrow but sheltered **beach** below El Capitolo, which is just a short walk from the old town. Steps opposite the legislative building lead down to the beach, a thin strip of sand that's rarely busy. At the far eastern end of the district, the **Balneario El Escambrón** (facilities open daily 8.30am–5pm; parking $3) incorporates one of the city's better beaches, with golden sand, a decent restaurant, toilets, and plenty of shady palm trees. Separated into two sections by a headland topped by the **Batería del Escambrón**, a small gun emplacement completed in 1801, the western end of the beach is popular with surfers (see opposite), though most of it is protected from the waves by a barrier of rocks. The eastern section shares a small lagoon with the *Hilton's* private beach and is ideal for swimming.

El Capitolo

The impressive marble bulk of **El Capitolo** (daily 8.30am–5pm; free) is just a short walk east of Plaza de Colón along Avenida Juan Ponce de León. Constructed between 1925 and 1929, it remains the home of Puerto Rico's legislature and well worth a visit, not least to admire the lavish ornamentation inside and out. The official entrance faces the ocean on Avenida Muñoz Rivera: you should be able to pick up a guide here for a short but animated tour of the building (free).

Loosely modeled on the US Capitol in Washington, DC, El Capitolo is certainly an opulent piece of architecture, with 22 kinds of marble used inside and the dome lined with 24-carat gold leaf, originally costing $2–3 million in the 1920s – the estimated value of the building today is an astounding $100 billion. The most impressive section is the rotunda, which contains the original nine articles of the Puerto Rican Constitution in glass display cases. The carved marble panels that ring the walls represent key elements of Puerto Rican political history, beginning with the Taíno and ending with the signing of the 1952 Constitution, while the four giant mosaics in the dome above represent the arrivals of Columbus in 1493 and Juan Ponce de León in 1508, the abolition of slavery in 1873, and autonomy in 1898. The House of Representatives sits on the west side of the rotunda, the Senate to the east – both have public viewing galleries on the third floor where you can watch live sessions (Mon–Fri). The chambers are color-coordinated: the Senate has burgundy chairs and carpets, while the House uses green.

Condado

The once snazzy resort of **CONDADO**, just across the mouth of the lagoon from Puerta de Tierra, became an affluent suburb of San Juan in the early twentieth century and was the first part of the city to be developed for tourism. After a long period of stagnation, the area is undergoing a remarkable renaissance: though it still feels shabby in places, the whole strip is humming with new construction and vast, luxury resorts are being created in a bid to regain its former glory. Even so, behind the beach, Condado remains a relatively wealthy community of high-rise condos and there's not much to see.

Avenida Ashford is the main strip, running behind the beach from Puerta de Tierra to Ocean Park and lined with fast-food outlets, shops, and restaurants. The first beach you'll see coming from the old town is **Balneario Playa del Condado**, a small piece of sand facing the sheltered lagoon with clear water and a convenient place for a quick dip. Beyond here the narrow strip of hotels faces a rocky shoreline and, further along, **Playa Condado** proper starts at **Plaza de La Gran Ventana al Mar**, a new park opposite the junction with

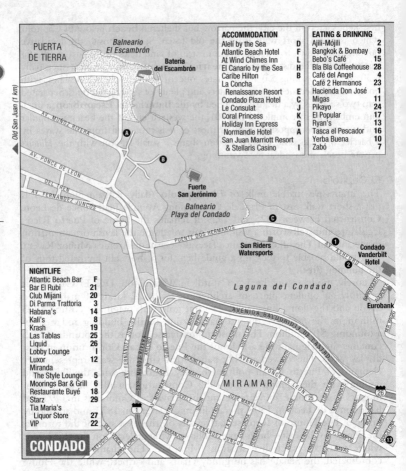

ACCOMMODATION

Aleli by the Sea	D
Atlantic Beach Hotel	F
At Wind Chimes Inn	L
El Canario by the Sea	H
Caribe Hilton	B
La Concha	
Renaissance Resort	E
Condado Plaza Hotel	C
Le Consulat	J
Coral Princess	K
Holiday Inn Express	G
Normandie Hotel	A
San Juan Marriott Resort	
& Stellaris Casino	I

EATING & DRINKING

Ajili-Mójili	2
Bangkok & Bombay	9
Bebo's Café	15
Bla Bla Coffeehouse	28
Café del Angel	4
Café 2 Hermanos	23
Hacienda Don José	1
Migas	11
Pikayo	24
El Popular	17
Ryan's	13
Tasca el Pescador	16
Yerba Buena	10
Zabó	7

NIGHTLIFE

Atlantic Beach Bar	F
Bar El Rubi	21
Club Mijani	20
Di Parma Trattoria	3
Habana's	14
Kali's	8
Krash	19
Las Tablas	25
Liquid	26
Lobby Lounge	I
Luxor	12
Miranda	
The Style Lounge	5
Moorings Bar & Grill	6
Restaurante Buyé	18
Starz	29
Tia Maria's	
Liquor Store	27
VIP	22

CONDADO

Avenida Magdalena. While the sand is thick and golden, it can get dirty and there's not much shade. Loungers can be hired for \$3 (per day).

Ocean Park

Beyond Avenida José de Diego, the hustle and high-rises of Condado peter out into the tranquil, residential community of **OCEAN PARK**. The **beach** here is far more attractive than Condado's: it's wider, less busy, and backed by a thin line of palm trees, though it also attracts its share of trash – it's still a city beach after all. The reef offshore means the water is usually far calmer here, making it ideal for **windsurfing** and **swimming** (see p.84); the only downside is that the beach is slightly harder to reach by bus and there are fewer amenities nearby. The beach starts to thin out as it reaches the Punta Las Marías headland – on the other side lies Isla Verde.

Isla Verde

Lining the coast along Avenida Isla Verde just beyond Ocean Park, **ISLA VERDE** is another brash resort of malls, self-contained hotels, and international

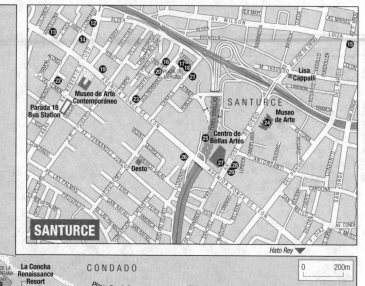

SANTURCE

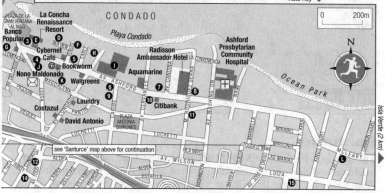

restaurants. While this is a highly sanitized version of Puerto Rico, it's newer and more upmarket than Condado, and the palm-tree fringed **beach**, split in half by the rocky Punta El Media headland, is the best in the city. It's wide with fine sand and gentle waves, and the proximity of so many stylish hotels and beach bars creates a party atmosphere at the weekends, attracting a diverse crowd of well-heeled locals, *reggaetón* fans, and plenty of cocktail-sipping tourists.

The beach can be accessed via passages between the condos (opposite the footbridges over the main road), or Calle Tartak halfway along. Once here, you can hire loungers for $4, or grab a jet ski at the eastern end of the beach from Water Toy Rental ($60/30min; over-21s only). Further east, beyond the *Courtyard* hotel, the beach merges into the **Balneario de Carolina**, the most popular public beach for local families. Though there are showers here, and weekends volleyball tournaments, the beach is otherwise marred by the steel poles sticking into the water (to deter jet skis) and the jets taking off from the airport across the road. From here it's a short bus ride into Piñones (see p.105). Isla Verde falls under Carolina municipality and is very close to the international airport, just to the southeast.

81

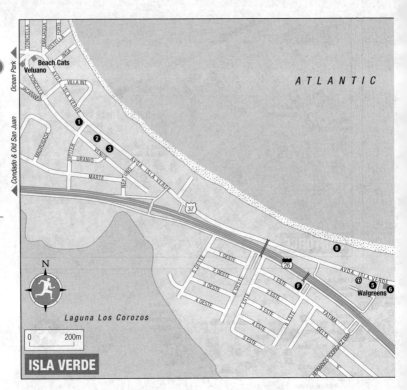

ATLANTIC

Beach Cats
Veluano

Laguna Los Corozos

N

0   200m

ISLA VERDE

Walgreens

Santurce

The working-class *barrio* of **SANTURCE** lies behind the main beaches, a gritty neighborhood that offers a refreshing contrast to the tourist zones on the coast. From the 1920s to the 1950s it was a thriving commercial district, home to one of the island's most successful baseball teams and crammed with fine Art Deco buildings. Hard times in the 1970s led to increased crime and the steady migration of its middle class to the suburbs, and by the 1980s it had become dilapidated and run-down. In recent years the area has been undergoing much needed regeneration, with a couple of excellent **art museums**, an exuberant **nightlife**, and plenty of cheap **places to eat** along central Avenida Ponce de León.

Museo de Arte Contemporáneo and around

The **Museo de Arte Contemporáneo** (Tues–Sat 10am–4pm, Sun noon–4pm; free; Ⓦ www.museocontemporaneopr.org), housed in the tastefully restored Edificio Histórico Rafael M. de Labra on the corner of Juan Ponce de León and Avenida Roberto Todd, holds temporary exhibitions of often bold and experimental post-1940 art from Puerto Rico and elsewhere in the Caribbean. Although the temporary shows sometimes take up every gallery, you may still see pieces from the museum's permanent collection, including the photography of Néstor Millán Alvarez and some of the best abstract work from José Morales. The building – a former public school built in 1918 – is an attraction in itself, its striking red-brick galleries surrounding a bright, glass-covered courtyard.

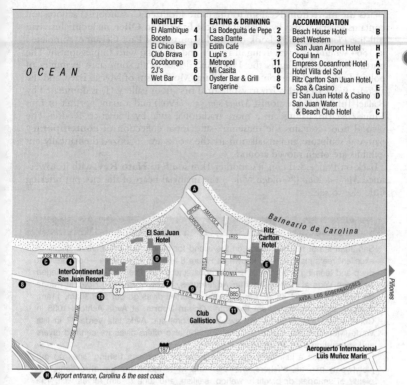

NIGHTLIFE		EATING & DRINKING		ACCOMMODATION	
El Alambique	4	La Bodeguita de Pepe	2	Beach House Hotel	B
Boceto	1	Casa Dante	3	Best Western	
El Chico Bar	D	Edith Café	9	San Juan Airport Hotel	H
Club Brava	D	Lupi's	7	Coqui Inn	F
Cocobongo	5	Metropol	11	Empress Oceanfront Hotel	A
2J's	6	Mi Casita	10	Hotel Villa del Sol	G
Wet Bar	C	Oyster Bar & Grill	8	Ritz Carlton San Juan Hotel,	
		Tangerine	C	Spa & Casino	E
				El San Juan Hotel & Casino	D
				San Juan Water	
				& Beach Club Hotel	C

OCEAN

Balneario de Carolina

El San Juan Hotel

Ritz Carlton Hotel

JOSE M. TARTAK

InterContinental San Juan Resort

Club Gallistico

Aeropuerto Internacional Luis Muñoz Marín

▼ ⓗ, Airport entrance, Carolina & the east coast

From the museum it's a short walk south along Juan Ponce de León then left up Calle Dos Hermanos to the **Plaza del Mercado**, where a vibrant indoor **market** (Mon–Sat 5am–5pm, Sun 5am–noon) is surrounded by a collection of fashionable places to eat and drink known as **La Placita** (see p.102). The market contains mostly fruit and vegetable stores and retains a distinctively local character despite the growing number of tours that come through here. Try the *Cocos Bien Frios* stall for fried snacks, *batidas* ($3), and *agua de coco* (coconut juice) sold by the half-gallon ($5).

Museo de Arte

Displaying the finest ensemble of Puerto Rican art on the island, the **Museo de Arte** (Tues & Thurs–Sun 10am–5pm, Wed 10am–8pm; $6, free Wed 2–8pm; Ⓦ www.mapr.org) is housed in another graceful structure blending Neoclassical styles, built in 1920 and originally serving as a hospital. The gallery is a short walk east of the market, on Avenida José de Diego. The museum's two floors are arranged thematically, in roughly chronological order from the seventeenth century to the present day. Start in Gallery 6, in the southern wing on the first floor, which has a modest display of *santos* (carved wooden figures representing the saints), followed by Gallery 7, featuring religious art of the seventeenth and eighteenth centuries. The highlight here is the piercing, anonymous image of the **black Christ**, *El Señor de Esquipulas* (1690–1710), recalling the sacred icon of the same name in Guatemala. Gallery 8 contains a few devotional paintings from eighteenth-century Rococo master **José Campeche**, while Gallery 10 charts the move from Realism to the more idealized Costumbrista school, and contains several works by celebrated artist **Francisco Oller**, including his vivid still-life *Plátanos* (1893). Look out for his portrait of Paul Cézanne, completed in 1864 when Oller was living in France and dabbling with Impressionism. The northern wing highlights the 1950s and 1960s, with some rare examples of political poster art, the sometimes chilling Modernism of Myrna Báez, and the abstract work of Carlos Irizarry. The final first-floor gallery (1) is dominated by Rafael Tufiño's Expressionist *Mujer son gato* (1968) and a giant portrait of Luis Muñoz Marín, painted in a more traditional style by Francisco Rodón. The second floor contains the museum's substantial collection of **contemporary** painting, sculpture, and installation art; the works are organized thematically, but exhibits are often moved around.

Back on Ponce de León, it's another 1km south to **Hato Rey**, with its tower-lined *Milla de Oro* ("Golden Mile") the financial heart of the city, but offering little else to see.

Watersports in San Juan

San Juan is not the best place on the island for **diving**, but there are a couple of excellent reefs just offshore, known as Figure 8 and the Horseshoe – both are 30ft deep and teeming with tropical fish, octopus, and squid. The best outfit is managed by Karen Vega at **Caribe Aquatic Adventures**, in the *Normandie Hotel* in Puerta de Tierra (☎787/281-8858). Pre-arranged escorted dives go out at 9.30am, 11am, 2.30pm, and 4pm daily from the hotel. **Ocean Sports**, at Avda Ashford 1035 in Condado (☎787/723-8513, ⓦwww.osdivers.com) and Avda Isla Verde 77 in Isla Verde (Mon–Sat 10am–6pm; ☎787/268-2329) also offers dives for certified divers and **snorkeling** trips off San Juan.

San Juan has a justifiably good reputation for deep-sea **fishing**: lines go out just twenty minutes offshore, with blue and white marlin the top attractions, but plenty of snapper, dolphinfish, wahoo, sailfish, and tuna to aim for as well. The most professional expeditions are arranged by **Mike Benítez' Marine Services** (☎787/723-2292, ⓦmikebenitezfishingpr.com) and depart the Club Náutico de San Juan on Avenida Fernández Juncos, at the eastern end of Puerta de Tierra. Charters for a maximum of six people cost $555 for a half-day or $185 per fisherman and $85 per passenger.

Laguna del Condado is ideal for **kayaking**: **Sun Riders Watersports** (Mon–Fri 1–6pm, Sat & Sun 9am–6pm; ☎787/721-1000) rents kayaks for $15/hr. You'll find it opposite the *Condado Plaza Hotel* on Avenida Ashford, behind the parking lot on the banks of the lagoon, though if it's raining hard they won't open.

For **windsurfing**, head to Punta Las Marías (east of Ocean Park) and the four-mile reef about half a mile out, which is one of the best wave-sailing spots on the island. To get started, visit **Velauno** at c/Loíza 2430 (☎787/728-8716, ⓦwww.velauno.com), close to the top end of Isla Verde and five blocks from the beach. This huge shop is the primary wind- and kite-surfing center in the city. Beginner lessons go for $100 for two hours while rental boards (full kit) are $75/day; kiteboards are $40/day. Nearby is **Beach Cats**, at c/Loíza 2434 (ⓦwww.kitesurfpr.com), another wind- and **kite-surfing** specialist that organizes lessons ($150/2hr) and rents boards.

If you fancy something less energetic, seek out **San Juan Waterfun** (☎787/643-4510, ⓦwww.waterfun-pr.com), which organizes all manner of beach activities, from parasailing and jet-skiing to snorkeling and kayak rides. Based on the beach in front of the *El San Juan Hotel* in Isla Verde, they offer free pick-up from other hotels.

On a final note, many companies that run **boat trips** from Villa Marina and Puerto del Rey on the east coast offer transport to and from San Juan (see p.133).

▲ Isla Verde Beach

Río Piedras

Founded in 1714 and incorporated into San Juan in 1951, **RÍO PIEDRAS** is a low-rise residential district south of Hato Rey (12km from Old San Juan), home to the main campus of the **Universidad de Puerto Rico** (Ⓦ www.uprrp .edu) and the city's largest **market**. Thanks to the university, you'll also find a high concentration of Spanish **bookstores** along Avenida Ponce de León, south of the campus.

The university is worth a visit for the illuminating **Museo de Historia Antropología y Arte** (Mon, Tues & Fri 9am–4.30pm, Wed & Thurs 9am–8.30pm; free), just inside the main entrance on Avenida Ponce de León (buses stop outside the gate). Though it's small, the galleries here contain a number of very significant artifacts, including some enigmatic **Taíno** finds from around the island. Exhibits from the permanent collection tend to rotate, but highlights include the mystifying stone collars, ritual objects thought to be connected to the ball game (see p.215), and the tiny carved seats known as *duho*. The museum also has an extensive collection of art, including **Francisco Oller**'s masterpiece, *El Velorio*, an agonizingly moving depiction of a wake in rural nineteenth-century Puerto Rico. Jumping continents, you'll find a rather gruesome pair of Egyptian **mummies** (with mummified cat) incongruously displayed in the reception area. Before moving on, check out the striking **Torre Franklin D. Roosevelt**, clearly visible above the main university buildings, a clock tower constructed in 1937 in Spanish Revival style with an ornate facade and intricately patterned ceiling.

It's a short walk southeast of the university to the **Plaza del Mercado** (Mon–Fri 6am–5pm, Sat 6am–1pm), an indoor market on the edge of the busy commercial centre of Río Piedras. Though it's primarily a collection of fruit and vegetable stalls, you'll come across fascinating *botánicas* selling all sorts of herbal remedies, as well as a collection of cheap **cigars** at *Tabaco Don Bienve* ($0.40 *petite*, $3.75 Churchills). The real highlight, however, is the **food court** at the back, where almost every Puerto Rican dish is served up at bargain prices: try *El Tropical* for *batidas* and *Doña Alice* for chicken and stews.

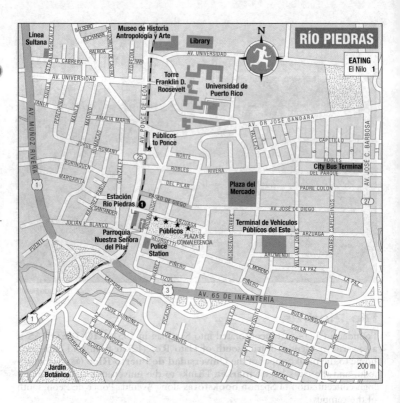

If you still have energy, hike over to the **Jardín Botánico** (daily 8am–5pm; free), a serene enclave of gardens and tropical flowers, especially noted for its magnificent orchids. The entrance is on the south side of the junction of PR-1 and PR-847, a ten-minute walk south of Río Piedras Tren Urbano station.

Eating

San Juan has a well-deserved reputation as the **culinary capital** of the Caribbean. The city is loaded with restaurants showcasing everything from international haute cuisine and classy Nuevo Latino cooking to American diners and humble canteens serving tasty *cocina criolla*, the perfect introduction to the island's own rich gastronomic traditions.

When it comes to food, **Old San Juan** offers the most diversity and some of the best restaurants on the island. Meals can be expensive here, but there are plenty of cheap options and the scene is by no means solely tourist oriented – most of the people eating here will be locals, especially in the mornings or evenings. The cheapest places are the stalls around **La Casita**, where you can usually pick up *alcapurrias* and *bacalaítos* for less than $2, or the *kioscos* in Plaza de Armas: *Kiosko 4 Estaciones* on the northwest side is open 24hr and sells pastas, sandwiches (less than $5), and excellent coffee. You'll also see stalls selling home-made ice cream and refreshing *piraguas* (shaved ice with flavored syrup) all over the old town: these items are safe to eat, though you might be charged $2 (locals rarely pay more that $1.50). The most fashionable restaurants in the city are located in Old San Juan's **SoFo** ("South Fortaleza") district, offering superb fusion and international cuisine in equally elaborate premises. For **self-catering** or picnics, stock up at the *Pueblo* supermarket on Plaza de Armas (Mon–Sat 6am–midnight, Sun 6am–6pm).

The beach areas of **Condado** and **Isla Verde** also boast a number of excellent and conveniently located restaurants, while cheaper, no-frills diners can be found in **Santurce**, and there are plenty of fast-food outlets if you get desperate, particularly along the main avenues in Condado and Isla Verde.

Note that most restaurants in SoFo and many of the hotels have some sort of **dress code**, especially in the evening – "casual attire" such as shorts for men and beach wear in general is frowned upon, though in practice women usually receive more leeway.

Old San Juan

Amadeus c/San Sebastián 106 ☎787/722-8635. One of San Juan's fusion cuisine pioneers, showing Spanish, Italian, and African influences with a Puerto Rican twist: try the fried plantain with caviar, dorado ceviche, or tempting range of fritters. Order mains ($20–30) or simply share the appetizers, tapas-style. The interior feels more Spanish than anything else, with local art and full-length mirrors on the walls, and the space morphs into a popular bar after 9pm. Reservations recommended. Closed Mon lunch.

Aquaviva c/Fortaleza 364. Small but stylish SoFo trend-setter with an eclectic menu of international seafood and an azure blue color scheme. Specialties include fresh oysters, ceviches, Caribbean coconut shrimp ($14), and sharp, perfectly mixed martinis. The presentation is sensational – try a seafood tower (from $34). No reservations, dinner only.

Ben & Jerry's c/Cristo 61. The Vermont ice cream franchise is a deservedly popular stop in the old town, offering all the usual, addictive flavors and high-quality ingredients in a cozy, relaxed environment. Cones and cups come in three sizes ($3–5).

Blend c/Fortaleza 309 ☎787/977-7777. This bar, lounge, and restaurant features an elegant interior of plush crimson seats and booths, and a blend of Mediterranean, Asian, and Puerto Rican cuisines: sumptuous tuna tartare, lamb chops, lobster ravioli, and sweet-soy steak. You'll spend at least $30. Live jazz Wed 8pm–midnight and DJs playing upbeat garage at the weekends. Dinner only, closed Mon & Sun.

La Bombonera c/San Francisco 259. Established in 1902, this is one of the city's most atmospheric and oldest cafés, with a long bar, diner-style tables, and waiters dressed in white shirts, red bow-ties,

▲ Plaza del Mercado

and jackets. The place gets packed at weekends, especially for breakfast, when scrambled eggs or *mallorcas* (toasted pastries filled with bacon, ham, or cheese and dusted with icing sugar; $1.50–5.25) are served with rich mountain coffee (check out the vintage steamed-milk machine).

Brickhouse c/Tetuán 359. Slightly scruffy US-style grill and bar that knocks out succulent ribs ($15–20), zesty wings, and juicy burgers ($7–10). The bar does specials on Miller beer ($2.75) and holds a decent range of rums, closing at 7am at weekends. Open from 4pm weekdays.

Café Puerto Rico c/O'Donnell 208. This cozy restaurant makes a fine introduction to *cocina criolla*, with attentive service, rich *asopaos* ($10–15), plenty of seafood, and 13 choices of *mofongo*: the national dish is served here as a giant hollowed-out bowl of cassava, plantain, or banana, stuffed with codfish, crab, prawn, or lobster. Jugs of potent *sangría* (made with rum) are $28 and the guava *flan* is fresh and bursting with fruit. The interior feels like a friendly Spanish *taverna*, and there are a few tables on the plaza.

Cafeteria Mallorca c/San Francisco 300. Open since 1961, this endearing diner is the less fusty cousin of *La Bombonera*, with uniformed but laid-back waiters and an army of loyal regulars enjoying the cheap breakfasts, fluffy *mallorcas* ($1.50–2.75), and solid, great-value meals at lunch (under $5). Eat at one of the small Formica tables or at the bar. Closes 6.30pm.

Dragonfly c/Fortaleza 364. One of the most innovative restaurants in San Juan, fusing Caribbean classics with Asian flavors. Try Mongolian beef *ropa vieja* ($18), Peking duck nachos with wasabi sour cream ($20), or marinated *churrasco* with "dragonflies" (shoestring potatoes). Order several dishes and share tapas-style. The ruby-red Chinese dining room was inspired by 1930s Shanghai. No reservations, so be prepared for a wait. Closed Sun.

Fratelli c/Fortaleza 310 ☎787/721-6265. SoFo's outstanding Italian restaurant is a stylish, romantic retreat, replete with Renaissance frescoes and giant mirrors on the walls, a lovely antique bar and a narrow patio with palm trees at the back – from around 10pm it becomes more like a hip lounge bar. Feast on *risotto di mare* with squid and assorted shellfish, and the luscious pork fillet with gorgonzola and pears (mains run from around $15–25).

La Mallorquina c/San Justo 207 ☎787/722-3261. Founded in 1848, this is the oldest restaurant in the city (and probably in the Americas). It's pricey, but the refined colonial setting, marble floors and antique-littered dining room make this place a must-try – check out the giant Czech vases made in 1810. *Asopao* is the specialty here, the soupy rice dish served with chicken or seafood in small "kettles" for $14–18, but don't miss the sensational vanilla *flan* ($5), *piña coladas* ($6), and jugs of *sangría* ($28). Closed Sun.

Mojito's c/Recinto Sur 323. An ideal spot for a hearty, good-value Puerto Rican lunch – try the *bacalao guisado* (codfish stew) for $9.50 or the ubiquitous *mofongo* served with chunks of fried pork. Close to the marina and extremely popular with local office workers. Despite the name, it's not a great place for a drink.

El Picoteo *El Convento Hotel*, c/Cristo 100 ☎787/723-9202. This refined Spanish restaurant overlooks the old convent's tranquil courtyard, justly popular for its pricey tapas such as *jamón serrano* ($13.50) and sardines ($11). It also serves the best *paella* on the island and a playful selection of "Spanish" pizzas such as the *Picasso*, loaded with Kalamata olives, anchovies, caramelized onions, and goat's cheese. Closed Mon.

Parrot Club c/Fortaleza 363. Always busy, the main draw here is the salsa-soaked party atmosphere, though the clientele tends to be an older tourist crowd. The kitchen serves up excellent Nuevo Latino combos from a menu that's written in "Spanglish" – Cuban and Mexican classics are given an American slant. Try the huge, succulent legs of roast pork or fabulous seared tuna. Service and presentation is top-notch, but it's pricey (mains $25–30) and the famous house *mojitos* ($7.50) are a little overrated. No reservations, so come early.

Restaurante El Jibarito c/Sol 280 ☎787/725-8375. Set in a quiet corner of the old town, this recreation of a rustic mountain diner offers a nostalgic slice of traditional Puerto Rico: a simple wooden interior, daily specials, and hearty *comida criolla* such as the oven-baked pork with sweet plantains, mouth-watering ribs, and plantain tamales filled with pork. Most mains are under $10.

Sonné c/Fortaleza 358 ☎787/721-0136. Trendy SoFo restaurant that doubles as a fashionable lounge bar at the weekends, with an extensive list of tropical martinis such as "key lime pie." The food is "international creative," which means just about any dish given a Puerto Rican touch: chicken curries, shrimp risotto, soba noodles, and tuna tacos. Mains are reasonably priced at $17–25, but the space is best for couples, as tables are small. Live jazz Sat 9pm–midnight. Dinner only.

Spanglish c/Cruz 105 ☎787/722-2424. For delicious Puerto Rican food, away from the crowds in more intimate surroundings, try this cozy, unpretentious little restaurant, with photos of salsa stars on the walls and a small menu that includes house specials *serenata de bacalao* (cod with vegetables), *chuletas* (pork chops), and *cazuela de garbanzo* (bean stew) from $6.95.

Tío Danny's c/Fortaleza 313. Welcoming restaurant with a small wooden bar and dining room facing the street, with more space in the attractive *patio interior* at the back. The menu offers a mixture of solid Mexican food and beautifully crafted local classics such as *mofongo* ($12–19), but this is also a popular place for a drink – *sangría* is $5 and draft *Medalla* is $2.50.

Trois Cent Onze (311) c/Fortaleza 311 ☏787/725-7959. Posh French restaurant with a striking facade of Mudéjar tiling, a stylish interior embellished with white drapes and a slightly 1920s colonial feel. The menu is Provençal, with tongue-tingling classics such as *foie gras* ($19), mango and crab salad ($11), and the perfectly seasoned *Bouillabaisse 311* ($26), as well as a fabulous French wine list. Dinner only, closed Sun.

Puerta de Tierra

🏃 **El Hamburguer** Avda Muñoz Rivera. Since it opened in the 1940s, just up the hill from Escambrón beach, this local barbecue shack has built up a loyal cult following thanks to its flame-grilled burgers, the best in the city. The home-made main event comes in several varieties, the patties roasted over an open fire and served with skinny fries ($2.50–3). Gets jam-packed at weekends.

Condado

🏃 **Ajili-Mójili** Avda Ashford 1006 ☏787/725-9195. One of San Juan's true culinary gems, the place to come for a boldly upmarket interpretation of traditional Puerto Rican food, set in an opulent Spanish Revival villa. The large, seasonal menu is heavy on seafood, and the weekend buffets are superb. Try the *mofongo* specials, *asopaos*, or more substantial grills such as the *lechón asado* (roast pork); mains run $25–30.

Bangkok & Bombay c/Caribe 58 ☏787/721-1390. Anyone craving Indian or Thai food should make for this smart restaurant, just off Avda Ashford. You can't go wrong with the *tom kha gai* (soup) or *murgh tikka masala*, though everything here is fairly authentic. Sat dinner only, closed Mon.

🏃 **Bebo's Café** c/Loíza 1600 ☏787/726-1008. Another neighborhood institution, this Dominican-owned cafeteria sits behind the beaches on the edge of Ocean Park. The menu includes hearty portions of *comida criolla* classics such as *mofongo*, but also an incredibly filling *pastelón de amarillos* (fried plantain pie stuffed

with meat) for under $10. It's also a good place for Mexican-style breakfasts (under $5). The buzzing dining room is large and air-conditioned, but always packed at lunchtime.

Café del Angel Avda Ashford 1106. One of the best bets for reasonably priced Puerto Rican food on the main strip, though it's worthwhile only if you haven't got time to venture further afield. Decent choice of the usual *mofongo* (from $9.95), rice dishes and a large menu of more substantial island favorites (mains from $8.95). Closed Tues.

Hacienda Don José Avda Ashford 1025. Mexican and Puerto Rican standards are served in an open dining room overlooking the ocean at this spot at the western end of Condado. It's a smart choice for an early breakfast, and the lunch specials ($6.95) are good value, but otherwise it's rather overpriced (*burritos* $15, *fajitas* $17.95) – you're paying for the waterside location.

Migas Avda Magdalena 1400 ☏787/721-5991. Located in the most dazzling building in Condado, a Mudéjar-inspired mansion decorated with ornate carvings and Moorish tiling. The sophisticated menu offers haute cuisine and fusion dishes such as coffee-and black-pepper-crusted lamb chops, and crispy duck breast with coconut curry. Mains are $15–30, but trendy *sanjuaneros* also come here just for drinks.

Yerba Buena Avda Ashford 1350 ☏787/721-5700. Popular bistro knocking out Caribbean and Cuban classics such as *ropa vieja* (shredded beef) and yam fritters with creole hot sauce, but best known for its authentic *mojitos* and live Cuban music Thurs–Sat. Dinner only, closed Mon.

🏃 **Zabó** c/Candina 14 ☏787/725-9494. Easily the most enticing place to eat and drink in Condado. It's set just off Ashford, in a rustic wooden *criollo* house away from the traffic, with an inventive, snappy menu of international dishes created by lauded chef Paul Carroll. Highlights include the Puerto Rican Sampler, the smoked fish blinis, mini beef Wellingtons, and steamed pork dumplings, but there are also burgers, pastas, and local classics (mains $15–27). Closed Mon.

Ocean Park

Dunbar's Avda McLeary 1954. This Ocean Park stalwart opened in 1982 and serves lunch and dinner (sandwiches, pastas, burgers from $8), sushi on Wednesdays and a great brunch on Sundays. It doubles as a lively pub with pool tables and lots of cozy nooks and crannies; check out the happy hour Mon–Fri 5–7pm.

Kasalta Avda McLeary 1966. This venerable bakery and café has long self-service counters where you can choose various pastries, cakes, and local snacks (from $1), though real aficionados come here for the legendary coffee. The *Cubano* sandwiches ($7.25) and Spanish-style *tortilla* (omelet) are excellent $3, and there's good-quality *jamón serrano* from Spain.

Pamela's c/Santa Ana 1, *Número Uno Guest House* ☎787/726-5010. This is one of the most appealing (and romantic) places to eat in the city, with an indoor section and tables right on the beach. The menu comprises delectable Caribbean- and Puerto Rican-inspired dishes with a contemporary edge: gems such as jalapeño- and ginger-sautéed shrimp, and marinated chicken sandwiches with cheese and roast red peppers.

Pinky's c/María Moczo 51 ☎787/727-3347. Perfect for a wholesome brunch before hitting the beach, this bright café is justly popular with expats and locals alike, all addicted to the playful, eclectic menu of comfort food such as pork plantains, hummus, vegetarian specials, and various wraps: check out the Porno Surfer (turkey, salami, and Swiss cheese sandwich) and Bondage Burrito.

Isla Verde

La Bodeguita de Pepe Avda Isla Verde 35. Worth a try for its tempting *comida Cubana* (Cuban food such as *palomilla* steaks), as well as the vast range of cocktails and *mojitos* on offer. It's a modern, trendy place with live music Fri & Sat, and happy hour Tues–Thurs 5–9pm. Closed Mon. Lunch Thurs, Fri & Sun only.

Casa Dante Avda Isla Verde 39 ☎787/726-7310. A simple dining room just off the main road, but an excellent place for *comida criolla* and especially the house specialty, *mofongo* – this is the self-styled "Casa del Mofongo" after all. The *camarones* (shrimps) and wine list aren't bad either. Closed Mon.

Edith Café Avda Isla Verde (near the *El San Juan Hotel*). This basic cafeteria is the best choice for solid Puerto Rican food in the eastern end of Isla Verde. Cooks up huge breakfast plates ($3.50), *chuletas* (pork chops, $7.95), and lip-smacking *carne frita con arroz y habichuelas* (fried pork with beans and rice, from $9.95). Don't get confused: the pictures of Guilin, China, on the walls were a gift and having nothing to do with the cuisine. Open 24hr.

Lupi's Avda Isla Verde 6369. It's a bit touristy, and doubles as a sports bar, but this lively Tex-Mex-style restaurant is an easy option near the big hotels, offering an appetizing array of *fajitas*, *nachos*, and *burritos*. Expect live music and a raucous crowd most evenings.

Metropol Avda Isla Verde, next to *Club Gallistico* ☎787/791-4046. Local institution, established in Santurce in 1965, specializing in Cuban and Puerto

Rican food. The menu is littered with mouth-watering dishes, but try the avocado salad, *gallinita relleno* (guinea hen stuffed with a rice-and-black-bean mixture called *congri*), or the *Fiesta Cubana* ($13.95) for a taster of several Cuban favorites (*tamales*, pork, cassava). The *asopaos* ($16.95) are also excellent.

Mi Casita La Plazoleta shopping court, Avda Isla Verde (near the *El San Juan Hotel*). A genuinely good-value Puerto Rican café, with ham and egg breakfasts for under $4 and all the *comida criolla* favorites ($5–12), but don't overlook the substantial octopus salad and selection of soups, especially the sublime garlic shrimp. Tends to get swamped with guests from nearby resorts at lunch, looking for a local experience.

Oyster Bar & Grill Avda Isla Verde 6000. New Orleans-inspired restaurant, serving up substantial bowls of jambalaya ($15.95) and decent burgers ($6.95), as well as the signature oysters (flown in from the mainland) from $11.95 per half-dozen. Open daily from noon till 2 or 3am weekdays and 7am weekends, when it transforms into a lively bar and salsa club.

Tangerine *San Juan Water & Beach Club Hotel*, c/Tartak 2 ☎787/728-3666. Best place to splurge in Isla Verde: chic contemporary decor, attentive service, and Asian-American fusion cuisine conjured up by award-winning chef Nelson Rosado. Expect delights such as green banana roll of beef, crab tempura, or sumptuous Tribal Mongolian ribs (mains $22–30). Closed Mon.

Santurce

Café 2 Hermanos Avda Juan Ponce de León 1317. No-nonsense local diner, popular for its live music Fri & Sat from 9 or 10pm, usually salsa or *merengue*. Seafood and hearty plates of *comida criolla* staples dominate the menu, though the crispy barbecue chicken makes a satisfying lunch ($4.50). Open 24hr.

Bla Bla Coffeehouse Avda José de Diego 353. Friendly, modern café, conveniently located in between art museums and perfect for a pre-visit breakfast, coffee break ($1), or light lunch (salads, sandwiches, and burgers from $5). The refreshing strawberry, papaya, and melon *batidas* ($3.50) are superb. Mon–Fri 7.30am–3.30pm.

Pikayo Avda José de Diego 299, Museo de Arte ☎787/721-6194. Stylish restaurant serving exquisite Caribbean fusion cuisine concocted by award-winning chef Wilo Benet. Be mesmerized by dishes such as halibut with mashed apio (celeriac) and sautéed Japanese squid, served in chic dining rooms embellished with modern art. Mains run from $30–40. Closed Sat & Sun, Mon dinner only.

El Popular c/Capitol 205. One of the best cafés in La Placita, its Spanish-style dining room lined with old photos of the island's political *illuminati*. Service is slow, but the food is fresh and it dishes out some of the best *chicharrones de pollo* (fried chicken) and *olla Española* (Spanish beef stew) on the island. Beers are $1.25, and happy hour is 7–10pm. Closed Mon.

Ryan's Avda Juan Ponce de León and c/Barcelona. This renowned mobile food stall specializes in tangy buffalo wings ($5.25 for six) and fries, and is usually parked opposite the new Energy Department building. Closed Sat & Sun.

Tasca el Pescador c/Dos Hermanos 178 ☏787/721-0995. Another excellent restaurant in La Placita, with an antique wooden bar temptingly laden with all manner of exotic bottles. The Spanish-style menu specializes in fresh fish (try the fabulous salmon in guava sauce; $17.50), but this place is best for lunch or a very early dinner, as it closes at 6pm. Closed Mon.

Río Piedras

El Nilo Avda Ponce de León 1105. If the market stalls don't appeal (see p.85), try this down-to-earth cafeteria close to the Tren Urbano station in the heart of Río Piedras. It cooks up the best *comida criolla* in the area, and is an old student favorite. Try the sumptuous roast pork. Open for lunch and dinner Mon–Sat.

Drinking and nightlife

Going out in San Juan can be a raucous, all-night affair, with things especially crazy on weekends when **Calle de San Sebastián** in Old San Juan becomes jam-packed with revelers. It tends to get busy around 11pm and winds down after 3am, though many **bars and clubs** – especially in the beach districts – keep going well beyond dawn. Lovers of rum, cocktails, salsa, and, not least, thumping *reggaetón*, are particularly well catered for; in addition, the **gay scene** is the most sophisticated in the Caribbean. If you want something a little less intense, the large **resorts** offer plenty of activities as well, and you can always hit the **casinos** (see p.97).

Bars

Bars are scattered all over **Old San Juan**, but the highest concentration of late-night boozers can be found on **Calle de San Sebastián**. Note also that most of the SoFo restaurants double as fashionable lounge bars (see p.87). To get really local, hit **El Callejón** at the top of Calle de Tanca, where dive bars such as *El Adoquin del Patio* host an eclectic mix of oddballs and party-goers, or *Colmado Bar Moreno* at Calle del Recinto Sur 365, a Dominican liquor store that doubles as a bar, pumping out salsa and *merengue* most days and nights.

In **Condado**, the hotel bars overlooking the beaches are the best places for drinks (see p.64), but there are several pubs inland, and **Santurce** is just a short drive or walk away, home to some of the biggest clubs, a thriving gay scene, and the lively bar and restaurant area known as **La Placita**, centered on the Plaza del Mercado. Come here on a Thursday or Friday night, when the whole area becomes a wild salsa party. **Isla Verde** nightlife is fairly self-contained but just as animated, with most bars open until dawn, especially on weekends – here also many **restaurants** (notably the *Oyster Bar & Grill*) double as bars and discos (p.90).

Old San Juan

Amapola c/Norzagaray 280. Fairly quiet bar at the end of *El Callejón*, with a fantastic upstairs terrace overlooking the Atlantic – it's one of the best views in the city and a great place to start your evening. Serves *mojitos*, beers, and frappes, as well as a range of American and local food. Closed Thurs.

El Batey c/Cristo 101. This dive bar ("batey" is the Taíno word for ball-court) is a San Juan institution, with the walls plastered in graffiti and an eclectic clientele that ranges from cruise-ship tourists to wannabe *reggaetón* gangsters. Incongruously located across from the refined *El Convento*, it tends to get busy in the early hours. Daily 2pm–7am.

Café Celeste Callejón de la Capilla. A genuine *chinchorro*, or tiny hole-in-the-wall bar with a couple of tables outside, popular with workmen for breakfast and lunch, and open late for cheap drinks in the evenings. Pop in for a quick can of Medalla ($1.50) before hitting the posh restaurants on c/Fortaleza, or *Nuyorican* across the alley.

Café Hijos de Borinquen c/San José 151. This classic old town bar opened in 1954, and is the best place to get a sense of the area's Puerto Rican roots and culture, with plenty of faded memorabilia on the walls. Expect it to be empty till 10pm, but overflowing 1–2am. Closed Mon.

Café Seda c/San Sebastián 157. One of the most alternative bars on this busy strip, with a different theme every night, notably hip-hop (Mon), ska and reggae (Thurs), and a variety of live acts weekends.

Candela c/San Sebastián 110. A lounge bar that's worth a peek for its cool retro theme alone: each room is plastered with German-designed wallpaper reminiscent of 1960s pop art, in vivid tangerine and crimson shades, and the furniture is minimal – there are a few sofas and benches at the back. It gets busy late, and there's a resident DJ on Sat. Closed Sun.

Ku Lounge c/Fortaleza 314. Stylish lounge bar with comfy sofas, resident DJs, and a mix of mellow house and trance on weekends, when it becomes more like a club. Open from 10pm.

Maria's c/Cristo 204. This small bar has been around for over 40 years and is noted for its quality *piña coladas* and *margaritas* ($6). A former haunt of actor Benicio del Toro (his tipple of choice was banana frost cocktails), it's quite touristy these days, but serves decent Mexican food and a wickedly potent cocktail, *La Norta*.

Nono's c/San Sebastián 100. Basic *cantina*-style bar in a colonial building with high wooden ceilings, TVs, and a pool tables. It's often crammed with expats and boozing tourists on weekend afternoons, and late nights on Fri when it plays predominantly rock music.

Old Harbor Brewery c/Tizol 202. Only micro-brewery in town, just up from the dockside, with beers freshly brewed German-style in the

Home of the piña colada?

Synonymous with both tropical languor and the high-life, the **piña colada** was adopted as the national drink of Puerto Rico in 1978, thanks to the widely held view that it was created here over fifty years ago. The official claimant (recognized by the Puerto Rican government) is bartender Ramon "Monchito" Marrero, who is said to have created the drink while working in the former *Beachcombers' Bar* of the **Caribe Hilton** in 1954. However, if you visit the **Barrachina** restaurant at c/Fortaleza 104 in Old San Juan, a marble plaque on the street claims that Don Ramon Portas Mingot created the drink there in 1963.

The truth is that no one really knows who invented the cocktail – "piña coladas" were being made in **Cuba** at the turn of the century, where they literally were just non-alcoholic "strained pineapple". However, some aficionados claim the alcoholic version was mentioned in travel magazines as early as 1922 with reference to Cuba. The latter is definitely the home of the *mojito* and *daiquiri*, and perhaps the *piña colada* too – but just don't say that when you're in Puerto Rico.

Gay nightlife

San Juan is generally gay-friendly, and most clubs have gay nights. Much of the explicitly gay nightlife in the city once revolved around the gay-oriented hotels and bars in **Condado**, with the **Atlantic Beach Bar** (c/Vendig 1) especially popular on Sunday afternoons (after 4pm). These days, though, you need to head behind the beach to **Santurce** for a more cutting-edge club scene. Grab a drink before (or after) hitting the dance floor at **Tia Maria's Liquor Store**, Avda José de Diego 326, a dive bar with a small pool table, which is packed at weekends. You could also try *VIP* (formerly *Junior's Bar*), a gay-friendly local pub at Avda Condado 613 (Thurs–Sun 9pm–late), recognizable by its rainbow facade. Of the best clubs in the area, **Starz**, at Avda José de Diego 385 (Sat only), pulls in an overtly gay, extremely fashion-conscious crowd while **Krash** (Wed–Sat from 10pm), at Avda Ponce de León 1257, has been around for years (formerly *Eros*), with two levels and a metallic, industrial theme: look out for the rainbow flag and TV screens outside. Check out ⓦ www.orgulloboricua.net (Spanish only) or ⓦ www.gayfriendlytravel .com for the latest in gay news, events, and nightlife in the city.

copper-and-steel vats on site. You can order a decent spread of tapas and more substantial meals at either the small bar or from one of the tables. The beers, ranging from lagers and hoppy pale ales to robust, creamy stouts, are $4.50. Popular with locals and tourists alike.

Condado

Di Parma Trattoria Avda Ashford 1901, at Plaza de la Gran Ventana al Mar. This Italian restaurant serves reasonable food, but is best as a fashionable place to start or end your evening. Sip drinks on the terrace overlooking the park and beach, accompanied by suitably *Café del Mar*-inspired sounds: jazz (Thurs), house (Fri), and Afro-Cuban (Sat) – live music played Sat only.

Kali's Avda Ashford 1407. Extremely hip, dimly lit lounge bar, with minimalist chairs and sofas, a vaguely Asian theme, and stylish clientele. Closed Mon.

Miranda The Style Lounge Avda Ashford 1131 ☏ 787/723-8625 ⓦ www.mirandathestyelounge .com. It might seem odd dropping in to the local hairdressers for a house *sangría* ($5), but this trendy beauty salon doubles as a popular bar, made chic after pop diva Olga Tañón shot her video for *Bandolero* (2005) here. Closed Mon.

Moorings Bar & Grill Avda Ashford 1214 (across from the *Marriott*). US-style bar popular with tourists and college students (it's a big spring break venue). Though it's got two levels, drinking sometimes spills onto the street outside. Music ranges from hip-hop and disco to techno and pop: it becomes very club-like Thurs–Sat.

Isla Verde

El Alambique c/Tartak 102. If you're looking for a bar that overlooks the beach, but want to avoid

resort prices, try this no-frills place near the *Water Club* hotel. It's located at the base of a high-rise condo, but looks out onto the sand – grab a Medalla beer ($2 on Sat) or *piña colada* in a plastic cup. Hard to believe, but this was a hugely popular club in the 1970s, and the beach opposite is still known as "La Playa del Alambique."

Boceto Avda Isla Verde 2480. This restaurant opens for Spanish-inspired lunches and dinners, but after 11pm it morphs into an attractive lounge bar with live music. Inside are several elegant rooms decorated in different styles: there's a Neoclassical dining area, an Art Deco room with a colonial bar, and an outdoor terrace.

Cocobongo Avda Ashford 5940, corner of c/Hermanos Rodriquez Ema. Not quite as raucous as the legendary Cancún nightspot, but still a top place for drinking and dancing till the early hours, not far from the main resorts. Beer is $2.75 Thurs– Sun 11pm–2am, while at *El Taquito*, underneath, basic and cheap Mexican fare is served 24hr (*tacos* from $1.50). Closed Mon & Tues.

🏃 **Wet Bar** *San Juan Water & Beach Club Hotel*, c/Tartak 2 ☏ 787/728-3666. Seductive rooftop bar and lounge, with an excellent sushi bar and panoramic views of the city and beaches below – it's worth having at least one drink here in the afternoon, just to lounge on the white double beds. High prices keep the riff-raff out: it's $7.50 for beers and $10 for spirits. Latin nights on Thurs from 9pm, club nights Fri & Sat.

Santurce

Bar El Rubi c/Canals 213. This languid bar is a real slice of Caribbean mellow in the heart of the city, serving tapas and cocktails on weekends. Not as intense as places around the Plaza del Mercado. Thurs–Sat 7pm–3am.

Restaurante Buyé c/Canals 202 ☎787/725-4826. Cozy bistro serving *comida criolla*, but more popular as a basic bar with a small outdoor terrace and wooden tables. Good option if La Placita is too crowded.

Las Tablas (Centro de Bellas Artes), Avda Ponce de León 299. Theater restaurant that reverts to a lively bar most evenings, with stylish, contemporary decor. Closed Mon.

Clubs

The major **clubs** in San Juan tend to serve up the usual mix of hip-hop and house variants, but as elsewhere in Latin America, almost all of them splice in (or have nights dedicated to) Latino sounds such as **salsa**. This being Puerto Rico, there's also plenty of **reggaetón** around. *Club Brava* (formerly *Babylon*) at the *El San Juan Hotel* (Avda Isla Verde 6063; Thurs–Sat 10pm–3am; ☎787/602-8222, ⓦ www.bravapr.com; cover $8–15, free for hotel guests) is a good place to start, with its two floors, a main room, a more relaxed "ultra lounge" and a steady stream of glamorous clients. You'll need to dress up and bring ID to get in (over-21s on Fri, over-23s Sat).

Liquid, at Avenida Ponce de León 1420, is the latest club incarnation to grace this corner of **Santurce**, and not to be confused with the bar/club of the same name at the *Water Club* hotel in Isla Verde. As with many clubs in San Juan, the theme is Latino/Cuban, with aspirations to create a South Beach, Miami, vibe. The club is open on Friday and Saturday but also on Thursdays, when its infamous "Release" parties get going from 9pm ($11 entry). In **Old San Juan**, resident DJs at *Pink Skirt*, at Calle de la Fortaleza 301 (Mon–Sat 8pm–6am), spin upbeat electro-house throughout the week.

Reggaetón

You'll hear **reggaetón** booming out of SUVs, stores, and apartments all over San Juan, and though almost every nightlife venue will play the major hits, there are several places noted for the genre. Clubs are generally safe, though fights occasionally break out and *reggaetón* does attract its fair share of gangsters – but that's part of the appeal to hardcore fans. In **Old San Juan** try *Club Lazer* at Calle de la Cruz 251 (ⓦ www.clublazer.com), with three packed floors and *reggaetón* now dominating the DJ line-up Fridays and Saturdays; cover is usually $15, but women can get in free before midnight (Fri–Sun 10pm–4am). *The Noise*, in an old colonial-style house at Calle de Tanca 203, also has a popular Friday night party that attracts *reggaetón* celebrities. In **Isla Verde**, make for *2J's*, at Avda Isla Verde 5930, a small, edgier place specializing in hip-hop and *reggaetón* (Thurs 11pm–2am, Fri & Sat 11pm–5am). *Luxor*, at Avda Roberto Todd 1 (☎787/721-6129), is a large club in **Santurce** (but just a short walk from **Condado**) with a kitsch Egyptian tomb-like exterior replete with pharaonic statues. *Reggaetón* has become the staple here, with a very hardcore crowd: if you're a real fan it's worth checking out for a more raw experience, but things have got violent in the past (near closing time), so be careful. Note that many of the most innovative venues, such as *Club Dembow* at Avenida Campo Rico, are located in **Carolina**, but you'll need to be very committed (and preferably have a local friend in the know) to check these out – the scene changes monthly and places are hard to find, especially without a car.

Salsa

San Juan is one of the world's great centers of **salsa**, and if you love Latin dance you're in for a real treat. **Lessons** are a good way to get warmed up for **clubs** that specialize in salsa beats, but there are also **shows** and **live** performances,

Salsa lessons

If you're in town for a short visit but want to learn to dance salsa, your best bet is to call Coral del Mar Cruz at ℡787/507-1807 or 787/722-8810, who gives excellent lessons at the *Nuyorican Café* in Old San Juan (see below) for $10 per hour, $15 for a couple. Classes are usually held just before the club gets going, so you can put your newly learned moves into practice. With more time, you can visit one of the many salsa schools in the city, which are popular with locals and expats. The **Unique Style Dance Studio**, at Avda José De Diego 812 in Caparra Terrace, Guaynabo (℡787/299-9500), specializes in all styles of Latin dance, including salsa, *merengue*, and tango. Lessons for beginners cost $8 and usually run Tuesday and Thursday at 8pm; it's open Monday to Friday 3–10pm and Saturdays 11am–6pm (you'll need to take a taxi here). **Salzuumba** (℡787/342-6964, ⓦwww.salzuumba.com), in Santurce at Avda Ponce de León 1418, is easier to reach by bus and offers ten salsa lessons for $75. It's open Monday to Friday 6–9pm, and Saturday 10am–4pm. You can usually join **free lessons** on weekdays at the **Coliseíto Pedrín Zorrilla** on Avenida Eleanor Roosevelt (℡787/753-7845), near Plaza las Américas, but check times with the tourist office first.

many in the resort hotels, where you can watch popular salsa bands and professional dancers do the work. It's also worth checking with the tourist office for upcoming events and salsa **festivals**: the annual **Salsa Congress** (ⓦwww .puertoricosalsacongress.com) is usually held at the *El San Juan Hotel* every July. You can usually get tickets to watch the main competition for $10, while other performances cost $10–25. Note also that the *Oyster Bar* in Isla Verde (see p.90) turns into an energetic salsa club on Sunday nights.

Clubs and live music

El Balcón del Zumbador PR-187 km 5.2, Piñones ℡787/791-9902, ⓦwww.elbalcondelzumbador.com. It's worth heading out to Piñones for this jumping salsa joint alone, which hosts some fabulous live acts from the salsa and rumba worlds. It's usually open Fri–Sun from 6pm; you'll need to arrange taxis or drive to get here.

El Chico Bar *El San Juan Hotel*, Isla Verde ℡787/791-1000. The *El San Juan* is a hive of activity in the evenings, but the *Chico Bar* is the prime spot to hear live salsa, Latin dance, and assorted pop tunes; professional dancers often mingle with the crowds to show them how it's done. Popular with an older (and affluent) clientele.

Club Mijani c/Dos Hermanos 252, Santurce. This club, catering primarily to a 30-something crowd, is tucked in amongst the action in La Placita, absorbing the overspill of salsa-lovers from the restaurants and bars in the plaza from midnight on. Thurs is the main salsa night, while Fri feature a variety of Latin sounds. Arrange a taxi pick-up in advance if you want to hang out in this neighborhood.

El Criollo Expreso Martinez Nadal (PR-20) km 3.2, Guaynabo ℡787/720-0340. Renowned for showcasing the best salsa on the island, the live bands that play here every Wed & Fri (at 8 or 9pm) certainly get the crowds worked up into a dizzying salsa sweat. Cover is usually $5–10, but the real downside is the location: it's a long drive or taxi ride from the main tourist zones.

Habana's Avda Condado 303 ℡787/722-1919. This two-story, vibrant Santurce club is a much-loved stalwart of the salsa scene. Live bands play most Fri nights and free salsa lessons are offered on occasion (call to check). Tues–Sat 4pm–6am.

Lobby Lounge *San Juan Marriott Resort*, Condado ℡787/722-7000. The vast lobby of this usually packed hotel offers an accessible but slightly sanitized introduction to salsa. Live music, with salsa usually featuring heavily, is heard most nights, with accomplished house bands performing Fri–Sun at 10pm from a repertoire of various Latin styles.

Nuyorican Café c/San Francisco 312 (entrance on Callejón de la Capilla; no sign; ⓦwww.nuyoricancafepr.com). If you only visit one salsa club in San Juan, make it this one. Small, intimate, and extremely energetic, it's crammed most nights with loyal devotees enjoying the live salsa (Wed, Fri, & Sat), Latin dance (Sun), and a fusion of everything (Thurs), from samba to Spanish-guitar music (poetry readings feature on Mon.)

It's open from 7pm most nights, but there's not much point in getting there before 9pm: things wind down after 3am. Entry is free.

Rumba c/San Sebastián 152. Slightly bigger than *Nuyorican* and just as popular, pulling in a mixed crowd of locals, expats, and tanked-up tourists. It has live salsa most weekends from 10.30pm, but unlike *Nuyorican Café* relies on DJs spinning Latin sounds at other times: this is more like a traditional club where people come to drink and hook-up as much as dance. Open Thurs–Sat 9pm–4am. Cover is normally $15.

Entertainment

San Juan is one of the most important **cultural centers** in the Caribbean, with a hectic program of concerts, shows, and festivals year round. **Casinos** play a big part in the city's tourist industry, while **cinemas** show all the US blockbusters as well as Spanish-language films.

Performing arts

Everything from classical music and theater, to folk music, hip-hop concerts and cutting-edge performance art takes place in San Juan on a weekly basis. To get an idea of what's happening, check the local newspapers or ask at the tourist office. You can also check the websites of the two primary ticket vendors: **Ticket Center** (☎787/724–8321, ⓦ www.tcpr.com), and **Ticketpop** (☎787/294–0001, ⓦ www.ticketpop.com), which has an office opposite the Centro de Bellas Artes in Santurce (Banco Popular Bldg, Avda Ponce de León 1500).

▲ Le Lo Lai performance

Folk dance for free

The **Le Lo Lai** cultural program has been organizing performances of traditional Puerto Rican dance and music for over thirty years, and though it's aimed squarely at tourists, the performers are usually extremely proficient and fun to watch. It's also **free**, making it one of the best deals in town. The performances provide a taster of all the island's rich musical traditions from salsa and *danza*, to *bomba* and *plena*. Check with the tourist office or call ⓣ787/721-2400 (ext 2715) to ask about current programs. At the time of writing there were four performances in San Juan per week: Castillo de San Cristóbal, Old San Juan (Mon 6–6.45pm; included in castle entry fee; see p.77); Plaza de la Gran Ventana al Mar, Condado (Thurs 7–8pm & Sat 8–9pm); and Isla Verde Beach, c/Tartak (Fri 7–8pm).

It's definitely worth checking out at least one of the special **Le Lo Lai** performances (see above), but you should also catch the free concerts of traditional music held every Saturday (6–8pm) at the tourist office in Old San Juan, dubbed **La Casita Festival**. On Sundays you can watch the primarily elderly crowd of locals enjoying a more sedate afternoon of *bolero* and *trios* music as they dance gracefully on Paseo de La Princesa.

There are numerous concert and performance **venues** in San Juan, but the one with the most character is **Teatro Tapia** in the old town (see p.77). The **Centro de Bellas Artes**, on Avenida Ponce de León in Santurce, is a lavish, modern arts center with three theaters, and home of the Puerto Rico Symphony Orchestra (ⓦwww.sinfonicapr.gobierno.pr).

Cinemas

Caribbean Cinemas (ⓣ787/727-7137, ⓦwww.caribbeancinemas.com) operates several movie theaters in Greater San Juan. The closest to Old San Juan and Condado is the **Fine Arts Cinema**, at Avda Ponce de León 654, which shows independent or alternative films, and the **Metro** at no. 1255 in Santurce, featuring all the Hollywood blockbusters. Head to the screens at **Plaza las Américas Shopping Center**, Avenida Roosevelt (ⓣ787/767-4775), for a larger selection of US and international choices. Tickets are usually around $6–7.

Casinos

All the major hotels and resorts in San Juan have **casinos**, with flashing lights and vast swathes of Las Vegas-style slot machines. Note that many places don't offer much more than this, however, and only the fancier hotels provide the full range of card games, roulette, and the like. Top of the list is the 24-hour **Ritz-Carlton Casino** (ⓣ787/253-1700), inside the hotel in Isla Verde, with elegant 1940s decor, the largest floor in Puerto Rico and all the major games on offer. The **El San Juan Hotel & Casino** (daily 10am–4am; ⓣ787/791-1000) down the road comes a close second: this cavernous and opulent wood-paneled palace has the highest number of slot machines (336) and gaming tables (27) in the city, where you can indulge in craps, roulette, and Caribbean stud poker till the early hours. Cocktail service is available throughout the casino.

In Old San Juan make for the **Sheraton Old San Juan Hotel Casino** on the waterfront (c/Brumbaugh 100; daily 8am–4am; ⓣ787/721-5100), a welcoming place with similarly endless rows of slot machines and plenty of table games. Note that most casinos have a dress code for men (don't wear shorts).

Festivals

The most festive period to be in San Juan is over the **Christmas** holidays, when you'll hear **live music** everywhere: it's the best time to catch *cuatro* players and performances of *aguinaldos*, a type of Christmas folk music unique to the island, but based on traditional Spanish carols. *Aguinaldos* are performed by groups of singers known as *parrandas*, going from house to house much like carol singers in Europe or North America. On **New Year's Eve** half the city descends on the *campo* in front of El Morro to watch the sun rise amidst a real party atmosphere – bring a blanket and plenty to drink. On January 6 crowds gather in Old San Juan for **Three Kings Day**, featuring concerts and the governor handing out presents to children, while the official end to the exhaustive holiday season is marked by the **San Sebastián Street Festival** (Jan 18–21), with processions, craft stalls, and traditional food.

One of the city's biggest religious festivals – the **Fiestas Patronales de San Juan Bautista** – honors its patron saint St John the Baptist, with dancing, feasts, bonfires, parades, and more. At midnight on June 23 (the day before St John's Day itself), half the city can be found on the beaches, where revelers march backwards into the Atlantic three or seven times, to ward off bad luck and evil spirits. For a list of festivals see Basics p.35 and the *Festivals of Puerto Rico* color section.

Shopping

San Juan is a decent place to pick up general souvenirs, but it also attracts serious collectors looking for contemporary Puerto Rican art. The best streets for browsing in **Old San Juan** are **Calle del Cristo** and **Calle de La Fortaleza**, while for a more conventional experience, **Plaza Las Américas** (ⓦwww .plazalasamericas.com), on the western edge of Hato Rey, is the largest mall in the Caribbean, with JC Penney, Macy's, and Sears department stores, as well as all the other major US chains.

Antiques, arts, and crafts

The narrow streets of **Old San Juan** offer the best opportunities for **crafts and antiques**. You'll find everything from high-quality gifts, prints, and carvings, particularly *santos*, to colorful *vejigante* masks, and the usual line-up of tacky T-shirts and souvenirs. Unless stated otherwise, shops tend to open Monday to Saturday from 10am to 6pm.

El Alcázar c/San José 103. Lovely old store crammed with all sorts of antiques, including wooden carvings and *santos*, Spanish tiling, paintings, and even Asian and African statues.
Butterfly People c/Cruz 257, ⓦwww .butterflypeople.com. This unique shop sells mounted tropical butterflies from all over the world (gathered by humane means, not hunted), and displayed in stunning ensembles that range $40 to $1000 and more. Mon–Sat 10am–6pm, Sun 10am–2pm.
Le Calle c/Fortaleza 105. Enticing alley jam-packed with stores selling carnival masks, paintings, and all sorts of gifts, as well as the *Café El Punto* at the back, great for a quick coffee or snack.

El Galpón c/Cristo 154. Small place selling primarily Panama hats ($45), fine cigars, high-quality festival masks, and *santos*.
Ole c/Fortaleza 105. Next to the entrance of *La Calle* and specializing in Panama hats (from $40), as well as traditional string puppets and Puerto Rican posters.
Puerto Rican Arts & Crafts c/Fortaleza 204. This spacious two-story store is the most comprehensive repository of local arts and crafts in town, selling everything from hammocks, carvings, and cookery books to paintings and festival masks. Mon–Sat 9.30am–6pm, Sun noon–5pm.

Spicy Caribee c/Cristo 154, ⊛www .spicycaribbee.com. The owner of this store hails from St Lucia, and offers a taste of the West Indies through her home-made sauces (try the Banana Ketchup) and seasonings ($6–9 per bottle), as well as locally sourced Puerto Rican vanilla.

Art galleries

In recent years San Juan's **contemporary art** scene has really taken off, with a strong base of talented local artists and growing international interest. Many of the cutting-edge galleries are in **Santurce**, but there are plenty of showrooms in **Old San Juan**. For any galleries in the former, it's important to call in advance, as opening times tend to be irregular.

Old San Juan

Galería Botello c/Cristo 208 ⊛www.botello .com. This spacious, well-restored former home of Galician artist Angel Botello is now one of the best galleries in Old San Juan, with work from the Spanish painter and local, modern artists on display: Jorge Zeno, Myrna Báez, Nora Rodríguez Vallés, and others.

Mora c/San José 54 ⊛www.galeriamora.com. One of the most exciting galleries in the old town, displaying the bold, exuberant work of local artist Enrique Mora.

OBRA Galería Alegría c/Cruz 301 ☎787/723-3206, ⊛www.obragaleria.com. An extremely plush gallery dedicated to high quality Puerto Rican art, including the work of Domingo Garcia, Nick Quijano, Félix Rodríguez Báez, and Paris-based Ricardo Ramírez. You'll occasionally see gems from Francisco Oller here also.

Santurce

Desto c/Américo Salas 1400 ☎787/633-3381. Experimental collective founded in December 2005 and run by the three artists Raquel Quijano, Jason Mena, and Omar Obdulio Peña Forty. Call ahead to see what's being shown.

Espacio 1414 Avda Fernández Juncos 1414 ☎787 725-3899. Housed in a former tire warehouse, this is one of the most fashionable and avant-garde galleries in the city, though it only opens for special events or viewings arranged in advance. Featured artists include Jennifer Allora, Guillermo Calzadilla, Piotr Uklanski, and Peter Halley.

Galería Comercial Avda Fernández Juncos 1600 ☎787/726-1065 ⊛www.galeriacomercialpr.com. Another innovative gallery, housed in a pink concrete building, showing fresh, contemporary work from primarily young, local artists, but also painters from around the region. Exhibitors have included Michael D. Linares, Carolina Caycedo, and Fernando Pintado.

Books and CDs

Bookworm Avda Ashford 1129, Condado. Small bookshop selling titles in English and Spanish, with a special focus on gay interests and authors. Mon–Sat 10am–9pm, Sun 1–9pm.

Borders Plaza Las Américas. This megastore has by far the best selection of books in English and Spanish, with plenty on Puerto Rico: check the history and Latin American studies sections for a decent selection (including local fiction). Mon–Sat 9am–9pm, Sun 9am–5pm.

La Gran Discoteca Plaza Las Américas. This CD shop stocks a wide selection of both salsa and

reggaetón, as well as Latin pop, rock, and international music.

Librería Cronopios c/San José 255, Old San Juan. Quiet, cozy bookshop with a small selection of English titles, including some by Puerto Rican authors and books on various aspects of the island, including its history. Also sells local CDs.

Librería la Tertulia c/O'Donnell 204, Old San Juan, ⊛www.tertulia.com. Thoughtful selection of books in Spanish and English, including plenty on Puerto Rico. The main store is in Río Piedras at Avda Ponce de León 1002. Daily 9am–8pm.

Noche de Galerías

On the first Tuesday night of the month (usually Feb–May and Sept–Dec), San Juan's art galleries open their doors till late for the **Noche de Galerías**. It's become something of a party night, with gallery visits followed by drinking and eating till the early hours. Most galleries stay open till 11pm, but in Old San Juan places often close at 1 or 2am. Call ☎787/721-2400 or check at the tourist office for details.

Cigars

Puerto Rican cigars may not be as prized as their Cuban counterparts, but they're almost as good. Don Collins (ⓦwww.don-collins.com) is part of the Puerto Rico Tobacco Corporation, with a shop at Calle del Cristo 59 that sells some wonderful varieties, though like everything else here, they're not cheap. The *Puros Indios* are dipped in rum ($12.99 each) and taste sensational, while the *Lonsdale CF* are cured in vanilla. You can buy a selection box of their whole range from $19.80 for four and even tour the factory in Bayamón if you contact them in advance. *El Galpón* also stocks a good selection of Puerto Rican and Dominican cigars (see p.98).

Fashion

Young Puerto Rican designers are making quite a name for themselves, and San Juan is the best place to get a taster of the latest trends. For more information check out ⓦwww.sanjuanfashion.com, or attend **San Juan Fashion Week**, which usually runs twice a year, in March and September.

Bounce Plaza Las Américas. This is the most popular store in the city for *reggaetón* fans, selling all the hippest street fashions, including hand-painted graffiti T-shirts by US label Miskeen Originals.

David Antonio Avda Condado 69. Flashy eponymous boutique of a top local designer, with an eclectic range of stylish clothes for men and women. Antonio is best known for his loosely cut tunics, and "Neoclassical" designs.

Lisa Cappalli Avda José de Diego 151. The main boutique of one of the island's top female designers,

noted for her chic, diaphanous couture. It's a short walk south of c/Loíza and central Condado.

Nono Maldonado 2/F Avda Ashford 1112, Condado. Boutique offering elegant clothes for men and women, designed by the former fashion editor of NYC-based *Esquire* magazine and doyen of the local fashion scene.

Polo Ralph Lauren Factory Store c/Cristo 201. Popular with visitors looking to buy up items from this major US designer, at heavily discounted prices.

Listings

Airlines Air Canada ☎877/321-0173; Air Flamenco ☎787/724-6464; Air Sunshine ☎787/791-8900; American Airlines ☎800/981-4757; Cape Air ☎787/253-1121; Continental Airlines ☎800/231-0856; Copa Airlines ☎787/722-6999; Delta Airlines ☎800/221-1212; Dolphin Airlines ☎787/253-1005; Isla Nena Air Service ☎787/863-4447; JetBlue Airways ☎800/538-2583; Liat ☎787/791-1030; Northwest Airlines ☎787/253-1505; Seaborne Airlines ☎787/977-5044; Spirit Airlines ☎800/756-7117; United Airlines ☎800/426-5561; US Airways ☎800/622-1015; Vieques Air Link ☎888/901-9247.

Banks Finding banks and ATMs is easy in San Juan. Try Banco Popular at c/Tetuán 206 in Old San Juan, or at Avda Ashford 1060 in Condado; Citibank is opposite La Casita at c/Tanca 500 in Old San Juan (Mon–Fri 8.30am–5pm; ATM 24hrs; ☎1800/360-2484).

Bicycle rental B Bikes at Avda Isla Verde 4770 (☎787/727-1233) sells and repairs bikes, while

Hot Dog Cycling at Avda Isla Verde 5916 (☎787/791-0776, ⓦwww.hotdogcycling.com) rents mountain bikes for $30 per day and arranges guided tours.

Car rental Numerous companies rent cars in San Juan. The best deals are usually at Budget (daily 24hr; ☎787/791-0600, ⓦwww.budget.com) at the airport; and Charlie Car Rental at Avda Isla Verde km 0.7, Isla Verde (daily 24hr; ☎787/728-2418; ⓦwww.charliecarrentalpr.com) and Avda Ashford 890, Condado (daily 8am–5pm; ☎787/721-6525). Note that Charlie Car will pick you up from the airport for free, but the cars are all at the Isla Verde office. Avis is at the airport (☎787/253-5925) and in Condado, at Avda Ashford 1052 (☎787/721-4499; ⓦwww.avis.com); Hertz has 24hr desks at the airport (☎787/791-0840), in Condado at Avda Ashford 1365 (daily 7am–5.30pm; ☎787/725-2027), and at the *Marriott*, *Caribe Hilton*, and *Sheraton* hotels (daily 7am–noon & 1–4pm); National (☎787/791-1805, ⓦwww.nationalcar.com)

and Thrifty (☎787/253-2525, ⊛www.thrifty.com) are both at the airport. Local outfit AAA Car Rental (☎787/726-7350; ⊛www.aaacarrentalpr.com), in Isla Verde at Avda Isla Verde 5910, also offers good deals.

Consulates Canada, Avda Ponce de León 268, Hato Rey (☎787/294-1205); UK, Avda Chardón 350, Hato Rey (☎787/758-9828). For other countries contact your embassy in Washington, DC: Australia (☎202/797-3000), Ireland (☎202/462-3939), New Zealand (☎202/328-4800), and South Africa (☎202/232-4400).

Emergencies Dial ☎911.

Hospitals and clinics The most convenient hospital is Ashford Presbyterian Community Hospital at Avda Ashford 1451 in Condado (☎787/721-2160, ⊛www.presbypr.com), with a large emergency room and outpatient clinics.

Internet Old San Juan is littered with Wi-Fi hotspots where you can check the Internet for free, if you happen to have a laptop (*Starbucks* on c/Recinto Sur is the most congenial place); otherwise, try the Seafarer's House at c/O'Donnell 161 (Mon & Tues 1–8pm, Wed 10am–6pm, Thurs 10am–8pm, Fri 10am–6pm, Sat & Sun 11am–7pm; $0.08/min, $4.80/hr). This is a seaman's foundation and sailors get priority, but the computer terminals are open to the public. *Ben & Jerry's* also has two terminals ($3/15min, $5/30min). In Condado, try *Bookworm* at Avda Ashford 1129 ($9/hr or $3/20min) or *Cybernet Café* at Avda Ashford 1128 (daily 9.30am–11.30pm; $3/20min, $9/65min). In Isla Verde, try *Cybernet Café* at Avda Isla Verde 5575 (daily 9am–10.30pm; $3/20min, $9/65min).

Laundry In Old San Juan the *Lavanderia Café* at c/Sol 201 serves coffee ($1) and does your washing for just $2 for 18 pounds (daily 8am–8pm; closed Wed). In Condado try Condado Cleaners at Avda Condado 69 (Mon–Fri 7am–7pm, Sat 8am–5pm; $2.50 per pound, minimum $4).

Left luggage In Old San Juan, Audio Guía on the marina in front of the bus station will hold bags daily 8am–5pm, while the *Barrachina* restaurant at c/Fortaleza 104 will look after bags for free,

weekends only. Car rental companies will usually let you leave bags in their offices for a few hours if you want to look around before your flight.

Pharmacies Walgreens (⊛www.walgreens.com) has big stores at Plaza de Armas (corner of c/Cruz and c/San Francisco) in Old San Juan (Mon–Fri 7am–10pm, Sat & Sun 8am–10pm), Avda Ashford 1130 in Condado (24hr), and Avda Isla Verde 5984 (24hr).

Police ☎787/343-2020.

Post office Old San Juan Branch, Paseo de Colón 100 (Mon–Fri 8am–4pm, Sat 8am–noon); in Condado, Avda Magdalena 1108 (Mon–Fri 8.30am–4pm, Sat 8.30am–noon).

Scooter rental San Juan Motorcycle Rental has locations in Old San Juan (Covadonga Parking Lot 6, opposite Pier 4, ☎787/722-2111) and Isla Verde (Avda Isla Verde 6779, next to the *Ritz*, ☎787/791-5339). Scooters are $20/hr or $70/day, and can be useful if heading out to Piñones for the day, though you'll feel safer in a car for trips further afield and buses are better for trips within the city.

Taxis Atlantic City Taxi ☎787/268-5050; Metro Taxi ☎787/725-2870; Rochdale Taxi Cabs ☎787/721-1900.

Tours La Rumba (☎787/375-5211, ⊛www.larumbapr.com) organizes party cruises around San Juan Bay, Fri–Sun evenings ($12), while Captain Duck Tours (☎787/447-0077, ⊛www.captainduck.com) offers 80–90min spins around the city and harbor in an amphibious bus ($24). Tours usually run Mon–Wed, Sat & Sun 11am, 1pm, and 3pm from outside the bus station in Old San Juan, but call to confirm. Several companies offer tours further afield, but while these are certainly hassle free, they tend to be expensive: try Sunshine Tours (☎787/647-4545, ⊛www.puerto-rico-sunshinetours.com), which offers day-trips to Camuy Caves ($60), Yunque ($48–68), and Ponce ($65). Tours leave daily, but they need at least four people to go, and entrance fees, tax (7 percent) and tips for the driver/guide (15 percent) are not included. Legends of Puerto Rico (☎787/605-9060, ⊛www.legendsofpr.com) offers excellent thematic tours of San Juan on foot (from $30) and the island (from $100–125).

Around San Juan

Greater San Juan is a vast, often bewildering mish-mash of residential areas and modern commercial development, but there's plenty to see before you move on. **Bayamón** and **Caparra** offer small but important historical attractions, while the bike trails and celebrated *kioscos* of **Piñones** are great fun on weekends. Failing that, you should definitely make a pilgrimage across the bay to the **Casa Bacardi Visitor Center**, one of the great shrines to rum-making.

Moving on from San Juan

By air

Domestic flights from San Juan are often serviced by small aircraft and it's usually pointless turning up without a ticket – try and make reservations two weeks in advance if possible. Vieques Air-Link operates five daily flights to **Vieques** from Aeropuerto Isla Grande and three from Aeropuerto Internacional Luis Muñoz Marín, while Air Sunshine operates an additional four flights daily. To **Culebra**, flights are operated "on demand" to set timetables by Air Flamenco, Vieques Air-Link, and Isla Nena, though this isn't as expensive as it sounds (under $100 one-way). From Aeropuerto Internacional Luis Muñoz Marín, Cape Air operates daily flights to **Mayagüez** and **Ponce**. There are currently no domestic flights to **Aguadilla**. Heading to either airport, it's usually easiest to get your hotel to call a **taxi**, though you can catch **bus C45** from Isla Verde to the international airport. Note that the only places to eat at the latter after 11pm are Subway and McDonald's.

By car

Most people touring the island leave San Juan by car. Heading **east** to El Yunque or Fajardo is straightforward on PR-66 ($3 in tolls) and PR-3 (this road is the worst on the island for traffic – try to leave early). The lengthy Teodoro Moscoso Bridge ($1.75) cuts right across Laguna San Juan from Isla Verde and the airport, to Río Piedras and all routes **south** – PR-52 is the main *autopista* to Caguas and Ponce. There are several tolls along the way ($1–1.75; around $5 total to Ponce), but you'll save lots of time taking this road. Heading **west** from the airport you'll need to cut across the city to PR-22 via Avda De Diego or Kennedy. This *autopista* goes all the way to Arecibo, with six tolls on the way ($6 total).

By taxi

Taxi turísticos will drive long distance, though prices are expensive and, unless you have a group or can't drive yourself, not really worth it. The exception is the run to the **Fajardo ferry terminal**, which is $80 (or $50–60 if you call Fajardo drivers in advance, see p.136), and saves a lot of hassle if you're heading straight to Culebra or Vieques by ferry.

Casa Bacardi Visitor Center

Visit the slick **Casa Bacardi Visitor Center** (Mon–Sat 8.30am–5.30pm, last tour 4.15pm; Sun 10am–5pm, last tour 3.45pm; free; ☎787/788-8400, Ⓦwww .casabacardi.org) inside the "cathedral of rum," the vast Bacardi distillery across San Juan Bay in Cataño, and you'll enter another world – Cuba, to be precise. It's a series of fun and illuminating interactive exhibits that emphasizes Bacardi's Cuban roots, and involves not just watching and listening, but sniffing the products on display. **Guided tours** (the only way to visit the site) depart every 15 to 30 minutes and last around 45 minutes.

Established in Santiago de Cuba by Catalan expat Don Facundo Bacardí Massó in 1862, the Bacardi empire now dominates the global rum market, supplying 75 percent of rum sold in the US alone. The Puerto Rican plant was established in Old San Juan in 1936 and moved to this location – when it received its "cathedral" sobriquet from then-governor Luis Muñoz Marín – in 1958. The move here proved timely, as Castro seized the Bacardi assets in Cuba shortly afterwards, precipitating exile in 1960 – the family remain vehement opponents of what they term a "totalitarian" regime.

Today Bacardi is a true multinational organization, headquartered in tax-free Bermuda, and with massive operations in the Bahamas, Mexico, and Puerto Rico

By bus

With a few exceptions, the main *líneas* and *público* terminals for San Juan are all in **Río Piedras**, so you'll need to take a city bus or taxi from other parts of the city (see Basics, p.23, for general information on *públicos*). Taxi-type *públicos* operated by Choferes Unidos de Ponce (℡787/764-0540) depart for **Ponce** ($15) from Calle 2, just off Avda Gandara near c/Saldana, though this service can be erratic: Mondays and Fridays seem to be busiest, but call ahead to confirm. Minibus services to **Fajardo** ($4) run fairly frequently and depart the Terminal de Vehiculos Públicos del Este (℡787/250-0717) on c/Arzuaga near c/Vallejo, though not all of them go to the ferry port, so check before you go. Línea Sultana (℡787/765-9377) on c/Esteban Gonzalez (near Avda Universidad) runs buses every two hours to **Mayagüez** (daily 7.30–5pm; $15). The driver will drop you off on the road along the way, and anywhere in Mayagüez beyond the terminal for an extra charge. For other locations head to Plaza de Convalecencia: on the north side there are frequent buses ($1.15) and *públicos* ($1) to **Caguas** (℡787/744-8833), and far fewer services operated by Línea Arecibeña (℡787/751-6178) to **Arecibo** ($10), as well as Choferes Unidos de Aguadilla (℡787/751-7622) and Blue Line (℡787/250-0717) to **Aguadilla** ($15). Slightly more frequent buses head for **Humacao** ($3) and **Juncos** ($2.40) further along the square, though as usual, drivers will be reluctant to depart without a decent load of passengers. Línea de Utuado (℡787/894-3512) runs to **Utuado** ($15), but call in advance.

Several *líneas* operate from **Santurce**, but here too you'll need to call in advance; in most cases they will pick you up from your hotel. Línea Yaucana runs from Parada 18 (℡787/725-4393 or 787/594-0943) for **Yauco** and the Porta del Sol ($30); Línea Lajeña runs buses to **Lajas** ($35; ℡787/722-1206) from Parada 15 in Santurce; Línea San Germaña (t℡787/722-3392) runs nearby from Avda Las Palmas and c/Cerra to **San Germán** ($30), and Línea Caborrojeña (℡787/723-9155) arranges rides to **Cabo Rojo** ($35) from the same place. For **Dorado**, buses depart Terminal Kuilan in Bayamón.

– the last outpost has the capacity to produce 100,000 gallons of rum every 24 hours and is the biggest taxpayer on the island.

Equipped with a hand-held audio guide and accompanied by enthusiastic docents, you'll pass through seven different zones introducing both the history of the company and the rum-making process. Special barrels allow you to "nose" the effects of wood barreling, ageing, and finishing, as well as the various Bacardi brands on offer: sweetly scented apple and melon flavors and the rich, addictive aroma of coconut-laced rum – *piña colada* in a bottle. Mercifully, there are two **free drinks** waiting for you at the end of the tour (and as many soft drinks as you like).

Note, however, that you don't get to visit the actual distillery – for security reasons the real rum-making facilities have been off limits since 9/11 and are likely to remain that way for the immediate future. The **store** is open throughout the day; the most expensive bottle on sale is the **Reserva Limitada** ($69.95), a cognac-like rum, aged for 10–16 years and only available here.

To get to the Visitor Center, take the ferry from Pier 2 in Old San Juan ($0.50; every 20min; 10min), which provides fine views of the old town, and catch bus C37 on the other side ($0.75; every 30min; 5min). You can also flag down *públicos* for $1. Either will drop you at the main gate from where it's a five-minute walk to the visitor center. Note that in high season, particularly early in the week, up to 1500 visitors come here each day: arrive early. A **taxi** direct from Old San Juan will be at least $30 one-way.

Bayamón

Well off the tourist trail, 15km from Old San Juan, **BAYAMÓN** is the second largest municipality in Puerto Rico after the capital, and though it's usually regarded as part of Greater San Juan, it tries hard to maintain a distinct identity. Established in 1772, today Bayamón is noted as the home of the best rum in Puerto Rico, **Ron de Barrilito** (see p.67), the celebrated fried pork snack **chicharrón** and, more recently, pop superstar **Ricky Martin** (see p.374).

Due largely to enterprising former mayor **Ramón Luis Rivera** (mayor 1976–2000), central Bayamón is an attractive area of colonial architecture containing several small but engaging museums; chief among them is the **Museo de Arte y Historia de Francisco Oller** (Mon–Fri 8.30am–4pm; free), which commemorates Bayamón's best-known son, born here in 1833 (see p.371). The museum occupies the former city hall built on the central Plaza de Recreo in 1907, and holds a handful of portraits by Oller and a collection of sculptures by Tomás Batista, as well as temporary exhibits by local contemporary artists. Highlights include Oller's earliest surviving painting, a portrait of his grandfather from 1847 (copied from a José Campeche original), and Batista's image of Agüeybaná, "El Bravo," (paramount *cacique*, or ruler of the island in 1508, see p.355), and other Taíno leaders. Behind the museum, on Calle de Degetau, the **Museo de Archivo Histórico** (Mon–Fri 8.30am–4pm; free) contains a fairly dry collection of old photos and scale models of the city on the first floor, and a shrine-like exhibition dedicated to Ramón Luis Rivera upstairs. One of the city's more off-beat museums can be found at Calle de Degetau 18, the **Museo de Muñecas** (Mon–Fri 8.30am–4pm; free), with its collection of around 1240 Puerto Rican and international **dolls**, including some slightly disturbing creations with human teeth and fixed grins.

Two blocks east, at Calle de Barbosa 16, the charming wooden *criollo* home and birthplace of José Celso Barbosa (1857–1921) has been preserved as the **Museo de Barbosa** (Mon–Fri 8am–noon & 1–4.30pm; free). Barbosa was a medical pioneer and father of the "Statehood for Puerto Rico" movement (see p.362), but while the modest displays inside are a stimulating introduction to his life and work, everything is written in Spanish only.

Practicalities

The fastest way to reach Bayamón is to take a **bus** to Estación Sagrado Corazón (M1 from Old San Juan or C10 from Condado) and transfer to the Tren Urbano. There are no direct buses to Bayamón from Old San Juan: take B8 and transfer to M2 at Sagrado Corazón or at the San Patricio shopping mall (final stop) in Guaynabo (usually a much slower option). The bus station and the Tren Urbano terminal in Bayamón are close to each other, three blocks northeast of Plaza de Recreo. **Taxis** from Old San Juan or the beaches will be around $30.

The best place **to eat** near Plaza de Recreo is *Restaurante La Mia* (Tues–Sat 7am–5pm), a cozy place on Calle Maceo just off the square, where you can get hearty *cubano* sandwiches, *chuletas*, or burgers for under $5. Coffee, *mallorcas*, or *kanelles* (brownies) are available for less than $2 at *Kanelle* (Mon–Fri 7am–3.30pm), Calle de Barbosa 43, one block away. To try the local *chicharrónes*, look for the **Pacheco** brand in the *Farmacias Plaza* on the northeast corner of Plaza de Recreo – the city also holds a **chicharrón festival** in April each year.

Museo y Parque Histórico Ruinas de Caparra

In 1508, Juan Ponce de León hacked his way into the swampy jungles south of San Juan Bay to establish Caparra, the first settlement on the island, today preserved as the **Museo y Parque Histórico Ruinas de Caparra** (Tues–Sat 9am–noon & 1–4.30pm; free; ☎787/781-4795). The ruins are extremely modest, but if you're interested in the history of Puerto Rico (and indeed, the whole Caribbean), this spot has special significance: it contains some of the oldest Spanish remains in the New World. When the settlement was moved to Old San Juan in 1521, Caparra was dismantled and its location lost – it wasn't until 1935 that these remains were uncovered. The foundation stones on display follow the outline of the large mansion-cum-fortress built to house Ponce de León and his government, and were moved here from their original location under the adjacent highway.

There's a small **museum** on site, with English-speakers on hand to translate the Spanish explanations if required. Artifacts found here, such as the large wine jars and pretty Moorish tiles, are displayed along with Spanish armaments of the time.

Caparra is wedged between condos in a posh part of Guaynabo on PR-2 (km 6.4), halfway between Bayamón and Hato Rey. **Getting here** is a pain without a car: several buses stop outside the ruins but none runs from the main tourist areas, which means you'll have to change at least once. M2 runs past Caparra on its way to Bayamón from Hato Rey and Sagrado Corazón, where there are several connecting buses to Old San Juan and Condado. **Taxis** will charge around $25–30 from Old San Juan.

Fundación Luis Muñoz Marín

Revered by most (but by no means all) *puertorriqueñas* as the man who created modern Puerto Rico, former governor Luiz Muñoz Marin's home has been preserved as the **Fundación Luis Muñoz Marín** (daily 10am–4pm; tours $2; ☎787/755-7979, ⓦwww.munoz-marin.org) in Trujillo Alto, southeast of San Juan. The house is just off Expreso Trujillo Alto (PR-181), on PR-877 at km 0.4. **Guided tours** (daily 9am, 10.30am, 1.30pm & 3pm; ☎787/755-4506 or 787/761-7442) are offered, but you must call in advance to reserve a space. It's well worth taking the tour of the house (the only way to get inside), though the guards will let you wander around the gardens if you show up at other times. Muñoz Marín was the island's first elected governor (see p.362) and spent much of his retirement here in the 1970s; after his death in 1980, his wife, Inés María Mendoza, lived in the house for another ten years. Today the beautifully maintained property offers subtle insights into the life and routine of the influential leader, beginning with an introductory video in the main residence. His office and library are also preserved much as he left them, and the garage contains his favorite vintage car. The adjacent Sala Luis Muñoz Marín is crammed with memorabilia, documents, photos, and the like, charting his illustrious career.

Taxis from Old San Juan and the beaches should be around $30; it's best to negotiate a round-trip fare, as taking the bus involves a long wait and changing in Río Piedras.

Piñones

Just 2km beyond central Isla Verde, **PIÑONES** is an entirely different world, a languid, low-rent community of shacks, houses, and a couple thousand tenants scattered along the coast and PR-187. At the weekends the whole area comes alive with salsa and *sanjuaneros* looking to connect with their traditional roots,

The Land of Giants

The municipality of **Carolina**, Puerto Rico's third largest, is a predominantly industrial suburb of Greater San Juan (though it also includes Isla Verde) 19km east of Old San Juan, with the rather grand epithet of **Tierra de Gigantes**, "Land of Giants." Ostensibly, the nickname refers to the tallest ever Puerto Rican (Felipe Birriel, 7ft 11in), who was born here in 1916, but the city has also been home to several eminent islanders: **Julia de Burgos** (1914–53), one of the greatest ever Latin American poets; **Jesús Piñero** (1897–1952), first Puerto Rican governor of the island; and, more recently, **reggaetón** superstars such as **Héctor El Father** and **Don Omar**. But the real "giant" has to be **Roberto Clemente** (1934–72), one of the world's greatest ever baseball players and someone who's afforded saint-like reverence in Puerto Rico, even today. Clemente started playing with the Santurce Crabbers, and was picked up by the Brooklyn Dodgers in 1954. In 1955 he joined the **Pittsburgh Pirates** and stayed with them throughout his career, winning the World Series in 1960 and 1971 and becoming the most valuable player in 1966: a skilful batsman, Clemente is also widely regarded as the greatest right-fielder of all time. He was the first Puerto Rican initiated into the National Baseball Hall of Fame (1973), in Cooperstown, NY, and the first Latino to reach 3000 hits. Today two stadiums in Greater San Juan are named in his honor and there's a statue and monument in Carolina, but he's equally remembered for his legacy off the field. A dedicated **philanthropist**, Clemente died in a tragic plane crash in 1972, just off Isla Verde, as he was traveling to deliver aid to earthquake victims in Nicaragua. He also helped to change the nature of baseball in the US: in the 1950s he had to deal with widespread racism in the sport, but after his success attitudes changed and today over 28 percent of Major League players are Latino.

drink beer, and enjoy the *cocina en kiosco*. The food and party atmosphere are the obvious attractions, but in 2007 a new project was launched to develop the area's cultural and ecotourism potential, which includes the largest mangrove swamp in the Caribbean. In addition, the beaches here are excellent for **surfing**, especially in winter (see p.78).

Bus B40 (and C45 weekdays) runs into Piñones from Río Piedras via Isla Verde: from elsewhere take a bus to Isla Verde and change outside the cockfighting arena. On Sundays it runs every hour until 8pm, and unless you have your own transport this is the only way to get back, as taxis are hard to find. Get off the bus as soon as you cross the bridge into **Boca de Cangrejos**, the first part of Piñones, crammed with cheap restaurants, and head to **La Paseodora** information center (daily 7am–6pm), just off the road on the right.

Piñones is home to the descendants of freed African slaves as well as more recent immigrants from the Dominican Republic, making for a vibrant cultural mix. The area became a rich farming community in the eighteenth century, and its citizens played a crucial role in the defeat of the British in 1797 (see p.359). La Paseodora, run by the **Corporación Piñones se Integra** (COPI; ☎787/253-9707, ⓦwww.copipr.com), acts as a focus for activities to commemorate events like this, and also manages the area's ecological attractions. To explore the latter, **rent a bicycle** here ($5/hr; photo ID required) and follow the **Paseo Piñones** bike trail.

Paseo Piñones

The well-marked **Paseo Piñones** bike trail cuts through several contrasting environments, from the ramshackle villages and scrubby vegetation that hug the coast, to the **Bosque Estatal de Piñones**, a reserve of thick mangrove swamps around the Laguna de Piñones, and finally to some pristine, palm-lined beaches. There are plans to eventually extend the route to Loíza, but for now the trail is around 9km long (one-way). It can be completed in two hours, but it's best to take the whole morning and stop along the way.

From La Paseodora, the first section snakes around the headland in Boca de Cangrejos and follows the coast to the **Torre Maldonado** on the promontory of the same name (an excellent lookout point). Beyond here there are two rows of *kioscos*, in front of a small lagoon ideal for paddling. The *kioscos* are only open weekends, selling delicious *alcapurrias* and *bacalaítos* fried over wood fires, for around $1. From here the trail crosses the road and splits: the left-hand fork takes a shorter route along the coast while the trail on the right slices 2km through dramatically different terrain, a vast forest of twisted mangroves shading hordes of crabs and other tiny mud-dwelling creatures. The trail passes the DRNA Center (Department of Natural Resources) on the lagoon in the heart of the reserve (where you should be able to rent kayaks by the end of 2008), and rejoins the shortcut near PR-187. The route runs along the south side of the road for another 1.8km before heading into the dunes: grab a snack where it crosses the road at *Las Dos Palma*, a popular *kiosco* (weekends only). The final stretch is 1.2km along the coast to the "Fin de Paseo," where you'll find **Playa Tres Palmitas**, a fabulous beach that's never crowded.

Eating and drinking
In addition to the weekend *kioscos* that line PR-187, Piñones is home to some rustic open-air restaurants and trendy beach bars that do business all week. Most can be found in Boca de Cangrejos, or along the main beach on the other side

St James, Yoruba-style

The town of **Loíza**, 30km from Old San Juan and a short drive east of Piñones, is best known for its **Fiestas Tradicionales de Santiago Apóstol**, the ten-day carnival held every July to honor St James (his feast day is July 25). What makes the festival so special is the town's rich **African heritage**: the religious ceremonies are enhanced with *bomba* music and dancers, and with multicolored spiky **vejigante masks** made from coconut shells.

Like Piñones, Loíza became a refuge for runaway and freed slaves in the seventeenth century, most of them Yoruba people from West Africa, and the festival is the result of a gradual blending of Spanish and African cultures over the years. Santiago (St James) is the **patron saint of Spain**, where he became known as Matamoros ("Moor-slayer") in the Middle Ages for his supposed help in defeating the Moors, and in the sixteenth century Spanish colonists brought his cult to Puerto Rico (the festival masks symbolize the "heathen" Moors). African slaves began to pray to Santiago for help in fending off pirates and enemy attacks, and gradually St James became associated with Yoruba deities such as **Ogun**, the spirit of iron and war. Ironically, St James evolved into a symbol of resistance *against* the Spanish ruling classes, the festival a potent act of defiance against the oppression leveled at slaves and their descendants. Following an influx of Irish settlers in the nineteenth century, the Church made **St Patrick** the town's patron saint, but that only served to make the worship of Santiago more intense. The town's main church is called **Iglesia San Patricio** (Mon–Fri 8am–4pm, and during services at weekends), and is the oldest in continuous use on the island (established in 1670).

Most of the festival action takes place in Plaza de Recreo, Loíza's main square: call the local tourist office (☎787/876-3570) for details. The town gets jam-packed at festival time, so you'll need to get there early, preferably with your own car (or via bus C45 from Isla Verde, Mon–Fri, last departure from Loíza 6.30pm). You can purchase masks from **Artesanías Castor Ayala** at PR-187 km 6.6 (daily 9am–6pm), just outside the town, throughout the year.

of the headland. Salsa fans should make for *El Balcón del Zumbador* (see p.95), which hosts outstanding live salsa bands most weekends.

Bamboobei PR-187 km 4.5. Facing the main beach (1.5km from La Paseodora on the bike trail, closer by road), this is a fashionable spot for drinks and food, with a cozy indoor area and a breezy open-air deck. The menu offers plenty of seafood, and there's live music (jazz, salsa) Fri & Sat. Closed Sun.

El Farol PR-187 km 5. This pink-and-green building just off the main beach is a big local favorite, identified by the sign saying "El Palacio de las Frituras" (Palace of Fritters). There's a pool table at the back, as well as roosters ambling around, but people line up here for delicious *bacalaítos*, *alcapurrias*, *pionono* (plantains stuffed with ground beef) and *relleno de papa* (stuffed potato).

El Pulpo Loco PR-187 km 4.5. A beach bar and no-frills restaurant, just a short ride or walk along the road from La Paseodora; located in the second collection of eateries near the main beach. The *arroz juegos* (crab rice) is excellent and there's thumping salsa at weekends.

Reef Bar & Grill Boca de Cangrejos, PR-187 km 1. The highlight here is the spectacular view over the ocean and San Juan coastline, shaded by pine trees at the end of the Punta de Cangrejos. There's a pool table, lots of music, and happy hour at 6–7pm weekdays – the appetizing *comida criolla* classics on the menu are also worth a try. A short walk from La Paseodora. Closed Mon & Tues.

Soleil Beach Club PR-187 km 4.6 ☎787/253-1033. This two-story wooden house just off the beach is the most fashionable bar and restaurant in Piñones, with plenty of seafood and live music at the weekends. It's especially congenial for a relaxed beer or two on Sun afternoon, when the Piñones party scene is at its peak.

La Terrazza Boca de Cangrejos, PR-187 km 1. Opposite *Reef*, the specialty at this large, open-air diner is the *carne al pincho*: pork, beef, and chicken kebabs barbecued on the street in front. Backs onto adjacent *Puerta del Mar*, with its highly rated *mofongo*, and has pool tables for additional amusement.

Travel details

Note that **públicos** depart various locations in Río Piedras and Santurce. For most destinations, the number of trips per day varies depending on demand: journey times may also vary according to traffic and the number of stops made.

Buses

San Juan to: Aguadilla (infrequent; 2hr); Arecibo (infrequent; 1–2hr); Caguas (frequent; 35–45min); Gurabo (daily; 45–50min); Fajardo (frequent; 1hr); Humacao (daily; 1hr 20min); Juncos (daily; 45–50min); Las Piedras (daily; 1hr); Mayagüez (6 daily; 3–4hr); Ponce (daily; 2hr).

Flights

San Juan International to: Culebra (on demand; 30min); Mayagüez (5 daily; 35min); Ponce (5 daily; 25min); Vieques (7 daily; 25min).

San Juan Isla Grande to: Culebra (on demand; 30min); Vieques (5 daily; 25min).

2

El Yunque and the east coast

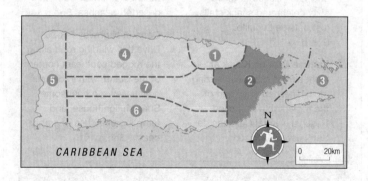

CARIBBEAN SEA

N

0   20km

CHAPTER 2 # Highlights

* **El Yunque National Forest**
Climb the jungle-smothered
slopes of El Yunque or
bathe in the seductively cool
waters at Mina Falls. See
p.112

* **Balneario de Luquillo**
Splash, swim, or simply
lounge on one of the most
dazzling beaches on the
island, backed by picture-
perfect coconut palms.
See p.126

* **Luquillo kioscos** Gorge on
the best of Puerto Rico's
cocina en kiosco at these
sixty celebrated snack stalls
just outside Luquillo.
See p.127

* **Laguna Grande** Kayak at
night across this mesmerizing
bioluminescent bay, part of
the remarkably unspoiled
Reserva Natural Cabezas de
San Juan. See p.131

* **La Cordillera** This string of
alluring cays east of Fajardo
is a desert island fantasy,
with powder-fine sands
ringed with banks of coral
and a rich panoply of marine
life. See p.131

* **Cayo Santiago** Take an
entertaining boat ride around
the world's oldest monkey
reserve, and snorkel above
a shipwreck teeming with
tropical fish. See p.137

* **Rancho Buena Vista** Ride
one of Puerto Rico's beloved
Paso Fino horses along wild,
deserted beaches. See p.140

* **Coastal Highway PR-901**
Drive this winding road along
the rugged southeast corner
of the island, with intoxicating
ocean views, a handsome
Spanish lighthouse, and
tempting stretches of empty
beach. See p.141

▲ El Yunque Peak

El Yunque and the east coast

Eastern Puerto Rico is a microcosm of the whole island, at times brash, modern and touristy, but also rural, remote and achingly beautiful. Being so close to San Juan, and on the route to Vieques and Culebra, the coastline is sprinkled with luxury resorts, condos and exclusive marinas, while in between you'll find long stretches of primitive beach, festooned with nothing more than the flotsam blown up by the trade winds. Looming over the whole region, the forest-drenched hills of the **Sierra de Luquillo** were the last parts of Puerto Rico to be settled by the Spanish, thanks to indomitable Taíno resistance and the wet, hurricane-prone climate. In the nineteenth century the area did succumb to sugar and coffee plantations like the rest of the island, but here they did not prosper, leaving nature to reclaim much of the land.

The most captivating evidence of this turnaround is **El Yunque National Forest**, a protected reserve of mist-draped mountains and bubbling cascades. The forest receives over one million visitors each year, but you can escape the crowds by **hiking** one of its well-maintained **trails**, enveloped by little more than the chirping of frogs, rustling palms and the soothing murmurs of distant running water. You'll need at least two days to do it justice. **Luquillo** is the highlight of the northeast coast, a low-key resort town best known for its spectacular beach and legendary snack food, while **Fajardo**, the gateway to the Spanish Virgin Islands, is all about boats. **La Cordillera**, just offshore, encapsulates most dreams about the Caribbean: uninhabited islands with sugary white sand, piles of multicolored coral, fish and the odd turtle. Nearby, the **Reserva Natural Cabezas de San Juan** is another protected area of untrammeled mangrove swamp and dry forest, also containing **Laguna Grande**, one of Puerto Rico's spellbinding bioluminescent bays.

The east coast proper offers a real contrast, a blend of sleepy villages and a wilder, cliff-backed shoreline laced with secluded beaches. **Playa Naguabo**, noted for its seafood, is also the best embarkation point for **Cayo Santiago**, a private monkey reserve surrounded by sparkling sapphire waters, while the sprawling condo development of **Palmas del Mar** contains one of the best **horse ranches** on the island. Finally, **highway PR-901** snakes along the vertiginous southeast coastline, a twisting route lined with scenic viewpoints and a handful of modest but absorbing sights.

If you know where to look, **eating** in this part of the country can be just as rewarding, with a number of enticing local specialties to enhance the usual menus of Puerto Rican staples and fresh *dorado* or red snapper: *frituras* in Luquillo, johnny cakes and sauce "*a la Rosa*" in Fajardo, *pastelillos de chapín* and lobster in Playa Naguabo, and shark meat in Punta Santiago.

As with the rest of the island, you're better off exploring the region **by car**, as *públicos* are a slow and unreliable way to get around. Be warned however, the main highway between San Juan and Fajardo (PR-3) is one of the worst in Puerto Rico: congested and accident prone, it's also plagued by traffic lights, making large sections of it frustratingly slow, so avoid rush hour if you can. One alternative is to take *autopistas* PR-52 and PR-30 between San Juan and Humacao, a slightly less harrowing route and much faster to the east and southeast coasts. Heading this way it's worth stopping to visit the historic towns of **Caguas** and **Juncos**, with the former in particular boasting a spread of engaging museums and galleries.

El Yunque National Forest

Sacred to the Taíno long before the Spanish conquest, the rich, emerald green slopes of **El Yunque National Forest** dominate eastern Puerto Rico like a protective wall, absorbing most of the rain hurled into the island by the trade winds. Much of the reserve is untouched wilderness, crowned by 3000ft peaks – when the clouds clear it can seem like the whole island is visible. The frequent (but brief) showers haven't stopped El Yunque from becoming the island's top attraction. Justifiably so: part of the US National Forest system, its well-paved roads, enlightening visitor centers, and a network of clearly marked trails make it the most accessible reserve in the Caribbean.

You can **drive** right into the heart of the forest, but to really appreciate the area you need to get **hiking**. The Forest Service maintains thirteen trails ranging from easy, concrete paths to more challenging dirt tracks, but even the trek up to the peak of **El Yunque** itself (the name refers to both the reserve and the mountain) is manageable for anyone of moderate fitness, and well worth the effort for the momentous views from the top. Less taxing highlights include a series of plunging **waterfalls** and natural **swimming pools**, perfect for cooling down in the summer, and a smattering of whimsical structures created by the Civilian Conservation Corps in the 1930s.

El Yunque's thick, primeval forest is a precious ecosystem of 240 tree species and four distinct zones: 70 percent of the reserve is smothered in **tabonuco forest**, found on slopes below 2000ft and characterized by *tabonuco* trees that can grow up to 100ft tall. **Palo colorado forest** extends from 2000ft to about 3000ft, featuring wider but shorter *palo colorado* trees, some of them over 1000 years old, with the canopy topping out at around 50ft. **Sierra palm forest** can be found at the same elevations, but mainly in steep and wet areas, heavily dominated by delicate *sierra* palms. Up here you'll pass clumps of aromatic white ginger flowers, wild papaya, banana and date palms, breadfruit, and vivid orchids. **Cloud** or dwarf forest clings to the highest peaks, dense vegetation that rarely tops 10ft, the stunted trees draped with mosses and vines.

Most tourists visit El Yunque on day-trips, which is a shame – you'll get a lot more out of the place by staying at one of the enticing **guesthouses** nearby. Half the visitors to the forest are Puerto Ricans, who typically come in the hot summer months of July and August when the northern section is often bursting with traffic. More foreigners tend visit in the winter and early spring, making mid-April to mid-June and September through October the quietest periods,

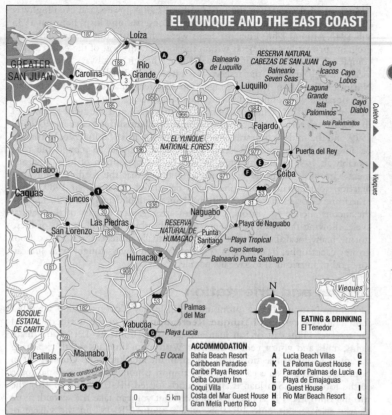

EL YUNQUE AND THE EAST COAST

RESERVA NATURAL CABEZAS DE SAN JUAN

GREATER SAN JUAN

Loíza

Carolina

Río Grande

Balneario de Luquillo

Luquillo

Balneario Seven Seas

Cayo Icacos

Cayo Lobos

Laguna Grande

Isla Palominos

Cayo Diablo

Isla Palominitos

Fajardo

Puerta del Rey

EL YUNQUE NATIONAL FOREST

Gurabo

Ceiba

Caguas

Juncos

Las Piedras

San Lorenzo

Naguabo

Playa de Naguabo

RESERVA NATURAL DE HUMACAO

Punta Santiago

Playa Tropical

Cayo Santiago

Balneario Punta Santiago

Humacao

Palmas del Mar

N

Vieques

BOSQUE ESTATAL DE CARITE

Yabucoa

Playa Lucía

Patillas

Maunabo

El Cocal

under construction

0   5 km

EATING & DRINKING
El Tenedor   1

ACCOMMODATION
Bahía Beach Resort	A	Lucia Beach Villas	G
Caribbean Paradise	K	La Paloma Guest House	F
Caribe Playa Resort	J	Parador Palmas de Lucia	G
Ceiba Country Inn	E	Playa de Emajaguas	
Coqui Villa	D	Guest House	I
Costa del Mar Guest House	H	Río Mar Beach Resort	C
Gran Melía Puerto Rico	B		

but it's relatively easy to escape the crowds at any time. The average temperature of the forest is 73°F (21°C), but in winter, the highest peaks can be 20 degrees cooler than the coast (53°F, 12°C). And be prepared for **rain**: El Yunque is a rainforest after all, with an average deluge of 160 billion gallons each year. In general, the higher you are, the more it will rain: annual rainfall can total 250in (6350mm) on the peaks, but just 50–60in (1270–1525mm) lower down.

Some history

The Taíno regarded El Yunque as a sacred mountain, the place where Yokahú or **Yukiyú**, their chief god, made his home (*yuké* meant "white lands" in Taíno, referring to the clouds). For years after the Spanish conquest, the **Sierra de Luquillo** was a base for resistance against the invaders. As late as the 1580s, Taíno hiding in El Yunque were hampering efforts to develop the area, but over the following three centuries, farming gradually made headway, and much of the lower slopes was converted to fruit or coffee plantations.

In 1876, desperate to conserve valuable timber resources for shipbuilding, Puerto Rico's Spanish rulers turned most of the Sierra de Luquillo into a protected zone, and in 1903 (after the US had occupied the island), this became the **Luquillo Forest Reserve**.

Much of what you see in the forest today – cabins, towers, and even highway PR-191 – was constructed by the Civilian Conservation Corps between 1935 and 1943. Around 2400 Puerto Ricans were enrolled in this US public works program, primarily on projects within the forest, with most of the construction completed by back-breaking manual labor. Though it's always been known locally as "El Yunque", the reserve was given the official title of **Caribbean National Forest** in 1935, a designation that remained until 2006 when its current name was confirmed by presidential decree.

Highway PR-191, which had linked the northern and southern sections of the forest, was seriously damaged by four major **landslides** between 1970 and 1979, and the mid-section was closed permanently in 1972. In 1976, El Yunque became a UN Biosphere Reserve, and several attempts to rebuild the road (notably in 1993) were thwarted, in part by the opposition of local environmental groups – virtually everyone now agrees that the road is simply not practical to maintain. Hurricane Hugo devastated the forest in 1989, while Hurricane Georges caused an additional $5m worth of damage in 1998. Despite the inconvenience to visitors, hurricanes are regarded as part of the natural cycle, allowing the forest to regenerate. By absorbing the full impact of these storms, many locals believe that El Yunque actually protects Puerto Rico from greater catastrophe: in the Taíno tradition, Yukiyú always fought with Juracán (the god of hurricanes) to save his people.

Arrival and orientation

El Yunque National Forest (pronounced "El Junkay") covers 28,000 acres, but most visitors focus on **El Yunque Recreation Area** in the northern half of the reserve, 43km east of San Juan and accessible from PR-191; all the main sights, trails, and visitor centers are here. With more time, it's worth exploring the quieter southern section of the forest, in the area known as **Cubuy**, but in both cases you'll need a car as public transport is nonexistent. The usual route to the forest from San Juan is along traffic-clogged PR-3 (45min to 1hr): the turning onto PR-191 is poorly signposted but you can take the second, more clearly marked exit onto PR-955, which rejoins PR-191 in the village of Mameyes, just off the highway. For Cubuy, stay on PR-3 till it becomes the PR-53 *autopista* and take exit 22 west (right) along PR-31, then head north on PR-191. Note that if you are approaching from the south on PR-53, you'll have to take exit 20 and turn around.

Entry to the forest is **free**. The steel gate across PR-191 at La Coca Falls (km 8.1) opens 7.30am–6pm daily, and as most of the reserve lies above this area, visiting outside these hours is pointless. The southern sections and trails are ostensibly open 24 hours, while most information offices, sights, and food stalls get going after 9am. English and Spanish are used equally in the park.

Information

There are two principal information centers for El Yunque, both on the northern section of PR-191: **El Portal** (see p.118) and the much smaller **Palo Colorado Visitor Center** (daily 9.30am–5pm), further along the road at km 11.8. The Catalina Service Center near El Portal is primarily an administrative office and of little interest to visitors. To **camp** in the park you'll need to apply for a permit (free) by filling in a form available at any of these offices, though rangers prefer campers to use the Palo Colorado center. Permits are usually issued on the spot (or at least the same day), as long as you submit a completed form by 4pm and provide ID (driver's license and passport is best).

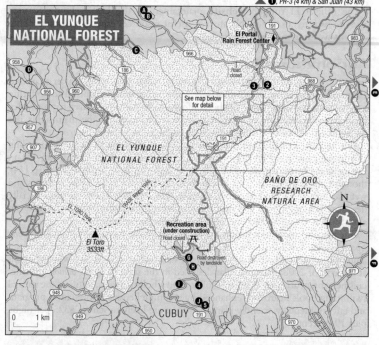

EL YUNQUE NATIONAL FOREST

▲ ❶, PR-3 (4 km) & San Juan (43 km)

A
B
C
D

El Portal
Rain Forest Center

Road closed

See map below
for detail

❸ ❷

191

EL YUNQUE
NATIONAL FOREST

EL TORO TRAIL
TRADE WINDS TRAIL

BAÑO DE ORO
RESEARCH
NATURAL AREA

N

El Toro
3533ft

Recreation area
(under construction)
Road closed

G
H
Road destroyed
by landslide

I   ❹
J ❺

CUBUY

0   1 km

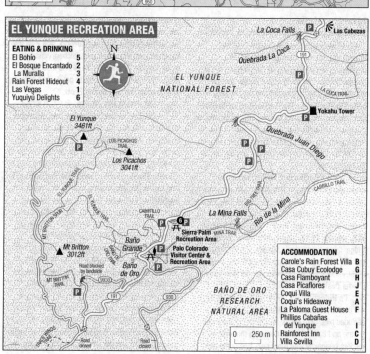

EL YUNQUE RECREATION AREA

EATING & DRINKING
El Bohío   5
El Bosque Encantado   2
La Muralla   3
Rain Forest Hideout   4
Las Vegas   1
Yuquiyú Delights   6

N

La Coca Falls   P   Las Cabezas

Quebrada La Coca

EL YUNQUE
NATIONAL FOREST

LA COCA TRAIL

Yokahu Tower

El Yunque
3461ft

LOS PICACHOS
TRAIL

Quebrada Juan Diego

Los Picachos
3041ft

CARRILLO TRAIL

CAIMITILLO
TRAIL

La Mina Falls

Río de la Mina

Mt Britton
3012ft

Sierra Palm
Recreation Area

Baño
Grande

Palo Colorado
Visitor Center &
Recreation Area

Baño
de Oro

Road blocked
by landslide

MT BRITTON TRAIL

TRADE WINDS TRAIL
Road
closed

191

Road
closed

BAÑO DE ORO
RESEARCH
NATURAL AREA

930

ACCOMMODATION
Carole's Rain Forest Villa   B
Casa Cubuy Ecolodge   G
Casa Flamboyant   H
Casa Picaflores   J
Coqui Villa   E
Coqui's Hideaway   A
La Paloma Guest House   F
Phillips Cabañas
  del Yunque   I
Rainforest Inn   C
Villa Sevilla   D

0   250 m

The official El Yunque **website** maintained by the USDA Forest Service at ⓦ www.fs.fed.us/r8/caribbean is a useful resource, especially for checking current weather and fire conditions.

Accommodation

In recent years several **guesthouses** and **rental villas** have sprung up in or around El Yunque, most owned by enthusiastic *Americanos* from the mainland and offering a more intimate experience of the rainforest than the average day-trip provides. Stay on the **north side** of the forest and you'll be closer to the main sights, but the southern slopes of **Cubuy** are just as inviting and much quieter.

Although most of El Yunque Recreation Area is off-limits to campers (including El Yunque peak and PR-191 between La Coca Falls and the gate at km 13), in theory you can **camp** anywhere else provided you have a **permit** (see p.114), though rangers prefer the area just beyond the gate at km 13, as steep slopes and wet weather make finding other suitable sites difficult. There are no officially designated campgrounds and no facilities, so bring everything with you. You can also camp at *Casa Picaflores* and *Phillips Cabañas* (see below).

One place to watch out for on the north side of the forest is *Yuquiyú Resort and Spa* (PR-966 km 1.2 Interior, ☎212/787-0500, ⓦ www.yuquiyuresort.com), an ambitious project which hopes to set new standards in eco-luxury when it opens at the end of 2008: spacious villas designed in the style of Taíno *bohíos*, gourmet cuisine, vibrant art from Raphael Collazo and a holistic spa that utilizes the natural swimming pools nearby, all enhanced by a comprehensive reforestation program and environmentally-friendly planning. Rates are likely to start at $325 per night, plus 19 percent.

North side

Carole's Rain Forest Villa PR-966, ☎787/809-4172, ⓦ www.rainforestvillas.com. Rent this appealing three-bedroom guesthouse (❽), presided over by friendly host Carole Severn, the two-bedroom main living space (❼) or just one double room (❹): all rooms have double beds with bath. You also get a cozy shared living room with comfy sofas and a funky tropical kitchen located on the terrace outside, with fabulous views. It's close to the northern border of the forest, at an elevation of 1000ft. No children under eight, and minimum 2–3 night stay.

Coqui Villa PR-984 km 2, ☎787/889-2098, ⓦ www.coquivilla.com. This rustic, two-bedroom *casita* is hidden away in three acres of lush tropical gardens close to Fajardo, with three verandas overlooking the forest. Rooms come with bathroom, VCR, satellite TV, CD player, microwave, stove, and fridge. It also has a pool, Jacuzzi, and charcoal grill, the only catch being you must rent by the week ($750–900 according to season): call to negotiate shorter deals. ❹–❺

Coqui's Hideaway PR-966 km 3.6, ☎787/396-4470, ⓦ www.coquishideaway.com. Set in a secluded nine-acre estate, this is one of the most private and tranquil rental homes in the area, a modern bungalow with three cozy bedrooms and

gorgeous ocean views from the back terrace. Rooms (all with a/c) are simply but thoughtfully decorated with different color schemes, artwork, and vivid wall hangings, and it boasts a pool, kitchen, washer/dryer, satellite TV, and WiFi. You'll find it south of PR-3 off PR-966, but it's best to get directions from affable hosts Ray and Gwenn Bentz. ❺

🏃 **Rainforest Inn** PR-186, ☎1-800/672-4992, ⓦ www.rainforestinn.com. Real gem of a B&B, with two plush and very unique suites beautifully finished with exposed brick, pine, and cedar, in a gorgeous five-acre estate at the edge of the forest. Each unit contains two bedrooms and a kitchen. The views are phenomenal, and hosts Bill and Laurie Humphrey are a mine of information, especially on the local flora – they also cook up gourmet breakfasts (included). There's WiFi but no TV, a/c, or radio. It's at the end of a 1.5km-long gated driveway off PR-186: get directions on booking (3-night minimum). ❺–❻

Villa Sevilla PR-956 km 7.9, ☎787/887-5889, ⓦ www.villasevilla.net. This inviting rental property comprises three separate units: a large three-bedroom wooden chalet sitting above the garden like a giant treehouse, with enough space for six (5-night minimum; ❻); a rustic two-bedroom clapboard cottage, decorated in tropical bamboo style (4-night minimum; ❻); and the more modern and spacious

El Yunque wildlife

Most day-trippers visit only the busiest sections of the reserve and leave El Yunque seeing very little **wildlife**, yet the forest is home to over thirty species of amphibian and reptile, eleven types of bat (the only native mammal), and 68 species of **bird** – it's the last that get naturalists most excited. Early morning (before 10am) and late afternoon (after 4pm) are the best times to hear and see them.

Symbol of the island's growing conservation movement, the **Puerto Rican green parrot** or *Cotorra Puertorriqueña* is the most celebrated and endangered inhabitant of the forest. When the Spanish arrived in 1508, it was estimated that one million parrots lived on the island: after years of hunting, deforestation, and devastating hurricanes, there are thought to be around 44 in the wild, all here in El Yunque (up from a record low of 13 in 1975), thanks to a rehabilitation program founded in 1968. The program also established **aviaries** in Luquillo In 1973 (now located within El Yunque) and in the Bosque Estatal de Río Abajo (see p.216) in 1993, which collectively shelter over two hundred parrots (both are closed to the public). As you can imagine, you need the eyes of a hawk and lots of luck to spot one. The parrot has a distinctive bright green color with a red forehead, and is usually around 12in long. Nesting season runs from February through June.

You should have more luck with the **Puerto Rican tody** (*san pedrito*), a small bird with bright green feathers, lemony white breast, and scarlet throat, and the **bananaquit** (*ciquita*), a tiny warbler with a black-and-white striped head and yellow breast. You might also hear the "cow cow, kuk krrk" of the **Puerto Rican lizard cuckoo** (*pájaro bobo mayor*), which feasts on lizards and has a long striped tail. The **green mango** (*zumbador verde*), a type of hummingbird, is also common. From higher peaks you might spy the **red-tailed hawk** (*guaraguao colirrojo*) or **broad-winged hawk** (*guaraguao de bosque*), hovering above the trees. You'll find plenty of information on other bird species in the forest visitor centers.

One creature you'll have no trouble hearing, if not seeing, is the **coquí frog** and its repetitive "ko-kee" call, the official national symbol of Puerto Rico: thirteen species live in the forest, with the **grass coquí** (*coquí de las yerbas*) being one of the smallest, measuring just 0.6in and extremely hard to spot.

Geckos and **lizards** are everywhere: you'll see them scuttling through the bush as you hike along the trails. There are also several species of **snake** in the forest, but these are rarely seen, non-poisonous and not dangerous. The largest is the **Puerto Rican boa** (*culebrón*), which can grow up to 7ft in length and is occasionally spotted near Yokahu Tower.

Note that you should avoid contact with **feral cats** and **dogs**, and **mongooses** in the park, as they can carry rabies. See Contexts p.379 for more on wildlife.

---

one-bedroom garden apartment (2 night minimum; ⑤). It's perfect for families and has a pool on site.

South side and Cubuy

Casa Cubuy Ecolodge PR-191 km 22.4, ☎787/874-6221, ⓦwww.casacubuy.com. Marianne and son Matthew Kavanaugh have owned this wonderful hillside property since the early 1970s, converting it into a tranquil guesthouse in 2000, just within the forest boundary at an elevation of 1500ft. Rooms are simple but comfortable with private bathrooms: no TV or a/c, but it's cool enough with a fan and the views across the Cubuy valley are mesmerizing. Breakfast (9am) is included, while hearty dinners can be

booked in advance (6.30pm; $18.50) and the terrace features a small honor bar. ③–④. They also rent *Villa Sierra Palms* (⑥), a modern three-bedroom apartment down the road.

Casa Flamboyant PR-191 (just before *Casa Cubuy*), ☎787/874-6074, ⓦwww.rainforestsafari .com/flamboy.html. This pretty pink B&B offers magnificent views from three stylish rooms and one suite overlooking the Cubuy valley, the perfect romantic hideaway for couples (no kids allowed). Each room has slightly different decor, though an elegant nineteenth-century theme dominates overall – ask for the Ginger Room, which has wood furnishings, antiques, and a comfy double bed that looks out onto a private terrace. Extras include a small heated pool and hostess Shirley's celebrated breakfasts. ❻

Casa Picaflores off PR-191 at km 25.9, ☏787/874-3802, ⓦwww.casapicaflores.com. This enticing B&B is often booked months in advance, set in a five-acre former fruit farm with three bedrooms, two bathrooms, a shared kitchen, and *El Bohío* on site (see p.123). You get satellite TV, DVD, laundry, and whirlpool, but much of the appeal comes from the simple but elegant rooms, all with tiled floors, the incredible variety of exotic fruits grown on site, and the dynamic hosts, Matt and Karen Needham (the exquisite banana bread also helps). You can also stay at their rainforest cabin, *Casita Zumbador*, or camp nearby. ❻

La Paloma Guest House PR-975 km 8, ☏787/ 885-4040, ⓦwww.lapalomaguesthouse.com. This simple family-run guesthouse is halfway between El Yunque and Fajardo, but tends to be favored by those exploring the former. The biggest draw here is

the price – it's one of the few budget guesthouses, with adequate rooms and fridge, pool, a/c, and satellite TV thrown in. It's also a rare opportunity to meet a Puerto Rican of Taíno ancestry: host Nilda offers fascinating insights into the culture and history of her people. ❷

Phillips Cabañas del Yunque PR-191 km 24.2, ☏787/874-2138, ⓦrainforestcabin.web1000. com. The only budget option in Cubuy, this no-frills wooden cabin, perched 300ft above the parking area on the road, is owned by local guide Robin Phillips. Other than camping, this is the closest you'll come to sleeping in the jungle, but you still get a double bed, sheets, blankets, hammocks, outdoor toilet, and barbecue grill (bring the charcoal). You can also pick fruits at the Phillips' farm. It's basic but a rare bargain: just $35 for the first two nights and $25 thereafter (for 2 people; $5 per extra person). You can camp for $12.

North side: El Yunque Recreation Area

It's a good idea to start your visit at the El Portal Rain Forest Center near the northern entrance of the forest, but if you only have one day and want to hike, skip this and head straight to the trailheads in the **El Yunque Recreation Area**. All the sights listed below can be reached via PR-191, which cuts into the heart of the forest from PR-3 – note, however, that with the road blocked halfway down (see p.114), you can no longer drive across El Yunque to Cubuy on this route.

El Portal Rain Forest Center

Surrounded by flourishing *tabonuco* forest in what was once a coffee plantation, **El Portal Rain Forest Center** (daily 9am–5pm; $3) provides the best introduction to El Yunque, with its soaring white roof sheltering several thought-provoking exhibits. This is the first point of interest inside the forest boundary on PR-191, 4km south of PR-3, and also contains a small café, gift shop, and information desk, with a fifteen-minute introductory video narrated by actor Jimmy Smits (whose mother is Puerto Rican) screened continuously throughout the day.

The exhibition rooms are laid out as a series of open pavilions, each furnished with interactive displays; the first floor provides a basic introduction to the forest while the upper level galleries focus on "Understanding the Forest", "Managing the Future", and "Connections" – the last showing how the rainforest impacts our daily lives, and how materials from the forest are used to produce commonly used household items.

Afterwards you can tackle the short (and usually empty) **El Portal nature trail** (770yds), which makes an easy fifteen-to-twenty minute loop through the *tabonuco* trees down to the wetlands beneath the center. Information boards explain what you see en route: a rich panoply of tree and flower life, with plenty of red ginger, breadfruit, and false birds of paradise.

La Coca Falls and around

For a magnificent panorama of the Atlantic and lower slopes of El Yunque without leaving the car, **Las Cabezas Observation Point** is at km 7.8, just before La Coca Falls. Parking is available here, but the site is unmarked and located on the left side of the road, on a nasty bend: on busy days it's wiser to stop here on the way back down the mountain.

The first major attraction on PR-191 beyond El Portal, **La Coca Falls** tumbles over an 85ft cliff right by the road, a wispy veil of water that folds into the rocks like delicate silk thread. You can glimpse the falls from your car window, but for a more leisurely look, dump your vehicle in one of the parking lots either side. You'll find them on PR-191 at around the 8km mark, at an elevation of 1500ft and just beyond the steel gate (which closes at 6pm; see p.114). Kids like to paddle in the rock pools here.

Another 400m beyond the falls, at km 8.5, is the start of **La Coca Trail** (1.8 miles), named after the area's former banana plantation owned by Spanish settler Juan Diego de La Coca. The trailhead has space for just four cars, otherwise you'll have to walk up from the falls. The main appeal of this trail is the relative ease with which you become immersed in the forest: few people hike here, and the sounds of the road soon melt away. It's steep and rocky in parts and involves crossing two streams via a series of boulders and stones. Rather than return the same way, it is possible to extend the hike by following the **Carrillo Trail** (1.9 miles), which continues upstream to La Mina Falls (see below) – note, though, that the trail has been officially closed for years because of minor landslides, and signs (along with park officials) discourage use of this path. At the time of writing the trail was relatively easy to follow, but restoration work has been slow and heavy rain can change things fast – check at one of the visitor centers if in doubt.

Yokahu Tower

Providing stupendous views of the forest, the north coast and, on a clear day, the peak of El Yunque itself, **Yokahu Tower** at km 8.8 is a popular stop along PR-191, with a parking lot and gift shop at its base. Named after Yokahú, the Taíno's chief deity, the castle-like observation tower was constructed in 1963 to mimic the style of the sham medieval turret built on Mount Britton (see p.122). It's 66ft tall, with 98 steps leading to the top for a total elevation of 1575ft above sea level.

Just over 1km south of the tower, at km 9.5, the natural pools and gentle cascades where the road crosses the **Quebrada Juan Diego** lure plenty of families with paddling kids in summer – it's a relatively underwhelming sight, however, and often difficult to park along the roadside.

La Mina Falls

Thousands of Puerto Ricans throng into El Yunque in the summer, their towels and swimsuits a sign most of them are heading for just one place. **La Mina Falls** is a relatively modest 35ft waterfall on the Río de la Mina, but it's surrounded by pools of cool mountain water and thick swathes of sierra palm deep inside the forest, perfect for a refreshing dip or a meditative afternoon of lounging on the rocks – you can also swim underneath the waterfall. In July it seems half of San Juan is here, but at other times, especially weekdays, you should have it to yourself. Reaching the falls involves a short, energetic walk; the most popular route is the **Big Tree Trail** (0.7 miles), which starts at km 10.2 with its own small parking lot, and is marked by interpretative panels along the way. The trail snakes through *tabonuco* forest and up and down several flights of steps before ending in around 35 minutes at the small footbridge in front of the falls. **La Mina Trail** (0.7 miles) starts at the Palo Colorado Information Center (see p.120) and follows the river downhill like a concrete ribbon, through a *Jurassic Park*-like landscape of giant palms, rustic barbecue pavilions, and *palo colorado*

Tours and activities

Forest adventure tours (1hr; $5 adults, $3 children) run by the Forest Service are available on a first-come-first-served basis from 10.30am until 3.30pm daily, from the Palo Colorado Visitor Center (☎787/888-1810). Guides lead short, fairly easy hikes around the area, providing background on local history and ecology. Ecoquest Adventures and Tours (☎787/616-7543, ⓦwww.ecoquestpr.com) arranges **hikes** through sections of El Yunque (half-day $89; full day $119) accompanied by informative, experienced guides, not a bad option if you are staying in San Juan and don't want to drive (they'll pick you up from your hotel). If you're staying in the area, try knowledgeable local **Robin Phillips** (☎787/874-2138, mobile 787/414-9596, ⓔphillips@east-net.net), who organizes illuminating hiking excursions on the south side of the forest, usually starting at 9.30am and taking in several rivers, the falls on the Río Prieto, and the Taíno petroglyphs (minimum $110 for up to five people, $22 per additional person; exclusive tours $135).

If you are more of a thrill seeker, get in touch with Aventuras Tierra Adentro (☎787/766-0470, ⓦwww.aventuraspr.com), which arranges **canyoning** trips to El Yunque every Sunday ($160), with rappelling, a couple of *via ferratas*, rock-climbs and zip-lines across the river – on-the-spot training is provided and expert guides are on hand throughout. Tours run from 5.45am to 5pm.

Team Spirit Hang Gliding (☎787/850-0508, ⓦwww.hangglidepuertorico.com) is based southwest of El Yunque, on PR-9948 (near the end of PR-186), offering various **hang-gliding** options from four-hour beginner classes ($50) to full four-month programs ($750) and intensive ten-day courses ($999). Paragliding is $100.

Ornithologists should contact AdvenTours (☎787/530-8311, ⓦwww.adventourspr .com) for custom-made **bird-watching tours** ($40/hr, regardless of group size). Tours are a minimum three hours and must be booked 48 hours in advance.

Though **swimming** in rivers and mountain pools is one of the most popular activities in the reserve, especially in the summer, note that heavy downpours can cause flash floods and turn the water an uninviting muddy brown color. **Fishing** is banned throughout the forest.

---

forest – the only steep section is the steps down to the falls at the end, where it connects with the Big Tree Trail. You can make a loop by hiking both trails, but this would include a 1.8km stretch along the road – appealing only if traffic is light. Along the section of PR-191 between the two trailheads you'll pass the **Sierra Palm Recreation Area** (km 11.3), which has small snack stall but nothing to see.

Palo Colorado Recreation Area

Serious hikers should make for the **Palo Colorado Recreation Area** at km 11.8, the hub of a network of easy-to-find trails shooting off all over the forest. The **information center** (see p.114) is a small hut with a shop, basic maps, and a ranger on hand to provide advice, with two small parking lots on either side. La Mina Trail zips off to the falls (see p.119) from here, while the **El Yunque Trail** starts opposite (see opposite). Before tackling the latter, take a look at the forlorn waters of the **Baño Grande**, up the steep flight of steps opposite the information center. Another legacy of the 1930s, this 18-foot deep swimming pool was created by a stone and masonry dam, with the old bathhouse beyond. It was used until 1976, when it became too difficult to maintain.

El Caimitillo picnic area is just below Palo Colorado (but with not much parking) at km 10.4, while the **Caimitillo Trail** (0.2 miles) provides a small loop between here and the Yunque Trail if you fancy a shorter walk.

South of Palo Colorado and higher up the mountain, PR–191 is blocked by a metal gate just beyond km 13: you can continue on foot from here (see El Toro, p.122), making sure your car doesn't block the road, but you'll have to return the same way unless you're attempting to cross the whole forest. Just before the metal gate, cars can turn right on PR–9938 for another 400m to the cramped parking area at the end of the road. This is the trailhead for the **Mount Britton Trail** (0.8 miles), popular as the shortest route to one of the loftiest observation points in the forest (see p.122) – you can continue on to El Yunque from there, but it's best to start back at Palo Colorado.

Climbing El Yunque

Although it's only the second highest peak in the forest, the Taíno holy mountain of El Yunque (3461ft) dominates the region, making a tempting target for an exhilarating half-day hike. The well-marked trail to the summit is lined with some of the richest forest in the reserve, a mostly gentle climb rewarded by scintillating views from the top.

From the Palo Colorado Visitor Center you have two options: the direct route via the Baño Grande along the El Yunque Trail (2.4 miles), or the small detour via the Baño de Oro Trail (0.3 miles), which starts further up PR–191 at km 12.2. The latter passes the sadly dilapidated Baño de Oro bathhouse and pool (which the Forest Service is planning to rehabilitate), built in the mid-1930s as a children's swimming pool (it means "bath of gold") and long since closed to the public. The gravel path rejoins the main Yunque trail beyond the abandoned fish hatchery pools (a failed attempt to introduce trout to the forest), further up the hill. From here El Yunque Trail climbs slowly through lush sierra palm forest for just under two miles, and you should reach the spur to the rugged peak of Los Picachos ("the peaks") in a leisurely sixty to ninety minutes. It's just 0.2 miles to the top, reached by 45 short, steep steps at the end of the trail. The flat

▲ Mount Britton Tower

grassy summit of Los Picachos (3041ft) is enclosed by a concrete wall built in the 1930s, providing a taste of what's to come – practically the whole of eastern Puerto Rico is visible on a clear day. Hawks hover above the precipitous drops on all sides, and the peaks of El Toro and El Yunque loom beyond. Return to the main trail and you should reach the peak of El Yunque, sprinkled with communication towers, in under thirty minutes. On the way up you'll understand why the cloud forest is also known as dwarf forest, as the vegetation is increasingly twisted, stumpy and wind-blown. When you reach the road on top, turn left for the summit, marked by a stocky observation tower also built in the 1930s – check out the remains of the fireplace inside, still used by chilly hikers. Clouds often submerge the peak, but you'll see a stunning panorama unfold through the mist, including stellar views of San Juan to the west.

Rather than retrace your steps, make a loop by returning along Forest Road 10, which drops past the police communication towers and Roca El Yunque, another jagged outcrop off the main trail. Follow the sealed road and you'll eventually come to the trailhead for Mount Britton (the short path that veers off to the right of the information board), a 3012-foot peak topped with a turret-like observation **tower** built in 1935. It's named after US botanist Nathaniel Lord Britton (1859-1934), founder of the New York Botanical Gardens, and keen student of Caribbean ecology. Return to the road and continue down to the next trail that drops off to the left (the lower section of the Mount Britton Trail), snaking down the mountain to the parking area below. Though maps suggest otherwise, you cannot turn left at the parking area – follow the road back to where it meets PR-191 and walk another 1 mile down to Palo Colorado. The whole loop can be completed in three hours, depending on stops and fitness level.

El Toro

Crowned with dense cloud forest and grand vistas that take in half of Puerto Rico, **El Toro** is the highest peak and most challenging hike in the reserve, though unless it's exceptionally wet, not as draining as some rangers make out. The peak tops out at between 3474ft and 3533ft, depending on who you believe.

The path is sometimes overgrown, so dress accordingly and get an early start. The **Trade Winds Trail** (3.9 miles), which begins on PR-191, around 0.25 mile beyond the metal gate at km 13, is the best route up. The path should be easy to follow, but does get muddy and strenuous in places, making for an arduous three- to four-hour ascent. It's possible to pitch a tent near the summit, and you can continue down the other side of the mountain on the steep and generally unmaintained **El Toro Trail** (2.2 miles) to PR-186, assuming you have some way of getting picked up. Otherwise the hike back to PR-191 should take under three hours: if you start in the morning it's easy to complete the return trip in one day.

Cubuy

The southern section of El Yunque, known as **Cubuy**, offers a completely different experience to the busy northern half, with PR-191 slicing through a wilder, more rugged landscape of steep river valleys, raging waterfalls, and towering trees. To appreciate this area you really need to spend the night in one of the local guesthouses: places such as *Casa Cubuy* and *Casa Flamboyant* are a wealth of information and have their own network of trails fanning out across the four mountain streams that water the **Río Blanco**: the Cubuy, Sabana, Icacos, and Prieto rivers.

If you just want a taste of the area, drive half a kilometer beyond *Casa Cubuy* to where PR-191 is blocked by a metal gate on the bridge over the Río

Cubuy (park on the roadside). From here a narrow, short concrete path leads upriver to a series of invigorating pools fed by the stream, popular for swimming and barbecues at the weekends. You can also continue walking along the road, which remains in surprisingly good condition and is lined with great clumps of bamboo and sierra palm forest, to a **recreation area** being built by the Forest Service at the **Río Sabana**, around 1km further on, though it's not clear when this will be officially open. This area was smothered in coffee plantations before the 1930s, and what you see today is almost all secondary growth forest. Beyond here, the road rises and is quickly gobbled up by the giant landslide that destroyed it in the 1970s. Hardy climbers with a decent map can negotiate the landslide and rejoin the road on the other side, from where it's a long slog to the El Yunque Recreation Area, but you'll need to camp or arrange transport before making the return journey. Don't try it in wet weather.

Other highlights include the enigmatic Taíno **petroglyph sites** located along the **Río Icacos** and **Río Blanco** (inscribed onto large boulders in the river) and the secluded falls on the **Río Prieto**, but these are hard to find on your own – ask at your guesthouse or join a tour (see p.120).

Eating

Eating options within El Yunque might seem limited at first, but there are several places to fill up on local food, and plenty of restaurants nearby offer a smarter experience. You can get snacks within the forest on PR-191, but once you hit the trails you're on your own.

North side

El Bosque Encantado PR-191 km 7.2. Convenient pit-stop halfway into the forest, a no-nonsense food shack that serves fresh *batidas*, juices, and fried snacks such as *alcapurrias* ($1–3). Puerto Ricans tend to hit this place in the late afternoon, on the way home. Park your car along the roadside nearby. Daily 9am–5pm.

La Muralla PR-191 km 7.4. Just up the hill from *Bosque Encantado*, this canteen and souvenir shop sells similar fare, with a wider range of fried treats: beef or crab *alcapurrias* ($1.50), *empanadillas*, and occasionally *bacalaítos*. Lunch tends to be busiest here: park on the road nearby if you can. Daily 9am–5pm, closed Thurs.

Las Vegas PR-191 km 1.3, ☎787/887-2526. Upscale restaurant specializing in Puerto Rican dishes such as prawn *mofongo* and juicy *chuletas*, as well as appetizing fresh fish such as red snapper and mahi-mahi (mains $20–22). Just outside the village of Mameyes, on the way to El Portal, and a convenient choice for a sit-down dinner after a day exploring the forest. Has a/c and plenty of parking. Wed–Sun noon–midnight.

Yuquiyú Delights Sierra Palm Recreation Area, PR-191 km 11.3. This welcome food shack sits in what used to be the forest visitor center, with a popular picnic site nearby. Handy for lunch, it knocks out decent burgers (from $6) and grilled

meats from its outdoor barbecue, as well as local *frituras*, pizza, and hot dogs (from $2.25).

Cubuy

El Bohío ☎787/874-3802 or mobile 787/463-6640. This little culinary gem is a private dining room attached to *Casa Picaflores*, not far from PR-191, in a tranquil valley that seems a million miles from San Juan. Inside you'll find a table which seats ten, a small bar and nourishing, home-style cooking. The dinner menu is set daily: the person who makes the first reservation (you must call in advance, before noon on the same day) decides the time and the main entrée to be served (only one is served each day, usually from a choice of five dishes such as paella, steaks, and pastas), while the home-made desserts such as banana bread and key lime pie are heavenly. Open daily by appointment, dinner $30 (no credit cards), and breakfasts for $10.

Rain Forest Hideout PR-191 ☎787/526-0131. Small local roadside diner, serving filling sandwiches and no-frills home-cooked Puerto Rican classics such as giant *relleno de papa* (potato fritters stuffed with meat) from a simple menu including fried chicken or pork, cod, and pasta ($9). The *Paradores* dive bar on site offers cold Medalla ($1) and juices ($1). Tues–Sun lunch & dinner.

Luquillo and the northeast coast

Perched on the balmy Atlantic coast in the shadow of El Yunque, 45km east of San Juan, **LUQUILLO** combines three of Puerto Rico's most appealing pastimes: lounging on picture-perfect palm-fringed **beaches**, world-class **surfing**, and gorging on celebrated *cocina en kiosco*. While it can get insufferably busy on weekends, it's well worth a pit-stop during the week, and a couple of attractive hotels mean you can stay the night (and use it as a base for El Yunque). Alternatively, the sparsely populated **northeast coast** between here and San Juan is graced by some of the island's most exclusive **resorts. Getting here** involves an straightforward 45-minute drive from San Juan along PR-3, or a shorter twenty-minute hop from El Yunque. Taxis from San Juan's Aeropuerto Internacional Luis Muñoz Marín will charge $70.

Accommodation

Much of Luquillo's seafront is dominated by holiday homes and condos, rented primarily by *sanjuaneros* on weekends or over the summer. **Rental apartments** can be a good deal, especially if you stay a week or longer (the minimum stay is usually a weekend). Check ⓦ www.playaazulpr.com or call ⓣ 787/435-1825 for a current sample of what's available.

The most inviting **hotel** is the ⚜ *Luquillo Sunrise Beach Inn* (ⓣ 787/409-2929, ⓦ www.luquillosunrise.com; ❹) at Calle Costa Azul A2, with twelve clean, new rooms with tiled floors, TV, air-conditioning, and balconies overlooking the ocean. Full breakfast is included. The location is perfect, facing La Pared beach on the edge of the town center. *Hotel Yunque Mar* (ⓣ 787/889-5555, ⓦ www.yunquemar.com; ❸) is also right on the seafront, but several kilometers west of town at Playa Fortuna (Calle 1, no. 6). It's still a great deal though, with spacious rooms equipped with cable TV, air-conditioning, and balconies, so book ahead. If you have a tent, you can **camp** at the Balneario de Luquillo (ⓣ 787/889-5871), facing the beach ($17 with or $13 without utilities in camping area, or $10 in open areas).

Beach resorts

The north coast between San Juan and Luquillo is the preserve of the most luxurious **resorts** on the island. Frequented primarily by Puerto Rican professionals and wealthy visitors from the US, these giant five-stars also monopolize some of the best stretches of **beach** in the region, and often feature top-class **restaurants**. Many visitors like to end their trips to Puerto Rico with a night or two of pampering here, within caviar-throwing distance of El Yunque and Luquillo, but unless you're an avid **golf** fan with plenty of cash, it's not worth visiting for the day, and parking fees are often exorbitant.

The *Gran Meliá Puerto Rico* (ⓣ 787/809-1770, ⓦ www.paradisus-puerto-rico.com; ❽) is an all-inclusive resort at the end of a spur off PR-955, on **Coco Beach**, one of the most alluring stretches of sand on the north coast and handy for the exclusive *Coco Beach Golf and Country Club* (ⓣ 787/657-2000, ⓦ www.cocobeachgolf.com; day rates $140-160). You get suites not rooms, set in two-story villas on the beach with flashy contemporary design and all the extras. Despite the 11 percent resort fee, online deals can reduce prices considerably. The Wyndham-owned *Río Mar Beach Resort and Spa* (Blvd Río Mar 6000, 3.5km off PR-3, ⓣ 877/636-0636, ⓦ www.wyndhamriomar.com; ❾) is like a self-contained island covering five hundred acres, with a secluded beach, six hundred rooms with balconies and luxury baths dripping with marble, and

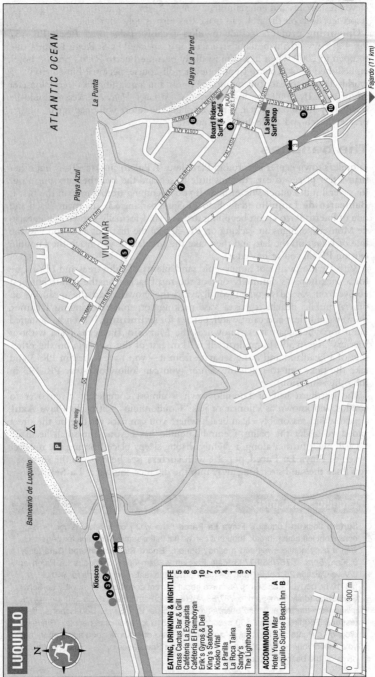

ATLANTIC OCEAN

La Punta

Playa Azul

VILOMAR

Playa La Pared

La Selva

Fajardo (11 km)

Board Riders
Surf & Café

La Selva Surf Shop

Balneario de Luquillo

Kioscos

San Juan (45 km)

EATING, DRINKING & NIGHTLIFE

Brass Cactus Bar & Grill	5
Cafeteria La Exquista	8
Cafeteria El Flamboyan	6
Erik's Gyros & Deli	10
King's Seafood	7
Kiosko Vital	3
La Parilla	4
La Roca Taina	1
Sandy's	9
The Lighthouse	2

ACCOMMODATION

Hotel Yunque Mar	A
Luquillo Sunrise Beach Inn	B

0   300 m

EL YUNQUE AND THE EAST COAST

125

eleven restaurants and entertainment venues. Again, despite the hefty 14 percent resort fee, deals on the web can make this surprisingly affordable.

Upcoming projects include the ultra-exclusive *Bahía Beach Resort* (PR-187 km 4.2, ⓦwww.bahiabeachpuertorico.com), operated by St Regis Resorts, due to open in 2009 when it will most likely become Puerto Rico's poshest hotel, embellished by a Robert Trent Jones Jr golf course, personal butler service, a world-class spa, oceanfront swimming pools, and a magnificent three-kilometer arc of sand. By 2009, the long-delayed *Cayo Largo Hotel and Resort* should be opened by Intercontinental. When finished, the resort will encompass another pristine beach and an 18-hole golf course.

The beaches

Luquillo's town center lies around Plaza Jesús T. Piñero, just off PR-3, but other than a few places to eat, contains little to see and the **beaches** are spread out for several miles either side of here. If you're coming from San Juan the first is **Balneario de Luquillo** (daily 8.30am–5pm; parking $3), the main beach and one of Puerto Rico's most beguiling strips of sand, formally known as Balneario de Monserrate. Signs are lacking on PR-3: take the first exit after you pass the line of *kioscos* on the left, and then take the first left (if you reach the Luquillo exit on PR-3, you've missed it).

With a wide swathe of honey-gold sand, plenty of palm trees and El Yunque for a backdrop, it's definitely one of the top beaches on the island, but best enjoyed on weekdays when you'll avoid the crowds (and the trash). As an official public beach, it has a vast parking lot, toilets, changing facilities, showers, and clear and calm water, perfect for **swimming**. It even has a staffed ramp for wheelchair users known as the **Mar Sin Barreras** ("sea without barriers", see p.50). Luquillo itself is 1km east of the *balneario* on the other side of a headland and quite separate from it – you have to rejoin PR-3 and take the next exit to reach the center (you can follow one-way PR-193 in the other direction).

The northern half of Luquillo town is almost completely given over to condos, and known as Vilomar or just "Condominio" – it backs **Playa Azul**, a narrow but reasonably clean beach where you can park for free on the street and doze under the palms. Central Luquillo lies beyond the small headland ("La Punta") further along, a slightly shabby, sleepy place fronting the rougher beach of **Playa La Pared**, popular with **surfers** (see below). To the southeast you'll see the sand stretching away into the distance: known as **La Selva**, this is

---

Luquillo watersports

Surfers flock to Luquillo's **Playa La Pared** ("the wall") on weekends for its fairly consistent left beach-break, though it can go flat in the summer: it's fine for beginners, with a fairly gentle swell and a sandy bottom. **Board Riders Surf and Café** (daily 9.30am–5pm, ☏787/889-7793, café Fri–Sun 7.30am–6pm) overlooks La Pared at c/Veve Calzada 25, not far from the main plaza, and rents **surf boards** for $40 per day ($8–10/hr, bodyboards $6/hr). Ask here about current conditions, or stop by **La Selva Surf Shop** (daily 9am–5pm, ☏787/889-6205) at c/Fernández García 250, one block inland from the plaza, where boards are just $35 per day. Owner Bob Roberts offers **lessons** ($60 first person, $30 second person, $15 for additional people). The reefs around La Punta dividing Playa Azul and La Pared offer some good **snorkeling**, but you'll need your own gear. Note also that Sunset Snuba (see p.132) organizes **Snuba** dives off the beaches at Luquillo.

hard to access by car and often sprinkled with debris, but almost always deserted. Conservationists have dubbed the undeveloped stretch of coast between here and Balneario Seven Seas (see p.130) the **Northeast Ecological Corridor**. With **turtle** nesting sites threatened by the construction of mega resorts, the area has attracted a coalition of various groups campaigning for its protection: see ⓦ www.sierraclub.org/corridor for more details.

Eating and drinking

Luquillo contains a handful of decent **restaurants** and **bars**, but is more famous throughout Puerto Rico for its **kioscos**, sixty *friquitines* (food stalls) that stand along the north side of PR-3, just before the turning to the *balneario* (coming from San Juan, exit the highway as if heading to the latter, and turn left at the beach). As you'd expect, this isn't food for the health-conscious: *alcapurrias*, *bacalaítos*, and other deep-fried delights are the staples here (typically $1–3). If you visit Luquillo in November check out the **Festival de los Platos Típicos**, held in the main plaza to celebrate local dishes, which tend to contain coconut.

Kioscos

Only a handful of *kioscos* are open in the mornings or early in the week; you'll get a bigger choice later in the day or on weekends. *La Roca Taina* (*kiosco* no. 60) is a solid choice for fried snacks, while *The Lighthouse* (no. 20) knocks out excellent crab *tacos*, various *pinchos*, and delicious fried fish – try the red snapper ($12). Many locals claim *La Parilla* (no. 2) is the best on the block, though it's a little overpriced compared to its neighbors. More like a sit-down restaurant, with bar and grill overlooking the beach, the seafood *mofongo* ($22) is worth sampling. *Kiosko Vital* (no. 15) is the place for **vegetarian food** and fresh juices, as well as occasional live music on weekends, when most *kioscos* stay open till midnight.

Restaurants and bars

Brass Cactus Bar & Grill PR-193 km 1.3. This Tex-Mex grill is a good choice for lunch or evening drinks, just off the highway in the Vilomar/Playa Azul section of town. The seven types of juicy half-pound burger, and tender baby-back ribs in home-made sauce ($7–9) are mouthwatering, but the selection of sandwiches, Angus steaks, and pastas is also excellent, and the margarita menu is well worth sampling. Take the first exit into Luquillo and turn left on the main street. Happy hour Mon–Fri 5–7pm.

Caféteria La Exquisita Avda 14 de Julio, Plaza Jesús T. Piñero. Cheap takeaway on the plaza, serving Puerto Rican staples such as rice and beans, *arroz con pollo*, and cakes for around $2, as well as juices ($1.75) and potent coffee ($0.60). Also has a few plastic tables and chairs inside. Daily 10am–2pm.

Caféteria El Flamboyan PR-193 km 1.2. Close to *Brass Cactus*, this is a no frills open-air bar and canteen with pool tables and a basic menu of *comida criolla*, though cheap beer ($1.50 during happy hour Sun 8–10pm) and live music on weekends are the main attractions. Open Thurs–Sun.

Erik's Gyros & Deli c/Fernández García 352. Handy for a last-minute stop on the way out of Luquillo (it's just off PR-3, on PR-193 at the southern end of town), this cheap diner serves all the Greek favorites (gyros, lamb kebabs, and lots of feta cheese) but also burgers, sandwiches, and breakfasts ($5–7). Closed Mon & Tues.

King's Seafood PR-193 (c/Fernández García 352). Just down the road from *Brass Cactus,* this is the best place in town for fresh seafood. With its own parking lot, the small dining room with wooden tables is packed at lunch with a loyal clientele. The freshly cooked fish dishes are superb, as is the *mofongo*, crammed with lobster, prawns, octopus, and fish broth (mains from $8). Closed Mon.

Sandy's c/Fernández García 276. Simple, clean restaurant specializing in seafood and finely grilled steaks, a short walk from the central plaza (with small parking lot). Expect giant portions of shellfish, chicken, *paella*, and plenty of lobster. Opening in 1984, it's been popular with the island's *glitterati* ever since, though mains range an affordable $6 to $20. Usually opens daily 11am–9pm, but sometimes closes early on weekdays.

Fajardo and around

Justly regarded as the boating capital of Puerto Rico, it's no surprise that the real appeal of **FAJARDO** lies along the coast. Numerous boat operators provide ample opportunity to explore the glittering waters and islets of **La Cordillera** just offshore, while the nearby **Reserva Natural Cabezas de San Juan** is an unexpectedly wild reserve containing one of the island's extraordinary **bioluminescent bays**. The city itself has become something of a boomtown in recent years and is best avoided, a wholly unattractive mess of strip malls, clogged highways, and rampant property development.

Coming by car, it's easy to drive right through all this, and most *públicos* will drop you elsewhere if you ask – get a taxi or another bus if you get stuck at the downtown terminal. The *reserva* is 5km north of the city on PR-987, near the fishing village of **Las Croabas**, which also contains some of the best places to stay and eat. Most boat excursions depart **Villa Marina**, just east of the center on PR-987, or **Puerto del Rey**, several kilometers to the south. The majority of visitors head straight to the grubby port district of **Puerto Real** (referred to locally and on *públicos* as "La Playa"), to catch the ferries to Vieques and Culebra (see p.136), but it's worth lingering a couple of days to appreciate the area's natural wonders.

Accommodation

Some of Puerto Rico's most reasonably priced hotels can be found in Fajardo municipality, though most of them are thankfully outside the city center, and close to the coast. Many lie close to PR-987, on the way to the *reserva*, and in the village of Las Croabas beyond. You can **camp** at Balneario Seven Seas (☏787/863-8180) for $10 if you have your own tent: there are toilets, showers and 24-hour security, making this one of the safest places to pitch tents on the island.

Anchor's Inn PR-987 km 2.7 ☏787/863-7200, ⓦwww.anchorsinn.net. Despite the nautical theme inside, this budget hotel was built in a bizarre red and white Spanish Revival style, a bit like the Ponce fire station. Rooms are fairly plain and worn around the edges, but come with aging a/c, bathroom, cable TV, and spotless tiled floors. Check out the excellent restaurant downstairs. Small parking lot on site. ❷

Ceiba Country Inn PR-977 km 1.2 ☏787/885-0471, ⓦwww.geocities.com/countryinn00735. This former hacienda lies a short drive south of Fajardo (3km from PR-53), on a wonderfully scenic and tranquil ridge surrounded by forest. The nine rooms are simple, clean and comfortable, and decorated with bright, flowery murals. Each has a/c and fridge, but no TV. Breakfast is included. Take PR-975 from the highway (exit 5), then follow the signs on PR-977. ❸

El Conquistador Resort Avda Conquistador 1000 ☏866/317-8932, ⓦwww.elconresort.com. This vast town-like resort sprawls over the 300-foot cliffs above Puerto Real, with casino, the plush Golden Door Spa, five "villages" including the luxury *Las Casitas Village* (ⓦlascasitasvillage.com), 21 restaurants and lounges, and its own private island. Even the cheapest of its 983 elegant rooms have balconies and five-star amenities, and though staying here sometimes feels a little too isolated from the outside world, online deals can be good value. ❻–❽

Fajardo Inn c/Parcelas Beltrán 52, Puerto Real ☏787/860-6000, ⓦwww.fajardoinn.com. Despite looking like a big motel, this is more like a mini-resort, with 100 rooms, family-oriented *Coco's Park* (swimming pools, mini golf etc) on site, and a couple of decent restaurants. All rooms are relatively spacious, with queen-sized beds and cable TV, though it's $20 extra for a balcony. You can check email in the computer room. ❹

Lighthouse at Las Croabas Inn Calle 2, no. 84, Las Croabas, ☏787/860-8753, ⓦwww.lascroabasinn.net. Two-story motel-like guesthouse, perched in a hill-top residential section of Las Croabas. Rooms are simply but warmly decorated with a/c, partial ocean views, bathroom, microwave, and cable TV; some have kitchenettes and patios. Internet is available and they have parking – look for the signs off PR-9987. ❷

Passion Fruit Bed & Breakfast PR-987 Int PR-9987 km 4.8, Las Croabas ☏787/801-0106, ⓦwww.passionfruitbb.com. Best of the budget hotels in Las Croabas, this three-story villa just off PR-987

FAJARDO & AROUND

EATING & DRINKING
Anchor's Inn	F
A La Banda	6
Blue Bahía Seafood Restaurant	2
Cremaldi Ice Cream	5
Mar Adentro	1
Ocean View	3
Rosa's Seafood	4

0 —————— 500 m

ATLANTIC OCEAN

RESERVA NATURAL CABEZAS DE SAN JUAN

Laguna Grande

Playa El Convento

Laguna Aguas Prietas

Balneario Seven Seas

LAS CROABAS

A
B P
C
D P
2
3 P
1
E

Entrance to El Conquistador

N

987

AV. EL CONQUISTADOR

F

CARIBBEAN SEA

Sun Bay Marina

CAMINO CABEZAS

AV. B

Villa Marina

Isleta Marina

Cayo Zancudo

194

AV. GENERAL VALERO

987

PUERTO REAL

G

UNION

195

Ferry Terminal

4

FAJARDO

5

194

3

Río Fajardo

Luquillo (11km) & San Juan (50km)

Fajardo Airport (2km)

H, 6 & Puerto del Rey

Culebra

Vieques

ACCOMMODATION
Anchor's Inn	F
Ceiba Country Inn	H
El Conquistador Resort	E
Fajardo Inn	G
Lighthouse at Las Croabas Inn	D
Passion Fruit Bed & Breakfast	A
Seven Seas Campsite	B
Yamil's Guest House	C

has large, simply furnished rooms with tiled floors and satellite TV, great breakfasts, super-friendly owners, and a small pool. ❸–❹

Yamil's Guest House PR-987 km 6.1, Las Croabas ☎787/860-8601. No-frills budget accom-modation right on the main road, with good deals on singles and doubles, and cable TV and a/c in each room. Near to a cluster of shops and close to the beach. ❷

Around Fajardo

Lingering in Fajardo itself is pointless; focus instead on the varied ecosystems of the **Reserva Natural Cabezas de San Juan** and **Laguna Grande** before exploring the reef-encrusted islands of **La Cordillera**. While plenty of travelers visit on day-trips from San Juan, staying in the area means you won't have to pay additional transport charges or get up at the crack of dawn.

Balneario Seven Seas

The only public beach in the Fajardo area, **Balneario Seven Seas** (daily 8am–6pm; parking $3) is 4.85km north of the city center on PR-987, a sheltered arc of sand famed for its brilliant, multi-hued waters, though you'll need a vivid imagination to identify all seven colors alluded to in the name. With a reef just offshore, it's better for snorkeling than swimming, and because it's generally calm, popular with families. Note however that the facilities here tend to be a little more run-down than at Luquillo, and the sand not as clean (it has lots of seaweed year round, and trash on public holidays). Alternatively, hike to the western end of the beach (left side) where the rocky area begins, and look for an overgrown trail up to the left. Follow this trail until it ends, and turn right to reach **Playa El Convento**, a more remote, secluded beach, home to turtle nesting sites and the location of the governor's beach house. It's also part of the **Northeast Ecological Corridor** (see p.127).

Note that the scrappy bit of sand east of the *balneario* is popular with locals who park their cars along the road nearby for free (the private parking lot opposite is $3.50): you can scramble northeast along the coast into the *reserva* (see below) from here and eventually to **Playa Escondida**, a far more appealing place to spend a few hours.

Reserva Natural Cabezas de San Juan

Wonderfully preserved by the Conservation Trust (🌐www.fideicomiso.org) since 1975, the **Reserva Natural Cabezas de San Juan** (Wed–Sun, tours 9.30am, 10am, 10.30am, 2pm; $7; over-65s and 5- to 11-years-olds $4; weekdays ☎787/860-2563 or 787/722-5834, weekends ☎787/860-2560) comprises 321 acres of untamed scrub and mangroves, and five miles of reef-lined coast on the north-eastern tip of the island. You'll pass the gated entrance to the reserve just beyond the Balneario Seven Seas parking lot, but the guard will only let you in if you have a reservation: **reserve a tour** in advance, by phone: English tours depart at 2pm.

Laguna Grande (see opposite) dominates the lower half of the reserve, while the bush-smothered hill that rises over the northern section is topped by **El Faro**, the old Spanish lighthouse completed in 1882. It now houses a small visitors' center with exhibits showcasing the reserve's marine and coastal ecosys-tems, including the bio bay – the highlight being bags of dinoflagellates (see p.167) that glow in the dark when shaken. Be sure to soak up the magnificent views from the observation deck on top.

General tours (by trolley bus; 2hr 30min) provide a brief taste of some of the diverse environments preserved here, starting with the **mangrove forests** that surround the lagoon (30 percent of the reserve), where a short boardwalk passes red, black, white and buttonwood mangroves, and hordes of crab scuttle for cover. At Playa Lirios you get a chance to see the **rocky coast** and scrub, and the three headlands that give the reserve its name (*cabeza* means "head"), before ending up at the lighthouse. Other than birds and insects, the only other wildlife you may encounter are giant **iguanas**, plodding through the undergrowth. To experience the **dry forest** (40 percent of the reserve) you'll have to join the edifying guided tours at 8.30am (2hr 30min, Spanish only), which follow the trail south of the lighthouse.

Laguna Grande

Lying just inside the reserve, the placid waters of **Laguna Grande** look fairly ordinary by day, but when night falls everything changes. Thanks to creatures known as dinoflagellates (see p.167), kayaks and boats leave glowing trails in the dark, while water falls like sparks of light from paddles and trailing arms. Puerto Rico has several places where heavy concentrations of microscopic plankton create this mesmerizing phenomenon: Vieques is home to the most celebrated example, but on a dark (and moonless) night, Laguna Grande is almost as magical. Optimum days for viewing are based not only on the phases of the moon but also the actual time the moon rises – check before you go.

Laguna Grande tours

The only way to experience the lagoon is to take a tour, preferably by **kayak**. As of April 2007, it is forbidden to swim in the bay, and cutting through the mangroves by kayak is now the best way to appreciate its bizarre luminescence – it's not as taxing as it looks and easy for beginners. One of the most eco-friendly and informative operators is **Las Tortugas Adventures** (T787/809-0253, Wwww.kayak-pr.com), which tends to have smaller groups and earlier excursions (Mon–Sat 6.30pm & 9pm; 2hr). You don't need prior kayak experience. The cost depends on group size, but is normally around $45 per person. **Kayaking Puerto Rico** (T787/435-1665, Wwww.kayakingpuertorico.com) is another professional outfit that can arrange trips for $45 per person (daily 7 & 9pm; 2hr). Try to book at least three days in advance.

For those that really cannot kayak, **Captain Suárez Cruise Boat** (T787/655-2739 or 787/556-8291) is the only operator licensed to pilot motor boats in the lagoon, usually making ninety-minute trips (Mon–Sat at 7pm, 9pm & 11pm; $45 per person). All tours start at the Las Croabas quay, and guides tend to be bilingual; taking unlicensed boat tours is a bad idea and adds to the pollution of the lagoon.

La Cordillera

While the modern city of Fajardo has all the charm of a giant shopping mall, the real Caribbean starts in earnest just offshore. La Cordillera is a chain of around ten uninhabited, reef-encrusted white sand cays, paradise for anyone interested in snorkeling, diving, or just lazing on the beach. Turtles nest here each year, and the sprawling coral reefs are home to a variety of marine life. Many of the islands are now protected within the Reserva Natural La Cordillera, managed by the DRNA.

To reach the islands you'll need a boat: the easiest way to get one is to find or call Captain Domingo "Mingo" Nieves (T787/383-6509) at the Las Croabas pier. He'll take you to **Icacos** or **Palominitos** for $100 (maximum 6 people), and pick you up anytime. For $30 per person (minimum 4 people) he'll take you snorkeling off Palominitos for a couple of hours. If you fancy kayaking out to the islands, contact Las Tortugas Adventures (see above). If you're lucky enough to be a guest at the *El Conquistador Resort* (see p.128), you'll get ferried over to Isla Palominos for free, and failing that, numerous boats operating out of Villa Marina and Puerto del Rey (see opposite) visit the islands every day.

The islands

Cayo Icacos (163 acres) is the biggest island in the chain, coated in a thick layer of scrubby bush, seagrape, and coconut palms, and fringed by incredibly seductive beaches of floury white sand and vivid, turquoise waters. Being relatively close to shore (though still 4.5 miles from Villa Marina), it's a particular favorite of boat operators, which means the best beach areas (on the calmer, leeward side) can get crowded on weekends, but at other times it's easy to find a secluded spot. The ocean side of the island is rough and rocky, while the reefs between Icacos and the rock known as "Cucaracha" have the best snorkeling.

Diving La Cordillera

Join any dive trip from Fajardo and you'll almost certainly be heading for La Cordillera. Unless conditions are perfect, experienced divers may be disappointed with the level of coral and marine life on display, much reduced in the last twenty years or so – hardcore divers should insist on **Cayo Diablo** (or just head to Culebra, p.175). For casual or beginner divers, it's still worth a look, and it's not overly expensive.

La Casa del Mar Dive Center (daily 8am–6pm; ☏787/860-3483) inside *El Conquistador Resort* is open to non-guests, and offers two-tank dives for $99 ($69 for one tank). Trips to Culebra start at $125 for two tanks, while the Discover Scuba program for beginners is $119. They also run daily **snorkeling** trips to Palominos ($50) and Culebra ($85), and offer a popular **kids' program** (for 8- to 9-year-olds) known as Bubblemakers ($49) – call for details.

Sea Ventures Dive Center (Mon–Sat 8am–noon & 1–5pm, Sun 8am–1am; ☏787/863-3483, ⓦwww.divepuertorico.com) at Puerto del Rey is the other main operator in the area, charging $99 for two-tank dives with equipment and $89 if you bring your own ($55–65 for one-tank). Non-certified beginners can dive for $150, or sign up for a PADI certification course for $425 (minimum four days). Smaller operators such as **Caribbean School of Aquatics** (see opposite) tend to be more flexible about destinations. Their dives include all equipment, and cost $119 for two tanks.

For **Snuba** (see p.134) contact **Sunset Snuba** (☏787/354-0999, ⓦwww.sunsetsnuba .com). They run excursions to Palominos, Icacos, and Lobos three times daily ($79) from **Sun Bay Marina**, the newer dock not far from Villa Marina, a bit further along PR-987. Trips last two and a half hours. They also conduct beach-based Snuba dives ($59) all over Puerto Rico.

Where you end up diving is largely in the hands of your divemaster and the weather/ sea conditions on the day – note also that heavy rain in El Yunque can decrease visibility (which normally ranges 20–70ft) dramatically, as heavily silted rivers flow into the sea near here. Beginners usually end up at **Pyramid** (30ft), a coral rise teeming with small fish and reef lobsters, but often disappointing for seasoned divers. **Cayo Lobos** has three main sites, with **Lobos** itself (up to 33ft) having the greatest variety of fish: yellowtail snapper, blue tang, the ubiquitous sergeant major, and sometimes dolphins and stingrays. **Isla Palominos** has five main dive sites, with **Sandslide** (15–70ft) one of the most popular, a gentle sandy slope that leads to a large reef crawling with enormous lobsters and all sorts of coral. You might also see dolphins, turtles, barracudas, small tuna, and octopus here. **Spurs and Grooves** (10–70ft) comprises spur-and-groove fingers that slope down to a sandy bottom. Turtles and dolphins sometimes hang out near the reef. Finally, **Cayo Diablo** (45–50ft) has several sites and some of the best diving on the east coast, though swells and high winds often prevent visits. The island is surrounded by brilliant hard and soft corals, schools of barracuda, and occasional rays – the water is always extremely clear.

From here, smaller islets stretch east towards Culebra: **Cayo Ratones**, **Cayo Lobos**, and further out, **Cayo Diablo** (30–40min by boat), are popular dive and snorkel sites (see opposite), and it's rare to go ashore. Five-acre Lobos is 1.7 miles east of Icacos and actually a private island, though it's permitted to dive or snorkel off its reef. A posh hotel was built here in the early 1960s, but went bankrupt soon after and now serves as a luxury vacation home for the owners.

To the south is the larger, rockier **Isla Palominos** (3 miles offshore and 15min by boat). Most of the island is leased by the *El Conquistador Resort* and officially off-limits to everyone else, though people do come here to snorkel off the northern shore, and dine in the restaurant. Resort guests get whisked across in minutes to enjoy the lavish facilities on the 104-acre island, which include swimming, snorkeling, diving, windsurfing, and horseback riding. It also has a bar, café, and plenty of loungers on the smallish but pristine beach. **Isla Palominitos** covers just one acre, 500 yards off the southern tip of Isla Palominos, and surrounded by a reef perfect for snorkeling. Though it's tiny, it also has wide, sugary sand beaches – a real desert island.

Villa Marina and Puerto del Rey

The two biggest boating centers on the east coast are **Villa Marina** (☏787/863-5131, ⓦwww.villamarinapr.com) and **Puerto del Rey** (☏787/860-1000, ⓦwww.puertodelrey.com), and the only reason to visit either is to pick up a boat excursion.

Villa Marina was built in 1975 and occupies a small harbor just off PR-987 at km 1.3. Assuming you've made a reservation, the guard will open the gate and you should be able to park inside: if you drive past you can also park further up the road and reach the moorings for the *Salty Dog*, *Traveler* and *Barefoot IV* boats through a side entrance. The marina is barebones, but you'll find a small row of shops, including a supermarket, on the road before the main entrance.

Opening in 1988, Puerto del Rey is now the largest marina in the Caribbean with 1100 slips, a few kilometers south of Fajardo at PR-3, km 51.4: take exit 2 off PR-53. The large free parking lot is just inside the main entrance, with a convenience store (which also does cheap meals), Westernbank ATM, and a couple of places to eat nearby. The marina office (daily 8am–5pm) has maps and information about the area, while a 24-hour coin-operated laundry stands opposite ($1.25). Thrifty (daily 8am–noon & 1–5pm; ☏787/860-2030) **car rental** also has an office here.

Boats

Most of the boats listed below offer similar routes and services: departing at around 10am, most head out to the reefs of La Cordillera (invariably Icacos) before a buffet lunch and afternoon snorkeling further offshore, returning 3–4pm. Note that many locals refer to these boats disparagingly as "cattlemarans": that's a little harsh, but at peak times on the big boats you might find yourself sharing the deck with over forty people.

Villa Marina

Caribbean School of Aquatics ☏787/728-6606, ⓦwww.saildiveparty.com. Captain Greg Korwek organizes snorkeling trips on his self-built catamaran *Fun Cat* ($69, extra $20 for pick-up), and also diving for certified divers.
Castillo Tours/Barefoot IV ☏787/791-6195 or 787/726-5752, ⓦwww.castillotours.com. Captain

José (and José Jr) take catamarans *Stampede* and *Barefoot IV* out to La Cordillera daily, usually anchoring off Cayo Icacos for snorkeling. Picnic lunch and *piña coladas* are served on board, with a 45-people maximum ($65 or $79 with San Juan pick-up).
Fajardo Tours Traveler ☏787/863-2821 or 787/396-0995, ⓦwww.travelerpr.com. Fajardo

Snuba

Created in the 1980s, **Snuba** is fast gaining popularity all over the world, but especially in the Caribbean. Essentially, Snuba is cheat scuba diving: air tanks usually strapped to the back are instead set on rubber pontoon rafts that float on the water's surface and are connected to the diver by air tubes. The major advantage is that anyone (aged 8 and above) can get into the water almost immediately, without any kind of training, as all the stuff that real divers must learn to master – direction, air pressure, depth – is monitored by someone else. Usually, two people share one raft and descend gradually until they are 15–20ft below the surface. Once comfortable, guides will lead you on an underwater tour of the area, usually lasting around forty minutes. In Puerto Rico at the time of writing, the only outfit franchised to use Snuba International's (@www .snuba.com) patented equipment was Sunset Snuba (see p.132). You must be eight years old or over.

native Captain Antonio and family take their catamaran *Traveler* out to Icacos and other islands, providing new snorkeling gear and a "snorkeling instructor" on board. The salad-style lunch buffet with cold cuts and cheeses is top-notch, accompanied with plenty of cocktails, and the fun crew is popular with families. Day-trips are $65 per person including lunch and drinks. Maximum 48 people.

Salty Dog ☎787/717-6378, @www.saltydreams .com. This 46ft catamaran makes regular trips out to Icacos, Lobos, and Palominitos, its young and enthusiastic crew, led by Captain Saso, making it something of a party boat popular with twenty-somethings. Snorkeling breaks up the cocktails and salsa. Day-trips are $59 per person.

Spread Eagle II ☎888/523-4511, @www .snorkelpr.com. This 51ft catamaran is one of the most popular in Fajardo, running daily trips out to Icacos for snorkeling and dive trips, with gargantuan sandwich buffet lunches. All tours include complimentary *piña coladas* and tropical fruit punch, as well as snorkel equipment. Daily trips (10am–3.30pm) are $70 ($50 for under-12s) and they'll provide return transport from San Juan for $12. Maximum 49 people.

Puerto del Rey

Deep Sea Fishing ☎787/547-4851, @www .deepseafishingpr.com. Captain Osva Alcaide leads half- or full-day fishing charters (maximum six people), supplying equipment and bait on his nippy *Topaz Royal* or *Hatteras*. Rates for the whole boat are $500 for a half-day (4hr) or $750 for six hours and $800 for a full day (8am–4pm). All trips include

beers, sodas, water, and snacks, with full days also coming with a light lunch (sandwiches). The cost can be split between different parties if you have fewer than six in your group.

East Island Excursions ☎787/860-3434, @www .eastwindcats.com. One of the most professional operations in the area, the 62ft sailing catamaran *East Wind* visits Icacos and La Cordillera for $69, while speedy power catamarans are used for excursions to Culebra, Culebrita (both $89), Vieques (for the bio bay; $109), and St Thomas ($109, minimum twenty people) – these boats are the most efficient way to visit the outer islands for the day.

Erin Go Bragh Charters ☎787/860-4401, @www.egbc.net. Captain Bill Henry (who has been here since 1990) sails to Palominos, Icacos, Lobos, and Palominitos for snorkeling and a sumptuous barbecue lunch of chicken, ribs, and salad, with the real draw being the small groups of two to six people on board his 50ft Gulfstar Ketch yacht. He also offers charters to Vieques, Culebra, and the Virgin Islands. Day-trips are $85 per person, while you can hire the whole boat for $510 per day. Sunset cruises are $95.

Ventajero Sailing Charter ☎787/645-9129, @www.sailpuertorico.com. Captain Domingo Garcia runs day-trips to La Cordillera for up to six people in this beautiful 52ft sloop, but also overnight charters to the Virgin Islands where you get to bunk up below deck. He prefers to deal with groups: the whole yacht is $570 per day, with overnight excursions $750 (you'll need at least seven days to see the best of the Virgin Islands).

Eating and drinking

The waterfront in **Las Croabas** has the greatest concentration of Puerto Rican seafood restaurants in the area, while cheap fast-food chains are scattered all over central Fajardo and easy to spot from the highways. **Nightlife** is fairly subdued, with many of the restaurants listed here and in Las Croabas doubling as bars and venues for live music on weekends, but not much happening during the week. If you really want to splurge, you're better off heading to the **casino** and posh **restaurants** like the *Strip House* inside the *El Conquistador Resort* (see p.128).

Anchor's Inn PR-987 km 2.7 ☎787/863-7200. French flair meets Puerto Rican cuisine in this appealing restaurant with a vaguely nautical theme, plastic tables and chairs, wooden bar, and superlative food. Highlights include the zesty French onion soup, *paella*, beautifully cooked snapper fillet (mains $16–24), seven types of *mofongo* ($19–24), lobster *asopao* ($18), and a special children's menu. Officially open daily except Tues 11am–10pm or 11pm, but tends to get going at 5pm on Monday, also morphing into a lively bar and music venue on weekends.

A La Banda Puerto del Rey. Facing a forest of gleaming white masts across the marina, this is the smartest place to eat at Puerto del Rey, with *cocina criolla* classics such as *asopao* ($14.95), fresh fish of the day, a tempting selection of Spanish style seafood ($22–25), and even Italian favorites in honor of Columbus (try the *linguini con salsa* for $11.95).

Blue Bahía Seafood Restaurant Las Croabas ☎787/863-6509. This indoor dining room overlooking the park and harbor beyond is a sound choice for seafood: try the *camarones de ajillo* (garlic prawns), *paella marinara*, and filling *arepas rellenos* (all $7–8). For a real treat, order the *ruedas de mero* (red grouper; $9). They also do a mean *asopao* with prawn ($13) and the ever present *mofongo* ($14) is a specialty.

Cremaldi Ice Cream c/Unión 62. This venerable ice cream parlor is the best reason for a detour into downtown Fajardo, where home-made ices in tangy fruit flavors are sold beneath faded historical photos of the town. Open daily.

Mar Adentro Las Croabas. Beach-type bar and grill right on Las Croabas harbor, perfect for a cheap meal or cocktail on the water, assuming you can handle the aroma of salt fish and sea-spray wafting over your beers and assorted local snacks ($3). Happy hour Wed–Fri 5–7pm, open Wed–Sun 11am–midnight.

Ocean View Las Croabas ☎787/863-1164. Another harbor-front restaurant, with a lime-green open-fronted terrace, specializing in fresh fish, *mofongo*, grilled lobster, and prawns – a worthy alternative to *Blue Bahía* if you prefer sitting outside. Open 11am–11pm, closed Tues.

Rosa's Seafood c/Tablazo 536, Puerto Real, ☎787/863-0213. This lauded restaurant was founded in 1968 by Rosa Ayala, and overlooks the Río Fajardo on the edge of Puerto Real, not far from the ferry terminal. Try anything "*a la Rosa*", the house sauce (mayonnaise with garlic, onions, and peppers), but especially conch ($17.95) or lobster ($25.95). Other highlights include the tasty cornmeal *arepas* (johnny cakes; $0.40) and mango margaritas ($4). Open 11am–10pm, closed Wed.

The east coast

Heading south along the east coast, you eventually lose the cars, condos, and tourists and enter a rural, slower-paced, and infinitely more appealing part of Puerto Rico. The main towns here, Naguabo and Humacao, hold little of interest for most visitors and are best ignored. Once again, it's the coast that provides the real allure, throwing up a series of modest but entertaining attractions as you head south, the highlights being the boat trip to **Cayo Santiago** (Monkey Island), and some exceptional seafood **restaurants** at **Playa Naguabo** and **Punta Santiago**, before ending up at the **beaches** and staggering vistas of PR-901, one of the most scenic roads on the island. Along the way, nature lovers should check out the tranquil **Reserva Natural de Humacao** and the thoroughbred Paso Fino **horses** at Palmas del Mar.

Playa Naguabo

The first place of any interest south of Fajardo, the laid-back seaside village of **PLAYA NAGUABO** (not to be confused with Naguabo town, and also known as **Playa Húcares**, after the local tree) is a welcome reminder than Puerto Rico

Moving on to Vieques and Culebra

Ferries to Culebra and Vieques depart from the run-down port area of **Puerto Real**, at the end of PR-195. You'll see the ample, secure **parking lot** (daily 6am–midnight; $5/24hr) on the right as you arrive at the wharf. World Car (c/Unión 466 ☎787/860-4808) **rents cars** from its office a short walk back along the main road from $35/day. The **Terminal de Lanchas** (ferry terminal) is a basic affair with a snack bar, toilets, and some seating, while tickets are sold on the other side of the road. Note that ferries can fill up quickly at weekends or holidays – you can't reserve tickets but you can buy them in advance. Schedules do change, so check times before arrival. Note that the ferry service between Vieques and Culebra was canceled in 2006 (you have to come back to Fajardo to travel between the two) and that scheduled ferries between Fajardo and St Thomas (in the US Virgin Islands) no longer run.

Ferries

Ferries **to Vieques** ($2 one-way, kids and seniors $1) depart Mon–Fri at 9.30am, 1pm, 4.30pm, and 8pm, and 9am, 3pm, and 6pm weekends. Coming back, ferries leave Vieques at 6.30am, 11am, 3pm, and 6pm weekdays, and 7am, 1pm, and 4.30pm weekends. The journey takes around 1hr 15min. **Ferries to Culebra** ($2.25 one-way) depart 9am, 3pm, and 7pm daily, returning 6.30am, 1pm, and 5pm. The trip takes around 1hr 30min.

Flights

Flying to Vieques or Culebra from tiny **Fajardo Airport** is relatively cheap and much faster than the ferry – you'll also get magnificent views of La Cordillera, and Playa Flamenco if heading for Culebra. The airport lies on PR-976 on the west side of the city, but it's poorly signposted from PR-3. Parking (daily 6am–7pm) is $1 for the first hour

---

isn't all shopping malls, cars, and fast-food chains. Other than soaking up the soporific atmosphere (though as always, it gets busy on weekends), the main draw is the plethora of seafood **restaurants** on the small *malecón* (promenade), and the celebrated local snack, **chapín** (see opposite).

The village also has a few charming leftovers of *criollo* and Spanish colonial architecture, notably the **Villa del Carmen**, the stately white building with yellow trim (a private colonial mansion) next to the tourist office, and just beyond the *malecón*, on the left overlooking the sea, the ruinous **Castillo Villa del Mar**. Built in the 1880s by Spanish landowner Luciano Fuertes, and once the most elegant villa in town, it's now a national monument and is slowly being restored.

Playa Naguabo is on PR-3 a short drive off the PR-53 *autopista* (exit 13; once off the highway, don't take the right fork on PR-31 to Naguabo itself). You can park along the main road that runs along the harbor, or in the parking lot behind the *kioscos* at the end of the *malecón*. The helpful **Naguabo Information Center** (Mon–Fri 8am–4.30pm) on the *malecón* usually has English-speakers on hand and plenty of information on Naguabo municipality, but little else. You'll learn that *naguabeños* are nicknamed *enchumbaos* ("the soaking wet ones"), as it tends to rain a lot more here than in other parts of the island, but showers are brief and thankfully sunshine is just as plentiful.

Continue 2.5km south from Playa Naguabo (which doesn't really have a beach, despite the name) on PR-3, and you'll reach **Playa Tropical**, a small collection of ramshackle houses facing a white-sand beach backed by coconut palms. Very quiet midweek, it's not bad if you want a quick dose of sun and surf, and there are basic snack stalls on the road.

and $0.50 per hour thereafter, or $8.50 for 24 hours. World Car Rental (☎787/863-9696) has a desk inside, but otherwise it's just airline counters (no ATM). For snacks and drinks try the food stall outside.

Vieques Air Link (☎787/863-3020, reservations ☎1-888/901-9247) flies to **Vieques** for $42 return or $23 one-way: flights depart fairly regularly Mon–Sat 6.15am–5.30pm, and though you can just turn up, it's best to call ahead to check the schedule. Flights on Sundays are usually limited to two in the morning. There are usually three flights to **Culebra** daily ($54 return, $28 one-way) starting at 6.45am, last flight 3pm. You can also fly to **St Croix** (US Virgin Islands) every day except Wednesdays, ($163 return, $83 one-way). Air Flamenco (☎787/801-8256) also flies to Culebra "on demand" several times daily ($54 return, $27 one-way) but you must reserve in advance. Isla Nena Air Service (☎787/863-4447) offers flights to both islands, but you'll also need to make advance reservations.

By taxi

Though taxis and *públicos* do typically wait for ferry and air arrivals, **moving on to San Juan** from either the ferry terminal or the airport, it's best to arrange transport in advance. Reliable drivers include Zoriada's Taxi (☎787/432-1572 or 939/475-4164, ✉alexisa_2001@hotmail.com) and Mary and Angel (☎787/863-8224 or 787/649-9155). The latter have mini-buses with air-conditioning and charge $65 to Old San Juan and just $50 to San Juan's **Aeropuerto Internacional Luis Muñoz Marín** (plus a few dollars extra for additional people, luggage, and evening drives).

Traveling between Fajardo airport and the ferry terminal, you should pay no more than $6 – Luciano Rivera (☎787/556-2061) is usually on hand at the airport, and also charges $70–90 to San Juan.

Cayo Santiago (Monkey Island)

The main reason to visit Playa Naguabo is to take a trip out to **Cayo Santiago**, just offshore. In 1938, the University of Puerto Rico established a colony of 409 Indian Rhesus **monkeys** on the 39-acre cay (now thought to number 900 to 1000) to study their behavior, and as such it's the oldest monkey colony in the world.

Trips (2hr 30min) on *La Paseodora*, the motorboat captained by the sprightly Frank (Paco) Lopez (☎787/316-0441 or 787/850-7881), cost just $35 per person, a real bargain. Though it's forbidden to actually go ashore, Lopez regales his passengers with facts and amusing yarns about the island throughout the voyage. Trips also include snorkeling nearby, spiced up by the wreck of a cargo ship that sank in 1944 and is now a haven for tropical fish. Lopez goes out every day, but make sure you call in advance to reserve a space (the boat can take up to twenty people, but he prefers to take groups of between six and ten).

Eating and drinking

Each February Playa Naguabo hosts a **Festival del Chapín** to honor its savory fish *empanadas*, deep-fried turnovers usually stuffed with local trunkfish. You'll find them all over Puerto Rico but this is where they were first created, and the festival features boat races, market stalls, and arts and crafts, as well as the mouthwatering snack itself. At other times, most of the restaurants along the seafront offer their own versions of *chapín,* and if you have access to a kitchen, you can buy freshly made, raw versions at *Pastelillos Nitza* (daily 8am–6pm), a short walk back up PR-3 from the waterfront ($8 for fourteen, but you need to cook them before eating).

The best **restaurants** are on the left as you hit the waterfront, while those that face the *malecón* itself are a little dilapidated and tend to function as **bars** that open later in the day. *Griselle Seafood* (Mon, Tues, Thurs & Sun 11am–8pm, Fri & Sat 11am–midnight; ☎787/874-1533) is a fabulous family-run seafood restaurant right on the corner of the *malecón*, with chef Miguel Castro specializing in Caribbean spiny lobster (*viveros de langosta*): pick out one of the hapless crustaceans from the tank inside ($25–30). The front deck is a good place to enjoy a cocktail and views of the sea. *El Makito* (Wed–Sun 11am–11pm; ☎787/874-7192) occupies the second floor of the building above the dock (turn left when you reach the seafront on PR-3), with air-conditioning and rustic decor. It specializes in lavish plates of lobster stuffed with seafood, and offers a range of fresh fish and Puerto Rican staples – you also get sweeping views of the bay and Cayo Santiago. If you fancy something cheaper, *El Botecito* (☎787/630-0994), near *Makito*, is one of the cheapest cafés on the waterfront, with filling tacos ($1.50), hamburgers ($3), *carne frita* ($4.25), and *chapín* ($1.50). It also sells bottles of beer for $2. Failing that, at the far end of the *malecón* (heading south out of the village), *kioscos* deliver all the classic *frituras* for $1–3, usually open weekends only.

Punta Santiago

Five kilometers south of Playa Naguabo lies the small seaside town of **PUNTA SANTIAGO**, another former fishing village now associated with some top-notch **seafood restaurants**, but with little else in the way of attractions. Around 3km further south at PR-3 km 72.4, **Balneario Punta Santiago** (Wed–Sun 8.30am–5pm; $3 parking) is a long strip of public beach also known as Balneario Público de Humacao, containing a kids' water park ($5 kids, $4 adults) and the *Centro Vacational Villa Punta Santiago* (☎787/852-1660; cabañas ❷, villas ❹). Accommodation is fairly basic and primarily targeted at local families (six people to each villa): you need to contact the Compañía de Parques Nacionales in advance to stay (see p.28). The beach is relatively clean and usually empty during the week, if you fancy a quick swim.

Eating

The most inviting **places to eat** in Punta Santiago are both *mesones gastronómicos*. *Tulio's Sea Food* (closed Mon; ☎787/850-1840) at Calle Isidro Andreux Andreu 5, just off PR-3 at km 76.6, specializes in lobster and garlicky dressings from its vast seafood menu, though its desserts are equally as tempting (try the pound cake). *Daniel Sea Food* (closed Tues; ☎787/852-1784) is at Calle Marina 7, the road that runs along the seafront parallel to PR-3, with an open-front and indoor seating,

▲ Cayo Santiago

though views of the sea are blocked by thick vegetation here. It offers a similar menu of fresh fish and local specialties such as *arroz con jueyes* (crab rice); call ahead to be sure it's open. *Panaderia La Familia* on the main road sells lip-smacking barbecue chicken and fresh bread daily, if you want something cheaper for a picnic. One local specialty is **shark meat**: at weekends, *kioscos* south of the town sell *pastelillos de tiburón* (shark turnovers), a surprisingly rich and tasty snack best experienced at the *Bajo El Arbol de la Frescura kiosco* (ask someone if you can't find it on PR-3). In July the local shark fishermen celebrate the **Festival del Tiburón**.

Reserva Natural de Humacao

Bringing together several diverse ecosystems scattered around the estuary of the Río Anton Ruiz, the **Reserva Natural de Humacao** (Mon–Fri 7.30am– 3.30pm, Sat & Sun 7.30am–5pm; free; ☎787/852-6088) is a remarkably unspoiled patch of wetland, tropical jungle, and lagoon. The swamps were drained in the 1920s and converted to sugar cane plantations, until Hurricane David flooded the area in 1979. In a salutary example of nature taking revenge, the newly created lagoons were soon colonized by vegetation and wildlife, but it was only after the protests of local environmental groups that attempts to re-establish sugar cane were abandoned, and the reserve was established in 1984. Covering 3000 acres, the Santa Teresa section is the most accessible, with a small parking lot, office, and trail at PR-3 km 74.3, 2km beyond Balneario Punta Santiago. If you don't have time to join a tour (see below), you can park your car and stroll along the main trail through the old coconut and sugar cane plantation, ending up at a lagoon and beach in around fifteen minutes. The lagoon was once a sugar field, now surrounded by white mangroves, and you can also explore an abandoned observation tower and bunkers from World War II. The reserve is noted for its **birdlife** (over 100 species reside here including the ruddy duck, white-cheeked pintail, and West Indian whistling duck), but come very early if you want to see anything. **Turtles** sometimes nest on the beach. **Fishing** and **camping** are free, but you need a permit from the DRNA in advance (see p.28).

Tours

On weekends (or Wed & Fri with reservations), the reserve office organizes guided hikes ($3.50/hr) and boat rides ($5) between 9am and 4pm, and you can also rent **kayaks** on the lagoon for $5 per hour. Ecoquest Adventures and Tours (☎787/616-7543; ⊛www.ecoquestpr.com) organizes guided tours of the reserve ($129) that include kayaking across the lagoon and a light lunch, worthwhile for those short of time and without transport from San Juan.

Palmas del Mar

Just over 11km south of Humacao lies the upscale "club community" of **PALMAS DEL MAR** (⊛www.palmasdelmar.com), a 2700-acre Neverland of landscaped putting greens, pristine condos, country clubs, and 9km of beaches. More like an affluent suburb of southern Florida than Puerto Rico, it's nevertheless one of the best places to go **horseback riding** on the island, and the local **dive** and **boat** operators tend to be less swamped than their Fajardo rivals.

Practicalities

The gate-guarded main entrance is on PR-906, a short drive from *autopista* PR-53 (exit 35). Grab a map at the **information center** (daily 8am–5pm) just beyond here. At present, the suitably opulent *Four Points by Sheraton* (☎787/850- 6000, ⊛www.fourpointspr.com; ⑥–⑦) at 170 Candelero Drive is the only

Los Caballos de Paso Fino: the horses with the fine walk

Puerto Ricans are among the most passionate horseback riders in the world, immensely proud of their unique, island-bred **Paso Finos**. Despite rapid modernization, you'll come across locals (often sporting baseball caps and mobile phones) steering their horses along busy roads in towns and villages all over the island, families joining *cabalgatas* (group day rides) organized on weekends in mountain towns, and serious international competitions held here every year.

Horses were introduced to Puerto Rico by the Spanish, the Paso Fino evolving as a cross-breed of the Andalusian, North African Barb, and Spanish Jennet, and although the horse also emerged in Colombia, only the Puerto Rican Paso Fino has the tantalizing **four-phase gait** that makes it so valuable: other show horses have to be taught the walk, but Paso Finos are born with it. Bred all over the world today, Paso Finos are fast learners and extremely responsive to their riders, making them a pleasure to ride.

Unless you have local horse-loving friends, the best way to experience the smooth, fine walk of a Paso Fino is to visit a ranch such as Rancho Buena Vista (see below), where experienced guides take groups out on well-trained horses. You can also check out *4 Tiempos* (℡1-888/4843-6767; ⓦwww.4tiempos.com), the world's largest Paso Fino magazine, for the latest reviews of horses, shows, and events from around the world, and including what's going on in Puerto Rico.

hotel on site, replete with casino and super-luxurious rooms. In addition to the 11 percent tax, you'll pay an 11 percent resort fee. Although it might not look it, the pleasant (and generally deserted) **beach** here is open to the public, and you can simply walk through the hotel grounds and stake out a spot on the sand (follow the signs for "3 Tee Palm Course" from the hotel entrance). You'll have to leave your car in the parking lot opposite the hotel ($0.50/hr, $12/day valet at the hotel). To get to the **marina** (formally known as Anchor's Village Marina) and the best restaurants, follow Palmas Drive (the main road) past Candelero Drive, turn left on Coral Way, then right on Harbor Drive.

Rancho Buena Vista

Tucked away on the edge of Palmas del Mar (turn left on Academy Drive opposite the information center), **Rancho Buena Vista** (℡787/479-7479, ⓦwww.ranchobuenavistapr.com) provides a fabulous opportunity to ride **Paso Fino horses** along tropical sandy beaches. The **regular trail rides** (10am, 1pm, & 3pm; $45) are perfect for beginners, lasting around one hour and covering 4 miles (no minimum, but maximum thirty people). Experienced riders can opt for the **expert trail ride** (9am; $75, minimum two people, maximum ten) which lasts two hours and covers over 6 miles of trail. Both routes include local beaches where turtles nest (the beaches are regularly inspected so that nothing is disturbed). Longer rides (with lunch) can be arranged for $125. Riders must be eight years or older, but ponies are available for children aged three to seven. The ranch is open daily from 8am, but sometimes closes September and October. Christmas is peak season, so book ahead.

Diving, snorkeling, and fishing

Palmas del Mar is a worthy alternative to Fajardo as a base from which to explore the rich waters of the east coast, with local operators here less focused on the San Juan day-trip brigade, and diving more suited to intermediate and advanced levels. The water tends to be clearer and the corals healthier: there are 35 recognized dive sites within five miles of the marina, most located along the two-mile

Basslet Reef System. **Medusa** is a popular site with up to 100ft visibility, while **Rooms** has barracuda and dolphins in the spring, the reef cut through by interlocking channels and a bit more interesting for experienced divers. **Cracks** is a labyrinth of caverns, home to giant lobsters, while at **Drift** you might see nurse sharks and angelfish. **Red Hog** is the highlight for seasoned divers, an awe-inspiring wall that drops from 80ft to 1140ft.

The only dive outfit here is **Sea Ventures Dive Center** (Mon–Sat 8am–noon & 1–5pm, Sun 8am–1am; ☎787/863-3483, ⓦwww.divepalmasdelmar.com), which organizes daily trips to all the primary dive sites, and snorkeling trips to Cayo Santiago (p.137). Two-tank dives are $99 ($89 with your own equipment). They can also arrange PADI Open Water Diver courses here ($425), and offer trips for non-certified divers for $150.

The other main attraction is **fishing**. **Karolette Charters** (☎787/850-7442, mobile 787/637-7992, ⓦwww.karolette.com) is run by Captain Bill Burleson, who has been fishing these waters since 1964. He offers fishing and snorkeling trips to Vieques ($110 per person, or $650 whole boat). Ocean fishing is $680 for a half-day, and $1250 for a full day. **Maragata Charters** at Slip 14 (☎787/850-7548 or mobile 787/637-1802, ⓦwww.maragatacharters.com) is run by Captain Matthew, who leads daily snorkeling trips to a variety of destinations, according to demand: Cayo Santiago (8am & 1pm; 3–4hr; $65 per person), Vieques (4hr; $75), and Culebra (8hr; $175): and also four-hour fishing charters (7am & 1pm) from $100 per person in his 38ft power catamaran. Minimum two people required for all trips.

All the operators are based at the **Anchor's Village Marina** at the end of Harbor Drive, though they work off their boats and there are no offices or dive shops here, so call in advance to arrange trips.

Eating and drinking

Being a self-contained universe, it's no surprise Palmas del Mar has twenty **restaurants** on site. *Costa Nova* at Palmanova 116 (☎787/656-7171), inside the central shopping mall, does American breakfasts with eggs ($3-8), pastas ($5) sandwiches and wraps (from $4).

For something special, aim for *Chez Daniel* (Mon, Wed & Thurs 6.30–10pm, Fri–Sun noon–3pm & 6.30–10pm; ☎787/850-3838), a French restaurant run by acclaimed chef Daniel Vasse, right on the marina at 110 Harbor Drive (near the charter boats), with indoor and terrace seating. Everything on the menu is exquisite (mains $27-38): try the *bouillabaisse de Marseille* ($36.50), grilled duck breast ($29.95), and wickedly rich desserts like profiteroles ($11.50). The choice of quality wine is overwhelming. Nearby you can also try the *Tapas Bar* (six oysters for $10.50), or *Bistro Rico*, which serves a selection of sandwiches and salads for under $10 (closed Sun). Both belong to the *Daniel* stable. Next to the marina parking lot, *Shipyards Restaurant* (closed Mon) is a bright café and bar serving American staples like burgers.

Coastal highway PR-901

Coastal highway **PR-901** is one of Puerto Rico's most scenic roads, winding around the rugged southeast corner of the island where the mountains of the Central Cordillera collapse gracefully into the sea. Though only a short drive south of Palmas del Mar, the towns and villages here seem unusually remote, and despite jaw-dropping vistas and a smattering of windswept beaches, see far fewer tourists.

Autopista PR-53 ends abruptly at the long causeway over the Río Guayanés wetlands, near the former sugar town of **Yabucoa**, though by the end of 2009 an extension should continue south via a series of tunnels blasted out of the rocks. Yabucoa has been struggling with twenty percent unemployment since the sugar plants started closing in the 1960s, and through the current mayor is gradually improving things, the town is marred by the Shell Chemicals oil refinery on the outskirts and contains nothing to warrant a visit. Follow PR-901 along the coast instead, towards **Maunabo** and the heart of sugar country (see p.310). You can also head inland on the **Ruta Panorámica** from here (see p.323) – the first section of this mountain highway actually follows PR-901, before looping back to Yabucoa on PR-3.

Playa Lucia and around

Your first stop heading south should be **PLAYA LUCIA**, just off PR-901 on PR-9911, 5km from Yabucoa a thin arc of reddish sand backed by coconut palms and cooled by the brisk trade winds that whip across the waves from the Virgin Islands. The beach is often deserted on weekdays, and has a slightly rougher, raw feel – Playa Lucia is a natural debris basin, and sometimes the washed-up timber, seaweed, and assorted jetsam can be quite extensive. The beach is cleaned on a regular basis, however, and with a couple of decent hotels it makes an appealing place to break a journey or use as a base for longer stays.

Accommodation

Parador Palmas de Lucia (☎787/893-4423, ⓦwww.palmasdelucia.com; ❸) is the oldest hotel on the beach, offering reasonable rates for standard doubles, and package deals that include meals. It has a small pool and tends to get very busy with families at weekends and holidays.

🎍 *Lucia Beach Villas* (☎787/266-1111, ⓦwww.luciabeachvillas.com; four people ❺, six people ❼) opened nearby in 2007, a series of luxury two-floor villa units tastefully furnished and equipped with air-conditioning, satellite TV, DVD players, kitchenette, and balcony with sea views. The landscaped garden features another small pool, and it's all just off the beach. Check the website for special deals, but note that meals are not served here. Both hotels here have plenty of parking.

▲ Faro Punta Tuna

A short drive further along PR-901 at km 5.6, the *Costa del Mar Guest House* (☎787/266-6276, ⊛www.costadelmargh.com; ❹) is a convenient alternative, a bright three-story place perched on the hillside with sixteen simple but comfortable doubles. The real highlight here is the spectacular view down to the coast: twelve rooms have sea views, and you can see Vieques from the small pool and sundeck.

El Cocal

Beyond Playa Lucia, PR-901 temporarily cuts inland across the Punta Yeguas, rising high above the Caribbean and away from the actual coastline. **El Cocal** is a local secret and can be tricky to find, but being well off the beaten path, it's a secluded, wild, and blessedly undeveloped beach. Popular with surfers, it's also a favorite with Puerto Rican families who like to lounge on the reddish sand in between the palm trees and scrub, especially in summer.

To reach it, take the narrow, unmarked lane off PR-901 at around the 8.5km mark, opposite *Club Tropical*, a snack stall and bar. Follow the lane steeply down towards the coast, for almost 3km to the end, before turning left just before it becomes a private drive – this side road ends a short distance ahead, at a craggy, pot-holed parking area behind the beach.

Eating and drinking

Eating options at Playa Lucia are restricted to *Coco Mar*, the beach bar, usually open from noon Thursday to Sunday for snacks and drinks, with live salsa on Sundays, and the mediocre restaurant in the *Parador Palmas de Lucia*: open daily from breakfast through till early evening, the lunch menu comprises basic American comfort food (such as burgers and ribs) while dinner sees a greater choice of fish and Puerto Rican dishes from around $12.

Better **restaurants** are scattered along PR-901. For spectacular views, nothing beats *El Nuevo Horizonte* (☎787/893-5492; Thurs–Sun noon–10pm) at km 8.8, 4km from Playa Lucia. It's worth stopping here for a quick look, even if you don't intend to eat, as it's the highest point on the road with magical vistas across the Punta Yeguas headland and along the coast. The seafood is usually fresh, but the steep prices primarily reflect location: six types of *mofongo* range $12–22, while mains such as *dorado* fillet or marlin start at $24, and the house special, the aromatic *asopao de langosta* (lobster rice soup) is $22. You can also grab a quick drink at the small terrace bar overlooking the cliffs by the restaurant parking lot, the *Balconcito del Cielo*. *Bella Vista* (open daily; ☎787/861-1501) is the local favorite at PR-901 km 4.6; it offers seven types of filling *mofongo* from $9–18 (the best being lobster), as well as the usual *cocina criolla* classics.

For **self-catering**, *Ralph's Food Warehouse* is a big supermarket on PR-901, back on the edge of Yabucoa. *Walgreens* and several **fast-food** options are on the same stretch of road.

Maunabo and around

Like Yabucoa, 9km to the north, the town of **MAUNABO** holds little interest for travelers, but the coastline nearby is exceptionally pretty, dusted with heavy mango and vivid *flamboyant* trees in summer, and boasting several enticing places to stay and visit.

Around Maunabo

Around 12km from Playa Lucia, PR-901 rejoins the coast at the *barrio* of **Emajaguas**. The beach here is relatively tranquil and fringed with trees, but often littered with seaweed. Just under 2km further along the road is the turning to the **Faro Punta Tuna** (Wed–Sun 9am–4pm; free), a striking ninety-foot Neoclassical lighthouse completed in 1893 – take narrow PR-7760 and then PR-760 to the end of the road (parking is limited). It's one of the most attractive Spanish-era lighthouses on the island, but as it's still working, you can't go inside. Instead, you can wander around the grounds, admiring the French-designed octagonal tower and lantern, as well as the views of the coast and overgrown **Playa Larga** to the north: you can reach this beach by taking the path to the left of the lighthouse entrance, along the fence, but strong currents can make it a dangerous place to swim. Better is **Playa Los Bohíos**, 2.5km from the lighthouse on PR-760, a 2km stretch of grayish sand shaded by palms with the *faro* standing guard in the distance. Though plenty of seaweed and flotsam gets blown onto the beach, the cooling breezes and lack of people make this an attractive spot, and the restaurant is excellent (see below). The turning to the beach is signposted on PR-760 at the 2.7km marker, but easier to spot coming from Maunabo.

Practicalities

The best budget **accommodation** in the area is *Playa de Emajaguas Guest House* (☎787/861-6023; ❷–❸) at PR-901 km 12.6, signposted off the road just before the village of Emajaguas. Overlooking the sea in rustic gardens replete with overgrown tennis courts, and with roosters ambling around, this milky-white guesthouse offers simple, clean, and very tranquil studio apartments with kitchenettes. Smarter options can be found west of Maunabo along PR-3: once the road drops down from the hills, the south coast stretches on towards Arroyo and Ponce, a quiet, thinly populated area reminiscent of sleepier Caribbean islands. In the *barrio* of Guardarraya, 6km from Maunabo at km 112.1, the ⚑ *Caribe Playa Beach Resort* (☎787/839-6339, ⓦwww.caribeplaya.com; ❺) faces a narrow strip of sand, with a sundeck right over the waves and an excellent café. The spacious beachfront studios have fridge, air-conditioning, cable TV, and balcony or patio, and you can use the pool and barbecue grills. Two kilometers further along PR-3 at km 114.3, the *Parador Caribbean Paradise* (☎787/839-5885, ⓦwww.caribbeanparadisepr.com; ❸) is a cheaper alternative, set on the hillside above the coast just off the main road. It's a bit like a motel, but has a nice enough pool, landscaped grounds, and a restaurant open daily for breakfast (8–10am) and dinner (5–9.30pm), and for lunch weekends only (noon–2.30pm). Rooms have two full-sized beds, air-conditioning, and basic cable TV, though you'll pay an extra $20 for a balcony and view.

For a place **to eat**, it's hard to beat *Los Bohíos* (☎787/861-2545; Wed & Thurs 11am–3pm, Fri–Sun 11am–8pm), overlooking the beach of the same name, a chilled-out restaurant that specializes in Puerto Rican seafood. Dishes are satisfying but standard fare (fried fish, *mofongo* and the like), and the main attraction is the chance to relax in the open dining area facing the beach, soaking up a truly languid Caribbean atmosphere. Note that the *Seaview Terrace Restaurant* at the *Caribe Playa Beach Resort* offers moderately priced lunch and dinners overlooking the sea, and there are additional waterside restaurants a short drive along PR-3 near Arroyo (see p.320).

Caguas and Juncos

From San Juan, most travelers take the direct route to Fajardo and the east coast along PR-3, and although this makes sense coming from the airport, it can be faster to take the PR-52 and PR-30 *autopistas* from other parts of the city: it's certainly the most efficient route for all points south of Humacao. Along the way, the towns of **Caguas** and **Juncos** are worth a look for their quirky museums, history, and traditional architecture.

Festivals of Puerto Rico

Puerto Rico is an island of immigrants, its dynamic *criollo* blend of African, European, Taíno and American traditions expressed through a seemingly endless list of festivals celebrated with passion by the whole community. Though many have Spanish roots, Puerto Rican *fiestas* have become deliciously localized: parades, *kioscos*, tropical music and street parties are marked with an unmistakable Caribbean twist.

The Catholic calendar

Most Puerto Ricans are Catholics, and the Church lies at the core of almost every major festival on the island. The liturgical year begins with Advent and the **Christmas season** (Dec & Jan), celebrated longer and harder in Puerto Rico than almost anywhere else in the world. Parties herald the lighting of Christmas trees all over the island, and traditional carols, *aguinaldos*, echo around town plazas. Though some gifts are exchanged on Christmas Day, most kids receive their main presents on January 6, known as the **Festival de los Tres Reyes** (Three King's Day or Epiphany) which is marked with great processions in Culebra, Guayama, Juana Díaz, Jayuya, Lares, and Old San Juan. **Lent** is preceded by carnivals while **Easter** or *Semana Santa* (Holy Week, usually in March or April) is the most important Catholic festival, marking the crucifixion and resurrection of Jesus. Good Friday sees processions re-enacting the Stations of the Cross, most notably at the Old San Juan Cathedral, led by a cross-bearing Jesus (played by a real person). After church, most families head to the beach and party all weekend.

The saints

Every town in Puerto Rico honors its **patron saint** with an annual *fiesta patronal*, a boisterous celebration that always includes parades, dancing, games, traditional food and plenty of live music. Infused with West African traditions, Loíza's Fiestas Tradicionales de Santiago Apóstol commemorates St James, a mesmerizing display of *bomba* music and dancers, enhanced with gaudy,

San Sebastian Festival ▲

At the Fiesta Tradicional de Santiago Apóstal ▼

multicolored **vejigante masks** made from coconut shell (see p.107). The **Día de San Juan Bautista** ends week-long festivities all over the island in June for St John, particularly in San Juan, where crowds assemble on the beaches at midnight to stumble backwards into the ocean for good luck (see p.98). In Ponce, Nuestra Señora de la Guadalupe is remembered every December by **Las Mañanitas**, a massive procession led by Mexican *mariachis* (see p.285). The procession celebrating San Pedro (St Peter) in La Parguera each June takes to the water after touring the town, a fleet of boats making the rounds of the nearby cays (see p.272).

Carnaval

Carnaval is the week-long festival (Feb & March) that heralds the start of Lent, traditionally the last opportunity to party before the forty-day fasting period leading up to Easter. In Puerto Rico, **Ponce** holds the oldest and most dazzling *carnaval,* though the emphasis is on family-fun rather than the raunchy hedonism of Rio. Others include the Carnaval de Cristóbal Sánchez held in Arroyo (named after the famous writer), the Carnaval del Plata in Dorado, the Carnaval Mabó in Guaynabo (named for a Taíno chief) and Carnaval Vegalteño in Vega Alta. All follow essentially the same structure, opening with a procession led by King Momo (the "King of Carnivals"), and like Loíza, Ponce has its own **vejigantes**, sporting elaborate, devilish masks. The fun ends on Shrove Tuesday with the Entierro de la Sardina (Burial of the Sardine), a mock funeral procession symbolizing the purging of sins.

▲ Parade in Old San Juan

▼ Street parade at Ponce Carnaval

Taíno traditions

Puerto Rico's pre-Columbian inhabitants, the **Taíno**, had a rich cultural tradition that was systematically destroyed during the Spanish colonization of the island. Today the Taíno are remembered at the **Festival Nacional Indígena**, held every November in the mountain town of Jayuya. The festival recreates Taíno dances and rituals, and features craft stalls, live folk music, and plenty of deep-fried *criollo* food, though the Miss Taíno Indian pageant is a very modern Puerto Rican innovation. In recent years, Yauco's International Arts festival (Dec) has also featured authentic Taíno music and dancing.

Fiesta patronales in Old San Juan ▲

Salsa dancer ▼

Dance nation

Puerto Rico is steeped in vibrant dance and musical traditions that reach far back into the Spanish colonial period, from sultry salsa to the refined elegance of *danza*. Though almost every festival will feature dance performances, the annual **Puerto Rico Salsa Congress** is the premier showcase for professionals from all over the world. Usually held at the *El San Juan Hotel* every July, the week-long convention features nightly salsa shows and a fiercely-fought competition. **Puerto Rico Danza Week** usually takes place in Old San Juan in May, a celebration of the island's softer but equally absorbing national dance – Ponce hosts its **Semana de la Danza** at around the same time. **Bomba y Plena** are traditional music and dance genres inspired by the island's African and peasant farmer populations, celebrated at special festivals held in Juana Díaz (Aug), Aguas Buenas (Aug & Sept) and Ponce (Nov).

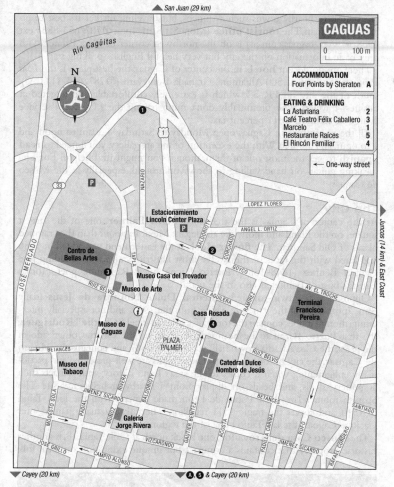

▲ *San Juan (29 km)*

CAGUAS

0   100 m

ACCOMMODATION
Four Points by Sheraton   **A**

EATING & DRINKING
La Asturiana	2
Café Teatro Félix Caballero	3
Marcelo	1
Restaurante Raíces	5
El Rincón Familiar	4

← One-way street

▶ *Juncos (14 km) & East Coast*

Río Cagüitas

N

33

P

P Estacionamiento
Lincoln Center Plaza

LOPEZ FLORES

ANGEL L. ORTIZ

Centro de
Bellas Artes

Museo Casa del Trovador

Museo de Arte

CELIS AGUILERA

GOYCO

AV. EL TROCHE

Terminal
Francisco
Pereira

Casa Rosada

RUIZ BELVIS

ℹ

Museo de
Caguas

PLAZA
PALMER

RUIZ BELVIS

BETANCES

Catedral Dulce
Nombre de Jesús

Museo del
Tabaco

BETANCES

SANTIAGO

JIMENEZ SICARDO

Galería
Jorge Rivera

VIZCARONDO

JIMENEZ SICARDO

JOSE GRILLO

CAMPIO ALONSO

▼ *Cayey (20 km)*   ▼ **A**, **5** & *Cayey (20 km)*

Caguas and around

Formally established in 1775 near the site of a far older Taíno village, the thriving community of **CAGUAS** is the fastest growing metropolitan area in Puerto Rico, and currently its fifth largest city. The historic core is a compact, attractive area easily explored on foot, surrounded by a great swathe of suburbs and strip malls. Parking is easy and it's only 29km and 25 minutes' drive from San Juan, making the city a tempting day-trip or first stop on the routes south or east. It's also one of the few places served by regular *públicos*, so you won't need a car to get here.

Arrival, information, and accommodation

Arriving by **car**, there are several places to park on the edge of the historic center – the best is Estacionamiento Lincoln Center Plaza (Mon–Fri 6am–7pm, Sat 7am–8pm; $1.50 first hr; $0.75 thereafter) at the end of PR-1, on the north side of town.

By **público** you'll be dropped at the Terminal Francisco Pereira, two blocks northeast of central Plaza Palmer. Moving on, it's easy to take *públicos* from the bus station to nearby towns such as Juncos, but traveling further it's best to go back to San Juan. The **tourist office** (Mon–Sat 8am–4pm; ☎787/653-8833 ext 2908, ⓦ www.caguas.com.pr) is on the northwest corner of Plaza Palmer, with only basic information on the city but very helpful English-speaking staff.

There are no decent **hotels** in the center of Caguas: the best place is the *Four Points by Sheraton* at 500 Alhambra, Granada Boulevard (☎787/653-1111; ❾), south of the city off PR-52, which is extremely comfortable and targeted at business travelers who presumably don't mind paying the 11 percent service charge in addition to 11 percent tax.

All the **museums** in Caguas open Monday to Saturday 8.30am to noon and 1 to 4pm, and are free. With the exception of the art gallery, you'll need to **read Spanish** to get the most out of them, though you might find helpful English-speaking guides on hand willing to show you around, especially at the Museo de Caguas.

The City

At the center of Caguas is the tree-filled **Plaza Palmer**, one of the largest squares on the island and more like an elegant Mexican *parque* than the cramped plazas of Old San Juan. The **flower clock** at the eastern end was added in 1966 and lined with the faces of the twelve most illustrious *cagüeños*, including José Gautier Benítez (1848–1880), Puerto Rico's finest Romantic poet (Tomás Batista's bust of Benítez is also in the plaza).

Opposite is the twin-towered **Catedral Dulce Nombre de Jesús** (daily 6am–7pm), most of the structure dating from the 1930s and not especially interesting, though it does contain the tomb of Carlos Manuel **"Charlie" Rodríguez**, the first Puerto Rican to be beatified (see box, p.148). On the other side of the plaza, the Casa Alcadía (town hall) was built in 1887 and contains the **Museo de Caguas**, the city history museum. The exhibits are well-presented and particularly enlightening when it comes to the area's Taíno history, with artifacts such as pottery, shells, and beads on display from a nearby archeological site. The Spanish room relates how Ponce de León made contact with the local Taíno in 1510, and covers the tragic 1511 rebellion. The city is actually named after Cacique Caguax, the last Taíno chief of the region.

The **Museo Casa del Trovador**, one block north at Calle Tapia 18, is another historic property that contains a compact but unique exhibition on local folk

▲ Flower clock in main plaza

singers and troubadours, charting the important role Caguas has played in the development of Puerto Rican folk music.

One block west of here, on the corner of calles Ruíz Belvis and Padial, the modest **Museo de Arte** contains three spacious exhibition rooms housing mostly local, contemporary art: the abstract work of Caguas-born painters Carlos Osorio (1927–84) and Orlando Vallejo (b. 1955) is well represented, and you can admire *Las Tradiciones Puertorriquenas*, the vivid seven-panel mural by Alfonso Arana (1927–2005).

The museum faces the **Centro de Bellas Artes**, a modern art center completed in 1993 – check at the box office inside for what's showing if you intend to stay the night. Walk one block south and you'll find the **Museo del Tabaco** at calles Padial and Betances, testament to the area's central role in the Puerto Rican **tobacco industry**, especially between 1890 and 1930. In addition to exhibits and information panels, the museum contains a replica of an old tobacco factory, where aging but dextrous workers demonstrate how to roll cigars by hand. Today there are only a handful of factories in the area.

Art fans should head south to Calle Muñoz Rivera 40 and the **Galería Jorge Rivera** (T787/539-3840), a respected showcase for up and coming Puerto Rican painters such as Luis Alvárez and Miguel Angel Cruz (call to check opening times), while back towards the bus station, **Casa Rosada** at Calle Alejandro Ramírez 14 was the former home of Charlie Rodríguez and local writer Abelardo Díaz Alfaro (1916–1999), beautifully restored in 2007 and housing a small exhibition on both men.

Eating and drinking

Eating options in Caguas are fairly typical for a provincial Puerto Rican city, with predominantly cheap local restaurants in the center, plenty of fast-food outlets around Plaza Palmer, and stalls selling Puerto Rican snacks in the square most days. You'll find a handful of modern and international restaurants on the main highways outside the center.

La Asturiana c/Goyco 58. Cheap snacks and cakes (under $5) can be found at this no-frills bakery with heaps of character, open since 1932. Takeout or eat at a couple of tables inside. Open 24hr.

Café Teatro Félix Caballero Centro de Bellas Artes T787/258-4045. For a drink, check out this bar in the art center, with outdoor tables and a respectable cocktail menu. Expect live *nueva trova* (progressive folk music) on Thurs, and salsa Fri & Sat. Closed Mon, Tues & Sun.

Marcelo PR-1 and Avda Jose Mercado T787/743-8801. This is the top place to eat in the center of Caguas, just on the edge of the old town, facing the monument to Taíno women. The oldest restaurant in the city, in business since 1969, it's nothing special inside but the menu of Cuban and local *comida criolla* is first-rate. Try the house specialties *jamón*

de pollo (smoked chicken), smoked pork loin and *paella* (mains from $12). Closed Sun.

Restaurante Raíces Urb Villa Turabo H-31 T787/258-1570. If you have a car, check out this restaurant south of the center on PR-172, opposite the Plaza del Carmen mall. It's a fun place to eat with a kitsch "old Puerto Rico" theme and a range of creative *criollo* dishes such as *mofongo* stuffed with *churrasco* (steak) in *chimichurri* sauce. You can also get *chuleta Kan Kan* (pork chops), and *dorado a la criolla* (mahi-mahi) here. Mains range $8–25.

El Rincón Familiar c/Manuel Corchado Juarbe 11. Just south of the plaza, this is a solid choice for a cheap sit-down meal of local classics: rice and sausage combos and *mofongo* go for $6–7, but you can also order sandwiches and pizza. Closed Sun.

Juncos

Founded in 1797 and known as the "Ciudad de Valenciano" after the river that snakes around the town, **JUNCOS** is 14km from Caguas along speedy PR-30 and worth another brief stop before hitting the coast. Driving into the old town center can be a little confusing, however, thanks to the one-way system, and it's hard to

St Charlie

Born in Caguas in 1918, few would have believed **Carlos Manuel Rodríguez Santiago** was destined to become the island's **first Catholic saint**. Known as "Chali" (which later became Anglicized as "Charlie"), he was an earnest but initially shy boy who struggled with ill health from an early age, seeking solace in scripture and the rituals of the Church. He became a Catholic lay minister while at university in the 1940s, preaching all over the island and especially active in the **revival of traditional Catholic customs** such as the Easter vigil. Tragically, this burgeoning Church career was cut short in 1963 when Rodríguez died of intestinal cancer. Though he was certainly regarded as a deeply spiritual man, it takes more than that to become a Catholic saint, and what got the Vatican's attention was a **miracle**: in 1981, a local woman (and former friend) claimed to have fully recovered from cancer after praying to Charlie. Brought to the attention of the Pope in 1992, the miracle was deemed genuine and the normally tortuously long process of canonization was initiated. Pope John Paul II beatified Rodríguez in April 2001, and he's well on the way to becoming a fully-fledged saint, though the Vatican must confirm one more miracle before that can happen – until then he's known as the "Blessed". Not only the first Puerto Rican to be beatified, Charlie was the first layperson in US history, and only the second in the Western Hemisphere to receive that honor.

park along its narrow streets. If you don't mind walking, just leave your car outside *El Tenedor* (see below), which lies on PR-189 on the edge of the center and is easy to locate by its tall brick chimney. The **Terminal de Carros Públicos** is centrally located on Calle Muñoz Rivera, near the plaza: buses to Caguas are $1.

Juncos's tree-filled **plaza** is smaller and not as impressive as the one in Caguas, but it's surrounded by a handful of attractive Art Deco and Spanish Revival villas. You can usually peek inside the impressively restored **Teatro Junqueño** on its southeast corner, a working Art Deco theater, before walking along Calle Martínez on the opposite side. This pretty street leads to **Paseo Escuté**, a wider tree-lined boulevard containing the stately Casa Alcaldía (town Hall) and **Biblioteca José M. Gallardo**, a gorgeous light-blue library, built in Spanish Revival style.

To eat, your best option is ⚘ *El Tenedor* (c/Emilia Principe 1, ☎787/734-6573), one of the most enticing restaurants in the region. Until 1942 this was a rum factory owned by Destilería del Ron Caray, and the charming dining room features original brickwork and wooden beams reminiscent of northern Europe. The menu is heavy on succulent steaks (from $18) and other grilled meats, supplemented by a huge wine selection. It's open daily from 11am, closing at 10pm Friday and Saturday and 9pm other days. Cheaper food can be found in the old town center, though nothing particularly stands out.

Travel details

Públicos

The following gives a rough idea of duration, though heavy traffic at weekends can add more time:
Fajardo to: San Juan, Río Piedras (frequent; 1hr 15min).
Caguas to: Juncos (frequent; 20min); San Juan, Río Piedras (frequent; 1hr).

Ferries

Fajardo to: Culebra (3 daily; 1hr 30min); Vieques (Mon–Fri 4 daily, Sat & Sun 3 daily; 1hr 15min).

Flights

Fajardo to: Culebra (5 daily; 12min); St Croix (on demand; 35min); Vieques (5 daily; 9min).

3

Vieques and Culebra

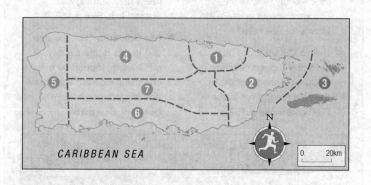

CARIBBEAN SEA

N

0   20km

CHAPTER 3   # Highlights

✱ **Museo Fortín Conde de Mirasol** This distinctive museum was one of the last Spanish forts to be built in the New World, with superb views across Isabel II. See p.162

✱ **Beach-hopping** Rent a car and explore the pristine coastline of Vieques, from the silky sands of Sun Bay to the reef-rimmed coves of Green Beach. See p.166

✱ **La Reserva Natural de la Bahía Bioluminiscente** Be mesmerized by the otherworldly glow of the bioluminescent bay at Puerto Mosquito. See p.167

✱ **Diving Culebra** The offshore cays and rugged coastline of Culebra shelter some of the finest reef dives in the Caribbean. See p.182

✱ **Turtle-watching** Volunteer to patrol Culebra's beaches at night and witness the magic of a giant leatherback turtle laying her eggs. See p.183

✱ **Playa Flamenco** Lounge on one of the world's most spellbinding stretches of sand. See p.184

✱ **Kayaking the Reserva Natural Canal de Luis Peña** Paddle through the calm, clear waters of this marine reserve, home to multicolored reefs, rays, turtles, and tropical fish. See p.185

✱ **Isla Culebrita** Take a water-taxi to this gorgeous cay off Culebra, topped by a crumbling Spanish lighthouse and fringed with bone-white beaches. See p.186

▲ Playa Flamenco

Vieques and Culebra

C learly visible from Fajardo and the east coast, the offshore islands of **Vieques** and **Culebra** are in many ways the most alluring parts of Puerto Rico, and definitely the most stereotypically Caribbean. If you're yearning for laid-back, tropical islands and dreamy landscapes of empty, palm-fringed beaches, this is where to find them.

Politically and culturally part of Puerto Rico, Vieques and Culebra are also known as the **Spanish Virgin Islands**, though they were only brought under direct Spanish control in the nineteenth century. The US Navy occupied both islands for over half of the twentieth century, and as a consequence they avoided the rampant development endemic to much of the region: with the navy long gone, the area has the potential to become an **ecotourism** paradise. Today you'll find some of the most unspoiled **beaches** in the Antilles, clear skies (perfect for stargazing), and a chilled-out mix of locals and *Americanos* running a simple but sophisticated infrastructure of guesthouses and eateries. Both islands are rimmed by vivid coral reef and hordes of tropical fish, with Culebra in particular a haven for **sea turtles**.

Though the islands are very similar, there are some differences and it's worth experiencing both if you have time. Vieques is far larger (around 21 miles long and 3 miles wide), and with a population of around ten thousand it can seem much busier at times, though it's relatively easy to find a secluded strip of sand. In contrast, the three thousand or so *culebrenses* can be disarmingly friendly, and unlike Vieques, crime is virtually unknown on their island, much of which shuts down in the afternoons for a siesta. High season is the same on both islands (November to May), but Vieques goes into semi-hibernation over the summer, while Culebra sees a second boom in Puerto Rican tourists – rental cars and hotels can be booked solid in July.

Vieques

Lying just 7.5 miles off the east coast of Puerto Rico, **VIEQUES** is blessed with great sweeps of savagely beautiful **beaches**, the world's brightest and healthiest **bioluminescent bay** (or just "bio bay"), and a tourist industry that remains stubbornly low-key and underdeveloped. Most of Vieques was occupied and sealed off by the **US Navy** in 1941, and by the time the military was forced out sixty years later, much of the coastline had reverted to a wild, natural state. Despite a steady stream of new arrivals from the US mainland, and house prices quadrupling since 2000, Vieques has been spared large-scale resort and condo development – for now.

Vieques is undoubtedly one of the highlights of Puerto Rico, but as with many seemingly idyllic islands, life here has a darker side. The US Navy presence, though long gone, overshadows everything; although the public beaches are clean and perfectly safe, much of the island remains contaminated and off-limits (see p.154), and while the small scale of tourism is appealing for outsiders, it has had little impact on the **local economy**, the poorest in Puerto Rico. Petty crime is a problem, and unemployment regularly hits sixty percent, the major sources of work being a small General Electric factory and the hundred or so fishing boats that ply the local waters. You'll rarely see any expression of these frustrations on the streets, however: like most Puerto Ricans, *viequenses* are a friendly, easy-going bunch who welcome visitors and generally live amicably with newcomers.

Most travelers arrive at **Isabel Segunda** (or just Isabel II), the workaday capital of the island, with its spread of modest sights and shops guarded by the old Spanish fortress, **Museo Fortín Conde de Mirasol**, now the an absorbing history museum. From here the windswept north coast is sprinkled with a series of rougher, thinner beaches, broken up by the **Rompeolas** (Mosquito Pier), a World War II folly that juts into the sea like a road to nowhere. **Esperanza**, on the south coast, is more geared up for the tourist trade, with its lazy *malecón* lined with restaurants and bars, and excellent snorkeling just offshore. Nearby, the sands at Sun Bay, Media Luna, and Playa Navío offer an enticing introduction to the island's southern coastline, while more beaches lie within the **Vieques National Wildlife Refuge**. If you rent a car, you should spend most of your time exploring the potholed roads that crisscross this reserve, though the other obvious highlight is the bioluminescent bay, a truly mind-blowing spectacle (assuming the moon cooperates). If you visit in summer, check out the **Fiestas Patronales de Nuestra Señora del Carmen**, which takes place around the Virgin's feast day on July 16, with live music, plenty of games, and *kioscos* in various parts of the island.

Some history

Vieques has been inhabited by humans for at least three thousand years, colonized by a series of **Arawak** migrations much as Puerto Rico itself (see p.355). Archeologists have discovered evidence of an Archaic settlement in the Caño Hondo area, dating from 1680 BC, and a more sophisticated Igneri village at Sorcé, established around two thousand years later, but the first written account of any of these peoples comes from **Christopher Columbus** in 1493, who spotted **Taínos** as he sailed past modern Esperanza. The Spanish named the island *La Isla Nena* ("little girl island"); "Vieques" comes from a Spanish transliteration of *bieques* or **Biéké** in the Taíno language, meaning "small island." Initially ignored by Ponce de León, the Taíno of Biéké, led by cacique **Cacimar**, aided the rebels on the main island in 1511 (see p.357). Cacimar was killed on Puerto Rico, and in the aftermath a punitive Spanish force was sent to Vieques, where his brother and successor **Yaureibo** was also killed along with most of his warriors. The Taíno villages on Vieques were razed to the ground, the island virtually abandoned.

In 1685 the **English** established the first colony on the now empty Vieques (they called it "Crab Island"), but the Spanish, nervous about their proximity to Puerto Rico, transported the three hundred settlers to Santo Domingo four years

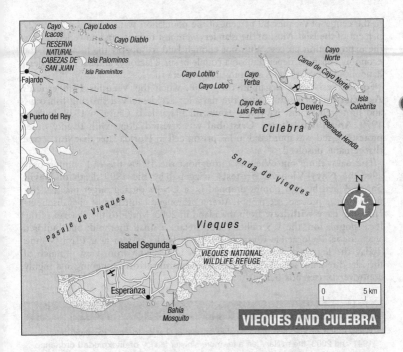

Map labels:

Cayo Icacos
Cayo Lobos
Cayo Diablo
RESERVA NATURAL CABEZAS DE SAN JUAN
Isla Palominos
Isla Palominitos
Fajardo
Puerto del Rey
Cayo Lobito
Cayo Lobo
Cayo Yerba
Cayo Norte
Canal de Cayo Norte
Isla Culebrita
Cayo de Luís Peña
Dewey
Culebra
Ensenada Honda
Sonda de Vieques
N
Pasaje de Vieques
Vieques
Isabel Segunda
VIEQUES NATIONAL WILDLIFE REFUGE
Esperanza
Bahía Mosquito
0   5 km
VIEQUES AND CULEBRA

later, thwarting further English attempts in 1718 and 1752. For much of the subsequent hundred years the island remained a wild place, the domain of fugitives and pirates such as **Captain Kidd**, who visited Vieques in 1699 (and is supposed to have buried treasure here) and **Roberto Cofresí** (see p.360), who picked up his last bloodthirsty crew on Vieques in 1824 and is also said to have stored his loot somewhere on the island.

The Spanish established their first formal outpost on Vieques in 1811, but the governor was ineffectual and order was eventually restored by an enterprising Frenchman, **Don Teófilo Le Guillou**. A former planter from Haiti, he arrived on Vieques in 1823 and persuaded the governor in Puerto Rico to allow him complete authority in return for bringing the island under control. By 1828 he had achieved his aim and introduced **sugar cane** to the island, retaining the position of military and political governor until his death in 1843. **Sugar plantations**, manned mostly by slaves from Tortola, soon dominated the island's economy, and the forests that had once covered the island were gradually cleared.

Even after the US occupation in 1898, little changed on Vieques: sugar production continued to grow and the sugar barons maintained their grip on local affairs, despite a landmark **strike** by sugar workers in 1915. At its peak in 1920 the population reached 11,651, mostly concentrated around **Central Playa Grande**, the largest of four sugar mills on the island. The end came when US sugar quotas and an eight-hour day forced Playa Grande into receivership in 1939 – in 1941 it was sold to the US Navy, by which time sugar production was dead on the island.

In 1941, with war looming, the **US Navy** essentially occupied Vieques, a cataclysmic event that led to three-quarters of the island being sealed off. Thousands of locals emigrated to St Croix and many were resettled, many forcibly with minimal notice, on eight hundred acres of razed sugar-cane fields in the center of Vieques: 89 percent of the population was squeezed into just 27 percent of the land. Most of the islanders were just **tenants** and powerless to stop the expropriation process. With not enough land to support the population, the economy collapsed, dependent on a couple of small factories and navy and federal handouts. Drunken brawls and prostitution were rife.

Formal **resistance** began in the 1970s, when the **Vieques Fishermen's Association** successfully sued the navy for accidentally destroying fish traps, and protested against navy war games off Playa de la Chiva in 1978. In May 1979, **Ángel Rodríguez Cristóbal** was arrested along with twenty other protestors, and was murdered in his prison cell in Florida later that year, a case that remains unsolved.

The navy clung onto Vieques throughout the 1990s, the end coming only after the **Navy–Vieques protests**, triggered by the 1999 death of **David Sanes**, killed by two bombs dropped by a US jet during target practice (for more on the protests, see p.365). After a prolonged campaign of civil disobedience, the navy **withdrew** from the island in 2003. Much to the chagrin of the local population, the US military does retain a small foothold: one hundred acres for its Relocatable Over the Horizon Radar system near Playa Grande. Today, the legacy of the navy occupation is never far from view – much of the island remains sealed off and the **decontamination** is ongoing and highly controversial (see box below).

The big clean-up

While much of Vieques' untrammeled appeal is thanks to navy isolation between 1941 and 2003, the military left a far more sinister legacy of **unexploded ordnance** and **contamination** by arsenic, cyanide, depleted uranium shells, lead, mercury, napalm, and other toxins. Some doctors have linked this to **cancer rates** that are 27 percent higher here than in the rest of Puerto Rico, and the ongoing **clean-up operation** remains controversial.

Vieques was never really a base – Roosevelt Roads on the main island was the US Navy headquarters, and Vieques was used primarily for target practice. The navy used the western half of the island for **munitions storage** until 2001, when 3100 acres were transfered to the US Fish and Wildlife Service, four thousand acres to the Municipality of Vieques, and eight hundred acres to the Conservation Trust. The eastern side of Vieques was used for amphibious training exercises and air-to-ground maneuvers: this included **Camp García** (which housed three hundred Marines until the 1970s) and a **Live Impact Area**, where explosives were tested. All 14,600 acres were handed over to the US Fish and Wildlife Service in 2003, but since then only tiny portions of this area have been opened to the public, and many residents of Vieques are unhappy with the apparently slow pace of decontamination. The Live Impact Area, nine hundred acres at the eastern tip of Vieques, has been declared a wilderness zone and may never be open to the public – it's that dangerous.

The navy has two clean-up operations on Vieques: the **Munitions Response Program**, to decontaminate 63 munitions sites, and the **Environmental Restoration Program**, to tackle environmental threats. Thanks to pressure from former governor Sila Calderón, in 2005 eight sites on Vieques were placed on the **Superfund National Priorities List**, a compilation of the most hazardous waste sites in the US, requiring the Environmental Protection Agency (EPA) and navy to prioritize decontamination. Things do seem to be changing for the better: in 2007 the navy published their **Community Involvement Plan** to facilitate greater communication between the military and local people. However, with the estimates for clean-up ranging as high as $450 billion, critics claim that handing most of the land to the Wildlife Service was a ruse to allow superficial cleaning.

Arrival, orientation, and information

Flights arrive at tiny **Aeropuerto Antonio Rivera Rodríguez**, around 7.5km west of Isabel II. *Públicos* operating like taxis usually meet flights, but you can also arrange a pick-up in advance. Drivers waiting at the airport usually charge $9 (or $3 per person) to Isabel II, and $15 (or $5 per person) to Esperanza. Note that the airport has no bank or ATM, and nowhere much to eat. Rental car offices are based elsewhere on the island, but will usually pick you up if you arrange it in advance.

The **ferry** docks in the center of Isabel II. If you haven't arranged a pick-up in advance, minibus *públicos* will drive you to Esperanza for around $15 (or $5 per person), or anywhere in town for $2–3, but note that unless you want to hire the whole vehicle, buses are shared and leave when full.

Orientation

Vieques has an area of around 52 square miles, but large swathes of the island within the **Vieques National Wildlife Refuge** remain off-limits to the public – only the central third of the island is open land, much of it covered with small farms and *barrios*. On the north coast, the capital **Isabel II** is home to the ferry port, most services and businesses, and plenty of decent places to eat and stay. The south coast lies beyond the central ridge of tropical highlands, with tourist-oriented **Esperanza** closer to the best beaches and the bioluminescent bay.

Information

The **tourist information office**, at Calle Carlos Le Brum 449 (daily 8am–4.30pm; ☎787/741-0800), faces the main plaza in Isabel II, and sometimes closes between 11.30am and 1pm for lunch, especially on weekends. You'll find plenty of local information and English-speaking staff inside (though English is widely spoken on the island in any case). There is a profusion of **websites** on Vieques, including Ⓦwww.islavieques.com and Ⓦwww.enchanted-isle.com. **Gay travelers** should check out Ⓦwww.gayvieques.net.

Getting around

Vieques has no public transport as such, so visitors are reliant on *públicos* (which act more like taxis than on the main island) and rental cars and scooters. **Car rental** in Vieques is expensive, but it's the most efficient option if you want to see a lot of the island. If you're staying in one of the towns and plan to visit just one or two beaches, *públicos* can be economical, or you could opt for a slightly cheaper (if uncomfortable) scooter. To save money, rent a **bike** (see Listings, p.175).

Públicos

Minibus **públicos** in Vieques serve as buses and taxis, charging per person on busy routes from the airport or ferry dock, when you may have to share. At other times you can call drivers to take you to a specific place, which tends to be more expensive. Drivers typically charge $5 (or $15 for the whole bus) between Isabel II and Esperanza, $2–3 for journeys within the Isabel II area, and $20 per hour to visit the principal beaches – in practice, it's much cheaper to rent a car if you intend to do a lot of exploring. See p.175 for a list of reliable drivers.

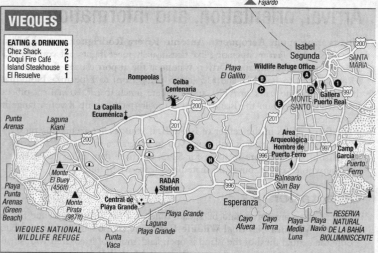

VIEQUES

EATING & DRINKING
Chez Shack	2
Coqui Fire Café	C
Island Steakhouse	E
El Resuelve	1

Car rental

Renting a car is a good idea on Vieques, though charges can be steep ($50–60/day) and **insurance** can add up to $25 per day. All the rental firms are locally owned (there are no major chains) and scattered across the island, but they will usually pick you up from the airport or ferry pier if you call in advance (see p.175 for numbers). To access the wilder beaches, you'll need an off-road Jeep or SUV, and a steely disposition – some of the unsealed roads (*camino de tierra*) are bone-jarringly rocky when dry, or scarred with potholes knee-deep in water when it rains.

Sadly, **theft** can be a problem in Vieques: never leave anything of value in your car. Rental firms usually prefer that you leave windows open and doors unlocked to save the car from smash-and-grab damage. Otherwise driving is easy and hassle-free – just take care at night, and watch out for **horses**. There are three Esso **gas stations** on the island, all on PR-200 outside Isabel II: one near the intersection of PR-997, and the other two opposite each other closer to the airport in Playa Monte Santo district. Speed limits are usually 35mph outside built-up areas.

Accommodation

Vieques' **accommodation** options are growing in number, though the island is mercifully devoid of large chain hotels, major resorts, and casinos. The boom sector is **apartment and villa rentals**, which can be a good deal for groups, or for those looking to stay one week or longer. Start at Crow's Nest Realty (℡787/741-3298, ⓦwww.enchanted-isle.com/crowsnestrealty) for a wide selection.

Hotels and guesthouses range from fairly basic budget options (though there are no hostels), to smart, boutique hotels. Many are clustered in or around **Esperanza**, convenient for the southern beaches, though staying on the *malecón* itself can be noisy, especially on weekends. Hotels in **Isabel II** are more

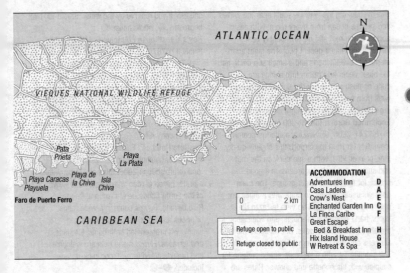

ACCOMMODATION

Adventures Inn	D
Casa Ladera	A
Crow's Nest	E
Enchanted Garden Inn	C
La Finca Caribe	F
Great Escape	
Bed & Breakfast Inn	H
Hix Island House	G
W Retreat & Spa	B

convenient for the airport, ferry, and services, while the handful of options in **central Vieques** offer a quite different, more rustic experience, surrounded by hills and tropical forest. You can **camp** right on the beach at *Balneario Sun Bay*, near Esperanza (☎787/741-8198; $15), a pleasant site maintained by the Compañía de Parques Nacionales, with showers and toilets.

Isabel II and the north coast

Adventures Inn PR-200 (across from second gas station), Playa Monte Santo ☎787/741-1564, ⓦwww.adventuresinn.com. Often empty in the summer, this bed and breakfast, contained within a large, colorfully painted villa with breezy roof deck, is managed by the owners of *Casa Cubuy* (☎787/874-6221, see p.117) – you must call in advance. The three simple but spacious rooms on the first floor are a great deal, with private baths, a/c, TV, and DVD, and shared fridge and microwave, with a larger one-bedroom apartment ($95) upstairs. ❸

Bravo Beach Hotel North Shore Rd 1 ☎787/741-1128, ⓦwww.bravobeachhotel .com. Smart, contemporary styling makes this one of the island's hippest hotels, overlooking the north coast with no beach but a gorgeous pool. The ten rooms sport a minimalist, bleached-white color scheme with mahogany beds, Italian Frette linens, satellite TV, PlayStations for games and DVDs (which you can rent), and iPod docking stations, creating a glamorous, boutique feel, and you can indulge in the gourmet restaurant and bar on site (see p.171). ❻

Casa de Amistad c/Benitez Castaño 27, Isabel II ☎787/741-3758, ⓦwww .casadeamistad.com. The best budget option in town, a charming two-story guesthouse with seven modern, cozy rooms, all with a/c, a shared lounge with satellite TV, tiny but attractive pool, patio garden, and wooden roof deck for lounging. You can also use the kitchen and Internet. ❷–❸

Casa Ladera Off PR-200, Playa Monte Santo ☎917/570-7558, ⓦwww .casa-ladera.com. This bright and comfy modern villa is a great deal, especially for families, containing three two-bedroom units with kitchens (each sleeping four adults), washing machines, and a host of thoughtful extras; there's a large pool, tranquil gardens (shaded by mango trees), DVDs, satellite TV, and a library of books and games in each unit. Playa Monte Santo is just two minutes away on foot. Save hassle by renting an SUV or Jeep from the owners ($50/day) – they'll pick you up on arrival and get you oriented. Normally rented for the week ($1300–1700), or four-night minimum. ❼

Casa La Lanchita North Shore Rd 374 ☎787/741-8449, ⓦwww.viequeslalanchita.com. Three-story, whitewashed Mediterranean-style

villa overlooking the water – you'll hear the waves
and see the ocean from every room, with easy
access to the reef and narrow, pebbly beach
below. It also has a decent pool. The eight apartments all have kitchens and a small sun deck, but
the basic decor and rattan furnishings are not
quite as posh as the exterior suggests. You can
walk from central Isabel II, though parking spaces
are plentiful outside. Four-night minimum. ⑤
Enchanted Garden Inn PR-200 km 2.6
☎787/741-2805, ⓦwww.enchantedgardeninn
.com. Not far from the airport, this slightly quirky,
pink-painted villa, with a sun deck on the roof
and surrounded by lush gardens, is a good
choice for families or larger groups. The main
house is usually rented in units with a minimum
of two bedrooms, jazzed up with terrazzo tile
floors, hand-painted furnishings, and whimsical
murals on the outside walls. Guests share the two
kitchens and two bathrooms. Each unit has a/c
and satellite TV, with a separate studio cottage for
couples with kitchenette and shower. Rates are

cheaper if you reserve by the week. Studio ⑤, two
bedrooms ⑦, whole house ⑨
Roy's Guesthouse c/Antonio G. Mellado 355,
Isabel II ☎787/741-0685, ⓔscotty2@bellsouth
.net. This striking, Neoclassical pink house on
the main street contains a coffee shop and
third-floor apartment for rent, perfect if you want
somewhere central in town. Decked out with
bright, bold colors and two queen-sized beds, it's
equipped with outdoor shower, washer/dryer, and
large balcony. ⑦
SeaGate Hotel c/El Fuente ☎787/741-4661,
ⓦwww.seagatehotel.com. Established in 1977
and refurbished in 2006, this hotel is set within
a pretty hilltop garden with stupendous views
of the Fortín Conde de Mirasol and Puerto
Rico beyond. Rooms come in a wide range
of prices and sizes, but are all clean and
simple with remodeled bathrooms, kitchens,
and terraces. Families and pets are welcome,
and breakfast and ferry/airport pick-up are
included. ③–⑥

Watersports

If lazing on an empty beach isn't enough, Vieques offers the usual range of **watersports**. **Surfers** should make for La Lanchita, north of Isabel II in the Bravos de Boston
neighborhood, a beach with big waves when the north swells are running in winter.
For **bio bay** tours see p.167.

Diving
Vieques isn't as rewarding as Culebra when it comes to **diving**, but there are plenty
of worthy targets just offshore, particularly around Rompeolas (Mosquito Pier), the
headland near Playa El Gallito (Gringo Beach), and in the shallow lagoons on the south
coast (perfect for beginners). Anchor, Bucky, and Patti Reefs are also popular, not far
from Esperanza: Bucky Reef is around sixty feet deep with a diverse population of
corals and fish, while Patti Reef, at thirty feet, attracts a plethora of multicolored but
smaller fish.

Black Beard Sports (Mon, Tues & Thurs–Sat 8am–5pm, Wed 8am–3pm, Sun noon–
3pm; ☎787/741-1892, ⓦwww.blackbeardsports.com), at Calle Muñoz Rivera 101 in
Isabel II, runs night dives or two-tank day dives for $80, boat dives for $120, and
half-day "discover scuba" PADI courses for $150. They also rent snorkeling gear for
$15 per day ($10/day for minimum four days). Dave Evans at **Nan-Sea Charters**
(☎787/741-2390, ⓦwww.nanseacharters.com) offers half-day two-tank dives for
$100 (maximum six people) or one-tank beach dives for $50.

Snorkeling
Abe's Snorkeling Tours (☎787/741-2134, ⓦwww.abessnorkeling.com) organizes
two-hour trips (by kayak) to Cayo Afuera off Esperanza ($35), and two-hour excur-
sions off Mosquito Pier ($30) for beginners. Ernie and Kathy Diaz run the popular
Vieques Charters (☎787/741-1389, ⓦwww.viequescharters-pr.com) snorkeling
trips ($75/half-day) via powerboat. **Blue Caribe Kayaks** (☎787/741-2522) rents
snorkels for $12 for 24 hours and organizes short snorkeling trips for $35. **Fun
Brothers** (daily 7am–5pm; ☎787/556-5966) rents snorkels for $10 per day, and

Tropical Guest House E41 Apolonia Gittings, c/Progreso ⓣ787/741-2449, ⓦwww.viequestropicalguesthouse.com. The cheapest option in Vieques and a bit dorm-like, a plain, two-story white house in a quiet residential area off the main road. Singles ($5 cheaper) or doubles are basic but adequate and clean, and come with private shower, a/c, and TV. ❷–❸

Esperanza and the south coast

Acacia c/Magnolia 236 ⓣ787/741-1059, ⓦwww.acaciaguesthouse.com. A good choice for couples who want self-catering near the beaches, this three-story guesthouse at the back of the Esperanza residential zone contains four spotless and spacious apartments with kitchens – the main differences are the fabulous views from the upper levels, with the third floor $50 extra. The first-floor rooms are still a good deal, and you can enjoy the same vistas sunbathing on the roof deck. It's a short walk to the *malecón*, but not signposted from the main road. The free washing machine is handy. ❸

Bananas Guesthouse c/Flamboyán 142 ⓣ787/741-8700, ⓦwww.bananasguesthouse.com. This guesthouse was one of the first to open in the 1980s and retains a backpacker feel, though the twelve basic rooms (with bath and fridge but no TV) are more comfortable than a hostel. Set at the back of the bar and restaurant on the ground floor, it's the best place to stay for easy access to booze and the main strip. Non-a/c rooms are much cheaper. ❷–❹

Casa Alta Vista c/Flamboyán 297 ⓣ787/741-3296, ⓦwww.casaaltavista.net. A small hotel at the far end of the strip, close enough to all the action but not as noisy at night. It's also convenient for activities, with daily rentals of snorkel masks ($5), fins ($5), bikes ($15–20), and scooters ($50), and has a small *colmado* on site. The eleven comfortable rooms (four renovated in 2006) offer plenty of choice: all have bath, fridge, and tiled floors, some with balcony, and the larger

Vieques Tours (ⓣ787/447-4104 or 939/630-1267, ⓦwww.vieques-tours.com) runs daily trips from the front of *Trade Winds Guest House* in Esperanza (see p.160) at 10am and 1pm, and can arrange kayaking trips and historical tours on demand. *Casa Alta Vista* (see above) also rents snorkeling equipment for just $10 per day.

Kayaking

Blue Caribe Kayaks, at Calle Flamboyán 149 in Esperanza, rents kayaks for $10 per hour or $55 per day – perfect for the cays and mangroves just offshore. **Fun Brothers** charges $45 for 24 hours, and Garry Lowe at **Vieques Adventures** (ⓣ787/692-9162, ⓦwww.viequesadventures.com) rents for $45 per day and will drop you off at the best locations – he also leads guided fishing trips by kayak for $150 per half-day.

Fishing

The waters around Vieques are rich in tarpon, bonefish, permit, and snook, with marlin, barracuda, kingfish, and amberjack also common. **Caribbean Fly Fishing** (ⓣ787/741-1337) is managed by twenty-year fishing veteran Captain Franco González (ⓣ787/450-3744), while experienced US expat Captain Greg McKee runs **Wild Fly Charters** (ⓣ787/435-4833, ⓦwww.wildflycharters.com) in his Maverick Mirage. Both charge $300 for a half-day excursion.

Sailing and jet skiing

Kris and Barbara Dynneson run **Marauder Sailing Charters** (ⓣ787/435-4858) with the 34-foot yacht *Marauder*, charging $95 for day-trips. **Captain Bill Barton** sails the 30-foot *Willo* out of Isabel II (ⓣ787/508-7245, ⓔbillwillo@yahoo.com), offering sunset cruises ($30), half-day cruises ($45), and all-day excursions ($95), which include snorkeling, a beach visit, and lunch.

Fun Brothers rents **jet skis** from the tiki hut in the parking lot at the eastern end of the Esperanza *malecón*. Rates are $80 for one hour or $40 for thirty minutes.

family rooms (for up to five people) have TV and microwave. The cheapest are singles with no TV ($75). ❸

🏊 **Hacienda Tamarindo** PR-996 km 4.5 ☎787/741-8525, ⓦwww.haciendatamarindo .com. Gorgeous colonial plantation house (named after the giant tamarind tree in the lobby), on a bluff high above the south coast, offering sixteen individually designed rooms with a charming, nineteenth-century theme: wooden shutters open to create light and airy interiors, enhanced with antique fixtures, rattan chairs, and tiled showers. Rates include breakfast and use of an attractive pool shaded by palms. No TVs or kids under 15. ❻

🏊 **Inn on the Blue Horizon** PR-996 km 4.2 ☎787/741-3318, ⓦwww .innonthebluehorizon.com. With a magnificent, breezy location overlooking the sea, this is a perfect romantic getaway for couples, the colonial-style rooms embellished with four-poster beds, art, and antiques. It's off the main road at the end of a dirt track, all very exclusive and extremely quiet, with no phones or TVs (and no a/c). Three-night minimum (much cheaper in low season). ❻

Jaime's Escondite c/Magnolia 239 ☎787/741-7937, ⓦwww.enchanted-isle.com/byowner/jaimes .htm, ⓔmimpop@aol.com. This is the best of several appealing rental properties in the area, a cozy *casita* for two, but unmarked from the street – you must reserve in advance. The tiny modern cottage has a queen-sized bed, bathroom, a/c, fridge, microwave, and coffee maker. Genial owners Mimi and Joe Popp live nearby and offer a wealth of tips and information about the island. ❸

Mi Pana Vacation Apartments c/Acacia 222 ☎787/741-1564, ⓦwww.mi-pana.com. Another venture from the folks at *Casa Cubuy* (☎787/874-6221), these six rental apartments lie within a handsome, two-story, lemon-colored wood and concrete building with balconies, in the residential section of Esperanza. All rooms have fridges, microwaves, and a/c, and are dressed in a simple, beach cabin style with basic furnishings. ❸–❻

Trade Winds Guest House c/Flamboyán 107 ☎787/741-8666, ⓦwww.enchanted-isle.com /tradewinds. Another budget favorite on the strip, this solid-looking house perched at the western end of the *malecón* offers reasonable rates. Rooms are rather plain (no TV), but come with ceiling fans (some with a/c), mini-fridges, and private bathroom. Singles pay $10 less. Ask for a front room with a balcony overlooking the sea, and eat breakfast on the open-air veranda. ❷

Villa Coral Guesthouse c/Gladiola 485 ☎787/741-1967, ⓦwww.villacoralguesthouse .com. One of the best bargains on the island, this

upscale guesthouse has six compact but plush rooms equipped with a/c, mini-fridge, multicolored bedspreads, ceiling fans, and stylish bathrooms. You get fine views of Sun Bay from the roof deck, beach towels and ice coolers are provided, and bikes are just $10/day. Minimum three nights. ❸

Central Vieques

Crow's Nest PR-201 km 1.6 ☎787/741-0033, ⓦwww.crowsnestvieques.com. Another Vieques institution with a homey atmosphere, tucked away in the foothills and enveloped by five acres of tropical flower-filled gardens. The rooms come with kitchenette, bathroom, TV, and Spanish touches such as alcoves and arches, and rates include breakfast, use of coolers, beach chairs, boogie boards, and towels. Rates are $30 less in summer. ❺

La Finca Caribe PR-995 km 2.2 ☎787/741-0495, ⓦwww.lafinca.com. In the jungly hills in the middle of the island, this is a bit like a wilderness lodge and the most rustic place to stay on Vieques, a world away from the surf and sand. Life here is basic: rooms and *cabañas* have fans, mosquito nets, cotton sheets, reading lamps, and little else, and the hammocks and solar-heated outdoor showers add to the *Survivor* feel. It's on a narrow lane signposted off the main road, and has a small pool and communal kitchen. Rooms (three-night min) ❸, cabañas (one-week min) ❹–❺

Great Escape Bed & Breakfast Inn Puerto Real Rd, off PR-201 ☎787/741-2927, ⓦwww .enchanted-isle.com/greatescape. Only a short drive from Esperanza, this big white house feels lost in the countryside, containing ten spacious, spotless rooms with old-fashioned beds, tiled floors, ceiling fans, and private balconies – it's cool enough at night without a/c. Continental breakfast is served by the pool. ❹

🏊 **Hix Island House** PR-995 km 1.6, ☎787/741-2302, ⓦwww.hixislandhouse .com. This is the most original hotel in Puerto Rico, but you'll have to be into the concept to enjoy it, and it's not cheap. Tucked away in a forest of pines and palms (up a dirt track off PR-995), these thirteen modernist and rather spartan open-plan studios have one side completely open to the forest (the modest can roll down a garage-like screen). Each room comes with kitchenette and outdoor shower, and the beds are covered in mosquito nets, the all-cement gray interiors brightened by some choice contemporary art. The Zen-like ethos is backed up by yoga classes, home-made bread, and the isolated location, magical at night when it's a bit like sleeping outside; it's also solar-powered and uses recycled water. ❻–❼

The Island

Most travelers arrive at **Isabel II** – home to a handful of sights associated with the island's rich past, notably the **Museo Fortín Conde de Mirasol** – but soon gravitate towards a tempting array of **beaches** for the rest of their stay on Vieques. The south coast boasts the most spectacular stretches of sand, as well as the laid-back village of Esperanza, with the **Vieques Conservation and Historical Trust** and nearby **Area Arqueológica Hombre de Puerto Ferro** offering a break from the surf and sun. Further east, the **bioluminescent bay** is one of the highlights of Puerto Rico.

Isabel II

The island's political and commercial heart, **ISABEL II** looks deceptively plain upon arrival, a mishmash of modern low-rise buildings thrown up around the harbor and promptly ignored by most travelers. While Isabel II is very much a working town, elements of its short but varied history spring to life upon closer

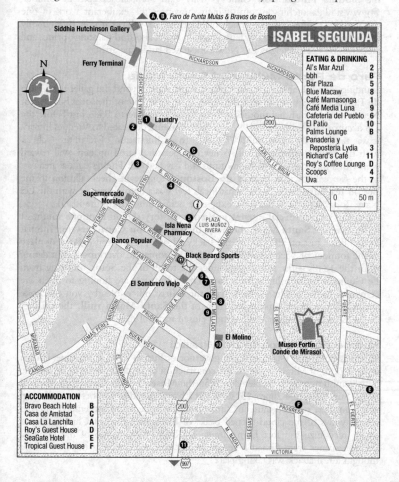

▲ Ⓐ, Ⓑ, Faro de Punta Mulas & Bravos de Boston

ISABEL SEGUNDA

Siddhia Hutchinson Gallery

Ferry Terminal

RICHARDSON

RICHARDSON

GERMAN RIECKEHOFF

N

❶ Laundry

❷

BENITEZ CASTANO

Ⓒ

200

CARLOS LE BRUM

❸

B. GUZMAN

❹

VICTOR DUTEIL

Supermercado Morales

BALDORIOTY DE CASTRO

MUÑOZ RIVERA

PLINIO PETERSON

ⓘ

❺

Isla Nena Pharmacy

PLAZA LUIS MUÑOZ RIVERA

Banco Popular

65 INFANTERIA

CARLOS LEBRUM

A. MOLANDO

Black Beard Sports

⑫

❻
❼

El Sombrero Viejo

ANTONIO G. MELLADO

Ⓓ ❽

JOSE A. SUERO

❾

PRUDENCIO

EL FUERTE

El Molino

❿

Museo Fortín Conde de Mirasol

TOMAS PEREZ

BRIGNONI

BUENA VISTA

EL TAMARINDO

MIRAMAR

CANON

Ⓔ

Ⓕ

PROGRESO

EL FUERTE

200

M. NADAL

IGLESIAS

⓫

VICTORIA

997

EATING & DRINKING
Al's Mar Azul **2**
bbh **B**
Bar Plaza **5**
Blue Macaw **8**
Café Mamasonga **1**
Café Media Luna **9**
Cafeteria del Pueblo **6**
El Patio **10**
Palms Lounge **B**
Panadería y
  Repostería Lydia **3**
Richard's Café **11**
Roy's Coffee Lounge **D**
Scoops **4**
Uva **7**

0   50 m

ACCOMMODATION
Bravo Beach Hotel **B**
Casa de Amistad **C**
Casa La Lanchita **A**
Roy's Guest House **D**
SeaGate Hotel **E**
Tropical Guest House **F**

VIEQUES AND CULEBRA | Vieques: The Island

161

investigation: Spanish Neoclassical houses, often with unique English and Danish touches (influences from the Virgin Islands) are scattered along the streets, a couple of historic bars and bakeries remain, and there are plenty of more formal if dilapidated remnants of the Spanish colonial period to explore.

Founded in 1843 by Francisco Saínz, the first Spanish governor of Vieques after the death of Le Guillou, the town is named after Queen Isabel II of Spain, who came of age that same year. Though the ferry dock sees more action these days, the historic heart of the town is **Plaza Luis Muñoz Rivera**, created around 1860 and bounded by the old city hall or **Casa Alcaldía** (dating from 1844), the tourist office, venerable *Bar Plaza* (see p.174), several aging schools, and a dull, modern church. Note, opposite the tourist office the bust of South American liberator **Simón Bolívar**, whose ship ran aground here in 1816 while escaping from Venezuela – Vieques was the only part of Puerto Rico visited by the legendary general.

The fort (see below) is a short stroll uphill from the plaza, but it's also worth wandering north to Calle German Rieckehoff, beyond the ferry dock, and the **Siddhia Hutchinson Gallery** (daily 9am–3pm, closes 2pm in summer; Ⓦwww.siddhiahutchinson.com), which showcases the exuberant work of one of the island's gifted artists – much of Hutchinson's subject matter is frequently the people and landscapes of Vieques. Inside you'll also find paintings, prints, and tapestries by Glen Wielgus, the New York-based landscape artist.

Faro de Punta Mulas and Santa María

Standing on a hill above the ferry pier, a short walk beyond the gallery, the **Faro de Punta Mulas** was completed in 1896, a fine example of the squat but elegant Neoclassical Spanish lighthouses thrown up all over Puerto Rico just before the US occupation. Restored in 1992 as a small museum dedicated to Vieques history, it was temporarily closed in 2007 thanks to an infestation of termites – check with the tourist office to see if it's been reopened. A stroll up here will reward you with a fine view across the rooftops and bay beyond. The residential area east of the *faro* is known as **Bravos de Boston**, a tongue-in-cheek allusion to the Boston Tea Party of 1773, and what locals feel was a heroic struggle with the US Navy. Today it's one of the most expensive neighborhoods on the island.

Anyone with a special interest in Vieques history should continue southeast to the *barrio* of **Santa María**, home to the **Le Guillou Cemetery** (or Tumbas Le Guillou), just off PR-200 in the backyard of a private house. Resting place of the founder of Vieques and his family, it's a romantic, overgrown ruin dating from the 1840s – the site also includes the tomb of the Sotos, offspring from Le Guillou's relationship with a slave. The authorities are hoping to open the cemetery to the public – check with the tourist office. Nearby you can poke around in the jungle-smothered ruins of the **Santa María mill**, the smallest of the island's four sugar mills, which closed in the 1920s.

Museo Fortín Conde de Mirasol

When Isabel II was established, the governor of Puerto Rico at the time, known as the Count of Mirasol, ordered the construction of a brick fortress to defend the new Spanish outpost. Completed in 1855, the **Museo Fortín Conde de Mirasol** (Wed–Sun 8.30am–4.20pm; $3) served as a barracks and prison before ending up as a beautifully restored museum, surrounded by gardens and battlements offering distant views of the cloud-topped peaks of El Yunque. Fans of Clint Eastwood might recognize the fort from *Heartbreak Ridge* (1986): some of the Grenada invasion scenes were filmed here, apparently without notifying the locals, who thought a real attack was taking place.

▲ Museo Fortín Conde de Mirasol

Although the collection inside is fairly modest, displays are enhanced by original wood floors, exposed brick walls, and timbered ceilings. Upstairs you'll find local artwork and artifacts from the prehistoric and Taíno periods: ceramics and stone tools, the esoteric *cemí*, striking jade amulets, and information on **El Hombre de Puerto Ferro**, the remains of a 35- to 40-year-old man who lived on the island around four thousand years ago. Currently on display at the Parque de las Ciencias in Bayamón, the bones are the oldest human remains found in the Caribbean. Little is known about *el hombre* other than that he was killed by a strong blow to the jaw. Museum officials hope one day to secure his return to Vieques, but until then you'll have to be content with a visit to the discovery site on PR-997 (see p.165). Other exhibits include historic photos of the town, old Spanish weapons and coins, an explanation of the fort's restoration, and a short **video** highlighting aspects of the island's history that runs throughout the day (Spanish with English subtitles). Note that captions in the museum are in Spanish only. From the plaza take PR-989 up the hill to get to the fort – you can park on site.

The north coast

The Atlantic-facing **north coast** of Vieques tends to be rougher than the Caribbean south coast, and its beaches less enticing, though there are a few attractions dotted along PR-200 before you reach the snorkeling haven of Punta Arenas (see p.169).

The most appealing beach is **Playa El Gallito** (also known as Gringo Beach), just beyond the *W Retreat & Spa*, a small bay with a narrow strip of soft sand and good swimming on calm days – you can also snorkel around the rocky point on the west side. Further west, beyond the airport, you'll pass the **Ceiba Centenaria**, an ancient kapok tree in a grassy clearing on the right side of the road. Said to be over 400 years old, the short but incredibly distended trunk is buttressed by broad, ridge-like roots, its thorny branches heavy with a dense canopy of leaves.

Not far from here is Mosquito Pier, more accurately known as **Rompeolas** in Spanish, meaning "breakwater" – it's actually a solid sea wall of rubble and stone jutting a mile into the ocean. Visible all along the north coast, it was recently dubbed Puerto de la Libertad David Sanes in honor of the security guard killed in 1999 (see p.365). The breakwater is the vestige of what now seems a ludicrous scheme to create a giant naval base linking Vieques with the main island during World War II, in part to create a safe haven for the British Navy should the Germans occupy the UK. With fortunes changing, work stopped in 1943 – if completed, according to most experts it would have been an environmental disaster. The pier was handed over to the municipality in 2001, and today it's a convenient staging post for divers and fishermen, with particularly good **snorkeling** towards the end. Though the road at the tip of the pier is fenced off, you can descend the concrete steps on the calmer western side and swim further up to where the reef widens out to a ledge, with plenty of starfish, big fish, and all sorts of coral. Non-snorkelers can still enjoy the **best views** of Vieques from here, a panorama of the whole north coast from Isabel II to Monte Pirata. The end of the pier is being turned into a **terminal** for ferries from the main island (see p.174). The pier lies off PR-200, about a mile beyond the airport, though the turning is not signposted: look out for a wide road branching off to the right, passing what looks like a white, abandoned weighing station.

Continuing west on PR-200, the road passes through a wide, grassy clearing containing **La Capilla Ecuménica**, the simple wooden chapel and bell tower

Cockfights

Cockfighting (see p.41) is one of the most controversial of Puerto Rico's traditional sports, and remains popular on Vieques. Fights take place at the **Gallera Puerto Real** most Sunday afternoons and usually Friday evenings – check with the tourist office. If you've been to the ring in San Juan (see p.76), this will be a rawer experience, though the same time regulations apply. Culturally fascinating, the fights are just as violent and blood-spattered here, so animal lovers should stay well away. The *gallera* is the pink building on the left as you leave Isabel II on PR-200, not far beyond the intersection with PR-997. Admission is usually $10 and you can buy food and drink inside.

built by activists during the Navy-Vieques protests (see p.365). The original chapel was built on Playa Icacos in 1999 (which is still off-limits), becoming the spiritual center of the protest movement before being bulldozed by the authorities in May 2000. In 2002, a replica was built in front of the Capitolio in San Juan, but this was transported to Vieques a year later to mark the departure of the navy: the chapel was supposed to be erected in Camp García, but due to a logistical foul-up it ended up here. Heading west, it's a short drive to the Vieques National Wildlife Refuge (see p.168).

Área Arqueológica Hombre de Puerto Ferro

Known as the "Stonehenge of Puerto Rico," the **Área Arqueológica Hombre de Puerto Ferro** (daily; free) is a mystifying circle of giant boulders: whether they were assembled into a mini-mountain of rock by prehistoric man, or just fell that way naturally, is still a matter of fierce debate. The discovery of **El Hombre de Puerto Ferro** (see p.163) here in 1990 added weight to the theory that the site had mystical or ceremonial significance in prehistoric times, though it seems impossible that such bulk could be maneuvered by anything less than a twenty-ton excavator. The site can be reached from PR-997 via a heavily rutted dirt track marked only by a small bronze plaque: it's about a half-mile from Esperanza, on the left just after the turn to the bio bay.

Esperanza and around

Facing the Caribbean on the south side of the island, the village of **ESPERANZA** is far more inviting than the capital, its cheerful *malecón* (Calle Flamboyán, or just "the strip") the preserve of independent travelers since the 1980s. With its guesthouses remaining low-key, and bars and restaurants ranging from casual to super-hip, it just about retains its backpacker ethos, though Esperanza attracts a far more eclectic range of visitors these days, with prices to match.

The narrow beach in front of the *malecón*, **Playa de Esperanza**, is a little scruffy, with some mildly interesting snorkeling around the rusting **Muelle de la Caña**, the old sugar-cane pier. Things get much better if you wander east towards **Cayo de Tierra** (you can stroll to the tip of the headland, or cut across to Sun Bay), or snorkel in the calm waters around **Cayo Afuera** just offshore, where you might see turtles. You can leave your car in the parking area at the eastern end of the beach, featuring a bust of murdered activist **Ángel Cristóbal** (see p.154), or right in front of the restaurants if you can find a space.

On the *malecón* itself, the **Vieques Conservation and Historical Trust** (shop & museum Tues–Sun 11am–4pm; office Mon–Thurs 8am–1.30pm; free; ☏787/741-8850; ⓦwww.vcht.com), at Calle Flamboyán 138, was founded in 1984 to preserve the bioluminescent bay and delicate coral reef systems that surround the island. Inside, the **Museo de Esperanza** is a small room housing a collection of Taíno bracelets, ritual masks, and tools, as well as old photos and other historical bits and pieces. At the back a mini-aquarium comprises pools of starfish and coral; a room highlights the ecology of Vieques (targeted principally at children); and the **gift shop** sells books, local crafts, and jewelry. Captain Mark Martin of Island Adventures (see p.167) gives talks on local ecology Thursday to Saturday between 1 and 3pm – ask at the shop. You can also bring in your seashells for identification, and use the **Internet**.

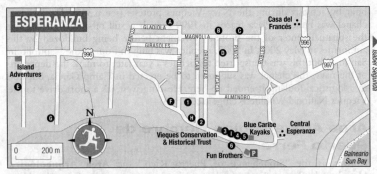

ACCOMMODATION				EATING, DRINKING & NIGHTLIFE	
Acacia	B	Jaime's Escondite	C	Bananas Beach Bar & Grill	I	La Dulce Esperanza	1
Bananas Guesthouse	I	Mi Pana Vacation Apartments	D	Belly Buttons Café & Grill	2	La Nasa	6
Casa Alta Vista	F	Trade Winds Guest House	H	Bilí	4	El Quenepo	5
Hacienda Tamarindo	E	Villa Coral Guesthouse	A	Duffy's	3	Trade Winds	H
Inn on the Blue Horizon	G				

Esperanza was established in the 1820s, and was the site of one of four big **sugar mills** that dominated Vieques in the early twentieth century. You can see some of the ivy-smothered brick ruins of **Central Esperanza** on the right side of PR-996 as you leave the *malecón* towards Isabel II. Also known as Puerto Real, the mill closed in 1927.

Balneario Sun Bay

Just east of Esperanza on PR-997, **Balneario Sun Bay** (daily 8.30am–5pm; parking $3) is a dazzling mile-long crescent of sugary white sand, perfect for swimming and easy to reach. The only official public beach on Vieques, the Compañía de Parques Nacionales upgraded the facilities in 2007, including the cheap cafeteria *(Arena y Mar)*, showers, and toilets, along with gazebos on the beach to escape the sun – the handful of coconut palms add character but little shade. You can use the main parking lot or drive along the tracks to park at the eastern end of the beach.

Playa Media Luna and Playa Navío

Keep driving along the bumpy sand road at the eastern end of Sun Bay, and you'll find the route to two of the best beaches on Vieques. After another stretch of spine-jarring track, **Playa Media Luna** (Half Moon Beach) is signposted to the right (the left fork cuts across to the bio bay), a beguiling cove of fine, powdery white sand and shallow water – ideal for paddling and swimming, especially for families. Portia trees with bushy yellow flowers, bay cedar, and sea grape bushes provide limited shade, while underwater the outer reaches of the bay are thick with turtle grass.

Playa Navío lies at the end of the dirt road, a quarter-mile or so beyond Media Luna, another gem of a beach and location for the final scenes of Peter Brook's powerful movie *Lord of the Flies* (1963). It retains the same wild, raw appeal captured in the film, a small bay of coral sand, coconut palms, and sea grape, hemmed in by jagged cliffs on both sides. It's rougher than Media Luna, so a bit more fun for swimmers (you can surf here in summer), and with a snorkel you can explore the underwater caves, sponges, and corals beneath the cliffs.

La Reserva Natural de La Bahía Bioluminiscente

One of the world's most enchanting natural wonders, **La Reserva Natural de La Bahía Bioluminiscente** at Puerto Mosquito is definitely the richest example of a **bioluminescent bay**. Boats leave glowing trails in the darkness, while swimmers are engulfed by luminous clouds, the water spilling off their hands like glittering fireflies – it's like something out of a fantasy movie.

The effect is produced by millions of harmless microscopic **dinoflagellates**, most commonly a protozoa known as *pyrodinium bahamense*. These release a chemical called luciferin when disturbed, which reacts with oxygen to create light. Experts think that this is a defense mechanism (the glow drawing bigger predators that will eat the creatures feeding on the protozoa) or a way to attract food. Dinoflagellates are found all over the tropics, but Puerto Mosquito has a particularly intense concentration: it's shallow, has a narrow mouth that acts like valve, the salinity is perfect (with no freshwater source or human contamination), and the mangroves provide a crucial nutrient boost. Though you can visit the bay on your own, it's much wiser to use one of the local **tour operators**, at least at first, to get a thorough introduction to the site.

Surprisingly, most of the land around the bay is private, and the main threat for now is **artificial lighting**, which limits the bioluminescent effect: the Vieques Conservation and Historical Trust (see p.165) is leading the campaign to reduce public and private light sources nearby. Neighboring Puerto Ferro, and Laguna Kiani in the wildlife refuge, are also bioluminescent, but closed to the public after dark.

Bio bay tours

Tours of the bay run all year, but **moonlight** has a huge impact on bioluminescence – it's crucial to avoid full moon cycles, when it's impossible to appreciate the effect, and ideal if you can visit during the new moon phase. Though most operators don't run tours when the moon is full, they tend to play down its impact – business is business. Another problem is **jellyfish**, which collect in the bay and sometimes sting hapless swimmers. Again, tour operators are reluctant to make too much of this, though to be fair, the stings are rarely serious, affect only a handful of visitors, and are easily treated with vinegar spray.

Conservation-minded **Island Adventures** (☎787/741-0720, ⓦwww.biobay .com; $30) is the best operator, and has a useful **moon calendar** on its website. Tours (8–10pm) begin at their office, west of Esperanza on PR-996 (near *Inn on the Blue Horizon*), with an informative talk, followed by a rickety bus ride to the waterside. From here one of their expert guides takes a boat around the bay (around 1hr), stopping for at least twenty minutes for a swim and pointing out all the major stars and planets along the way, with plenty of local history and botany thrown in. They have a café (daily 6–11pm) at the office serving Puerto Rican and Mexican food, and plenty of parking.

Abe's Snorkeling Tours (☎787/741-2134, ⓦwww.abessnorkeling.com) in Esperanza organizes daily **kayak trips** to the bay at 2pm, paddling through the mangroves for just over an hour, followed by snorkeling and a beach visit, before returning to the bio bay after dark ($90). They also do night trips around the bay only (with swimming; 1hr 30min; $30). **Blue Caribe Kayaks** (☎787/741-2522), at Calle Flamboyán 149 in Esperanza, also organizes kayaking trips for $30 per person. **Vieques Tours** (☎787/447-4104, ⓦwww.vieques-tours.com) offers nightly tours of the bay at 7–11pm for $25 ($15 children) from the front of *Trade Winds Guest House* in Esperanza, and also tours by **kayak** on demand.

Vieques National Wildlife Refuge

Vieques National Wildlife Refuge, a trove of spellbinding beaches, tropical forest, and flourishing mangroves, was occupied by the US Navy before being handed over to the US Fish and Wildlife Service between 2001 and 2003. Covering almost two-thirds of the island (17,771 acres), much of the reserve remains closed for fear of contamination (see p.154), which is a shame: Puerto Diablo is said to be the most stunning beach on the island. Nevertheless, the public areas, open daily between sunrise and dusk and best accessed by Jeep or four-wheel drive, are well worth exploring, epitomizing the raw, untouched aspect of Vieques that makes it so unique.

Visit the **refuge office** (Mon–Fri 8am–3pm), just outside Isabel II at PR-200 km 0.4, for the latest information. It's not signposted on the road and can be irritatingly hard to find: look for the long, single-story, light-green building on the left as you leave Isabel II, after the junction with PR-997 (opposite a small electricity booster station on the edge of a housing estate). Inside you'll find information on the varied **habitats** in the reserve, including beaches, lagoons, mangrove wetlands, and upland forest areas, as well as some of the best examples of subtropical dry forest in the Caribbean. The refuge is also home to at least five plants and ten animals on the **Federal Endangered Species list**, including the Antillean manatee, the brown pelican, and four species of sea turtle (green, loggerhead, hawksbill, and leatherback). Note that reserve security guards have been known to dish out stiff **fines** ($100–200) for sunbathing nude and driving or parking on the sand.

The southern beaches

The only part of the vast eastern section of the refuge open to the public lies along the ragged **south coast**, sprinkled with wonderfully tranquil beaches. Many have English names based on colors, a legacy of when the navy used them for assault practice. All the beaches can be accessed from the former entrance to **Camp García** on PR-997, halfway between Isabel II and Esperanza – a small plaque here recalls the **Campamento Justicia y Paz** (Camp of Justice and Peace) that became a focal point for the navy protestors. Most of the beaches are signposted off the gravel roads that run through the camp, along much rougher potholed mud tracks.

The first right turn off the main camp road, 2.7km from the entrance, is a gravel track that leads another 1.2km to **Playa Caracas** (Red Beach), a small bay north of Punta García. Justifiably popular with locals, its shady pavilions and palm trees face a wide arc of ivory sand – waves tend to be weak, and with a soft sand bottom throughout the bay it's excellent for swimming and safe for small kids. You can **snorkel** around the small cay about three hundred feet offshore.

Before you reach Caracas you'll see another turn to the right: take this road and it splits again, the right-hand track ending up at a landing site on Puerto Ferro known as **Tres Palmitas** (an excellent tarpon fishing spot), while the left branch ends at **Playuela** (García Beach), a wilder strip of sand with choppy waves, backed by a thick screen of scrub and bushes, and flanked by rough limestone cliffs – it's often deserted.

Back on the main road through the camp, the next right turn is narrow, steep, and littered with jagged rocks, ending happily at **Pata Prieta**, an exceptionally isolated beach: take the right fork when you get to the end of the track. Also known as **Secret Beach**, this is one of the prettiest spots on the island.

At the end of the main gravel road through the camp (5.6km) is Bahía de la Chiva, a wide, sun-drenched bay facing Isla Chiva just offshore. The set of three beaches here is known collectively as **Playa de La Chiva** (Blue Beach) or

Manuelquí (after a man who once lived on the island), another wild and windy stretch of coast and the place to come for glorious isolation. The beach is very scrubby, with bushes merging into the bone-colored sand, but the long, narrow stretch facing the island is a fine place to lounge. The second, middle section is the only one with shady *bohíos*, or "huts," and cover is otherwise lacking – the once abundant coconut palms here were cleared by the military in the 1950s. Isla Chiva is a prime target for snorkeling, with turtles and rays often gliding through the waters nearby, and plenty of pelicans, egrets, and herons nesting onshore. **Playa La Plata** (also known as Silver or Orchid Beach) is as far as you can go beyond here, another idyllic splash of bleached-white sand and almost always empty.

Note that the ruined **Faro de Puerto Ferro**, completed in the 1890s and set on a dramatic headland at the end of an unsealed road from Camp García (the first right turn after the entrance), is officially closed while plans are made for its restoration – locals regularly ignore the ban, however, and enjoy its magnificent perch overlooking the south coast. The lighthouse was closed in 1926.

Laguna Kiani

Rich in mangrove forests, the **Laguna Kiani** conservation zone covers 1058 acres, and is the first point of interest in the western section of the refuge. The lagoon itself is around 1.5km along a gravel track (usually in reasonable condition) at the end of PR-200, just after the metal bridge. Park at the information boards here and take the short **boardwalk** to lookout points on the murky stretch of water and through a dense forest of red, black, white, and button **mangroves**, the muddy floor carpeted with swarms of **land crab**. Kiani is **bioluminescent**, but is closed at night – note also that fishing and swimming are forbidden (though some locals flout the former rule) as the water may still be contaminated by toxic waste.

Punta Arenas (Green Beach)

Continue west from Laguna Kiani for around 1.5km and the road ends at the coast – turn right to **Punta Arenas** itself or left to run behind **Playa Punta Arenas**, also known as Green Beach. In reality the "beach" is just a series of thin strips of sand shaded by clumps of coconut palms, and the real attraction is world-class **snorkeling**. The reef starts right off the beach (which also makes it a bad place to swim), with patches of rare soft corals you'd normally only see on much deeper scuba dives: delicate Christmas tree coral and elegant, wavy fan corals, swaying with the current. Plenty of tropical fish dart around the reef, and spiny sea urchins are also plentiful, so be careful. Punta Arenas was once an important dock for sugar exports, and is only six miles from the main island,

---

Not-so-wild horses of Vieques

Though the herds of unkempt, shaggy-haired horses roaming around Vieques are essentially wild, local tradition maintains that they all have owners, who will famously appear only if any attempt is made to corral or control them. Local environmentalists bemoan this apparent lack of responsibility, and say that something must be done – eventually. For now they remain a romantic, if slightly hazardous slice of Vieques life. If you want to ride horses on Vieques, contact the *SeaGate Hotel* (see p.158), which can arrange two-hour **horseback rides** around the island for $65 per person through local expert Penny Miller, including guide. Call the hotel (☎787/741-4661) or Penny directly (☎787/667-2805) a few days in advance.

the vast bulk of El Yunque looming over the horizon. Lying on the sheltered leeward side of Vieques, the beach also attracts swarms of **sand flies** in the early mornings and evenings – be prepared.

Monte Pirata

The slopes of **Monte Pirata** (987ft) are open to the public, but the summit itself is officially sealed off, though locals regularly ignore this ban. The road to the top (turn left just before you enter the Laguna Kiani conservation zone) is blocked halfway up, so you must leave the car and walk up: it's an energetic but pleasant hike along the paved road, and the view from the summit takes in both sides of Vieques, the Puerto Rico mainland, and Culebra. The conservation zone

▲ Old sugar mill ruins near Playa Grande

around the summit covers 1826 acres of rare and unusual trees, but it's the land below (actually just outside the reserve) that has the most appeal. A loop road cuts through this area from PR-200, passing over a hundred concrete **bunkers**, mostly abandoned navy stores and munitions depots. Most are eerily empty or locked, like overgrown relics of a lost civilization, but some have been decorated by local artists and are occasionally used for exhibitions. Adding to the sense of surrealism, you might also encounter herds of Vieques' famed "wild" horses in the jungles around here.

Playa Grande

The southwest corner of Vieques is mostly barred to visitors, save for the desolate stretch of **Playa Grande**, at the end of PR-201. This steeply inclined beach runs for a couple miles between the sea and swampy Laguna Playa Grande, the haunt of herons, ducks, frigate birds, and brown pelicans. Strong currents, choppy water, and submerged rocks make this a poor choice for swimming, but it's perfect for *de vagabundo*, or **beachcombing** (shells and all sorts of flotsam get washed up here), or just lolling on the sand – you'll usually have it to yourself. You can hike all the way to rugged **Punta Vaca**, the sea cliffs that mark the most southerly point on the island, but don't stray any further west. The really adventurous can explore the decaying, jungle-covered ruins of the once-mighty **Central de Playa Grande** sugar mill, which lie behind the lagoon near the navy radar station (by car, the ruins are best approached from the north coast). The largest and last mill to be built on the island, the crowning glory of the Benítez sugar empire closed in 1942.

Eating and drinking

Traditional **food** on Vieques is identical to the *cocina criolla* found on the main island, with a handful of cheap but enticing diners knocking out rice and beans, *frituras*, and fresh seafood, and an eclectic choice of creative **restaurants** catering primarily to visitors. Some of these offer extremely high standards, with prices to match, and a fascination with fusion cuisine that equals San Juan's. Things quiet down in the summer, when many places operate at reduced hours (most are closed Monday or Tuesday throughout the year), and several shut down altogether between September and October.

For **self-catering**, try *El Molino* (Mon–Sat 7am–11pm, Sun 10am–11pm) in Isabel II at Calle Antonio G. Mellado 342 (next to *El Patio*), or the *Supermercado Morales* at Calle Baldorioty de Castro 15. In Esperanza, *Colmado Lydia* on Calle Almendro sells a good selection of groceries.

Though the island has few culinary specialties, bottles of locally made **Coqui Fire Hot Sauce** (Ⓦwww.coquifire.com; $6) make great gifts, available at the *Coqui Fire Café* (see p.172) and some of the shops in Esperanza. Created by Patty and Jim Cochran in 2002, these zesty concoctions are made with natural ingredients in wacky flavors such as Passionate Frog and Komodo Dragon. If you can find it, you should also try **bilí**, locally made rum fermented with *quenepas* (Spanish limes), especially popular during the fiesta in July.

Isabel II and around

bbh at *Bravo Beach Resort*, North Shore Road 1 ☎787/741-0490. This stylish restaurant overlooking the ocean offers posh sandwiches and salads for lunch (like smoked chicken, $11) and exquisite tapas for dinner: try the trio of dips (eggplant, garbanzo bean, and green olive) with pita bread, or steamed mussels in red coconut curry ($8). More substantial dishes include pan-roasted grouper ($15), watermelon gazpacho with seared tuna ($12), and the luscious three-onion risotto (green, caramelized, and *confit*, $13). Sunday brunch (11am–3pm; $20) is a bargain. Wed–Sun 11am–3pm & 6–9.30pm.

Blue Macaw c/Antonio G. Mellado 358. The owners of this long-term favorite, Rick Gallup and Honor Stanley, offer high-quality Caribbean fusion cuisine with a distinct Asian twist: try the exceptional clam chowder or crispy duck with ginger-flavored plum sauce. Mains from $18. Tues–Sat 5–10pm.

Café Mamasonga c/German Rieckehoff ☎787/741-0103. Isabel II stalwart, opposite *Al's*, with an upper deck providing picture-perfect views of the bay. Breakfast features fluffy omelets ($8) and more exotic German apple or potato pancakes ($6) created by the German-born chef and owner Ute (*Mamasonga* to the locals). Lunch offers the usual American staples such as burgers, nachos, and quesadillas (all from $6). Wed–Sun 7am–5pm.

Café Media Luna c/Antonio G. Mellado 351 ☎787/741-2594. Set in a bright yellow house with a mellow interior of tiled floors and batik wall hangings, this is one of the best (and most expensive) venues for fine dining on the island. Classic Italian cuisine is conjured up by Chef Drew: try the *ossobuco* (braised veal) and linguine with fresh clam sauce (entrees from $19). Grab a romantic table on the second-floor balcony if you can. Thurs–Sun 11am–2pm & 6–11pm.

Cafeteria del Pueblo c/Muñoz Rivera. A real hole-in-the-wall place and ever popular with locals looking for tasty fried snacks, and coffee that packs a punch, right at the top of the main street. The chicken tacos are a good choice for lunch ($2–3). Daily 8am–6pm.

Coqui Fire Café at *Enchanted Garden Inn* ☎787/435-1411. Run by the makers of Coqui Fire Hot Sauce, this homey restaurant serves up Mexican breakfasts (Mon, Tues, Thurs & Fri) and sumptuous Mexican dinners on Tuesday and Thursday nights (5–9pm). Options include seasoned baked pork ($9), stuffed chilis ($8), home-made enchiladas ($10), and the legendary "King Kahuna" burrito ($10). Medalla is $1.50 and margaritas $4. Reservations suggested.

Panadería y Repostería Lydia Avda Benítez Guzmán 63. Local sandwich shop not far from the ferry, drawing long lines at lunchtime for all the usual Puerto Rican snack favorites, breads, and cakes. Breakfast is also worth a try for the egg specials and spine-straightening coffee. Everything is under $10. Daily 7am–5pm.

El Patio c/Antonio G. Mellado 340 ☎787/741-6381. Cheap, no-frills *criollo* food, cooked up in a roadside diner with exposed brick walls, TV blaring all day, and a small veranda. Local workers swarm here for breakfast ($3–6) and lunch ($5–20): lots of seafood, fried snacks, and plates of richly stewed rice and beans grace the menu. Mon–Fri 7am–5.30pm, Sat 9am–4pm.

Richard's Café c/Antonio G. Mellado 35. Another local diner offering all the Puerto Rican staples, but one of the few that keeps the kitchen open all afternoon and all evening. Don't let the cheap decor and Formica tables put you off: the seafood, *mofongo*, and ever popular rice and beans are skillfully prepared and just as good as anything on the main island (mains $6–18). Look for the red-brick building right on the intersection of PR-997 and 200, just before the Esso gas station – it can be hard to park.

Roy's Coffee Lounge c/Antonio G. Mellado 355. Expat favorite and the closest thing on the island to a cozy American coffee house, with snacks (including the only decent bagels on Vieques), cocktails, and free Wi-Fi complementing the full range of lattes and iced and flavored coffees ($1–5). The pink Neoclassical exterior is easy to spot, a gorgeous colonial building with Spanish touches and an outdoor patio at the back. Daily 8am–8pm, closes 2pm in low season.

Scoops Avda Benítez Guzmán 53 ☎787/741-5555. The best pizza on the island ($1.95 a slice), made fresh on the premises, New York-style with a super-thin crust and rich cheese and tomato base. Choose from seven types of medium ($11.95) or large ($17.95) pizzas, pastas ($7.95), hot sandwiches (from $3.95), and calzones ($7.95) that melt in the mouth. Also serves wickedly good Häagen Dazs ice cream, smoothies, and fresh carrot, apple, and spinach juices. Mon–Fri 10am–10pm, Sat & Sun 10am–11pm.

Uva c/Antonio G. Mellado 359 ☎787/741-2050. With a fresh, contemporary interior right in the heart of town, this is the place for upscale Caribbean fusion cuisine. The food is pricey (mains from $35) but impressive: fresh sea bass served with a fennel cream sauce, a rich seafood *cassoulet* (with octopus, squid, scallops, and local fish), and fresh salmon with a Chinese five spice glaze. The jointly owned *Next Door* bar and lounge serves tapas ($10–12) and more casual fare: kebabs, burgers, and fries. Wed–Mon 7–10pm.

Esperanza and the south coast

Bananas Beach Bar & Grill c/Flamboyán 142 ☎787/741-8700. This wooden beach house with an open front is a Vieques institution, always packed with expats and travelers. The menu is crammed with juicy US staples such as chicken wings ($7–12), the celebrated half-pound Paradise burger ($5.75), and hot dogs ($4), and spiced up with hearty Caribbean comfort food: crab cakes ($7), jerk chicken ($15), and red snapper and El Cubano sandwiches ($8). Daily 11am–1am, 2am Fri–Sat.

Belly Buttons Café & Grill c/Flamboyán. Great open-air place for a cheap breakfast of *pan de agua* sandwiches and pineapple pancakes. Lunch features a wider choice of sandwiches, cheap American diner food (enhanced by the full range of Coquí Fire Hot Sauces), and zesty home-made lemonade. Tues–Sun 7.30am–2.30pm.

Bilí at *Amapola Inn*, c/Flamboyán 144 ☎787/741-1382. This oceanfront restaurant with a bright, cheerful interior offers a flamboyant take on Puerto Rican classics, but really stands out for its vegetarian options prepared by lauded chef Eva Bolívar. Try the yucca salad with bay leaves or cheese-stuffed enchiladas; meaty highlights include fresh sea scallops, crab pasta, and crispy red snapper (mains $8–20). Morphs into a salsa-soaked bar at night – try the fruity "Amapola" cocktails. Wed–Sun 11am–4pm & 6–11pm.

Duffy's c/Flamboyán 140. This relaxed bar and restaurant is named after the son of the *Chez Shack* owner and serves a solid choice of deli-style sandwiches such as the *cubano* and reuben, as well as meaty, flame-grilled burgers (from $7), and tasty veggie burgers. At night, sip a fresh *piña colada* or *parcharita*, a margarita made with *parcha* juice (passion fruit). Daily noon–midnight.

La Dulce Esperanza c/Almendro. This local bakery, a short walk behind the *malecón*, sells breakfast sandwiches (egg, ham, and cheese), slices of pizza, calzones, and larger subs, as well as basic bread, muffins, and cakes, though opening times vary. Usually open daily 7.30–11am and 5–9pm, and occasionally lunchtimes Wed–Sat.

El Quenepo c/Flamboyán 148 ☎787/741-1215. The most stylish bistro on the strip and a fabulous place for dinner, with a tantalizing menu inspired by local and Caribbean cuisine: dishes like Thai-style snapper, pineapple-guava pork ribs, and tuna with noodles in a shellfish broth. Owned by Kate and Scott Cole, who utilize home-grown herbs such as lemongrass and ginger, and even sugar cane (used as swizzle sticks in cocktails – try the coconut martini or

Quenepo martini with local fruit). Mains from $20. Daily 5–11pm, close Tues.

Trade Winds c/Flamboyán 107. The best thing about this guesthouse restaurant is the raised outdoor terrace, providing sweeping views across the bay. Gorge on the filling egg breakfasts ($7–9), lunches featuring salads and burgers ($10–18), and dinners of local fish ($18), three kinds of *mofongo* (pork, chicken, or shrimp, $16–18), Caribbean lobster (priced per ounce), coconut curry shrimp ($18), and *churrasco* served with fresh papaya salsa and mash ($19). Mon–Fri 8am–2pm & 6–9.30pm, Sat 6–9.30pm.

Central Vieques

Chez Shack PR-995 km 1.8 ☎787/741-2175. This ramshackle wooden house with an open terrace is literally in the middle of nowhere, surrounded by lush, tropical forest. Booths and benches provide fittingly rustic surroundings for slabs of barbecued pork, ribs (slathered with tongue-tingling dressings such as dark rum mustard, black bean, and *chorizo*), and mahi-mahi – portions are big, but still a bit pricey ($20–24). Don't miss the signature crab cakes or West Indian duck with mango *piña* marmalade and grilled banana ($24). Owner Hugh Duffy is real character, so expect steel drum bands and other eclectic entertainment on weekends. Mon & Wed–Sun, 6–11pm, Sun 6.30–11pm.

Island Steakhouse at *Crow's Nest*, PR-201 km 1.6 ☎787/741-0011. It's hard to imagine a more soothing, tropical setting for a restaurant, an open-air treehouse surrounded by great swathes of green. Hefty steaks include the succulent rib eye ($32) and tenderloin filets ($27), served with a smorgasbord of sides and salads, while other highlights include lamb chops with mango chutney ($27), Vieques lobster ($30), and a plethora of sumptuous US-style desserts: try the key lime pie ($7). Mon, Tues & Fri–Sun, 6–10pm (happy hour Tues 5–7pm).

El Resuelve PR-997 km 1 ☎787/741-1427. This open-air roadside diner between Isabel II and Esperanza is justly acclaimed for its hearty plates of Puerto Rican food, such as *arroz con pollo* and crab *empanadas*. You can eat well for under $10 (with beer). Locals congregate here to dance salsa and play the slot machines on weekends. Wed 9am–6pm, Thurs–Sat 9am–9pm, Sun 9am–7pm.

Bars

Nightlife on Vieques is low-key, and tends to center on restaurants and a cluster of **bars** in Isabel II and Esperanza – the latter is favored on holidays and weekends by bar-crawling locals as much as tourists. Most nights out involve

You can usually pick up a **flight** back to **Fajardo** or **San Juan** with a few hours' notice, though you'll need to book ahead for services at peak times (weekends and holidays). Cape Air (☎1-800/352-0714) and Vieques Air-Link (c/Antonio G. Mellado 358, ☎787/741-8331) operate several regular daily flights to **Aeropuerto Internacional Luis Muñoz Marín** in San Juan, with the latter also flying five times a day to Isla Grande Airport and on demand to Fajardo. One-way prices range $25–30 to Fajardo, $80–90 to San Juan international, and around $50 to Isla Grande. Both airlines fly twice a day to **St Croix** (US Virgin Islands). Air Sunshine (☎787/741-7900) also flies to San Juan international airport and St Croix, as well as **St Thomas** (US Virgin Islands) twice a day. Air Flamenco (☎787/741-8811) and Isla Nena Air Service (☎787/741-1577) run flights on demand to Fajardo and further afield – the latter will fly to **Culebra** for around $55.

You can buy **ferry** (*la lancha* in Spanish) tickets to Fajardo at the *embarcadero* in Isabel II, the office (☎787/741-4761) usually opening 8–11am and 1–3pm ($2 one-way). You can buy tickets in advance, but reservations are not accepted. Ferries depart Mon–Fri 6.30am, 11am, 3pm & 6pm; Sat, Sun & holidays 6.30am, 1pm & 4.30pm. Note that a faster service (*La Ruta Corta*) between Ceiba and Rompeolas (Mosquito Pier) may replace the Fajardo ferry in the next few years, and that with the cancelation of the inter-island ferry, the only way to travel between Vieques and **Culebra** by boat is to go via the main island.

Regardless of traveling by ferry or plane to **Fajardo**, it pays to arrange your onward travel in advance (see Moving on from Fajardo, p.136).

at least a few drinks at *Bananas Beach Bar*, *Bilí*, and *Duffy's* on the *malecón* in Esperanza, while the *Blue Moon Bar and Grill* at the *Inn on the Blue Horizon* has live Latin jazz every Saturday night. In Isabel II, *Next Door* is also worth checking out (see p.172).

The best place to buy your own booze is *El Sombrero Viejo* at the corner of Calle 65 Infantería and Calle José Suerio in Isabel II (daily noon–midnight).

Isabel II

Al's Mar Azul c/German Rieckehoff 577 ☎787/741-3400. One of the most popular bars on the island, with an enticing wooden deck overlooking the ocean and ferry pier nearby, a couple of tatty pool tables, and a notorious karaoke night (known locally as "scareoke"), from 9pm on Sat (the more you drink, the more the singing improves). The best place for rum cocktails at sunset, and mingling with an amicable blend of locals and tourists on weekends. No food, just snacks. Mon, Wed, Thurs, Sun, 11am–1am, Fri & Sat 11am–2.30am.

Bar Plaza Plaza Luis Muñoz Rivera. Exuding a run-down, raffish charm, this dive bar in the center of town is the only remaining Spanish *cantina* on the island, with peeling murals, high ceilings, swinging doors, and nothing but local beer on the menu ($3). Savor the atmosphere with the motley group of locals slumped at the bar or around the aging pool table.

Built in 1903, the bar was originally a pharmacy, amusing considering the state of its patrons most Friday nights. Daily 9am–9pm.

Palms Lounge at *Bravo Beach Resort*, North Shore Road 1. The ultra-hip lounge bar inside the *Bravo Beach Resort* opens to the public on weekends only, well worth at least one cocktail (try the icy mangotinis) to check out the candlelit pool, stylish interior, and romantic vistas across the ocean. Fri & Sat 5.30–11pm.

Esperanza

La Nasa c/Flamboyán. It doesn't get more local than this shack on the beach side of the *malecón* – you'll be drinking cheap Medalla beers with fishermen and other well-oiled locals, so brush up on your Spanish. Especially busy on Sun afternoons, but the fairy lights stay on and the radio blasts salsa all week. The name hasn't anything to do with the space program – it means "fish trap." Closed Tues.

Listings

Banks Banco Popular (☎787/741-2071) at c/Muñoz Rivera 115, open Mon–Fri 8am–4.30pm, Sat 9am–1pm, has the island's only ATM (24hr). The line for the ATM can be very long in the morning, and occasionally it runs out of cash over weekends.

Bicycle rental Black Beard Sports (☎787/741-1892, ⊛www.blackbeardsports.com), at c/Muñoz Rivera 101 in Isabel II, rents mountain bikes for $25–35/day. Open Mon–Sat 8am–5pm, Sun noon–3pm. La Dulce Vida Mt Bike & Adventure Co (⊛www.bikevieques.com) runs excellent guided cycling tours around the island for $75 for a half-day (book via the website). Garry Lowe (see p.159) also rents bikes for $25/day and will deliver to your hotel, while *Casa Alta Vista* (see p.159) rents mountain bikes for just $20/day.

Car and scooter rental Acevedo's Car Rental, PR-201 km 1.3, Barrio Florida (daily 7am–10pm; ☎787/741-4380); Extreme Scooters (☎787/741-8141); Island Car Rental (☎787/741-1666); Maritza's Car Rental, PR-201, Barrio Florida (☎787/741-0078, ⒺDmaritzascarrent@aol.com); Martineau Car Rental, PR-200 km 3.4 (☎787/741-0087, ⊛www.martineaucarrental.com); Steve's Car Rental (☎787/741-8135); and Vieques Car and Jeep Rental (☎787/741-1037, ⊛www.viequescarrental.com). *Casa Alta Vista* (see p.159) also rents scooters.

Emergencies For serious emergencies call ☎911, for fire ☎787/741-2111.

Hospital The Centro de Salud de Familia is south of Isabel II on PR-997, open Mon–Fri 7am–3.30pm, with a 24-hour emergency room.

Internet Black Beard Sports (see opposite) offers high-speed access for $3/30min (Mon–Sat 8am–5pm, Sun noon–3pm). In Esperanza, you can access the Internet at the Vieques Conservation and Historical Trust (Tues–Sun 11am–4pm; for $3/30min or at La Luz de la Esperanza (Mon–Fri 9am–7pm; $3 donation), the small library at c/Orquidea and c/Almendro. Students get priority 3–7pm.

Laundry Familia Ríos at c/Benítez Castaño 1 (☎787/438-1846) has self-serve washers, dryers, and parking (Mon, Wed–Fri & Sun 6am–7pm, Sat 6am–5pm).

Pharmacy Isla Nena Pharmacy (Mon–Fri 7.30am–7pm, Sat 8am–6pm, Sun 11am–3pm) is at c/Muñoz Rivera 112 in Isabel II. Farmacia San Antonio is nearby at Avda Benítez Guzmán 52 (☎787/741-8397, Mon–Sat 8.30am–6pm).

Police The police station is at PR-200 km 0.2 (intersection with PR-997 in Isabel II), ☎787/741-2020.

Post The post office (Mon–Fri 8.30am–4.30pm, Sat 8am–noon) is at c/Muñoz Rivera 97 in Isabel II, near Banco Popular

Taxi Recommended *público*/taxi drivers include Ana Robles (☎787/313-0599 or 787/385-2318), Ángel (☎787/484-8796), Eric (☎787/741-0448), Henry (☎787/649-3838), and Luis González (☎787/608-6894).

Culebra

Effectively occupied by the US Navy until the 1970s, **CULEBRA** is an unapologetically raw Caribbean island that, like Vieques, has resisted high-impact tourism and shrugged off attempts at large-scale development. There are no casinos, tour buses, mega-resorts, or traffic lights, crime is virtually unknown, and the **beaches** are simply staggering – **Playa Flamenco** is consistently voted one of the world's most awe-inspiring stretches of sand, while the turtle-rich sapphire waters and shallow reefs offshore make **diving** and **snorkeling** a real treat. St Thomas, clearly visible to the east, is a choking metropolis in comparison: the last official census, in 2000, found Culebra's population at just under two thousand, though neither foreign condo-owners nor illegal workers were counted (at the time, locals estimated an additional one thousand Dominicans lived here).

But behind the calm veneer – and *culebrenses* are undeniably chilled out – paradise has an edgier side. Though the US Navy is long gone, chased out in 1975, the spirit of **activism** remains strong, vividly expressed in the energetic campaigns to protect the local **reef ecosystems** and **turtle populations**, as well as resistance to looming **development** and attempts to limit **beach access**. Indeed, many locals feel that Culebra stands at a crossroads, as more and more land is sold for posh condos and holiday villas, and hard drugs have begun to creep into the community, raising the specter of serious crime for the first time. **Tourism** is booming, and at times parts of the island can get uncomfortably busy, especially in July when it's become the favored retreat for Puerto Rican day-trippers from the main island. For now, though, it's still easy to avoid the crowds, and the island remains untainted by **cruise ships** – just make sure you bring plenty of bug spray, as the flies and mosquitoes are voracious.

Some history

Little is known about the early inhabitants of Culebra, though evidence has been found of a prehistoric people known as the **Cuevas** (part of the Igneri culture; see p.355), who settled in the Lower Camp area in around 640 AD and occupied the site for between one hundred and two hundred years. The Spanish initially called the island Isla Pasaje, but were unenthusiastic about setting up a colony, and it wasn't until Spanish adventurer Don Cayetano Escudero founded the village of **San Ildefonso de Culebra** in 1880 (in honor of the then Bishop of Toledo, Spain) that a formal Spanish presence was established. The name Culebra, meaning "snake," was eventually applied to the whole island (although there are no snakes, and its shape bears no resemblance to a serpent).

The colony was short-lived, as the US assumed control in 1898 and the US Navy took charge of the island five years later, promptly sealing off large areas for marine exercises and forcing the abandonment of San Ildefonso, or "Pueblo Viejo." The majority of islanders were resettled on the other side of Ensenada Honda: leaving no doubt as to who was now in charge, the new town

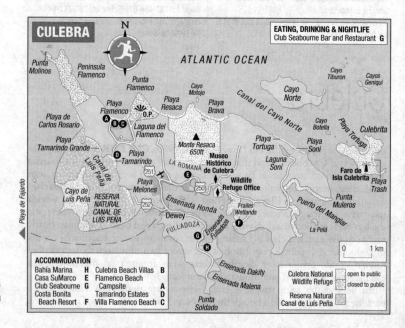

What bombs?

As in Vieques, the clearance of **unexploded ordnance** and military contamination continues in Culebra, over thirty years after the navy left the island. It's perhaps because of this inexplicably long time lag that the subject is rarely discussed here, and is usually ignored altogether by the tourism industry.

In 2004, the US Army Corps of Engineers said it would implement a "Plan of Action," coordinated with the Puerto Rican government, to expedite the clean-up of the island. Removal of explosives is ongoing on Cerro Balcón, Isla Culebrita, and other cays, with work on more parts of Culebra planned in future. Don't stray off well-worn paths or trails, and when snorkeling or kayaking, be on the lookout for rusty bombs lodged in the coral – all the main tourist zones are perfectly safe, but check with the Wildlife Refuge if ranging further afield (see p.186).

was named **Dewey** after Admiral George Dewey, a US Navy hero from the 1898 campaign. The island was dominated by the navy thereafter, and non-military development was minimal.

In 1936, the navy began to use Culebra as a munitions testing site, operations reaching their peak in 1969 as the fleet trained pilots for Vietnam. In 1970 the formal campaign to remove the US Navy began with a feisty coalition of locals known as the **Culebra Committee**, led by **Mayor Ramón Feliciano**, **Rubén Berríos**, the leader of the Puerto Rican Independence Party (PIP), and several US senators. In January 1971 Playa Flamenco, which was closed to the public at the time, was occupied by protestors – one month later their makeshift chapel was torn down by the authorities, following a violent clash on the beach and the arrest and imprisonment of Berrios and other activists. Finally, in 1973, with the help of Governor Colón, a coalition of respected ex-governors, and US Senator Howard Baker, the US government agreed to **withdraw** the navy from Culebra in 1975 – all navy activity ended on September 30 of that year.

In 1975 the population was just 575, and after the navy left Culebra became a sleepy backwater inhabited primarily by the elderly. **Tourism** developed gradually, boosted in 1996 when the new **car ferry** initiated a surge in new arrivals and **property development**. Contrary to what you might expect, most *culebrenses* either work for the government, for construction companies, or at the RD Medical factory on the edge of town. Surprisingly few fish for a living, though the establishment of a futuristic **fish farm** operated by Snapperfarm (Ⓦwww .snapperfarm.com) is expected to create more jobs on the water.

Arrival, orientation, and information

Culebra is an exhilarating ten-minute **flight** from Fajardo or 35 minutes from San Juan, ending up at tiny **Aeropuerto Benjamín Rivera Noriega**, around half a mile north of the main settlement, Dewey. Inside the terminal you'll find the small *Café Delizioso*, selling snacks, drinks, and coffee, and the main airline and car rental desks (see p.191). If you are not renting and your accommodation is not providing a pick-up, you'll need to take a *público* to your hotel for $3–5, depending on where it is: if none is around, call one (see p.191). The airport has no ATM – you have to go into Dewey for cash. **Ferries** from Fajardo dock in the center of Dewey, and are met by a cavalcade of *públicos* that will take you to any of the hotels ($2–3) when full, though at peak times their main business is running day-trippers back and forth between here and Playa Flamenco.

Orientation

Culebra usually refers to the hilly main island of an archipelago that includes 22 smaller cays. The main settlement is **Dewey**, known locally as Pueblo, a typically laid-back island village whose torpor is punctured only by the arrival of the Fajardo ferry and a flurry of activity in the early morning, as the island's tiny workforce lumbers into motion. A jumble of low-rise, mostly modern houses, restaurants, and bars, it's not especially attractive, and the only reason for a wander, other than to use the services, is to do a bit of **shopping** (see p.191).

Dewey sits on a narrow isthmus on the west coast of the island: the main street is Calle Pedro Márquez, which cuts across the village from the ferry pier (facing the open sea) to the great natural inlet on the other side, the **Ensenada Honda**. The settlement is bound by Laguna Lobina and a narrow canal to the south, which connects the two sets of water and separates the main part of town from the southern **Fulladoza** district and **Punta Soldado**. To the north, PR-251 connects Dewey and the *barrios* of central Culebra, near the airport, with **Playa Flamenco** and access to the **Reserva Natural Canal de Luis Peña**; PR-250 follows the northern edge of the Ensenada Honda from the airport, ending up at **Playa Soní** on the east coast. The main island has an area of around ten square miles, and is easily covered in a couple of hours by car.

Information

The friendly **tourist information office** (Mon–Fri 7am–4.30pm; ☎787/742-3521) faces the harbor close to the ferry pier, and can supply basic information and maps. Staff usually speak English, but note that they sometimes close at lunch (1–2pm). In the future they hope to open on weekends. When you arrive, try to pick up a copy of the island newspaper, *Culebra Calendar* (Ⓦwww.theculebracalendaronline.com), published monthly by Jim Petersen (who also rents kayaks; see p.182). **Online resources** are plentiful and include Ⓦwww.culebra-island.com and Ⓦwww.gotoculebra.com.

Getting around

Culebra is a compact island, but unless you want to spend all your time near your hotel, you'll need some form of transport to get around. If you're feeling fit, you can **rent a bike**, though considering the heat and swarms of flies on the island, cycling is definitely the most uncomfortable option – see p.191 for numbers.

Públicos

Privately operated **públicos** (usually minibuses) serve as buses and taxis on Culebra, and can be useful if you just want to get into town or go to the beach a couple of times – if you're staying in Dewey, you might prefer this over renting a car. Daily buses run back and forth between the ferry pier and Playa Flamenco ($2 one-way) via the airport (also $2) when full, but will make detours to drop off at hotels ($2–3) near Dewey. The last *públicos* start to leave Flamenco at around 4pm.

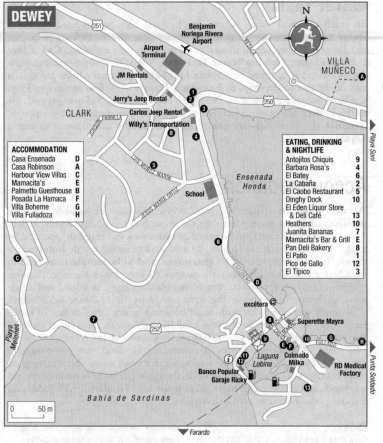

▲ Playa Flamenco (2 km)

DEWEY

Benjamin
Noriega Rivera
Airport

Airport
Terminal

JM Rentals

Jerry's Jeep Rental

CLARK

Carlos Jeep Rental

Willy's Transportation

VILLA
MUÑECO

Playa Soní ▶

Ensenada
Honda

School

ACCOMMODATION
Casa Ensenada   D
Casa Robinson   A
Harbour View Villas   C
Mamacita's   E
Palmetto Guesthouse   B
Posada La Hamaca   F
Villa Boheme   G
Villa Fulladoza   H

Playa
Melones

excétera   @

Superette Mayra

Punta Soldado ▶

**EATING, DRINKING
& NIGHTLIFE**
Antojitos Chiquis   9
Barbara Rosa's   4
El Batey   6
La Cabaña   2
El Caobo Restaurant   5
Dinghy Dock   10
El Eden Liquor Store
 & Deli Café   13
Heathers   10
Juanita Bananas   7
Mamacita's Bar & Grill E
Pan Deli Bakery   8
El Patio   1
Pico de Gallo   12
El Típico   3

Laguna
Lobina

Banco Popular
Garaje Ricky

Colmado
Milka

RD Medical
Factory

Bahía de Sardinas

0   50 m

▼ Farardo

VIEQUES AND CULEBRA | Culebra: Getting around

At other times, most drivers will pick you up on demand, charging $2–3 per person for most trips to the airport or ferry and $5 to places such as Playa Soní – traveling in the evening requires advance reservations and is much less reliable. See p.191 for numbers.

Car and scooter rental

If you want to really explore the island it's best to **rent a car or scooter**, though the latter can be uncomfortable on some of the bumpier roads. Most firms have offices in or close to the airport terminal, but will usually pick you up from the ferry pier if you call in advance. Rates range $45–60 per day depending on the season and company, and **insurance** can add up to $25 per day: unless you plan to drive like a madman the latter isn't really necessary (even with insurance, you are usually liable for the first $1000 in damages).

Driving rules are casually enforced by Culebra's tiny police department, but limits are 25mph in town, and 40mph elsewhere. There are only two **gas stations**: Garaje Ricky (8am–6pm) opposite the ferry pier, and Villa Pesquera (8am–noon & 1–3.30pm) on the south side of Dewey, across the canal.

Water taxis

To reach Culebra's more isolated beaches and islets, you'll need to take a **water taxi**, operated by a handful of private boat owners. Pick-up points are usually near Dewey, but in theory you can ask to start anywhere. Call at least a day in advance. **Culebra Water Taxi** (T787/360-9807, E culebraoceanview @yahoo.com) is operated by Captain Luis Grundler (usually from *Mamacita's*) and offers various day-trips to **Ensenada Dakity** as well as services to Playa Carlos Rosario, Cayo de Luis Peña, and Isla Culebrita ($45 per person). He normally departs at 9.30am and returns at 3pm, for a minimum of three people. **Tanamá** also does pick-ups (see p.182). The healthy alternative is to rent a **kayak** (see p.182).

Accommodation

Accommodation is plentiful in Culebra, and you are unlikely to have problems finding a place other than on major holidays and weekends in July. Most of the options are family-owned **guesthouses** and many are operated by long-term expat residents. There's also a handful of small, upscale **hotels** and a varied choice when it comes to **apartment and villa rentals**: these tend to be a better deal than the relatively overpriced alternatives. Vacation Planners (T787/742-3112, W www.culebravacationplanners.com) is a local real estate agent with an office opposite the ferry pier (daily 10–11.30am, 4–5.30pm & 7.30–9pm) that also helps with hotel bookings and a large choice of rental properties – check their website for a full listing. You can also contact Culebra Brava al Natural (T787/742-0007, W www.escapetoculebra.com).

In terms of **location**, Dewey is convenient for food, transportation, and services – if you want to save on renting a car, it's best to stay here. Staying on Playa Flamenco has an obvious plus side, though it can be busy on holidays and weekends, and if you prefer more solitude the island is littered with hideaways featuring equally magnificent ocean views.

Dewey

Casa Ensenada c/Escudero 142 T787/742-3559, W www.casaensenada.com. Basically a cute rental home overlooking the bay on the north side of Dewey, divided into three units (all with a/c, satellite TV, kitchens, and bathrooms). The property and amenities are a little worn in parts, but Jackie and Butch Pendergast are thoughtful hosts, offering use of the waterside patio and BBQ, free kayaks, beach chairs, towels, and coolers: make sure they are in Culebra when you visit. Prices vary considerably according to room size and how long you stay. ⑤-⑥

Harbour View Villas PR-252, Barrio Melones 1 T787/742-3855, W www.harbourviewvillas.com. Flowing down the hillside above Playa Melones, these A-frame chalets have been managed by Jane and Druso Daubon since the 1970s. Town is a short walk away, but the real draws are the gorgeous views and jaw-dropping sunsets. Be warned, however: this is a rustic experience, with

aging open-air kitchens and showers and living areas in need of renovation. Hot water can be erratic and because it's so open there are plenty of bugs. ⑤-⑦

Mamacita's c/Castelar 64–66 T787/742-0090. Small guesthouse with rooms overlooking the canal in the center of town, above the celebrated bar of the same name. Each has a veranda, though Room 3 is at the top (third story) and has by far the best views across the water and palm trees. Though you get satellite TV, DVD, a/c, and spotlessly clean rooms, this is fairly basic, hostel-like accommodation, and a bit pricey unless you expect to be hanging out in town most nights. Be prepared for noise on weekends. ④

Posada La Hamaca c/Castelar 68 T787/742-3516, W www.posada.com. Albert and Mary Custer run this guesthouse next door to *Mamacita's*, with a deck overlooking the canal, small doubles, and larger apartments for two to eight people. It's another dorm-like place, and also a bit pricey considering the level of amenities. Rooms have clean tiled floors, sinks, and kitchenettes, and the free beach towels, coolers, and ice are nice touches: it's an extra $5 for a room with TV. ❸

🏃 **Villa Boheme** c/Fulladoza 368 ☎787/742-3508, ⓦwww.villaboheme.com. A modern and cheery place on the waterfront south of the center, run by the amiable Rafy, with eleven spacious, bright rooms (all with a/c and bath), always spotlessly clean, three of which have kitchens (others have access to a shared kitchen). The second-floor rooms have balconies, and the waterside sun deck also has stellar views across the Ensenada Honda. It's right next to *Dinghy Dock* and, overall, this is the best deal in town. ❸

Villa Fulladoza c/Fulladoza ☎787/742-3576. Seven apartments set within a pretty, white wooden house with pink and blue trim, in a tranquil spot at the end of town, right on the Ensenada Honda near *Boheme*. This is more like a villa rental – you get clean sheets, towels, bathroom, and basic kitchen, and are left more or less to yourself. Rooms are simple but cheap – it's just $455 for the week. ❷

Central Culebra

🏃 **Casa Robinson** La Romana, off PR-250 ☎787/742-0497, ⓦwww.casarobinson .com. Modern, super-comfortable, three-story house on a fabulous hilltop perch overlooking the Ensenada Honda and Vieques beyond. Cooled by the trade winds, it's surrounded by pomegranate and *nopales* bushes and buzzing with hummingbirds. The immaculate rooms come with kitchenette, satellite TV, and bathroom, while your host, local ex-policeman Elias Robinson, is a mine of information and will usually pick you up from the dock or airport. ❹

Casa SuMarco La Romana, off PR-250 ☎917/848-0054, ⓦwww.casasumarco.com. Another panoramic, breezy deck overlooking the *ensenada*, this cozy two-bedroom, one-bath rental home is a great deal for families, comfortably sleeping up to four people. Amenities include kitchen, washing machine, a/c in bedrooms (ceiling fans in all other rooms), indoor and outdoor showers, TV (DVD only), and stereo. Three-night minimum. ❻

Costa Bonita Beach Resort Punta Carenero, PR-250 ☎787/742-3000, ⓦwww.ahappyvacation .com. This resort, reminiscent of a Costa Brava holiday village, is a collection of colorful villas set on the hillside. After years of controversy (see p.184), the project was completed in 2004 and assumed new management in 2007, pledging to work more closely with the local community. It remains one of the most luxurious places to stay on Culebra, with plush studios or one-bedroom apartments with all the amenities including satellite TV – the site has a restaurant, the best pool on the island, and a bar. ❼–❽ (plus $50 housekeeping fee).

🏃 **Palmetto Guesthouse** c/Manuel Vasquez 128 (behind Carlos Jeep Rental) ☎787/742-0257, ⓦwww.palmettoculebra.com. This comfy inn has been fully renovated by its friendly owners, and the compact but spotless rooms sport tiled floors, a/c, fridge, and sparkling bathrooms. You get the use of two shared kitchens and a lounge, free bikes, boogie boards, beach towels, chairs, and coolers, and a DVD and book exchange for when you want to remain idle. ❸–❹

Playa Flamenco and around

Culebra Beach Villas ☎787/754-6236, ⓦwww.culebrabeachrental.com. Whether you stay at this unique hotel depends on how much you value the incredible location, right on the beach. Though the views are spectacular, and the chalets running back to the parking lot are slightly better, rooms in the four-story wooden beach house are spartan and showing their age. Avoid public holidays (especially the summer), when it's overrun with families. Options range from studios to three-bedroom apartments. ❺

🏃 **Flamenco Beach Campground** Playa Flamenco is the only legal place to camp on the island, offering a truly enchanting night under the stars. Avoid July, weekends, and holidays if you value solitude, however, as the beach gets mobbed and a party scene ensues, despite the segregation of "teenage" campers by the warden. You need to fill in an application form for the Culebra Conservation and Development Authority (6am–7pm; ☎787/742-0700), which you can do on arrival at the beach, though it's best to reserve a space in advance. Tents are $20 (maximum six people), with a seven-day maximum. You can rent four-person tents from *Joe's Ice Shack* for $20/night, and queen-sized air beds for $10. There are toilets, barbecue pits, and showers (4–7pm) on site, but the food options are limited. Don't forget the bug spray.

Tamarindo Estates c/Tamarindo Final ☎787/742-3343, ⓦwww.tamarindoestates.com. This collection of hillside villas sits on the west side of the island facing Playa Tamarindo (and the sunset), three minutes' drive from Playa Flamenco and a half-mile off PR-251 at the end of a sealed road. It's an upscale place, but not as luxurious as the newer hotels on the island – the twelve villas are neat and simply furnished with small kitchen, the TV has local channels only, and staff are rarely around. If you just turn up you'll have to use the phone at the entrance to call the manager. ⑤–⑥

Villa Flamenco Beach ☎787/742-0023, ℮esmer@coqui.net. These six units, all with kitchenettes, in a two-story pink concrete building just off the beach, are much nicer and quieter than the *Culebra Beach Villas*. Maintained by the sociable Max and Esmeralda Gutiérrez, there are two large apartments for four people each, and four studios upstairs that accommodate two people. Note the one-week minimum Dec 15–May 30, four-night

Watersports

The inviting cays and reefs off Culebra make ideal targets for **diving, snorkeling**, and **swimming**, but remember to check the latest tide and weather reports before setting out – currents, waves, and riptides offshore can be treacherous, and people drown here every year. One of the best sites is **Ensenada Dakity** (Dakity Bay), a sparkling stretch of cobalt blue water at the mouth of the Ensenada Honda, accessible only by boat.

Diving

With no freshwater runoff (drinking water is pumped in via a pipeline from the mainland), the pellucid waters off Culebra offer some of the best **diving** in the Caribbean, and are certainly its best-kept secret. With up to fifty sites to choose from, including a plethora of shallow locations perfect for beginners and plenty of more challenging dives, you won't get bored. Highlights include **Impact Reef** in the Reserva Natural Canal de Luis Peña; **Cayo Lobito**, whose 75-foot drop-off is the best place to see big fish and nurse sharks; **Cayo Yerba**, an underwater arch where you can swim with stingrays; **Cayo Raton**, a 55-foot reef that is literally swarming with incandescent marine life; and **Tug Boat**, a cool wreck dive around the *Wit Power*, which sank in 1984. Everywhere you'll see forests of fan coral, sponges, sea urchins, and great clouds of tropical fish; turtles, barracuda, stingray, and puffer fish are also common.

Culebra Divers, just across from Dewey's ferry terminal at Calle Pedro Marquez 14 (daily 10am–1pm & 3.30–5pm; ☎787/742-0803, ⓦwww.culebradivers.com), is run by Walter and Monika Rieder and is currently one of only two dive operators in town (the Culebra Dive Shop on the edge of town just sells gear). They run daily **dive trips** (8.30am–2pm; $65 one tank, $90 two tanks) for a maximum of six divers. In the afternoons they offer **snorkeling trips** (2.30–4.30pm; $50, minimum two people). You can **rent** snorkeling equipment for $12.50 per day.

Friendly competition is supplied by **Aquatic Adventures** (☎787/742-0605, ⓦwww.culebradiving.com), operated by Captain Taz Hamrick, with morning and afternoon dive trips ($50 one tank, $85 two tanks), as well as snorkeling excursions for $45. He also runs two-tank day-trips ($120) to **Sail Rock**, a celebrated deep-water pinnacle between Culebra and St Thomas, and PADI courses ($500). You can rent snorkels fromJerry's Jeep Rental (see p.191; $10/day) and Culebra Bike Rental (see p.191; $15/day).

Boating and kayaking

Glass Bottom Boat Tanamá, operated by captains Jack (☎787/397-7494) and Pat (☎787/501-0011), offers glass-bottom boat tours (2hr) for a minimum of two people and maximum of six, as well as snorkeling (3–6hr) and Isla Culebrita trips (4–8hr).

Jim Petersen's Oceans Safaris, at Calle Escudero 189 (☎787/379-1973), rents **kayaks** for $60 per day for two (first time, $40 thereafter), usually starting at Playa Tamarindo. Rates include orientation and instruction if necessary.

Fishing

Contact local expert Chris Goldmark at **Culebra Fly Fishing** (☎609/827-4536, ⓦwww .culebraflyfishing.com) for boat and off-beach fly fishing for bonefish, permit, and tarpon (equipment included). He charges $60 per hour on the boat, $50 for the beach, and $400 for a full day.

Save the turtles!

Culebra is one of the few places on earth where the nesting population of **giant leatherback sea turtles** is on the increase, as well as hawksbill, and a smaller number of green turtles. Leatherbacks can nest at any time between February and August, though the peak season runs April to July, while hawksbills visit the beaches from September to December. Watching one of these ancient reptiles crawl up the beach and lay eggs in the middle of the night is a truly magical experience, but never go wandering around turtle beaches on your own: contact **CORALations**, an innovative NGO founded in 1995 that's dedicated to conserving the turtle population through **Proyecto Tinglado**. For a small donation (suggested $10, children $5), you can help patrol nesting beaches at night. After making camp (usually on Playa Brava, Resaca, or Soní), you'll take turns scouring the beach in groups until dawn, notifying one of the experts on hand of any activity: you'll usually be able to watch the turtles digging a nest from a safe distance, before coming in closer to watch them lay eggs. Leatherback females are huge, averaging five feet in shell length and weighing a thousand pounds. Participation is limited to ten people per night, and kids must be over ten years old.

CORALations also works to conserve Culebra's **coral reef ecosystems**, through establishing marine reserves (see p.185), supporting relevant legislation, using artificial concrete reefs such as Reef Ball (ⓦwww.reefball.org), and by growing corals more resistant to thermal stress. For more **information** and **volunteer** opportunities, contact director Mary Ann Locking (ⓣ787/556-6234, ⓦwww.coralations.org).

---

minimum June 1–Dec 14, and closure Sept 3–Oct 31. Balconies cost an extra $10–25. ⑤

Fulladoza

🏃 **Bahía Marina** c/Fulladoza km 2.4 ⓣ787/742-0535, ⓦwww.bahiamarina .net. This luxury "condo-resort," tucked away in the hills above Ensenada Dakity, offers fabulous views over the water and real tranquility, with sixteen one- or two-bedroom apartments with balconies, kitchens, tiled floors, and lounge areas. Eat in the posh *Dakity Restaurant* (Wed–Sun 6–10pm) or *Shipwreck Bar & Grill* (Mon–Wed & Sun 4–10pm, Thurs–Sat noon–10pm) on site, explore local trails, or slump in the pool and Jacuzzi. At the end of

a narrow lane off the main road, opposite *Club Seabourne*. ⑤–⑥

Club Seabourne c/Fulladoza km 1.5 ⓣ787/742-3169, ⓦwww.clubseabourne.com. Culebra's first luxury hotel and the one with the most character, overlooking the Ensenada Honda amidst lush, landscaped gardens and a fine pool. With just fourteen units, it feels exclusive and clubby, and the Spanish plantation-style rooms are decked out with dark wood beds and furniture, cozy sofas, and vintage fixtures – there are no phones or TVs, however, and some rooms are showing their age. Rates include breakfast, 1hr free kayak rental (otherwise $40/day), airport and ferry pick-ups, and beach towels. ⑥–⑦

The Island

The real charms of Culebra are its rugged coastline, wild beaches, and warm, enticing waters, and there are very few cultural or historical sights. The justly celebrated highlight is **Playa Flamenco**, but there are plenty of other empty and equally appealing stretches of sand, notably **Playa Soní**. Some of the most precious parts of the island are contained within the **Reserva Natural Canal de Luis Peña** and the **Culebra National Wildlife Refuge**, but to really appreciate your surroundings, you need to get onto the water. Aim to explore at least one of the offshore islands by kayak or water taxi – **Isla Culebrita** has the most to offer, but **Cayo Norte** will almost certainly be deserted.

Playa Melones

The only **beach** within easy walking distance of Dewey is **Playa Melones**, near the end of PR-252, a fifteen- to twenty-minute walk west of the center. The sand here is meager and the primary appeal is the easy **snorkeling** just offshore; watch out for the giant **long-spined sea urchins** here (reef shoes are essential). Melones, which gets its name from the abundance of melon cactus in the area, is the southernmost section of the protected **Reserva Natural Canal de Luis Peña** (see opposite) and perfect for watching **sunsets**.

Playa Flamenco

For most visitors, **Playa Flamenco** (24hr; free) is the real highlight of Culebra, and the main reason so many of them pile across the straits in the first place. To be fair, it doesn't get much better than this: a brilliant white crescent of coral sand, lapped by glittering waters of turquoise and azure blue, and fringed with the same low-lying scrub and palm trees that Columbus would have seen five hundred years ago. Staggeringly beautiful, it's worth a day of swimming, lounging, and simply soaking in the idyllic scenery. The name comes from the **flamingos** that once flourished in the lagoon behind the beach – local legend has it that navy shelling scared them off, and it's unlikely they'll ever return. The beach can get busy at the weekends, but it's wide enough to handle the crowds, and at other times is remarkably tranquil. Check out the rusting **Pershing tank** half-buried in the sand at the northwestern end of the beach. Once used as target practice, it's decorated with murals and has been adopted by *culebrenses* as a symbol of their struggle against unfettered development.

Flamenco lies about a mile and a half north of Dewey at the end of PR-251, with the large parking lot behind the sands home to a *Joe's Ice Shack*, selling T-shirts, swim suits, tents, and other beach essentials. Besides a couple of drink stalls serving *piña coladas* and snacks, eating options include *Kiosko de Mami*, in the parking lot behind the beach, frying up crispy *frituras* and *arroz blanco*

Free the beach

The beach plays a central role in Puerto Rican life, and **beach access** has become a highly emotive subject, especially on Culebra. Throughout Puerto Rico, all beaches are **public**, but access is another matter – owners of coastal property can effectively close beaches by claiming that access routes cut across private land.

The problem on Culebra is exacerbated by the rampant **land speculation** of developers who build million-dollar apartments and condos that only outsiders can afford. One of the largest is the fifteen-acre *Costa Bonita* resort (see p.181), completed in 2004 and nicknamed *Costa Feíta* ("ugly coast") by frustrated locals, but the most recent clash concerns the **Muellecito** (also known as the "shark pen"). This rocky outcrop with natural saltwater pools on the far eastern side of Playa Flamenco has been a family favorite for years, but in 2005 cement importer Victor González bought the nearby farm and promptly closed the access road to the area. The dispute has proved one of the nastiest so far, with González refusing to back down and taking several protestors to court. As of early 2008, after repeated efforts by locals (with the support of Culebra mayor Abraham Peña and a couple of bulldozers), the road was finally cleared.

As a guest on Culebra be mindful of private property, but remember that you have as much right to the beaches as anyone else.

most days, and the *Coconut Bar & Grill*, facing the beach at *Culebra Beach Villas* and usually open for basic lunch and dinners.

For information about **camping** here, see p.181. To access **hotels** (see p.181), turn right along the signposted dirt track just before the parking lot. Lifeguards are on duty daily 9am–5pm.

Reserva Natural Canal de Luis Peña

To escape the relative hustle of Flamenco, walk to the back of the parking lot and look for the trail to **Playa Tamarindo Grande** and **Playa de Carlos Rosario** on the other side of the metal fence – the gate is chained, but it's never closed and there's a sizeable gap to squeeze through (it's perfectly acceptable to walk here). Both beaches lie on the western side of the peninsula, about fifteen to twenty minutes' walk up the hill and down the other side. The trail is easy to follow despite the lack of signs, but can be overgrown in parts.

This stretch of coastline is part of the DRNA's **Reserva Natural Canal de Luis Peña**, which covers the channel between Culebra and Cayo de Luis Peña (see p.186), clearly visible offshore. The reserve was established in 1999 to protect the fragile **reefs** here, though the narrow sandy beaches are pleasant enough and good for some secluded sunbathing. Fishing was banned in the reserve in 2003, and the area is an encouraging example of cooperation between government agencies like the DRNA, the local municipality, and community organizations: the reserve was actually proposed by the local Asociación de Pescadores (fishermen's association) to preserve fish stocks, and involves the Fundación Culebra and CORALations. For more information on reef conservation or guided tours, contact the latter (see p.183). Sadly, corals here have been severely depleted thanks to a combination of water contamination and coral bleaching in 2005, brought on by the highest sea surface temperatures ever recorded in this part of the Caribbean. Worryingly, the reef showed no sign of recovery in 2006. You are free to **snorkel** here, but take care: the slightest touch of hands, feet, or fins can damage the coral.

Playa Tamarindo and Playa de Carlos Rosario

The first beach you'll reach is **Playa Tamarindo Grande**, usually deserted and named after the tamarind trees that once flourished here – you can see the **mooring buoys** marking the coral just offshore, used to deter anchor damage. Walk a little further north, past the headland (Punta Tamarindo Grande), and you'll reach **Playa de Carlos Rosario**, named after the area's first Spanish inhabitant and now the best **snorkeling** site on the island, with a far larger reef stretching out from the shore with only shallow areas for swimming at the northern end. Flitting amongst the giant brain and pink fan coral are angelfish, stingrays, blue tangs, and the occasional green sea turtle. The narrow pebbly beach is often empty, but you'll probably share the bay with boats of day-trippers from Fajardo. Keep walking north for a quarter-mile and you should see a stretch of chromatic reef just offshore, known as the **Wall**. Stretching for about a mile, the corals here are particularly bright and vigorous.

If you follow the coast south of Tamarindo Grande you'll reach **Playa Tamarindo**, also accessible via the road to *Tamarindo Estates* (see p.181). Information boards here describe the **Ruta de Snorkel**, marked by yellow and green buoys, that takes a safe passage through the delicate offshore reef and constructed **coral farms**. In theory, you could keep walking south from here to Playa Melones and Dewey, but there are a couple of rocky headlands to negotiate, so start early. All the beaches on this side of the island are backed with scrubby vegetation, with little shade.

Culebra National Wildlife Refuge

President Theodore Roosevelt created the first wildlife reserve on Culebra in 1909, but the modern **Culebra National Wildlife Refuge** was established in 1976. Covering 25 percent of the archipelago, its 1510 acres are divided between several different areas on the main island and many of the offshore cays. Only some of this is accessible to the public, however, so to find out what's currently open, stop at the **visitor center** (Mon–Fri 7.30am–4.30pm; ☏787/742-0115), signposted off PR-250 at km 4.2, on the north side of Ensenada Honda. The sealed road ends at the Conservation Authority office – follow the dirt track to the left and you'll see the center ahead. Set in an area of the reserve known as Lower Camp, it has plenty of information, leaflets, and usually helpful English-speakers on hand, though you might have to wait a bit to catch someone.

Lower Camp is where prehistoric ceramics and other artifacts belonging to the **Cuevas** culture were found in 1992, but it's now being developed primarily for **bird-watching** – a short interpretive trail leads from behind the center to the mangroves of the **Frailes Wetlands** below. Birds are the big draw in the refuge: more than fifty thousand seabirds from thirteen species breed on Culebra each year, and Peninsula Flamenco contains one of the largest **Sooty Tern** nesting sites in the Caribbean. **Sea turtles** are also important visitors. Areas open to the public include highlights Isla Culebrita and Cayo de Luis Peña, Laguna del Flamenco and Laguna Soní for bird-watching, and the Puerto del Manglar wetlands on the eastern side of the island. Visitors aren't normally permitted to enter the rest of the refuge, including the bird haven of Peninsula Flamenco, all of Monte Resaca (the island's highest point at 650ft), and Punta Flamenco. **Live bombs** still litter these areas, jammed into the reefs or buried in sand. The public areas are open daily sunrise to sunset.

Cayo de Luis Peña

Cayo de Luis Peña is a 350-acre island off the west coast of Culebra, topped by a small hill and crisscrossed by a couple of hiking trails. The island was initially known as Cayo del Oeste by the Spanish; the current name derives from the island's first caretaker, a fisherman and farmer from Vieques who was hired to look after the place by Don Cayetano Escudero. Other than **snorkeling** the reef-rich channel between here and the main island, you can relax on one of the cay's narrow beaches. The most popular is **North Beach**, though the southwest side of the cay also has a sandy beach bordered by coral, and you'll see **tropicbird** nesting sites all over the island.

Isla Culebrita

Don't leave Culebra without spending some time on **Isla Culebrita**, the inviting cay off the east coast. Like Luis Peña, the 300-acre island is only accessible via water taxi or kayak (see p.182). The main attraction here is the **beach**, but you can also hike up the 300-foot hill in the center to the half-ruined **Faro de Isla Culebrita**. The Spanish lighthouse opened in 1886, and, after a spell as a navy observation post, was closed in 1975. Its current dilapidated state makes the interior officially off-limits – the **Fundación de Culebra**, a nonprofit organization founded in 1994 to restore the lighthouse, continues to raise money to fix the building.

▲ Old lighthouse on Isla Culebrita

The best beach on Culebra is actually on Culebrita: **Playa Tortuga** is a cove on the northern side of the island and one of the most picturesque arcs of milky white sand you'll ever see, backed by the odd coconut palm and scrub. It's often deserted, and never crowded (though boats from Fajardo do come here, especially on weekends), and you'll often spy stingrays and turtles playing in the water just offshore, the latter munching on seagrass beneath the surface. Nearby are the **Jacuzzis**, shallow pools of warm saltwater big enough to bathe in, while rougher waves can be found at **Playa Trash** on the eastern side of the island, though shelter is lacking here (being on the windward side, debris is often blown onto the beach). It takes about twenty minutes to walk across the island. To kayak to Culebrita from Culebra, start at Playa Soní.

Playa Brava and Playa Resaca

The isolated beaches along Culebra's north coast are great for **surfing** in winter, but most of them fall under the Monte Resaca section of the wildlife refuge and are prime turtle breeding sites, with access limited from April to July – check with the refuge before you go.

Reaching either beach can be a bit of an adventure: access **Playa Brava** by taking a side road off PR-250 (turn left just after the museum, opposite the turn to the refuge office). The sealed road ends at a house where a trail continues downhill to the beach – this is technically private farmland, though locals simply park their cars here and start hiking. There are a couple of routes to **Playa Resaca**: the easiest follows the now disputed road to the Muell-ecito (see p.184), off PR-251 (on the right), just before Laguna del Flamenco. Take the track that splits off this road to the right before the beach, up to the abandoned navy **Observation Post**, currently owned by the Fish and Wildlife Service. The "OP" overlooks Resaca and affords stunning views of the north coast – the trail down from the adjacent helipad is rough and very overgrown. Note also that in addition to big waves, there are strong riptides and under-currents at both beaches.

Museo Histórico de Culebra

Another spirited community project supported by the Fundación de Culebra and Friends of the Museum, the **Museo Histórico de Culebra** is a noble attempt to create a history museum for the island and a focus for cultural activities. The museum is housed in the barn-like Polvorín, the former US munitions warehouse, built in stone in 1905 on the edge of what was then the village of San Ildefonso (it's also known as the Museo de San Ildefonso). The area later became a camp for US troops, and all that remains of the village is the old cemetery. Inside you'll find a core collection comprising over two hundred historic photographs, old navy items, and Taíno artifacts discovered on the island. After years of work and restoration, the museum was expected to open by the end of 2008, but it's best to contact Juan Romero (T787/742-3832, @jjromero@coqui.net) in advance for the latest updates. You'll pass the museum on PR-250 as you head towards Playa Soní – it's on the left just after the turn to the refuge office.

Playa Soní and Playa Tortuga

Right at the end of bumpy PR-250, on the eastern side of the island and below a hillside flowing with expensive, secluded condos, **Playa Soní** (or "Zoni") is a gorgeous beach that stretches for about a mile. It's another nesting site favored by leatherback turtles, with nests roped off with yellow tape and the beach closed after dark from February to September. Try to avoid making footprints in the sand between June and September, which can trap hatchlings. If you wander to the far northern end of the beach and clamber over the rocky headland, you'll discover another pretty cove known as **Playa Tortuga**, a small but picture-perfect patch of sand that's usually deserted. As with most beaches on Culebra, shade is lacking on Soní, but you get fine views of Cayo Norte, the lighthouse on Culebrita, and usually St Thomas in the distance. Strangely enough, the beach is said to be named after an Englishman who once lived here.

Cayo Norte

The only privately owned island in the archipelago, 500-acre **Cayo Norte** lies off the north shore of Culebra, and is the second largest cay in the chain. It was ceded to Don Leopoldo Padrón, one of the last of the Spanish special delegates to Puerto Rico, during the initial colonization of Culebra. In 2006, with Leopoldo's descendants unable to agree about what to do with the island, one of the family members managed to auction off Cayo Norte to property developer Spanish Virgin Island Investments for $10.1m, without the consent of the others – the legality of the sale is still being disputed. The island is still technically closed to casual visitors, though its beaches (including the long, beautiful stretch of sand on the south side) are public and you can kayak, snorkel, and fish just offshore. The easiest way to visit is to take the **Cayo Norte Water Taxi** (T787/742-0050 or 646/924-6362, @kidcayopr@aol .com), operated by Captain Louis Padrón ($30–50 for 2–3hr), great-grandson of Leopoldo.

Punta Soldado

Beyond *Club Seabourne*, south of Dewey, PR-252 (also known as Calle Fulladoza) weaves along the banks of the Ensenada Honda towards the southern headland of **Punta Soldado** (Soldier's Point), named after a Spanish soldier who went missing (or deserted) and later turned up here. After the sealed road ends, follow the rocky track for another half-mile to the small parking area: on the left, the reef just offshore is suitable for snorkeling (this bay is known as Ensenada Malena), while the stony coral beach on the right is known as Playa Punta Soldado. It's a tranquil if unspectacular spot, with decent views of the actual headland, topped with an old navy observation tower, and Vieques beyond. Come later in the day to swim with schools of trumpet fish off the beach, and enjoy the blazing pinks, ambers, and ruby-reds of a tropical sunset.

Eating and drinking

Most of the **eating** options on Culebra are within Dewey or on the roads nearby, comprising a mix of American and Puerto Rican family-run diners and upscale restaurants serving more creative cuisine. The island doesn't really have any specialties to try, though **Culebran Cobia**, a tasty white fish raised at the Snapperfarm, should start to grace more menus.

As you'd expect, **nightlife** is fairly subdued, but locals and tourists mingle at a few cheery bars, with plenty of salsa-inspired dancing on weekends. For **self-catering** try the *Superette Mayra* mini-market on Calle Escudero in Dewey (Mon–Sat 9am–1.30pm & 3.30–6.30pm), which sells groceries, bug spray, and sun cream. *Colmado Milka* (Mon–Sat 7am–7pm, Sun 7am–1pm), across the canal near the gas station at Calle Escudero 374, also has a decent selection of groceries and booze. If you are in desperate need of takeout beers when these are closed, try Garaje Ricky opposite the ferry pier, or local dives such as the *Hotel Puerto Rico* and *Golden China* restaurant in town.

Dewey

Antojitos Chiquis c/Pedro Márquez. Local hole-in-the-wall on the main street selling life-saving *piraguas*, ice cream, milkshakes, *batidas*, and sundaes ($1.25–2). Daily 11am–4pm & 5–9pm, but hours can be erratic.

Dinghy Dock c/Fulladoza, just across the drawbridge ☎787/742-0233. Great restaurant and bar with a deck of plastic chairs overlooking the Ensenada Honda – check out the hungry tarpon gliding below – and a solid menu of Angus beefsteaks and fresh local seafood (also a salad bar and choice of Puerto Rican staples). The bar's theme nights pull in plenty of locals, with Thurs karaoke ever popular. Happy hour runs 3–6pm daily, and covers beers and tropical cocktails. Daily 8am–9pm (later on weekends); food served daily 8–11am, 11.30am–2.30pm & 6.30–9.30pm.

🏃 **El Eden Liquor Store & Deli Café**
☎787/742-0509. The wooden shack exterior hides a hip, a/c-cooled deli-cum-bar with a fine wine cellar, managed by the energetic Richard Cantwell and Luz Rivera. Highlights are the big choice of deli sandwiches, the freshly baked breads, salads, soups, and espresso coffee (mains from $8). It also sells fresh cheddar, cold cuts, and provolone. Eat at the tables or take away. Mon–Sat

9am–6pm, Sun 9am–5pm.

Heathers c/Pedro Márquez 14. Easily identified by its striking crimson facade on the main street, this restaurant and bar serves up the best home-made pizzas on the island, with a wide variety of toppings, as well as subs, salads, pasta, and scrumptious desserts (mains $9–12). The bar can be loads of fun on weekends, with satellite TV normally showing all the major US sports events. Mon & Thurs–sun from 6pm.

🏃 **Juanita Bananas** Barrio Melones 1
☎787/742-3171, ⓦwww.juanitabananas .com. Buried in lush gardens on a hillside above the road to Playa Melones, just outside town (follow the yellow arrows if there are no signs), this is an incredibly romantic setting for Chef Jennifer Daubon's innovative island cuisine. Ingredients plucked from the garden enhance dishes such as citrus-marinated salmon, rich *sofritos* lobster limojili (cooked in garlic and lime juice), fried fish St Thomian (lightly battered triggerfish), and citrus snapper cakes. Mon is sushi night. Mains run $22–32, cash only. Oct/Nov to April/May, Mon & Fri–Sun 5.30–10pm.

🏃 **Mamacita's Bar & Grill** c/Castelar 66
☎787/742-0322. This bar and restaurant on the canal is celebrated for the posse of iguanas

that sunbathe on the deck every morning. The menu changes daily, but always features fresh local fish, salads, burgers, Puerto Rican classics, and vegetarian dishes (mains $9–15). Things are livened up by DJs on Fri and live conga drummers on Sat, while a large-screen TV provides relief for sports-starved fans. Breakfasts are served weekends only, while lunch (11am–3pm) and dinner (6–9pm) are available daily. The bar (Mon–Thurs & Sun 4–10pm, Fri & Sat 4–11pm) is justly acclaimed for its frozen cocktails: try the passion fruit *coladas*, bushwhackers (a toxic blend of Baileys, Kahlua, rum, Amaretto, and vodka), the equally potent *culebrita* (invented here), and the comparatively prosaic *piña colada*.

Pan Deli Bakery c/Pedro Márquez 17. Come here for a cheap early morning breakfast (under $5) of buns, Danish, *mallorcas, quesitos*, and *pastel-litos*, or sandwiches ($3–4) and salads ($4–5) for lunch. Welcome a/c and seating inside. Mon–Sat 5.30am–5pm, Sun 6.30am–5pm.

Pico de Gallo c/Pedro Márquez. This bright, modern Mexican restaurant on the main street is the best place for a fix of hearty tacos, burritos, and other international Mexican favorites (mains from $7). Daily 4–11pm.

North of Dewey

Barbara Rosa's c/Escudero 189 ☏787/742-0773. Congenial atmosphere and great home-cooked American comfort food by Barbara Petersen: the crab cakes ($9) are some of the best you'll ever taste, while the equally crisp fish and chips ($7), bacon burger ($6), or Philly steak ($7) make a bargain lunch, and the dorado ($14)

or fisherman's platter ($19) are great choices for dinner. Order at the kitchen, then grab a table outside – you can bring your own wine. Wed–Sun 11.30am–9.30pm.

El Batey PR-250 km 1.1 on c/Escudero, towards the airport. This roadside bar is little more than a wooden shack with a few tables, pool table, and long bar inside, but it serves the best burgers and cheeseburgers ($3–5) on the island, and is the closest thing to a club on Culebra, packed with a salsa-loving crowd late on Fridays and Saturdays. Daily 8am–2am.

El Caobo Restaurant c/Luis Muñoz Marín ☏787/742-0505. No-frills traditional *comida criolla* restaurant offering hefty grilled meats ($8–10) and seafood (mains $15) for dinner, and served in a small house in a residential area off the main road (turn left at the Escuela Nueva). Known locally as *Tina's*, highlights include the roast chicken and grilled pork cutlet, but don't pass on the aromatic rice and beans. It's cheap but bright and clean, with a tiny bar and extra room at the back. Mon–Sat 4–10pm.

El Patio PR-251 at PR-250. Close to the airport, this local bakery and snack stall (daily 5.30am–6.30pm) sells bread and sandwiches ($4–5) all day, as well as cheap breakfasts of eggs or *frituras* ($2–3), highly popular with local workers. The wooden shack next door is *La Cabaña* (daily until midnight or 2am), where the same crowd enjoys beers and mellow salsa after work.

El Típico PR-251 at PR-250. This *kiosco* serves some of the best Puerto Rican snack food on the island, including *alcapurrias* and mouthwatering *bacalaítos* ($1–2). It's open most days from 10am

Moving on from Culebra

You can usually pick up a **flight** back to **Fajardo** or **San Juan** with a few hours' notice, though you'll need to book ahead for services at peak times (weekends and holidays). Air Flamenco (☏787/742-1040) and Vieques Air-Link (☏787/742-0254) are the most reliable, while Isla Nena Air Service (☏787/742-0972) runs flights only when booked well in advance. Prices are roughly $28 to Fajardo and $55–75 to San Juan (one-way). Get your hotel to arrange a *público* ride to the airport. Note that there are no scheduled flights to Vieques, though you can reserve an "on demand" charter flight from Isla Nena Air Services (☏787/863-4447).

You can buy **ferry** tickets to **Fajardo** ($2.25) at the dock in Dewey in advance, the office usually opening daily 8–9.30am, 10.30–11am, and 1–3pm (no reservations; ☏787/742-3161). Ferries depart daily at 6.30am, 1pm, and 5pm and take around 1hr 30 min. Delays are common, and during July and holiday periods the ferry fills up well in advance, so try to buy tickets ahead of time.

With the cancelation of the inter-island ferry, the only way to travel between Culebra and Vieques by boat is to go via Fajardo. Regardless of traveling by ferry or plane to **Fajardo**, it pays to arrange your onward travel in advance (see p.136 for taxi numbers).

to 4pm or 6pm – even if this one closes, you'll almost certainly find some sort of *kiosco* here.

Fulladoza

Club Seabourne Bar and Restaurant c/Fulladoza km 1.5 ☏787/742-3169. The Caribbean gourmet cuisine concocted by Chef Yamil Sanchez keeps discerning *sanjuaneros* happy at this posh hotel restaurant overlooking the bay. The lobster bouillabaisse and award-winning duck *patacón* are sublime, but leave room for the chocolate spring rolls. Count on spending at least $40 per head, without wine, and follow up with a *mojito* at the bar (open from 3pm) – it tends to attract an older, well-heeled clientele. Wed–Sun 6–10pm.

Listings

Banks Banco Popular (☏787/742-3572) is at c/Pedro Márquez 10, open Mon–Fri 8.30am–3.30pm (ATM 24hr).

Bicycle rental Culebra Bike Rental (☏787/435-1779) no longer has a shop, but rents mountain bikes for $20 per 24hr. You can also try Dick & Cathie's Bike Rentals (☏787/742-0062) and Culebra Bike (☏787/742-2209).

Car and scooter rental Carlos Jeep Rental (☏787/742-3514, ⊛www.carlosjeeprental.com) has a desk at the airport (Mon–Sat 8am–4.30pm, Sun 8am–noon; ☏787/742-1111). New Jeep Wranglers are around $60/day. There are a couple of cheaper options across the road from the terminal: Jerry's Jeep Rental (☏787/742-0587) is cheapest, with battered but perfectly roadworthy Suzuki Samurais with no a/c ($45–50/day); JM Rentals (Mon–Sat 8.30am–6pm, Sun 9am–5pm; ☏787/742-0110, ⊛www.scooterspr.com), PR-251 no. 67, a bit further up the main road opposite the airport, is part of the Thrifty franchise and offers midsize cars for $35–50/day, depending on the season, and Wussi Sport 150cc scooters (☏787/717-7583) from $15/hr, $25/half-day (suitable for ferry day-trippers), and $45/24hr. Culebra Scooter Rental (daily 9am–6pm; ☏787/742-0195, ⊛www.culebrascooterrental.com) has a desk inside the airport, and offers Yamaha Zuma scooters for $45/24hr (with a $100 deposit). You have to be at least 23 years old at this place (21 elsewhere).

Emergencies For serious emergencies call ☏911; for police call ☏787/742-3501, for fire ☏787/742-3530.

Hospital The small island clinic (☏787/742-3511) is in Dewey on the road to Playa Melones (c/William Font) and open Mon–Fri 7am–4.30pm. It has a 24-hour emergency service (serious cases are airlifted to the main island).

Internet Unless you have a laptop, the only place to check email or surf the web is excétera (Mon–Fri 9am–5pm, Sat 9am–1pm; $5/15min), on c/Escudero in Dewey (this is also the Western Union office, with fax and phones).

Laundry Ricky's Laundry is behind the gas station opposite the ferry pier ($1.50 per wash). *Mamacita's* also has a laundry, and Exquisite Laundry Service does same-day drop-off and pick-up (☏787/742-0722).

Pharmacy The clinic has the only official pharmacy, but *Superette Mayra* and *Colmado Milka* (see p.171) stock basic over-the-counter remedies.

Post office At c/Pedro Márquez 26 (Mon–Fri 8.30am–4.30pm, Sat 8.30am–noon).

Shopping Dewey has a smattering of absorbing shops selling gifts and local art. Butiki (daily 9am–6pm; ⊛www.butikiculebra.com), up the hill by *Superette Mayra*, sells vivid Culebra T-shirts ($20) and usually closes for lunch. Culebra Gift Shop & La Cava at c/Escudero 138 (daily 9am–6pm), across from the school on the way to Playa Flamenco, stocks gifts, music, handicrafts, T-shirts, caps, and various kitsch bits and pieces. On c/Pedro Márquez, Galeria Souvenirs Shop (daily 9.30am–5.30pm) sells clothes, carvings, and other trinkets, as well as "República de Culebra" T-shirts. Taller Fango, c/Castelar 56 (⊛www.artefango.com), showcases the vibrant art of Jorge Acevedo.

Taxi The following *públicos* serve as taxis: Fontáñez Transportation (Adriano, ☏787/590-1375); Juanito's Taxi (☏787/556-1334); Kiko's Transportation (☏787/514-0453); Viangel's Services (Angel, ☏787/505-2246); and Willy's Transportation (☏787/742-3537 or 396-0076).

Travel details

Ferries

Culebra to: Fajardo (3 daily; 1hr 30min).
Fajardo to: Culebra (3 daily; 1hr 30min); Vieques
(Mon–Fri 4 daily, Sat & Sun 3 daily; 1hr 15min).
Vieques to: Fajardo (Mon–Fri 4 daily, Sat & Sun
3 daily; 1hr 15min).

Flights

Culebra to: Fajardo (5 daily; 12min); San Juan
(5 daily; 30min); Vieques (on demand; 9min).

Fajardo to: Culebra (5 daily; 12min); Vieques
(5 daily; 9min).
Vieques to: Culebra (on demand; 9min); Fajardo
(5 daily; 9min); St Croix (4 daily; 30min); St Thomas
(daily; 35min); San Juan (10 daily; 30min).

The north coast and karst country

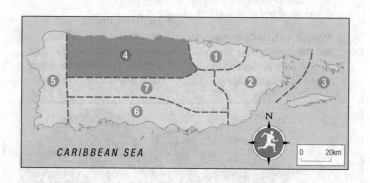

CARIBBEAN SEA

0   20km

THE NORTH COAST AND KARST COUNTRY

193

CHAPTER 4 # Highlights

✳ **Playa Mar Chiquita** Swim, snorkel, or just laze in the sun on the north coast's most dazzling beach. See p.203

✳ **Bosque Estatal de Guajataca** This forest reserve is one of the best on the island for hiking, with well-maintained trails snaking past jungle-smothered outcrops of limestone karst See p.209

✳ **Observatorio de Arecibo** Take a dizzying look at the world's biggest radio telescope, a vast window into outer space suspended above the tropical forest. See p.211

✳ **Parque de Las Cavernas del Río Camuy** Tour the largest cave system on the island, a maze of gaping sinkholes, dimly lit caverns, and twisted pillars of limestone. See p.212

✳ **Lares** Soak up the spirit of independence at this proudly Puerto Rican town, home of the *Grito de Lares* and some of the best ice cream in the region. See p.213

✳ **Centro Ceremonial Indígena de Caguana** One of the most important Taíno sites in the Caribbean, a series of ancient ball-courts inscribed with mystifying petroglyphs. See p.214

✳ **Lago dos Bocas** Feast on superb Puerto Rican food overlooking the water at this picturesque, mountain-ringed lake. See p.216

▲ Karst country

4

The north coast and karst country

B eyond the sprawling suburbs of San Juan, much of northern Puerto Rico remains refreshingly rural, a region of small coffee towns, untouched nature reserves and dozing cattle. The **north coast** is endowed with spectacular **beaches** and a ragged coastline punctured by blowholes, caves and lagoons, while **karst country**, its hilly hinterland, is a sparsely populated, ethereal landscape of overgrown limestone peaks, quite unlike anything else on the island.

The north remained a relative backwater until **Operation Bootstrap** (see p.364) brought rapid industrialization to the coast after World War II, and today many of its larger communities are dominated by pharmaceutical plants, and serve as little more than overspill towns for the capital. Proximity to San Juan partly explains the lack of hotels in the area, and though day-tripping *sanjuaneros* flood the coast at weekends and holidays, fuelling a mini-construction boom in condos and second homes, large stretches of oceanfront remain wild and unspoiled. The small settlements tucked away in the folds of karst country are far more inviting, remnants of the island's once great **coffee** industry, while the hills themselves are best experienced on foot, hiking in one of several pristine **forest reserves**. This region also contains three of Puerto Rico's most popular attractions: the gigantic radio telescope at the **Observatorio de Arecibo**, the subterranean wonderland of the **Cavernas del Río Camuy**, and the **Centro Ceremonial Indígena de Caguana**, an evocative remnant of ancient Taíno culture.

The north coast

The secret to making the most of Puerto Rico's rugged **north coast** is to skip the towns and head straight for the **beaches**: the exceptions are **Dorado**, a golfer's paradise boasting a modest collection of museums and galleries, and **Vega Baja**, a gracious old town slowly remodeling itself as a haven for ecotourism. *Autopista* PR-22 is a fast and efficient route west, but if you have time you're better off following the coast roads, a leisurely alternative rewarded by long, deserted stretches of sand. The trinity of Balneario Cerro Gordo, Playa Los Tubos, and Playa Mar Chiquita represent the best of Puerto Rican **beach life**,

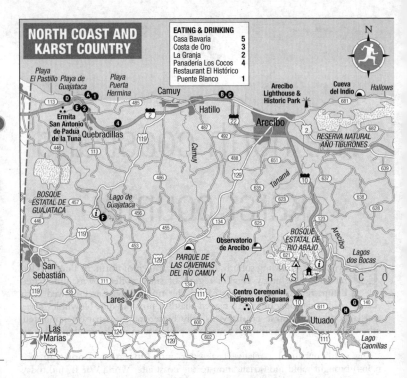

EATING & DRINKING

Casa Bavaria	5
Costa de Oro	3
La Granja	2
Panadería Los Cocos	4
Restaurant El Histórico	
Puente Blanco	1

while the Reserva Natural de Hacienda La Esperanza and Bosque Estatal de Cambalache offer some wilder, off-road relief. **Quebradillas** is the gateway to the Porta del Sol (see p.223), well off the beaten track despite some celebrated culinary attractions, a compelling beach area and some low-key but enigmatic ruins. Toa Baja, Toa Alta, Vega Alta and Manatí hold little appeal, while even the region's largest city, **Arecibo**, is best avoided.

Dorado

DORADO means "golden" in Spanish, but **golf** adds the lustre here these days, with four of the town's superlative courses designed by Robert Trent Jones, and the other conceived by Chi Chi Rodríguez, the legendary Puerto Rican golfer. As the first coastal town beyond Greater San Juan (27km from Old San Juan), it's worth a look even if you're not into thwacking balls between bunkers, as beyond the condos, clubs and resorts lies a compact historic core with a cluster of absorbing museums.

Condo-land stretches out along PR-693 west of downtown Dorado, principally a playground for rich *sanjuaneros* and well-heeled North American tourists, following in the footsteps of billionaire **Laurance Rockefeller**. The wealthy conservationist arrived in 1955, buying property owned by Alfred Livingston and his daughter (the first Americans to settle here fifty years earlier). In 1958, Rockefeller created the first of several mega hotels along the coast, the original *Dorado Beach Resort,* and today the town is part-resort, part-San Juan suburb. Other than downtown, which is small enough to explore on foot, Dorado is spread out and you'll need your car to get around. From San Juan, the fastest way

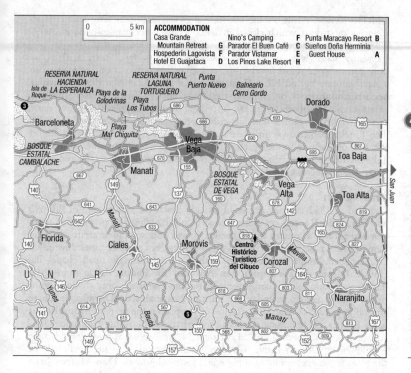

to get here is to take PR–22 to junction 22 then PR–165 north, but you can also follow PR–165 along the coast.

Públicos travel between Bayamón and Dorado, but for most visitors the only practical way to get here is to rent a car.

Accommodation

There are several **places to stay** in Dorado, making it a more convenient base than San Juan to explore the north coast. Coming direct from San Juan's Aeropuerto Internacional Luis Muñoz Marín, Dorado Tours (☎787/796-3000 ext 7023) will take you to any of these hotels for $60 (or $30 each for two people, $25 for three).

The most luxurious option is the *Dorado Beach Resort* (☎787/796-1234, ⓦwww .doradobeachclubs.com), essentially a vast exclusive club with access to four golf courses at PR-693 km 10.8. In 2007 it opened the *Su Casa Cottages* (❾) on the premises, extremely plush villas overlooking the ocean and decked out in expensive beds, drapes and stylish furniture. The villas face Rockefeller Point (Punta Mameyes), good for snorkeling, have a quiet pool and are a short walk from the resort's usually deserted West Beach. Note that this is no longer a Hyatt hotel (the whole thing is managed by KemperSports): the only Hyatt resort in Dorado is the *Hyatt Hacienda del Mar* (☎787/796-3000, ⓦhyatthaciendadelmar .hyatt.com; ❼), a bit further along PR-693 at km 12.8, which is a collection of luxury condos rather than a traditional hotel, but with units rented to temporary visitors. Amenities include kitchen, balcony, washer and dryer, cable TV and DVD player, but the real highlight is the astonishing 1776-foot **freshwater river pool** with fourteen waterfalls, hot tub, and slides (this was part of the now defunct *Hyatt Cerromar* next door, which closed in 2003; a new hotel may re-open in 2009). The beach here is fabulous.

Embassy Suites (Ⓦwww.embassysuitesdorado.com, ☎787/796-6125; ❼) is the only conventional resort hotel in town, a sprawling property on the seafront in a gated community off PR-693 (at the end of Dorado el Mar Blvd). **Cheaper accommodation** is on offer at the *Costa de Oro Hotel* (☎787/278-7888, Ⓦwww.costadeorohotel.com; ❷), a relaxed motel-like place with modern, clean, and bright rooms with air-conditioning, fridge, shower, and local TV. The hotel is tucked away in a residential area and a little tricky to find: it's off PR-697 on the way to the beach, but there are no signs, even when you arrive. Take the first left after you turn off PR-693, and keep driving to the end of the street (the address is Calle H, B-28).

The Town

Founded in 1842, the tidy center of Dorado lies at the eastern end of PR-693 and **Plaza de Recreo**, a compact zone of old buildings, shops, and businesses that makes quite a contrast to the invasive sprawl of development nearby. Parking here can be a problem, especially in the mornings, but at other times downtown Dorado seems more like a village, with a correspondingly small chapel-like church, **Iglesia de Parroquia San Antonio de Padua**, dating from 1848. The town's patron saint, San Antonio, is honored with a bronze statue in front of the church and celebrated at the **Fiestas Patronales de Dorado**, held here around June 13 each year. In the center of the plaza is the grander **Monumento a las Raíces**, commemorating the *criollo* heritage of the island with bronze life-size statues of a proud Taíno, "El Africano Negro," and a Spanish conquistador – sculpted by Dorado native Salvador Rivera Cardona. On the north side of the plaza is the enchanting birthplace and former home of **Don Marcos Juan Alegría** (1916-1992), the respected painter, maintained as the **Museo Marcos J. Alegría** (Mon–Fri 8am–4pm; free). With pale yellow clapboard walls, polished wooden floors and ceilings, and the bedroom preserved in 1920s simplicity, the *criollo*-style residence is immaculately kept, though apart from some odd bits of memorabilia, paintings, and a bust of the artist, has little to see inside.

Walk one block behind the church along Calle Méndez Vigo, the main street, and you'll see the **Museo Histórico del Dorado** (Mon–Fri 8am–4pm; free) on the left, a local storehouse of historical treasures with three small exhibition rooms. The first contains archeological remains and **Taíno** artifacts, notably some vivid petroglyphs dating from 1200 to 1500, and the skeletal remains of a fifteen-year-old

Teeing off in Dorado

They might appear to be exclusive clubs, but it's still possible to play a round of golf in Dorado if you're not a member – assuming you have plenty of cash. The *Dorado Beach Resort* charges $160 for its 18-hole **East** and **West** courses (hotel guests pay $60) and $120 ($55 for guests) for its two 18-hole Plantation Club courses (**Sugar Cane** and **Pineapple**) – all four were designed by Robert Trent Jones. Club rental is an additional $59. To book tee times call the Dorado Beach Pro Shop (☎787/796-8961) or the Plantation Club Pro Shop (☎787/626-1010).

Chi Chi Rodríguez designed the stunning 18-hole course at the **Dorado Del Mar Beach and Golf Resort** (☎787/796-3070) in 1998, as part of the *Embassy Suites* complex. Rates range $22–120 according to a sliding scale for guests and non-guests. Tee times are available daily 6.30am–4pm, but you must call in advance. The driving range is open Tuesday to Sunday 6.30am–9pm.

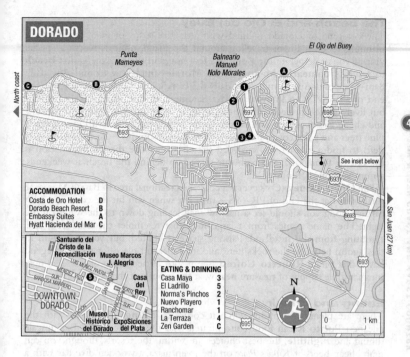

Taíno found at nearby Ojo de Buey in 1984, one of the richest archeological sites on the island. The collection of tools, pottery, stone collars, necklaces, and *cemís* from the site is relatively big – it's unusual to see so many Taíno objects in one place. The second room has a collection of *santos* carvings and paintings of local VIPs, while the final display tackles the short history of Dorado itself through old photos and antique furniture. Most of the latter comes from the **Casa del Rey**, an exquisite colonial stone house a little further along Méndez Vigo. Built in 1823 to house the local Spanish garrison, it more recently served for twenty years as a period furniture and art museum, until damaged by Hurricane Georges in 1998. Keep walking to the bottom of the hill and turn right for the **Exposiciones del Plata** (Mon–Fri 8am–4pm; free) on Calle Industria, a small gallery displaying art and sculptures by prominent local artists. The temporary exhibits are a mixed bag, but there are usually a few gems inside.

Santuario del Cristo de la Reconciliación

The world's largest indoor image of Jesus rests inside the **Santuario del Cristo de la Reconciliación** (Tues–Sat 8am–5pm, Sun 9am–6pm; free), an arresting 25-foot-tall creation by well-known Puerto Rican sculptor, Sonny Rodríguez. Cast in gray cement and acrylic polymer, the towering installation is quite unique, measuring 8.75ft across and dominating the altar and interior of the main church building. The whole thing is over 40ft high and commemorates the resurrection of Christ, including images of his tomb and four accompanying angels – it probably is the "biggest indoor sculpture suspended from a wall," as the church claims.

The church itself is a modern structure with plenty of parking at the end of Paseo del Cristo, off PR-693 just west of the center – the *paseo* is marked by the bronze **Monumento al Cristo**, another striking statue of Jesus.

The beach and El Ojo del Buey

The coastline of Dorado is lined with attractive strips of sand, but if you're planning to do a lot of traveling around the island, none is worth a special visit. If you're desperate for a dip or a few hours in the sun, the easiest **beach** to reach is **Balneario Manuel Nolo Morales** (mid-May to mid-Aug daily 8am–6pm; mid-Aug to mid-May daily 8.30am–5.30pm; free; parking $3) at the end of PR-697, also known as Playa Sardinera, or just "playa." It's a no-frills but lively place on weekends, with changing rooms, toilets, plenty of parking, and cheap *kioscos* nearby. The beach is a bit scruffy but wide, with lots of shady pine trees and palm cover, and good swimming in summer – keep walking west (left) to find a cleaner, less crowded stretch. Otherwise the main attraction is the **cheap food**, salsa, and barbecue served up behind the beach at weekends, a mini version of Piñones.

The **Ojo del Buey** (Ox's eye) is a coastal recreational area in Barrio Mameyal, further east at the end of PR-698 – turn left when you hit the coast and a bit further along you should see a narrow road leading down to the water on the right. The name comes from a large rock that resembles the head of a bull, sprouting from the headland. Parking space is limited, but you can swim in the lagoon between the rocks here, and it's a pleasant place for a stroll. Legend has it that pirate **Roberto Cofresí** (see p.360) buried some of his seemingly inexhaustible supply of treasure nearby, at the mouth of the Río La Plata.

Eating and drinking

There are plenty of options when it comes to **eating** in Dorado, with the cheapest Puerto Rican food concentrated near the public beach. For upscale dining and **nightlife**, the best choices are within the resorts, though you can grab cheap beers at *Kuky's Place* on the main plaza, a wooden dive bar with a small veranda that sells $1.25 Medalla and snacks. Note that non-guests at the *Embassy Suites* will pay $1.50 per hour for parking.

El Ladrillo c/Méndez Vigo 334 (PR-693) ☎787/796-2120. This attractive old villa houses the best restaurant downtown, its exposed brick walls embellished with vibrant local art. The specialties are prime Angus beef and lamb steaks, with perfectly grilled sirloin and T-bones, as well as Puerto Rican seafood such as rich shrimp and lobster stews (mains $18–28). Closed Mon.

Norma's Pinchos Calle G, Balneario Manuel Nolo Morales. This homely *kiosco*, right at the end of the beach road near the car park, sells huge chicken, beef, and pork *pinchos* (kebabs), a bargain for just $2. Closed Mon–Wed.

Nuevo Playero Balneario Manuel Nolo Morales. Lively salsa beach bar with pool tables and great snack food: try the fresh octopus, or *croquetas de marlin* ($2–3). Opposite *Ranchomar*. Closed Mon–Wed.

Ranchomar Calle G 146, Balneario Manuel Nolo Morales (where PR-697 hits the seafront), ☎787/796-3347. This large wooden bar and restaurant has a big menu of home-cooked Puerto Rican food to eat in or take onto the beach. Locals go for the freshly caught fish (mains $6–25), *carne fritas*, and filling *mofongos* here. It's an appealing spot, with a kids' menu, lots of space, pool table, and large open terrace. It also has free parking, a real bonus. Closed Mon–Wed.

La Terraza c/Marginal C-1, PR-693 ☎787/796-1242. This is the best of a small strip of restaurants on the north side of PR-693, next to the PR-697 turn-off, with a wooden terrace and a menu of upmarket versions of Puerto Rican classics such as *mofongo* (stuffed with octopus and lobster) and fat, juicy steaks ($20–45). The second floor acts as a sports bar on weekends, with live music. Open daily from 5pm.

Zen Garden *Hyatt Hacienda del Mar* ☎787/796-1234. This posh restaurant is a little past its prime, but still a solid choice for a splurge, with a high-quality selection of sushi and sashimi supplemented by a variety of tasty Chinese and Japanese dishes – try the grilled halibut with miso sauce. Dishes $10–30. Mon–Sat 6–11pm, Sun 1–10pm.

Balneario Cerro Gordo

The first **beach** that merits attention as you head west from Dorado is **Balneario Cerro Gordo** (mid-May to mid-Aug daily 8am–6pm; mid-Aug to mid-May daily 8.30am–5.30pm; free, parking $3), a small curving bay with thick golden sands, clumps of palm trees, and a rocky headland at the end of PR-690. You can snorkel along the reef just offshore, and the usually calm, crystalline waters are perfect for swimming: in the summer it gets mobbed on weekends. You can also **camp** here (℡787/883-2730; $13 per night); there are showers and toilets on site.

To eat, try *Solymar* opposite the beach on the main road, a bar and restaurant that does a good trade in cold beers and Puerto Rican staples ($5–15), and has a couple of pool tables to boot. Further back along PR-690, at km 7.2 just before the junction with PR-6690, *El Batey del Indio* (Thurs–Sun noon–10pm) offers fresh fish, crab soup, and filling *mofongo* in a rustic shack, with mains from $12, while at the junction itself the stylish *El Corzo Sports Bar & Grill* is an open terrace bar and restaurant with pool tables, open every day. Grilled meats such as *churrasco* are the specialty here ($7–10), as well as succulent roast chicken dishes.

Vega Baja

Established in 1776, **VEGA BAJA** is one of the few towns worth seeing along the PR-22 corridor, its gracefully aging center enhanced by the **Museo Casa Alonso**, a charming museum. With five **natural reserves** accounting for forty percent of the municipality (two accessible to the public), the town is also desperately trying to promote the area's **ecotourism** potential (see box below).

The Town

At the heart of Vega Baja is **Plaza de Recreo José Francisco Náter**, the animated central square containing the imposing **Casa Alcaldía** (town hall). Built in US Neoclassical style in 1925 and painted a vivid tangerine color, it boasts a precious clock beneath the dome on top, created by master New England clockmaker Seth Thomas. Next door is **Teatro Fénix**, a Greek Revival theater built in 1917 with slender Doric columns. The **Iglesia Nuestra Señora del Rosario**, a simple colonial church dating from 1867, sits on the other side of the plaza near the **Teatro América**, an Art Deco cinema completed in 1942 – renovated in 2000, it's still used to show movies in the evenings. Both theaters are usually locked up during the day.

The real highlight of the town, however, is the **Museo Casa Alonso** (Wed–Fri 9am–noon & 1–4pm, Sat & Sun 10am–4pm; $2), a sumptuous nineteenth-century

---

Vega goes eco-friendly

Brushing off local concerns about funding, Vega Baja is attempting to win the seemingly unlikely title of **ecotourism capital** of Puerto Rico, embarking on an ambitious scheme to open up its mangrove swamps, local cave systems, and other natural resources. Future plans include kayaking tours, campgrounds, botanical gardens, night tours of the lagoon, an ecological park for kids, "eco-cabins" along the beach, and even reviving an old train route. To learn more, contact the **Oficina de Ecoturismo** (Mon–Fri 7.30am–4pm; ℡787/807-1830 or 787/858-6617, ✉ecoturismovb@yahoo.com), at PR-687 km 1, which has plenty of information and arranges organized tours of the area (Tues–Fri 9am–noon & 1–3pm), including special **bird-watching** excursions, provided you make reservations at least one week in advance – note though, that a lack of English-speakers means you need to speak Spanish fairly well to get much out of this.

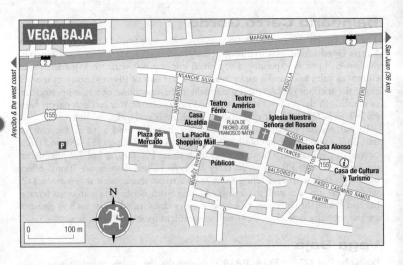

townhouse with typical *criollo* touches: wooden doors and shutters, a tranquil inner patio, timbered ceilings, and ornate wrought-iron railings along the verandas. Originally owned by Don Pablo Soliveras, a former mayor, it was bought in 1912 by Don Ramón Alonso Dávila and the Müller family, and finally acquired by the city in 1982. The interior has been restored in flawless nineteenth-century style, with one room honoring satirical writers **José Gualberto Padilla** (who died in Vega Baja in 1896) and **Trina Padilla de Sanz** (born in the town in 1863) with a few personal effects and assorted memorabilia. The room called the Sala de la Música contains a collection of dusty 78rpm vinyl records and the first guitar of **Fernandito Alvarez**, born in Vega Baja in 1914 and leader of the Trío Vegabajeño, one of the most beloved Puerto Rican *bolero* groups (see p.372). The entrance is on Calle José Julián Acosta, a short walk east of the plaza.

Continue walking east and at the junction of Calle Betances and Calle Tulio Otero is the **Casa de Cultura y Turismo** (Mon–Fri 8am–4.30pm; ☎787/858-6447), another attractive colonial house which has plenty of information about the town and environs, though mostly in Spanish.

Practicalities

You'll find plenty of **parking** at the western end of Vega Baja, off PR-155 beyond the modern Plaza del Mercado building, but there are no **hotels**. The Plaza del Mercado itself, on Calle Betances, is the best place for cheap **food**, cooked up at the snack stalls facing the street – *Cafeteria Pablon* on the western side does the best *bacalaítos*. Otherwise the choices in town are fairly uninspiring – head to Punta Puerto Nuevo instead.

Punta Puerto Nuevo

Jutting into the Atlantic a few kilometers north of Vega Baja, the pockmarked headland of **PUNTA PUERTO NUEVO** also gives its name to the adjacent beach and seaside village, best known for its enticing snack stalls. The action takes place at the junction of PR-692 and PR-686 (km 12), where a one-way road runs along the beach – head east along PR-692 and look for the left turn. You can park along the beachfront (easier weekdays) or in the free car park back on the main road. Known as the **Playa de Puerto Nuevo** (or just Playa de

Vega Baja), the beach is backed by pine trees, faces a calm bay with gentle waves, clear water, and a small reef offshore, all said to be inspiration for a much-loved song by local crooner Fernandito Alvarez.

Good choices for **food** include *Kiosko La Merlaza* overlooking the beach, for crispy fried tacos and *empanadillas*, or *Kiosko Ricky Mar* further along the seafront, for *pulpo* (octopus) and *camarones* (prawn) tacos, *pastelillos de Chapín* (fish turnovers), crab *alcapurrias*, and potent "coco whiskey" cocktails, and cold beers – everything here will be under $5. *Restaurante Costa Norte*, on Calle Joaquin Rosa Gomez (daily 9am–9pm), is back at PR-686 at the turn-off to the beach, a canteen with an outdoor patio and a simple menu of classics such as fried chunks of *dorado* (mains under $10) and the usual *frituras*.

Reserva Natural Laguna Tortuguero

The marshy wetlands northwest of Vega Baja are protected within the **Reserva Natural Laguna Tortuguero** (Wed–Sun 6am–5pm), a DRNA-managed reserve at PR-687 km 1.2. You can drive up to the serene lagoon at the center of the swampy reserve, bordered by a picnic area, gazebos, and, short boardwalk (fishing is permitted), but to get the most out of the area contact the **Oficina de Ecoturismo** (see p.201), based nearby at PR-687 km 1. The reserve is a wildlife magnet, attracting plenty of bird species including skylarks, but the most exotic natives of the lake are **spectacled caiman** (a type of alligator), with more than a thousand thought to be lurking beneath the water – swimming is not encouraged, though the crocs rarely grow bigger than 6ft and it's unusual to see one.

Playa Los Tubos and Playa Mar Chiquita

The stretch of coast north of **Manatí** is graced by some of the most memorable beaches in Puerto Rico. Heading west along PR-686, the first is **Playa Los Tubos** (Tues–Fri 8am–4pm, Sat & Sun 9am–5pm), a thick, beautiful wedge of sand with a big car park and basic amenities, embellished with unusual and quirky touches: a children's playground which incorporates oversize models of brightly painted animals, and picnic shelters with step-pyramid rooftops. Los Tubos gets some heavy **surf** in winter, while for the week of July 4 the beach plays host to the **International Playero Los Tubos de Manatí Festival**, featuring a series of concerts by well-known artists from Puerto Rico and all over Latin America.

Beyond here the road follows a narrow strip of beach known as **Playa Tortuguero**, enticing on weekdays when the lack of people means you can simply pull over and stake out your own private stretch. Keep driving west along PR-685 and you'll come to PR-648, the road to stunning **Playa Mar Chiquita**. This cove is an almost perfect horseshoe shape, hemmed in by jagged arms of coral on both sides and lined with a silky strip of sand. Most of the water here is calm and perfect for swimming, though you'll find bigger waves surging through the narrow gap into the lagoon itself, further off the beach. The area remains wild and undeveloped, with no facilities or food on site, though you'll be sharing the beach with the usual hordes on weekends and holidays.

To find two much quieter beaches, return to PR-685, turn right and make the short drive to the turning for PR-6684. At the end of this road you'll find **Playa La Poza de Las Mujeres** and **Playa de Las Golondrinas**. The latter is home to La Cueva de Las Golondrinas (Cave of the Swallows), a small tunnel at the edge of the beach, cutting through the rocks to the bay on the other side. To reach the cave, cross the fence at the end of the road and turn right at the sign for the Reserva Natural de Hacienda La Esperanza: you should reach the beach in around five to ten minutes. Playa La Poza is off to the right, with no actual well (*poza*), but a tiny, sheltered cove.

Reserva Natural de Hacienda La Esperanza

Formerly one of the largest sugar plantations on the island, holding 152 slaves at its peak, the **Reserva Natural de Hacienda La Esperanza** (Fri–Sun 8am–6pm; free) contains over two thousand acres of unsullied grassy plains, karst forest, wetlands, and coastline, as well as a Taíno ceremonial site and the original hacienda building in the center.

The plantation was established in the 1830s, but it's been owned by the Conservation Trust since 1975. The main entrance is at the end of PR-616, off PR-685 and inland from Playa Mar Chiquita. From here a bone-jarring dirt track leads 6km through the reserve, before ending at a small **beach** zone, the most accessible area for visitors. You'll pass several places to pull off along the way, but be warned that on weekends it can get jam-packed, making it hard to find a space (despite the 175 vehicle limit). The two principal beaches are rocky coves, making natural pools ideal for swimming and snorkeling, with a thick bank of trees and tropical bush right up to the water providing plenty of shady cover. You'll see the actual **sugar mill** and hacienda on the way, fine colonial buildings dating from the 1860s, with outhouses containing a rare beam steam engine constructed in New York State in 1861. The mill is being restored and should be open as a visitor center and hub for a network of trails by sometime in 2009.

Barceloneta to Arecibo

The former port of **Barceloneta** was founded in 1881, one of the last towns to be established by the Spanish on the island. Today it's surrounded by ugly pharmaceutical plants and, though the center is pleasant enough, bereft of attractions. Instead, aim for coastal road PR-681, which winds between here and Arecibo, a less-traveled route that in part resembles southern California: beyond the pineapple groves just inland, the beaches start to get emptier and the waves get bigger. At km 16.2 you'll pass the **Isla de Roque**, actually a rocky promontory with some good places to swim, a beach, and *kioscos* selling filling snacks on weekends. Beyond here there are numerous places to pull over and lounge on the sands: **Hallows** is a popular surf break at km 11.8, opposite the *Hallows Apartments* and a small café, while at around km 9.7 you'll find another secluded beach protected by a headland, just beyond the Gulf gas station. Turn off next to the abandoned building and park behind the dunes.

Finally, the **Reserva Natural Cueva del Indio** at km 7 is a sea cave filled with ancient Taíno **petroglyphs**, though when the waves are fierce, the dramatic surroundings are more thrilling than the symbols themselves, and it's easy to believe that this was a sacred Taíno site. The cave is signposted on the right around 50m before the Esso gas station. Drive up the sandy trail and you can park for $2 on land owned by the affable Richard, who will usually offer to give a quick introduction and point you in the right direction. The site itself is public property (the DRNA has yet to decide what to do with it), and if you drive on to the next bay, you can park just off the road for free and clamber along the rocky coastline back to the cave, though this will take much longer. Beyond the trees at the back of Richard's house you emerge onto a headland honeycombed with dead coral arches and blowholes. The cave is essentially a large overhang underneath the headland, a spectacular location with waves slamming into the rocks and roughly hewn steps leading down to the water. You need a flashlight and a good sense of balance to explore the cave properly, but you can spot some of the petroglyphs without going too far down: a series of simplistic, almost alien-like figures and shapes, daubed in white paint.

The best place **to eat** on this stretch of coast is *Costa de Oro* (Tues–Sat 2.30–9.30pm, Sun noon–8.30pm; ☎787/815-5632) at km 12.2, a friendly place right on the ocean and serving a mix of spicy Peruvian food, *ceviches*, and Tex-Mex favorites ($8–22).

Bosque Estatal de Cambalache

Inland from the coast, the **Bosque Estatal de Cambalache** is a magnet for **mountain bike** enthusiasts as one of the only places on the island to maintain a decent bike trail (though hardly a technical ride). The major problem for most visitors is you must bring your own bike – if you don't have one there are still 6km of well-marked **hiking trails** to try. The reserve is at the end of a badly potholed side-road off PR-682 (next to the Job Corps complex): from the coast you have to swing back through Barceloneta or Arecibo to get there. The main trails lead off from the parking lot and picnic tables at the *area recreativa* at the end of the road, with a small **information office** (Mon–Fri 8am–4.30pm) nearby. The 3.5km **Ruta Recreativa de Bicicletas** is clearly marked, as is the **Vereda Interpretativa** a short nature trail, a little further along.

Arecibo Lighthouse and Historic Park

The coastal city of **Arecibo** is one of the fastest growing in the region, but with little to offer in the way of sights except the **Arecibo Lighthouse and Historic Park** (Mon–Fri 9am–6pm, Sat & Sun 10am–7pm; $9, kids $7, parking $2; ⓦ www.arecibolighthouse.com), a theme park probably only worth a look if you're traveling with kids. The park hinges around the old lighthouse, the **Faro de Los Morrillos de Arecibo**, built in 1898, and now containing a small exhibition on marine life – it's one of the few lighthouses on the island which you can explore inside, and offers stellar views of the coastline from its upper deck. The park also includes a small petting zoo and five areas with historical themes, notably the recreation of a small Taíno village, a fairly candid reproduction of a barebones nineteenth-century slave quarters, and replicas of the *Niña*, the *Pinta*, and *Santa María* (one-third of the actual size), the first fleet of Columbus, ideal for clambering around and exploring (with small displays about the admiral inside). Finally, kids will love the creepy pirate's cave and Blackbeard's pirate ship. The park is at the end of PR-655, off coastal road PR-681, just before you hit Arecibo proper.

Practicalities

The most convenient **places to stay** on this stretch of coast lie just beyond the end of the PR-22 *autopista*, on other side of Arecibo. *Parador El Buen Café* (☎787/898-1000, ⓦ www.elbuencafe.com; ❹) at PR-2 km 84 is a busy roadside hotel with comfortable but rather pricey rooms considering the motel-like standard. The hotel has two **places to eat** in the building opposite: the cheap buffet-style cafeteria (daily 5.30am–10pm) on the right, serving great breakfasts (from $4), sandwiches, and hearty Puerto Rican dishes (under $10), and the posh *mesón gastronómico* and bar on the left, *El Buen Café* (daily 11am–10pm), noted for its *carne mechada* (stuffed pot roast), chicken rice, and red snapper (mains $18–28).

A newer alternative is the *Punta Maracayo Resort* (☎787/544-2000, ⓦ www.puntamaracayoresortpr.com; ❹) on the other side of the highway (km 84.6), which despite the name, is a wholly unglamorous modern hotel. Rooms are similarly priced with all the amenities (fridge, DVD players), and the pool is a decent extra – you can see the ocean from second- and third-floor rooms.

Quebradillas and around

Few visitors make it to **QUEBRADILLAS**, a typically languid provincial town best known in Puerto Rico for its legendary basketball team, the *Piratas*. While the center holds little interest, the town makes a decent base for visiting the surrounding countryside, littered with offbeat attractions and enhanced by some unusual places to eat – the overall lack of tourists makes this a fun place to explore.

Officially established as a *villa* in 1823 by landowner Felipe Ruiz, people had been settling here since the early eighteenth century, the name coming from the large number of streams or *quebradas* in the area. Today, downtown Quebradillas is 3km south of PR-2 on PR-113, but other than coming in to admire the twin-towered Neoclassical church on the central plaza and the nineteenth-century Casa del Rey (the old town hall), there isn't much to see in the town itself. If you visit during the week of October 24, check out the town's lively **Fiestas del Pueblo**, celebrating archangel and patron saint Raphael with a marathon, games for children, live music, and the usual spread of *kioscos*.

Accommodation

You have a choice of three **places to stay** in Quebradillas. The best option is the *Sueños Doña Herminia Guest House* (☏787/239-8893, ⓦ www.herminia-gh .com; ❹), a small, modern hotel with bar and restaurant, right on the cliffs north of town. The views here are extraordinary. The parking lot is tiny but there are just eight cozy rooms (with a/c, local TV, and spotless bathrooms), so you should have enough space. Ask for a room with a balcony overlooking the ocean. You'll often get a cheaper rate if you pay cash. To get here, take the exit to Area Recreativa Guajataca Merendero (see p.208) off PR-2, and keep driving along this road.

The most expensive place is *Hotel El Guajataca* (☏787/895-3070, ⓦ www .hotelelguajataca.com; ❹), signposted off PR-2 at km 103.8, above Playa de Guajataca. You get relatively compact but classy rooms (some with wood-frame, antique-looking beds), balconies overlooking the sea, and a nice pool, popular with local day guests. The *Restaurant Casabi* on site is a slightly overrated *mesón gastronómico*, but does at least enjoy stellar views across the choppy waves below.

Parador Vistamar (☏787/895-2065, ⓦ www.paradorvistamar.com; ❸) is better value, perched high above the coast on PR-113 (just over 1km from PR-2, north of town), with spectacular views across the whole of Guajataca bay and plenty of parking. The property itself is a modern, fairly characterless place with basic motel-like units that are showing their age, but all well maintained with cable TV and air-conditioning – you'll pay $30–40 extra for the larger rooms with ocean views.

Eating and drinking

Quebradillas has some intriguing places **to eat**, relics of the island's *criollo* and colonial past. *Panadería Los Cocos* is reputed to be the oldest **bakery** on the island (sometimes known simply as "Panadería Legendaria"), with a history going back 100 or 140 years, depending on who you believe, though the current premises look like typically modern Puerto Rico. It's also the only one still baking bread in wood-fired ovens, according to an original nineteenth-century recipe. Standout items include bread stuffed with *lechon asado* (roast pork) priced at $6 per pound, and the locally produced *queso del pais* (white cheese), but all the cakes ($0.75) and fresh breads are worth trying. They also do breakfasts (from $3.50) of eggs and pork combos, and various sandwiches from

$3.40. You'll find the bakery on PR-484, just north of PR-2, a few kilometers east of the town (PR-484 makes a short loop off PR-2 through the *barrio* of Cocos – the bakery is at the eastern end).

For another dose of history and excellent food, make for Restaurant *El Histórico Puente Blanco* (daily 11.30am–10pm; ☎787/895-1934) at the end of the narrow road (known as Calle La Estacion) beyond the *Sueños Doña Herminia Guest House*, 2km from PR-2. Noted for its vast menu of steak, seafood such as fresh snapper, and Italian dishes (mains $13–20, pastas around $10), the restaurant gets particularly lively at weekends and has stunning views of the ocean below. It's named after the "white bridge" built in 1922 to carry a railway over the nearby gorge – you can walk over the concrete replacement at the end of the road, 220yds further east.

Hard to spot, *La Granja* (daily 8am–8pm) is a large wooden shack on the southwest side of PR-2 – heading towards Hatillo (eastbound), you should see it just after the PR-4484 turn-off (it can't be accessed safely from the other side of the road). Just pull off and park nearby. The place is stuffed with Puerto Rican sweets, cakes, fried snacks, and local *queso de hoja* (white cheese), all for well under $10. You can also buy local souvenirs, games, and postcards. Elsewhere, the *criollo* buffet (chicken, rice, and all the usual Puerto Rican dishes) at the *Sueños Doña Herminia Guest House* (Mon–Fri 11am–3pm) is excellent value at just $6.95.

Around Quebradillas

The coastline around Quebradillas is one of the island's most rugged, with plunging cliffs punctured by alluring coves such as the beaches at **Puerta Hermina** and **Guajataca**. The elegant ruins of the **Ermita San Antonio de Padua de La Tuna** are a modest reminder of the area's past, while the **Bosque Estatal de Guajataca** is laced with easy walks through enchanting woods, one of the most rewarding places to hike in Puerto Rico. From here you can head east into karst country via **Lago de Guajataca**, a tranquil lake with some rustic waterside accommodation, or head into the Porta del Sol (see p.223) on PR-2: it's just 7km to Isabela from Quebradillas, and 28km to Aguadilla.

Playa Puerta Hermina

In the eighteenth century, pirates would offload contraband at **Playa Puerta Hermina**, a narrow beach buried deep between soaring cliffs. Reminiscent of the Cornish coves favored by English smugglers, it's a wild and windswept place, at the bottom of a very steep one-track road (PR-4485), off PR485 east of town. Despite the waves and the wind, it's an atmospheric spot for a picnic, and you can clamber around the ruins at the end of the beach (around the corner from where the road ends), said to be the pirates' storehouse.

Guajataca

The Taíno kingdom that covered this part of the north coast was known as **Guajataca** (Taíno for "the water ladle"), commemorated in a host of place names including the Río Guajataca, the main river. When locals refer to Guajataca however, they're usually talking about the **beach**, a popular strip of sand 1km from PR-2, west of Quebradillas. **Playa de Guajataca** is hemmed in by cliffs on one side and fringed by a line of palms, though its location is more appealing than the shell-strewn beach itself, which has coarser sand and rough waves – swimming is discouraged thanks to strong currents. On the west side, the **Tunel del Guajataca** – an old sugar-cane railway tunnel built in 1911 – cuts through the cliffs for around 65ft. You can continue walking along the

▲ Cacíque Mabodomaca Monument

trail for another 230yds to a more secluded beach, and if you have time, on to Playa El Pastillo (see below).

Note that although you can access Playa de Guajataca from both directions on PR-2, coming back you can only rejoin the highway heading west, away from Quebradillas. Just up the hill from the junction, at the intersection of PR-113 and PR-2 at km 105, the **Monumento Cacíque Mabodomaca** or *Cara del Indio* ("Face of the Indian"), is a giant image of the last ruler of Guajataca carved into the rocks, facing north towards the sea. Mabodomaca was a key member of the 1511 rebellion (see p.357), and though this is a powerful reminder of Puerto Rico's Taíno roots, it can be tough to stop with traffic racing down the hill.

A short drive east along PR-2 from Playa de Guajataca, the **Area Recreativa Guajataca Merendero** (daily 8am–5.30pm; free) is a fabulous viewpoint just off the highway, in gardens overlooking a vast swathe of the north coast – keep driving down this turn-off to reach the *Puente Blanco* restaurant and the *Sueños Doña Herminia Guest House*.

Playa El Pastillo

Moving on to the northwest coast it's worth stopping at **Playa El Pastillo**, a beautifully wild and usually empty beach just off PR-113, a few kilometres west of Guajataca. With wide, powdery sand and plenty of space, the only downside is the lack of tree cover or shade. Look for the signs advertising *Ali Baba Pizza* and *Pa-Yu Sports Bar*, and take the narrow road here right down to the beach (Avda Noel Estrada) – leave your car along the side of the road.

Ermita San Antonio de Padua de La Tuna

One of the most important colonial sites on the north coast, the ruins of **Ermita San Antonio de Padua de La Tuna** will appeal primarily to history lovers, though the quiet location, incongruously squashed between the houses of a modern village, seems oddly symbolic of the struggle to preserve the island's rich

Spanish heritage. The hermitage or convent was established around 1725 near the Río Guajataca, and a settlement, known as San Antonio de La Tuna, grew up around it. Between 1818 and 1819 the village was relocated to be closer to the sea, eventually becoming the current town of Isabela, and the church was abandoned. Today the well-restored stone ruins are fenced off but easy to appreciate through the bars. Follow the signs off PR-2, just west of Guajataca, into Barrio Coto, then look for the tiny sign directing you along a street to the left, marked "Concierto Entre Ruinas" (leftover from a local concert). The ruins face a small plaza in the middle of the village.

Bosque Estatal de Guajataca

Head inland to the **Bosque Estatal de Guajataca** and you start to penetrate karst country (see p.210), the forest characterized by giant sinkholes and oval-shaped hills covered with a thick carpet of trees. Unlike many of the island's sadly under-used forest reserves, this one is well-organized, with a network of 46 short, interlinked trails making it one of the best for hikers. Like all state forests in Puerto Rico, entry is free.

The **information center** (℡787/724-3724) is 9km south of PR-2 on PR-446, in the heart of the forest: for the last 2km after the junction with PR-476 the road narrows to a single track. The center supplies basic **trail maps** and information, and is usually open Monday to Saturday 7.30am to 4pm, though the rangers occasionally step out for short periods. The **campground** is along Vereda 9 (trail 9), a short walk from the information center – you'll need the usual permit from the DRNA to camp here (see p.28).

The most popular and accessible trail is the **Vereda Interpretiva** (3.2km), an interpretive trail incorporating parts of Vereda 1 (2.6km) and others, which can be hiked at leisure in an hour and starts near the information center – grab an English leaflet here pointing out all the main flora and fauna along the way. You'll pass through groves of *pino Hondureño* (Caribbean pine), *majó* (blue mahoe), *moralón*, and *María* trees, and see bunches of white scented flowers sprouting from *cupey* trees in the summer, but to hear one of the 45 species of birds in the forest, get here early. Make sure you make the short detour to the **Torre de Observación** (400m from the start), providing magnificent views of haunting karst formations, before continuing onto the **Cueva del Viento** (2.5km and around 40min). The entrance to the cave itself is partially blocked by wire mesh and a staircase now takes you down into the cavern, along with several vines and hefty tree roots that reach right into the cave. If you have a flashlight, you can explore the large boreholes that lead off left and right: the latter contains spectacular dry limestone formations and flowstone walls, ending in around 120 metres.

Lago de Guajataca

One of the largest lakes in Puerto Rico, **Lago de Guajataca** is best known for **fishing**, though the rustic food stalls and simple places to stay at the water's edge make this a pleasant break from the beaches. The scenery is certainly soothing, if not spectacular, with a fringe of low hills smothered in lush vegetation circling the shore. Like all major lakes in Puerto Rico, this one is a reservoir, created in 1928 by flooding the narrow Río Guajataca valley for 6.4km.

Whether you approach the lake from Quebradillas (11km) or the Bosque Estatal de Guajataca, you'll end up on PR-119, which follows the western shore. Aim for the **Refugio de Vida Silvestre Lago Guajataca** (Tues–Sun 6am–6pm), at the end of a narrow road at km 22.1. The DRNA office and information center here has displays about the lake (especially ongoing conservation work), and live fish in tanks: the *tucunaré* (peacock bass) was introduced to the lake in 1967 from

South America and is the most prized fishing target, but there are also *lobina* (largemouth bass), *chopa criolla* (bluegill), and *barbudo* (white catfish) from the US, and *tilapia* from Africa. Anyone can have a go at fishing – you can borrow bamboo rods at the center (free) but you'll have to bring bait. It's also a tranquil spot for a picnic, with a few wooden tables near the shore – swimming is prohibited and there are no boats for rent.

You can **stay** at one of the simple guesthouses nearby for a taste of torpid Puerto Rican country life. *Nino's Camping* (☎787/896-9016, ⓦwww.ninoscamping .com; ❶) is a chilled-out backpacker-type place, with camping area and *cabañas* for four to twelve people, and kayaks to use on the lake. *Hospedería Lagovista* (☎787/280-5522, ⓦwww.lagovistapr.com) next door has cozy rooms in the main building (❸) and comfortable chalets (❻) right by the lake, with the *Tucunaré* restaurant offering local fish and Puerto Rican dishes, open daily for breakfast ($7.50) and dinner (6–9pm; $14.50). You can also rent kayaks here.

Elsewhere, for something **to eat**, try *Lechonera Crespo*, north of the refuge at PR-119 km 20.9, a simple shack open weekends serving crispy roast pork and assorted deep-fried delights (under $10). From the lake area you can continue driving into the heart of karst country via PR-455, or on to Lares (p.213), 9km south along PR-453.

Karst country

Squashed between the north coast and the peaks of the Central Cordillera, **karst country** is quite unlike anything else in Puerto Rico, a haunting landscape that resembles parts of China more than the Caribbean. Stretching between Quebradillas and Corozal, this is a region of crumbling limestone hills smothered in dense jungle, flashes of white stone poking through the vines like a lost city, the narrow gorges (*sumideros*) in between pockmarked by cavernous sinkholes. These striking formations, known as *mogotes*, were created over millions of years, the limestone bedrock worn away by seeping water: Kras (or "karst" in German) is the region in Slovenia where the phenomenon was first studied. Gazing over Puerto Rico's karst country from lofty viewpoints on the Ruta Panorámica (see p.323), it's easier to appreciate their surreal uniformity – a bit like a roughly made egg carton spreading across the horizon.

Hard to believe today, but by the 1940s much of the area had been deforested to make way for coffee plantations and fruit farms. By the 1960s most of these had closed, and with the forests restored, you'll find plenty of tranquil **reserves** nestled among the peaks, as well as some major attractions: you might recognize the vast **Observatorio de Arecibo** from movies such as *Contact* (1997) and *GoldenEye* (1995), while the **Parque de las Cavernas del Río Camuy** shows what happens beneath the surface, and the **Centro Ceremonial Indígena de Caguana** is an evocative reminder of the Taíno past. Make time for **Lares** if you can – spiritual home of Puerto Rico's independence movement – and the small hill towns further east, with **Ciales** a charming introduction to the island's lauded **coffee-growing** traditions.

Accommodation

You can see much of karst country on day-trips from the coast, assuming you have a car, but there is a handful of **places to stay** in the mountains.

One of the most popular, especially with jaded North American city dwellers, is *Casa Grande Mountain Retreat* (☎787/894-3939, ⓦwww.hotelcasagrande.com; ❸), a former coffee plantation with twenty spotless rooms in five wooden chalets, tucked away in a quiet valley engulfed by lush vegetation. Each room has a private bath, fan, balcony, and hammock, but not much else – you're paying for the serene location. The hiking trails, fresh-water pool, and 8am yoga sessions ($10) enhance the tranquility, and at night you'll be serenaded by the sound of a hundred *coquís*. Its restaurant, *Casa Grande Cafe*, serves high-quality Puerto Rican food and has a veranda with sublime valley views; on offer are heartly breakfasts ($6), dinner daily, plus lunch on weekends. The hotel is on PR-612, just off PR-140 to the north of placid **Lago Caonillas**.

South of *Casa Grande*, on the north shore of the lake at PR-140 km 28.1, just before the junction with PR-613, *Los Pinos Lake Resort and Spa* (℡787/894-3481; ❸) is really a collection of quiet chalets overlooking the lake, despite the grand name – you'll pay an extra $30 for a villa right by the water. Each has a small kitchen, bedroom, living room and bathroom. The mediocre on-site restaurant and bar is open Friday to Sunday.

Another former coffee plantation, *TJ Ranch* (Ⓦwww.tjranch.com; ❹) lies in the foothills off PR-22 between Arecibo and Utuado, with just three cozy *casitas*, all with bathrooms, a pool, and a restaurant offering a mix of international and local dishes. You can also **camp** in the grounds of the Parque de Las Cavernas del Río Camuy (℡787/898-3100; $5 per person), which has showers and toilets, and at the Bosque Estatal de Río Abajo (see p.216).

Observatorio de Arecibo

The world's largest radar and radio telescope, the **Observatorio de Arecibo** (Aug to mid-Dec & mid-Jan to May Wed–Fri noon–4pm, Sat, Sun holidays 9am–4pm; June, July & mid-Dec to mid-Jan daily 9am–4pm; $5, kids $3; ℡787/878-2612, Ⓦwww.naic.edu) is one of the most unusual sights in Puerto Rico, an immense 1000-foot concave dish surrounded by jungle-drenched limestone peaks. Scientists come here to gaze into the deepest corners of the galaxy, and the giant installation has an appropriately serene, isolated feel.

The **visitor center** contains an illuminating series of exhibits that help to explain the pioneering research that takes place here, as fun for adults as it is for children and budding astronauts. The first floor contains a range of multi-media displays divided into three sections, each examining aspects of space and the universe: the Earth and our solar system, stars and galaxies, and tools and technology. Short **videos** look at the Big Bang Theory, the birth and death of stars, and finally the Solar System, a mind-blowing imaginary journey that starts with the telescopic protons of a human being and ends at the outer limits of the universe. The second floor is crammed with absorbing exhibits shedding light on the work at the observatory, while the **auditorium** shows longer videos every thirty minutes in English, though the "Day in the life of the observatory," is rather dull.

Step outside onto the viewing deck and the vast size of the **reflector dish** is brought home. Below, 38,778 aluminum panels hang just over the jungle canopy, covering around twenty acres and supported by a network of steel cables. Suspended 450ft above the dish is a monitoring station and a series of precarious-looking walkways, held up by eighteen cables strung from three reinforced concrete towers (the tallest is 365ft). The whole site is surrounded by a typical karst landscape, thick with verdant outcrops of limestone, and enveloped with an almost eerie calm.

The telescope was conceived by Dr William E. Gordon at Cornell University, and constructed between 1960 and 1963, making it one of the oldest still in use. The location was chosen principally because of its proximity to the equator

4

Caving and rappelling

Karst country is riddled with caves, but most of them should only be tackled by professional spelunkers or on organized tours. Ecoquest Adventures and Tours (☎787/616-7543; ⊛www.ecoquestpr.com) runs standard trips to the Camuy caves and the Arecibo observatory ($95), but far more exciting are its tours of the Río Tanamá ($149), an area impossible to explore on your own. Hikes begin in Caguana, take in the Cueva del Arco, and involve **rappelling** down an 80-foot cliff into the river before body-rafting through El Portillo natural tunnel (exact routes depend on river flow). Thrill-seekers should also get in touch with Aventuras Tierra Adentro (☎787/766-0470, ⊛www.aventuraspr.com), which arranges **caving** trips to the Río Camuy every Saturday ($160). Tours (5.45am–5pm) involve an exhilarating 250-foot rappel into Angeles Cave. Expediciones Palenque (☎787/823-4354, ⊛www.expedicionespalenque.com) also runs caving excursions to the Camuy (Cueva Resurgencia) and Ciales (Cueva Yuyú) areas from $90 per day, as well as expeditions along the Río Tanamá.

(which provides the clearest views of the night sky) and the surrounding limestone formations, which provided a natural shell in which to build it. Unlike optical telescopes, it works by collecting radiation in the radio region of the electromagnetic spectrum – the dish concentrates the radio waves so that scientists can detect all sorts of objects in space, from pulsars and quasars to black holes and, one day perhaps, signs of extraterrestrial life. Cornell University still operates the telescope, under contract with the National Science Foundation.

Practicalities

The observatory is tucked away in the heart of karst country at the end of PR-625, 20km from Arecibo, and not hard to find – just follow the brown signs from PR-22. From the parking lot it's a short but steep walk up to the visitor center. The **gift shop** sells freeze-dried astronaut food, mugs that light up when hot liquids are added, and plenty of educational games and toys.

The only place **to eat** around here is the *Restaurante El Observatorio* at PR-625 km 1.1 (closed Mon & Tues; mains $7–18), a short drive from the main entrance. You'll get solid if unexceptional local food – the fried pork is a good choice and the *mofongo* worth sampling (entrees $8–15) – offering a pleasant open-air deck with views across the karst landscape.

Parque de Las Cavernas del Río Camuy

Tapping into one of the largest cave systems in the world, the **Parque de Las Cavernas del Río Camuy** (Wed–Sun 8.30am–5pm, last entry 3.45pm; ☎787/898-3100 or 787/763-0568) makes a dramatic contrast to the world of palm trees and beaches on the coast, a series of cool limestone caverns packed with dripping stalactites, flowstone walls that seem to collapse into the rock, and giant stalagmites crumpled like melted wax. Note, however, that the main cave is expected **to remain closed** until 2009, after a tourist was accidentally killed by falling rocks in January 2008. Call ahead or check with the PRTC for the latest situation.

The caves were known to the Taíno, but rediscovered by speleologists in 1958, and only opened to the public in 1986. The park is a tiny portion (290 acres) of a vast cave system that includes 15km of caverns, created by the world's third longest underground river, the Río Camuy, but most of this is inaccessible to casual visitors.

Operated by the Compañía de Parques Nacionales, the caves are clearly signposted at PR-129 km 20, with plenty of **parking** ($3 extra). Once inside, you must buy tickets for a **guided tour** ($12, kids $7) at the **visitor center** (which has a basic cafeteria and gift shop), the only way to visit the site – English-speaking tours should be available most days. Until the main cave reopens, tours will only visit **Sumidero Tres Pueblos**, a gargantuan sinkhole 650ft across and 400ft deep – you get to stand at the viewpoint on the crater edge for a glimpse of the subterranean Río Camuy, far below.

The real highlight is **Cueva Clara**, a vast cavern hidden beneath a soaring wall of white limestone at the bottom of a jungle-clad gorge, pockmarked with holes and straggling plants. Walking tours (45min) of the cave - a short trolley-bus ride from the sinkhole and visitor center – should resume in 2009. The entrance is strewn with ivy-and-vine-covered stalactites, with guides leading you down into the **Hall of Sculptures**, the dimly lit main chamber, 170ft high and 200ft wide. Plenty of **bats** live inside the caves, but you are unlikely to see them during the day. The trail runs for around 700ft, past some dimly lit but garish rock formations, and ends at the bottom of the **Sumidero Empalme** (419ft), and another look at the Río Camuy.

Eating

For something **to eat** nearby, try *Restaurante El Taino* (Wed–Sun 10.30am–7pm) at PR-129 km 21.1, a short drive south of the caves, a large, simple dining room just off the road. The best things on the menu are the specialty of the house, *arroz con guinea* (guinea hen with rice; $10.95) and *mofongo*, which comes in large wooden goblets with a variety of fillings ($15.95).

Lares

The mountain town of **LARES** is often bypassed by foreign visitors, its shabby center and weathered buildings evidence of prolonged hard times. Yet its citizens are some of the most welcoming on the island, proud of their central role in the **Grito de Lares** of 1868 (see p.360), the most significant Puerto Rican rebellion against the Spanish and commemorated solemnly here every year on September 23. Indeed, revered independence activist Pedro Albizu Campos is supposed to have said "Lares is Holy Land, and as such, it must be visited kneeling down." Lares isn't all serious, however: Campos would no doubt be mortified by the monument honoring the slightly less heroic (but equally famous) local girl **Denisse Quiñones**, who in 2001 became the fourth Puerto Rican to win the Miss Universe title, and even if the history doesn't interest you, the town's celebrated **ice cream** more than justifies a visit.

The Town

Drive straight into the center and park if you can near the main square, the **Plaza de la Revolución**. The helpful **tourist office** (Mon–Fri 8am–4pm; ☎787/897-3290) is next to the Casa Alcaldía at the southern end of the plaza, while opposite is a large Spanish Colonial-style church, the **Iglesia de Parroquia San José de la Montaña**. Its wide vaulted interior has antique tiled floors and a beautifully carved *retablo* – the rebels placed their revolutionary flags here to signal the beginning of the 1868 revolt. After the well-attended mass on Sundays, worshipers stuff down fried snacks ($1–2) at the *Kiosko de la Iglesia*, beneath the church on the plaza, only open Sunday mornings. In front of the church are the main memorials to the *Grito*: the **Obelisco**, an austere pillar flanked by flagpoles honoring the six heroes of 1868; the **Monumento a Betances**, a statue of the leader of the rebels, Ramón Emeterio Betances (see p.360); and the **Arbol de Tamarindo**, a tamarind tree from Simón Bolívar's estate in Venezuela, symbol of the struggle for freedom throughout Latin America. The plaza is the scene of two other major festivals: the **Fiestas Patronales de Lares** runs for ten days in December to honor the feast day (December 8) of patron saint La Virgen de la Inmaculada Concepción, while the **Festival del Guineo** (usually held in early June) celebrates pastries and other foods made from **bananas**.

Walk down the hill from the plaza (north along Calle Campos) and a couple of blocks on the right is the **Museo de Lares** (Mon–Fri 8am–noon & 1–4pm, Sat 11am–4pm; free; ☎787/563-7883), with a mildly interesting collection of old photos, documents, and artifacts relating to the history of the town and the *Grito*, as well as some local contemporary art.

Eating and drinking

Lares' **restaurants** are nothing special, and the real culinary highlight is ☆ *La Heladería de Lares*, a venerable **ice cream** parlor on the plaza selling some of the strangest flavors ever devised: bean, avocado, rice, *bacalao* (cod), and even *arroz con pollo* (chicken rice). Scoops are $1.

Lares is also home to one of the most highly respected brands of Puerto Rican coffee, **Alto Grande Super Premium**, though it can be irritatingly hard to buy in the town itself (it's primarily exported). The gourmet blend is produced by Garrido & Co at the **Hacienda Alto Grande** (☎787/897-6000, ⓦwww .altogrande.com), which was founded in 1839, south of Lares, at PR-129 km 6.2. The beans are grown at an altitude of up to 3000ft and need eight days to process (other beans take two). It's rare to be given a tour of the premises, but if you call in advance, you may be able to buy some freshly roasted coffee on site.

Centro Ceremonial Indígena de Caguana

One of the few remnants of Taíno civilization on the island, the **Centro Ceremonial Indígena de Caguana** (daily 8.30am–4pm, closed holidays; $2) was established between 1200 and 1270, and used well into the sixteenth century. Hidden within a tropical forest and backed by a majestic karst ridge known as *Montaña Cemí*, a Taíno holy mountain, the site's palpable sense of antiquity, unusual in Puerto Rico, is just as appealing as the ruins themselves. As with Tibes (see p.295), you'll find none of the awe-inspiring monuments of Mesoamerica here, just stone foundations and outlines of a series of **ball-courts**

El Grito de Caguana

Contrary to the widely held view that the Taíno were wiped out or fully integrated by the Spanish population in Puerto Rico, a small but active **indigenous movement** does exist on the island, run by those who claim Taíno ancestry (see p.341). In 2005, activists **occupied the Caguana ceremonial site** for seventeen days, tired of what they consider daily insults to Taíno culture: women walking in high heels that "pierce the ground" of the sacred site, when ideally everyone should be barefoot; the display of Taíno skeletal remains in the museum; Taíno people being refused free entry; and park guides having little or no knowledge of Taíno traditions or protocols. The protest received scant attention in the international media, and the Puerto Rican government (along with many citizens) tends to regard the group as embarrassing, if not wholly ridiculous. But **El Grito de Caguana** ("the cry of Caguana"), as it came to be known, did help to bring some awareness, and also created links with North America's native populations.

▲ Centro Ceremonial Indígena de Caguana

known as *bateyes*, as well as some valuable **petroglyphs**, but thought-provoking nonetheless. The true purpose of Caguana remains a mystery, though it's evidence of a level of social complexity brushed over by early Spanish accounts, a sort of Caribbean Olympia, built purely for ceremonial games rather than as a settlement: people would gather here at special times, but very few lived here. The **ball-game** (also known as *batey*), which was played with two teams of ten to thirty males and a rubber ball, is thought to have had great symbolic signifi-cance, the outcome influencing important tribal decisions – some experts believe the site was also used to make **astronomical observations**. If you've seen any of the ancient ball-courts in Central America, the similarities will be obvious, and though most academics agree that the ball game probably spread across the Caribbean from Mesoamerica, it remains a contentious theory.

Ten courts have been excavated, including the central plaza, a circular plaza, and eight smaller *bateyes*, revealing thick paving stones around the edges and some remnants of walled enclosures. Some of the **standing stones** are engraved with worn **petroglyphs**, geometric designs, and arcane depictions of human faces and animals. The largest plaza, the **Batey Principal**, is also known as the *Batey del Cacique Agüeybana* in honor of the last great overlord of the Taíno (see p.355), though it seems unlikely he spent time here. The small **museum** at the entrance (closed until late 2008 for renovation) exhibits Taíno artifacts garnered from all over the island – very little has been found at Caguana itself.

Practicalities

Caguana is around 14km east of Lares, at km 12.3 on PR-111. On the way you can grab something **to eat** at *Matias BBQ* (Sat & Sun 9am–4pm), which sells fabulously crispy roast chicken ($4–10) from a roadside stall just before the junction with PR-602. From Caguana it's another 11km to the dreary mountain town of **Utuado**, along an increasingly windy road. From here you can head to *Casa Grande* and **Lago Caonillas**, picking up some sumptuous *lechón* (roast pork) at *El Fogon de Georgie* (Thurs–Sun 9am–9pm), along with other grilled meats, veggies, and bananas for under $10 – it's at the junction of PR-111 and PR-140. To continue your tour of karst country, head north from Utuado on PR-10 towards Arecibo (27km), stopping at the **Bosque Estatal de Río Abajo** (8km) and **Lago dos Bocas** on the way. Adjuntas (see p.344) on the Ruta Panorámica is 20km south of Utuado via PR-10.

Bosque Estatal de Río Abajo

For a slice of sylvan tranquility and the chance to see karst country on foot, visit the **Bosque Estatal de Río Abajo**, a reserve of dense woodland created in 1943 from old logging plantations. You'll see it signposted on the west side of PR-10 – note that this route (PR-6612) is the only way into the forest from the main highway. A short drive from PR-10 you'll hit PR-621: turn left into the forest or right to the **Centro de Visitantes** (hours are erratic). Head into the forest and you'll pass the ranger station (call in for maps here), and around 3km further on, beyond a small village, the road ends at the *Area de Acampar María Soto* (☎787/817-0984), where you can pitch a tent for $4 a night (per person) assuming you have a DRNA permit (see p.28). You'll also find picnic tables and several trailheads nearby. There are supposed to be 24 hiking trails in the area, but only two are recommended by rangers, both offering a fine introduction to the inner forest: **Las Perdices** (around 2km one-way), which starts at the campground, and **La Juanita**, which makes a shorter loop around the same area. Note that the photocopied trail maps are very poor, and weekdays you won't see a soul. Beyond the camping area is the **José L. Vivaldi Aviary**, created in 1993 as an extension of the El Yunque program to save the endangered **Puerto Rican Parrot** (see p.117), but currently off-limits to visitors. Back at the Centro de Visitantes, if you keep driving along PR-621 you'll eventually hit PR-123, the main road down to **Lago dos Bocas**.

Lagos dos Bocas

Puerto Rico doesn't have many mountain lakes, but **Lago dos Bocas** is one of its most captivating, hemmed in by karst cliffs draped with tenacious fern-green vegetation. Created as a reservoir in 1942, its three snaking arms cover 25 square miles, making it the third largest lake in Puerto Rico. You might see a few pelicans on the water, but other than soaking up the impressive scenery, the main reason for a visit is to dine at one of several inviting lakeside **restaurants**, only accessible by boat and open only on weekends.

The lake is signposted at PR-123 km 68, a short drive from PR-10. Park your car at the *embarcadero* (dock) and catch a *lancha* (small boat) across the lake to a restaurant of your choice. At weekends the restaurants will ferry you across in their own boats, but you can also use the public *lanchas* that operate from 6.30am and run every hour between 10am and 5pm (free), though it's supposed to be locals only from 3pm. These boats also run **weekdays** and you can hop on for a free spin around the lake, a round-trip taking around an hour.

Eating

Weekend mornings you'll be amiably accosted by representatives of each **restaurant** at the *embarcadero*: all offer a similar experience, but the best is ⚘ *Rancho Marina* (☎787/894-8034; Sat & Sun only 10am–6pm), set in tropical gardens on a quiet stretch of the lake, with a friendly, rustic atmosphere and fresh food cooked in nouvelle Puerto Rican style. Try the *albondigas* (meat balls in creole sauce, $5) or fried cheese with guava sauce ($5) to start, followed by *conejo a la naranja,* fried rabbit in orange sauce ($13.95), or *churracsco*, sumptuous skirt-steak strips, Rancho style ($14.95). *Otoao* (☎787/312-7118; Fri–Sun) comes a close second, specializing in *fricasés* (thick stews served with rice; $12.95) of rabbit, lamb, and veal.

Ciales

The first of three beguiling hill towns on the eastern side of karst country, **CIALES** straggles prettily over a hillside above two rivers, encircled by low karst peaks, though the center is dominated by the usual hodgepodge of architectural styles and only a few elegant but run-down old buildings remain. Despite increasing modernization, Ciales remains remarkably old-fashioned, more akin to Cuba or the Dominican Republic than towns on the coast: farmers in straw hats chat at street corners, vendors knock out rice and beans for a couple of dollars, and the paint peels gracefully off brightly colored *criollo* homes. The town is particularly well-known for its high-quality **coffee**, and is an excellent place to buy freshly roasted beans.

Ciales lies 27km east of Lagos dos Bocas along PR-146. Use the **free parking** near the Mercado Agricola (agricultural market) building on PR-649, which runs into the center from PR-146, on the west side of town.

The Town

From the market, walk up Calle Betances towards the main plaza and you'll pass **Casa Corretjer** (Mon–Sat 8am–4pm; ⓦwww.casacorretjer.com) on the right, a library and small museum dedicated to celebrated poet and independence activist **Juan Antonio Corretjer** (1908–1985). The building really functions as more of a community center, but the first-floor museum has a painting of the artist, some of his old books, personal effects, and newspaper cuttings – call city hall in advance if you want to see it (☎787/871-3500) as the place is often closed. The **Cantata a Corretjer**, held every March in the poet's honor, features poetry contests, shows, artisans, classes for children, and troubadours.

Turn right at the plaza and walk up the main street, Calle Palmer, for a couple of blocks to the indoor market and **Paseo Aroma de Café**, really just a small street and home to the cultural center and **Museo del Café** (Mon–Fri 8am–4.30pm; free) next door (no sign). The museum is part of an ambitious community project to chart the history of coffee production on the island, and also to catalog a library of forty thousand precious documents associated with two local coffee giants: **Café Pintueles**, which operated between 1850 and 1967 – a portrait of the Spanish founder, Fernando Pintueles, is at the entrance – and **Café Cialitos**, established in 1939 and closing in 1983. The museum is run by English-speaking Pedro Maldonado, grandson of the founder of the latter company. Inside you'll find the library and a small display room containing tools, old coffee baskets, signs, a bean press, and antique coffee grinders, while old processing machinery and an aging roaster from 1928 can be viewed at the back. Enthusiastic volunteers staff the museum, some speaking English. The **ruins** of the vast Pintueles plant can still be seen on Calle Muñoz Rivera, off Calle Palmer back towards the plaza – the government may restore the site, but for now it remains abandoned.

Around 250 farmers in the area still produce coffee as part of the Cooperativa Agro-comercial, contributing to local gourmet brand **Café Cibales** (ⓦwww .cafecibales.com), sold at the museum ($5.99 for 12oz). You can also try **Finca Cialitos** (ⓣ787/807-5248, ⓦwww.fincacialitos.com), another exceptionally fine coffee (10oz for $10), produced locally. Contact friendly owner Joaquin Pastor González (ⓔjguayacan@yahoo.com) to visit the plantation and buy direct.

Eating

Restaurant options are limited in Ciales, but *Cafeteria Misitio* on the plaza sells decent coffee, sandwiches and snacks (under $10) from a small bar with a few tables, and nearby *Mi Chyn* (daily 10.30am–10pm) offers a break from Puerto Rican food with its Chinese staples, ranging $5–20. For cheap and cheerful *comida criolla*, try *Cafeteria El Nuevo Cocoloco* at the market on Calle Palmer,

The great coffee comeback

Still regarded by many connoisseurs as the home of the world's best coffee, Puerto Rico is undergoing a remarkable **coffee renaissance** after decades of stagnation. Coffee was introduced to Puerto Rico in around 1736, most likely from the French colonies of Martinique and Haiti, and boomed in the nineteenth century. In 1887, **Don Angel Agostini**, a Yauco (see p.297) resident of Corsican descent, went to Paris to begin a hugely successful marketing campaign that resulted in the Pope becoming a regular customer of Puerto Rican *café*, along with half the salons of Europe. By the time the US occupied the island in 1898, Puerto Rico was the coffee capital of the world. Disaster struck in 1899 in the form of **Hurricane San Ciriaco**, which destroyed sixty percent of the island's coffee crop. International coffee prices collapsed the same year, and with the US encouraging the production of sugar over coffee, production was slashed further. After years of consolidation the local market is now dominated by just two companies: **Grupo Jiménez** (which produces the most profitable brand, Café Yaucono) and **Garrido & Co**, but their monopoly is being challenged by an enthusiastic ensemble of small, **gourmet coffee producers**, many of which sell high-quality roasts direct from the farm (see *Puerto Rican food and drink* color section).

Puerto Rican coffee is exceptional for lots of reasons: its high quality **arabica** beans (*borbon* and *porto rico* varieties) are grown at high altitudes, watered by over one hundred inches of rain per year, while a unique blend of clay-based soils provides the crucial nutrients; micro-nutrients blown in from the Caribbean are also thought to add character.

which sells bargain ham and cheese ($1.25) and tuna sandwiches ($2.50), various *frituras* (from $1.25), and burgers ($2.50). It has a small bar-style counter and a few chairs facing the street.

Morovis

If you're really feeling hungry, make for **MOROVIS**, another hill town 14km east of Ciales via PR-145 and PR-156. *Panadería La Patria* (daily 5am–10pm) is one of the **oldest bakeries** on the island, said to have roots in 1862, and much admired for its *pan de la patita echá*, freshly braided French bread ($1.40), crunchy on the outside and pillowy soft inside. You can also order egg and ham breakfasts ($2.60), sandwiches ($3–4), roast chicken (from $4), and other assorted cakes and snacks – there are a few tables inside. You'll find the disappointingly modern premises on PR-155 in the center of the town. Squeeze your car into a space right outside or further south on the same road, where you'll find **free parking**. You can grab zesty **ice creams** from *New King Cream* on Calle Ruiz Belvis, just off the main road through town (PR-159) and a short walk from the bakery. Flavors include cookies and cream, coconut, pistachio, *maní* (peanut), *bizcocho* (biscuit), and *guineo* (green banana). Cones are $1.25–2.

The best **restaurants** in the area can be found on PR-155 south of town, many of them rustic diners set on rolling wooded hills. *Casa Bavaria* (PR-155 km 38.3, ☎787/862-7818; Thurs, Fri & Sun noon–8pm, Sat noon–10pm) is one of the more unusual places, around 8km south of Morovis in the *barrio* of Perchas. As the name suggests, the theme here is German, with an eclectic menu featuring *schweinshaxe* (pork knuckles) and hearty *goulasch* (stew), as well as classics such as *bratwurst* and *schnitzel*, and Puerto Rican favorites such as *amarillos* (fried plantains). It's a two-story modern place that doesn't look particularly German, but the views from the terrace at the back are phenomenal, stretching over clusters of *mogotes* to the north, and a verdant canopy of trees in the valley below.

Corozal

A swift 14km drive from Morovis on PR-159, **COROZAL** is the last hill town of any interest before hitting the dreary San Juan suburbs, a much busier place surrounded by karst outcrops swamped in emerald-green. Founded in 1803, the town is known as the "city of plantains" in honor of its chief crop, celebrated at the end of October at the **Festival Nacional del Plátano**, when plantain exhibitions, over sixty craft stalls, and plenty of music and dance fill the main plaza.

The town's premier attraction, however, is a small theme park 2.5km outside the center on PR-818, the **Centro Histórico Turístico del Cibuco** (Thurs–Sun 9am–5pm; $5, under 12s $3), a firm favorite with Puerto Rican families and once part of a large sugar plantation. Facing the car park is **Hacienda Aurora**, a handsome wooden mansion built between 1934 and 1940 in colonial style for the wealthy Bou family (maker of the much loved Melao Cibuco syrup). The rooms inside have been decked out with nineteenth-century furniture and also house two museums. The **Museo de La Caña de Azúcar** is an enlightening exhibition on the history of sugar cane, as well as the back-breaking process of sugar extraction in the nineteenth century, while the **Sala de la Historia de Corazal** is a collection of old photos and documents relating to the history of the town – note the bills of sale used for slaves in 1850 and the wooden bowl used to pan for gold.

Beyond the house is a kids' playground and a rather provocative bronze **statue** symbolizing Puerto Rico's creole roots: a Taíno warrior and a Spanish man holding an African slave by the chain. A trolley-bus runs through the park's fifty-acre grounds, where you can stroll on a nature trail through woods of graceful *ceiba*, *guayacán*, and *panapén* trees, see Taíno petroglyphs, and paddle boats on an artificial lake.

You won't find much in the town itself, though if you enjoy delving into island history the **Museo de la Antigua Barbería** (℡787/859-8079) on the plaza is worth checking out. This tiny barber shop, little more than a wooden hut, is wonderfully preserved in a rustic, early twentieth-century style – it's more evocative of the period than many fancier museums, but you need to call ahead to take a look. You'll find a large multi-story **parking lot** near the plaza, a **bank** (with ATM), and plenty of simple places **to eat**: *El Gran Café* is a basic cafeteria selling coffee, sandwiches, and solid Puerto Rican food (under $10).

Porta del Sol

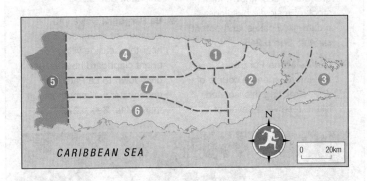

CHAPTER 5 # Highlights

* **Playa de Jobos** The northwest coast is littered with exceptional surf breaks, but this is the best for beginners, a picture-perfect bay with soft sand and consistent waves all year round. See p.225

* **Rincón** The surf capital of the Caribbean boasts killer waves, spectacular sunsets, and Isla Desecheo, an underwater paradise just offshore. See p.234

* **Mayagüez** Soak up the colonial charm of this once grand city, best known for its stock of majestic buildings, cream-filled cakes, and potent *sangría*. See p.246

* **Isla de Mona** For true adventure, spend a couple of days exploring this isolated island reserve, a haven of unique wildlife and untouched beaches. See p.260

* **Cabo Rojo** This scenic cape topped by a Spanish lighthouse looms high above pounding waves, a seductive beach, and a shimmering expanse of salt flats. See p.265

* **San Germán** Wander the beguiling streets of this remarkably well-preserved town, its mansions, churches and neat, empty plazas frozen in seventeenth-century splendor. See p.266

* **La Parguera** Delve into the labyrinth of mangrove cays near this seaside village of bright clapboard houses, or dive down to La Pared, an underwater wall smothered in marine life. See p.272

▲ Boats along the beach

Porta del Sol

When Christopher Columbus reached Puerto Rico in 1493, he staggered ashore somewhere on the balmy west coast, a sun-soaked region of glittering beaches known today as the **Porta del Sol** (ⓦwww.gotoportadelsol.com), "gateway to the sun." This is Puerto Rico's playground, with an enticing coastline rimmed by low-key resorts offering sensational snorkeling, diving, and surfing. Yet tourists rushing to the beaches miss out on a traditional hinterland steeped in colonial history, with rickety old towns, crumbling ruins, and mango trees bursting with fruit. Indeed, the past is serious business in the west, with the Puerto Rican passion for historic pedigree taken to extremes: towns compete not just for Columbus bragging rights but also for the honor of being the first or second town on the island. It's this blurring of beach and culture – crab cakes and conquistadors – that makes the region so appealing, with a diverse landscape that runs from the forest-drenched northern mountains to the arid saltpans of the south.

The **northwest coast** begins at Isabela and **Playa de Jobos**, a gorgeous arc of sand and the perfect place for surfers to get warmed up, while **Playa de Shacks** is equally renowned for **snorkeling**. **Punta Borinquen** marks the start of Puerto Rico's prime **surfing** real estate, a chain of nonstop breaks that peaks in **Rincón**, one of the world's most revered surf centers but just as inviting for divers, horseback riders, and beach bums. Inland, the French elegance of the **Palacete Los Moreau**, the delicate lace of **Moca** and the historic towns of **Aguada** and **Añasco** provide aesthetic relief from the coast, while serious divers and adventure seekers should target **Isla Desecheo** and **Isla de Mona** further offshore. **Mayagüez** is the underrated capital of the west, slowly recovering some of its former glitz and loaded with fine colonial architecture, plus the best zoo on the island. The southwest is vacation central for Puerto Ricans, dominated by unpretentious resorts with heaps of character: **Playa Joyuda** has the seafood, **Playa Buyé** and **Boquerón** the beaches, and **La Parguera** an intriguing patchwork of canals and mangrove cays. Towering **Cabo Rojo** and its nineteenth-century lighthouse guards an otherworldly landscape of lifeless salt flats and reserves thick with bird life, while **San Germán** is a colonial pearl of a city with quiet, narrow streets and cobbled plazas, perfect for idling away an afternoon.

PORTA DEL SOL

Playa de Shacks **D**
Playa de Jobos **A** **B**
Playa Montones **C**
Playa Punta Sardinera

Ramey

Aeropuerto Rafael Hernández

Isabela (459) (472) (474) (113)

Quebradillas

San Juan

Playa Crash Boat (107) (459)

Aguadilla (464)

Palacete Los Moreau

(446)

(112)

BOSQUE ESTATAL DE GUAJATACA

Balneario de Aguada (443)

Aguada (110)

Ermita Espinar

Moca

Museo del Mundillo (444) (445)

(446)

Lago de Guajataca

(115) (414) (411) (110) (404) (495)

Rincón (4412) (412) (411) (420)

Culebrinas

San Sebastián (109) (111) (435)

(2) Añasco (405) (109)

Añasco (119) (433)

Balneario Añasco (406)

Aeropuerto Eugenio María de Hostos (342) (108) (354)

Las Marías (120) (124)

Cañas (106)

Museo Eugenio María de Hostos

Mayagüez (102) (349) (105) (357) (105)

(348) Rosario

Maricao (120) (365)

(102)

Basílica Santuario Nuestra Señora de la Monserrate (119)

Hormigueros

Cupeyes

Ruta Panorámica

Joyuda (103) Guanajibo

San Germán (362) (120) (364)

Cabo Rojo (114)

(308) (102)

(312) (314)

Sabana Grande (118)

(307) (100)

(103) Lajas (117)

Boquerón (101) (116)

(305)

(121) (2)

(304)

El Combate (301) (303) La Parguera (323) (116) Ensenada

(324) (325)

Bahía de Fosforescente

N

Cabo Rojo

Santo Domingo (Dominican Republic)

Pasaje de la Mona

Ponce

0   5 km

ACCOMMODATION
Costa Dorada
  Beach Resort   **C**
Ocean Front Hotel   **A**
Pelican Reef
  Apartments   **A**
Villas del Mar Hau   **B**
Villa Montana
  Beach Resort   **D**
Villa Tropical
  Beachfront
  Apartments   **D**

The northwest coast

The windswept **northwest coast** of Puerto Rico is redolent of Hawaii's North Shore, a series of empty **beaches** and sandy dunes set between small, laid-back beach communities. In the winter, the **surfing** here rivals Rincón, and as always, you'll need a car to enjoy the best breaks. Many pros claim that the municipality of **Aguadilla** contains the finest surf on the island, though the city itself holds little appeal unless you're traveling with kids (see p.51). Towns are not major attractions here, the notable exceptions being the lace-making center of **Moca** and the cultural diversions of **Aguada**, so stick to the more rural stretches of coast, pulling over wherever you see a tempting sweep of sand.

Arrival and information

The only **international airport** in the region is **Aeropuerto Rafael Hernández** in Punta Borinquen, 5km north of Aguadilla and part of the former Ramey Air Force Base. Arrivals are primarily from the mainland US (see p.19), and there are no domestic flights.

Inside you'll find **car rental** desks (turn right as you exit), a Banco Popular ATM machine, and a café. The regional **tourism office** (daily 8am–4.30pm; ℡787/8903315) is also located here. Some **taxis** do meet flights, but it's best to call ahead if you're not renting a car: Boriquen Taxi (℡787/431-8179) is a reliable operator. Aguadilla's Blue Line (℡787/891-4550 or 787/765-7733) provides intermittent **público** services to San Juan and the surrounding area, but again you'll need to call ahead if traveling this way. **Driving** is straightforward, with most of the roads around the coast blissfully free of heavy traffic as far as Punta Borinquen and the airport, though the main highway, PR-2, is often badly congested.

Playa de Jobos and Playa Montones

The coast is littered with dazzling beaches west of Isabela, but the most appealing is **PLAYA DE JOBOS**, a sumptuous crescent of sand facing a shallow, protected bay perfect for swimming, surfing, and simply fooling around in the waves. Though the beach avoids a serious hammering, even in winter, heavier waves roll steadily into the bay throughout the year, making Jobos hands down the best **surf** beach for beginners on the island. More experienced surfers can try the right-hand reef break off nearby **Punta Jacinto** – this was the scene of the first Pro-Am Surf-Sail competition in 1989.

You can park on the *punta* itself at the east end of the beach, a bumpy, sandy patch of ground right on the water – you'll see the parking area as PR-466 emerges at the coast after cutting across the headland. The headland itself is a jagged cape of dead coral, with sweeping views across Playa Jobos and **PLAYA MONTONES** on the other side, a long expanse of honey-gold sand usually deserted during the week. From the parking lot you can clamber up to the tip of the headland, where you should spy the natural arch and blowhole known as **Foso Jacinto** (or El Pozo de Jacinto), a few precarious inches from the crashing waves below.

Not far from the beach at PR-466 km 6.3, the friendly and experienced crew at **La Cueva Submarina Dive Shop** (Mon–Sat 9.30am–5.30pm, Sun 9am–4pm; ℡787/872-1390, ⓦ www.lacuevasubmarina.com) offer **snorkeling** ($25) and various **dives** in the area from $45 (9.30am and 1.30pm), as well as diving certification courses.

Surfing the northwest coast

Northwest Puerto Rico is **surf** heaven, its numerous breaks catching more swell than Rincón during the peak Nov–March season, and some decent waves lingering through summer. The best spots lie to the north of Aguadilla in the area known as **Punta Borinquen**, host to the 1988 world surfing competition, though **Playa de Jobos** is a magnificent beach for beginners. Assuming you have a car you could base yourself at any of the beaches or towns covered below, as distances are short – make sure you visit one of the following shops if you intend to spend a lot of time in the area.

Aquatica Dive & Surf PR-110 km 10, near Gate 5, Ramey Base ☏787/890-6071, ⓦwww.aquatica.cjb.net. This small shop rents boards for $25/day and offers 90min lessons for $65. Groups of four or more pay $55 each, and intermediate coaching is $90 for 4hr.

Hang Loose Surf Shop PR-4466 km 1.2, near Playa de Jobos ☏787/872-2490, ⓦwww.hangloosesurfshop.com. Owned by legendary board-shaper Warner Vega, this shop sells and rents top-notch boards ($25/day), accessories, and gear. Private lessons are $55/hr. Tues–Sat 10am–5pm.

Playa Brava Surf Underground Calle E, no. 135, Ramey Base ☏787/431-8055, ⓦwww.playabravasurf.com. Managed by veteran surfer Tupi Cabrera, who offers lessons ($40/person, or $35 each for two) and board rentals ($20/24hr). A good choice for beginners.

El Rincón Surf/Beach Shop Ramey Shopping Center ☏787/890-3108, ⓦwww .elrinconsurfshop.com. The friendly English-speaking staff here have been selling surf gear, handing out surf maps, tide charts, and advising on current conditions, offering rentals and lessons for over thirty years. Mon–Sat 9am–6pm, Sun 11am–5pm.

Surf Zone Cliff Road Bldg 704, on the way to Playa Surfers, ☏787/890-5080, ⓦwww.surfzonepr.com. Compact but hip place for gear, owned by surf pro Rebeca Taylor – also has the best website for up-to-date surf conditions. Mon–Sat 9am–6pm, Sun 9am–4pm.

Accommodation

Playa de Jobos makes an attractive base for touring the region, with plenty of options when it comes to accommodation.

Costa Dorada Beach Resort PR-466 km 0.1 ☏787/872-7255, ⓦwww.costadoradabeach.com. Just west of Isabela, this hotel is a bit past its prime, catering primarily to Puerto Rican families on weekends. Rooms range from standard pool-side suites (❹) to the posh *Villas de Costa Dorada* (❻), fully equipped apartments with partial sea views, overlooking a palm-fringed beach.

Creach Guest Houses ☏787/412-5673, ⓦwww .creachatthebeach.com. These three fully equipped homes, with space for up to eight people (all a short drive from the beach), are only worth considering if traveling with a big group. ❸–❼

Ocean Front Hotel PR-4466 km 0.1 ☏787/872-0444, ⓦwww.oceanfrontpr.com. This budget option is just a short walk from the beach and is popular with surfers, offering simple rooms equipped with a/c, shower, cable TV (only a few channels), and small balcony. ❷, $25 extra Fri & Sat.

Pelican Reef Apartments PR-4466 km 0 ☏787/872-6518, ⓦwww.pelicanreefapartments .com. Near the *Ocean Front* but a step up in comfort, with modern, smart studios and larger one-bedroom apartments available for long or short stays. All rooms come with microwave, cable TV, fridge, a/c, and balconies that face the sea, though it's a short walk away from the actual beach. ❸

Villas del Mar Hau PR-466 km 8.9 ☏787/872-2627, ⓦwww.hauhotelvillas.com. Cluster of flower-studded *cabañas* facing their own wild stretch of sand at Playa Montones. The cheapest rooms are basic doubles, but other cabins have kitchens and the most expensive sleep six. All are decked out with slick, modern furnishings, a/c, and decent cable TV, while extras include a pool and laundry. ❺–❼

Eating and drinking

The best places **to eat** line the coastal road behind the beach, particularly the strip known as Punta Jacinto on PR-4466.

Happy Belly's PR-4466 Playa de Jobos ☎787/872-6566. This Jobos institution is little more than a large wooden shack right on the sand, serving cheap drinks and a voluminous menu of US and Puerto Rican comfort food (such as burgers, buffalo wings, fajitas, and *mofongo*) for under $10, with a raucous party scene and dancing till 4am Thur–Sat nights. You can hang out at the bar inside, but unless it's raining most people lounge on the open-air deck on the beach.

Mi Casita Tropical PR-4466 Playa de Jobos ☎787/872-5510. Next door to *Happy Belly's*, with a similar but slightly younger crowd on weekends and regular karaoke nights (Wed). The specialty is seafood, including stuffed *mofongo* and fresh fish. Closed Mon & Tues.

Ocean Front Hotel PR-4466 km 0.1 ☎787/872-0444. This smart hotel restaurant offers a surprisingly upscale menu of Puerto Rican fusion cuisine, such as dumplings de *langosta* (lobster) and grilled salmon (mains $12–20). Closed Mon & Tues.

Playa de Shacks

With a wide reef riddled with tunnels and underwater caves just yards offshore, **PLAYA DE SHACKS** is perfect for **snorkeling** and **diving**, a quiet coral beach backed by unassuming private villas. Note that while you can happily sunbathe here, swimming is difficult. To explore the reef, contact Aquatica Dive & Surf (see opposite) in Punta Borinquen: two tanks are $75 for non-certified and $60 for certified divers, while you can rent snorkeling equipment for $35 per day. You can also go **horseback riding**: Tropical Trail Rides at PR-4466 km 1.8 (daily 9am–4pm; ☎787/872-9256, ⓦwww.tropicaltrailrides.com) offers two-hour treks along the beach starting at Playa de Shacks. In January and February, when the blustery weather can make snorkeling difficult, the beach attracts **wind** and **kite surfers**.

Practicalties

Playa de Shacks is at the end of a narrow road off PR-4466 km 1.9, a short drive west of Jobos – look out for signs to Villa Montaña and Tropical Trail Rides. As you approach the sea you'll come to a crossroads: the beach is straight ahead. Note that **parking** is extremely limited at the end of the road – most of the seafront is occupied by private homes. Turn right at the junction and you'll come to *Villa Tropical Beachfront Apartments* (☎787/872-7172, ⓦwww.villatropical.com; ❹) right on the beach, all with full kitchens, cable TV, free use of snorkeling equipment, surf boards, and kayaks. Tropical Trail Rides and *Villa Montaña Beach Resort* (☎787/872-9554, ⓦwww.villamontana.com; ❻) are left at the junction, the latter a plush **resort** on the best stretch of sand, with rooms decorated in colonial plantation style. The resort's *Eclipse* **restaurant** (open daily for breakfast, lunch, and dinner), with its open terrace, is the best place to splurge on the coast, while *tapas* is served Tuesday to Saturday evenings at the hotel's "*O*" restaurant. The only other option for drinks is the *Ola Lola Garden Bar* (Fri–Sun 3–9pm), set in blooming gardens on the road coming in.

Punta Borinquen

Best known today for its network of dreamy **beaches**, plunging cliffs, and slamming winter waves, **PUNTA BORINQUEN** lies at the strategic northwest corner of Puerto Rico. Between 1939 and 1973 the headland was occupied by **Ramey Air Force Base**, home to B-52 bombers and hundreds of US airmen. Since closing (the US Coastguard retains a small station here), most of the base

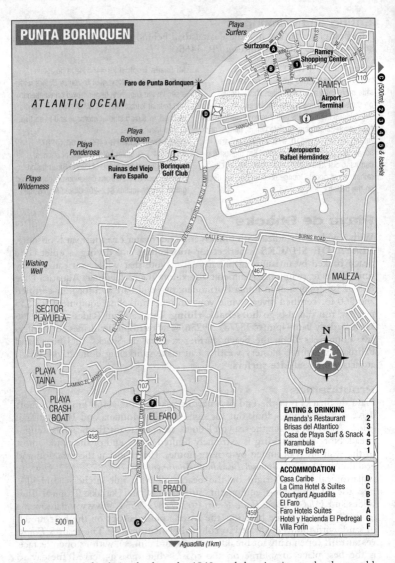

PUNTA BORINQUEN

Playa Surfers

Surfzone

Ramey Shopping Center

Faro de Punta Borinquen

RAMEY

ATLANTIC OCEAN

Airport Terminal

Playa Borinquen

Playa Ponderosa

Ruinas del Viejo Faro Españo

Borinquen Golf Club

Aeropuerto Rafael Hernández

Playa Wilderness

CALLE-E

BURNS ROAD

Wishing Well

MALEZA

SECTOR PLAYUELA

PLAYA TAINA

CAMINO-EL-MANGO

PLAYA CRASH BOAT

EL FARO

N

EL PRADO

EATING & DRINKING
Amanda's Restaurant	2
Brisas del Atlantico	3
Casa de Playa Surf & Snack	4
Karambula	5
Ramey Bakery	1

ACCOMMODATION
Casa Caribe	D
La Cima Hotel & Suites	C
Courtyard Aguadilla	B
El Faro	E
Faro Hotels Suites	A
Hotel y Hacienda El Pedregal	G
Villa Forin	F

0 ___ 500 m

▼ *Aguadilla (1km)*

housing, some of it dating back to the 1940s and showing its age, has been sold off to locals and ex-Federal employees, creating a slightly institutional-looking community that retains the layout and road system of the old base.

Heading west on PR-110 you'll enter the Ramey area through Gate Five, and here it gets a little confusing. Within the former base signs are rare, but follow traffic through the maze of streets and you'll eventually emerge on the west side and PR-107, which heads south towards Aguadilla. This is where you'll find the golf course and the airport (see p.225), which uses the main base runway. Other landmarks include the **Ramey Shopping Center**, off Belt Road in the center of the base (where you'll find Banco Popular, shops, and restaurants), and the Faro de Punta Borinquen on the coast. Constructed in 1920 at the tip of the headland, it remains a working lighthouse and is closed to visitors.

If you'd prefer to explore the area by **mountain bike**, contact Aquatica Dive & Surf (see p.226), which rents bikes for $10 per hour and $25 per day. Serious divers should check out the Puerto Rico Technical Diving Center (☏787/997-3483; ⓦ www.technicaldivingpr.com) south of the base at PR-107 km 4, which offers recreational and technical diving courses – check the upcoming events page for local dive trips (sometimes free).

Accommodation

Given the slightly odd surroundings, staying in the base is less appealing than Playa de Jobos or points south, but there are plenty of economical **hotels** and all are extremely convenient for nearby beaches. Alternatively, **rent a bungalow**: Ramey Guest Houses (☏787/890-4208; ⓦ www.rameyguesthouse.com ❸–❺) rents three vacation homes in the old base area, all with air-conditioning and cable TV.

Casa Caribe Avda Borinquen 131 (in front of the tennis club), ☏787/314-3227, ⓦ www.casacaribepr .com. This three-bedroom property (❺) comes with kitchen, a/c, washer/dryer, phone, outdoor shower, TV, barbecue, and plenty of parking. You can also rent the adjacent studio, *Casa Sunset* (❸).

La Cima Hotel & Suites PR-110 km 9.2 ☏787/890-2016, ⓦ www.lacimahotel.com. One of the best options here, just east of the base. It looks like a featureless motel from the outside, but the interior is quite hip, with contemporary art, tiled floors, and dark wood furnishings. All rooms have a/c, cable TV, and fridge, while the business center has Internet access. ❸

Courtyard Aguadilla West Parade at Belt Rd ☏787/658-8000, ⓦ www.marriott.com. This Marriot-run hotel opened in 2008 and is a more expensive but far more appealing alternative to the nearby *Faro*, with spacious rooms and plush facilities (though parking is $3/hr or $10/day). ❺–❻

Faro Hotels Suites West Parade at Wing St ☏787/890-9000, ⓦ www.farohotels.net. This is a fairly characterless business hotel behind the Ramey Shopping Center. Rooms are comfortable enough, with the usual cable TV, a/c and plenty of free parking on site, as well as an attractive pool. ❸

Playa Surfers

Some of the wildest waves can be found at **Playa Surfers**, a classic reef break rather than a beach, on the rugged northern side of the old base. The road hugs the rocky shoreline here, under a swaying line of palms, and ends at a storm-battered clump of rocks; park along the verge. Surfers is sometimes compared to the legendary break point at Lower Trestles (in California), with a long right and a short, hard-hitting left, but unless things are unusually fierce, it should be OK for beginners. Equally respected breaks nearby include Survival, Table Tops, and Roettger Reef, but even for non-surfers they make a dramatic spot for a picnic lunch. **To get here**, drive behind Ramey Shopping Center and *Faro Suites* on 4th Street, turn right on Cliff Road and pass *Surf Zone*: where the road appears to end at a residential estate, turn left through the metal fence and follow the road downhill.

Playa Borinquen to Wishing Well

The secluded **beaches** that lie west of the base offer some of the best **surf breaks** on the island, as well as the chance to laze on usually empty swathes of sand. **To get here**, take the unmarked narrow lane that cuts across the golf course from PR-107, just beyond the turning for the club house and opposite the airport runway – this winds through bunkers and sombrero palms before dropping steeply through the cliffs to the shoreline. As you near the sea you'll pass a small turnoff to **Playa Borinquen**, a soothing carpet of fine sand and ideal for swimming in the summer. The main road continues along the coast for a short distance until it's replaced by an extremely battered dirt track laced with potholes. The beach here is known as **Playa Ponderosa**, and you should be able to spot the remains of **Las Ruinas del Viejo Faro Españo** poking through the scrub – the old lighthouse was constructed in 1886 but flattened by the earthquake and tsunami of 1918. The two breaks offshore are known as **Ruinas** and the hard-to-forget **Shithouse**. More intrepid (or well-insured) drivers rattle a little further along to **Playa Wilderness**, a pro surf beach where groundswells of 30ft are possible. At the end of the track lies Playa Peña Blanca and the equally challenging **Wishing Well** break, just north of Playa Crash Boat (see below) – you'll have to return to PR-107 to reach the latter, however.

Eating and drinking

Ramey Bakery inside the Ramey Shopping Center is best for cheap cakes, coffee, and bread, while plenty of **restaurants** line PR-110 just east of the base.

Amanda's Restaurant PR-110 km 8.8 (just beyond *La Cima Hotel*), ☎787/890-7378. This is a relaxed place with a sports bar (open to 2am weekends) and spacious dining room serving upscale *cocina criolla* (mains from $10).

Brisas del Atlantico PR-110 km 7.4 (opposite the junction with PR-4466), ☎787/890-1441. This bright diner offers similar quality and prices to *Amanda's*, with a side-splitting *criollo* buffet lunch.

Casa de Playa Surf & Snack PR-110 km 7.4 ☎787/890-3351. Just next door to *Brisas*, with surf boards and gear for sale but also a small bar for sandwiches and coffee.

Karambula PR-110 ☎787/890-1392. Back on PR-110 towards the base, this is a popular roadside shack serving local staples from $4, with a small area for parking.

Aguadilla: Playa Crash Boat

Despite a spate of beautification projects along its seafront in recent years, downtown **Aguadilla** has a justly unglamorous, gritty reputation and it's the **beaches** that line the jagged coast between the city and Punta Borinquen that get most attention. **PLAYA CRASH BOAT** is the best and most accessible, with a festive atmosphere on weekends and some decent surfing.

Practicalities

The cluster of **hotels** north of downtown Aguadilla make convenient bases for the nearby beaches and northwest coast, though none is particularly special. All the hotels below have rooms with air-conditioning and cable TV. *El Faro* at PR-107 km 2.1 (☎787/882-8000, ⓦwww.farohotels.net; ❸) is a comfy but standard business hotel with pleasant gardens, while *Hotel y Hacienda El Pedregal* at Calle Cuesta Nueva, PR-111 km 0.1 (☎787/891-6068, ⓦwww.hotelelpedregal.com; ❷), is a better budget choice, with clean tiled floors, bright decor, and small balconies overlooking landscaped gardens on a hillside. Ask for a room with a whirlpool bath. *Villa Forin* at PR-107 km 2.1 (☎787/882-8341, ⓦwww.villaforin.com; ❷) is cheapish roadside motel on the other side of the highway from *El Faro*, two minutes from Crash Boat. Rooms are simple but adequate, and singles pay $20 less. The best of a fairly uninspiring bunch of **restaurants** are located within these hotels, while PR-107 is lined with fast-food chains and local bakeries.

The beach

Sandwiched between two rocky headlands and plummeting cliffs, **Playa Crash Boat** is a wide, fine stretch of sand at the end of PR-458. The concrete piers that jut into the sea here are an unsightly remnant of Ramey Air Force

Base, built in 1956 for fuel tankers, when "crash boats" (fast rescue launches) would speed out to save pilots that had overshot the runway. Today, multi-colored fishing boats are dragged up onto the sand, tables and snack stalls lodge between the palm trees, and the lively weekend scene attracts plenty of families, and sadly, a fair amount of trash. The surprisingly clear waters around the piers make for diverting if unspectacular **snorkeling**, while further offshore, an artificial reef 60–100ft down provides a greater spread of marine life for **divers** (contact Aquatica Dive & Surf – see p.226, or La Cueva Submarina Dive Shop – see p.225). Serious shredders should aim for the world-famous break to the right of the beach known as **Gas Chambers**, home to Puerto Rico's best right tube.

Palacete Los Moreau

For a welcome time out from surf and sand, head inland along PR-2 from Aguadilla to the **Palacete Los Moreau** (daily 8am–3.30pm; free; ☎787/830-2540), lording it over a swathe of parkland like a mini French castle. The house is tucked away 2–3km along PR-464 from the highway (follow the signs), and is now the artfully restored cultural center and museum for Moca municipality.

This enchanting mansion was once at the heart of Hacienda Irurena, one of Puerto Rico's largest **coffee plantations**, established by the Peugeot family in the nineteenth century. The estate was inherited by Frenchman **Juan Labadié** in 1860, but it wasn't until 1905 that the mansion you see today was complete, a grand *criollo* adaptation of French château style. Graceful balconies surround both floors, with towers and cupolas on each corner, and the whole thing is set rather majestically in a manicured garden. Known as the **Hacienda Labadié**, it became a sugar plantation after the US occupation, ensuring immortality by appearing in the 1935 best-selling novel *La Llamarada* by **Enrique Laguerre** – the house was renamed in 1993 to honor the fictional Moreau family from the book, and the author was buried in the garden on his death twelve years later. Inside, the first-floor museum contains bits and pieces related to Moca, while a more absorbing collection of black-and-white plantation photographs can be found on the second floor. The house and grounds are far more engaging than the collections on display, however, and the beautifully restored wooden floors, stairs, rails, and upstairs bedrooms give a rough idea of what it must have been like to live here.

Moca

Founded in 1772, 8km inland from Aguadilla, **MOCA** is best known for its delicate, handmade bobbin **lace** or *mundillo*, used to embellish collars and handkerchiefs, linens, pillows, bridal veils, and baby clothes. The town's *mundillo*-making roots are hazy: the craft was imported from Spain and became popular among the island's elite in the nineteenth century, when it seems to have become the established trade of the town.

The Town

Though lace-making remains an important cottage industry here, with around nine thousand primarily female lace-makers, you won't see much evidence of this on the streets: it's a fairly typical Puerto Rican country town, with a sleepy center of aging clapboard houses and newer concrete buildings. The busy main square, Plaza Don José de Quiñones, contains a small statue of female lace workers, the **Monumento a la Tejedora de Mundillo**, but is overshadowed by the pretty pink Spanish Colonial-style church. Dating from 1841, the **Iglesia**

de Nuestra Señora de la Monserrate y San Juan Nepomuceno, perches on a small hill, reached by a stone stairway framed by palms. Unless there's a service, it tends to be locked.

Eating options in town are unexceptional, and you're better off heading elsewhere.

Museo del Mundillo

To learn more about the craft and history of *mundillo* visit the **Museo del Mundillo** (Wed–Sun 9am–4pm; free; Ⓦ www.museodelmundillo.org), a short walk east of the plaza at Calle Barbosa 237 (PR-125). Housed in the old public health building dating from 1928, the modest collection of antique bobbins from nineteenth-century shirts, dresses, lace patterns, and baby clothes is primarily for aficionados, but retains a degree of quirky charm nonetheless. Labels are in Spanish only (with English leaflets), and a Spanish-only video explains more about the lace-making process. Be sure to pick up the museum's list of the **top lace-makers** in the municipality – you have to call ahead to arrange a viewing of their work, but prices are much cheaper than retail outlets. The museum is forbidden to recommend individual lace-makers, but two of the most respected are Gladys Hernández (Ⓣ787/877-2285) and Ada Hernández Vale (Ⓣ787/877-3800): the latter runs *Juliany's Mundillo Lace* (Ⓦ www.mundillomoca.com), near the plaza at Calle Américo Miranda 126, which sells clothes for adults. Enter at the Farmacia San José and ask for Ada or Mokay Hernández (Ⓣ787/487-7924).

The **best place to buy** *mundillo* nearby is *Artesanía Leonides* and *Pequeño Angelito* at Calle Blanca E. Chico 200 (Mon–Sat 9am–5.30pm, Sun noon–5pm), on the Añasco road. You can pick up lacy purses, place settings (from around $15), and cute dresses and booties for baby girls here ($30–40). Otherwise the **Festival del Mundillo** (Ⓣ787/818-0105) is held at the end of June, when stalls in the main plaza overflow with fine lace products.

Aguada and around

Most travelers speed past **AGUADA** on the way to Rincón, missing out on one of the most historically significant towns in Puerto Rico, boasting enigmatic ruins, an array of unusual snacks, and a tempting beach beyond the often traffic-choked center. While Aguada can claim to be one of the **earliest Spanish settlements** in Puerto Rico, its muddled history often blurs with that of San Germán, Añasco, and Rincón. The town claims to be the **landing site of Columbus**, celebrated each November 19 with a huge parade, and also the location of Villa Sotomayor, the antecedent of San Germán and the second oldest settlement in Puerto Rico (see p.266); both associations are disputed by scholars.

Coming from Moca (10km away) on PR-416, you can bypass the worst of Aguada's jams by taking Avenida Nativo Alers, which cuts across to PR-115 for Rincón, another 10km west.

The Town

Central Aguada has little to offer, but south of the main plaza, on Avenida Nativo Alers (just off PR-411), the **Museo Agricola Aguada** (free; Ⓣ787/868-3960) occupies the weathered former train station and contains a whimsical collection of old farm tools, a rusty train engine, and other oddly engaging bits and pieces. It's nominally open Monday to Friday 8am to noon and 1 to 4pm, but in practice you'll have to call to make an appointment. Park at the supermarket opposite.

Around Aguada

Heading west on PR-115 you'll pass the first of the region's spellbinding beaches, **Balneario Pico de Piedra de Aguada** (parking $3). Continuing west to Rincón, the **Ann Wigmore Natural Health Institute** (Ⓦ www.annwigmore .org) is dedicated to teaching the late Dr. Ann Wigmore's "Living Foods Lifestyle" through its two-week program – see the website for details. **Wiggie's Shop** (Mon–Fri 9am–4pm, Sat 10am–2pm) on site sells all sorts of health foods, books, and related products.

Ermita de Nuestra Señora del Espinar

The humble remains of the **Ermita de Nuestra Señora del Espinar** (Mon–Fri 8am–noon & 1–5pm; free), sheltered within the hushed nave of a modern church, offer a tiny window into the early, tremulous years of Spanish colonization. Like Caparra in San Juan (see p.105) these ruins are small, but unlike that abandoned settlement, Espinar is still used today, making it an extremely evocative site.

The hermitage was built by Franciscan friars in 1526 and dedicated to Nuestra Señora de la Inmaculada Concepción; destroyed by Taíno raiders in 1528, five out of the eight Spanish friars were murdered and are still regarded as martyrs. The church was rebuilt between 1590 and 1600, and today the ruins are protected within the shell of the newer tin-roof church, the pink outer walls designed to replicate its original Spanish Colonial style. All that remains are sections of crumbling stone walls around the altar, with a tree trunk sprouting from one corner, and some of the original floor tiles. Carvings of the Franciscan martyrs are on the far side.

▲ Ermita de Nuestra Señora del Espinar

The church is a short drive along PR-442 off PR-115, but has no signs – you'll see it on the right at a sharp bend in the road. The church tends to be closed throughout July and August.

Eating

Even if nothing else inspires you, Aguada's quirky **eating** options are worth a try, with ✹ *El Plátano Loco* (☎787/868-0241, ⊛www.platanoloco.com; closed Mon–Wed) top of the list. You'll find it south of town off PR-411 at km 5 – look out for the signs to "Universidad del Plátano" and turn right beyond "Parada 5." As befits the name, everything on the menu features **plantains**, the savory green banana: a bizarre but satisfying array of lasagne, pizza, sandwiches, and the *isla de plátano*, the signature *mofongo* shaped like Puerto Rico and stuffed with meat. Try the sweet *flan de plátano* for dessert.

Near the Ann Wigmore Institute, don't miss the celebrated roadside stall on PR-115 (around km 20) known as ✹ *El Original Kioskito de la 115*, a popular vendor of sweets, cakes and snacks for over 25 years. Try the *limber de coco*, frozen coconut milk cake, (or the *piña*, *uva*, *maiz*, or "cheez-cake" versions) for less than $1.

Rincón and around

Hemmed in between the coast and a ridge of lush, flower-strewn hills, **RINCÓN** has managed to hang on to its small town roots, despite being one of the most popular resorts in Puerto Rico and justly celebrated for its *bellos atardeceres*, beautiful sunsets. Perhaps best known to outsiders as the premier **surfing** destination in the Caribbean, its northern *barrio* of **Puntas** is a maze of narrow lanes and steep slopes dotted with chilled-out guesthouses, bars, and cafés, all booming thanks to "surf tourism." US expats (many of them surfers) dominate businesses in the area, providing an easy-going, international feel similar to Vieques. In contrast, the southern beaches of the **Caribbean Coast** area are lined with gleaming beach resorts, condos and hotels attracting thousands of overseas and Puerto Rican sun-seekers. This area in particular has been experiencing a mini-construction boom, prompting some disapproving locals to refer to the town as "**Rin-condo**". Development has not gone unprotested however, and thanks to environmental groups, particularly the local chapter of the **Surfrider Foundation**, Rincón is at the forefront of ecological activism on the island.

In addition to some serious surfing, you can do just about any outdoor activity here, with nearby **Isla Desecheo** offering some of the best **diving** in the region, and **horseback riding** along the beach for those who prefer to stay dry. Be warned: during the **winter season** hordes of surfers descend on the town, and at this time Rincón can seem more like a small city, its tiny roads often jammed with traffic. The blazing **summer** months are dominated by Puerto Rican vacationers who tend to huddle in the southern resorts, and many of the expat-run activities go into hibernation – with the waves flattening off, this is the best period for **snorkeling** and **swimming**.

Some history

Rincón is one of several municipalities to have a decent claim on **Columbus**'s first encounter with Puerto Rico in 1493: the admiral may have waded ashore at Playa Córcega, known for its freshwater springs. Although the word Rincón means "corner" (describing the shape of the headland it occupies), the town is thought to take its name from one of the first Spanish landowners in the area,

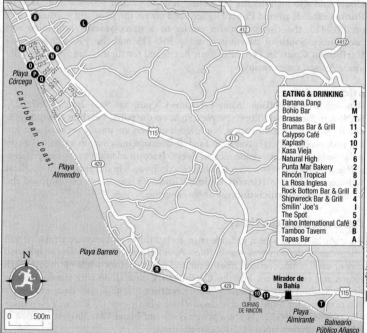

RINCÓN

Aguada, Aguadilla & Moca ▲

Isla Desecheo (19 km) ◄

Sandy Beach Ⓐ
Pools Beach
Ⓑ
Spanish Wall
ⒹⒺ
Ⓕ
● BONUS
Ⓖ
BARRIO PUNTAS
DOMES TRAIL
CSN A
CSN B
Playa Domes ▲
Area Recreativa del Faro
Ⓗ
4413
413
②ⓘⓣ
Indicators Beach
③
Playa Marias
Sunset Coast
4400
115
413
Ⓙ
115
Steps Beach
⑤④
Black Eagle Marina
JOSÉ PÉREZ
Centro Cultural de Rincón
414
Sunset Village ⓘ
N
Balneario de Rincón
Mercado Venta al Mar
⑥
DOWNTOWN
⑦
MUSCO RIVERA
115
412
Ⓚ
0   500m

MAP CONTINUES BELOW

ACCOMMODATION

Bello Horizonte	H
Beside the Pointe Inn	B
Bunger's Bon-Accord Inn	F
Caracol Ché Private Retreat	C
Casa Isleña Inn	A
Casa Serena	O
Casa Verde Guest House	E
Coconut Palms Guest House	P
Horned Dorset Primavera Hotel	R
Lazy Parrot	I
Lemon Tree Oceanfront Cottages	S
Pool's Beach Cabañas	D
Rincón Beach Resort	T
Rincón Inn	N
Rincón Surf & Board	G
Pineapple Inn	Q
La Rosa Inglesa	J
Surf 787	L
Tropical Treehouse	K
Villa Cofresi	M

⑧
Ⓛ
412
ⓂⓄ
⑨
Ⓝ
ⓅⓄ
CS16 CS15 CS20
CS13
CS12
CS11
CS10 CS9 CS7 CS6 CS5
Playa Córcega
Caribbean Coast
115
411
Playa Almendro
429
Playa Barrero
Ⓡ
N
Ⓢ
429
Mirador de la Bahía
⑩⑪
CURVAS DE RINCÓN
Playa Almirante
Balneario Público Añasco
Añasco & Mayagüez ▶
0   500m

EATING & DRINKING

Banana Dang	1
Bohío Bar	M
Brasas	T
Brumas Bar & Grill	11
Calypso Café	3
Kaplash	10
Kasa Vieja	7
Natural High	6
Punta Mar Bakery	2
Rincón Tropical	8
La Rosa Inglesa	J
Rock Bottom Bar & Grill	E
Shipwreck Bar & Grill	4
Smilin' Joe's	I
The Spot	5
Taíno International Café	9
Tamboo Tavern	B
Tapas Bar	A

5

PORTA DEL SOL

235

Don Gonzalo Rincón. He allowed a small community to grow here in the sixteenth century, dubbed Santa Rosa de Rincón in his honor. The village finally received *villa* status in 1771, but remained a sleepy backwater well into the twentieth century. In the late 1950s, construction of the exclusive beachfront community of *Sea Beach Colony* (near Playa Córcega), followed in the 1960s by *Villa Cofresí*, the first hotel, heralded the arrival of mass tourism. The **1968 world surfing contest** cemented Rincón's growing reputation as a surf center, the area north of the town swiftly evolving into a relaxed beachside community increasingly inhabited by foreigners. Today it's the tourist trade as much as the lifestyle which lures outsiders, the majority of whom live in peaceful coexistence with Puerto Rican locals; you'll hear an easy mix of English and Spanish on the streets, and with a population of just 15,000, Rincón is now the richest municipality outside Greater San Juan.

Arrival, orientation, and information

The nearest airport to Rincón is at Aguadilla (see p.225), about 25km and thirty minutes drive to the north – San Juan is 150km and around two and a half hours by car. Most visitors drive here, but depending on the time of year and on what day you arrive, the roads into Rincón can be frustratingly congested, particularly around Aguada and Añasco. PR-115 is the main route from PR-2 heading south or north, making a loop along the coast.

Downtown Rincón, known simply as *pueblo*, is the busy commercial heart of the area, though the *barrios* of most interest to visitors lie several kilometers to the north and south along the coast. These have recently been given touristy but easy to remember designations by the local authorities. North of downtown, along PR-413, the most venerated stretch of surf has been dubbed the **Sunset Coast**, and also includes the lighthouse and old nuclear power station. **Barrio Puntas** extends around Punta Higüero and covers the plunging northern coast off PR-413, the closest Rincón comes to a stereotypically bohemian surf community. South of downtown, along PR-115 and the PR-429 loop, the **Caribbean Coast** incorporates some hotels and restaurants that are technically inside Añasco municipality.

Information

Rincón's **tourist office** (Mon–Fri 8am–4.30pm, Sat 9am–2pm; ☎787/823-5024) is in the Sunset Village complex, right on the public beach in downtown. It doesn't have much information, but English speakers are usually on hand and you can park nearby. When it comes to English-language information sources, Rincón is the best served of any destination in Puerto Rico: in addition to the free *El Coqui of Rincón* newspaper (@www.coquirincon.com), you'll find a plethora of excellent websites, notably the **Rincón Online Guide** (@www.rinconpr.com), and the official **tourism association** site at @www.rincon.org.

Accommodation

Rincón's laid-back vibe is genuine enough, but this is no backpacker paradise and prices can be steep in peak season (Nov-April). **Barrio Puntas** offers an informal mix of small hotels, cottages, apartments, and private houses, while more traditional resorts and beach hotels line the **Caribbean Coast**, along with condos, beachfront villas, and inns. As always, consider **renting** private homes or apartments if you're staying for more than five days or have a big group: try Property Resources West (☎787/420-5227, @www.prwest.com) and Island West Properties (☎787/823-2323, @www.rinconrealestateforsale.com).

Barrio Puntas

Amelia's House Vista Linda Rd 4133 (PR-413 km 4.3) ☏786/546-6653, ⓦwww.ameliahousepr.com. This gorgeous rental home opened in 2008, with four bedrooms, three bathrooms, and a rooftop ocean-view terrace with spa. Extras include a flat-screen TV with cable and stereo with iPod connection. Minimum three nights. ❼

Bello Horizonte PR-413 km 4 ☏787/890-3584, ⓦwww.a1vacations.com. This private three-bedroom hilltop home is one of the most inviting rental properties in Rincón, tastefully furnished and painted with soothing orange and aqua shades. The small pool and patio are perfect for lounging, and it's just a short drive from the beach. Comes with two bathrooms, satellite TV, and half an acre of gardens, just off the road. ❼–❾

Beside the Pointe Inn PR-413 Interior km 4.4, ☏787/823-8550, ⓦwww.besidethepointe.com. Basic inn accommodation on two floors above the *Tamboo Tavern*: it's ideal for Sandy Beach but can be noisy at night. Rooms are spacious and airy with plenty of murals and tropical colors to brighten things up, and all units come with a/c, cable TV, fridge, and bathroom. ❸

Bunger's Bon-Accord Inn PR-413 Int km 3.3 ☏787/823-2525, ⓦwww.bonaccordinn.com. Most stylish hotel in Rincón, with a minimalist contemporary design and ten rooms with pool or sea views, a/c, cable TV, and fridge, though the coolest features are the all-white deck and pool, funky metallic furniture, and glass tables. The restaurant also has excellent Sunday brunch from 10am. This is one for couples: no kids under 12. ❹

Casa Isleña Inn PR-413 km 4.8 ☏787/823-1525, ⓦwww.casa-islena.com. One of the newest properties in the area, with an attractive pool terrace and upscale beach villas overlooking the ocean. Rooms are light and breezy, with shiny red Mexican tiled floors, wooden beds, and cable TV. Rates usually include breakfast. ❺–❻

Casa Verde Guest House PR-413 km 4 ☏787/823-3756, ⓦwww.enrincon.com. Completely renovated in 2007, just back from Sandy Beach, with eight simple but comfy, spotlessly clean rooms and the *Rock Bottom Bar & Grill* on site: the studios are a real bargain off-season, while the three-bedroom apartments with kitchen (❼) are a good deal for groups. ❷–❸

Lazy Parrot Inn PR-413 km 4.1, ☏787/823-5654, ⓦwww.lazyparrot.com. Popular hotel with eleven rooms whimsically dressed in bright tropical colors, duvets, and art, all with a/c, cable TV, fridge, and spotless tiled floors. Breakfast is included (8–10am). Perched high on La Cadena ridge, 5km from town, its lush back terrace slopes down to a restaurant, pool, and *Smilin' Joe's* bar – the parrot lives in a cage at the entrance. Can be pricey, but will do deals for longer stays in summer. ❹–❺

Pool's Beach Cabañas off PR-413 ☏787/823-8135, ⓦwww.poolsbeach.com. Mid-range accommodation for a mostly hardcore surf crowd, off the narrow road that fronts Pool's Beach – turn left at Puntas Bakery on PR-413. Choose from one-, two-, and three-bedroom cabins with a/c, kitchenettes, and basic cable TV. Extras include a laundry and even a small pool with bar and grill. Great weekly rates. ❻

Rincón Surf & Board off PR-413 ☏787/823-0610, ⓦwww.surfandboard.com. Laid-back guesthouse doubling as surf school managed by Dez and Garret Bartelt, and the only place with dorms ($20). Other rooms are simple but equipped with a/c and TV, all set in a ramshackle but comfy three-story clapboard house high in the hills above Sandy Beach. Note that it can be tricky to find, and parking is tight. From PR-413 heading west, take the lane next to the *Vista de la Bahia* signs, past Colmado Bonet. ❷

La Rosa Inglesa PR-413 Int ☏787/823-4032, ⓦwww.larosainglesa.com. The winding, potholed lane up to this enticing B&B is rewarded by mind-blowing views of the coast and the best breakfast in town. The hilltop property has just three suites with satellite TV, sparkling tile floors, and basic kitchenettes, 1.5km from PR-413: the road up starts opposite the turnoff to Playa Escalera, and rejoins PR-413 on the other side of Puntas, just beyond the Speedway gas station. ❹

Tropical Treehouse ☏541/482-6357 or 787/365-3296, ⓦwww.tropical-treehouse.com. The most original and eco-friendly lodging in Puerto Rico is a real jungle fantasy, a central bamboo treehouse (that sleeps eight) and two separate bamboo "hooches" sheltered by mango trees. Once a private home, the *casa de bambu*, the Scheer family now rent out the main house (❼) with two bathrooms, a kitchen, two doubles, and two singles, and the treehouses with bathrooms and basic cooking facilities (❹).

Caribbean Coast

Coconut Palms Guest House Calle 8, no. 2734 ☏787/823-0147. This modest white villa offers rooms right on the beach, without the glitz or fuss of a resort: it's set in a quiet residential area, with plenty of terrace space for lounging and a garden full of palms, while the beach is narrow but usually empty. ❸

Horned Dorset Primavera Hotel PR-429 km 3 ☎787/823-4030, ⓦwww.horneddorset.com. Exclusive resort of Mediterranean-style villas set in cliff-top gardens overlooking a very thin strip of secluded beach. Thanks to a recent upgrade, guests can choose between "non-electronic" rooms and suites with all the extras: LCD TVs, iPod docks and Bose speakers, Internet, and phones. All rooms feature luxurious old world Puerto Rican interiors, but this remains a pricey option, even for the Caribbean. ❾

Lemon Tree Oceanfront Cottages PR-429, km 4.1 ☎787/823-6452, ⓦwww.lemontreepr.com. The best thing about these apartments is their waterside location, with spacious terraces literally hovering right over an extremely peaceful stretch of sand (it also has an on-site PADI dive center). Rooms are fitted out with flat-screen TVs, contemporary furniture, and soothing lights, the only gripe being occasional problems with hot water and the relatively pricey rates. ❻

Pineapple Inn Calle 11, no. 2811 ☎787/823-1430, ⓦwww.thepineappleinn.net. Charming family-owned place, with extra-helpful owners and cute pool, just behind a beach shaded by a giant mango tree. Prices differ according to room size, but all contain plenty of amenities, including a handy microwave, and there's fresh coffee, pastries, and fruit for breakfast. ❸–❺

Rincón Beach Resort PR-115 km 5.8, Almirante Beach ☎787/589-9000, ⓦwww.rinconbeach.com. Another exclusive seaside resort that looks like a modern condo, with plush facilities and swanky

infinity pool overlooking a beach that's effectively private to the hotel. It's just off the main road, but a bit of a trek from Rincón's main drag. Rooms come with smart antique furniture, giant beds, tiled floors, and lots of drapes. ❼

Rincón Inn Avda Pedro Albizu Campos 2231 (PR-115 km 11.6) ☎787/823-7070, ⓦwww.rinconinn.com. Best of the budget options, with comfy dorm beds (four per room) as well as barebones singles and doubles – stay more than two nights for discounts. All rooms come with a/c, basic cable TV, bathrooms, free use of Internet, cheap surfboards ($12/day), and the small pool, making this exceptionally good value, though the road can be noisy. ❷

Surf 787 off PR-115 (right at *Angelo's*) ☎787/448-0968, ⓦwww.surf787.com. This spanking new guesthouse doubles as surf school and resort, with packages including full board and lessons – you can also just stay at one of the four simple but clean and spacious rooms (one with private bath), cooled by mountain breezes, and enjoy the stellar ocean views. ❹–❺

Villa Cofresi PR-115 km 12.3 ☎787/823-2450, ⓦwww.villacofresi.com. Grand dame of Rincón resorts and still popular with Puerto Rican families, though it's struggling to match the posh new resorts nearby. Rooms are large but standard motel fare, though most bathrooms have been renovated. The staff is helpful and you get access to a lovely beach and lively bar. If you're looking for a resort-style experience, this is good value out of season or on weekdays. ❹

The town and beaches

Downtown Rincón has little to offer in the way of sights, and the real allure lies along the coast. Most of Rincón's **beaches** are easy to find: just look for the whale-shaped signs. Assuming you have transport it's not hard to get around, and though the narrow and generally unmarked lanes of Puntas can be confusing at first, you won't get lost if you keep heading downhill.

Downtown

The local government has some ambitious plans to boost the appeal of **downtown Rincón**, primarily by creating the **Mercado Venta al Mar**, a small plaza for craft stalls and restaurants, facing the sea and those stunning sunsets. You'll find it where PR-115 turns inland, on the edge of central Rincón. The town has little else to recommend it, however, with shops and services lining congested PR-115 from for several kilometers south, and parking difficult. If you turn off PR-115 and keep following the coast from Mercado Venta al Mar, you'll pass the **Balneario de Rincón** (free parking), the town's modest public beach, backed by a strip of condos. At the far end, **Sunset Village** is a modern shopping center which contains the main **tourist office** (see p.236), a decent seafood restaurant, and water sports and beach rentals (see p.240). The beach isn't very wide but is popular with families for swimming and snorkeling, has

Rincón is surf central in winter, though come in summer (May–Sept) and the waves are a lot calmer. To avoid the crowds, aim for September to October, when the surf starts to get rough, and the town is virtually deserted – you'll get the best deals at hotels at this time, though some places do shut down. **Beginners** should start at María's Beach or Parking Lot, though when the swell gets up, even these require caution: surfers die almost every year in Rincón. Unsurprisingly, the town is loaded with surf **instructors** and **surf shops**: learners should also consider *Surf 787* and *Rincón Surf & Board* (see p.237). The latter is a good place to make friends, though classes tend to be bigger here in peak season, so it doesn't appeal to everyone.

Elsewhere, entertaining (and qualified) teachers include Ramses Morales (☏787/617-4731, ⊛www.surflessonspuertorico.com), and Melissa Taylor, a certified lifeguard and surf instructor (☏787/823-3618 or 904/315-4304) who runs lessons from $30/hr with groups of a maximum four people.

At Playa María's, **Desecheo Surf & Dive Shop** (☏787/823-0390, ⊛innsurfanddiveshop .com) is usually open daily 9am–7pm, for rentals of snorkel gear ($10/4hr, $15/8hr, $20/24hr), and short, long, fun, and boogie boards from $10–20 for 4hr, $15–25/8hr and $20-30/24hr. **Surf lessons** are $45 per hr, per person, plus tax.

Hotwavz Surf Shop (daily noon–6pm) was opened by veteran surfer Cindie Rice in 1989 as part of *Calypso Café* (see p.243) and sells all the surf and beach accessories as well as **renting** surf and boogie boards (all $8 first hr, $2/hr thereafter; 11am–6pm $15; 24hr $20). *Rincón Inn* (see opposite) also rents shortboards ($12/day guests, $20 non-guests).

plenty of parking, toilets, and changing rooms with showers, and is normally deserted on weekdays.

Just outside the center, at PR-413 km 0.2, the **Centro Cultural de Rincón** (☏787/823-5120) acts as the local history museum (nominally Tues & Thur 9.30am–2.30pm, Sat & Sun 9am–2pm). You need to call in advance to make sure it's open or ask the tourist office to make an appointment, though the collection is only worthwhile for real history enthusiasts: a small ensemble of Taíno artifacts dug up from nearby condo building sites, and old maps and documents outlining the town's Spanish past.

Steps Beach and the Reserva Marina Tres Palmas

Heading north from downtown, PR-413 shoots towards the Sunset Coast, passing La Marina and then Playa Escalera or **Steps Beach**, named for the unsightly stub of concrete steps washed up on the sands. In winter this is prime surf country, with both Steps and the adjacent outside break of **Tres Palmas** generating some of the meanest waves around, with 20-foot swells over a rocky reef bottom. In summer the beach is much calmer, ideal for **snorkeling** the precious waters of the **Reserva Marina Tres Palmas**. Established in 2004 after years of local activism, the reserve stretches along the coast from La Marina to Dogman's Beach, protecting its endangered banks of **elkhorn coral**. Essentially, this means **no fishing**, in addition to things you shouldn't be doing anywhere: littering, damaging or touching corals, and collecting anything from the reef. You can swim, snorkel, surf, and dive in the reserve, as long as you stick to these rules.

In addition to the dominant elkhorn, you'll see clumps of brain, star, and mustard hill corals along a dense reef that begins about 15ft offshore and extends seaward 60 to 100ft. Fish life is gradually increasing, and the deeper you get the more sea fans, soft corals, and shellfish you'll see, as well as the occasional hawksbill and leatherback **sea turtle**.

Sunset Coast

The biggest, gnarliest winter waves slam into the **Sunset Coast** north of Steps Beach, where the Atlantic meets the Caribbean at Rincón's "corner", the **Punta Higüero**. The action takes place off PR-4413, a short, clearly signposted spur of PR-413 which dead-ends at the old power station, 2.5km from downtown. Surf central is **Playa María's** behind the *Calypso Café*, a reef break with long, fast waves, and though it can get rough, usually OK for beginners because of its depth. Just to the south is the break known as **Dogman's**, named after the dog-loving old man who once lived here and for experienced surfers only. In summer things are completely different, with María's becoming a gentler place to soak up the sun.

Area Recreativa del Faro

Drive a little further and you'll reach Rincón's beloved lighthouse, the **Faro de Punta Higüero**, built by the Spanish in 1892 and reconstructed in 1922 after the big earthquake and tsunami (see p.362). Today it's part of the **Area Recreativa del Faro** (daily 8am–midnight; free), which was given a comprehensive $2m facelift in 2007. The unstaffed *faro* is something of a local landmark, though it's fairly stubby and not particularly impressive – the lighthouse is still in use so the inside is closed, but the surrounding gardens and low-rise cliffs make ideal viewing points for the surfers at Domes (right) and Indicators (left), and if you're lucky, **humpback whales** (in the winter). With plenty of **free parking** on site, you can leave your car and head off to nearby beaches.

Just below the lighthouse is one of the most famous surf breaks in Rincón, known as **Deadman's** for the jagged rocks jutting out from the cliffs, while **Indicators** is to the left, another surf favorite but strewn with pebbles

Activities and watersports

In addition to surfing, Rincón offers **diving**, **snorkeling**, yacht **cruises**, humpback **whale-watching** (Jan–April, but peaks in Feb), **fishing**, and **horseback riding** along the beaches. Many outfits are based at Black Eagle Marina (or just La Marina) off PR-413, now almost completely silted up with sand – boats depart from a concrete slip nearby.

Taino Divers at 564 Black Eagle Rd (La Marina, ☎787/823-6429, ⊛www.tainodivers .com) is open from 8am and offers daily **scuba** excursions to **Isla Desecheo** (see p.243) and whale-watching (two-tank dives $109, snorkeling $75). Moondog Charters (☎787/823-3059, ⊛www.moondogcharters.com) offers a similar line up of activities, plus fishing excursions and trips to Mona and further afield. For a pleasant day of **cruising** by catamaran, contact Katarina Sail Charters (La Marina, ☎787/823-7245, ⊛www.sailrinconpuertorico.com; from $60). **Fishing** enthusiasts should seek out Makaira Fishing Charters (☎787/823-4391, ⊛www.makairafishingcharters.com), which runs half- ($575) or full-day ($850) excursions. You'll find Capital Water Sports X-treme Rentals (☎787/431-2741) at Sunset Village on the public beach downtown, renting kayaks and windsurfers and offering half-day dive trips ($50 for two tanks) and snorkeling ($35) into the Reserva Marina Tres Palmas for six people at a time.

Landlubbers can try Pintos R Us (☎787/361-3639), which organizes daily **trail rides** on high-spirited Paso Fino horses; find them opposite the turnoff to La Marina on PR-413. **Yoga** fans should check out the **Secret Garden** (☎787/431-2962, ⊛www .yogainparadise.net) at PR-429 km 3.7. You can usually drop in for classes ($25), but check times first. Finally, for $55 you can zip above the waves with Flying Fish Parasail (daily 9am–5pm; ☎787/823-2359, ⊛www.parasailpr.com).

▲ Playa Domes

and usually deserted in summer. Experienced surfers should make for **Point**, literally at the Punta Higüero, where you'll find consistently heavy but highly unpredictable waves.

Playa Domes

Beyond the lighthouse, PR-4413 eventually ends at **Playa Domes**, named after the dome of the **decommissioned nuclear power plant** looming behind it, and another legendary surf break: it's also one of the most crowded beaches, as the waves are normally very consistent. Often littered with seaweed and bits of trash, Domes nevertheless remains popular for swimming in the summer, and there's usually enough space for parking.

Hard to believe given its precious natural surroundings, but the nuclear plant, also known as **BONUS** ("Boiling Nuclear Superheater"), was a sort of experiment, a prototype nuclear station built in 1960-64. Decommissioned by 1970 after technical difficulties terminated operations, many contaminated materials were simply entombed in concrete on site, and additional cleanup activities were conducted in the 1990s and early 2000s. After a long wait, the main dome should be open as a science center and museum in 2009, tentatively entitled the **Museo Nuclear** and **Museo Rincón**, recounting the history of the station and the town, as well as housing displays on electric and nuclear power – some locals grumble that the delay in opening is due to continued radioactivity at the site, despite an official US Department of Energy report in 2003 concluding it was safe.

Nearby is Rincón's "secret beach," **Spanish Wall**, approached from Domes on the **Domes Trail**, though this is slated to be resurfaced as part of the controversial Bike Trail project (see box, p.242).

Barrio Puntas

Beyond Punta Higüero, PR-413 climbs into the hills above Rincón's alluring northern **beaches**, a labyrinth of lanes known as **Barrio Puntas**. It's not quite Goa, but the low-rise community that clings to the slopes all the way down to the shore exudes a tropical languor wholly distinct from the downtown area. The **beach breaks** here are perfect for beginners, though the swells can really thicken up in winter and it pays to seek local advice before paddling offshore.

Pools Beach is at the western end of Puntas, the first beach you come to if you turn down the hill at the *Puntas Bakery* on PR-413. Pools is sandy and relatively calm, so ideal for swimming and snorkeling: park on the road and climb down a small rise to get to the beach. To the right, the jagged headland known as **Siete Barrasos** is where pirate Roberto Cofresí (see p.360) supposedly carved a map locating his seven stashes of loot, while beyond here is **Sandy Beach**, the main Puntas strip, where most of the action takes place. With a sandy bottom, it's justifiably enticing for beginner surfers, but be careful – it has a brutal undertow and a steep drop-off. The beach can get trashy at times, but is one of the widest in town and a mellow place to simply loll in the sun. Sandy Beach ends at **Parking Lots** (in front of *Casa Isleña*), another fine and less crowded spot for beginner surfers, with waves breaking over a flat reef. Further on, **Antonio's Beach** was named after the owner of the land that borders the coast. It tends to be much quieter here, with just the odd sunbather or beachcomber looking for sea glass. Finally, **River Mouth** is a thinner stretch of sand at the eastern end of Puntas, location for the new *Punta del Mar Beach Resort*. Families with small kids should wander out here to swim or paddle in the inviting tidal pools on the beach.

Caribbean Coast

South of downtown, the **Caribbean Coast** is far calmer, marked instead by long swathes of palm-lined beaches and serene turquoise waters, perfect for lazing, swimming, and a variety of watersports. You can access **Playa Córcega** at *Villa Cofresí*, though a better place to spend an afternoon is **Playa Almendro**, off PR-429 just after it splits from PR-115 – look for the blue whale sign next to the Sol y Playa condo. Named after almond trees nearby, the beach is wide and usually clean, the favorite haunt of local families enjoying the gentle waves and palms in between the condos. It can be a squeeze, but you can usually park at the end of the road.

Back on PR-115, just beyond the collection of restaurants at km 6.7, the road passes the **Mirador de Añasco** (daily 7am–6pm; free), also known as the **El Mirador de la Bahía**, a three-story lookout tower over Añasco Bay. The tower is often locked up despite the listed opening times, but it's still worth stopping to gaze over the glassy waters of the bay, distant Mayagüez, and the hazy mountain-choked interior on the other side.

A Rincónvenient Truth

Rincón might seem like a tie-dye tropical paradise, but trouble's brewing under those drooping coconut palms. The gradual expansion of Rincón over the years – the building of more hotels and condos – is nothing new, but many in the community feel that a tipping point has been reached. The qualities that make Rincón such a success – the blend of small-town, relaxed attitudes with comfortable, modern facilities – are being jeopardized. Projects that have been floating in the pre-approval stage include **condos** and **hotels** near Steps Beach; the much-hated **Sandy Beach Apartments project**; the building of ecologically damaging **seawalls**; and the even more vilified **Rincón Bike Path**. This project has garnered particularly harsh opprobrium because on the surface it seems like such a decent, eco-friendly idea. Not so say critics, who have set up a web campaign dubbed the **Rincónvenient Truth** (W rinconbikepath.blogspot.com): slated to link downtown with Playa Domes (6.6km), the path was initially expected to be more like a paved road, actually harming the beaches, limiting beach access and damaging water quality. And the price tag of $17.3m does seem a tad excessive. Opposition has been led by local community groups, fishermen, and the Surfrider Foundation – a less damaging version of the path is now expected, but visit the blog or W www.surfrider.com (go to the Rincón chapter page) to learn more.

If you're looking for a wider beach with easier access and more facilities, drive on to the **Balneario Público Añasco** (daily 8am–5pm; parking $3) at Tres Hermanos, a sleepy village at PR-401 km 1, off PR-115, a few kilometers beyond the *mirador*. Usually empty on weekdays, it's a dazzling stretch of sugary sand, the Caribbean feel augmented by lilting palm trees and striking views across the bay towards the hills of Rincón – you can also **camp** here ($10–17).

Isla Desecheo

Clearly visible around 19km off the coast of Rincón, **Isla Desecheo** is a barren 370-acre hunk of rock that became a national wildlife refuge in 1983, off-limits to casual visitors. The real draw lies beneath the sapphire waters that surround the island, an underwater wonderland with consistent 100-150ft visibility, open for **diving** and **snorkeling**. Amidst the shimmering corals, swim-through tunnels, and caverns just offshore you'll spot nurse sharks, giant lobster, and a plethora of tropical marine life: porcupine fish, spiky scorpion fish, and schools of flounder, snappers, and triggerfish. Sea fan gardens shelter eel and turtles, while the celebrated dive site known as Yellow Reef comprises a mesmerizing underwater pinnacle teeming with activity. Boats take around 45 minutes to reach the island – see p.240 for details.

Eating and drinking

Most **restaurants** in Rincón double as bars ranging from simple Puerto Rican canteens to American-style diners with full international menus. The scene gets lively during peak season, fuelled by an amicable mix of locals and tourists, though things quieten down considerably in the summer. The coolest surf bars and cafés lie, not surprisingly, in **Puntas** or along the **Sunset Coast**, while **downtown** and especially along PR-115 is where you'll find all the chains and a cheaper range of options. On the **Caribbean Coast**, head for the cluster of restaurants on the hilltop at PR-115 km 7 (known as **Las Curvas de Rincón**), perfect for cheap snacks, spectacular views, and meeting locals – there's also a choice of upmarket restaurants along the shore. For **self-catering**, *Econo* supermarket (Mon–Sat 7am–9pm, Sun 11am–5pm) is on PR-115 just south of downtown.

Downtown

Kasa Vieja c/Union 164. Cozy dive bar in the center of town, a wooden clapboard house with plenty of character, popular with expats hoping to catch the latest sports event from the mainland. Open most days, but hours can be erratic. Happy hours 4–7pm.
Natural High c/Sol 99 (PR-115 km 14.3) ☎787/823-1772, ⊛www.naturalhighcafe.com. This juice bar and café is currently the only organic restaurant in town. Try the mouthwatering smoothies, salads, and soups, or more filling Thai green curry, veggie BLT sandwich, and items from the zesty "raw and living foods" menu. Prices are set daily, but mains start at around $7. Closed Wed.
Shipwreck Bar & Grill 564 Black Eagle Rd, La Marina ☎787/823-578, ⊛www.rinconshipwreck .com. This large shack-like place near the marina is becoming a Rincón institution, with an open-air deck and fabulous pig roast on Sundays. At other times try the local fish specials, or indulge in the $2 rum punch and beers at happy hour (3–6pm). Closed Tues & Wed.

🏃 **The Spot** La Marina ☎787/823-3510. This funky waterside restaurant is best after dark, when flaming tiki torches and crashing waves accompany exceptional dishes such as mahi with a canela almond crust ($24), and the crispy chicken-breast paella ($24). Finish off with a seasonal dessert, freshly made on site. Tends to close in the summer months.

Sunset Coast

🏃 **Calypso Café** PR-4413, Playa María's ☎787/823-1626. Favorite surfer bar just off the beach, the terrace and palm-shaded veranda making for a classic Caribbean hangout. The legendary happy hours run 5–7pm to take in the vivid sunsets, with the special calypso rum punch just $2.50. Fri & Sat see live music and dancing 10pm–2am, with full moon parties every month, and you can order a range of grilled snacks throughout the day.

Barrio Puntas

Banana Dang PR-413 km 4.1 ⓦwww.bananadang .com. New coffee house near *Lazy Parrot*, serving the best organic coffee and tea in town, and scrumptious banana smoothies from $2. You can also use the Internet here. Closed Tues.

Punta Mar Bakery PR-115 km 4.1. Next to *Lazy Parrot* and the best bet for a cheap bun, cake, or snack in this part of *Puntas*, especially in the early morning ($1–3). Also sells freshly-baked bread (ask for the *pan de agua*).

Rock Bottom Bar & Grill *Casa Verde Guest House* ☏787/823-3756. Another surfer stalwart, a "treehouse-style" bar offering different themes every night: Wed is margarita madness ($3), Thurs is jam night, and on Sun there's surf videos and *sangría* pitchers for $16. The menu of finger-licking bar snacks like chili cheese fries ($7.95) is irresistible, and you can build your own burger ($7.95).

🏃 **La Rosa Inglesa** off PR-413 ☏787/823-4032, ⓦwww.larosainglesa.com. Best place for a full breakfast in Rincón (and possibly Puerto Rico) at the B&B that bakes its own bread, fries bubble and squeak, and stuffs its own sausages. The winding ride up is rewarded with a fabulous menu: Eggs Benny Hill (eggs Benedict with salmon, $9), the Full Monty (full English, eggs, bacon, sausage, bubble and squeak; $7), and classic American with pancakes ($6). See p.237 for directions.

Smilin' Joe's PR-413 km 4.1 ☏787/823-5654. Bar and grill inside the *Lazy Parrot*, with an inventive menu that includes *piña colada* shrimp, mango-chipotle glazed chicken breast, tempura mahi tacos, or just good old-fashioned burgers. Also has a decent list of sandwiches and wines. Mains – $9-18.

🏃 **Tamboo Tavern** PR-413 Interior km 4.4 ☏787/823-8550. This legendary beach bar and surfers' haunt, with its wide wooden deck jutting over the beach, is almost as well-known as in Manhattan as Rincón, reflecting its surprisingly cosmopolitan clientele. Cocktails are $5–6, while the *Tamboo Seaside Grill* serves relatively upscale steaks and seafood ($10–15) and sandwiches ($7–10). Live music gets things fairly animated on Fri while DJs spin Sat – happy hours run 7–9pm weekdays.

Tapas Bar *Casa Isleña Inn*. If you're looking for something a little more sophisticated at reasonable

rates, it's worth checking out this small Spanish-style place right on the beach, offering an appetizing selection of authentic tapas, fruity *sangría*, and sandwiches (from $4). Dec–April closed Mon & Tues; May–Nov closed Mon–Fri.

Caribbean Coast

🏃 **Bohío Bar** *Villa Cofresí Hotel*, PR-115 km 12. This venerable resort hotel has one of the best beach bars in town, with heart-melting sunset views, pool tables, and an awesome line-up of drinks, including the infamous "Pirata Special," a blend of four kinds of rum, cacao milk, coconut juice, and milk, served in a coconut shell for $7.50. Happy hours Mon–Fri 5–7pm (wine $3, beers $2.50).

Brasas *Rincón Beach Resort*, PR-115 km 5.8. For a splurge, try this posh hotel restaurant overlooking the water, a romantic location with delectable seafood and fresh fish – try the local snapper or Chilean sea bass. You can even order a super-swish seafood *mofongo* for $22. Mains $20–27. Daily 5.30–10pm.

Brumas Bar & Grill PR-115 km 7 ☏787/826-6315. Large bar with spectacular balcony, big TVs, and pool tables. Wed is ladies night ($1 drinks), Fri karaoke, and Sat live music and salsa. The menu is heavy on comfort food such as fish bites, burgers, and a delicious shrimp basket, and there are several other places to try within stumbling distance. Closed Tues.

🏃 **Kaplash** PR-115 km 7. No-frills diner tucked away in the cluster of restaurants here (on the bay side of the road) and extremely popular for its seafood *empanadillas*. For $1.50–2.95 you can feast on lobster, crab, octopus, or prawn fillings; or join the genial mix of locals and expats in the evenings as they enjoy beers on the back terrace, with fabulous views of the ocean.

Rincón Tropical PR-115 km 12.4. One of the best Puerto Rican restaurants in town, in a small residential block just off the main road, with its own parking lot and open-front dining area. Plenty of fresh fish gets fried up here, along with all the *criollo* favorites, and in case you're missing it, decent *mofongo*. Mains under $10. Daily 11am–9pm.

Taíno International Café PR-115 km 11.5 (Rincón Shopping Center). Bright, modern US-style coffee shop off the main road – the location opposite the parking lot is hardly inspiring but you can slump in a sofa for an hour or so, and enjoy the rich Puerto Rican coffees. Breakfast specials start at around $2, lunches (salads, burgers, sandwiches) at $5.95.

Listings

Banks Westernbank (Mon–Fri 7.30am–5pm, Sat 8.30–11.30am) has a branch and 24hr ATM on the central plaza in downtown Rincón (c/Muñoz Rivera Esq Unión), while Banco Popular is at PR-115 km 12.4 (Mon–Fri 8am–4pm, Sat 9am–noon).

Car rental Angelo's (☎787/823-3438) at PR-115 km 12.3 is a local outfit that rents cars from $35/ day, while Hertz (☎787/823-4646) is at PR-115 km 11.7.

Hospital Rincón Health Center (Mon–Fri 8am– 4.30pm, Sat & Sun 8am–4pm emergency only) is on PR-115 in the middle of downtown.

Internet Wi-Fi is widely available in Rincón, but Internet cafés with computers are thin on the ground. Try the *Backup Computer Store*, PR-115 km 12, in Plaza Bonet near downtown (☎787/823-4990, ⓦwww.backupcomputerstore.com), which charges $1 for 10min or $6/1hr (Mon–Sat 8.30am–5.30pm), or *Rincón Inn* nearby, which has two computers (Mon–Sat 10am–7pm, Sun noon–5pm; $1/10min), though guests get priority.

Laundry Try the coin laundry at Plaza Bonet south of downtown on PR-115, open daily 8am–7pm ($1.50 per load).

Pharmacy Farmacia del Pueblo (Mon–Sat 8am– 9pm, Sun 10am–6pm) is opposite the Rincón Health Center on PR-115 in the center of downtown.

Post The post office (Mon–Fri 7.30am–4.30pm, Sat 8.30am–noon; ☎787/823-2625) is north of downtown on PR-115.

Shopping Blue Bay Art Gallery at PR-413 km 3.7, Barrio Puntas (☎787/823-8006), is best for local art; Mango Beach Shop (☎787/823-2100) at Sandy Beach (near *Tamboo Tavern*) sells home-made crafts, T-shirts, local artwork, and sea glass. Caribbean Casuals (daily noon–6pm) sells tropical beach wear, sarongs, bags, and general attire at the *Calypso Café*, while Taina's Souvenir on PR-115 in downtown (c/Luis Muñoz Rivera 43) sells perfumes, bamboo crafts, T-shirts, and other souvenirs.

Taxi Rincón Tours & Taxi ☎787/823-0906.

Around Rincón: Añasco

Heading south from Rincón towards Mayagüez it's worth making a brief detour to **AÑASCO**, a small town with a rich history and some unusual snack food. In the city "where the gods died," Taíno *cacique* Urayoán had a Spanish soldier drowned in the nearby Río Grande de Añasco to prove the white men weren't gods, precipitating the rebellion of 1511 (see p.357). The Añasco river mouth may also be the location of Villa Sotomayor and all the early incarnations of San Germán, challenging the rival claims of Aguada (see p.232). San Germán was re-established in the south in the 1540s and 1550s, and Añasco was officially founded in 1733 by wealthy landowner José de Santiago. He selected land once owned by Captain Luis de Añasco, a companion of Juan Ponce de León and mayor of the first San Germán in the 1520s – naming the town in his honor, Santiago was also ensuring that Añasco would have a distinguished historic lineage.

The Town

Añasco is a hard-working blue-collar town 17km from downtown Rincón, laid out around **Plaza José Adolfo Pesante**, the second largest plaza in Puerto Rico. It's often gridlocked with traffic on weekday mornings, but plan to arrive at other times and you should be able to park somewhere around the square. On the west side of the plaza, the **Iglesia de Parroquia San Antonio Abad** is a relatively grand church built in Spanish Colonial style, its graceful twin towers embellished with Baroque and Mudéjar elements, particularly the spires on top. Founded in 1728, the current structure dates from 1801 and has a striking eight-foot stained glass window above the main entrance – times tend to be erratic, but the church is open most evenings and early mornings for mass. Inside you'll find a revered image of the **Virgen de Monserrate** in a side chapel, with its *mestiza* (racially mixed) skin, and a rare image of the **Nuestra Señora de la Divina Providencia**, the patron of the island. In front of the church, look out for the small **bronze statue** depicting the unlucky Spanish soldier drowned in 1511, and the **war memorial** in the plaza beyond, with two names added in 2003 from the war in Afghanistan.

The plaza is surrounded by some shabby but charming examples of early *criollo* architecture and several decent places **to eat** and **drink**, but don't leave without trying the local specialty, **hojaldre** cakes (literally "puff pastries," filled with brandy and spices), sold from a tiny shop east of the plaza: **Fábrica de Hojaldres** (Tues–Fri 7am–1pm, Sat 7.30am–noon) is tucked away in a commercial building off Calle Principal (PR-109) opposite the old Plaza de Mercado – walk through the passage towards the parking lot at the back and look for the yellow sign. The official address is Calle 65 Infantería no. 50.

Otherwise, stick to the cheerful local places around the plaza, such as *La Taberna de Añasco* (☎787/826-0960) for thick steaks and *criollo* food, or *El Yunque Bar* for a beer. The town is also renowned for its *pitorro*, **home-made rum**, now sold mostly by word of mouth over the Christmas holidays (it's technically illegal – see p.33).

Mayagüez and around

After years of decline, **MAYAGÜEZ** is finally starting to feel like Puerto Rico's third city again, a willfully provincial place that has always stuck its nose up at posh Ponce and the brash wealth of the capital, desperately proud of its historic reputation as "La Sultana del Oeste" (Sultan of the West). Long ignored by tourists, central Mayagüez is a surprising treasure trove of ornate **architecture**, a legacy of the boom years of coffee and sugar, and home to some oddly endearing edible attractions: the cream-stuffed *brazo gitano* and zesty home-made *sangría*. Now just the eighth largest municipality on the island after years of migration, the city's impressive center is being spruced up, and a palpable sense of optimism pervades the streets. The no-nonsense *mayagüezanos* spirit is on full display at **festival** time, the most important being the **Fiestas Patronales de Mayagüez**, held the week leading up to February 2 to honor patron saint La Virgen de la Candelaria. The **Fiesta Nacional del Mango** is held in June, a celebration of the ubiquitous local fruit through recipe contests, exhibitions, music, and market stalls.

Some history

Mayagüez was founded in 1760 by a group of settlers from the Canary Islands, the name deriving from the Taíno word for the Río Yagüez, "Maygüex." In the nineteenth century the city became the unofficial capital of the west, a major port and commercial center serving the rich **coffee** plantations in the western mountains. This was despite a series of catastrophic **natural disasters**: the great fire of 1841 destroyed most of the city, while the **1918 earthquake** and tsunami leveled it yet again with seven hundred stone buildings and over a thousand wooden homes destroyed – much of what you see today dates from the massive rebuilding program that followed. The University of Puerto Rico Mayagüez Campus (UPRM) was founded in 1911 (🌐www.uprm.edu), and today the city remains a major **education** center, students making up a large proportion of its population.

With the decline of the coffee industry in the early twentieth century, Mayagüez turned to other trades to support its economy. The city was an important **rum producer** between the 1930s and 1970s, and Cervecería India, which opened in 1937, still produces **Medalla beer** here, the only remaining mass-produced Puerto Rican brew. After World War II, **textile** factories boomed, and between 1962 and 1998 Mayagüez was a major **tuna-canning center**, supplying 80 to 90 percent of all tuna consumed in the US – now only one factory remains, supplying the Bumble Bee brand. In a hopeful sign of renaissance, Mayagüez has been selected to host the 2010 **Central American and Caribbean Games** (Ⓦ www.mayaguez2010.com), meaning investment in a new stadium, new hotels, highways, and the development of Mayagüez Port to accommodate cruise ships.

Arrival and information

Mayagüez's airport, **Aeropuerto Eugenio María de Hostos**, is located 6.4km north of the city on PR-342 (off PR-2). Four car rental companies have desks at the terminal: Avis (Ⓣ 787/833-7070), Budget (Ⓣ 787/831-4570), Hertz (Ⓣ 787/832-3314), and Thrifty (Ⓣ 787/834-1590). They usually open daily 8am to noon and 1 to 5pm. The terminal also contains a Westernbank ATM, but nothing else. To get into the city take a taxi ($8–10); if none is around, get the airline desk to call one. If you call in advance, driver Ariel (Ⓣ 787/644-3001) offers cheaper rates to locations in the region.

Ferries from the Dominican Republic dock at the **Puerto de Mayagüez** (Mayagüez Port), north of the city off PR-64. Inside the terminal you'll find a small shop, toilets, and a basic café (no bank or ATM). Ferries del Caribe (see p.256) can arrange for Línea Sultana *públicos* to meet you at the terminal before driving on to **San Juan** (Río Piedras), but only when you buy the ferry ticket. Take a **taxi** ($7) into the city – if you can't find any, ask the ticket office to call one.

Most **públicos** should pull in at the **Terminal de Vehículos Públicos** at the end of Calle Peral, a few blocks north of the plaza and a short walk from most of the central hotels.

Driving into Mayagüez is fairly straightforward, though there is a one-way system and the streets in the city center tend to get clogged with traffic during the week. The **parking lot** ($1.25 first hr, $0.85/hr thereafter) on Calle Méndez Vigo, near Calle Del Río and the *Howard Johnson* hotel, is convenient for the plaza, but most hotels have their own parking.

The new **tourist office** (Mon–Fri 8am–4pm; Ⓣ 787/832-5882) is in the center of the city on Plaza Colón at c/Candelaria 53, and can provide maps and information on the region as well as walking tours of the city. Note that on **Sundays**, downtown Mayagüez virtually shuts down, and almost everything is closed.

Orientation

Downtown Mayagüez is the oldest part of the city and the most interesting place to explore. It's fairly compact and arranged on a grid system, so it's easy to navigate around the central point, **Plaza Colón**. To the north, across the Río Yagüez, lies the sprawling campus of the Universidad de Puerto Rico, the Tropical Research Station, and the city zoo, while 2km west of downtown, at the end of McKinley and Méndez Vigo, the old, run-down port area (known as **Mayagüez Playa**) is also being slowly revitalized with new shops and businesses, though there's not much to see other than *Brazo Franco Gitano* (see p.252). The rest of the modern city and its suburbs are spread out along the sides of PR-2, the main north–south highway on the west coast, with strip malls lining the road from the airport in the north to **Hormigueros** in the south.

City transportation

Public transportation in Mayagüez is limited to a free but infrequent **trolley-bus system**, similar to the service offered in Old San Juan. Check with the tourist office for the latest schedule, or wait at the central terminal on the north side of Plaza Colón (Calle Peral).

MAYAGÜEZ

0   250 m

ACCOMMODATION

Holiday Inn Mayagüez & Tropical Casino	B
Hotel Colonial	F
Hotel El Embajador	D
Howard Johnson Inn	C
Downtown Mayagüez	A
Mayagüez Resort & Casino	A
Western Bay Mayagüez	E

EATING, DRINKING & NIGHTLIFE

Bleu Bar & Tapas	4
Brazo Gitano Franco	1
Buffalos Café	13
Cafetería La Nueva Victoria	12
Galerías en el Estoril	11
El Estoril	10
El Garabato	2
Red Baron Pub	2
Restaurant Vegetariano	6
La Familia	8 & 9
Rex Cream	7
Ricomini Bakery	3
Sangria de Fido	10
Siglo XX	5

Map labels

❸ & Museo Eugenio María de Hostos

Maricao

Ⓐ (2km), Ⓑ (5km) & Rincón Airport (6km)

Mayagüez Zoo (1km)

Puerto de Mayagüez (2km)

Ⓐ (2km), Ⓑ (5km)

N

Río Yagüez

Bahía de Mayagüez

Ponce, Mayagüez Mall & Hormigueros

Universidad de Puerto Rico

Cervecería India

Tropical Agriculture Research Station

Parque de los Próceres

Entrance

Terminal de Vehículos Públicos

Supermarket

Museo Casa Grande

Catedral Nuestra Señora de la Candelaria

Teatro Yagüez

Westernbank

Casa Alcaldía

Casa de los Cinco Arcos

Plaza de Mercado

Plaza Colón

Taxi

Street names

AVE HOSTOS, MÉNDEZ VIGO, DR. RAMÓN EMETERIO BETANCES, JOSÉ DE DIEGO, PERAL, BASORA, PABLO MUÑOZ, PALOMITA, DEL BOSQUE, LAS FLORES, LAS ACACIAS, SULTANA, LOS MILLONARIOS, SOLIMAN, MCKINLEY, RAMOS ANTONINI, SANTA ISABEL, RIVERA, ESTACIÓN, DUFRESNE, PILAR DEFILLÓ, LEÓN, PABLO CASALS, AGUILA, PALMER, SAN VICENTE, MUÑOZ RIVERA, SANTIAGO R. PALMER, MÉNDEZ, FERIA, DE AGOSTO, DEL PILAR, TETUÁN, LIBERTAD, DE DIEGO, ST. THOMAS, MAYAGÜEZ ABRIL, MATEO FAJARDO, POST, PERAL, CRUZ, SAN JURJO, BETANCES, LA PAZ, FLORIDA, CATALINA, ALMENDROS, CALIFORNIA, DR. ISLABI, DR. LASSISE, DR. PEDRO PERA, MARTÍNEZ NADAL, MEDITERRÁNEO, BORINQUEN, LICEO, AGUILA, CULTO, PLUMA, O. POLANCO, SAN RAFAEL, SAN JOSÉ, MERCEDES SÁNZ, JACINTOS, EUGENIO DE HOSTOS, MARIANO RIERA PALMER, KENT CORONEL CABR., A. QUINTANA, BALBOA, ROIG, LIS LASCHER TORRES, MIRAMAR, CARACAS, BLANCO, ARGENTINA, SAN JUAN, ADUANA, COMERCIO, MANUEL PIRALLO, MELÍCO, LEVITTOWN, BENIGNO CONTRERAS, PEDRO PÉREZ, PERAL, M. NADAL, MARÍN MONGE, CASA VICTORIA, UNIÓN, BUENOS AIRES, CONCORDIA, COMERCIO, SAN PEDRO, SAN JORGE, MANUEL M. SANTOS, AVE JOSÉ GONZÁLEZ CLEMENTE, EDISON, H. LUCHETTI

102

105

106

65

2R

AVE HOSTOS

Taxis are easy to find downtown: White Taxi (daily 6.30am–midnight; ☎787/832-1154) operates from a small office at Calle José de Diego 18 Este, while Westernbank Taxi (daily 6am–midnight; ☎787/832-0562) is based just south of the plaza on Calle Del Río. Both usually charge $8 for the airport, $7 for the ferry terminal, and $5 for the zoo.

Accommodation

Staying in Mayagüez can be good value, its hotels ranging from basic but comfortable one-star inns to luxurious mini-resorts. Your options fall into two principal groups: the collection of hotels in **downtown**, some set in historic buildings, and all handy for the central sights and restaurants; and the two upmarket hotels on PR-2 north of the center, convenient for drivers but a little isolated from the rest of the city. Most of the hotels listed here have **wireless Internet**, but unless you have a laptop this isn't much use: only the *Holiday Inn* and *Mayagüez Resort* have computers for guests' use.

Hotel Colonial c/Iglesia 14 Sur ☎787/833-2150, ⓦwww.hotelcolonial.com. This excellent budget option is a charming sand-colored building built around 1920, and used as a convent for forty years. Its 29 rooms include triples and quads, and all come with a/c, cable TV, and bathroom; private parking is available nearby. Breakfast is included and singles get great deals (from $39). ②

Hotel El Embajador c/Ramos Antonini 111 Este ☎787/833-3340, ⓔhotelembj@hotmail.com. Aging but friendly hotel, with new management in 2007 improving its somewhat lackluster reputation with a decent restaurant and simple but clean rooms equipped with cable TV, bathrooms, and breakfast included – you even get a welcome drink. Currently no parking, but singles pay $20 less. ②

Holiday Inn Mayagüez & Tropical Casino PR-2 km 149.9 ☎787/833-1100, ⓦwww.holidayinn .com/mayaguezpr. Sizeable mini-resort 5km north of downtown, popular with locals attracted by the casino and nightclub on site. Rooms are comfortable if standard hotel-chain fare, with cable TV and a/c, while the fitness center and outdoor pool make pleasant extras. ④

Howard Johnson Inn Downtown Mayagüez c/Méndez Vigo 70 Este ☎787/832-9191, ⓦwww.ihphospitality.com. This five-story building oozes historic charm, with wide balconies that wrap each level and 39 comfortable rooms fitted out with wooden bed frames, clay tile floors, old chests and furniture, and cable TV. Extras include a 24hr self-service laundry, free parking across the street, and breakfast at *Ricomini Bakery*. The stately building was constructed in 1902 by a Catholic order, and survived the 1918 earthquake. ④

Mayagüez Resort & Casino PR-104 km 0.3, Barrio Algarrobo ☎787/832-3030, ⓦwww .mayaguezresort.com. Another large resort hotel, just off PR-2, 3km north of the city and set in twenty acres of gardens. In addition to a decent pool, fitness center, and tennis courts, you get breezy sea views and a posh restaurant, *El Castillo*, on site. Rooms are smart but a little overpriced, though bargains are available via the Internet. ⑥

Western Bay Mayagüez c/Santiago Riera Palmer 9 Este ☎787/834-0303, ⓦwww .westernbaymayaguez.com. The former *El Sol* has improved considerably, now offering a variety of renovated rooms from singles to quads (prices go up $10 each size), each with spotless tiled floors, a/c, and cable. The hotel has a small pool and private parking. ③

The City

The most appealing parts of Mayagüez lie around central **Plaza Colón**, but Puerto Rico's best **zoo** and the shady walkways of the **Tropical Agriculture Research Station**, both just outside downtown, are modest but equally worthwhile sights.

Plaza Colón and around

The heart of downtown Mayagüez has been **Plaza Colón** since the foundation of the city in 1760, though the current name and elegant design date from 1896. The gracious monument to Christopher Columbus in the center was dedicated

▲ Mayagüez Cathedral

in 1892, but four years later a series of fountains and sixteen small bronze statues were added to embellish the square, all made in Barcelona. The area around the plaza remains shabby in places, but life is returning and many of the old buildings are being restored. The **Catedral Nuestra Señora de la Candelaria** (Mon–Sat 6.30am–5pm, Sun services only) dominates the plaza, its majestic twin towers and pale yellow, Neoclassical facade dating from 1922 and the lavish restoration completed in 2004 – the city's first church was constructed of wood on this spot in 1763. The interior is relatively opulent for Puerto Rico, with timbered ceiling, marble floors, and impressive *retablo* depicting scenes from the life of Jesus. Don't miss the statue of Mary to one side, always surrounded by reverent worshippers and known here as **Nuestra Señora de la Candelaria** (see p.368).

The flamboyant building on the northwest corner of the plaza (with a restaurant at its base) is the **Antiguo Casino Español**, a blend of Neoclassical, Mudéjar, and *modernisme* elements. Constructed in 1874, it was rebuilt after the quake and completed in 1930 by Francisco Porrala Doria, one of the key architects of the post-1918 city. On the western side of the plaza stands the impressive **Casa Alcaldía**, a US-inspired Neoclassical building with clock tower dating from 1926. The original was constructed in 1845 but, like almost everything else, was destroyed in 1918.

One block west of the plaza on Calle McKinley is one of the most exuberant buildings on the island, **Teatro Yagüez** (Mon–Fri 8am–noon & 1–4.30pm; free), the city's main theater and a playful concoction of Neoclassical pillars and elaborate, multi-patterned Art Nouveau windows and dome. Completed in 1909, it survived the quake only to get tragically (and suspiciously) gutted by fire in 1919. The current theater was reopened in 1923, and the latest restoration project was completed in 2008.

Walk three blocks south of the theater, along Calle Betances, and you'll see the single-story **Casa de los Cinco Arcos** (House of the Five Arches) on the right, now sadly neglected but marked with a special plaque. Built by celebrated nationalist Ramón Emeterio Betances (see p.360) in 1865, it's a wonderful example of an upscale clapboard *criollo* house, with a four-arch veranda and finely crafted pillars and iron railings – the "father of the nation" lived here for two years before the Grito de Lares, having spent much of his successful medical career in the city.

Museo Casa Grande

Two blocks east of the plaza at Calle Méndez Vigo 104 Este, the **Museo Casa Grande** (Mon–Fri 8am–4.30pm; free) was built in 1890 and is a rare survivor of the quake, a pristine example of nineteenth-century "Neoclassical criollo" architecture. The graceful facade features four half-point arches with delicate iron railings on a raised stone veranda (the windows in the base are known as "bull's eyes"), while the main rooms are arranged around a cooling *patio interior* with gallery. Built as the private home of Don Guillermo Santos de la Mano, it temporarily hosted the Audiencia de Mayagüez (the judicial court), and is now a museum and cultural center, retaining much of the original interior – wooden floors, ornate plaster ceilings, and odd pieces of period furniture. You'll see paintings of former mayors and various Puerto Rican politicians on the walls (many by respected portrait artist Tulio Ojeda), and a room dedicated to **Oscar Garcia Rivera**, the first Puerto Rican to hold public office in the US – he was born in Mayagüez in 1900 and served in the New York State Assembly 1937–1940. One of the most interesting sections is the gallery of old black-and-white photos of Mayagüez, labeled in English, and the only place you'll get a sense of the city's rich history.

Tropical Agriculture Research Station

If you've always wondered what cocoa, vanilla, ginger, or coffee looks like before ending up in the supermarket, check out the US Department of Agriculture's **Tropical Agriculture Research Station** (Mon–Fri 7am–noon & 1–4pm; free), a series of beautifully maintained gardens north of downtown. As the staff is likely to emphasize, however, this is not a botanical garden or public park; the 127-acre estate was once part of the Hacienda Carmen, but since 1902 it's been a center for experimental research with over two thousand species of tropical plants on site, and you must stick to approved paths at all times. On arrival you have to check-in at the information center in the main building, a charming structure completed in 1909. A pamphlet details the best route around the grounds, passing 76 tropical trees, shrubs, and bushes including sugar palms, cacao, nutmeg, fig, lychee, camphor, teak, and breadfruit. The route takes thirty minutes to one hour, and you must sign out before leaving. The research station is next door to the university (but is completely separate from it) at Avenida Pedro Albizu Campos 2200, and overlooks Parque de los Próceres on PR-65. It's a short 1km walk or cab ride from the center.

Parque Nacional Zoológico de Puerto Rico Dr. Juan A. Rivero

More simply referred to as Mayagüez Zoo, the **Parque Nacional Zoológico de Puerto Rico Dr. Juan A. Rivero** (Tues–Sun 8.30am–4pm, closed Tues in low season; $6, $4 for children 11-17, $2 for 5-10s, free for under-5s) is the only real zoo in Puerto Rico, and has tried hard to get away from cages by constructing "savannah-style" enclosures, protected by moats and walls. Some of its 75 species are native to the island and the Caribbean (especially birds such as the red-tailed hawk and wide-eyed owl), as well as the usual crowd-pleasers: lions, tigers, leopards, elephants, snakes, rhinos, and giraffes. The new **Aviario** (aviary), has a high walkway through tropical forest, and features macaws, parrots, and flamingos, while the **Mariposario** is an enchanting butterfly house. You'll find the zoo 2km northeast of the city center, off PR-108, and too far to walk – drive or take a taxi. Parking is an additional $3.

Eating and drinking

Mayagüez is home to some of the most celebrated snacks and drinks on the island, and it can be a fun place to eat. The most famous locally and certainly the most addictive is the **brazo gitano** (literally "gypsy arm"), a sweet and slightly crumbly Swiss roll (or jelly roll), loaded with a variety of creamy fillings. You can buy it from several sources in town, as well as roadsides all over the west coast. Other than grabbing a locally produced *Medalla* beer, don't leave Mayagüez without sampling the local **sangría**, a snappy cocktail which has an almost cult following in Puerto Rico.

For **self-catering**, *Mr Special Supermarket* (Mon–Sat 7am–9pm) is on Calle Balboa at the eastern end of downtown, just across the Río Yagüez. For a fast food fix, head to the junction of Calle Post and PR-65, or *Subway* and *Quiznos* on the plaza.

Cafés and restaurants

Brazo Gitano Franco c/Méndez Vigo corner of Manuel Pirallo 3, ⊛www .brazogitano.com. Bakery and cafeteria founded in 1850 by Don Enrique Franco Rey, best-known for bringing the *brazo gitano* to Mayagüez from Spain. The shop and small eating area occupy the end of an old brick warehouse, with tiled floors, ceiling fans, and timbered ceilings. The kitchen doles out all the *criollo* staples for lunch (rice and beans, grilled meats, sandwiches, and *frituras*) while the shop sells cakes, *sangría*, and other snacks: the *brazo gitano* comes in 29 flavors ($4.28 7.50).

Cafeteria La Nueva Victoria c/McKinley 6 Oeste, ☎787/833-1999. Unpretentious *comida criolla* in the downtown area, with plastic tables and chairs,

a *menu del día* written up on a whiteboard, and hearty cod stews, *arroz con Jamón* (ham rice), and *pechuga*; also does breakfasts. Closed Sun.

El Estoril c/Méndez Vigo 100 Este ☎787/834-2288. For a proper sit-down dinner, this is the best choice in downtown, a charming dining room in a red-brick, blue-trim colonial building with high ceilings, wood beams, and fountains in the corner. Though the chief influences are Spanish and Portuguese, there are plenty of Puerto Rican favorites. The *caldo Gallego* is always excellent (Galician soup with beans and *chorizo*) and the buffet on Wed is great value ($9.75). Closed Sun; reduced hours June & July.

Restaurant Vegetariano La Familia c/José de Diego 151 Este ☎787/833-7571. Only real vegetarian restaurant in town, another no-frills place that offers outstanding value: for $6 you can stuff yourself with rice, tofu, fresh salads, lasagne, pasta, and *empanadas* from the sumptuous daily lunch buffet. Lunch only, closed Sat & Sun.

Rex Cream c/Méndez Vigo 60. Established by Chinese immigrants in the mid-1960s, this ice cream chain has two branches in the city (the other one is on c/McKinley near the plaza), each knocking out a plethora of refreshing and often imaginative natural flavors ($1.75 per cone): coconut, maize, *guanabana* (soursop), *uva* (grape), and the bitter-tasting *tamarindo*.

🏃 **Ricomini Bakery** c/E. Méndez Vigo 101. Bakery and basic canteen open for over 100 years, selling its trademark *brazo gitano* (large/small $6.42/$4.01) and *pan de flauta* (fresh bread), in addition to offering breakfast and light meals from $4. The *brazos* come in cream, cheese, pineapple, coconut, or regular guava jam flavors. You can also buy *Sangría Fidos* here ($12/litre).

Order at the counters first and then grab one of the tables.

🏃 **Sangría de Fido** c/Duliebre 78. This acclaimed home-made brew is sold in a residential area off PR-106, east of the city center. Wilfrido Aponte started bottling the stuff in the 1950s, though his *sangría* ($10.70/750ml, $21.40/1.5 litres) is actually a potent blend of fruit juice, Bacardi 151 rum, and red wine. Choose from *La Tradicional*, *Albina* (white wine), or *Juan 23* (non-alcoholic). Look for the small sign beyond the Texaco gas station on the right (c/Belisario del Valle), then take the third right.

Siglo XX c/Peral 9 Norte ☎787/265-2094. This *Gran Café* was founded in 1973 in another handsome building oozing character, with a wooden upper deck, cozy booths, and stools at the bar. You can get all the usual *criollo* dishes for under $10: stews, *chuletas*, *pechuga*, snapper, *mofongo*, and vanilla *flan*, as well as filling sandwiches. Closed Sun.

Bars and clubs

Mayaguez has a somewhat mixed reputation when it comes to **nightlife**, reflecting the fact that much of it depends on its large but restless population of students; come during the university vacation and things might seem completely dead. It's also true that places tend to go in and out of fashion fast, though there are always plenty of pubs and clubs in the streets between the university and the plaza, especially on Calle Post. Wednesday and Thursday nights tend to be the most animated during term time, as students usually head home or to the beaches at the weekends. If you just fancy a night on the slots, check out the **casinos** at the two resort hotels north of the city, which also have lively bars and clubs that tend to attract an older local crowd on weekends.

Bleu Bar & Tapas c/Jose de Diego 63 ☎787/831-1446. This popular club has a shiny industrial exterior and a big dance floor bathed in appropriately azure lights, featuring live Latin sounds and DJs. Tapas ($4–8) are served with cocktails ($4) and beers ($2.50). Cover is $5 on Sat. Closed Mon–Tues & Sun.

Buffalos Café 2/F, c/Post 252 ☎787/265-1395. This fun Southwestern chain pub offers cold beer, enthusiastic live bands, and notorious karaoke nights: gobble up the comfort food and wonder at the talent (or lack thereof) on display, before getting tanked up enough to have a go yourself. Weekends sees live salsa and rock replacing the amateurs, with plenty of frenetic dancing.

Galerías en el Estoril c/Méndez Vigo 100 Este. Stylish wine bar next to *Estoril*, with a wooden counter and lemony walls splashed with reproductions of the boldest paintings by Degas, Frida

Kahlo, and local artists. Most popular on weekends, with a friendly crowd that spills out onto the street. Closed Mon, Tues, & Sun.

El Garabato c/Post 102. If you just want a few beers, this is the most dependable choice in downtown and one of the few bars open all afternoon most days, marked by the unmistakable grin of the yellow face outside. Beyond the wooden doors and shutters it has a laid-back, sports bar feel, with TVs and plenty of older regulars mingling with student drinkers. Beers are $2. Closed Sun.

Red Baron Pub c/Post 102. Perched conveniently above *Garabato*, this is a late-night bar and dance club rather than a conventional pub, hosting raucous parties since 1984, karaoke on Tuesdays, and DJs spinning *reggaetón*, rock, and hip-hop on weekends – the usual form is to get happily lubricated at *Garabato* then stumble upstairs. Beers are $1–2. Closed Mon & Sun.

Listings

Banks Westernbank has a branch with an ATM on the plaza (c/McKinley 53 Este; Mon–Fri 7.30am–5pm, Sat 8.30am–11.30am), with its main branch at c/Méndez Vigo 15 (Mon–Fri 7.30am–6pm, Sat 8.30am–12.30pm). Citibank (24hr ATM) is at Plaza Sultana, PR-2 km 158 (Mon–Fri 8.30am–5pm, Sat 8.30am–12.30pm; ☎787/834-5353) or Mayagüez Mall.

Car rental Avis is at Sears at the Mayagüez Mall (Mon–Sat 9am–9pm, Sun 11am–5pm; ☎787/805-5911); Hertz (daily 8am–noon & 1–5pm; ☎787/832-3314) is at c/McKinley 153, downtown, near PR-2. For rental desks at the airport, see p.247.

Cinema Cine Vista is at Mayagüez Mall (☎787/833-3335, ⓦwww.cinevistapr.com), or downtown at c/Post 252 (☎787/265-2600). You can also try Caribbean Cinemas Western Plaza on PR-2 (☎787/833-0315, ⓦwww.caribbeancinemas.com).

Consulate Dominican Republic, c/McKinley 30, 2/F, ☎809/833-0007.

Hospital The main city hospital is Hospital Dr. Ramón Emeterio Betances with a 24hr emergency room and various day clinics (PR-2, Barrio Sabalos ☎787/834-8690). In town, Hospital Perea (☎787/834-0101) at c/Basora 15 is more convenient.

Internet access To check email or surf the web, try the business centers in the two resort hotels on PR-2, or the computer section in the main library at the University of Puerto Rico (Mon–Wed 7.15–11.30pm, Thurs 7.15am–9.30pm, Fri 7.15am–4pm, Sat 12.15–4.30pm, Sun 3.15–11.30pm).

Laundry Laundry Puerto Rico, c/Méndez Vigo 166 (near PR-2); ☎787/832-4012) is open Mon–Sat 8am–5pm.

Pharmacies Walgreens (24hr; ☎787/805-4805) is located on PR-2 (Avda Hostos 2097), north of the city (and at the Mayagüez Mall); in the center try Farmacia Luciano (opposite the *Howard Johnson*), open Mon–Fri 8am–7pm & Sat 8am–5pm.

Police ☎787/831-2020.

Post office The main branch is at c/McKinley Oeste 60 (Mon–Fri 7am–5pm, Sat 7.30am–1pm).

Shopping Paseo Georgina Morales (c/Peral) is being developed as a pedestrianized street of art and craft stalls near the plaza. Mayagüez Mall (Mon–Wed 9am–7pm, Thurs–Sat 9am–9pm, Sun 11am–5pm) is south of the city on PR-2 and the third largest shopping mall in Puerto Rico, with Sears, JC Penney, Wal-Mart, and all the major US chains, including a Borders book store.

Sports The city's professional basketball team, the Indios de Mayagüez (ⓦwww.indiosdemayaguez .com), plays at the Palacio de los Deportes on Avda Pedro Albizu Campos. The local baseball team has the same name, and at the time of writing had the most championship wins on the island. Their home base is Isidoro García Baseball Stadium (south of downtown on PR-63), currently being rebuilt for the 2010 games – check at the tourist office for where to catch them in the meantime.

Around Mayagüez

Anyone with an interest in Puerto Rican history should make time for a couple of absorbing cultural diversions in the hilly country beyond Mayagüez, the modest **Museo Eugenio María de Hostos** and revered Catholic shrine at **Hormigueros**.

Museo Eugenio María de Hostos

Tucked away in the lush mountain slopes east of Mayagüez, the **Museo Eugenio María de Hostos** (Tues–Sun 9am–5pm; free) honors one of Puerto Rico's most respected political heroes (see box, p.257). Hostos was born here in the *barrio* of Río Cañas in 1839, and this ambitious project acts as a community and arts center as well as memorial to the great man. Inside is a theater, a library, and several exhibition rooms decorated with period Spanish colonial furniture, while the Sala Hostos contains memorabilia such as letters, photos, and other documents. The work of **José Alicea** is also on permanent display, one of the island's foremost print-makers and creators of poster art. The museum is a long and winding drive from the city, and only worthwhile for real aficionados, but the route is well-signposted and the tranquil, rustic location is certainly evocative of traditional Puerto Rico, making an appealing excursion in its own right. From Mayagüez head east along PR-106 to PR-354 – it's a further 3.7km to Río Cañas, and then another 2km along a narrow lane to the museum.

Hormigueros

The unassuming town of **HORMIGUEROS** has become a virtual suburb of Mayagüez in recent years, but its semi-deserted, compact center retains a certain charm, bolstered by some aging colonial buildings and the main attraction, the **Basílica Santuario Nuestra Señora de la Monserrate** (daily 8am–noon & 1–5pm; free). Perched majestically on a small hill right in the center of town, the church dates back to 1775, and is today a major pilgrimage site for Puerto Ricans. Several legends are attached to the shrine: it was supposedly founded by a local landowner, who was miraculously saved from a charging bull by praying to the Virgin Mary (Our Lady of Monserrate). Later, his daughter, who had been missing for several days, claimed Mary had taken care of her. The otherwise simple interior is embellished by a silver altar and ornate *retablo*, while behind the church sits the handsome **Casa de los Peregrinos**, built in 1676 as a hostel for pilgrims and now the rectory. At the bottom of Calle Mateo Fajardo you'll find **Casa Marquéz**, an enchanting two-story wooden hacienda with wraparound balconies and flourishing mango trees in the garden – it's a private residence but you can still take pictures.

Eating

There are a few **places to eat** on the main street below the shrine (Calle Mateo Fajardo), all serving up the same combination of fried snacks and Puerto Rican food. *Gloria's Café* at no. 32 has a large seating area, burgers, sandwiches, and *comida criolla* for well under $10. It's usually easy **to park** on one of the side streets in the center.

For a treat, seek out *Cilantro's* (closed Wed; ☎787/849-1170), on PR-344. Chef Carlos Rosario worked at *Mark's at Melia* in Ponce, and is now recognized as one of the best cooks on the island, serving imaginative Puerto Rican food with contemporary flair – menus change but he's especially creative with fresh fish (mains from $22). It can be hard to find, so call if you get lost: from PR-2 take PR-3344, drive past two intersections to a funeral parlor and turn right, then immediately left behind it, where you should see signs to the restaurant.

Cabo Rojo and around

Puerto Rico's rustic southwest corner is entirely taken up by the municipality of **Cabo Rojo**, a region of mellow seaside resorts, sprawling marshland, and a coastline smothered in tangled mangroves, easily accessible by car from Mayagüez or the south coast. While El Yunque gets slammed with the full tropical force of the trade winds, Cabo Rojo (and neighboring Lajas and Guánica) is protected by the Central Cordillera and sees relatively little rain, making the area a prime target for sun-hungry tourists. The city of Cabo Rojo, known simply as *el pueblo*, boasts a few low-key historic attractions, but don't confuse this with the actual **cape** (the name means "Red Cape") further south, where crusty saltpans provide a startling contrast to the warmer tropical landscapes of the north.

Some history

Cabo Rojo has a fascinating history, indelibly linked to the exploitation of its valuable **salt fields** at the cape itself, though some of the local attempts to claim

Cape Air (☎1-800/352-0714) operates several daily **flights** between Mayagüez and the international airport in **San Juan** ($79): you can buy tickets at Mayagüez airport, one hour before departure, though planes are small so it's best to reserve in advance.

Ferries del Caribe (☎787/832-4800, ⓦwww.ferriesdelcaribe.com) runs three **ferries** a week (Mon, Wed & Fri) to Santo Domingo in the **Dominican Republic** from **Puerto de Mayagüez**, the port area north of the city ($7 by taxi). Services depart at 8pm and take 12 hours. You can buy tickets at the terminal (Mon, Wed, Fri 8am–8pm, Tues, Thurs & Sat 8am–5pm, Sun noon–4pm), and pick up useful information about traveling in the DR; parking is limited. Summer (June–Aug) prices range from $219 round-trip for an armchair seat, and $238 return for a berth in a 4-bed cabin, to $325 round-trip for a single cabin with sea view (plus tax). At other times prices are around $30–40 cheaper. Note you'll also have to pay $10 for the Dominican **Tarjeta de Turista**.

The **Terminal de Vehículos Públicos** is at the bottom of Calle Peral, a short walk north of the plaza, but as elsewhere on the island, long-distance services are becoming hard to find these days. The exception for now is Línea Sultana (☎787/832-1041), which operates a regular hourly service to **San Juan** (Río Piedras) for $15 (daily 7.30am–5pm). Taxi-type *públicos* charge $15 to Rincón, but are erratic. You can usually pick up a ride to **Añasco** anytime, but if traveling to other destinations, aim to get to the terminal as early as possible, and definitely before 2pm.

Driving, the main route out of the city is PR-2, which can get gridlocked during rush hour: to the south it's gradually being turned into a freeway, which should help ease congestion. Ponce is 74km, Guánica 46km, and Cabo Rojo (town) 14km. To the north it's 13km to Añasco, 27km to Aguadilla, and 24km to Rincón. Mayagüez is the western terminus of the **Ruta Panorámica**, with a winding 28km to the first major stop, Maricao: take PR-105 out of the city.

historic bragging rights are absurd: you'll see information boards sponsored by the Mayagüez Rotary Club quoting Gavin Menzies's fanciful claim that Chinese admiral Zhao Wen made a brief stop here in 1421 (discredited by most academics), and stating that Sir Walter Raleigh made camp in El Combate in 1525 (some twenty years before he was born). It's generally agreed that salt has been extracted continually since that year, starting with the Spanish, and since the area was never properly defended it's also true that the French (in 1528) and English often stumbled ashore – Sir Walter Raleigh's mission to Roanoke (Virginia) did stop here in 1585 (though the explorer himself was absent), even making a rudimentary fort, and Sir Francis Drake took on water and supplies in 1595 after his bruising in San Juan.

As the salt industry grew in importance, rival groups from Aguada and Cabo Rojo clashed in a violent skirmish in 1769, now known as "El Combate" (see p.266), but it wasn't until 1815, when **Juan Comas Roig** arrived from Santo Domingo, that the saltpans were exploited in an organized way. In 1884 the Comas and Colberg families bought the salt fields outright, controlling a healthy trade in salt until the 1960s.

The City

The languid center of **CABO ROJO** retains a time-warped air despite encroaching modernization, worth a brief stop for its important monuments and remaining clapboard houses, quaint if rambling examples of *criollo* architecture squashed amongst ugly modern development. Settlers established the first community here in 1733, with the town formally created in 1771 with the help of lawyer Nicolás Ramírez Arellano. Today Perza Rodríguez Quiñones is one of the few mayors on the island to be a woman of *criollo* descent.

The eye-catching central square, **Plaza de Recreo Ramón Emeterio Betances**, is named after Ramón Emeterio Betances, the revered abolitionist, doctor, and independence activist who was born here in 1827. Betances died in exile in France in 1898, but his ashes were taken back to Puerto Rico in 1920 and buried in the Cabo Rojo cemetery; two years later his remains were placed inside the **Monumento Ramón Emeterio Betances** on the plaza, topped with a bust of the great man by Italian sculptor Diego Montano, and backed by the Grito de Lares revolutionary flag (see p.360). Nearby is a striking steel sculpture of a broken chain by Alberto Fernandez Zequeira, commemorating the abolition of slavery in 1873.

The plaza is dominated by, the pale yellow **Iglesia Católica San Miguel Arcángel** (Mon–Fri 8am–11.30am & 2.30–4.30pm), originally completed in 1783 but constantly added to and rebuilt since then. It retains its basic Spanish Colonial structure, and despite its relatively large size often overflows during mass. Elsewhere on the plaza you'll see the **Monumento Salvador Brau**, a white marble statue of poet, historian and Cabo Rojo native Salvador Brau (1842–1912), backed by a soaring Art Deco pillar. The needle-like **Obelisco** in the southeast corner is a memorial to the 128 families (led by Arellano) who founded the town.

Just outside the center, the **Museo de Los Próceres** (Mon–Sat 8am–4.30pm; free) is an unexpectedly grand memorial to famous *caborrojeños*, a bit overblown considering the modest nature of the displays inside, though everything is well-presented and you can pick up useful information on the area here – it doubles as the headquarters of the local culture and **tourism department** (☎787/255-1560, ⓦwww.ciudadcaborojo.net). The main rotunda is lined with portraits of the city's most illustrious citizens, while the room dedicated to Betances contains his old piano and a collection of paintings. The room commemorating Brau also features portraits, documents, and another sculpture, while the Sala Indígena has a quirky ensemble of Taíno pottery, ceremonial objects, tools, and other bits and pieces, the most illuminating being a couple of stone petroglyphs. Temporary exhibitions of local art fill up the other galleries. The building stands in parkland at PR-312 km 0.4, just south of the center, with plenty of parking, and you can usually access the Internet inside.

El Ciudadano de Las Americas

Remembered today as "The Citizen of the Americas," **Eugenio María de Hostos** was one of several Puerto Rican rebels exiled from the island in the nineteenth century, admired all over Latin America for not just promoting independence from Spain, but also the integration of Latin American states, education, and women's rights. Born to wealthy parents in 1839, he was educated in Spain where he joined the **Puerto Rican independence movement**. In 1869, disillusioned by the failure of the Grito de Lares (see p.360), he moved to the US where he continued to fight for the independence of Puerto Rico and Cuba, and the idea of an **Antillean Confederation** uniting the two islands with the Dominican Republic. In a peripatetic career that saw him travel all over South and Central America, he established schools and wrote numerous essays on social topics: ultimately disappointed by the US invasion of Puerto Rico in 1898, he died in the Dominican Republic in 1903 and was buried in Santo Domingo's National Pantheon. His last wish was to be reburied in Puerto Rico, should the island ever become independent.

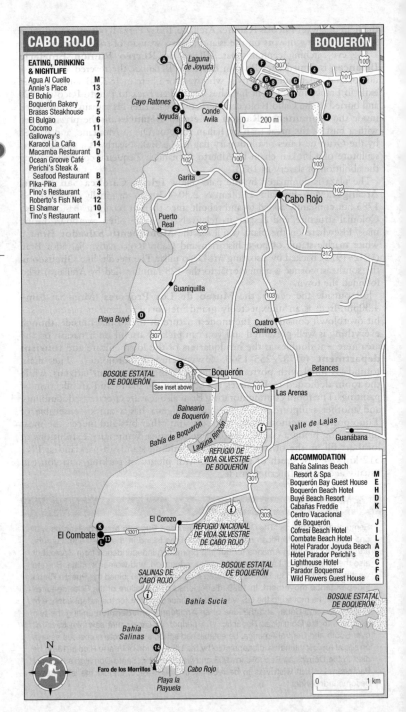

CABO ROJO

EATING, DRINKING & NIGHTLIFE

Agua Al Cuello	M
Annie's Place	13
El Bohío	2
Boquerón Bakery	7
Brasas Steakhouse	5
El Bulgao	6
Cocomo	11
Galloway's	9
Karacol La Caña	14
Macamba Restaurant	D
Ocean Groove Café	8
Perichi's Steak & Seafood Restaurant	B
Pika-Pika	4
Pino's Restaurant	3
Roberto's Fish Net	12
El Shamar	10
Tino's Restaurant	1

BOQUERÓN

See inset above

ACCOMMODATION

Bahía Salinas Beach Resort & Spa	M
Boquerón Bay Guest House	H
Boquerón Beach Hotel	E
Buyé Beach Resort	D
Cabañas Freddie	K
Centro Vacacional de Boquerón	J
Cofresí Beach Hotel	I
Combate Beach Hotel	L
Hotel Parador Joyuda Beach	A
Hotel Parador Perichi's	B
Lighthouse Hotel	C
Parador Boquemar	F
Wild Flowers Guest House	G

Practicalities

The city is best visited as a day-trip from somewhere else, but if you get stuck in Cabo Rojo, the motel-like *Lighthouse Hotel* (☎787/255-3887, ⓦwww .lighthousehotel.net; ❸) is a reasonable fall-back option, just outside the center at the intersection of PR-100 and PR-102. Otherwise, try to park where you can in the center, or aim for the ugly **multi-story** east of the plaza, on Calle Salvador Mestre between Betances and Baldorioty. Cabo Rojo's *público* terminal is a short walk from the plaza at the southern end of Calle Salvador Brau (PR-103). You can pick up taxi-type *público*s from here to Puerto Real ($1.25) or Boquerón ($1.45) – Boquerón beach is five cents extra. For **San Juan** ($35), look for the small phone box belonging to Línea Caborojeña (☎787/851-1252), on Calle Muñoz Rivera a half block north of the plaza, next to no. 36. to operates weekdays 5am–7pm, but call ahead. Banco Santander has a 24-hour ATM on the main plaza. **Eating** options arc unexciting in Cabo Rojo, but the *kioscos* in the central plaza serve up rich coffee and light snacks, while *Friends Café* on the east side of the square is a welcoming US-style coffee shop with a *Starbucks*-like menu of cakes, snacks, and drinks.

Playa de Joyuda and Cayo Ratones

One of several proudly traditional Puerto Rican seaside resorts on the southwest coast, **PLAYA DE JOYUDA** isn't really a beach but a string of seafood restaurants, fishing shacks, and faded hotels. Running for 2km along PR-102 south of Mayagüez, between a ragged shore of bleached coral and the mangrove-fringed nature reserve of Laguna Joyuda, it's as unattractive as it sounds (most of the coral is dead and erosion has whittled away the seafront), but while its sobriquet of *Milla de Oro del Buen Comer* ("golden mile of good food") is a little exaggerated, some of the **seafood** restaurants are genuinely excellent value and the tiny islet of **Cayo Ratones** just offshore makes an appealing target for a lazy afternoon. The island is completely undeveloped and is actually part of the Bosque Estatal de Boquerón (see p.263), a protected nature reserve, with silky white sands and excellent snorkeling. You have to hire a boat to take you across: contact **Adventures Tourmarine** (☎787/375-2625, ⓦwww.tourmarinepr.com) at the small dock between the *Vista al Mar* and *Vista Bahía* restaurants. Captain Elick Hernández García runs out to Cayo Ratones ($5, minimum four people), around the bay ($10) and even to Boquerón ($20, 1hr). He also does fishing charters from $375 for a half-day and diving/snorkeling day-trips to **Isla Desecheo** (see p.243) for $75 (minimum ten people) and **Isla de Mona** (see p.260).

Accommodation

There are plenty of **hotels** in Playa de Joyuda, but although you can get basic doubles for $75-100, none a particularly good deal and you're better off staying elsewhere. If you do end up here, the best of the bunch is *Hotel Parador Joyuda Beach*, PR-102 km 11.7 (☎787/851-5650, ⓦwww .joyudabeach.com; ❷), at the more secluded north end of the strip, with simple but large and clean motel-style cabins, stretching back from a seafront of palms and a healthier reef just offshore. Rooms come with the usual cable TV and air-conditioning, and plenty of parking, but it gets packed on weekends. *Hotel Parador Perichi's* at PR-102 km 14.3 (☎787/851-3131; ❷) is an unsightly place, over twenty years old and starting to look it, but remains one of the better hotels on the strip, with standard rooms arranged around a pool, all with air-conditioning, balcony, and cable TV.

Eating

All the action takes place on PR-102, with the best **restaurants** jutting out over the rocky fringe for incredible sunsets and views of Cayo Ratones. Note that the restaurant at *Hotel Parador Perichi's* (see p.259) serves decent breakfasts daily 7am between 11am, and other meals until 10pm.

El Bohio PR-102 km 13.9 ☎787/851-2755. For something a little more rustic, try this wooden stilt house with a timber deck that hangs right over the water. The menu offers the usual range of seafood, plus steaks and tasty *criollo* sides such as yucca and mini-*mofongo*.

Pino's Restaurant PR-102 km 14.6 ☎787/255-3440. Solid choice specializing in *biftec de chapín* (fish steaks), *salmorejo* (traditional Spanish tomato soup served cold), and the ever-present *mofongo* stuffed with seafood (from $11).

Tino's Restaurant PR-102 km 13.6 ☎787/851-2976. One of the most distinguished restaurants on the strip; its specialty is *mofongo* ($15–17) served in large goblets and stuffed with high-quality seafood including conch, octopus, and lobster – the last is superb value. Note that the restaurant stands on the landward side of the road, so you won't get the sea views here. Closed Tues.

Isla de Mona

One of the last true adventure destinations in the Caribbean, the **ISLA DE MONA** is a blessedly isolated nature reserve maintained by the DRNA, 45 miles off the west coast of Puerto Rico, and just 38 miles from the Dominican Republic. Staying on the island requires advance planning, though it's much easier to arrange day-trips to dive or snorkel off its deep, unbelievably clear waters and richly stocked barrier reef. It's worth the effort: although it's not quite the "Galapagos" made out in the tourist literature, it does offer the chance for a real wilderness, back-to-nature experience.

The island is roughly 7 miles long and 4 miles wide, and other than occasional groups of illegal immigrants from Cuba, completely uninhabited, though you can still see evidence of **Taíno** and early Spanish settlement: stone walls, graves, old trails, petroglyphs, bones, and other bits and pieces. The Taíno village was visited by Ponce de León in 1508 on his way to Puerto Rico (he sheltered from a hurricane here and was given cassava bread by the friendly natives), but the community had died out by the late sixteenth century. The island is essentially a raised plateau surrounded by 130-foot sea cliffs, with an extensive cave system and 5 miles of absolutely stunning pearly white beaches lining its southern shore. Other than enjoying the caves and these (usually) utterly deserted strips of sand, Mona's chief attraction is its wildlife. The Galapagos comparison was spurred chiefly by the colony of **giant rock iguanas** (*Iguanas de Mona*) that lounge on the shore, and can grow up to 5ft long. There are also wild pigs, goats, and cattle, left by Spanish colonists, and pods of Humpback whales offshore in winter. Between May and October turtles nest on the beaches and there are over 100 species of bird zipping around the island, including hawks, red-footed boobies, and pelicans. The DRNA maintains a basic ranger station, toilets, and showers at Playa Sardinera on the west side of Mona, but otherwise you're on your own – you must bring a tent and all your food and drink.

Practicalities

To visit, you must obtain **a permit** from the DRNA (see p.28), usually good for up to three days. Camping is $3 per night and you need to apply at least 45 days in advance. In practice, the company taking you to the island should arrange all this, and if you are just coming to dive or snorkel offshore, no permit is required – the trip takes about four to five hours by boat. Note, however, that most operators will be reluctant to take fewer than four or five people, so you may have to be flexible with dates (or cough up a hefty supplement).

Acampa (☎787/706-0695, ⊛www.acampapr.com) arranges all-inclusive packages from San Juan (four nights, three days) for a steep $979 per person, but this does include all food, transportation, tents, equipment, and guided tours of trails and caves – you might be able to negotiate a cheaper price depending on the size of your group. AdvenTours (☎787/831-6447, ⊛www.adventourspr.com) can arrange similar trips. You could also check with COPLADET (☎787/765-8595, ⊛www.copladet.com), which occasionally arranges tours to the island with an eco-friendly and educational angle.

Adventures Tourmarine in Playa de Joyuda (see p.259) departs at 4am for diving and snorkeling day-trips off the island, but they need a minimum ten people (usually around $120 per person). In Boquerón, Mona Aquatics also arranges dive trips to Mona (see p.265) and Oceans Unlimited at the Rincón Beach Resort (see p.238) runs dive trips (minimum six people) and three-day excursions to the island (minimum eight people).

Playa Buyé

One of the most alluring beaches in the southwest, **PLAYA BUYÉ** has a natural, unspoiled feel quite unlike anything else in the region. Though it can get crammed with families at weekends and the narrow strip of sand is backed by condos, development on low-key, the sea is a deep azure blue, and bushy Portia trees with bony limbs reach almost as far as the water, providing plenty of shade. You can **park** ($3) at the end of the potholed road to the beach, signposted at km 4.8 on PR-307, south of Cabo Rojo, and a small shop sells basic supplies and snacks.

Staying here is a good idea, especially during the week: the *Buyé Beach Resort* (☎787/255-0358, ⊜vctorramrez@yahoo.com) is a collection of sixteen simple beach cabins for three or four people, with hot water, air-conditioning, kitchen, and small verandas just behind the beach, but no TV. Bed sheets and towels are an additional $15 and you can eat fresh seafood at nearby *Macamba Restaurant*. Prices

▲ Boquerón water front

differ according to the seasons, the cheapest period being September to December when cabins start at just $65.40 – in the peak March to September season they cost $109, while December to March is $81.75. Add another $10 for the four-person cabins. You also get use of a coin-op laundry and free parking.

Boquerón

The ramshackle fishing village of **BOQUERÓN**, with its jumble of clapboard houses and slightly shabby seafront, is a magnet for Puerto Rican tourists on weekends, who pile in to soak up the carnival atmosphere and fresh seafood. For jaded *sanjuaneros*, this is a nostalgic throwback to a more simple, rustic Puerto Rico, though apart from the food, particularly the **fresh shellfish**, sold raw from stalls on the main road through town, the real draw is the **Balneario de Boquerón** (facilities and parking daily 8am–6pm; $3). One of the best beaches on the island, this three-mile horseshoe-shaped curve of velvety white sand is backed by a thick crust of palm trees. You can park here or stroll along the coast from the main village. Other distractions include two **nature reserves** nearby and, in the summer (usually June), Boquerón's very own **gay pride parade**, which has regularly attracted over five thousand revelers since it began in 2003.

Orientation

Central Boquerón is a compact area of shops, restaurants, and hotels lining the bay and wharf area along PR-101, 6.5km south of Cabo Rojo – the road makes a loop from PR-100 and rejoins PR-307 heading west to Playa Buyé. The **beach** is at the end of a wide road off PR-101, just before entering the main part of the village. Note that PR-101 is closed to traffic Friday to Sunday nights. The nearest **bank** is Banco Popular at Plaza Boquerón, PR-101 km 17.4, a ten-minute drive east of the village, but there's an ATM inside the *Boquerón Beach Hotel*.

Accommodation

Boquerón is overflowing with **hotels** and guesthouses, though it's best to call ahead on weekends and in summer. Note that anywhere on the central stretch of PR-101 (Calle José de Diego) will be **noisy** at weekends – in fact the whole village is best avoided at these times if you want peace and quiet, and weekday rates tend to be far cheaper. If your hotel doesn't have **laundry** facilities, try the public Laundromat (daily 7am–7pm) at the west end of the village, which has coin-operated machines ($1.50).

Boquerón Bay Guest House Quintas del Mar 10 ☏787/847-4325, ⓦboqueronbay.com /guesthousehome. This is a more intimate B&B option, a family-run house with lovely little pool, shared living areas, three rooms with kitchens, balconies, and all the amenities (including cable TV and a/c) – ask for an upper floor room. It's out of the village, in a more secluded area off PR-307 at km 7.6 (full directions on website). Weekly rentals only for $875 (no single-night rates).
Boquerón Beach Hotel PR-101 km 3.3 ☏787/851-7110, ⓦwww.westernbayhotels.com. Modern and characterless behemoth on the corner of PR-101 and the road to the beach, but worth considering for its proximity to the latter and its relatively cheap rates. Rooms are neat and tidy,

with red-tiled floors and bright bedspreads, all equipped with fridge, clean bathrooms, and TV. ❸
Centro Vacacional de Boquerón Balneario de Boquerón ☏787/851-1940. Despite the holiday-camp feel it's worth considering this government-run center – it's the only place where you can literally stay right on the beach. Avoid weekends and summer holidays, though, when the place is overrun with families. Each basic cinderblock *cabaña* (❷) sleeps six (two bedrooms) and has a kitchenette and bathroom, but bring your own cooking utensils and sheets (or rent the latter from the center) – it's all very sparse and a bit rough, but it's cheap and the proximity to sand and sunsets is priceless. Villas are slightly more comfortable (❹).

Cofresí Beach Hotel c/Muñoz Rivera 57
☎787/254-3000, ⊛www.cofresibeach.com. Smart place with Art Deco facade on the main road into the village, containing a series of compact one-, two-, and three-bedroom apartments, all with kitchens, tables, and living rooms. The furnishings are standard mid-range fare, but clean and comfortable, and good value if you're looking for a self-sufficient base. ❹

Parador Boquemar c/Gill Buyé, just off PR-101, ☎787/851-2158, ⊛www.boquemar.com. Another nondescript, modern three-story hotel, convenient for the bars and restaurants but noisy on weekends; rooms are a bit cramped, and it's worth paying $10–20 more for the top floor with views and balconies. The staff is adept at arranging activities such as kayak and snorkeling trips, *La Cascada* (daily 7.30am–noon & 5–8pm, closed Wed afternoon) is the only *mesón gastronómico* in town, and it's relatively cheap considering the location. ❸

Wild Flowers Guest House c/Muñoz Rivera 13
☎787/851-1793, ⊛www.wildflowersguesthouse .com. Two-story renovated wooden house on the road into the village, far more appealing than most of the hotels, with just eight small but cozy rooms all with cable TV, fridge, a/c, and attractive antique-style beds – ask for the rooms with outdoor seating and balconies overlooking the village ($25 extra), and check out the original artwork scattered throughout the hotel. ❹

Bosque Estatal de Boquerón

To escape the crowds, make for the **Bosque Estatal de Boquerón** (24hr; free) at the western end of PR-101, just before it meets PR-307. This is just a small section of the protected reserve, with a short but usually deserted boardwalk through marshes fringed with willowy sea grass and dense mangroves thick with scurrying land crabs. You can park in front of the information board on the left-hand side of the road, or walk from the village – the reserve office opposite nominally opens weekdays 7am to 3.30pm, but is often closed.

Refugio de Vida Silvestre de Boquerón

For a longer expedition into the untouched marshes around Boquerón Bay, head south to the **Refugio de Vida Silvestre de Boquerón** (☎787/851-4795), a 463-acre wetland preserve signposted off PR-301 at km 1.1, known simply as the Boquerón Wildlife Refuge in English. Wildlife here means **bird life** (the park was known as the Refugio de Aves when it was carved out of the Bosque de Boquerón in 1964), but it's also a spacious, breezy area covered in secluded trails and walks, perfect for biking, fishing, and hiking. The track into the refuge ends at the **visitor center** (daily 7.30am–noon & 1–4pm), which supplies basic leaflets and maps. The whole reserve is contained with three dykes that surround the Laguna Rincón and adjacent mangroves – the main trails follow the dykes. Over 120 species of bird have been recorded in the refuge, though you'll need to get up early to see most of them: the blue-winged teal, moorhen, and common snipe are most visible, while brown pelicans nest within the twisted arms of the mangroves.

Eating and drinking

After a trip to the beach, **eating** is perhaps Boquerón's most appealing activity, and despite appearances, hygiene standards are generally good. One of the best **kioscos** is ✳ *Happy Oyster*, usually found near the main pier: a dozen oysters or clams are sold raw, with a dash of lemon, for $4.50. It's open Friday to Sunday from around 11am till late, and occasionally on weekdays. Further along the main street you'll find more *kioscos* selling similar fare, along with *pulpo* (octopus), *carrucho* (conch), and *camarones* (prawns): *El Kiosko de la Abuela* sells tempting *empanadillas de mariscos*, *caldo de pescado*, and *pinchos de dorado y marlin* (mahi-mahi and marlin kebabs) for under $5.

Most **restaurants** double as bars, and come into their own on weekends when the village is usually crammed with revelers. Note it's illegal to drink from bottles or glasses in the street, but plastic cups or cans are OK.

Boquerón Bakery PR-101 km 18.3. Local favorite for an early breakfast, fresh bread, and cakes on the edge of the village, but also conjures up extra cheap burgers, hot dogs, and Puerto Rican dishes for $2–3.

Brasas Steakhouse c/Jose de Diego 210 ☎787/255-1470. Inviting restaurant located at the western end of the village, near the reserve, with a terrace shaded by trees. *Churrasco* steak is the main event here, but they also do pastas and local dishes (mains $13–25). Closed Tues & Wed.

🏃 **El Bulgao** c/José de Diego s/n. This shack is the self-proclaimed *casa de Viagra natural* for its libido-boosting *bulgao* (a conch-like shellfish also known as the West Indian Top-shell), as well as *pulpo* dishes from $5; their whiskey and vodka cocktails mixed with *agua de coco* and *piña coladas* from $8 are more likely to leave you flat on the floor.

Cocomo c/José de Diego 9. Reliable standby for breakfast, lunch, and dinner: solid breakfasts of pancakes or eggs are the best value (from $3), but the extensive menu of *comida criolla* staples for lunch is similarly priced, and you can also grab burgers and various alcoholic drinks. Closed Mon & Tues.

🏃 **Galloway's** c/José de Diego 12. This wooden shack right on the water has an enticing open-air veranda and plenty of parking. Nominally an Irish pub (though US license plates plaster the ceiling), the mix of *criollo* staples and comfort food isn't bad, and you can eat in the bar or in the separate dining area over a small bridge: choose the sauce for your fresh *dorado*, snapper and prawns

(creole, *fra diabla*, garlic butter or spicy creole). The main reason to visit is to enjoy the sunset over a cold beer or rum punch, the whole place reverting to lively boozer after 9pm on weekends.

Ocean Groove Café c/José de Diego s/n ☎787/851-4297. Slightly upscale bar and restaurant doubling as Internet café: customers get to use it for free, otherwise it's $5 for 30min (the maximum time allowed). The menu features plenty of Spanish and American classics, but the best dishes are the simplest – the rice and beans is heavenly.

Pika-Pika c/Estacion 224 (PR-307). Best bet for upscale Tex-Mex food, with all the usual burritos, tacos, and *fajitas* in a surprisingly refined dining room, though it's well-behind the seafront. Closed Mon & Tues.

🏃 **Roberto's Fish Net** c/José de Diego s/n ☎787/851-6009. Best seafood in town, with fresh, perfectly seared fish right on the waterfront at the east end of the village. Crab is the chief specialty: *salmorejo de jueyes* (crab stew), crab rice, or crab *empanadillas*. Closed Mon & Tues. You can also visit the more casual *Roberto's Villa Playera*, a little café around the corner (Fri–Tues 11am–9pm), which has a nicer view of the canal.

El Shamar (also *El Schamar*) c/José de Diego 1. Large, popular bar with pool tables that erupts with people, salsa, and *merengue* at the weekends, thanks in part to the cheap Medalla happy hours ($1) and friendly vibe. Also serves superb snack food: tacos, pizzas, and plump *empanadillas* stuffed with juicy fillings – try the lobster ($5–10).

Refugio Nacional de Vida Silvestre de Cabo Rojo

Much of the actual cape area, south of Boquerón on PR-301, is a rolling landscape of empty grassland and dry scrub, once the domain of cattle farms and denuded of much of its native vegetation by years of overgrazing. Today it falls within the 1836-acre **Refugio Nacional de Vida Silvestre de Cabo Rojo**, managed by the US Fish and Wildlife Service, but given the rather drab terrain, principally of interest to **bird-watchers** – species such as the Puerto Rican tody, Adelaide's warbler, and troupial thrive here.

The visitor centre, (Mon–Fri 7.30am–4pm; ☎787/851-7258), signposted off PR-301 at km 5.1, lies at the heart of the 587-acre original section of the refuge, established in 1974 and once used as a CIA "listening" unit. The center provides information about the ongoing work of the refuge, particularly the attempt to return the land to its original mature hardwood forest, and the twelve-mile network of trails that fans out across the plain: the two-mile interpretive trail provides a taster of the local ecosystem. If you have access to a bike, you can ride the **Cabo Rojo Refuge Bike Trail**, which starts in El Combate and skirts the whole area (see p.266).

Boquerón watersports

Captain Francisco "Pochy" Rosario's Light Tackle Adventure (☎787/849-1430, ⓦwww .lighttackleadventure.8k.com) runs **fly fishing** trips (normally 7.30–11.30am or 2–6pm for a maximum two people) from the public pier. He charges $275 for 4 hours and $325 for 6 hours. **Mona Aquatics** (☎787/851-2185, Ⓔmonaaquatics@choicecable .net), managed by Paco García and Captain Carlos Vélez, offers **diving** excusions to Mona and sites closer to shore. You'll find their office at the west end of the village, near Club Náutico.

Centro Interpretativo de Las Salinas de Cabo Rojo

Scorched mercilessly by the sun, the final section of the cape is a haunting moonscape of gleaming *salinas* – arid **salt flats**, a bizarre contrast to the tropical flora so familiar on the rest of the island. Considered the most important stopover for migratory and **shore birds** in the eastern Caribbean, the pinkish waters and heaps of rock salt blur into the Bahía Sucia on the eastern side of the road, an inhospitable environment more typical of Utah or Arizona. Salt is still produced here, though in much reduced quantities, and in 1999 an additional 1249 acres were added to the Cabo Rojo wildlife refuge (see opposite), made accessible by the **Centro Interpretativo de Las Salinas de Cabo Rojo** (Wed–Sat 8.30am–4.30pm, Sun 9.30am–5.30pm; free; ☎787/851-2999) at PR-301 km 11. Exhibits describe the ecology, history, and geology of the area, including the rich **bird life** of the reserve: nesting grounds for snowy plovers, terns, brown pelicans, and others, with 118 species recorded here in all. Outside, an interpretive trail highlights more of these with information panels, while the 40ft **Torre de Observación**, a five story wooden tower, provides a bird's-eye view of the saltpans and actual cape beyond.

Faro de Los Morrillos de Cabo Rojo

Cape Rojo itself is a narrow promontory of scrubby heathland and brackish salt flats, crisscrossed with trails and crowned by the **Faro de Los Morrillos de Cabo Rojo**, an elegant Spanish lighthouse completed in 1882. The *faro* stands on jagged limestone cliffs with the pinkish hue that inspired the cape's name, 200ft above the choppy waters below. PR-301 ends after 2km of bone-jarring unsealed road at a parking lot, from where it's a short walk to the lighthouse at the top of the headland. The lighthouse is still working and is closed to visitors, but you can wander around the grounds and drink in the blustery, dramatic views of the coastline.

Just east of the lighthouse, **Playa La Playuela** (sometimes referred to, incorrectly, as Playa Sucia) is one of the most scenic beaches on the island. Nestled between sheer cliffs, the short arc of floury sand is incredibly popular on weekends and in the summer, easy to reach from the lighthouse parking lot by following the dirt road that leads east – you can park behind the beach.

Practicalities

The 𝕏 *Bahía Salinas Beach Resort & Spa* (☎787/254-1213; ⓦwww.bahiasalinas .com; ❾) is a real gem of a **hotel** and the best place to stay in this otherworldly end of the island. It faces Bahía Salinas, on PR-301 at km 11.5, just as it becomes a gravel track, and though you can't really swim here (the bay is too shallow and lined with mangroves), the narrow strip of sand is pretty, and the sunsets magnificent. The hotel is surrounded by palms and designed in Spanish Mediterranean style, the cool white rooms equipped with smart wooden furniture, cable TV, and air-conditioning. The spa on site uses minerals from the nearby salt flats, and you can swim in the pool, rent mountain bikes, and choose from a long list of watersports.

The resort's swanky restaurant *Agua Al Cuello* is a lauded *mesón gastronómico* and the best place to eat in the region, serving contemporary Puerto Rican food with flair in a cozy wooden waterside terrace with rattan tables and chairs. Fresh fish (red snapper for $15 per pound, *dorado* for $19) comes with exotic sauces such as mango, pineapple, and almond, while the breaded crow fish ($22 per pound) and paella ($40 for two) are also exceptional. *Balahoo's Bar and Grill* offers slightly cheaper snacks and meals throughout the day.

Alternatively, cheap *comida criolla* can be found at *Karacol La Caña* (Sat & Sun 10am–6pm), one of a series of *kioscos* down the road knocking out seafood *empanadillas*, *tostones gigantes*, *caldo de pescado* (fish broth), and the more creative *vasos de pulpo de mollejas*, octopus sweetbread in a glass.

El Combate

Though it does possess a sort of down-at-heel charm, the resort village of **EL COMBATE**, at the end of PR-3301, is scruffy and run-down, gets packed out with families in the summer, and its modern, unattractive buildings have little of the rustic appeal of Boquerón and La Parguera (see p.272). On calmer days, however, the long, palm-fringed **beach** that runs for miles south of the village isn't bad, and the choice of cheap **restaurants** makes it a dependable choice for a budget lunch. Starting at the main beach parking lot, the **Cabo Rojo Refuge Bike Trail** leads south 5 miles through all the main sectors of the *refugio* (see p.264), though you'll have to come back the same way (inquire at the refuge visitor center or *Bahía Salinas Beach Resort* for rentals).

For **food**, *Annie's Place* (daily 11am–midnight) is a solid bet, the first spot on the seafront as you drive into the village, serving a basic menu of *comida criolla* and morphing into a popular bar in the evenings. Top picks include the *mofongo* stuffed with seafood ($7.95) and snacks such as *boletas de queso* (strips of cheese; $1.50) and slices of pizza ($2). You'll also find plenty of **cheap accommodation** in El Combate, comfortable but drab and uninspiring – you can do far better elsewhere. Of the guesthouses, *Cabañas Freddie* (☎787/851-7370; ❹) on the main seafront road has spacious two-bedroom apartments, while the *Combate Beach Hotel* (☎787/254-7053; ❸) is the best in town, essentially a motel on the seafront, south of the strip.

San Germán

Steeped in colonial history, **SAN GERMÁN** boasts a ravishing center of narrow streets and ornate mansions, adorned with stained glass and elaborate stucco. It's certainly the most beautiful provincial town in Puerto Rico, equally as precious as Old San Juan, but with a fraction of the visitors. Chief among its rare collection of graceful homes, churches, and museums is the **Museo Porta Coeli**, one of the oldest places of worship on the island and now an absorbing museum of religious art. Exceptionally quiet most of the year, the town bursts into life every July for the **Fiestas Patronales de San Germán**, honoring its patron saint.

Some history
San Germán has an odd and rather confusing history, compounded by a lack of historical records and, as always, the intense competition among Puerto Rican

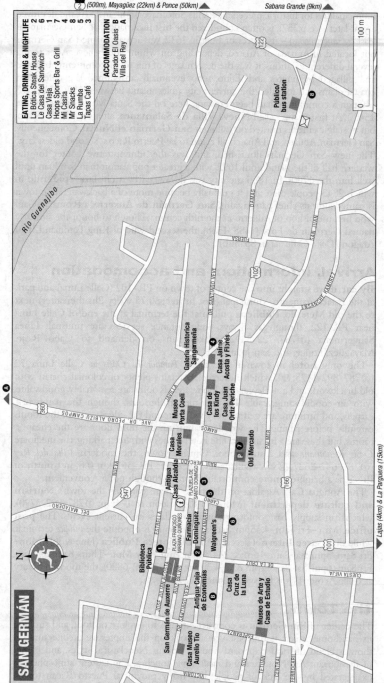

SAN GERMÁN

N

↑ (500m), Mayagüez (22km) & Ponce (50km) ▲   Sabana Grande (9km) ▲

100 m
0

EATING, DRINKING & NIGHTLIFE
La Botica Steak House   2
Le Casa del Sandwich   6
Casa Vieja   1
Hoops Sports Bar & Grill   7
Mi Casita   4
Mr Snacks   8
La Rumba   5
Tapas Café   3

ACCOMMODATION
Parador El Oasis   B
Villa del Rey   A

Río Guanajibo

Galería Histórica Sangarmeña

Casa Jaime Acosta y Forés

Museo Porta Coeli

Casa de los Kindy
Casa Juan Ortiz Perichi

Casa Morales

Antigua Casa Alcaldía

Old Mercado

Farmácia Domínguez

PLAZUELA DE SANTO DOMINGO

Walgreen's

Biblioteca Pública

PLAZA FRANCISCO MARIANO QUIÑONES

Antigua Caja de Economías

Casa Cruz de la Luna

San Germán de Auxerre

Museo de Arte y Casa de Estudio

Casa Museo Aurelio Tió

▲ Cabo Rojo (11km)

▼ Lajas (4km) & La Parguera (15km)

Público/ bus station

5

PORTA DEL SOL

267

municipalities for historic precedence. Villa Sotomayor, built in 1510 and destroyed a year later (see p.357), is often considered the first incarnation of San Germán (at least by *sangermeños*) – its successor, built in 1512, was actually named San Germán, but located in Aguada or Añasco, depending on whom you believe. After trying several different locations, it was the descendants of this town, consistently battered and pillaged by pirates and Taíno, who eventually abandoned the defenseless coastal plains and founded the current city miles inland between 1570 and 1573 (though a community had been growing here on the Santa Marta hills since the 1540s). At first it was called **Nueva Villa de Salamanca**, after the city in Spain, but nostalgic citizens insisted on calling it **San Germán el Nuevo**. Consequently, San Germán, Aguada, and Añasco all claim to be Puerto Rico's "second oldest city." The new San Germán flourished, and was the administrative center for the western half of the island until 1692, with a greater population than San Juan until well into the 1700s. In 1856 the city was devastated by a **cholera epidemic** in which 2843 people died, and it gradually became more of a backwater. The town is named after its chief patron saint, **San Germán de Auxerre**, a Romano-Gaul who became bishop of Auxerre in the fifth century, chosen to honor the similarly named Germain de Foix (1488–1538), the second wife of King Ferdinand II of Aragon (*Doña Germana* in Spanish).

Arrival, information, and accomodation

By car, drive straight into the center of town on PR-102 (Calle Luna) and park at the Estacionamento Municipal (first hr free; $0.75 every 2hr thereafter) next to the old Mercado. **Públicos** pull in at the terminal at the end of Calle Luna near PR-122, though as always, long-distance services are unusual: Línea Sangermeña (☎787/722-3392) makes runs on demand to Cabo Rojo, Mayagüez, Ponce, and San Juan.

The only **hotel** in town is the faded *Parador El Oasis* at Calle Luna 72 (☎787/892-1175; ❸), which nevertheless retains plenty of colonial charm with old brickwork and a 400-year-old lobby area. Rooms are reasonably good value, with air-conditioning, cable TV, and tiled bathrooms, though the paintwork, carpets, and furniture are getting very worn around the edges – check the rooms carefully before paying. The wooden cabins on the third floor are the cheapest rooms, but these are a bit smaller. The hotel comes with free parking, the mediocre *Oasis Restaurant*, and a small pool. Outside town, the modern *Villa del Rey* (☎787/642-2627, ⊛www.villadelrey.net; ❸) at PR-361 km 0.8, just north of PR-2, is a brighter, more comfortable option, though not as convenient.

The Antigua Casa Alcaldía on the main square contains the town's **tourism and culture department** (Mon–Fri 8am–noon & 1–4pm; ☎787/892-3790), which can supply basic information and updates on current events. The **post office** (Mon–Fri 7am–4.55pm, Sat 8am–4.30pm) is opposite the *público* terminal, while there's **free Internet** access at the **Biblioteca Pública** (June & July Mon–Fri 8am–5pm, Sat 8am–1pm & 2–4.30pm; Aug–May Mon–Thurs 8am–8.30pm, Fri 8am–6pm, Sat 8am–1pm & 2–4.30pm; ☎787/892-6820), the modern library at Calle Acosta 11 on Plaza Quiñones.

The Town

The center of San Germán is compact enough to explore on foot, and strolling its handsome streets is the best way to soak up the impressive architecture on show, a blend of local clapboard houses, various Neoclassical styles, and plenty of flamboyant Art Nouveau and *modernisme* touches. The austere atmosphere is exaggerated by the lack of people: like many provincial Puerto Rican towns, traditional street life has been sucked out by malls and suburban development, and other than a steady flow of customers to the incongruously located *Walgreens* on Calle Luna, at times it can seem a bit of a ghost town. Start at Museo Porta Coeli, on the eastern edge of town, San Germán's oldest and most iconic building.

Museo Porta Coeli and around

Rare example of the humble Spanish Mission style employed by the island's early colonists, the **Museo Porta Coeli** (Wed–Sun 8.30am–noon & 1–4.20pm; $3) was Puerto Rico's oldest church outside San Juan. Once part of a larger Dominican convent, it was originally known as the Capilla de Santo Domingo de Porta Coeli and today houses religious art work and statuary from around the region.

The church was established in 1606, but what you see today dates mostly from the 1690s. The Dominicans were forced out by government decree in 1838, and by 1874 the convent was so ruinous it was demolished. The chapel limped on until 1949, when the crippling costs of continued renovation led the Church to hand it over to the government. It reopened as a museum in 1961 and sits graciously above the plaza on steps of aged red bricks, its *ausubo* hardwood doors and weathered palm-wood pillars and beams making an atmospheric backdrop to the engaging collection inside. Highlights include a beautiful eighteenth-century wooden *retablo* (altarpiece), moved here from the cathedral and depicting the five patron saints of the city: Nuestra Señora del Perpetuo Socorro, San Germán, San Patricio, San Vicente Ferrer, and Santa Rosa de Lima. Similarly impressive are the *Estaciones del Via Crucis*, nineteenth-century carvings of the Stations of the Cross, and a more simplistic image of the *Virgen de la Leche* painted in 1864. You'll also find a small exhibition about the foundation of the church and the Dominican order, while outside in the terrace garden are the meager ruins of the convent.

Behind the church on Calle Javilla, the **Galeria Historica Sangermeña** is a series of inscribed tablets in a tidy garden facing the road, created in 1985 and listing all the key dates in the town's history. Nearby at Calle Dr. Santiago Veve 66, on the corner of Javilla, the **Casa Jaime Acosta y Florés** is a gorgeous example of late *criollo* architecture dating from 1917, a bright yellow clapboard house with veranda and ornate balustrade. Like most of the houses here, it remains a private

▲ Museo Porta Coeli

home and can only be viewed from the outside. Walk back towards the church along Santiago Veve and you'll see **Casa de los Kindy** on the left, built to impress in the early twentieth century, with a marble staircase, grand Neoclassical facade of Doric columns, and colorful *modernisme*-inspired glass in the windows. Before carrying on, nip down Calle Ramos to peek at **Casa Juan Ortiz Periche** at Calle Luna 94, constructed in 1920 in bombastic Palladian style, with a white entrance portico and staircase, the upper story topped with a tin roof, and more delicate stained glass in the doors.

Plazuela de Santo Domingo

The long and slender plaza that slopes gently uphill from Porta Coeli is the **Plazuela de Santo Domingo**, one of San Germán's two central squares. Originally a marketplace, the plaza is paved with cobblestones, its central brick-lined walkway (Paseo de Los Proceres) bordered with cast-iron benches and busts of illustrious *sangermeños*. Immediately opposite the steps below Porta Coeli is **Casa Morales**, San Germán's most photogenic house. Designed in an extravagant, gingerbread style, with turrets, pointed roof, and delicate pillars, it was built in 1913 for the family of Don Tomás Vivoni, and has been owned by Morales Lugo and his descendants since 1945. Note the multicolored glass in the windows, providing a pearly, shell-like effect.

Plaza Francisco Mariano Quiñones

One block west of Plazuela de Santo Domingo is the town's principal square, **Plaza Francisco Mariano Quiñones**, a more traditional space with a few trees and lined with terraces of clapboard housing. The **Antigua Casa Alcaldía** (old town hall) on the eastern side was built in 1844 and modified over the years, an impressively stately Spanish Colonial building that still houses government departments (including the tourist section). The main feature of the plaza is the grandiose **Iglesia Católica San Germán de Auxerre**, which looms regally over the western end of the square. The original was completed in 1573, with many subsequent enlargements, notably in 1842 when the current structure took shape, blending Spanish Baroque and Colonial styles, a gleaming facade, and decorative bell tower. As you enter, Las Capillas del Santo Cristo is on the left and the Baptistery is to the right, while hanging over the central nave is a crystal chandelier imported from Barcelona in 1866, said to be the largest in the Caribbean. Check out the stucco *trompe l'oeil* ceiling, restored in 1993 and mimicking wood beams, and the Carrara marble *retablo*, with a benevolent image of San Germán carved above it. The church is normally locked up and only opens for mass (Mon–Sat 7am & 7.30pm, Sun 7am, 8.30am, 10am & 7.30pm), but you can try the parish office nearby on Acosta (Mon–Fri 8–11.30am & 1–3pm, Sat 8am–11pm; T 787/892-1027) to see if someone will let you in at other times.

Back on the plaza, on the corner of Calle de La Cruz, **La Casona** was completed in 1871 as a luxurious home for Tomás Agrait, and for many years was the meeting place of local cultural foundation Círculo de Recreo, formed in 1880 and still going strong. It now houses the *Casa Vieja* restaurant (see opposite).

Calle de La Cruz

South of the plaza **Calle de La Cruz** is lined with more venerable structures, notably the **Antigua Caja de Economías**, the old Banco San Germán building from 1880, more recently a branch of Westernbank. Opposite is the captivating if slightly faded **Farmacia Domínguez**, originally a pharmacy founded in 1877, with walls of peeling pink stucco and heavy timber doors. Heading south, you'll pass the **Logia Masónica** on Calle Luna, a typically Greek Revival

Masonic lodge, now a small church on the lower floor but with the Masons' symbol still visible above. **Casa Cruz de La Luna** (Fri 2–6pm) on the other side of the road (c/Luna 67) is a private theatrical library and art space, with irregular events held on weekend evenings (check Ⓦ www.geocities.com /cruzdelaluna or call ☎787/264-4402).

Museo de Arte y Casa de Estudio

The lavish French-influenced villa housing the **Museo de Arte y Casa de Estudio** (Wed–Sun 10am–noon & 1–3pm; free) was built in 1903, and is one of only two mansions in San Germán you can actually enter. The house is more appealing than the collection inside, the upper story windows beautifully embellished with delicate filigree, and the carved-wood transoms and original wood floors providing a rare insight into the private world of the town's former elite. The museum displays the work of local artists and various aspects of the town's history – like many on the island, it has a small collection of Taíno artifacts, period furniture, and assorted bric-a-brac from the Spanish period, including old documents, photos, and religious items. The museum is a short walk west along Calle Luna from Calle de La Cruz, then south on Calle Esperanza to no. 7.

Casa Museo Aurelio Tío

One of Latin America's greatest poets, **Lola Rodríguez de Tío** (1848–1924) was born in San Germán and spent her youth in the family home at Calle Dr. Santiago Veve 16, west of the plaza, now preserved as the shrine-like **Casa Museo Aurelio Tío** (free). The name springs from the last owner of the mansion, one of Lola's descendants, though it's also known as the Casa de Los Ponce after Lola's mother, who was descended from Ponce de León. Parts of the villa date back to the 1840s, now comprehensively restored by the local Universidad InterAmericana, with a dignified Art Deco upper balcony jutting over the street contrasting with the typical *criollo* wooden doors and shutters on the first floor. This lower level contains an academic library, while the museum upstairs displays personal effects and memorabilia associated with the Tió-Nazario family, and the poet and independence activist herself. Lola became one of the most famous writers on the island after penning the patriotic lyrics to *La Borinqueña*, the national anthem. Like many *independentistas* of her generation, she spent most of her later life in exile, and died in Cuba. After closing for renovation the museum should reopen in 2009: call the university at ☎787/892-5634 for times.

Eating and drinking

San Germán has a rather unfair reputation as being a poor place to **eat** and completely dead at night, but there are some exceptional restaurants in the center and things are more animated on weekends. Businesses do seem to close with alarming frequency however, so call ahead to make sure.

La Bótica Steak House c/Santiago Veve 33 ☎787/892-5790. Housed in the elegant premises of the former Farmacia Domínguez, this restaurant offers juicy steaks and fresh seafood in historic surroundings – mains range $7–20.

Le Casa del Sandwich c/Luna 79 (opposite Walgreens). This classic hole-in-the-wall was established in 1930, with a weathered counter top and wobbly bar stools, crafting the eponymous sandwiches to order, with a variety of meat and egg fillings (from $3).

Casa Vieja c/Estrella corner of Cruz, ☎787/264-3954. Easily the most enticing place to eat in San Germán, housed in *La Casona* facing Plaza Quiñones (entrance is on c/Estrella), a magnificent two-story colonial house with a timbered upper balcony and bluish-green wooden doors. The menu features Spanish-influenced seafood, meat, and poultry dishes from $12. Wed & Thurs 5–10pm, Fri noon–11pm, Sat 5–11pm, Sun noon–7pm.

Hoops Sports Bar & Grill c/Luna, old Mercado building. This chain-like place turns out standard

US-style comfort food and beers, morphing into the hippest club in town at the weekends: DJs spin techno, hip-hop, house, jazz, and reggae at ever-popular club night *Da Bump* on Sat from 9pm ($3, women free before 11pm). Usually open Wed–Sun from 6pm till late.

Mi Casita c/Javilla y c/Santiago Veve. This friendly open-air shack is sandwiched between two roads, its handful of bar stools and plastic tables what you'd expect on a mountain road rather than in downtown. Solid Puerto Rican food is on offer here, with mouthwatering *pernil asado* (roast pork) and cheap *almuerzos* (lunches) of *arroz con grandules* (pigeon pea rice) from $3.25.

Mr Snacks c/Luna (near junction with PR-122). Locals flock to this handy *kiosco* to gorge on fried breakfasts, industrial-strength coffee, and lunches of gloriously deep-fried Puerto Rican favorites (around $0.75), pizza slices, and ham and cheese sandwiches for under $2.

La Rumba c/Carro (near c/Santiago Veve) ☎787/922-3340. The only Latin nightclub in the center of town, with vibrant salsa and *merengue* pumped out by DJs and occasional live acts: drinkers nod their heads over cold beers at the back until the dancing kicks off later in the evenings. Closed Mon, Tues & Sun.

Tapas Café c/Santiago Veve 48 ☎787/264-0610. This is a real surprise, delicate tapas with an authentic Spanish feel, emphasized by the high ceilings, terracotta floors, and small tables with Andalusian tile tops and wooden chairs. Choose from a carefully prepared menu of classics: *Jamón Serrano*, spicy *chorizo*, and *albondigas* (meatballs) from $6, washed down with tangy *sangría*. Things heat up with *flamenco* and salsa at the weekends. Dinner only Wed–Fri, lunch & dinner Sat & Sun.

La Parguera

Despite the tourist veneer, the former fishing community of **LA PARGUERA** has managed to retain a modicum of rustic charm, especially on weekdays, with its weatherboard housing and tightly packed streets resembling Boquerón. But the real draw lies along the coast: Parguera's unique offshore environment, a patchwork of placid lagoons, extensive coral reefs, and mangrove-smothered cays, is a water wonderland, known rather grandly as a "barrier reef-fringing mangrove ecosystem." Beyond this lies some of the best **diving** anywhere on the island, a huge drop-off known as **La Pared** (the wall) that runs for 20 miles parallel to the south coast. A short drive to the east is the **Bahia de Fosforescente**, the island's most accessible bioluminescent bay, though thanks to pollution, the least impressive. And at the end of the day, the ensemble of down-to-earth pubs serving hearty Puerto Rican snack food, and punchy local **sangría** makes for entertaining eating and drinking, especially on weekends.

La Parguera's transformation has been rapid, even by Puerto Rican standards. In 1945 it was a tiny backwater of just 24 fishing families; the first hotel was built in 1955, but as recently as the early 1970s it was best known for its mud-spattered streets and cavorting feral hogs. It now welcomes over 100,000 visitors a year and, as elsewhere, flashy condo development has arrived on the outskirts. If you're here in summer, try to catch the **Procesión de San Pedro** on June 29, honoring the local patron saint. Headed by an effigy of St Peter, the procession begins on foot before taking to a flotilla of boats and making a festive tour of the nearby cays.

Arrival and information

La Parguera is essentially a big village, and PR-304 ends at the compact seafront, where you'll find most of the restaurants and boats. When you hit the waterfront, turn left to reach the free **parking lot**. With no local tourist office, hotels are the best source of up-to-date tour information and conditions.

Most **services** can be found in the **Centro Comercial El Muelle**, the shopping mall behind the seafront on the way out of town. Here you'll find a gas

Puerto Rican food and drink

Traditional Puerto Rican food is known as *cocina criolla*, firmly rooted in simple but tasty Spanish cuisine and heavily influenced by the island's Taíno and African inhabitants. Puerto Rican cooking at its best is certainly no frills: served up on paper plates, at the beach or off the road, spit-roasted meats, fresh seafood and crispy fritters are tantalizing nonetheless, washed down with fine mountain coffee and the best rum in the Caribbean.

The staples

More than anything else, **plantains** are Puerto Rico's staple food, though the ubiquitous **rice and beans** (*arroz con habichuelas*) comes a close second, a richly seasoned dish served up in markets, canteens and restaurants all over the island. Plantains (*plátanos*) are savory bananas, used when green and too starchy to eat raw. Usually grilled or fried, they can be munched as a snack or as the base for something else, most famously **mofongo** (fried plantains mashed with garlic and olive oil, usually stuffed with meat), Puerto Rico's national dish (see p.31). Another traditional favorite is **asopao**, a delicately-flavored rice stew served with chicken or seafood. Grilled meats and fish grace almost every menu, with the most common items being chicken and rice (*arroz con pollo*) and red snapper (*chillo*).

Mofongo ▲

Lobster ▼

Deep-fried delights

One of the most wicked pleasures in Puerto Rico is spending an afternoon trawling **kioscos**, simple shacks that knock out mouth-watering fritters, *pinchos* (kebabs) and other slabs of sea-food for a handful of change. Common *kiosco* fare includes **bacalaítos**, a sort of plantain pancake deep-fried with mashed cod, and **alcapurrias**, a thicker, more substantial fritter made from mashed plantain and yautía root, usually stuffed with ground beef or various types of seafood such as crab. The best *kioscos* can be found in **Piñones** (see p.107), **Luquillo** (p.127) and **La Guancha** (p.292), but individual stalls grace roads, beaches and town plazas all over the island.

A regional sampler

▶▶ **The east** The sea is the main attraction on the east coast, so *mariscos* (seafood) and *pescado* (fish) dominate menus. *Pastelillos de chapín*, deep-fried turnovers stuffed with trunkfish, are the specialties of Playa Naguabo, while Punta Santiago is noted for its crab rice and *pastelillos de tiburón* (shark turnovers).

▶▶ **The north** The north contains the oldest *panaderías* (bakeries) in Puerto Rico, and the northwest produces rustic milk cheese known as *queso del país*.

▶▶ **Porta del Sol** Cakes and booze top the list of local specialties: *hojaldre* cakes filled with brandy and spices, cream-stuffed *brazo gitano* and lashings of potent *sangría*.

▶▶ **Porta Caribe** Dishes created in the south include *chuletas kan-kan*, pork chops with thick rinds, and *mojo isleño*, a piquant sauce made with tomatoes and garlic and smothered over fresh fish.

▶▶ **Ruta Panorámica** Dining in the Central Cordillera is all about barbecue, with smoked chicken, home-made sausages and **lechón** (roast pig) sold from smoky roadside stalls.

▲ Chuletas kan-kan

▼ Lechón

▼ Rum at Casa Bacardi

Rum

If you drink at all, you'll almost certainly be drinking **rum** (*ron*) in Puerto Rico, as even the most popular cocktails (not just *piña coladas* but Bloody Marys and *sangría*) will be made, religiously, with just one or two local brands. Available in light, amber or dark gold, rum is distilled from sugarcane all over the Caribbean, but Puerto Rico is the world's largest producer. While rum has been re-branded as a glamorous, exotic spirit in many parts of North America and Europe, it remains a drink of the people in Puerto Rico.

Ten coffees to try

Thanks to near-perfect conditions, fine Arabica beans and a tradition that goes back hundreds of years, Puerto Rico grows some of the best coffee in the world. Seek out the following: in most cases you can buy direct from the plantation.

▶▶ **Café Bello** (Adjuntas). Aromatic but mild, with buttery undertones and an exceptionally smooth finish. See p.346

▶▶ **Finca del Seto Café** (Jayuya). Organically grown, making it incredibly rich and nutty, with hints of caramel and chocolate. See p.343

▶▶ **Hacienda San Pedro** (Jayuya). Another potent roast, with rich, spicy overtones and a semi-sweet, chocolaty aftertaste. See p.338

▶▶ **Café Madre Isla** (Adjuntas). Made by the eco-friendly Casa Pueblo project. See p.345

▶▶ **Café Hacienda Juanita** (Maricao). Produced at the Hacienda Juanita (now a hotel) for over 170 years and once served at the Vatican. See p.349

▶▶ **Offeecay** (Maricao). Fresh, carefully crafted coffee from Hacienda Adelphia. See p.349

▶▶ **Café Concierto** (Maricao). Grown and hand-picked on the Hacienda Caracolillo. See p.349

▶▶ **Finca Cialitos** (Ciales). Unique flavor deriving from sweet, red coffee beans, roasted the day they're picked, providing a complex taste and intense aroma. See p.218

▶▶ **Café Cibales** (Ciales). Blend of buttery and smoky flavors, with a caramel-like after taste. See p.218

▶▶ **Mi Café del Pais** (Yauco, NUPCAY). Perhaps the most potent coffee, especially the *selección catador*, made with sun-dried beans grown over 2600ft. See p.301

A worker sorting coffee beans ▲

Yauco coffee ▼

station, post office (Mon–Fri 7.30am–4pm, Sat 7.30am–noon), Westernbank ATM, Centro Ahorros supermarket (daily 7am–10pm), Farmacia San Pedro (daily 7am–9pm), and several places to eat. Note that many shops close for lunch (noon–1pm).

Accommodation

Many visitors zip down to La Parguera for the day from other parts of the region, but if you intend to explore the coast more thoroughly it's worth staying the night. Much of the town is given over to hotels and restaurants, so there's plenty of choice, especially during the week, though overall the quality is not high – the smaller guesthouses are generally better value. On weekends, especially in summer, the town morphs into a full-on Puerto Rican family resort, and while this definitely adds spice to the place, especially at night, prices jump dramatically and it can get uncomfortably swamped with people.

If you want to camp, contact **Parguera Camping** (℡787/899-0539), just east of the center and back from the water, on the way to Club Náutico.

Gladys Guest House Calle 2 no. 42B (just off PR-304), ℡787/899-4678. Excellent budget option, set in an old wooden house loaded with character and presided over by the affable Gladys Rodríguez. The eleven neat rooms and three apartments come with a/c, cable TV, and free parking. ❷

Hotel Torres de la Parguera PR-304 km 3.1 ℡787/808-0808, ℗www.torresdelaparguera.com. This Spanish-looking hotel is a solid mid-range option a short walk from the waterfront, though a little overpriced given the tiny pool and motel-like the rooms: ask for one of the higher floors with a balcony, and check for package deals on the website. Rooms are generally clean, with wooden furniture and bright tiled floors. Singles pay $10 less, and it has free parking. ❹

Lindamar Guest House Calle 7, no. 118 ℡787/899-7682, ℯrosadolinda@hotmail.com. This cheap but pretty guesthouse is one of the best deals in the village, a two-story family home with veranda set away from the waterfront in the sleepy residential area – rooms are plain but cozy,

and helpful host Linda Rosado is a font of local information. ❷

Parador Villa Parguera PR-304 km 3.3 ℡787/899-7777, ℗www.villaparguera.net. This extensive clapboard property is the best hotel in the village, with comfortable if unspectacular rooms overlooking the water, and lush gardens that run around the pool and along the shore. As with most places here, check the rooms first: some are showing their age, but you should get clean tiled floors and a balcony, the best feature. The old-fashioned cabaret show at the weekends can be fun (after a few *piña coladas*). ❹

Posada Porlamar PR-304 km 3.3 ℡787/899-4015, ℗www.parguerapuertorico.com. Opened in 1967, this waterside hotel looks like an old wooden warehouse, and is perennially popular with divers for the convenient dive shop on site. Ask for a room with a balcony on the third floor and check first: most are plain but adequate, and the real attraction is the location and outdoor deck, jutting over the water. ❸

Bahía de Fosforescente

The ethereal glow of Puerto Rico's **bioluminescent bays**, a mesmerizing night-time effect caused by microscopic dinoflagellates, is the island's most celebrated natural wonder, though pollution means that La Parguera's **Bahía de Fosfores-cente** is one of the poorest, and nowhere near as bright as those in Vieques (see p.167). The trade-off is that it's far cheaper to visit (around $5–6 per person), and if you skim across the bay on a cloudy or moonless night, the luminescent waves and sparkling drops of water are still magical – any amount of moonlight can severely dilute the effect. Rampant development nearby has also had a major impact: over-fishing, the construction of almost two hundred summer houses (with marshland filled in to provide access), a sewage treatment plant, and heavy boat traffic are all to blame. The **Parguera Nature Reserve** (℡787-899-7484) has been established to protect the bay and surrounding mangroves from further damage, but its powers are limited. Boats take around twenty minutes to get to the bay, and most stay for ten to fifteen minutes. **Johnny's Boats** and **Fondo de Cristal III** make trips (see below for both), as does **Paradise Scuba** (see opposite).

Exploring La Parguera's coast

One of the most pleasurable activities in La Parguera is exploring the more than thirty **mangrove cays** and winding channels (*Los Canales*) offshore, messing about on boats or swimming in the calm, balmy waters. Away from the crowds the bay supports a rich wildlife, with manatees drifting lazily in the water, and brown pelicans nesting in the bony tangle of mangrove branches. You can take a tour, rent your own boat, or simply pick an island and hang out for the day. To negotiate prices, aim for the booths and boat owners on the wooden pier and dock area in the center of the village – at weekends you will be approached by ticket sellers in the parking lot, but don't sign up until you see the actual boat. The large island just offshore is **Isla Magüeyes** (or "Lizard Island"), owned by the Universidad de Puerto Rico and off-limits to casual visitors, its English nickname deriving from the giant Mona iguanas that can be seen lazing on its shores. Further round to the east are the smaller **Cayo Caracoles**, **Isla Mata de la Gata**, and **Cayo Majimo**. Cayo Caracoles is fifteen minutes by boat, a popular choice for its protected swimming area and short boardwalk through the dense, creeping mangroves. Other options include **Playa Rosada**, a pleasant beach mainland accessed by boat, **El Laurel**, a wedge of reef and sand to the west of the village, and **Cayo Enrique**, a more secluded islet further offshore with a lagoon and coral sand beach.

Boat operators and activities

One of the more dependable operators is **Johnny's Boats** (☎787/460-8922), run by Johnny and Gina Cordero. They offer one-hour tours through the mangroves for around $25 per boat (or $5 per person), or tours of the bio bay at night for $6 (including time for a swim). Alternatively, for $30 you can have a boat drop you at the island or beach of your choice, and pre-arrange a time for pick-up (if there's more than five people the cost is $5.95 each).

Those short of time or requiring more comfort can try the **Fondo de Cristal III** (☎787/899-5891), a 72-foot two-deck catamaran with part-glass hull. Trips around the bay and the underwater gardens of Isla Gata take about one hour and cost just $5 – the catch is they need around thirty people to make the trip, which means on weekdays you could be waiting a long time. At weekends turn up at 9am and get a ticket. They also do trips to the Bahía de Fosforescente at 7.30–8pm for $6.

For a more edifying tour of the mangroves, contact **Aleli Tours** (☎787/899-6086, ⓦwww.alelitours.com). Snorkeling tours ($50/hr) feature expert commentary from local ecologist Captain Ismael Ramos – they also arrange guided kayak trips ($50 per person) and bio bay tours for $90 (max 6 people). **Kayak rental** is $10 per hour or $50 per day and a fabulous way to explore the cays. **West Divers** (see opposite) also rents kayaks ($10/hr, $15/hr for doubles) and runs guided kayak tours at the weekends for $50 – swimming included.

Anyone interested in **fishing** should contact Parguera Fishing Charters (☎787/382-4698, ⓦwww.puertoricofishingcharters.com), run by experienced Captain Mickey Amador, an ex-marine biologist who knows where to find the biggest dolphin fish (mahi-mahi), wahoo, and blue marlin. Day-trips usually run from 8am to 4pm and start at $500 for a half-day and $850 for a full day. Friendly competition and similar prices are provided by **Mahi-Mahi Tours and Fishing Charters** (☎787/642-2587, ⓔcharters@villadelrey.net), run by Captain Carlos Rivera.

Diving

Lying just a few miles off the south coast, **La Pared** is an astonishing underwater shelf that runs for 20 miles, its 60-120ft drop-offs, 100ft visibility and teeming marine life making this one of the **best dive sites** in the region. La Parguera is the ideal base to explore the reef, with around thirty sites nearby, though the most rewarding are only suitable for experienced divers: beginners often get taken to the **Enrique** reef a short ride from the pier, a 60-foot drop on the edge of dense seagrass beds, but with not much to see. **Black Wall** is far more riveting, with 65-150ft vertical drop-offs, while **Old Buoy** is a sloping wall dusted with moray eels and the odd ray. You'll see a kaleidoscopic range of soft and hard corals everywhere, rich with darting triggerfish, grunts, snappers, and plenty of angelfish.

West Divers at PR-304 km 3.1 (☎787/899-3223, ⊛www.westdiverspr.com), just up the main road from the waterfront, is a newish outfit with modern gear, offering a full range of dive courses and snorkeling excursions ($35 per person for 3hr). Dives off La Pared are $80 (for two tanks) between 8am and 1pm (three people minimum), while shallower dives to some of the closer reefs are $65. Competition is provided by long-established **Paradise Scuba and Snorkeling Center** (☎787/899-7611, ⊛www.paradisescubasnorkelingpr.com), which offers two-tank dives from $70 and snorkeling from $35 (daily 10am–1pm, or sunset 4–9pm). Trips around the bio bay by boat (with swimming) are $25 per person (minimum 6; daily 7.30–9pm) and they also do the full range of diving courses and rent snorkels from $10.

Eating and drinking

Like most seaside resorts La Parguera does a good line in **seafood**, but the real specialty is **sangría marca coño**, a potent blend of Argentine red wine and fruit juices that has a zestier kick than the usual Spanish version. The drink is said to have originated at *El Karacol* (see p.276), and is allegedly named after the *independentista* cry *Coño Despierta, Boricua!* ("wake up Puerto Rico"), popularized by an Andrés Jiménez song in the 1970s. Elsewhere there are plenty of cheap and cheerful places to eat and drink, though it tends to be dead early in the week. Most bars and restaurants cluster in the ramshackle buildings and shacks along the wharf area, close to the water, while the newly renovated *kioscos* at Plaza Mirador San Pedro nearby offer the usual range of snack food.

Agua Azul c/Magüeyes (opposite main parking lot) ☎787/899-7777. Standout dining option with a versatile seafood menu and accomplished gourmet chef – order the catch of the day breaded, *criollo* style, or with butter or garlic sauce. Lobsters (from $25) are a specialty, but the humble *mofongo* stuffed with octopus ($16) or lobster ($24), pasta of the day, and crab stew starter ($8) are all exceptional. Wed–Sun dinner only.

Los Balcones PR-304 (waterfront), ☎787/899-2145. This bar-cum-restaurant occupies the second story of a modern building, popular for the views, pool tables, live rock music, frenetic dance floor at the weekends, and fusion menu: the prawn pasta ($15.95), *dorado* ($15.95), and fresh snapper ($16.95) slip down with Medalla ($2.50), wine, or *sangría* ($5, pitchers $18).

La Casita PR-304 km 3.3 ☎787/899-1681. This large wooden shack has been knocking out home-style Puerto Rican seafood dishes since the 1960s, always busy with regulars and families stuffing down the fresh whole fish (cooked in seven styles) and perfectly seasoned *asopaos*, particularly the lobster and shrimp versions, all finished off with the luscious coconut *flan*. Mains $10–25. Closed Mon.

Golden City Centro Comercial El Muelle. If you need a break from *mofongo* et al, try this decent Chinese takeout in the shopping mall. All the usual American Chinese favorites grace the menu: fried rice, sweet and sour pork, and a variety of noodles and dumplings from $5.

La Jamaca Reparto Laborde, Solar 5 ☎787/899-6162. This restaurant and guest house is hard to find but worth the hassle for its special *Chuleta*

Can-Can (pork chops) and tasty *criollo* food from $7 – follow the signs from the waterfront, west of the village, past all the new condos, and you'll eventually get there.

El Karacol (behind the docks). Operating since the late 1960s, the proud inventor of *sangría marca coño* ($4.50) also offers a range of fresh seafood dishes to soak up the booze: the *pulpo* and *mofongo* are especially good, made daily and always fresh. At the weekends this remains primarily about the drinks, with a crowd that spills out onto the street.

Lucerna Bakery PR-304 km 4. This tiny bakery on the way into the village is a bargain for breakfast, with bar stools, just two indoor tables, and a few more outside: takeout is more popular with locals. Order from a simple but satisfying menu that

includes eggs and sausage ($2.50), pancakes ($2.25), and sandwiches ($2).

La Pared *Posada Porlamar*, PR-304 km 3.3, ☎787/899-4343. Occupying the second and third floors above the hotel, this is a fancy option for breakfasts or an evening meal, serving upscale versions of Puerto Rican staples: chicken breast glazed with a *guayaba* (guava) sauce, and pork loin with mango chutney (it's one of the few places to serve more meat than seafood). The views across the water make for a romantic night out, but the prices are high – expect to pay at least $50 each without drinks.

Yolanda's Bar & Grill PR-302 km 3.2. Just up the road from the waterfront this friendly bar in a wooden shack sells cheap beers, sandwiches, *empandillas*, hot wings, mozzarella sticks, and nachos.

Travel details

Públicos

Aguadilla to: Mayagüez (infrequent; 30–40min); Moca (infrequent; 15min); San Juan (infrequent; 2–3hr).

Cabo Rojo to: Boquerón (infrequent; 20min); Mayagüez (infrequent; 15–20min); San Juan (infrequent, 4hr).

Mayagüez to: Aguadilla (infrequent 30–40min); Añasco (frequent; 10–15min); Cabo Rojo (infrequent; 15–20min); Rincón (infrequent; 20min); San Germán (infrequent; 30min); San Juan (6 daily; 3–4hr).

San Germán to: Cabo Rojo (infrequent; 20min); Mayagüez (infrequent; 30min); Ponce (infrequent; 45min); San Juan (infrequent; 3–4hr).

Ferries

Mayagüez to: Santo Domingo, Dominican Republic (3 weekly; 12hr).

Flights

The region's only international airport is Aeropuerto Rafael Hernández in Aguadilla, with regular services to the US mainland.

Mayagüez to: San Juan (5 daily; 35min).

6

Porta Caribe

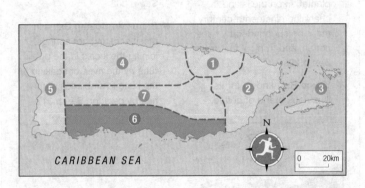

CARIBBEAN SEA

N

0   20km

CHAPTER 6 # Highlights

* **Ponce** This elegant city boasts romantic *criollo* architecture, an exceptional art gallery, and grandiose Castillo Serallés, legacy of the Don Q rum empire. See p.280

* **Centro Ceremonial Indígena de Tibes** Highly organized and utterly mystifying, the ruined ball-courts of Tibes are a fascinating reminder of the island's hazy pre-Taíno past. See p.295

* **Hacienda Buena Vista** Tour the most perfectly preserved plantation on the island, a charming nineteenth-century mansion surrounded by cacao, coffee, and tropical fruit trees. See p.296

* **Yauco** Best known for its illustrious brand of coffee, this beguiling rural town contains a gorgeous Belle Epoque villa and the creator of mouthwatering "*can-can*" pork chops. See p.297

* **Bosque Estatal de Guánica** Explore one of the world's most precious dry forests, a parched wilderness of gnarled trees and sandy hiking trails. See p.306

* **Guilligan's Island** Bask in the clear, waters of this pristine mangrove cay encircled by reef, just off the south coast. See p.308

* **Baños de Coamo** Bathe in these soothing hot springs, joining the locals in the public tubs by the river, or soaking up the historic ambience of the nearby *parador*. See p.312

▲ Museo Castillo Serallés, Ponce

Porta Caribe

P uerto Rico's balmy south coast is known as the **Porta Caribe** ("gateway
to the Caribbean"), a designation that neatly sums up its laid-back appeal.
The only part of Puerto Rico that actually faces the Caribbean Sea, the
waves here are calmer, the skies warmer and the air drier than elsewhere
on the island, but the lack of beaches means you'll see far fewer visitors. As a
result, traditional Puerto Rican culture remains vibrant here, towns and villages
exuding a strong Spanish identity closer in spirit to that of Cuba and Central
America. Ponce's genteel streets and exuberant carnival provide a total contrast
to fast-paced San Juan, while traditions such as mask-making and the rough and
raw business of cockfighting are enthusiastically preserved. Seafood is king, but
the region's long-established restaurants have a reputation for culinary innovation, from sumptuous *can-can* chops to delicate *mojo isleño* sauces.

Some of the most powerful **Taíno kingdoms** were based here, home to
Agüeybaná himself, overlord of the island when the Spanish arrived in 1508,
but the conquerors focused their efforts elsewhere and the south remained
thinly populated until the eighteenth century. **Sugar** changed everything, with
plantations rapidly colonizing the narrow strip between the Central Cordillera
and the coast, fueling a boom reflected in the ostentatious architecture that still
dominates the region. By World War II the sugar industry had collapsed,
attention shifting to the northern half of the island, and today great swathes of
the south are empty, overgrown prairies, a haunting reminder of a lost era.

Ponce is the capital of the south, Puerto Rico's second city and peppered
with ebullient architecture, a poignant legacy of those heady days of sugar. You
could spend a week soaking up the city, sprinkled as it is with mini-museums,
a romantic cemetery and its outlandish landmark, the Museo Parque de
Bombas. Highlights include the **Museo Castillo Serallés**, set in an opulent
mansion overlooking the city, and the **Museo de Arte**, a surprisingly comprehensive ensemble of European art history. Outside Ponce, make time for the
Centro Ceremonial Indígena de Tibes, one of the most important archeological sites in the Caribbean, and **Hacienda Buena Vista**, a lush coffee
plantation frozen in the nineteenth century. To the west, the humdrum town
of **Yauco** boasts a number of less-visited treasures to compliment its prestigious **coffee**, while **Guánica** is best known for its remarkable dry forest and
series of enticing beaches, the only section of the south coast mobbed by
tourists. To the east, the hot springs at **Coamo** are a pleasant novelty, but the
town itself is a fine product of **sugar country**, with nearby **Guayama** another
gracefully weathered example.

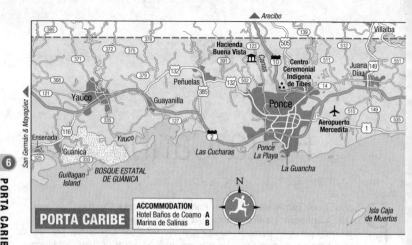

Known as *La Perla de Sud* ("the pearl of the south"), **PONCE** is a glittering showcase of *criollo* architecture, its lavish buildings a legacy of the golden years between the 1880s and 1930s, when the city was the hub of vastly profitable trades in rum, sugar cane and shipping. Ponce remains the **second largest city** in Puerto Rico outside Greater San Juan, and sometimes fierce rivalry exists between the two, *ponceños* often portraying themselves as a more sophisticated bunch than their money-minded northern cousins: as they say, *Ponce es Ponce, lo demás es parking* ("Ponce is Ponce, the rest is just parking"). San Juan is a far bigger and more modernized city, however, and Ponce feels surprisingly provincial despite its status, retaining a relaxed atmosphere long lost in the capital. Indeed, the city has struggled with serious economic and population decline since World War II, when industrial development focused on the north and the traditional plantation-based economy of the south collapsed. While Ponce remains relatively poor, things are improving, and since 1992 the government has earmarked over $400m to restore more than one thousand buildings in downtown, transforming much of the area around central **Plaza Las Delicias**. Several buildings act as small but fascinating museums, such as the exhibition commemorating the **Ponce Massacre,** while the collection of fine artwork on display at the **Museo de Arte** would be considered impressive in any European city. To get a feel for the old money that once dominated Ponce, visit **Museo Castillo Serallés** on the outskirts of town, monument to the great Don Q sugar and rum dynasty, and the sobering **Panteón Nacional Román Baldorioty de Castro**, the city's historic cemetery. In addition to the **carnival** (see p.285) and the vigorous **Festa de la Virgen de Guadalupe** (see p.285), the **Feria de Artesanías de Ponce** is held in Plaza Las Delicias in early May, a vast **craft fair** with music and food *kioscos*. Things also heat up in November during the **Fiesta Nacional de Bomba y Plena**, when drummers and dancers gather to compete.

Some history

Ponce was little more than a village until the mid-nineteenth century, evolving around a hermitage established in 1670. Ponce de León y Loayza (or Loíza), Juan Ponce de León's great-grandson, obtained official recognition for the

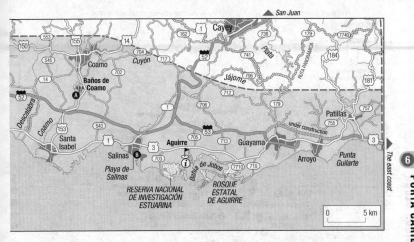

settlement in 1692, and the village was promptly named in his honor. Ponce remained a sleepy backwater until the 1820s, when the south became the center of the burgeoning **sugar economy** – the town rapidly grew wealthy as a port, trading, and smuggling center. Much of this new wealth was on display at the **Feria Exposición de Ponce** in 1882, an event which showcased the town's agricultural products via 440 exhibitors in the main plaza. The following year, Ponce was devastated by fire, valiantly brought under control by firemen operating from the **Parque de Bombas**, built for the *feria*. Despite a debili tating earthquake in 1918, the good times lasted well into the 1930s, the city home to scores of artists, politicians, and poets; *ponceños* are justly proud of their musical traditions, and claim that *danza* and *plena* (see p.373) were invented in the city. Ponce was also the home of the growing independence movement. In 1937, seventeen civilians were killed by police during a march celebrating the 64th anniversary of the abolition of slavery, a tragic event known as the **Ponce Massacre** (see p.288). After World War II the agrarian economy collapsed, and the introduction of new factories did little to alleviate the decline of the city. In October 1985, the *barrio* of Mameyes was destroyed by a tragic landslide triggered by Tropical Storm Isabel, killing 129 people and termed simply *la tragedia* to this day. The administration of Mayor **Rafael "Churumba" Cordero** began to turn things around in the 1990s, and although the popular leader died in office in 2004, successor Francisco Zayas Seijo has continued to revive downtown Ponce.

Arrival

Flights from the US (see p.19) and San Juan arrive at **Aeropuerto Mercedita**, 6km east of downtown Ponce (Ponce Centro). The terminal contains all the main **car rental** desks (see Listings, p.294) and a Banco Popular ATM, while the small **tourist information center** (daily 3.30–8pm; ☎787/842-6292), little more than a desk supplying basic information and maps, is usually open to meet incoming flights. If you're not renting a car or getting picked up by your hotel, you'll have to take a **taxi**. Most destinations have fixed tariffs: central Ponce is $13; the *Ponce Hilton* is $17; the *Howard Johnson Hotel* is just $7; and all other locations are $17–24. A taxi straight to the Yauco area is $40, while luggage will incur an extra charge of $0.50 per piece. Agree the price in advance for other destinations.

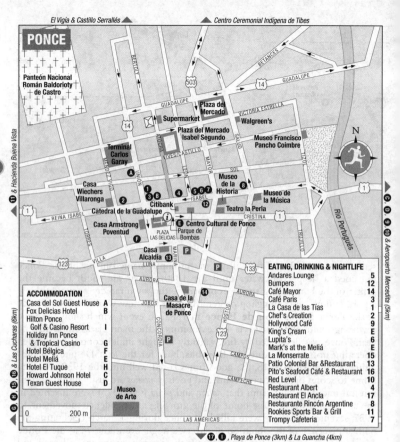

PONCE

El Vigía & Castillo Serrallés ▲   ▲ Centro Ceremonial Indígena de Tibes

Panteón Nacional
Román Baldorioty
de Castro

Plaza del
Mercado
Supermarket
Plaza del Mercado
Isabel Segundo
Walgreen's

GUADALUPE

503   14   GUADALUPE

BETANCES

VICTORIA ESTRELLA

Museo Francisco
Pancho Coímbre

Terminal
Carlos
Garay

Casa
Wiechers
Villaronga

Catedral de la Guadalupe

Citibank

Museo
de la
Historia

Museo de
la Música

Teatro la Perla

CRISTINA

Casa Armstrong
Poventud

Centro Cultural de Ponce
Parque de
Bombas

PLAZA
LAS DELICIAS

Casa
Alcaldía

Casa de la
Masacre
de Ponce

Museo
de Arte

0   200 m

EATING, DRINKING & NIGHTLIFE
Andares Lounge   5
Bumpers   12
Café Mayor   14
Café Paris   3
La Casa de las Tías   1
Chef's Creation   2
Hollywood Café   9
King's Cream   E
Lupita's   6
Mark's at the Meliá   E
La Monserrate   15
Patio Colonial Bar &Restaurant   13
Pito's Seafood Café & Restaurant   16
Red Level   10
Restaurant Albert   4
Restaurant El Ancla   17
Restaurante Rincón Argentine   8
Rookies Sports Bar & Grill   11
Trompy Cafeteria   7

ACCOMMODATION
Casa del Sol Guest House   A
Fox Delicias Hotel   B
Hilton Ponce
  Golf & Casino Resort   I
Holiday Inn Ponce
  & Tropical Casino   G
Hotel Bélgica   F
Hotel Meliá   E
Hotel El Tuque   H
Howard Johnson Hotel   C
Texan Guest House   D

▼ 17, 1 , Playa de Ponce (3km) & La Guancha (4km)

Ponce is 112.5km southwest of San Juan, around ninety minutes' drive along *autopista* PR-52 (there are four tolls along the way). Driving into the city is straightforward and traffic is far less congested than in the capital, especially in the center. Aim for one of the central **parking lots** – you'll find a couple on Calle Comercio east of the plaza (PR-133) and also on Calle Concordia south of the plaza under the *parque urbano* (all $0.75 per 1hr). **Públicos** pull in at Terminal Carlos Garay, four blocks north of Plaza Las Delicias on Calle Unión, between Calle Vives and Calle Estrella.

Orientation

Downtown Ponce, or **Ponce Centro**, is where most of the historic attractions are located and half of the hotels – others are scattered around the outskirts near the main highways, PR-52 and PR-2. To the south, **Ponce La Playa** is the old port district while **La Guancha** is a flashy new boardwalk and marina at the end of PR-12, both excellent places to eat but with not much else to do. West of town on PR-2, **Las Cucharas** is another cluster of inviting waterside restaurants, while overlooking Ponce Centro on the foothills to the north is **El Vigía** and **Castillo Serallés**.

Information

The main **tourist information office** (daily 9am–5pm; ☎787/284-3338, ⓦwww.visitponce.com) is inside the Parque de Bombas on Plaza Las Delicias. The office sells tickets for **tours** of the city, which are good value if you're short of time: for $2 you get a ride on the trolley-bus (see below); the rather kitsch "chu-chu train," and more enticing guided walking tours which take one hour and pass all the main sites in central Ponce. You'll also be given a book of discount coupons which can cut several dollars off meals and museum entry fees. There are usually seven tours per day, but not all in English: check at the office.

Getting around

Ponce Centro is easy to explore on foot, but if you don't have a car, take taxis or the trolley-bus tour for trips further afield. Note that Ponce is one of the few cities in Puerto Rico that now charges for its **trolley-buses**: these depart Casa Armstrong on Plaza Las Delicias at 9am, 9.30am, 10am, 12.30pm, 1pm, 1.30pm, 4pm, and 4.30pm, and make a loop around all the main sights, with stops and guided commentary. The bus is part of a $2 package available from the tourist office, and though you're supposed to stay with the same one until the end, the bus allows plenty of time at each site and it's the cheapest way to get to the Museo de Arte, barring a long, hot walk.

The easiest way to get a **taxi** from the center is to get the tourist office to call one for you, or find them near the central plaza, where you can set the fare in advance or persuade the driver to use the meter: it starts at $1, adding $0.10 per 1/13 mile thereafter. Prices to the main attractions are fixed: Castillo Serallés is $5 from Ponce Centro and $20 from the *Holiday Inn* or *El Tuque*, so use that as a guide when discussing fares elsewhere. Las Cucharas (*Pito's*) should be no more than $15, while La Guancha should be around $10.

Accommodation

Ponce offers two choices when it comes to **accommodation**: hotels within the central historic district, **Ponce Centro**, which has far more character and is more convenient; or hotels on the outskirts of the city, which include a couple of larger, more luxurious resort-style places. As with San Juan, there are few budget options, but the mid-range hotels are much better value here.

Ponce Centro

Hotel Bélgica c/Villa 122 ☎787/844-3255, ⓦwww.hotelbelgica.com. Established in 1872, this old-fashioned gem occupies a restored Neoclassical building with heaps of charm, and though it's fairly basic, the price makes it a good deal overall. Rooms are scrupulously clean, with high ceilings and wooden shutters, and some with balconies overlooking the plaza (though choose a windowless room to avoid noise at the weekends). All have a/c and local TV. ❷

Casa del Sol Guest House c/Unión 97 ☎787/812-2995; ⓦwww.casadelsolpr.com. This cozy hotel is in a small Ponce townhouse, with nine very plain but comfortable rooms with bathroom and TV. Downstairs you can relax or read in the

shady patio, enveloped with tropical plants, or soak in the bubbling hot tub. ❷

Fox Delicias Hotel c/Isabel 6963 ☎787/290-5050, ⓦwww.hotelfoxdelicias.com. The ornate facade of this former theater right on the main plaza, completed in 1931, converted first into a shopping mall and now a hotel, looks enticing, but it shouldn't be your first choice. Investment is required to fix problems with hot water and power, and the sterile rooms come with cheap fittings and tiny windows. They have cable TV but Internet only in the lobby, and the frozen escalators add to the sense of decline. ❷

Hotel Meliá Plaza Degetau y c/Cristina ☎787/842-0260, ⓦwww.hotelmeliapr .com. Facing Plaza Las Delicias, this is the best hotel in central Ponce, established by Mallorcan émigré Don Bartolo Meliá in 1895, but with no relation to the Spanish chain. The current property dates from 1915, the elegant rooms are tastefully decorated with smart new bathrooms and equipped with cable TV, free Internet, and Wi-Fi. Breakfast on the rooftop sundeck is included, and the small outdoor pool on the first floor is happily empty during the day. **④**

Greater Ponce

Hilton Ponce Golf & Casino Resort Avda Caribe 1150, ☎787/259-7676, ⓦwww.hilton.com. The most luxurious resort on the south coast is an eighty-acre self-contained universe facing the water, though the black-sand beach is poor and it's certainly not five-star. Rooms are spacious, with balconies and Internet access, and the relative isolation is compensated for by several restaurants, including the feted *La Cava*, and a large palm-fringed pool, but the real draws for most guests are the 27-hole golf course and tiny casino. Given its distance from central Ponce, you'll need a car to get around (parking is $4.50/day), though it's not far from La Guancha. **⑥**

Holiday Inn Ponce & Tropical Casino 3315 Ponce by-pass (PR-2), ☎787/844-1200, ⓦwww .holidayinn.com/ponce. This is a comfortable if fairly characterless option, convenient for the highway but a long trek from town (west of the city), and the restaurant on site is average and

there are far better eating options downtown. Rooms are modern, clean, and comfortable, but the best features here are the stellar views of the ocean and huge pool (they also have a gym). Plenty of parking, but fills up with 24hr casino traffic. Free Wi-Fi. **⑤**

Howard Johnson Hotel PR-1, 103 Turpo Industrial Park, just off PR-52, ☎787/841-1000, ⓦwww.hidpr.com. Convenient if you need somewhere to crash for one night, but this is a two-story, aging motel, built around a swimming pool courtyard. Its 120 rooms come with standard cable TV, and extras include a laundry, basic gym, and business center with Internet access (also Wi-Fi). Book on-line for the best rates. **⑤**

Texan Guest House PR-1 km 23.4 ☎787/843-1690. This no-frills motel option lies just off PR-1, beyond the junction with PR-52 – you must call in advance, as there's usually no one on duty. Rooms are acceptable, the cheapest ones with shared bathrooms. **②**

Hotel El Tuque PR-2 km 220.2, ☎787/290-2000, ⓦwww.eltuque.com. This is another cheap hotel that's best saved as a last resort, though families might appreciate the kids' water park and noisy speedway track on site. Most rooms are simple and showing their age, but adequate, and come with satellite TV, basic breakfast, and access to a small pool. It's a long way from the city center – again, you'll need a car or be prepared to spend most evenings at the friendly *Pub Club* nearby. **③**

The City

Ponce is an enchanting old city with plenty to see, but much of the allure comes from its ravishing architecture, actually a mishmash of styles employed between 1880 and 1940, and a complete contrast to the eighteenth-century streets of Old San Juan. **Ponce Creole** is a Spanish Colonial style, blending traditional clapboard *criollo* houses with exuberant balconies and layers of marble, while **Ponce Neoclassical** became vogue between the US occupation and the 1920s, a decorative form most associated with architect Alfredo Wiechers and influenced by Art Nouveau. You'll also see several Art Deco gems dotted around town, built in the 1930s. Almost all the main attractions lie within **Ponce Centro**, and the only reason to venture outside the center is to sample the city's full range of culinary delights.

Plaza Las Delicias

Ponce life once hinged around graceful **Plaza Las Delicias**, the central plaza that remains a hub of activity, though much of the commercial life of the city has migrated to shopping malls on the periphery. Anchored by Ponce's grand cathedral, the square is lined with Indian laurel trees, many dating back to the 1840s, and contains statues of former governor Luis Muñoz Marin and Ponce-born Juan Morel Campos (1857–1896), the acclaimed *danza* composer, as well as the **Fuente de los Leones** (Fountain of the Lions). The fountain was acquired at the 1939 World's Fair in New York to commemorate citizens who saved the city from a potentially deadly fire in 1899 – the lion is the symbol of Ponce, after the Ponce de León family.

The most arresting building here, and probably in all of Puerto Rico, is the cartoonish **Museo Parque de Bombas** (daily 9am–5pm; free), a bright red-and-white timbered hall with Mudéjar (Moorish) elements, constructed for the 1882 trade fair. In 1885 it became the fire station, and now houses the tourist office and a small exhibition on fire-fighting, far less engaging than the building itself. The **Catedral Nuestra Señora de La Guadalupe** (Mon–Fri 6am–2pm, Sat & Sun 6am–noon & 3–8.30pm) began life as a rustic chapel in 1670, but the current French-inspired Neoclassical structure was rebuilt in the 1920s after the 1918 earthquake destroyed much of its nineteenth-century core. Nuestra Señora de La Guadalupe, the earliest and most sacred aspect of Mary in the New World, is the patron saint of Ponce, and the annual **Fiesta de La Virgen de Guadalupe** is one of the most important festivals on the island (her feast day is December 12), involving candle-lit processions and special concerts. The exterior of the cathedral, with its stately towers and brickwork dome, is more attractive than the interior, though the stained-glass windows depicting saints are beautifully crafted, and an ornate alabaster *retablo* graces the altar.

On the south side of the plaza, the **Casa Alcaldía** (city hall) is the oldest colonial building in the city, dating from 1847 – you can pop inside the courtyard during office hours, but there's not much to see. Nearby are some truly grand Neoclassical structures: Banco de Ponce built in 1925 (now Banco Popular), and Banco Crédito y Ahorro Ponceño, constructed in Art Nouveau-style in 1924, now Banco Santander. Built by a Scottish banker in 1900, the **Casa Armstrong-Poventud** on the northwest side of the plaza has one of the most elaborate facades on the square, with sensuous caryatids flanking the main entrance.

It's also worth a quick peek inside **Casa Wiechers Villaronga** (Wed–Sun 8.30am–4.30pm; free) on Calle Reina Isabel at the corner of Calle Méndez

Carnival, masks, and the vejigantes

Ponce's flourishing *carnaval* starts one week before Ash Wednesday, a tradition that goes back officially to 1858, making it the oldest in Puerto Rico. It's nothing like the crazy celebrations in Rio or New Orleans (this version is more family oriented and a lot more local – you won't see many foreign tourists), but still loads of fun: just make sure you book accommodation well in advance.

The carnival opens with a procession led by King Momo (the traditional "King of Carnivals") and masked figures known as **vejigantes** (mostly local boys). The original purpose of the *vejigante* was to scare people (they traditionally represented Moorish warriors, as in Loíza, see p.107), and these days you'll see them merrily thwacking kids that line the streets with a *vejiga*, a dried, cow's bladder blown-up like a balloon. *Vejigantes* wear incredibly ornate and demonic **masks**, probably the most devil's aspect of the celebrations to outsiders: made of papier-mâché, each mask is embellished with outlandish colors and devilish horns.

The program of week-long festivities includes a *danza* competition, the unveiling of Miss Ponce Carnaval (chosen from a local high school), concerts, and special exhibitions in Plaza Las Delicias. The merrymaking ends on Shrove Tuesday with the **Entierro de la Sardina** (Burial of the Sardine), a mock funeral procession attended by hyperbolic cries and wails from everyone in sight. A dummy is symbolically burnt at the climax, signifying the purging of sins before the beginning of Lent. For more information call ☏787/841-8044 or check ⓦ www.ponceweb.org. To **buy masks** at other times, try **Utopia** (Mon–Sat 8am–6pm, Sun 11am–6pm) at c/Isabel 78 on Plaza Las Delicias, which sells all sorts of handicrafts including carnival masks.

Vigo, a short stroll west of the plaza. This was the home of local architect **Alfredo Wiechers**, who designed the house in 1911 in his signature Art Nouveau-inspired style, with pink rounded porticos, stylish Ionic columns, and undulating iron railings. The interior has been artfully restored, replete with period furniture and mosaic tiled floors, though alas, no air-conditioning. Wiechers, the Ponce-born son of the German consul to Puerto Rico, studied in Paris and Barcelona, where he was influenced by Gaudi's *modernisme*. Life became difficult for Germans living in Puerto Rico during World War I, and he sold his house to the Villaronga-Mercado family in 1918, before leaving the island forever the following year. Several of his distinctive designs still grace Ponce Centro, especially on Calle Salud.

East along Calle Cristina

The area east of the plaza is littered with tiny museums and galleries charting the rich history of the city. A short walk along Calle Cristina brings you to the **Centro Cultural de Ponce** (Mon–Sat 9am–4pm; free), exhibiting the work of local painters in its aging galleries. It also has an excellent literary **bookshop** (Mon–Sat 8am–11am) stuffed with the work of Puerto Rican writers, but only in Spanish. At the junction of Cristina and Calle Mayor you'll find the **Teatro La Perla** (Mon–Fri 8am–noon & 1–4.30pm; free; ⊙787/843-4080), a wonderfully restored Greek Revival theater adorned with Corinthian columns. English-speaking guides will show you around the polished interior for free, including a look at the vast stage and carved porticos. Built in 1864, the theater was destroyed by the combination of the 1918 earthquake and a fire in 1924, but rebuilt in this Neoclassical style between 1934 and 1940. The annual **Luis Torres Nadal festival** (Feb–March) sees a plethora of concerts and activities here, primarily for kids.

Museo de la Historia and Museo de la Música

Just around the corner from the theater, the **Museo de la Historia** (Tues–Sun 9am–5pm; free) on Calle Isabel also offers free English-speaking guides – it's best to wait for one, as the information given in the ten small galleries inside is solely in Spanish. Housed in a Neoclassical mansion designed by Blas Silva Boucher in 1911, the first series of exhibits tells the story of the city from the Taíno period to the modern day, while the next group tackles diverse themes such as health, the economy, and education, as related to Ponce.

Further down Isabel, at the junction with Calle Salud, the **Museo de la Música** (Wed–Sun 8.30am–4.30pm; free) was the former townhouse of the **Serrallés family** (see p.290), and another winning design by Alfredo Wiechers, with stained-glass windows, hand-painted floor tiles, carved mahogany louvers, and soaring 12-foot ceilings. Built in 1912, it was home to the family until they moved to the *castillo* (which was a summer house at first) and they eventually sold this house to the city in 1992 after a long period of abandonment. The interior decor is more interesting than the displays inside, essentially a collection of **musical instruments** (Spanish labels only), from the Puerto Rican folk, *bomba*, classical, and particularly *plena* traditions, the latest genre developing in Ponce in the early twentieth century. Look out for the florid mural by **Miguel Pou** depicting eminent musicians of the island, covering a whole wall.

Museo Francisco Pancho Coímbre

The next stretch of Calle Isabel is one of the prettiest in the city, a row of single-story houses dating from the colonial period. Baseball fans should turn left up Calle Lolita Tizol to the **Museo Francisco Pancho Coímbre** (Tues–Sun

El Cantante

One of the most talented yet tragic figures in the world of **salsa**, **Héctor Lavoe** was born in Ponce in 1946. He moved to New York in 1963, beginning a sparkling musical career that began with traditional *bolero* songs. Making his big break with band leader **Willie Colón** in 1967, he went solo in 1973, and had a string of catchy hits such as *Bandolera*, *Sóngoro Cosongo*, and *Joven contra Viejo*, but *El Cantante* ("the singer") became his signature tune, his eventual nickname, and title of the biopic movie released in 2007. Lavoe helped solidify the growing New York Latin sound of the era, soon to be known as **salsa** (see p.373), but despite his apparent success, he struggled with a largely unsupportive music industry, drug addiction, and depression for most of his career – after a suicide attempt in 1988, a penniless Lavoe died of AIDS-related complications in 1993. Initially buried in the Bronx, he was re-interred at the **Cementerio Municipal de Ponce** in 2002, along with his son Héctor Junior, and wife Nilda Rosado. In addition to laying flowers at the white marble headstone, fans can view the mural of Lavoe outside, and commemorate his birthday here on September 30. The annual **"Lavoe Weekend"** of concerts takes place on La Guancha boardwalk (see p.292) around the time of his birthday.

The **movie** *El Cantante* stars New York-born Puerto Rican **Marc Anthony** as Lavoe, alongside **Jennifer Lopez**, who was born in the Bronx to Puerto Rican parents from Ponce. Most of the Puerto Rican scenes were shot in San Juan, with just one concert filmed in Ponce.

9am–5.30pm; free), named after the talented batter who participated in the US "Negro League" in the 1940s and is regarded as the island's best ever player, prior to Roberto Clemente (see p.106). Coímbre died tragically in 1989, when a fire ravaged his home in Ponce – his baseball bat was saved from the flames and is displayed here. The museum is essentially a hall of fame and primarily for aficionados, the main gallery lined with the photos of famous sportsmen, mostly baseball players – you'll see portraits of Roberto Clemente and other memorabilia associated with the Ponce Leones baseball team, as well as more recent local stars such as Chaguín Muratti. From the museum, walk back into the center via Calle Castillo, another street of dazzling architecture.

Panteón Nacional Román Baldorioty de Castro

Ponce's tranquil old cemetery, the **Panteón Nacional Román Baldorioty de Castro** (Tues–Sun 8.30am–5pm; free), is the resting place of some of the city's most important citizens, fifteen minutes' walk northwest of the plaza at the top of Calle Torre. The cemetery opened in 1843, replacing an older graveyard built in 1808 where the *público* terminal now stands. Ponce's elite were buried here during the boom years of the nineteenth century, but the cemetery closed in 1918, and was gradually forgotten: vandals took their toll on the grandiose tombs; a period the site guardian calls "the poor's revenge on the rich." Marble was stripped and graves robbed. In 1980 the city started to restore the devastated site, and in 1991 renamed the cemetery after the energetic abolitionist who died in Ponce and was buried here in 1889 (see p.361). Now a preserved historic monument, its neatly manicured gardens are interspersed with ruinous brick tombs and the remains of grand monuments, hinting at its former glory. It may lack the grandeur of the great Latin American cemeteries, but is extremely poignant nevertheless.

The first plot on the main avenue is the tomb of **Antonio Paolí** (1871–1946), the accomplished Ponce-born tenor reburied here in 2005 under a circular white colonnade. Next is **Rafael "Churumba" Cordero Santiago** (1942–2004), the much-loved former mayor of Ponce, with a lion at the foot of his stately black tomb. You'll also see the resting place of **Roberto Sánchez Vilella** (1913–1997), who was governor of Puerto Rico 1965–69 and grew up in Ponce; the tomb and statue of **Román Baldorioty de Castro** himself; and **Manuel Tavarez** (1843–83), father of Puerto Rican *danza*, in a flat marble tomb. Beyond lie the ruins of other wealthy family vaults (mostly unmarked), the largest belonging to the **Serallés** family (see p.290) with room for twelve people – but only one body survived the pillaging. Somewhere are the graves of **Salvador de Vives**, mayor of Ponce and owner of Hacienda Buena Vista (see p.296), and **Francisco Parra Duperón**, one of the founders of Banco Crédito y Ahorro Ponceño, but you'll have to ask one of the caretakers to point them out. The small tomb in the far right corner belongs to Rachel Rudd (1895–99), daughter of a missionary who died tragically young. While the rich and famous took up the main plots, victims of the 1856 cholera epidemic were buried near the left-hand wall, and the poor were collected in mass graves at the back: on the right-hand side was a plot reserved for Protestants. The **Museo del Autonomiso Puertorriqueño** in the corner has a tiny exhibit dedicated to Castro's autonomy movement of the late nineteenth century, and information about recent mayors of Ponce (Spanish explanations only).

Casa de la Masacre de Ponce

Though the primary purpose of the small but thought-provoking **Casa de la Masacre de Ponce** (Wed–Sun 8am–4.30pm; free) is to commemorate the Ponce Massacre of 1937 (see below), it's really a spirited presentation of the whole history of the **Puerto Rican independence movement**. Beginning with Puerto Rico's struggles against foreign invaders in the early Spanish period, it traces the progress of the nationalist cause in the early nineteenth century, building up to the massacre itself. Pedro Albizu Campos and his Nationalist Party, and the events of the 1950s, are given special focus. The exhibition ends, somewhat optimistically, with the successful ousting of the US Navy from Vieques in 2003.

Ponce Massacre

One of the worst human rights abuses committed on US soil, the **Ponce Massacre** of seventeen civilians has assumed mythical status on the island, not just within the independence movement, but for many ordinary Puerto Ricans too, despite taking place over seventy years ago. The killings occurred amid growing tension: in the 1930s, the increasingly frustrated **Nationalist Party**, led by Ponce lawyer **Pedro Albizu Campos** and advocating full independence for Puerto Rico, became more militant, and relations with the police deteriorated rapidly. On Palm Sunday, 1937, the party organized a march in Ponce to commemorate the anniversary of the abolition of slavery, but at the last minute Governor Winship revoked their permit – he had surmised, correctly, that the march would also be an indirect protest against the recent incarceration of Albizu. Indignant, the marchers decided to continue as planned: in trying to break up the protest, police fired on the crowd with machine guns, killing seventeen people – men, women and one twelve-year-old girl – two policemen also died. Over one hundred people were wounded, many while trying to run away, and in the aftermath hundreds more were arrested. The massacre led to widespread anger across the island, especially when an official inquiry proved inconclusive and an investigation by the American Civil Liberties Union held the governor responsible. The massacre has only been taught in schools since 1990, and was largely covered up by the government. Now there are subdued ceremonies honoring the dead held every year at the Casa de la Masacre.

The museum is especially poignant because this is the former headquarters of the Nationalist Party, and the massacre took place just outside. If you ask, you'll usually find enthusiastic guides, many of whom are still politically active, willing to translate the predominantly Spanish information on display – this is a rare chance for visitors to meet some genuine independence supporters. The museum is on Calle Marina south of the plaza, near Calle Aurora.

Museo de Arte

With an impressive collection of over three thousand paintings, the **Museo de Arte** (daily 10am–5pm; $5, special exhibitions $2.50; ⓦ www.museoarteponce .org) is a real surprise, a treasure trove of fine European art in the heart of the Caribbean. Founded by former governor Luis A. Ferré in 1959, the museum is undergoing an ambitious **renovation** and extension, which means many of the following exhibits will move around, though the main galleries are expected to stay open throughout. At the time of writing the museum's rich ensemble of **Puerto Rican art** had yet to be allocated a permanent home, but you are likely to see the key works somewhere inside: as well as lauded paintings from **José Campeche** and **Francisco Oller** (especially *La Ceiba de Ponce*), Ponce artist **Miguel Pou** is well represented. Look out also for modern creations such as Rafael Tufino's *La Botella* (1963) and the moving *Barrio Tokio* (1962) by Myrna Baez. The museum is south of the Casa de la Masacre on Avenida Las Américas (PR-163), a twenty-minute walk from the plaza.

The collection

The initial first-floor galleries are dedicated to **French art** from the fourteenth to eighteenth centuries, mostly Baroque and fairly mediocre Rococo work. Through the passage on the right is a spacious gallery of international and more engaging French work from the nineteenth century, notably a bronze sculpture by **Rodin** and **Delacroix**'s *Study for the Two Foscaris* (1845), a small, sensitive painting of the Venetian Doge that laid the foundation for his exceptionally moving *Two Foscaris* ten years later.

Ponce is probably the last place you'd expect to find British nineteenth-century art, yet the last gallery is dedicated to an extraordinary collection of work from the **Pre-Raphaelite** school (1848–52) and its successor, the **Aesthetic Movement** (1870–80). Founded by John Everett Millais, Dante Gabriel Rossetti, and William Holman Hunt, the Pre-Raphaelites were inspired in part by an idealized view of the medieval period and a desire to create a more spiritual representation of nature, while the Aesthetics went further in proclaiming "art for art's sake" and advocating a cult of beauty. Millais, Hunt, and Rossetti are all represented here, with the last's *Roman Widow* (1874) a moving example of his later work: a widow of ancient Rome sits beside the urn containing her husband's ashes, playing two instruments in an expression of grief. Note the wonderful array of white shades, and the care taken with the fine details, such as the inscription on the urn. The crowning glory of this section, however, is *Flaming June* (1895), **Frederic Leighton**'s masterpiece, a sensuous depiction of a sleeping girl wrapped in a brilliant orange robe, an allusion to classic depictions of the goddess Venus, and simply unforgettable. The painting was famously acquired by Ferré in 1963 for a bargain price, thanks to the painter's low standing at the time. Elsewhere you'll see plenty of relatively lightweight stuff from **Edward Coley Burne-Jones** and **Ford Madox Brown**, though the gallery also has *Portrait of a Young Lady* from eighteenth-century portrait artist **Thomas Gainsborough**.

Don Q

The best-loved and most fiercely guzzled rum in Puerto Rico is **Don Q** (⊛ www.donq
.com), still proudly produced in Ponce by the **Destilería Serrallés** near the airport
(which was once its private airstrip). Like the Barcardís, the Serrallés family hail from
Catalunya in northern Spain, and it was patriarch **Juan Serrallés Colón** (1834–1897)
who emigrated to Puerto Rico and established Hacienda Mercedita in 1861 as a
sugar-cane plantation, still the location of the current distillery. In 1865 he began to
produce quality **rum**, using a French still you can see in the Castillo Serrallés, but it
wasn't until 1932 that the Don Q brand was launched, named after the much-loved
Cervantes character, Don Quixote. *Don Q Gold* and especially *Don Q Cristal* are now
staples in almost every home and bar on the island, and if you order a *piña colada*,
it will almost certainly contain the latter. Don Q is still owned by Destilería Serrallés,
which also produces the Ron Llave, Palo Viejo, and Granado brands, as well as
Ronrico and Captain Morgan for distribution in the Caribbean (Seagrams has US
distribution rights). Sadly, tours of the distillery are not available.

The second-floor galleries are arranged geographically, with a large collection of **Italian** work, including some medieval paintings from the **Sienese
School**, the oldest in the museum. Much of this is unremarkable, but the
galleries are small and offer an easy-to-digest history of Renaissance art. The
real highlights, however, are from **Spain**: look out for *Don Garpar*, attributed
to one of the world's great masters, **Diego Velázquez**; an adroit *Christ
Crucified* by **Francisco de Zurbarán**; and a portrait of *Martín Zapater* from
Goya (though this is a little drab, the jet-black background only hinting at
Goya's formidable talents). In the same section **El Greco**'s *St Francis in Medita-
tion with Brother Leo* is typically haunting, while other highlights include the
Head of the Magus by **Peter Paul Rubens** and a couple of minor paintings
by **Anthony van Dyck**.

Museo Castillo Serrallés and Cruceta del Vigía

Crowning the hills just to the north of Ponce Centro, the **Museo Castillo
Serrallés** (Tues–Thurs 9am–5pm, Fri–Sun 9am–5.30pm; $6, $2 gardens only;
☎787/259-1774; ⊛ home.coqui.net/castserr) was once the luxurious base of
the powerful Serrallés family, the sugar who that established **Don Q** rum (see
above). Plush mansion rather than fortress, it presides over the city like a
medieval castle nonetheless, its delicate Moorish arches, ornamental tower, and
terracotta tiling evoking Granada's majestic Alhambra palace. Built in Spanish
Revival style in 1930, the house served as the family's summer home until
1935, when it became their primary residence. Sold to the city in 1986, it's
valued at around $35m today.

Though a small exhibition room is dedicated to sugar and rum-making inside,
this isn't anything like Casa Bacardi – the mansion is a window into the life of
Puerto Rico's upper classes in the early twentieth century, the rooms perfectly
maintained with all the lavish accoutrements. Tours lead you through *salons*
crammed with period furniture and extravagant decor in pristine condition.
Highlights include the gorgeous Andalusia-inspired *patio interior*, and the most
expensive part of the house, the **dining room**, with a wooden ceiling carved
in an elaborate *artesenal* style.

The house can only be visited on guided tours that usually run every 30 to
45 minutes and take around one hour, beginning with a short **video** about the
family and Don Q. Times are not set and the language of the tour (Spanish or
English) depends on who turns up, so call in advance to avoid a wait. You can

also enjoy fabulous views of Ponce from the flower-filled gardens. Taxis charge $5 to drive up the hill from the plaza – you can walk back down in around forty minutes, but take lots of water. The trolley-bus no longer goes here.

Looming above the house is the **Cruceta del Vigía** (Tues–Sun 9.30am–5pm; $4 includes Jardín Japonés; $9 with Castillo), a 100-foot-high concrete cross offering another lofty view over the city and Caribbean beyond. Entry includes the elevator ride up to the observation area in the crosspiece, and the serene **Jardín Japonés** (Japanese Garden) at the back. An original wooden cross was built as part of a pirate warning station in 1801, and destroyed by Hurricane Georges in 1989. The concrete cross that replaced it was completed in 1984, in part to honor the security guard, Don Luis, who manned the station until his death in 1916.

Isla Caja de Muertos

If you visit Ponce on a weekend, take the ferry to **Isla Caja de Muertos** (Coffin Island), a sun-swept reserve of spotless beaches and dolphin-rich waters, five miles offshore. The island covers an area of 400 acres, and other than a few barbecue grills, gazebos, and a DRNA ranger station, is bereft of facilities. The main draw is the chance to lounge on the narrow but inviting stretches of white sand near the jetty (Balneario Pelicano and La Playa Larga), but you can also **snorkel** off the reef-encrusted shore, and hike along a surprisingly steep trail to the limestone outcrop in the center (almost 230ft straight up – take lots of water). At the top you'll find a **Spanish lighthouse** built in 1887 (automated but still working), and sweeping views of the main island. Small caves perforate the lower slopes, some with faint traces of Taíno petroglyphs, but these are hard to find without a guide. The rest of the island is relatively flat and covered in the same arid vegetation predominant in Guánica (see p.306).

Island Venture Water Excursions (☎787/842-8546, ⓦ www.islandventurepr .com; $17) runs a **ferry** to the island from **La Guancha** on Saturdays, Sundays, and most holidays. The first ferry usually leaves at around 8.30am and returns at around 3.30pm (45min one-way), but call in advance – a maximum of 325

▲ Isla Caja de Muertos

people are allowed on the island and the boat can take 125 people per trip. Take all the food and water you need, and a bag for garbage – leave nothing on the island. The same company offers daily **dive excursions** ($65 for two tanks) and snorkeling/beach ($35) trips to the island. For something a little more structured, contact Acampa Tours (℡787/706-0695, ⓦwww.acampapr .com), which runs expeditions to Isla Caja de Muertos for a total $1350 (plus tax) for up to six people, including a private catamaran to the island, lunch, and an expert guide to lead you along the trails. Unless it's a public holiday, the island is closed on Mondays.

Eating and drinking

Eating options in **Ponce Centro** are surprisingly poor compared to Old San Juan, limited to local cafeterias, a handful of upmarket restaurants and fast food on the plaza. *Ponceños* spend more time zipping around the outskirts in search of good meals, particularly along the section of PR-2 known as **Las Cucharas**, 6.5km west of the city. Restaurants here face the Caribbean on the southern (east bound) side of the highway, and though the quality of the seafood makes a trip worthwhile, you need to watch the manic traffic when getting back onto the road. **Playa de Ponce**, the slightly shabby former port area at the end of PR-123, 3.2km south of the center, also contains a handful of good-quality restaurants, while **La Guancha** is packed with families on weekends – parking here is easy, and the boardwalk (*tablado*) is lined with bars and *kioscos* selling all the usual Puerto Rican favorites. You'll also see giant tarpon and scores of brown pelicans being fed by the crowds at the southern end, near the Asoci-ación de Pescadores (see box opposite).

For **self-catering**, most of the larger supermarkets lie on the main highways outside the city, but the small *Super Mercado Atocha* (daily 7.30am–6pm) at Calle Atocha 104, four blocks north of the central plaza, has a basic selection of fresh and canned food.

Ponce Centro

Café Mayor c/Aurora 2638 (on the corner of c/Mayor). Also known as *Café Café*, this charming colonial house serves fresh juices indoors or in the leafy garden, as well as the best Puerto Rican coffee on the island. The secret: they expertly roast their potent, aromatic beans on the premises. You can also buy the raw product ($2–4 per bag), order sandwiches and local food (from $4), and admire the coffee-inspired murals on the walls. Turns into a cozy bar at night. Closed Sun.
Café Paris c/Isabel, on Plaza Las Delicias. The most convenient pit-stop on the plaza, a small bakery with a handful of tables inside. Grab coffee ($1), sandwiches ($2.50), or even a shaved-ice daiquirí ($4) to brighten up the afternoon. Closed Sun.
La Casa de las Tías c/Unión at c/Reina (just off the plaza) ℡787/844-3344. Refined Spanish restaurant, "the house of aunts" (aka the two owners), lures the town's elite with a menu of fine seafood (cod, red, snapper and mahi-mahi), excellent wine list, and historic, gallery-like ambience. The two fashionable bars on site are

also popular on weekends. Mains $20–30. Closed Mon.

Chef's Creation c/Reina 100. This crowd-pulling cafeteria is the best place to gorge on cheap, no-frills local food ($5–6): pick up a tray, select what you want, and grab a table indoors or on the patio at the back. It's standard stuff: fried chicken, rice and beans, stews and roast pork, but everything is fresh and perfectly cooked. Lunch only.

King's Cream c/Marina 9223, on Plaza Las Delicias. This venerable ice cream parlor sells around twelve refreshing home-made flavors, from tangy tropical fruits such as pineapple and coconut, to deliciously smooth chocolate, vanilla, and local favorites *tamarindo* and *guanabana* (soursop). Cups and cones range $1.10–1.60, while pints are $2.75.

Mark's at the Meliá *Hotel Meliá* ℡787/284-6275. The most upmarket place to eat in central Ponce, with carefully crafted cuisine from chef Mark French and prices to match. The food is a blend of international classics, grilled meats and pastas, with local seafood and Puerto

Snacking at La Guancha

La Guancha's harbor-side boardwalk at the end of PR-12 is crammed with locals on weekends, eagerly trawling the long line of Puerto Rican snack stalls. Stand-out *kioscos* include *La Mexicana* (no. 8) for its *pinchos*, *alcapurrias*, and *piña coladas* in plastic cups; *Miramar* (no. 2) for fried chops and steaks; *El Guanchero* (no. 10) for *frituras*; and *El Pilon Borincano* (no. 15) for *mofongo*, roast chicken, and *pulpo* salad. You won't pay more than $6 for anything. For a sit-down meal indoors (with a/c), head to *El Paladar* (daily 11am–11pm) in the center, which serves sumptuous *churrasco* ($9.50), lots of prawn dishes, and a decent paella ($19.95), though service is sometimes poor. The upstairs bar is the best place for a cold beer or cocktail with a view.

Rican classics: try the Caribbean shrimp *mofongo* ($26), creamy swordfish carbonara ($26), or sauteed codfish ($24), oozing with flavor. Closed Sun & Mon.

Restaurant Albert Plaza Isabel II, c/Isabel 66. This hole-in-the-wall dishes out hearty local fare in the courtyard just inside a renovated historic building, regularly attracting a hungry throng of office workers for lunch. The tempting range of sandwiches and combos of *tortillas*, *tostadas*, *mofongo*, burgers, rice, and *chuletas* costs less than $5. Takeaway or grab one of the tables outside. Closed Sun.

Restaurante Rincón Argentine c/Salud 69, at c/Isabel. For a welcome break from Puerto Rican food, try this Argentine steak house, set in a gorgeous colonial villa with shady patio, palm trees, and wrought-iron railings. Grilled meats are the focus of the menu, but you'll also have a good choice of fish and pastas (mains $15–30).

Trompy Cafeteria c/Isabel 56. Compact, no-nonsense canteen with plastic tables and a solid choice for cheap, filling breakfasts of ham and eggs ($3) and sandwiches (from $1.25). The *comida criolla* lunches are equally good value: *mofongo* for $2.50 and *chuletas* from $5.50. Closed Sun. *Café Tomas* next door is a smarter, sit-down affair.

Greater Ponce

La Monserrate PR-2 km 218, Las Cucharas ☎787/841-2740. Worthy alternative to *Pito's* with similar sea views and seafood menu, without the hype (mains $8–30). The attractive, wood-lined interior is reminiscent of a ship's galley, and you can dine on the open-air terrace at the back.

Pito's Seafood Café & Restaurant PR-2 km 218.7, Las Cucharas ☎787-841-4977. If you come to Las Cucharas just once, try this justifiably lauded seafood restaurant, a pretty pink wooden building right on the water. Locals grumble that it's become too touristy, but the food is consistently good quality, and the clean, open deck offers bewitching views across the Caribbean. Fri & Sat nights kick off with live music and plenty of cocktails, and the vast includes offers fresh lobster, shellfish, red snapper, and delectable house specialties such as trunkfish and shrimp wrapped in bacon (mains $8–30).

Restaurant El Ancla Avda Hostos 805, Playa de Ponce ☎787/840-2450. This award-winning but low-key restaurant is the best in the old port district. Ideal for lunch, the graceful, aging interior retains a loyal local following, with superb seafood (mains from $8), great pitchers of *sangría*, and punchy *piña coladas*. It faces the harbor, right on the water, but parking is limited. Closed Mon.

Bars and clubs

The streets of central Ponce might seem dead after 6pm, especially early in the week, but there are a few bars and clubs around, especially on **Calle Isabel**, just east of the main plaza, and it gets livelier at the weekends. **La Guancha** can also be fun, with dancing and drinking spilling out onto the boardwalk Thursday to Sunday nights. Other options are more spread out and not that practical unless you're used to driving around the city at night. Note also that local **resort hotels** *Holiday Inn* and the *Hilton* have casinos, popular bars, and discos (see p.284) and on weekends *La Tasca de los Sobrinos*, the second-floor bar at *La Casa de las Tías* (see opposite), attracts a smart, slightly older salsa-loving crowd.

Andares Lounge c/Isabel 62. One of the larger and more welcoming bars on this party-minded strip, with plenty of tables, large TV screens, and a range of cocktails and beers. Often hosts special party nights with guest DJs and live acts. Closed Mon.

Bumpers c/Isabel 59 ☎787/901-4780. Most happening nightclub in the center of town, open Thurs–Sat 10pm–5am: university night is on Thurs, the infamous *noche de Perreo* ("night of the doggie-style dance") takes place on Fri, and Sat is set aside for a hardcore *reggaetón* party. Cover charges are sometimes levied for special live sets or guest DJs, but beers are usually just $1, Bacardi shots $2.

Hollywood Café PR-1 km 125.5 ☎787/843-6703. Consistently packed out with younger *ponceños*, offering pub fare, pool tables, booming music, and live salsa at the weekends. On Wed college students pile in for *el party del pelao*, roughly "party of the broke ass," when drinks are dirt cheap ($1 rum shots). Closed Tues.

Lupita's c/Isabel 60. This former Mexican restaurant was operating solely as a bar at the time of writing, but will start cooking again once they find a chef. It's best for drinks anyway, with expertly mixed margaritas and genial bar staff. Closed Mon.

Patio Colonial Bar and Restaurant c/Luna 35 (at c/Marina). Another local place that's best for drinks rather than meals, although it does serve decent breakfasts and snack food. The patio is at the back, a spacious area filled with plastic tables. Beers are cheap ($1) during happy hour (most evenings), though the choice is limited. Closed Mon.

Red Level Los Caobos Industrial Park, Marginal Villa Flores (next to Edif. Froilan Alfrombras and Banco Popular). Top club in Ponce, with plenty of glamor and a pounding sound system. It's east of the center off PR-1; you'll need a car or taxi to reach it. Cover $12–20 at the weekends, depending on which top DJ or *reggaetón* star is performing. Doors usually open at 9pm.

Rookies Sports Bar and Grill Av Eduardo Ruberte 2313 (Centro de Convenciones) ☎787/844-1785. Every US city seems to have a *Rookies*, and the theme is extended here, with live sports, live bands, karaoke nights, happy hours (5–6pm), American bar food, and a fun local crowd. You'll find it west of the center: drive or take a taxi. Closed Mon.

Listings

Airlines Cape Air ☎787/844-2020; Continental Airlines ☎787/840-4680; Jet Blue Airways ☎1800/538-2583.

Banks Plaza Las Delicias has plenty of banks with ATMs, including Citibank at c/Marina 9641 (Mon–Fri 8.30am–5pm, Sat 8.30am–noon; ☎787/842-2160).

Car rental All the major firms are located at the airport: Avis ☎787/842-6154; Budget ☎787/848-0907; Hertz ☎787/843-1685; Thrifty ☎787/290-2525.

Emergencies General ☎911

Hospitals and clinics Hospital Damas, 2213 Ponce by-pass (PR-2) (☎787/840-8686); Hospital Manuel Comunitaro Dr Pila, Avda Las Américas, east of Avda Hostos (☎787/848-5600).

Internet access Internet cafés are lacking in the center of Ponce, though most hotels have Internet access. The Historic Archive office (Mon–Fri 8am–noon & 1–4.30pm) at c/Marina 9215, on the east side of the plaza, offers free use of computers and Internet, though it is expected to move to new premises outside the center in 2009 – check at the tourist office.

Laundry Caribbean Cleaners, Avda Las Américas 13; Express Laundromat, Avda Pámpanos 1; Hollywood Cleaners, c/Comercio 35; Zayas Laundry c/Victoria 425.

Pharmacies Try Farmacia El Amal at c/Unión 77 or Walgreens at c/Estrella 65 (Mon–Fri 8am–7pm, Sat 8am–6pm).

Post office The most convenient is at c/Atocha 93, four blocks north of the plaza (Mon–Fri 7.30am–4.30pm).

Taxis Ponce Taxi ☎787/842-3370; Boriquen Taxi Cab ☎787/843-6000; Best Union Taxi Cab ☎787/840-9126.

Around Ponce

Just north of Ponce are two of the most memorable sights on the island, both associated with the region's long and eventful history. The **Centro Ceremonial Indígena de Tibes** is one of the most significant **Pre-Taíno** archeological sites ever found, and a tantalizing window into the culture of this now lost civilization, while **Hacienda Buena Vista** is a captivating nineteenth-century plantation.

Cape Air operates four to five daily **flights** to San Juan (25min) from **Aeropuerto Mercedita** – take a taxi from the city ($13). Parking is free at the airport, and you can grab basic food and drinks at the *B52 Café and Sports Bar*.

The **Terminal de Carros Públicos Carlos Garay** (or just *"la terminal"*) is on Calla Vives and Calla Victoria, three blocks north of Plaza Las Delicias. Most of the *públicos* serve the surrounding area, and though signs suggest routes to Coamo, San Germán, Mayagüez, Guayama, and Jayuya, it's hard to find cars to these places in practice – turn up before 7am to be sure. The most useful and frequently used route is operated by Choferes Unidos de Ponce (☏787/842-1222) to Río Piedras in **San Juan** ($15 per person, or $45–60 for the whole car). Drivers will usually take you all the way to the beaches or Old San Juan for $25–30 per person.

Driving out of the city is easy, especially heading to San Juan (1hr 30min) or points east on the smooth PR-52 *autopista* (toll road). Unfortunately the *autopista* ends just west of the city, and PR-2 is much slower and often bristling with traffic – it's still a four-lane highway, however, and you should reach virtually anywhere in the southwest, beyond Mayagüez, within an hour or so.

Centro Ceremonial Indígena de Tibes

Evidence of pre-Columbian civilization has been rare in the Caribbean until relatively recently, but the **Centro Ceremonial Indígena de Tibes** (Tues–Sun 9am–noon & 1–4pm; $3) remains one of the region's greatest discoveries, proof of highly complex societies long before the Spanish conquest. The site was inhabited for 1500 years by a series of migrating peoples and primarily used as a burial ground and ceremonial center, littered with ball-courts and standing stones. Like Caguana (see p.214), this has none of the grandiose ruins of Central America, but the guides do their best to bring the site alive with illuminating facts and anecdotes, and if you visit early, you'll almost certainly have it to yourself. Tibes is clearly signposted off PR-503 at km 2.2, due north of central Ponce. Note that you can only visit the site with a **guide** (free; tours last up to 1hr): weekdays you should be able to pick up an English-speaking one at the entrance, though if the park is busy (unusual), you may have to wait. Note also that the site cannot be reached by public transport.

Some history

Tibes was discovered by accident. In 1975, a local farmer stumbled across ancient ruins uncovered by flooding in the wake of Hurricane Eloise, and archeologists finally got working on the site a year later. They found nine ball-courts, three plazas, and the largest indigenous **cemetery** ever discovered on the island, comprising 187 human skeletons (one of which is displayed in the museum) from the **Igneri** and **Pre-Taíno** periods (see p.355). The Igneri people established Tibes and used the site from around 300 to 600 AD as a sacred burial ground, but it was later re-inhabited by Pre-Taíno peoples, who constructed the ball-courts and seem to have used it primarily as a ceremonial and burial center (the remains of which survive today). The Igneri may have played an early form of the ball-game (see below), but just for sport, while it started to assume a more spiritual and symbolic meaning under the Pre-Taínos.

Our understanding of *el batey* or the **ball-game** (*pelota* in modern Spanish), is almost completely based on a few early Spanish accounts. Played with two teams, passing a rubber ball between them (with anything but the hands), it had many similarities to the game played in Mesoamerica, and had a serious ceremonial function. Plazas and ball-courts were also used to stage gladiatorial-style games between two teams, and important celebrations known as *areytos*, the recounting of oral histories through song and dance.

In around 1100 the site was abandoned after extensive **flooding** of the Río Portugués, and it remained lost for almost nine hundred years. The academic impact of Tibes was seismic: previously, little was known about Pre-Taíno cultures, and the ball-game was considered a relatively recent phenomenon, while the construction of so many stone structures implied a highly organized society able to plan, mobilize, control, and sustain many workers. Some experts go further, claiming that the plazas were positioned to reflect the seasonal solar equinox and solstice, making Tibes the oldest astronomical observatory in the Caribbean.

The museum

To get the best overview of the island's Pre-Columbian indigenous cultures, start at the enlightening **museum** at the entrance. Exhibits are arranged chronologically, beginning with the **Archaic** culture 4500 years ago (see p.355) and ending with the Taínos, embellished with displays of pottery, stone tools, and other artifacts. You'll also learn about the history of the site, and the **Cohoba ritual**, where Taínos would inhale powdered (and hallucinogenic) *cohoba* seeds in order to communicate with the gods. Don't miss the intricate Igneri shell amulets shaped like frogs, haunting Taíno idols, and the curious giant stone in the corner, carved over two thousand years ago – some of the guides think it was a musical instrument. Everything is labeled in English and the informative **video** has English subtitles.

The site

The site itself covers 32 acres along the banks of the Río Baramaya (officially the Río Portugués), a tranquil clearing in the forest that includes a small **botanical garden** containing native plants and trees: custard apple, silk cotton trees, *flamboyant*, *portia* trees, sweet potato, and yucca. The **rain tree** here is over three hundred years old, traditionally used to make canoes and furniture, while the bark of the *maví* tree is used to make beer. You'll also see wild *cohoba* – though stronger than most class-A drugs, the guides like to point out that sniffing *cohoba* is still perfectly legal.

Beyond the garden you'll pass a reproduction of a **Taíno village** (*Yucayeque*), comprising a *caney,* the or rectangular house used by the chief, and four *bohíos*, round huts used by the other villagers. Beyond here are the ruins themselves, clearly defined ball-courts and plazas lined with stones. The **Plaza Principal** is the largest structure and where most of the burials were found: the monolith in the center marks the spot where a baby was interred in a vase, obviously a location of great spiritual or ritual significance. Next door is the Sun or **Star Plaza**, comprising six triangular stone platforms and most likely used as a sort of astronomical calendar. Surrounding these core plazas are the main ball-courts, many very long and lined with standing stones, while paving stones denote where seating areas once stood. The most unusual is the **Batey de Herradura** (Horseshoe Ball Court, because of its shape), measuring 115ft long by 30ft wide and constructed by the Pre-Taínos. The largest is the **Batey de Cemí**, lining the Río Baramaya for 250ft, and another burial site also constructed by the Pre-Taínos. **El Batey del Cacique** is the oldest court, measuring 50ft by 35ft and located on the north side of the site, with two parallel rows of stones.

Hacienda Buena Vista

Coffee and sugar once dominated the Puerto Rican economy, a legacy beautifully preserved at the **Hacienda Buena Vista** (Wed–Sun tours at 8.30am,

10.30am, 1.30pm & 3.30pm; $7; ☎787/722-5882 Mon–Fri, 787/284-7020 weekends and holidays), offering a rare opportunity to tour one of the island's historic plantations. Note that you must **reserve a tour in advance** – don't just turn up. English tours normally run at 1.30pm and last around two hours, but call to check. You can take additional tours of the especially fertile grounds and Río Canas gorge – these last two hours (Wed–Sun 8.30–10.30am; $7) or four hours (Fri & Sat 8am–noon; $10), and are usually in Spanish only.

Some history
The hacienda was established as a small farm for *cacao*, corn, plantains, and coffee in 1833 by **Salvador de Vives**, a Spanish émigré from Venezuela, who had moved to the island in 1821 after the South American nation became independent. Between 1845 and 1847, his son Carlos Vives built the mill-course, most of the buildings you see today, and a corn mill, expanding production of coffee and corn meal so that the plantation was booming by the early 1870s. Technology and investment were important, but as in the rest of Puerto Rico, the real foundation of plantation wealth was the back-breaking labor of African **slaves**. The **abolition of slavery** in 1873 proved the first of many blows to the Vives empire, including **Hurricane San Ciriaco** in 1899, which devastated the plantation. In 1904 the hacienda started to produce oranges for the US market, a much smaller trade which nevertheless kept it going until the 1930s. By the 1950s the virtually abandoned estate was appropriated by the government, which distributed four hundred acres to landless *ponceños*, while the Conservation Trust acquired the remaining 86 acres preserved today.

The plantation
The core of the plantation retains the attractive, European-style of the main house. Running through the yard is a narrow but fast-flowing mill-course built in 1845, which leads back towards the river and an extremely lush gorge – the plantation was once powered by water. The tour starts inside the old coffee storage room and **main house** above, all painstakingly restored in 1890s style. From here you'll be led around the main outhouses (including the **slave house** that once quartered 57 slaves), before following the mill-course above the Río Canas to the gorge at the **Salto Vives** – the view through the bushes to the falls and pool below is the "Buena Vista." On the way back you'll visit the creaky wooden **roasting house** and the whirling millstones of the original **corn mill** built by Carlos Vives.

Come in March and you'll be able to take the special tour to mark the **chocolate harvest**, highlighting the process of making chocolate fresh from the *cacao* bushes on the property. In October the **coffee harvest** means a special focus on roasting beans (harvesting takes place September to January), concluding with the freshest cup of coffee you've ever tasted

The *hacienda* is around 17km from Ponce Centro, at PR-123 km 16.8. It's clearly signposted with a small parking lot on site.

Yauco and around

Many Puerto Rican towns claim to be the capital of coffee, but only **YAUCO** owns the franchise. For over one hundred years, the town has been synonymous with the island's most respected and eagerly sought brands – **Café Yaucono** remains the best-selling Puerto Rican coffee by a long margin. Yet the coffee-growing highlands of Yauco municipality lie far to the north of the actual town, which is part of the arid southwest and better suited to sugar cane. What really makes Yauco so appealing is its vastly underrated ensemble of dazzling *criollo* buildings, early colonial ruins, and culinary specialties, largely ignored by foreign tourists.

Since 1975, every February or March sees the **Festival Nacional del Café** pack the town plaza with coffee-related activities, while the **Celebración de la Fundación del Pueblo de Yauco** is held at around the same time, when music, dancing, artisan fairs, and *kioscos* in the main plaza honor the founding of the city on February 29, 1756.

Some history

No one has ever located the village of Guaynía, home to **Agüeybaná**, the great Taíno *cacique* who greeted Ponce de León in 1508, but the settlement is likely to have been somewhere in the vicinity of Yauco. Though the modern

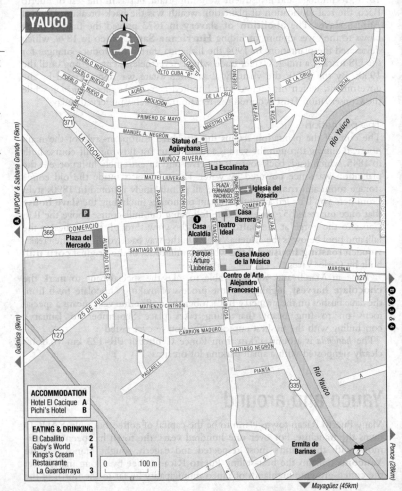

town of Guayanilla is named after the Taíno capital, experts have identified the *barrio* of Diego Hernández, at the intersection of the Yauco and Duey rivers, as a better candidate. The name Yauco derives from a Taíno word, *Coayuco*, meaning "long yucca."

The Spanish town grew up around the **Ermita de Barinas** on the banks of the Río Yauco in the early eighteenth century, but was officially founded in 1756 by Don Fernando Pacheco de Matos at its current location to avoid flooding. In the nineteenth century immigrants from southern Europe, particularly **Corsica**, poured into the area to take advantage of the booming **sugar** and **coffee** industries. In 1873 much of the town was destroyed by **fire**, while in 1896 and again in 1897, Yauco was the scene of small **armed risings** against Spain (the *intentona de Yauco*): both failed. After landing in Guánica during the 1898 Spanish-American War, the US army fought **El Combate de Yauco**, a small skirmish in which three Spanish (but no American soldiers) were killed. Hours later, Yauco was the **first town to be occupied** – legend has it that troops pinned a dollar bill, Washington-side up, onto a portrait of Queen María Cristina of Spain hanging in city hall, to show the locals who was now in charge. Yauco benefited from modernization programs in subsequent years, though its sugar and coffee industries faded away – the latter is experiencing a minor resurgence however, with local cooperatives leading the way.

Arrival, information and accommodation

Driving into Yauco, make for the free **parking lot** that covers the hill above the Plaza del Mercado on Calle Comercio (follow PR-368 to Sabana Grande). The municipal office of **art and culture** (☎787/267-0350) acts as a tourist office and has some enthusiastic English-speaking members: visit their office next to the Centro de Arte Alejandro Franceschi on Parque Arturo Lluberas. It's easy enough to walk around the center of town, but if you need to take a cab, try Yauco Taxi (☎787/267-5666 or 787/347-2675), opposite the parking lot.

Accommodation

Yauco is best seen by car as a day-trip from the coast or Ponce, but it does have one place **to stay**, *Hotel El Cacique* (☎787/856-0345, ⓦ www.motelelcacique .com; ❸), a simple motel-like place set in the rolling hills outside the town at PR-368 km 10.3.

Another convenient option nearby is *Pichi's Hotel* (☎787/835-3335, ⓦ www .pichis.com; ❹), a swish place just outside Guayanilla, at PR-132 km 204.6 (just off PR-2). Its two-story motel units were upgraded in 2008, and the rates include breakfast and access to a small pool and sun deck.

The Town

Yauco grew up around **Plaza Fernando Pacheco de Matos**, the central square surrounded by a plethora of graceful buildings. The **Iglesia Parroquial Nuestra Señora del Santísimo Rosario** (Thurs 8am–5pm; other days call ☎787/856-1222 or the art and culture office), the town's imposing church, was completed in 1934 in grand Spanish Revival style, on the site of the original established in 1754. The altar and baptismal font were both carved from Carrera marble in 1850. The most striking house on the plaza is **Casa Barrera** at Calle Comercio 19, built in 1884 by Tomás Olivari Santoni, with a bright pink wedding-cake facade embellished with an ornate stucco cornice and delicate iron railings. It remains a private home. Next door, the **Teatro Ideal** was built in 1919, a cinema with a grand Neoclassical arched front looking more like a French theater, a lavish building that seems utterly incongruous in provincial Puerto Rico. Currently under renovation, it's expected to reopen as a theater in 2009.

Walk north on Calle Betances from the plaza and you'll see **La Escalinata** one block ahead, a red-brick stairway built in 1910 and crowned by a statue of Agüeybaná. West of the plaza, the stretch of Calle Comercio as far as Calle Pacheco was pedestrianized and dubbed **Paseo del Café** in 1990, though it remains a fairly typical shopping street. Stroll one block south along Calle Betances and you'll hit the town's second plaza, **Parque Arturo Lluberas**, created around 1850 and serving as the local market till the 1920s. Named after a former mayor, it was given a slightly sanitized makeover in 2004, with palm trees and several stone monuments, as well as a rather kitsch representation of a coffee bush with giant, ruby red beans. The **Monumento a los Corsos** recalls Yauco's Corsican heritage, while the **Monumento a los Fundadores** commemorates the founders of the town. You'll also see two marble **war memorials** here, honoring locals killed in wars since 1898, including the Persian Gulf in 1991. The **Casa Alcaldía** (town hall) faces the *parque*, a fine two-story Spanish Colonial-style structure with arcades and balconies, originally constructed in 1864 but remodeled a couple of times since then. You can peek inside at the main staircase, preserved exactly as it was the day US troops marched in.

Centro de Arte Alejandro Franceschi

One of the most opulent *criollo* homes in Puerto Rico, the Casa Franceschi stands on the southeast side of Parque Arturo Lluberas, open to the public as the **Centro de Arte Alejandro Franceschi** (Mon–Fri 8am–3pm; free) since 1988. Gifted French architect André Troublard built the house in 1907 for Alejandro Franceschi, a local businessman and philanthropist. On the outside it looks like a pretty, pale blue *criollo*-style house, trimmed with Ionic columns, but what makes it truly unique are the florid French Beaux-Arts interiors, enhanced with fine stucco work, vivid frescoes, and bright oil paintings on the ceilings and walls – each room is different, giving the impression of a European palace in miniature (though the house has almost no furniture).

The first hall on the right contains a portrait of Franceschi and his wife, while the room with bright pink walls was their daughter's bedroom. The **bathroom** is the most impressive space in the house, bursting with exuberant frescoes painted by Polish artist H. Shoutka. Images of the Madonna and various angels grace the ceiling, while the walls boast three playful ocean-themed murals and a more unusual depiction of Dr. Faust, the legendary fictional German figure who sold his soul to the devil. Ponce-born artist Roberto Ríos worked on the warm landscapes adorning the **dining room**, inspired by Franceschi's rustic plantations, while pride-of-place in the **kitchen** goes to an original 1928 refrigerator, now a valuable antique. The house was the first in Yauco to have electricity – Franceschi built the first electric plant in the town in 1904.

Casa Museo de la Música

The Casa Veray-Torregrosa is now the **Casa Museo de la Música** (Mon–Fri 1–3pm, Sat & Sun 8am–noon; free), a much simpler wooden affair, far more typical of the humble but appealing *criollo* style of the time. Constructed in 1919, in 1922 it was the birthplace of local celebrity **Amaury Veray Torregrosa**, famous in Puerto Rico as the composer of the much-loved Christmas carol "Villancico Yaucano" (1951). In it, a poor boy from Yauco offers the baby

Jesus a rooster, as it's the most valuable thing he has. Exhibits are basic – a few old photos, sheets of music, and other memorabilia, but it makes a cozy, more intimate contrast to the Franceschi residence. You'll find the house at Calle Santiago Vivaldi Pacheco 15, around the corner from Casa Franceschi.

Ermita de Barinas and Hacienda María

The Ermita de Nuestra Señora del Rosario, more commonly known as **Ermita de Barinas** (24hr; free) after the southern *barrio* in which it stands, is where Yauco was born in the 1700s, though little more than a romantic, overgrown ruin today. The stone hermitage was constructed around 1706, but abandoned in 1760 after continual flooding. You can find the rarely visited remains off PR-335, south of the center (just before the PR-2 overpass), the peace disturbed only by creaking trees and a chorus of croaking frogs.

Another picturesque symbol of post-industrial decline, the old sugar mill at **Hacienda María** or just "Las Ruinas," lies further along PR-335 in Barinas. The hacienda was established in 1806 by Don Francisco Affrige, a French exile from Haiti, and the mill buildings were active from 1886 until the plantation was abandoned in 1912. It remains private property, rented for weddings and the like, but you can take pictures of the gracefully crumbling exterior.

NUPCAY coffee

Local officials hope to cement Yauco's reputation as coffee central by eventually creating a **Ruta del Café**, linking some of the five hundred *fincas* or farms in the mountainous north of the municipality. Until then, the closest place to buy **fresh coffee** is the warehouses of Nucleo Productores de Café Ahoras de Yauco, a cooperative of almost one hundred family-owned coffee farms, also known as **NUPCAY** (Mon–Fri 7.30am–4pm; ☎787/856-4121, ⓦwww.nupcay.com). The beans are dried, roasted, and packed here, and you can sometimes get an impromptu tour of the facilities – ask at the art and culture office in town (see p.299). The cooperative sells the **Mi Café del Pais** brand, a smooth, exceptionally aromatic coffee sold in 14oz packets in three grades: *comercial* ($3.69), *primera selección* ($5.88), and the acclaimed *selección catador* ($7.32), which is made with sun-dried beans grown at altitudes over 2600ft – prices here are much cheaper than retail. NUPCAY is on a side road off PR-368 km 2.1 in the La Palmita sector of *barrio* Susua Alta, a few kilometres west of town.

Selling Yauco

Branding in the coffee industry started long before Nescafé and Starbucks. Thanks to the pioneering marketing efforts of **Fraticelli, Bartolomei & Agostini**, a Yauco firm of Corsican immigrants who became rich exporting coffee to Europe in the 1800s, even the Pope was drinking **Yauco coffee** exclusively by the end of the century. The town became so closely associated with the product, much of the coffee grown throughout the island was simple labeled "Yauco" regardless of its origin.

The promotion of the Yauco brand in the twentieth century is mainly due to San Juan-based processor **Jiménez y Fernández**, who started marketing **Café Yaucono** (ⓦwww.yaucono.com) in 1916 – it's been an incredible success ever since, still controlling forty percent of the domestic coffee market, despite rivals claiming that much of the raw product hails from other parts of the island. Today **Grupo Jiménez** dominates coffee exports from Puerto Rico (it also owns popular mass market brand Café Rico), and in 1990 launched **Café Yauco Selecto** (ⓦwww.yscoffee.com) in cooperation with two farms in the mountains (one of them is **Hacienda San Pedro** in Jayuya, see p.338), a creamy, gourmet coffee with a hint of caramel.

Eating and drinking

Yauco has a modest array of **eating** options, with its most prestigious **restaurants** outside the center. For cheap eats, try the cheerful food stalls in the **Plaza del Mercado** (Mon–Sat 5am–5pm, Sun 6am–noon; closed most holidays) on Calle Comercio (opposite the parking lot), a fine example of Art Deco architecture built in 1924. *Cafeteria Jordán* usually has plenty of customers, offering hearty plates of beans, tuna, *pollo asado*, and *frituras* for around $5. For a cup of local **coffee**, try the *Kiosko Café Expresso* on Plaza Fernando Pacheco de Matos. For something cooler, *Kings's Cream* on Calle Comercio is an outpost of the popular Puerto Rican **ice cream** chain, with all the usual fresh fruit and chocolate flavors.

Nightlife is virtually nonexistent in the town, so hanging around after dark is pointless.

Restaurants

Puerto Ricans drive from as far as Fajardo to eat at ⨎ *Restaurante La Guardarraya* (Tues–Sun 11am–8pm, ☎787/856-4222), at PR-127 km 6, half way to Guayanilla from Yauco. The chief attraction is the house specialty, *chuletas can-can*, fried pork chop with thick rinds that resemble the can-can underskirts of the 1950s ($11.75). The dish was created here in 1959 by Don Juan Vera-Martínez and the restaurant is still owned by his family. Everything else on the menu is worth a try, such as especially rich rice and beans ($2.25), exquisite beef tenderloin with onions ($11), and sweet plantains ($1) – the classic vanilla *flan* ($2.25) is the best choice for dessert. The house *sangría* and special house cocktail (a blend of vodka, orange juice, grenadine, cherry, and pineapple juice) are both $3.50. The *criollo*-style wooden building nestles under a large rubber tree surrounded by gardens, with plenty of parking on site: you can also stop to buy bags of *Café La Guardarraya*, roasted at the restaurant.

El Caballito (daily 11am–8pm) at Gaby's World (see opposite) offers the only real competition, with its succulent "Kan-Kan Pork Chops" ($19.95 for two people, $9.95 single) and extensive menu of *criollo* food, notably its huge *churrasco* and *criollo* steaks.

Around Yauco: Santuario de La Virgen El Rosario del Pozo

The rural town of **Sabana Grande** is 18km from Yauco along PR-368, and though its soporific center is sprinkled with traditional clapboard houses, the main attraction here is the **Santuario de La Virgen El Rosario del Pozo** (daily 5am–11pm; ⓦ www.virgendelpozo.com), one of the island's most revered shrines. Tucked away in tropical gardens, halfway into the hills, the shrine is a rare opportunity to get beneath the veneer of Puerto Rican daily life and explore the spiritual side of the island, often at odds with the official Catholic Church.

The Virgin Mary is said to have miraculously appeared here on 33 occasions between April and May 1953, to three children aged seven to nine, precipitating several miracles and "healings" in the local community. The spot immediately became a sort of folk shrine, but since the 1980s the apparitions have become a deeply controversial issue, with the Catholic Church withdrawing its support, citing lack of evidence, and encouraging true Catholics to avoid the site, which it calls "degrading." Since then, despite a Vatican commission also finding no evidence of the "miracles," the shrine has continued to operate with local support and struggles for official recognition, maintaining a fiercely loyal base amongst ordinary Puerto Ricans – large festivals are held here each year.

The sanctuary comprises by leafy gardens, pretty pink buildings, and an appropriately hushed atmosphere throughout. The spot of the first apparition is marked by a large statue of the Virgin in a glass case, topped with a starry halo, and often surrounded by flowers. Next to it **La Capilla Nuestra Señora del Rosario del Pozo**, the shrine chapel, is a very humble affair with another smaller statue of Mary at the altar and plenty of flowers left as offerings. Behind the main statue outside you'll find the **well** (*pozo*) said to have been blessed by Mary, and now a font of "holy water," while representations of the Stations of the Cross line the garden to the left of the chapel. You'll often see small groups of (mostly elderly) Puerto Ricans reverently making a circuit of all the main sights, laying flowers.

The shrine is 2.4km north of Sabana Grande along PR-364. You are supposed to dress respectfully, which means no shorts, no sleeveless shirts, or bare shoulders, though as always, women should get more leeway in practice. From here it's only 10km to San Germán (see p.266).

Guánica and around

Blessed with one of the south coast's most flawless natural harbors, **GUÁNICA** is a once-prosperous sugar town with a typically torpid plaza and a couple of low-key sights. The real reason so many people flock here is the adjacent **Bosque Estatal de Guánica**, a unique dry forest of twisted trees and stumpy cacti, with well-maintained hiking trails winding down to a glorious coastline of sparkling **beaches** and sprawling mangroves. The coast is also accessible by road, its highlight the coral- and mangrove-smothered **Guilligan's Island** just offshore, where you can float in crystalline waters rich with fish and crab. With the Central Cordillera draining moisture from the trade winds, this area has the lowest annual rainfall on the island, meaning you are virtually guaranteed hot, sunny days.

Hard to believe given Guánica's current languid condition, but the town has been the scene of some of the island's most significant events. **Juan Ponce de León** may have taken his first steps on Puerto Rico on the shores of Bahía de Guánica in 1508 (this being Puerto Rico, you'll see some sources claim the town was "founded" in that year). The **US invasion** of the island began here in 1898, and for many years it was home to one of the largest sugar plants in the Caribbean, Guánica Central, which opened in 1909. Today its industrial presence is maintained by the singularly ugly Ochoa fertilizer plant, looming over the southern half of the town.

Guánica is 9km southwest of Yauco on PR-116: you'll pass the turning to the forest first (PR-334), before reaching the road to the beaches (PR-333), which

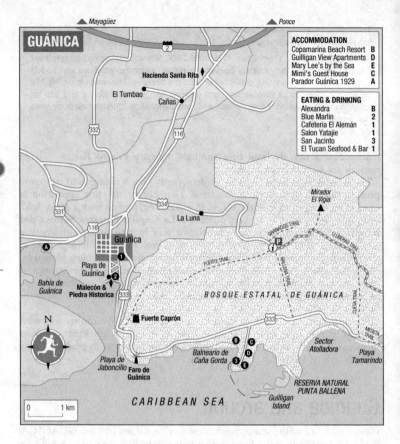

effectively bypasses the town. The main road to the center is PR–332, at the next junction. Needless to say, you need a **car** to get the most out of the area, as things are extremely spread out.

If you're here at the end of November, check out the **Fiesta de la Puertorriqueñiidad**, a celebration of Puerto Rican culture held in various parts of the town, with live music and folk dances and exhibits of local history. The main annual festival, the **Fiesta del Pueblo de Guánica** (☏787/821-5016), is held at the end of July.

Accommodation

The best places **to stay** lie along the coast, on the southern edge of the forest in the San Jacinto area, where you have access to all the main attractions right on the doorstep.

Copamarina Beach Resort PR-333 km 6.5 ☏787/821-0505, ⓦwww.copamarina.com. Guánica's only resort hotel, with tasteful, low-rise wooden villas lining a narrow strip of beach just beyond Caña Gorda, and set within 20 acres of leafy garden. Spacious rooms are decked out with rattan, tropical-inspired furnishings with cable TV and fridge, and all the extras are on site: tennis courts, watersports, spa, fitness center, and dive shop, as well as the posh *Alexandra* restaurant. Ocean views are $40 extra and like the big San Juan hotels, you'll pay a 7 percent "resort fee" in addition to the 9 percent tax. ❼

Guilligan View Apartments San Jacinto 27 ☎787/821-4901. Next to *Mary Lee's*, this large house right on the water contains two very basic apartments managed by the affable Rafael Rodríguez, both with kitchen and sea views; try here if everything else is full. ❹

Mary Lee's by the Sea San Jacinto 25, PR-333 km 6.7 ☎787/821-3600, Ⓦwww.maryleesbythesea.com. Fabulous ensemble of ten apartments and houses furnished in a whimsically florid style by sprightly octogenarian Mary Lee Alvarez, a US expat who settled here after fleeing Cuba in the 1960s. Spacious rooms and cozy bedrooms are lined with rattan floor tiles and bedecked with cheery multicolored hand-sewn towels, duvet covers, and cushions. Even the bathrooms feature installations of sand, plastic plants, fairy lights, and shells. The apartments below Mary's house overlook the cay-studded bay: all of them have kitchens and a/c, but only some can be rigged up for satellite TV ($10/day). Use of the washing machine is free. Take the turning off PR-333, just beyond *Copamarina*, and follow the signs. ❹–❻

Mimi's Guest House Sector Pitirre 11, PR-333 km 7 ☎787/366-2781, Ⓦwww.mimisguesthouse .com. This appealing modern villa is a great deal, tucked away off the main road, just beyond the turning to *Mary Lee's* and the ferry. The furnished studios or one-bedroom units are a little spartan but bright and fresh, and include fully equipped kitchenettes and baths. The gardens are ideal for barbecues, and you can walk to Punta Ballena in around fifteen minutes. ❹

Parador Guánica 1929 PR-3116 km 2.5, Ensenada, ☎787/821-0099, Ⓦwww.guanica1929 .com. The main alternative to the beach is this two-story colonial-style villa loaded with character in the neighboring town of Ensenada, with spacious verandas and 27 simply furnished, comfy rooms. Once serving as a private hotel for VIPs visiting Guánica Central sugar mill, it lies just off PR-116 and is convenient for touring the southwest. Note, however, that eating options are very limited and the hotel restaurant is poor. ❹

The Town

Downtown Guánica is an unassuming blend of modern and wooden *criollo* buildings, rarely explored by visitors. City officials are hoping to lure more to the central **Plaza Manuel Jiménez** with the opening of the **Museo de Arte e Historia de Guánica** (Tues–Sat 8am–4pm; $1), housed in an immaculately restored wing of the Antigua Casa Alcaldía (old city hall), on the south side of the plaza. It's more art than history, containing a series of galleries displaying the mediocre work of local artists, and a very small collection of aging photographs recalling the town's industrial ruins. The restored interiors are impressive, however, and it's expected that the exhibits will expand in future years. With its relatively humble lemon-colored church, the **Iglesia de San Antonio Abad** (dating from 1888), the plaza is otherwise fairly ordinary.

Head south along Calle 25 de Julio (PR-332) and you'll reach the **Malecón**, a largely deserted boardwalk facing the bay. Here you'll find **La Piedra Historica** ("historic rock"), which stands as the only memorial to the fateful **US landings** here in July 1898, arguably the most momentous event in Puerto Rico's modern history. Even then, the inscription on the rock simply recalls a battalion that came ashore in September (3rd Battalion, 1st U.S.V. Engineers), found during the construction of PR-333 in 1955 – it's a fairly vivid indication that most Puerto Ricans have no interest in commemorating the US occupation. The other monument further along is a bronze statue of an appropriately steely-faced Spanish conquistador, erected in 1992 to commemorate the 500th anniversary of the discovery of New World.

North of the town, **Hacienda Santa Rita** is testimony to Guánica's once booming sugar industry, the beautifully restored colonial plantation house now part of the Convento Hermanas Dominicas de Nuestra Señora del Rosario de Fatima, a convent and shrine. The two-story mansion is one of the finest on the island, richly adorned with wood and iron balconies and heavy mahogany doors and shutters – it's now used as sleeping quarters for the nuns. The plantation was sold to the Church in 1953 and restored in the 1990s: one of the nuns, Sor (Sister) Marianita (☎787/528-1673), offers free tours (Spanish only) of the historic premises on weekends, but you must call in advance.

Bosque Estatal de Guánica

Much of Guánica's seductive coastline falls within the **Bosque Estatal de Guánica** (daily 8am–5pm; free), a 37-square kilometer forest reserve that incorporates some of the driest and most unusual flora on the island. Its heart lies high above the coast, accessible via PR-334, which ends 3km from PR-116 at a parking lot and small information booth (daily 8.30am–4.30pm; ☎787/724-3724) supplying basic maps (if closed, check at the ranger station nearby). The reserve is crisscrossed by twelve well-kept and mostly signposted trails, with literally hundreds of species of **bird** flittering around the gnarled trees and bushes, in a withered landscape often reminiscent of outback Australia: spiky cacti poke out between bleached rocks and crumbling mounds of earth like twisted fingers, while the contorted limbs of bone-white trees slowly bake in the sun. Noting that Guánica is now the largest remaining tract of tropical dry coastal forest in the world, UNESCO made it a Biosphere Reserve in 1981.

It's important to remember however, that there are **four different forest types** here, with only one being truly exceptional: the **dry scrub forest** that lines the southern slopes, studded with the imaginatively named Spanish dildo cactus, squat melon cactus, and *gumbo-limbo* trees with peeling red bark. You'll also see a few rare *guayacán* trees, and groves of Dominican mahogany, planted here in the 1930s but still struggling to take hold. Two-thirds of the reserve is covered in **deciduous forest** (most of the area around the information booth, and containing most of the bird life), while one-fifth (mostly in the sinkholes and ravines of the east side) is **evergreen forest**. **Coastal forest** lines the shore, characterized by bonsai-like shrubs and mangroves.

Impressive as all this sounds, you might find the forest a little underwhelming: unless you have a keen interest in botany, the dry landscape can get monotonous and you'll have to be here at dawn to catch most of the birds. The best strategy

▲ Guánica dry forest

is to take a whole day and tackle one of the longer trails in order to appreciate the bizarre diversity of the area, combining the hike with a few hours on the beach. You'll need to bring plenty of water and preferably start early. December to April is the driest period, and you'll find the most color, flowers, and odd bouts of rain between September and January – the dullest time to visit is late spring and summer (July is especially hot).

The trails

Hiking is the best way to absorb the reserve's subtle charms, principally its unusual flora, coastal panoramas, and weather-beaten coastline. If you have a lot of patience (and luck), you might spot rare birds such as the tiny green Puerto Rican tody, lizard cuckoo, or Puerto Rican nightjar, but you'll definitely see plenty of lizards and geckos shooting across the trails.

One of the best hikes is the **Fuerte** trail (5.5km), which follows the ridges west from the information booth, providing stupendous views of the sea and Guánica bay. Towards the end it snakes around the stubby stone lookout tower known as **Fuerte Caprón**, backed by a long stone staircase. The tower was built in the 1930s by the Civil Conservation Corp on the site of a Spanish observation tower (destroyed by invading US troops), and is said to be named after one of the first officers killed in Cuba during the 1898 Spanish-American War – Captain Allyn Capron, one of the "Rough Riders." From here the trail drops down to the road (PR-333), from where you can keep going to Playa de Jaboncillo (see below).

Alternatively, trekking down to the easterly beaches you'll appreciate the transition from deciduous forest to the unique dry scrub zone, and finally the coastal littoral of twisted *gumbo-limbo* trees. The **Ballena** trail is the shortest (2km), but entails a stretch of road-walking at the end – you'll come out on PR-333 at km 8.6, about 500m from Sector Atolladora (turn left). On the way down, the trail passes a 200m detour to the **Guayacán Centenario**, a tree said to be between five hundred and seven hundred years old, but small and certainly not ancient-looking (it will take you an hour just to see the tree and walk back). For a longer and more energetic walk, follow the **Llúberas** trail (for around 4km), then the **Cueva** dirt trail (1.5km) to Playa Tamarindo and the parking lot at the end of PR-333. As you might expect, the latter trail passes a cave, home to two species of bat (though you can't go beyond the entrance), as well as a grove of ten-foot tall prickly-pear cacti near the coast. From the parking lot you can follow the shoreline via the **Meseta** trail (3.5km), one of the most enjoyable in the reserve – it climbs slowly from the beach along low-lying cliffs of *sebucán* and prickly-pear cactus, past rugged headlands of sea grape and purple milkweed, ending in a forest of dwarf white mangroves, buttonwood and cedar. Look out for pelicans and frigate birds along the way. You can also **drive** to the parking lot at the end of PR-333 to walk this trail – either way, you must retrace your steps to get back.

To just get a taste of the forest, make a shorter loop up to the **Mirador El Vigía**, a viewpoint on Criollo II, the highest hill in the forest. Use the Llúberas and Velez trails (1.5km in total), returning via the undulating Granados trail (1km) – the whole walk takes about an hour, and the climb up is not very steep. From the cliff edge at the top (walk through the undergrowth at the end of the trail), the forest spreads out beneath you, a carpet of densely packed vegetation stretching away to the hazy peaks of the Cordillera Central.

The beaches

While hiking down to the **beaches** from the hills of the dry forest is an enticing (if sweat-soaked) option, most visitors explore the coastline by car on PR-333. Heading south from Guánica, you'll see the turning to **Playa de Jaboncillo** at

Head to the **Dive Copamarina** shop in the *Copamarina Beach Resort* (daily 9am–9pm; free parking; ☎787/821-0505 ext 729) if you fancy getting deeper into the crystal-clear waters off Guánica. The shop is really a hut next to the resort beach, and offers popular **dive trips** ($95) for certified divers out to La Pared ("the wall"), the reef that lies 35 minutes by boat along the southwest coast (see La Parguera p.275). One-tank dives are just $50, while **snorkeling** trips are $45 (snorkel rentals are $10 for 3hr). **Kayaks** cost $12/hr or $60 for six hours, and are a great way to explore the cays offshore (it takes about 20min to reach Ballena), while small **sailing boats** are $40/hr or $55 for six hours. They can also arrange **fishing** excursions (6.30–11.30am; $500) and **sunset cruises** around the bay for $45 per person. *Mary Lee's* also rents kayaks ($10 for the first hour and $5/hr thereafter).

km 3.1, a steep, potholed gravel road, just about manageable with a normal car. The road leads down to a secluded cove with grills, toilets, gazebos, and usually fewer people than the other beaches. Back on PR-333 and just beyond the turning to Jaboncillo, the road passes the ruins of the **Faro de Guánica** at km 3.9, a Spanish lighthouse built in 1889. The site is abandoned and fenced off, though there are tentative plans to restore the building in the future.

Guánica's wildly popular public beach, the **Balneario de Caña Gorda** (mid-May to mid-Aug; daily 8am–6pm, mid-Aug to mid-May; daily 8am–5pm; parking $3) is at km 5.8, officially outside the reserve and managed by the Compañía de Parques Nacionales. Perfect for families, it has all the facilities (including toilets), a compact tree-lined stretch of fine sand, and clear, calm water. Be warned, however, the beach can get overwhelmingly busy on weekends and holidays, especially in the summer – the parking lot may look big, but at these times it fills up quickly and the road outside gets jammed with traffic.

Continue along PR-333 and you'll slip back into the forest reserve, a wilder, undeveloped coastline where you can simply pull off wherever you see an inviting strip of sand. At around km 9.1 you'll reach **Sector Atolladora**, which has several beaches with choppy water set around a headland, and a short drive further on, **Playa Tamarindo**, where PR-333 ends in a dusty parking lot. This attractive arc of sand is much better for swimming or lounging away the afternoon – when it cools down, tackle the **Meseta Trail**, which continues along the coast for another 3.5km (see p.307). With more time you can explore the western arm of the forest reserve, at the end of PR-325 beyond the town of Ensenada: **Playa Santa** is the most popular sandy beach, but further east **Playa Manglillos** ($1 entry) has clearer water, darting fish just offshore, and thriving mangroves.

Guilligan's Island

Officially known as Cayo Aurora, **Guilligan's Island** is one of the highlights of Puerto Rico, an idyllic outcrop of thick red mangroves bordered by white coral sand, just off the Guánica coast. The sobriquet recalling the US television series *Gilligan's Island* was added in the late 1960s as a marketing gimmick (but retaining a Spanish twist), and today it falls under the same DRNA management as the forest reserve.

A ferry plies back and forth from the main island, with short trails leading off from the jetty into the mangroves, and most day-trippers grab spots around the lagoon nearby. Here you'll find a few barbecue huts and plenty of shade, but this isn't really a beach – being completely hemmed in by mangroves is what makes the lagoon so magical. Swim or just drift around in the incredibly clear (and shallow) water, where shoals of parrot fish and crabs huddle beneath the roots, or snorkel over the reef just beyond the jetty. The "lagoon" is actually a channel that splits the dense vegetation in half, and you can wade across to the quieter far side of the island where a narrow strip of sand faces the Caribbean Sea.

The **ferry** (Tues–Sun 9am–5pm; $6.42 round-trip; ☎787/821-4941) sails from the pier in front of the *San Jacinto* restaurant, on the narrow road which splits off PR-333 towards *Mary Lee's by the Sea*. Departures are usually on the hour or every twenty minutes at busy times – the last sailing to the island is at 3pm (the last boat back is 5pm), the ferry taking ten to fifteen minutes to cross the bay. Note that on weekends and holidays, especially in the summer, cars begin to line up at the ferry parking lot at around 6am, and the island can get swamped (the ferry takes 45 people per trip, with a maximum 350 allowed on the island). Taking the **private launches** from *Copamarina* ($6.42) or *Mary Lee's* ($6) is a good idea, as you can set your own pick-up time and combine the trip with a visit to Ballena (see below). If you're not a guest at either place, *Copamarina* is the best bet, but call the dive shop in advance (see box opposite). Note also that the island is closed on Mondays.

Reserva Natural Punta Ballena

Administered by the Conservation Trust, but included within the same UN Biosphere Reserve as the forest, the **Reserva Natural Punta Ballena** is the flat, palm-covered headland beyond the residential area containing *Mary Lee's*. Once part of a failed coconut plantation, its 162 acres were earmarked for a controversial Club Med resort: the area is a haven for rare species such as the crested toad, the Puerto Rican nightjar, and the manatee, with the beach serving as a nesting area for hawksbill turtles, and in 1991 the Trust stepped in to quash the project. Confusingly, "Ballena" is used to describe the bay on the reserve's east side, the magnificent beach to the west, and sometimes the small mangrove island offshore – Cayo Ballena. When most locals talk about Ballena, they mean the **beach**, a treeless strip of soft, fine sand with a steep drop-off – the current between the beach and the mangrove cay is quite swift, though the water isn't deep, and it's a fun place to swim, especially with shoals of trumpet fish flashing past, and pelicans nesting in the mangroves nearby. The top of the beach faces the sea and a shallow reef, another ideal place for snorkeling.

When Guilligan's Island is full, the public ferry sometimes dumps passengers on Ballena beach – at other times it should be deserted, and easiest to reach by private boat from *Copamarina* or *Mary Lee's*. Otherwise it's a long walk from Sector Atolladora.

Eating and drinking

Other than the usual fast-food chains on PR-116 on the edge of town, eating options in Guánica are disappointingly sparse. The best place for an upmarket meal is the *Copamarina* resort, while Puerto Rican tourists grab snacks at the cluster of *kioscos* at PR-333 km 1.4, as the road bypasses Guánica on the way to the beaches – stick with simple things here, like the *frituras* or corned-beef *empanadillas*.

Alexandra *Copamarina Beach Resort*, PR-333 km 6.5 ☎787/821-0505. Only fine-dining option in the area, an elegant indoor restaurant facing the ocean, with floor-to-ceiling windows and billowing white curtains. The menu is a blend of Puerto Rican and Italian influences, with a special focus on seafood, but you can also order sizzling meats such as pork chops, with tropically inspired pineapple sauce (mains $20–45). For lunch or something a little less formal, try the resort's *Las Palmas Café.*

Blue Marlin Avda Esperanza Idrach 59 (Guánica Malecón) ☎787/821-5858. Old-fashioned *cantina*-style restaurant facing the bay right on the *malecón*, offering a reasonable seafood menu ($13–14) and cold Medalla ($2–3); in between meal times, the bar caters to a steady stream of loyal regulars and the odd tourist, though things get more animated on weekends when it hosts live music and salsa. Closed Mon & Tues.

Cafeteria El Alemán PR-333, km 1.3. This simple café is little more than a roadside shack, where local workers grab a greasy breakfast or cheap sandwich, and shoot the breeze over a few beers in the afternoons – all for under $3. Also sells fresh coconuts with a straw.

Salon Yatajie PR-333 km 1.4. This *kiosco* is best known for its *cocos frios* (chilled coconuts) and crispy *frituras* sold out the front: the chicken, prawn, and lobster *empanadillas* make for addictive snacks ($0.75–1.50) and attract a steady stream of

munching Puerto Rican tourists, stocking up before the drive home.

San Jacinto km 0.5, San Jacinto ☎787/821-4941. Restaurant that sees a steady trade from the Guilligan's Island ferry. The baked or fried fish, prawns ($18), and lobster ($25) are always fresh, while kids get a special menu of pizza and burgers. If you want to save money, opt for the rice and meat dishes ($3–4) sold from the self-service window outside, and eat at the tables nearby. The *chapín empanadillas* are the best choice, bursting with fish, and they also pour a mean *piña colada* ($3) and coffee ($0.75).

El Tucan Seafood & Bar PR-333 km 1.4. One of the better options among the cluster of *kioscos* on PR-333, with a large menu, plastic chairs, and a no-frills indoor dining room. Stick to classic *comida criolla* snacks such as *mofongo* ($2.25), *amarillos* ($1.50), and fried fish ($10.50), or enjoy the cheap *piña coladas* ($3), Medalla ($1.10), rum ($0.50), and boisterous salsa on Sun evenings. Locals eat here because it's cheap – expect fairly brusque service.

Sugar country

Once the heart of **sugar country**, the now empty plains between the southeast coast and the mountains show few signs of their former glory; this is a sparsely populated corner of Puerto Rico that seems somehow forgotten, struggling to catch up with the rest of the island. Yet the inviting hot springs at **Coamo** and the graceful sugar towns of **Arroyo** and **Guayama** are steeped in history, legacies of the great wealth created in the colonial and early American periods. The last in particular is a smaller, less pretentious version of Ponce, well-stocked with ramshackle but striking architecture, and a smattering of galleries and museums. The lack of beaches means you'll see few tourists here, and for once the coast is not the main attraction. **Salinas** is the modest exception, with a yacht-filled marina, seafood specialties, and a spread of tempting offshore cays to explore, while the information center for the wetland reserve at **Bahía de Jobos** is one of the most enlightening on the island. Access to the region is easy via PR-52 and PR-53, slicing through vast swathes of abandoned, overgrown plots of land that testify to the drastic collapse of not just the domestic sugar industry, but all Puerto Rico's traditional agriculture since World War II.

Coamo

Founded in 1579 at the foot of the Central Cordillera, **COAMO** is one of the oldest towns in Puerto Rico, best known today for its rustic outdoor **hot springs**, unique on the island and well worth a detour for some blissful soaking in mineral-rich pools. The town is about more than just bubbling waters, however: the **Battle of Coamo** was one of the most important engagements during the US invasion of the island in 1898, though it was more like a prolonged skirmish (seven men died), and Coamo was the last garrison to fall in the south. Today it's the **San Blás Half Marathon** (13.1 miles) held in early February that attracts northern invaders, the biggest race on the island, while the **Fiestas Patronales de Coamo** takes place over the last week of January in the main plaza, also dedicated to San Blás. The town itself is 34km from Ponce and a short drive from *autopista* PR-52, the oddly appealing cluster of aging buildings in the center evidence of its long history.

Accommodation

Hotels have been welcoming visitors to the hot springs since 1847, and though accommodation at the current incarnation is not spectacular, the *Hotel Baños de Coamo* (☎787/803-0207; ❸) offers a bucolic setting on the Río Coamo and the obvious bonus of hot springs on site. Rooms are set in slightly worn two-story wooden chalets in flowery, overgrown gardens above the river, with balconies, air-conditioning, and basic cable TV. Some rooms are in dire need of renovation – check yours before moving in. You'll have access to two pools, one fed by the hot springs and the other for swimming. The hotel is a short drive south of town, at the end of PR-546.

The Town

Downtown Coamo is often bypassed by visitors, but if you're visiting the hot springs it's worth a detour to soak up the bustling, no-nonsense atmosphere and pretty buildings around the central plaza. With the forest-drenched peaks of the Central Cordillera for a backdrop, spacious **Plaza Luis Muñoz Rivera** is studded with trees and dominated by the main church, the **Iglesia Católica San Blás de Illesca**. The first church was built in the 1570s, though the current building dates from 1784, with a typical Spanish Colonial facade crowned by three bells. The interior is unusually ornate, with high arched ceilings, tiled floors, aged timber doors, and a fine Neoclassical *retablo* – don't miss the vivid carvings of the Stations of the Cross, mounted on the walls. You'll also see some rare **works of art**, notably a painting by **José Campeche**, *El Bautisterio* – the artist originally had three paintings inside the church, but one was lost and the other, *Las Animas,* was so badly deteriorated it was copied and replaced by Francisco Oller in 1888. The latter is near the main entrance (on the right as you come in), the blond woman at the base said to have been Oller's mistress at the time.

Opposite the church on the southern side of the plaza, **Casa Florencio Santiago** was once one of the finest villas in town, now a dilapidated but slightly romantic, vine-covered ruin with peeling white paint. Born into one of the town's richest families (he was the son of Don Clotilde, see below), Florencio Santiago (1856-1924) was a farmer who went on to become mayor of Coamo and an enthusiastic philanthropist.

On the plaza's southwest corner, the **Museo y Archivo Histórico de Coamo** (free) occupies an eye-catching, reddish townhouse with tranquil *patio interior* that virtually drips with a sense of colonial Spain. The odd collection of bits and pieces inside reflects Coamo's checkered history, but it's normally open only on special days or by appointment – check at the Instituto de Cultura next door. The house was built in the nineteenth century by **Don Clotilde Santiago**, a wealthy landowner, businessman, and member of the Diputación Provincial, or Spanish colonial government, and much of his original mahogany and cedar furniture is on display inside. The living and dining rooms are decorated in a flamboyant Neoclassical style: the former contains four large Spanish paintings representing the four seasons, and a sculpture of Florencio Santiago. The main bedroom is stocked with religious paintings and icons, to demonstrate the earnest Catholic piety of the family.

Behind the museum on Calle Baldorioty, you can also admire the exterior of the **Casa del Rey**, a handsome Spanish Revival mansion built in 1927 and the former town hall, its tower and facade smothered in ornate stucco.

Eating and drinking

Unless you're **eating** at the hotel (see p.311), your choices in Coamo are restricted to the usual range of Puerto Rican diners and rustic restaurants outside the town. The two *kioscos* on the plaza serve cups of rich local coffee, snacks, cakes, and *frituras* throughout the day, while on the corner, *El Faro Deportivo* is a cheap dive bar, propped up by a colorful assortment of beer-nursing locals and open from early afternoon. Also on the plaza, *Los Domplines Coamo* (℡787/601-507) is a cheerful canteen with plastic tables and basic Puerto Rican food. *Domplines* are fried balls of dough, stuffed with meat, maize, and sometimes coconut.

The best local food can be found at the **kioscos** lining PR-14 south of town: *Don Pablo's* van specializes in roast chicken and is usually parked just outside the downtown area, while closer to the junction with PR-138 is *Kiosko de Guibo*, with cheap staples such as rice and beans for less than $2, and *Boulevar Hot Dog*, knocking out the eponymous snack along with burgers, *chicharrones*, and *frituras* for similarly bargain prices.

If you're looking for a sit-down meal, *La Guitarra* at PR-153 km 12.4 (℡787/803-2881) is the best of several restaurants between Coamo and the highway, a creaky wooden house serving *lechón* and other rural Puerto Rican favorites from $8.

Inside the *Hotel Baños de Coamo*, the *Aguas Termales* is a pleasant place to eat, set in historic brick building and open daily for breakfast (7–10am), lunch (noon–3pm), and dinner (5.30–9.30pm). The menu is principally upmarket *comida criolla*, with mains ranging $9-20. After eating, try the potent coffee, "*baños* style".

Baños de Coamo

Local legend has it that Juan Ponce de León's biggest (and fatal) mistake was to seek the fountain of youth in Florida, when the true source of eternal life was in Puerto Rico all along, at the **Baños de Coamo** (Coamo hot springs). The elderly locals hobbling down to the baths for a daily dip may appear to throw doubt on this claim, but even if you've been to hot springs elsewhere the sheer novelty of scalding hot mineral pools in the Caribbean makes them all the more enticing. The water shoots out of the ground at 110° Fahrenheit, but cools quickly in the baths: its therapeutic qualities stem from healthy doses of carbonic and sulphuric acid with magnesium carbonate.

You have two choices here: the smarter and larger pool within the *Hotel Baños de Coamo* (daily 9.30am–5.30pm; $5), lined with some of the brickwork from the original Spanish hotel and spa, offers a slightly more comfortable experience and is usually open to non-guests for a fee – check at reception first. Real aficionados can combine this with a jump into the regular (cold) swimming pool next door.

The free **public pools** (daily 8am–6pm) are at the end of the lane that continues to the right of the hotel, concrete and brick tubs that stick out incongruously near the marshy river, all shaded by a large tree. They may seem rather run-down and uninviting, but the water is genuinely hot and mineral-rich, and assuming you can avoid the crowds, a real bargain. Soaking is restricted to fifteen minutes, but on weekends local families hang out in the area for the whole day, taking turns – try to avoid visiting at these times. Normally you can park at the end of the lane nearby (you might get asked to leave if you try and park in the hotel), but note that the gate normally closes at 4pm. The hot springs are at the end of PR-546 and signposted off PR-153, which runs between Coamo and the *autopista*.

Playa de Salinas

Home of one of the island's most celebrated culinary innovations, **mojo isleño**, the small village of **PLAYA DE SALINAS** makes a convenient pit-stop on the drive along the south coast. Facing a bay of tiny, mangrove-swamped islands, it makes a useful hurricane hole for yachts, the marina and most of the restaurants clustered at the end of PR-701, a few kilometers south of the largely uninteresting agricultural town of **Salinas**. Proud home of **Zuleyka Rivera**, winner of Miss Universe 2006 (Puerto Rico's fifth victory), Salinas is more traditionally known as the **cockfighting capital** of Puerto Rico, and many locals still raise prize-winning roosters in cages outside their clapboard houses. Fights held here tend to be more brutal than in San Juan, but if you're still curious, visit **Club Gallístico de Salinas** (Wed & Fri–Sun afternoons; ☎787/824-0721) at PR-1 km 82.2, or **Gallera La Plena** (Fri–Sat; ☎787/839-8593) in the hills on PR-712 km 4.8. Salinas is around 15km from Coamo.

Accommodation

The aging *Posada El Náutico* (☎787/824-3185, ✉jarce@coqui.net; ❸), Marina de Salinas, at the end of PR-701 (c/Chapin G-8), is starting to look a bit frayed around the ages, but is still the best place **to stay** if you end up in Salinas. The basic motel-like rooms come with air-conditioning, fridge, and local TV, and the coin **laundry** serving the marina is open to guests (daily 8am–9pm). You'll pay $20 extra for a sea view.

The beach and cays

Despite the name, Playa de Salinas is essentially a cluster of low-rise homes and restaurants lining a bay thick with groping mangroves, with no actual beach as such. **Polito's Beach** (free parking) is just off PR-701 in the middle of the village, little more than a break in the dense wall of knotted mangrove roots, which nevertheless becomes inundated with salsa-dancing locals on weekends and holidays, enjoying the music, snacks, and drinks at the **kioscos** here. You'll also see hordes of private **jet skis** piled up at the jetty: if you're desperate to take a ride, ask around and someone will normally rent you one, though you'll have to fork out $70–75/hr.

Some of the cays offshore do have beaches, and make far more enticing targets: **Cayo Mata** is the largest, but the closest is **Cayo Matita**, around 200 yards from the jetty and surrounded by a narrow strip of sand. With more time and energy you can explore the **Cayos de Ratones** further out, but make sure you know exactly where you're going before setting off. The most enjoyable (and eco-friendly) way to explore the cays is to rent **kayaks** from the *Posada El Náutico* ($15/hr), but you can also take 35-minute boat rides around the bay on *La Paseodora* (Sat & Sun; $3–4). This small ferry sails from the Terminal de la Paseodora (☎787/824-2649), a little jetty next door to *El Balcón del Capitán*. The captain will normally drop you off on one of the cays if you ask, and pick you up later ($5 return).

Eating and drinking

Other than mucking around on the water, the main purpose of any visit to Playa de Salinas is **to eat**, and PR-701 takes you past several restaurants that hug the shore, most featuring **mojo isleño**, a piquant sauce made with tomatoes and garlic, usually added to fish or various *frituras*.

🍴 *Ladi's Place* (c/Principal A-86, PR-701; ☎787/824-2649; closed Mon) claims to have popularized the celebrated dressing, doling out a particularly tangy version faithful to the recipe concocted by Doña Ladi Correa in the 1940s: *mojo isleño* traditionally accompanies red snapper (around $25), while hearty pitchers of *sangría* ($24.95) slip down very easily from the breezy terrace overlooking the bay. The food quality and attentive service just about justifies the high prices, and you can park on site. *El Balcón del Capitán* (c/Principal A-54, PR-701; ☎787/824-6210) is a worthy alternative, specializing in grand lobster dishes and fresh fish with another outdoor terrace on the water. This place tends to be a bit cheaper (mains $7-30), and there are plenty of local snacks such as *empanadillas* stuffed with seafood on the menu. One of the most appealing restaurants lies in the *Posada El Náutico* complex, at the end of PR-701. *Restaurante Costa Marina* (☎787/752-8484) is on the second floor of a wooden boathouse, suitably adorned with nautical decor and wooden tables, all providing bird's-eye views of the marina and islet-studded bay. The expansive but fairly standard menu of Puerto Rican roast meats and seafood features exceptional lobster ($21.95) or prawn ($16.95) *asopaos*, and the usual red snapper and mahi-mahi dishes ($16-18), but it's also the best place for a coffee or the signature cocktail, *Flor de Mangle*, if you're not having a meal. You can leave your car in the hotel parking lot.

Aguirre and Bahía de Jobos

Much of the fragile coastline between Salinas and Guayama is protected within DRNA reserves, centered on the **Reserva Nacional de Investigación Estuarina de Bahía de Jobos**, established in 1981. The reserve covers around 2883 acres of mangrove forest and freshwater wetlands, including the Mar Negro and the Cayos Caribe, fifteen mangrove islets surrounded by coral reef and seagrass beds, habitats for the endangered brown pelican, peregrine falcon, hawksbill sea turtle, and West Indian manatee. The best place to get oriented is the **visitor center** in Aguirre (see opposite). Elsewhere, the **Vereda Jagüeyes** is a 1.5km hiking trail which follows the edge of the bay through the web of mangroves, via a series of wooden boardwalks and lookouts in the Bosque de Jagüeyes (the wooded western section of the reserve). To get there, head west on PR-3 and take the small road south at km 154.3 (Camino La Esperanza) – the turn off is before the junction with PR-703. The road ends at a farm but you can park before this at the brown sign marking the trail. Further east, the adjacent **Bosque Estatal de Aguirre** is another pleasant spot for a stroll: drive 2.7km on PR-7710, south of PR-3, to the **Area Recreativa El Toconal**. Here you can follow the Vereda Interpretiva, a signposted nature trail through thickets of shady scrub and patches of mixed woodland that surround the bay – a relatively cooler option on a burning hot day.

Aguirre

The sprawling **Central Aguirre Sugar Company** complex at the end of PR-705 was constructed between 1899 and 1902 by a US syndicate, becoming one of the largest sugar plants in the Caribbean and precipitating the development of **AGUIRRE** town, a self-contained community entirely dependent on the sugar factory. The company ceased operations in 1980, and the government maintained

The rise and fall of Puerto Rico's "white gold"

Sugar cane has had a bigger impact on Puerto Rico than any other commodity, at times utterly dominating the island's economy. Unlike a resurgent coffee industry, however, sugar is no longer produced here, a dramatic turnaround that has left vast tracts of the southern coastal plain wild and barren scrubland.

The first documented plantation was a short-lived venture established by Tomás de Castellón on the Río Anasco in the 1520s, and by 1582 there were eleven mills on the island. This **first era of sugar** lasted until the 1650s, when competition from the West Indies saw production in Puerto Rico dwindle. Thanks to a growing pool of slave labor, output began to increase again in the second half of the eighteenth century, and by the 1810s sugar had replaced coffee as the number-one export, spawning a thriving **rum** industry. By the 1820s the haciendas of the **southern coastal plain** were dominating production, making the towns of **Ponce** and **Guayama** rich in the process. Production peaked in the 1870s, but after the abolition of slavery, sugar slumped again in the 1890s. The third and **final boom** came after the US invasion of 1898 – thanks to US investment into new plants at **Aguirre** and **Guánica**, by the 1920s Puerto Rico was virtually a sugar island. Much of the sugar-cane crop was destroyed by Hurricane San Felipe in 1928, and the Great Depression proved a terminal blow. After World War II the remaining plants began to close as Operation Bootstrap took hold (see p.364). Today US industrial laws, particularly those that govern the treatment of waste from processing plants, ensure that growing sugar in Puerto Rico remains a wholly uneconomic prospect – rum-makers must import molasses from elsewhere.

a small sugar operation here until everything closed in 1990. Today Aguirre is not quite a ghost town, with many former employees still living in the houses nearby, though all the chief buildings are abandoned and the plant itself is locked up, a slowly decaying monument to the island's now moribund sugar industry.

PR-705 makes a loop through the town and past its only real attraction, the Jobos reserve's **Centro de Visitantes** (Mon–Fri 7.30–11.45am & 1–3.45pm; ☎787/853-4617) at PR-705 2.3km, occupying what was once the social club or "Casa Club" of the Hotel Aguirre. When it comes to ecology and the environment, this is the most illuminating information center on the island, with a large exhibition area covering every aspect of the conservation work in the Jobos estuary, as well as the rich array of marine and bird life in the area. Displays also cover the various habitats in the reserve, including coral reefs, and the history of Aguirre itself. The center is gradually establishing a network of trails, including an excellent **Ruta de Kayak** along the coast, but since you must provide your own kayak or canoe, this is of little use to casual visitors.

The rest of Aguirre holds little appeal unless you fancy a cheap round of golf: the **Aguirre Golf Course** (☎787/853-4052) at PR-705 km 1.7 is said to be the oldest on the island and looks it, but offers bargain rates for nine holes. Usually open Tuesday to Sunday from 7.30am to 6pm (call to check), it charges $20–25 on weekdays and $30–35 at weekends.

Guayama

In the nineteenth century **GUAYAMA** was one of the grandest towns on the island, overflowing with money garnered from nearby sugar-cane plantations. Though it remains a large, lively place, it's the legacies of that period, chiefly its fine **architecture**, that make a visit worthwhile today. The name comes from

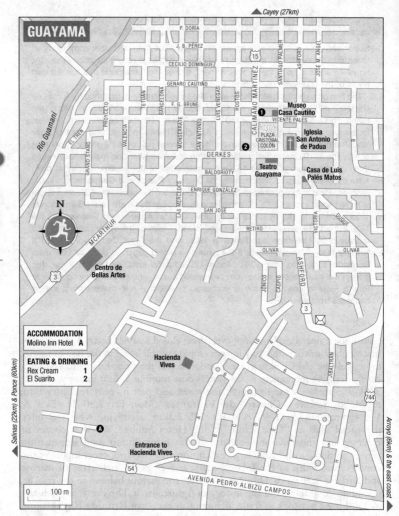

GUAYAMA

▲ Cayey (27km)

P. DORIA

J. B. PÉREZ

CECILIO DOMÍNGUEZ

GENARO CAUTIÑO

F. G. BRUNE

❶ Museo
Casa Cautiño

VICENTE PALES

Iglesia
San Antonio
de Padua

PLAZA
CRISTÓBAL
COLÓN

❷

DERKES

Teatro
Guayama

Casa de Luis
Palés Matos

BALDORIOTY

ENRIQUE GONZÁLEZ

SAN JOSÉ

RETIRO

OLIVAR

OLIVAR

N

Centro de
Bellas Artes

ACCOMMODATION
Molino Inn Hotel   A

EATING & DRINKING
Rex Cream   1
El Suarito   2

Hacienda
Vives

Entrance to
Hacienda Vives

AVENIDA PEDRO ALBIZU CAMPOS

0   100 m

Salinas (22km) & Ponce (60km)

Arroyo (6km) & the east coast

Guamaní or just Guayama, Taíno words for "large place." The Spanish formally established the town in 1736.

Currently the largest **Paso Fino** fair in the world and jam-packed with spectacular events, the two-day **Feria Dulces Sueños** (☎787/864-7765) is held in Guayama on the first weekend in March. In addition to the usual live music shows and local food stalls, the main arena hosts a varied program of performances and competitions involving Puerto Rico's famous Paso Fino horses (see p.140). More traditional festivities take place during the **Fiestas Patronales de Guayama** in June, to honor patron saint San Antonio de Padua; expect the central plaza to be crammed with arts, crafts, and snack stalls, a boisterous parade on June 12-13, fireworks, and lots of live music, salsa, and dancing (usually free).

Accommodation

If you get stuck in Guayama, aim for the tatty but bearable *Molino Inn Hotel* (⊤787/866-1515, ⓦwww.molinoinn.net; ❸) at PR-54 km 2.1, just outside the center. Its twenty motel-style rooms are a little faded, but adequate for a one-night stay, with rattan furnishings, air-conditioning, and basic cable TV.

The Town

Driving into town on PR-3, stop first at the **Centro de Bellas Artes** (Tues–Sun 9am–4.30pm; free), an imposing Neoclassical structure built in 1927 and

▲ Museo Casa Cautiño interior

formerly the Tribunal Superior (High Court). Today it houses an odd assortment of fine art, archeology, and sculpture, but you can also grab useful maps and **information** about the town here, and parking is free. The building itself is the real attraction, though some of the art and sculpture on display is engaging, and you'll find more abstract, contemporary work upstairs, mostly from local artists. The **Sala Taína** contains a couple of ghoulish Taíno petroglyphs and a small collection of the same types of Taíno tools, ceremonial objects, and ceramics you'll see elsewhere, while the **Sala de Simón Madera** is dedicated to the composer of the popular **danza** *Mis Amores*, containing his old violin, desk, and portrait. Madera supposedly wrote the piece in Casa Cautiño (see below), and died in Guayama in 1957.

Plaza Cristóbal Colón

In town itself, you should be able to park close to the central **Plaza Cristóbal Colón**, a wide square dotted with aromatic West Indian bay trees – check out the towering former cinema on the west side, built in 1920, and **Teatro Guayama** to the south, an Art Deco treasure built in 1938 and still in use. Built in a neo-Romanesque style in 1874, the **Iglesia San Antiono de Padua** graces the east side of the plaza, its soaring towers incorporating medieval influences such as *westwerk* (an entrance area with upper chamber) and an elaborate rose window of stained glass, though local comparisons with Notre-Dame are pushing things a bit. It's open for mass (Mon–Fri 6–7.30am & 4.30–7.30pm, Sat 6.30–8.30am & 6–8pm, and all day Sun), but tends to be locked up at other times.

On the north side of the plaza, the **Museo Casa Cautiño** (Tues–Sat 9am–4.30pm, Sun 10.30am–4pm; free) comes closest to capturing the refined opulence of the sugar era, a frost-white *criollo* villa, immaculately restored as a small period museum. The rooms feature some of the original furniture and European artwork collected by the former owners, but the real star is the house itself. The outer veranda is embellished with ornate plasterwork, lace-like filigree on the doors, and six slender iron columns, while the interior features checkered marble-tile floors, white mahogany ceilings, and a tranquil inner patio. One of the special features is the semi-elliptical "fanlight" windows that top each doorway. The house was completed in 1887 for Don Genaro Cautiño Vázquez, a local celebrity who was at various times the mayor, judge, and colonel of the local militia. His descendants lived here until 1981, when the house was donated to the state in lieu of taxes.

The Zona Histórica and Hacienda Vives

The best examples of Guayama's rich stock of clapboard *criollo* and Neoclassical buildings lie to the north and east of the plaza, an area dubbed the **Zona Histórica**. Many houses are in the process of being restored, and best taken in with aimless wandering: the town is arranged on a typical grid pattern and it's impossible to get lost if you keep to within two or three blocks of the square. At the time of writing the abandoned former birthplace of **Luis Palés Matos** (1898-1959), acclaimed author of poetry collection *Tun tun de pasa y grifería*, was in dire need of a savior – locals hope to turn the crumbling two-story wooden house into a **museum**, but funds have so far been lacking. You'll see it at Calle Ashford and Baldorioty. Matos created the poetry genre known as Afro-Antillano, a blend of Afro-Caribbean words and Spanish. The bust of the poet stands in the main plaza.

You'll see several ruins of old **sugar mills** around the town, notably the picturesque old mill tower (*molino*) of **Hacienda Vives**, constructed in 1828.

The ruins are maintained in park-like grounds off PR-54, not far from the *Molino Inn*, though the entrance can be hard to find: it's on a narrow service road on the north side of the highway. You can park near the gate, but take care as there have been muggings here in the past.

Eating and drinking

Guayama's central plaza is lined with plenty of unexceptional **places to eat**, serving Puerto Rican snacks, pizza, and sandwiches, but for historic ambience *El Suarito* (☏787/864-1820) at Calle Derkes 6 is hard to beat, a Spanish-style canteen lodged in an open-front colonial building dating from 1862. *Suarito* opened in the 1950s and while some of the clientele look like they've been regulars since then, the cheap *comida criolla* (dishes for $4–5) is tasty enough (roast chicken, pork chops), and the bar serves cold Medalla for $1.25 and sandwiches for $2.

Alternatively, cool down with one of the freshly made ice creams at *Rex Cream* (daily 9.30am–10.30pm) at Calle Derkes 24, which has all the usual innovative flavors from lime, tamarind, and *guanabana* (soursop), to chocolate and pistachio ($1–2.50). *Rex* also has a small branch on the northeast corner of the plaza.

Arroyo

Once a thriving port, bolstered by large wads of sugar-cane money, **ARROYO** is a ghost of its former self, a "Little Paris" lined with fancy mansions, where the local plantation elite would promenade in horse-drawn carriages. Though it attracts plenty of sentimental Puerto Rican tourists at the weekends, attempts to spruce up the town after years of decline have had mixed results, and the nearby beach resort at Punta Guilarte has little to offer foreign visitors. It's this undeveloped, no-frills Puerto Rican quality that makes it appealing, however, with a motley collection of pubs and canteens maintaining the raffish if not quite seedy charm of a small port district, and the main street still boasting some exquisite townhouses from its golden age. Rehabilitation continues at a snail's pace, but by 2009 the town may be looking a lot smarter.

The Town

Calle Morse (PR-178) runs through the heart of Arroyo from PR-3 to the *malecón*, lined with the most florid examples of wooden *criollo* architecture. The best stretch is the final section south of the tiny plaza, though it can be tough to park on the main road and you'll probably have to resort to one of the side streets. The town does have a **tourist office** (Mon–Fri 8am–noon & 1.30–4.30pm; ☏787/839-3500 ext 231), which has plenty of Spanish information about the town, and the latest updates about sights and events. The old office was located just north of the plaza on Calle Morse, but is expected to move into another building nearby by early 2009 – call or ask around if you can't find it.

The only real "sight" in Arroyo is the **Museo Antigua Aduana**, just south of the plaza on Calle Morse, though the most striking thing about it is the incredibly opulent entrance, crowned with a US shield and bald eagle glittering with Mayan-like splendor. The former customs house contains items related to the first telegraph line laid in Latin America, installed by Samuel Morse in 1859 at nearby Hacienda La Enriqueta (the ex-Lind family estate is now a forlorn ruin, 3km northeast of town). The museum is expected to be closed until 2009 for renovation.

The Casa Alcaldía (town hall) next door to the Aduana was completed in 1935, its simple Neoclassical design also showing US influence. Calle Morse ends at the **malecón** or seafront, also known as Paseo de Las Américas, a dusty, run-down, and usually deserted area, which only comes to life on weekends when the bars nearby fill up with boozing locals.

One of the town's biggest draws is **El Tren de Sur**, an old diesel train built in 1939 and once used to transport raw sugar cane. The train runs from a small parking area which can be hard to spot, on the north side of PR-3, in between the two PR-178 junctions at km 130.9. The train normally runs along a short length of restored track (25min) on weekends only (9am–4pm; $3–5), but is likely to be closed until 2009 for renovation.

Eating and drinking

Eating options in Arroyo are not particularly inspiring, and you're better off heading 10km east to the restaurants along the coast. The most inviting place to eat or spend a lazy afternoon on this stretch of road is *El Mar de la Tranquilidad* (closed Mon; ☎787/839-6469), a beachside restaurant in *barrio* Bajos, at PR-3 km 118.9. The wooden terrace sits over a rocky, crab-infested shoreline: unsurprisingly, crab rice ($7.50) is the house specialty, served with beans and plantains, but fried chunks of grouper ($13.50) and fried pork with *mofongo* ($12) are better (and bigger), while the cocktails and *sangría* ($4) are fairly potent. The food is OK considering the price, but the main appeal is the laid-back vibe and location.

In Arroyo itself the *malecón* sports a couple of unappealing dive bars and diners, while a better option is *La Familia* at the end of Calle Morse, at no. 53, next to the local *supermercado*. This canteen serves a choice of various local dishes (*mofongo* for $2) and cheap sandwiches ($2) in a small indoor seating area. *Danny's BBQ* at no.66, just off Calle Morse in a cul-de-sac, knocks up juicy *pollo asado* ($5.50).

For something sweeter, try *Jodymar Ice Cream* at Calle Morse 46, near the seafront. Tempting flavors such as butter rum and fresh coconut are $1.25-1.50 per cup.

For **a drink**, *El Trombon del Mar* nearby is normally open during the day, and is one of the more attractive options along the *malecón*, with a wooden bar, cheap local booze, and worryingly, a well-used karaoke machine.

Travel details

Flights

Ponce to: San Juan (5 daily; 25min).

Públicos

Públicos are not a reliable way to travel long distances in the south, mostly acting as local bus services.

Guayama to: Arroyo (infrequent; 10min); Ponce (infrequent; 1hr); Salinas (infrequent; 30min); San Juan (infrequent; 1hr 30min).

Ponce to: Coamo (infrequent; 30min); Guayama (infrequent; 1hr); Salinas (infrequent; 45min); San Germán (infrequent; 45min); San Juan (Mon–Sat; 1hr 30min); Yauco (infrequent; 25min).

7

La Ruta Panorámica

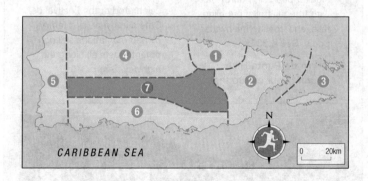

CHAPTER 7

Highlights

* **Lechoneras** Feast on a sumptuous meal of *lechón*, roast suckling pig, served at the rustic mountain shacks in Guavate, north of the Carite forest. See p.326

* **Cañón de San Cristóbal** Scale the precipitous, jungle-clad walls of this mesmerizing canyon, a jagged gash through the hills best explored with an experienced guide. See p.330

* **Bosque Estatal de Toro Negro** This beguiling forest reserve covers some of the highest peaks in Puerto Rico, with tranquil trails, bubbling falls, and cooling freshwater pools. See p.335

* **Cerro de Punta** Hike or grind your car up the potholed road to Puerto Rico's highest peak, an isolated, mist-drenched summit towering above the whole island. See p.337

* **Jayuya** Get to grips with Puerto Rico's Taíno soul at this sleepy mountain town, with its evocative museum, haunting petroglyphs and the annual Festival Nacional Indígena. See p.340

* **Coffee** The unspoiled hill town of Maricao is famed for its exceptional coffee, celebrated at the Festival del Café each year, and family-owned plantations sell rich, potent roasts all along the highway. See p.349

▲ Hacienda Juanita on La Ruta Panorámica

La Ruta Panorámica

Slicing across the physical and spiritual heart of Puerto Rico, the **Ruta Panorámica** follows the highest ridges of the Central Cordillera for 266km. This scenic highway cuts through some of the least explored but most rewarding parts of the island, snaking among mist-shrouded peaks, scintillating viewpoints, and dense, dimly lit forests. The road offers a hazy window into the rural past of Puerto Rico, a patchwork of small **coffee** farms shrouded in *palo colorado* forest, torpid villages of barefoot kids and horseback-riding locals where the *colmado* doubles as a bar, and smoky roadside barbecues of roast pork and thick wedges of banana. In the summer, the roads are framed with blazing *flamboyant* trees and ripe mangos pile up in the verges. It's a landscape inhabited by the descendants of the **jíbaros**, the hard-working peasant farmers who colonized the jungle-drenched slopes and who embody much of Puerto Rico's romantic ideas about its past: humble but wise, poor but proudly independent.

You can follow the route in either direction, but the further west you drive, the more rural and traditional things become. The **Bosque Estatal de Carite** is one of four **forest reserves** along the way, with basic camping facilities and trails in various states of use, while the **lechoneras** of Guavate roast succulent hunks of pork nearby. Keep heading west and you'll reach workaday **Aibonito**, host to an exuberant **flower festival** and the staging post for the **Cañón de San Cristóbal**, a dizzying gorge en route to **Barranquitas**, one of the region's most absorbing towns. Straddling the center of the island, the **Bosque Estatal de Toro Negro** is Puerto Rico's most alluring forest park; **Jayuya** has become the center of a mini-Taíno revival; and **Adjuntas** remains a conservative, traditional hill town, though it's home to **Casa Pueblo**, cultural center and hub of environmental activism. Finally, perched on the western end of the cordillera, sleepy **Maricao** is enveloped by some of the world's finest **coffee** plantations, and is home to the best of the mountain hotels, *Hacienda Juanita*.

Driving the Ruta Panorámica

The route, officially **La Ruta Panorámica Luiz Muñoz Marín** after the first elected governor of Puerto Rico, is really an interlocking network of around forty different rural highways, so you should follow the small brown "Ruta" signs throughout, not the actual road numbers. You'll need two or three days to see everything, and longer if you intend to stop for some hiking along the way.

On the east coast, the road begins as a loop between Yabucoa and Maunabo, incorporating scenic coastal highway PR-901 (see p.141). From Yabucoa, PR-182

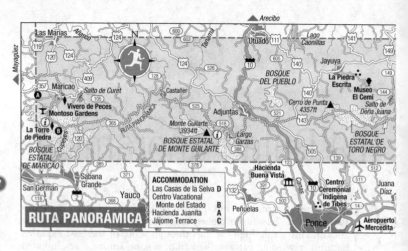

a narrow road that rarely sees much traffic, takes you into the mountains, and eventually, via PR-181 and PR-7740, into the **Bosque Estatal de Carite**.

Despite their somewhat hazardous reputation, driving the twisty roads up in the mountains is far less dangerous than the speeding highways of San Juan, assuming you stay within the fairly slow speed limits (usually 35mph), and take your time. All the roads are paved but heavy rain can cause problems, and there are some traffic black-spots around Aibonito. **Places to stay** are usually off the main route, and it's worth booking ahead as rooms are limited, though you should have no trouble finding **gas stations**. Note that to **camp** in any of the forests, you'll need to get permits in advance from the DRNA in San Juan (see p.28).

Bosque Estatal de Carite

Rising gently from the east coast, the Ruta Panorámica winds its way past isolated farms for 25km before running into the **Bosque Estatal de Carite**, a lush mountain forest of *pino hondureño*, subtropical *palma de lluvia*, and aged *palo colorado* trees. The reserve covers an area of around 6700 acres ranging 800–3000ft above sea level, making it several degrees cooler than the coast, and was once laced with 25 **hiking trails**, though Hurricane Georges washed most of these away in 1998. The most popular of those remaining is the half-mile trail leading to **Charco Azul**, an inviting freshwater swimming hole. Also home to a wide variety of bird species, the reserve was established in 1935 primarily to protect the watershed of three major rivers in the Sierra de Cayey: the Río Grande de Loíza, Río Grande de Patillas, and the Río de la Plata.

Practicalities

You can **camp** at Charco Azul or in the leafy confines of the **Area Recreativa Guavate** for $4 (see p.326). Both sites have toilets. You can also sleep at the wonderfully rustic 🎋 **Las Casas de la Selva**, an experimental forestry center (see box, p.326): a double room with bathroom in the center's main building is $50, while covered tents with airbeds cost $25 (with use of hot showers and toilet), though they are often fully booked with volunteers May to August – at

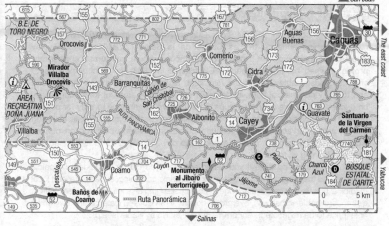

these times you can camp nearby for $10, if you have your own tent (no facilities). Use of shared kitchen facilities is an additional $5. Meals, using fresh organic produce from the gardens, can be arranged in advance.

The forest **information office** is on the north side of the reserve in **Guavate** (see p.326), which isn't really convenient unless you're driving from San Juan (coming from the east you'll have driven through the forest by the time you reach it). The more compelling reason to visit this area is to trawl the numerous *lechoneras* nearby, purveyors of magnificent barbecued meat all day long.

Santuario de La Virgen del Carmen

Also known as the Montaña Santa ("Holy Mountain"), the **Santuario de La Virgen del Carmen** (open 24hr; free; ☏787/736-5750, ⓦwww.santuariopr .org) is one of Puerto Rico's most revered **shrines**, a poignant reminder of the island's still potent folk beliefs, as well as its Catholic faith. The shrine lies on the eastern edge of the reserve, clearly signposted off PR-7740.

Little is known about the woman who lived here between 1901 and 1909, but **Elenita de Jesús** was undoubtedly a strong Catholic evangelizing presence in the region at a time when many feared that, under US control, Protestant faiths would swamp the island. Her intense devotion to God and extreme piety convinced local people that she was an incarnation of Mary herself, the **Virgen del Carmen** and after her death the mountain became a popular place of prayer and pilgrimage. Such practices have always sat uneasily with the Catholic Church, and in 1997 the Bishop of Caguas ruled that Elenita was definitely not Mary, only a woman "of extraordinary spiritual gifts and piety." Nevertheless, many Puerto Ricans continue to believe.

Across from the parking lot you'll find the Nuestro Templo del Santuario or just **La Capilla**, a simple single-story chapel constructed in 1985 on the site of three previous shrines dating back to the time of Elenita. Inside you'll find images of Mary and a small chapel dedicated to Charlie Rodríguez (see p.148). Beyond the parking lot, **El Arco de La Virgen** is a white gate that leads to a grassy trail up the hill, past representations of the fourteen Stations of the Cross to **Las Tres Cruces** (three wooden crosses), depicting the crucifixion. It's an especially venerated spot, with arresting views across the forest, often shrouded in mist in the early mornings.

Area Recreativa Charco Azul

Beyond the *santuario* the road widens, and when PR-7740 meets PR-184 it's worth leaving the *ruta* for the **Area Recreativa Charco Azul** (daily 9am–5pm), a short 1km detour south at PR-184 km 16.6. The "blue pool" is the most popular attraction in the forest, a freshwater pond at the end of the half-mile **Charco Azul Trail**. It's deep enough for paddling and usually swimming, and can get busy on weekends, but at other times you'll probably have it to yourself. The area is clearly signposted, with a parking lot and picnic area on the right, and the trailhead to the pool, campground, and toilets on the left.

Area Recreativa Guavate

From Chaco Azul, PR-184 climbs 5km through the forest to the junction with PR-179, the *ruta*'s highest point in the reserve, before curling around the **Area Recreativa Guavate** (Mon–Fri 9am–4.30pm, Sat & Sun 8am–5pm), a further 1.5km down the slopes at km 27.3. This is technically a spur of the Ruta Panorámica, as the main route follows PR-179 south, but worth a detour nonetheless. Named after the *barrio* of Guavate, the recreation area is a series of shady picnic spots along both sides of the road, with a **campground** off to the left. You'll also find a few muddy hiking **trails** in the area, but for the latest on conditions keep driving another 3km north to the tiny DRNA **Oficina Oficial de Manejo** (Mon–Fri 7am–3.30pm; ☎787/747-4545) on the left. Ask here for basic maps (it's usually staffed by Spanish speakers only). Beyond here the forest ends abruptly in *lechón* paradise.

Eating

No trip to Puerto Rico would be complete without sampling at least one **lechonera**, roadside grills that barbecue whole suckling pigs, traditionally over charcoal and wood fires, to produce mouthwatering roast pork with a crispy, fatty skin. Basted with *jugo de naranjas agria* (sour orange juice), *lechón* is normally devoured with plantains and **aji-li-mojili**, a local dressing. The undisputed home of professional roasters is **Guavate**, with the highest concentration of *lechoneras* on PR-184, just after the entrance to the forest in the Los Montañez sector, but you'll see plenty of them all the way to junction 31 on *autopista* PR-53. On weekends, and especially Sundays, these places double as salsa clubs, with thousands of *sanjuaneros* clogging the roads, drinking beer, and dancing till late. Most *lechoneras* operate canteen-style systems where you order from the counter: *lechón* is normally priced by weight ($7–8 per pound), while you can choose a variety of sides such as rice and beans, plantains, or bananas. *Pavochón* is roast turkey seasoned like *lechón*, and you'll also see plenty of equally addictive roast chicken on offer.

La Casona de Guavate PR-184 km 28.4 ☎787/747-5533. If you fancy a more traditional sit-down meal, keep driving north to this Art Nouveau villa (something of a local folly). *Comida criolla* staples start at $6.50, but with five *asadors* on the go *lechón* is also a key feature ($5 per pound), and live music adds a festive air. The curious but appetizing house "jam," a home-made sweet sauce, is added to most dishes. Open Sat & Sun noon–6pm.

Lechonera El Monte PR-184 km 27.5. Opposite *El Rancho*, this place is open similar times and offers similar fare (plates of roast pork for $5), but really gets rocking on Sun when its dance floor is packed with the salsa crowd.

🏃 **Lechonera El Rancho Original** PR-184 km 27.5. Though many places only open on weekends, this lauded shack starts roasting daily

for breakfast. A big plate of pork is $5, and they also do *morcilla* sausage ($5 per pound), roast chicken ($7 per pound), and a tangy home-made *flan* ($1.50). Choose chunks of violet-colored *yautía* and pearly white *yuca* to go with the main dishes. You can munch away sitting at benches and tables, and park out front (they even have an ATM), though on weekends you may have to use the parking lot nearby ($3).

Lechonera Los Piños PR-184 km 27.7. Further down the road from *El Rancho*, this *lechonera* is open longer hours and serves special sausages and *arroz con guinea* (rice with guinea hen) as well as the main event. Mon–Thurs 5am–8pm, Fri–Sun 5am–10pm.

Cayey

The prosperous town of **CAYEY** is the first major settlement on the *ruta*, a fast-expanding community thanks to the PR-52 *autopista* that sweeps right through it. The town was formally established in 1773 and is said to be named after the Taíno word for "place of many waters," though it's also sometimes known as *La Ciudad de las Brumas* ("city of the fog") due to its misty location sandwiched between the mountains. Despite being the birthplace of several Puerto Rican luminaries, including **Jesús Colón**, the founder of the **Nuyorican movement** (see p.378), it's only worth a brief pit-stop to grab some food and to check out the enlightening museum on the outskirts. If you're here around August 15, check out the **Fiestas Patronales de Cayey** celebrating patron saint La Señora de la Asunción, when the whole town turns out for processions, music, games, and special *kioscos*.

Accommodation

Set on a small hilltop just off the *ruta*, 9km from downtown Cayey, *Jájome Terrace* (PR-15 km 18.6; ☎787/738-4016, ⓦwww.jajometerrace.com; ❺) is a guesthouse and restaurant with spectacular views over the Jájome Valley and all the way to the Caribbean. Rooms are clean and comfy, with bright white walls and a balcony (the best feature), though some are starting to show their age and you won't get TV, air-conditioning (it's usually cool enough with ceiling fan), or phones (mobile reception is also bad). During the week you might feel a little isolated here, with the staff rarely around, though some guests prefer it that way. Ask for an upper floor room and remember that it's always busier on weekends. Singles save around $20 and a basic breakfast is included. You'll see the small parking area just off PR-15, around 500m after the junction with PR-741.

The jíbaro

The **jíbaro** has achieved iconic status in Puerto Rico, despite referring to the humble, hardworking, and generally poverty-stricken **farmers** that worked the island's rugged interior over the last four hundred years. The term was originally applied by the Spanish to runaway Taíno slaves, but by the end of the nineteenth century it had come to represent the agricultural working class, a *criollo* blend of all the early inhabitants of the island. The idealization of the *jíbaro* began in the 1920s, when artists such as Ramón Frade started to paint romantic images of the Puerto Rican countryside and what he considered its noble peasantry, and when the Popular Democratic Party (PDP) was founded in 1938, it adopted the *jíbaro* hat, the *pava*, as a symbol of its commitment to the common man. After World War II things started to change: the terms *jíbaro* and *jíbara* (for women) became more pejorative, equating to something like "bumpkin" or "hillbilly," a connotation vividly described by Esmeralda Santiago in *When I Was Puerto Rican* (see p.384). Today, in rapidly modernizing Puerto Rico, the true *jíbaro* has disappeared, and for many the word has regained its romantic associations, evoking nostalgia for a more traditional, stable, and simpler time. Few Puerto Ricans would be happy being called *jíbaro*, but most retain respect for what the word has come to symbolize: Puerto Rico's traditional roots.

The Town

Cayey is a typical Puerto Rican town, with strip malls on the outskirts and a jumble of low-rise buildings in its cramped center. It does, however, boast a small University of Puerto Rico campus, and here you'll find a real gem, the **Museo de Arte Dr. Pío López Martínez** (Mon–Fri 8am–4.30pm, Sat & Sun 11am–5pm; free), dedicated primarily to local boy **Ramón Frade** (somewhat confusingly, the museum is named after its founder, a university professor). Frade, who was born in Cayey in 1875, became part of what's sometimes termed the **Costumbrista school** of painters, with his idealized view of rural Puerto Rican life and particularly the *jíbaro* (see above). Inside you'll find temporary exhibits related to his work, as well as La Casa Frade, a faithful reproduction of the artist's childhood home, with clapboard walls, period furniture, and replicas of some of his most famous works, including *El Pan Nuestro* (now displayed in San Juan, see p.73). The museum also has a collection of *cartels*, the exuberant posters used to promote Puerto Rican festivals and musicals. Everything is presented beautifully, but labels are usually in Spanish only. The museum sits just inside the main entrance of the university on PR-14, heading out of Cayey towards Caguas. Use the free parking lot on site.

If you have time, check out the **Monumento al Jíbaro Puertorriqueño** ("Monument to the Puerto Rican Countryman") on *autopista* PR-52, a few kilometers south of Cayey. The bone-white statue of a standing peasant farmer or *jíbaro*, and his seated wife and baby, was sculpted by Tomás Batista. The statue is simple, but Batista has certainly added a noble, slightly haunting quality to the much-loved folk icon. Behind it, you should be able to make out the suggestively named twin peaks of **Las Tetas de Cayey**, something of a joke in Puerto Rico, and well-known landmarks.

Eating

The best **places to eat** in Cayey tend to lie on the main roads and mountains outside the town center. Failing that, you'll find all the usual fast-food chains on PR-1 as it skirts the town.

El Cuñao PR-1 km 65.5 ☎787-263-0511. Around 8km west of Cayey, conveniently positioned on twisting PR-1 and the Ruta Panorámica itself, this justly popular local lunch stop has simple tables and chairs, friendly staff and glorious *lechón asado* (less than $10), *morcilla* sausage, rice and beans, *mofongo*, and all the other core *criollo* dishes. Try and park on the road outside.

Jájome Terrace PR-15 km 18.6 ☎787/738-4016. This hotel restaurant is a solid option if you want to skip the town, right on the *ruta* with killer views from its terrace, serving a blend of upscale *cocina criolla* and Mediterranean food. Closed Mon–Wed.

El Mesón de Jorge PR-14 km 57 ☎787/263-2800. This modern dining room serves high-quality Puerto Rican cuisine: *asopaos* from $10, six types of *mofongo* from $11.50, *pechuga* ($12.75), and succulent *chuletas* ($22). The restaurant is located at the junction of PR-14 and PR-1, a few kilometers east of the town center: it's the wooden building off PR-14, behind the car dealership. Closed Mon & Tues.

Sand and the Sea PR-715 km 5.2 ☎787/738-9086. For a stunning location and convivial atmosphere, it's hard to beat this rustic perch overlooking the mountains, with awe-inspiring views of the south coast beyond. The food is fairly standard Puerto Rican fare, though (mains $15–20). Follow the signs to the much posher *Siempre Viva – Sand & Sea* is next door. Open Sat & Sun only.

Aibonito and around

One of the largest towns on the Ruta Panorámica, **AIBONITO** is known as *La Ciudad de las Flores* ("city of flowers"), a sobriquet marked by a giant **flower festival** every summer. Just to the north, the **Cañón de San Cristóbal** cuts across the hills like a narrow slit, its soaring, fern-smothered walls the ideal stomping ground for hikers and adrenaline junkies, while the **Mirador Piedra Degetau** offers a gentler but equally spectacular panorama of the region. Formally established in 1824 on the site of a ranch built in the 1630s, the town itself is better known today for its chicken factories and car dealerships. Despite the oft-quoted legend that the town's name stems from its beauty (an early Spanish visitor is said to have exclaimed "*Ay, que bonito*" on seeing the area), you'll see little evidence of this outside festival time, and it's a sprawling, unattractive place often choked with full-size SUVs barely able to pass through the narrow mountain roads. Aibonito's other claims to fame include being the highest town on the island (2400ft), and recording the lowest ever temperature: 40°F (4.5°C) in 1917. Gubernatorial candidate and all-around *independentista* **Rubén Berríos** is currently the most famous *aiboniteño*, president of the Puerto Rican Independence Party (PIP).

Accommodation

The *Posada El Coquí* (PR-722 km 7.3; ☎787/735-3150; ❸) looks unappealing from the outside, set above the "Happy Plaza" shopping mall and a fried chicken

---

The city of flowers

Since 1969, Aibonito's **Festival de las Flores** (held between the last weekend of June and the first weekend of July) has been a cornucopia of blooming orchids, flaming heliconias, ginger flowers, ornamental bananas, rambling bougainvilleas, floating lilies, and even miniature *flamboyant* trees. The festival has a permanent site on the outskirts of Aibonito, just off PR-722, where up to sixty booths sell all manner of blossoming plants and workshops are held by local experts, but *flores* are not the only feature of the festival. **Live music** is a big draw, with salsa and *merengue* stars flying in to attend, and there are plenty of arts, crafts, and food stalls to complement the flora. Parking is free, and entrance is usually around $3 for adults and $2 for children.

takeout, but it's surprisingly comfortable, with thirteen large, modern rooms equipped with kitchenette, cable TV, and air-conditioning. You can use the mall parking lot outside, but note that you might find the hotel door locked and no one on duty during the day – make sure you call in advance. *El Coquí* is located on the outskirts of Aibonito, not far from the junction with PR-14, and is convenient and fairly easy to find. The *Swiss Inn Guest House* (☎787-735-8500; ❷), on the other side of town at PR-14 km 49.3, is a cheap and friendly alternative, with small tiled rooms with showers, TV, and fans. Again, make sure you call ahead.

Around Aibonito

The Ruta Panorámica runs along the ridges south of Aibonito town center, and unless you need to visit the bank or stay the night, heading downtown is unnecessary. The **Mirador Piedra Degetau** is on the route itself, but the **Cañón de San Cristóbal** involves a short detour north: the congested town center can still be avoided if you take PR-14 then PR-162 towards Barranquitas, turning off towards the canyon on PR-725.

Mirador Piedra Degetau

Once the tranquil "thinking place" of writer and politician Federico Degetau, the **Mirador Piedra Degetau** (Wed–Sun 9am–5pm; free) is a 2400ft-high viewpoint offering jaw-dropping views of the island – on a clear day you can spy Ponce and the Caribbean to the south, and the edges of San Juan along the north coast. The *piedra* in the name refers to the large boulder where Degetau (1862–1914), who became the island's first resident commissioner in Washington, DC, between 1900 and 1904, was inspired to write some of his most philosophical prose – easy to imagine, despite the site being spoiled somewhat by the wooden observation tower that looms nearby. The tower is surrounded by a small landscaped garden with *bohíos* (gazebos) and the site has its own parking lot and toilets. You'll find the *mirador* around 16km from Cayey, just beyond the PR-722/162 junction south of Aibonito.

Degetau's actual house in the center of Aibonito (PR-162), **Casa Degetau**, is an impressive mansion with Art Deco and Spanish Revival elements, but has been derelict for years and is closed to the public. The city purchased the house with the intention of turning it into a museum, but so far nothing has been done, and a local campaign is aiming to save it from destruction.

Cañón de San Cristóbal

Just a few kilometers north of Aibonito, the **Cañón de San Cristóbal** is one of Puerto Rico's most tantalizing natural wonders, a rugged 9km-long gorge created by the raging waters of the Usabón, Aibonito, and Piñonas rivers. Tucked away in the folds of rolling hills and farmland, the canyon is hard to make out from above, its sheer sides smothered in dense subtropical foliage, clinging moss, and swaying ferns, but the drop down in places reaches a hair-raising 750ft. Exploring the gorge takes some effort, but that's part of the appeal: clamber to the bottom and you'll enter a lost world of plunging waterfalls (some the island's highest), churning pools, and a plethora of endemic Puerto Rican flora, freshwater fish, snakes, and rare birds such as the red-tailed hawk. In between the rocks it's still possible to see overgrown TVs and abandoned fridges, rusting and half-hidden in the jungle, a reminder that this was used as a municipal garbage dump for over twenty years. In 1974 the **Conservation Trust** stepped in to halt this shocking state of affairs, and today 1215 acres of the gorge are protected. The Trust originally bought lots on the northern side of the canyon, and continues to purchase land along the southern rim: the plan is to eventually build interpretive trails, a proper **visitor center**, and observation platform.

Exploring the canyon

The canyon can be difficult to reach on your own, and virtually impossible to make out from the road: Puerto Rican tourists sometimes battle their way down steep, overgrown trails from the side roads off PR-725, but these are unmarked and can be hard to find, and treacherous in wet weather. The main problem is that most of the land leading to the gorge is **private** and there are no official access points. One trail starts at *Bar El Cañon* at PR-725 km 4, while a better route can be found by taking the lane at km 5.1 (on the right side of PR-725 from Aibonito), downhill to the blue building on the corner: the trail leads down from here, but before you start, ask at the house if it's OK to leave your car (and trespass on their land). Though the trail is a little weathered and best tackled in a group, it is fairly easy to follow, and not that strenuous in dry weather for anyone in reasonable shape. Once on the canyon floor you can cross the river on stepping stones and walk upstream to the **Cascada la Nebina**, a majestic 100ft waterfall; downstream it can be tough going. Paths are slippery and overgrown, and the river spills over a series of hefty waterfalls, some of which need ropes to scale safely.

For a less energetic encounter, make for the **Vivero Árboles Más Árboles** (Mon–Fri 1–3.45pm; free; ☎787/857-3511) outside Barranquitas, the local Conservation Trust **office** and **tree nursery**. It can be tricky to find: leave Barranquitas on PR-156 towards Comerío, and take a right turn at around km 17.7 (Calle B). Follow this street to the end, turn left along Calle A and keep going a little further to where the road narrows – the office is up a drive on the right. You'll find plenty of information on the canyon, and staff can direct you to the best **viewing point** nearby.

If you still want to explore the base of the canyon, but don't want to waste time looking for trailheads and dealing with grouchy landowners, reserve a **guided tour** in advance. The Trust occasionally arranges half-day tours, often with a bird-watching theme ($40 adults, $20 children). Call ☎787/722-5834 ext 234, or email Lorena Matos (✉matosl@Fideicomiso.org) for details. At other

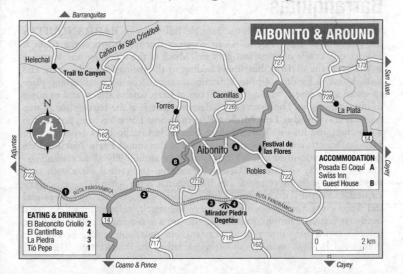

times, contact respected **local guides** Felix Rivera (☎787/735-8721) or Samuel A. Oliveras Ortiz at Cañón San Cristóbal Hiking Tour (☎787/857-2094 or mobile 787/647-3402, ⓦviajes.barranquitaspr.org), who can arrange hiking and rappelling in the gorge most weekends. Prices range $60–100 per person, depending on group size and activity. San Juan-based extreme sports outfit Acampa (☎787/706-0695, ⓦwww.acampapr.com) can also arrange custom-made tours.

Eating

As with many towns in the mountains, the best **restaurants** in Aibonito can be found outside the center, though there are plenty of US fast-food chains lining PR-14 on the eastern edge of town, should you get desperate.

El Balconcito Criollo PR-7718 km 3.1 (just before the junction with PR-14) ☎787/735-2005. This welcoming restaurant is a wooden building with veranda and eating area overlooking a small gulley. It does all the usual *criollo* dishes, as well as delicious roast pork and chicken, and there's plenty of parking. Closed Mon.

El Cantinflas PR-722, at the junction with PR-162. For a more casual experience, pull over at this no-frills place just before the *mirador*, specializing in spicy fajitas and other standard but filling Mexican fare like burritos and tacos for just $1.50–3. You can also get drinks at the bar (live music on weekends), and enjoy the views of Aibonito from the back.

🥾 **La Piedra** PR-7718 km 0.8 ☎787/735-1034. Right on the *ruta* (next to the Mirador Piedra Degetau), this is one of the most popular restaurants in the area thanks to its equally spectacular views, quality Puerto Rican food, and entertaining owner, radio talk-show host Joe Esterás. Try the perfectly grilled baby pork ribs with *tostones*, or the innovative "mountain and sea" blend of *pechuga* (chicken breast), veal, lobster, and shrimp in red wine and brandy, the *pollo a la monte* ($15.95). Don't leave without trying the exquisite home-made *flans*: ginger, vanilla, coconut, and cheese custard. Closed Mon & Tues.

Tío Pepe PR-723 km 0.3 ☎787/735-9615. This is a smarter, more refined place to eat, ideal for dinner after a hard day's driving, and set in lush gardens with its own large parking area. You'll get a posher version of all the *criollo* classics here: substantial *mofongo* stuffed with seafood, and seventeen dishes based on locally reared, plump *pechuga*, including the specialty, *Pechuga Rellena a la Tío Pepe* (mains from $10). Watch out for the sign on the left. Closed Mon & Tues.

Barranquitas

Since its foundation in 1804, the humble hill town of **BARRANQUITAS** has produced so many Puerto Rican *illuminati* that it's known as the *Cuna de Próceres*, the "cradle of important persons." Much of the old town was destroyed in the great fire of 1895, hurricanes adding to the damage over the years, and though only a handful of historic homes remain, it can be an absorbing place to spend a few hours, with a compact core of steep, narrow streets, and a couple of important sights. The town's chief claim to fame is as the burial place of two political heavyweights, **Luis Muñoz Rivera** (whose home has been turned into a museum) and his son, **Luis Muñoz Marín**, but it also has a reputation for high-quality arts and crafts, best appreciated at the annual **Feria Nacional de Artesanías**. Established in 1961, this takes place around July 17 to commemorate the birthday of Muñoz Rivera, livening up the central plaza with over two hundred stalls. More prosaically, Barranquitas is the self-proclaimed **celery capital** of Puerto Rico, so proud of this modest vegetable they have a **Festival del Apio** every April, though *apio* is more like starchy celeriac than the watery northern version. During Spanish rule the town was a major coffee producer, tobacco taking over under the Americans, but today's struggling economy is dominated by light industry and services rather than agriculture. The other

Río Barranquitas

0   50 m

Orocovis

MILTON PERELES

Moderna
Biblioteca
Municipal

FLORIDA

LA CRUZ

SANTINI

FONT

San Antonio
de Padua

Bank

Casa Museo
Joaquín de Rojas

Casa Natal
Luis Muñoz Rivera

BARCELÓ

PLAZA

PADRE DÁVILA

LUIS MUÑOZ RIVERA

Alcaldía

A. VÁZQUEZ

156

Museo de las Artes
y Antropología

PADRE BERRÍOS

ASUNCIÓN

Casa Pueblerina

162

65 DE INFANTERÍA

Mausoleo Familia
Muñoz Rivera

HERMANDAD

LUCIANA

719

N

EATING & DRINKING
Cafetería Plaza   2
El Coquí Here   1

ACCOMMODATION
Hotel Hacienda Margarita   A
Niaian Guest House   B

Comerío & Vivero Árboles Más Árboles

B & Aibonito

Aibonito

LA RUTA PANORÁMICA | Barranquitas

major annual street party is the **Fiestas Patronales de Barranquitas**, which takes place around June 13 to honor patron saint San Antonio de Padua.

Arrival and information

Driving into the center, look for the **free parking lot** on PR-156, near the garage and junction with PR-719, the road from Aibonito. To get to the central plaza, walk up the road behind the garage (which becomes Calle Barceló), and you'll reach the square in five minutes. On the way, stop by at the **municipal tourist office** (Mon–Fri 8am–4pm; ☎787/857-2065 ext 2300) to make sure everything is open: places can close without warning during festivals or: if someone is ill. The office is located inside the **Casa Museo Joaquín de Rojas**, a beautifully restored wooden house on Calle Ubaldino Font (just off Barceló), named after a former mayor and sporting vaulted ceilings, original Spanish tiles and a typically wide *criollo* veranda. You can have a peek inside during office hours, but the building is more engaging than the exhibits, a jumble of old photos, farm tools, and other bits and pieces.

Banco Santander (Mon–Fri 8.30am–4pm) has a branch at Calle Barceló 60, with a 24-hour **ATM** that accepts most cards. You can access the **Internet** at the public library (see p.334).

Accommodation

The best place to stay near Barranquitas is the *Hotel Hacienda Margarita* (☎787/857-4949; ❸), just north of town along a narrow lane off PR-152, in the *barrio* of Quebrada Grande. The turn-off is at km 1.7, but the signpost is hard to spot coming from town (it faces north, just before a huge car dealership). The hotel comprises a series of rustic *cabañas* on the hillside and a main building with seventeen standard rooms, with TV and air-conditioning in every unit, and terraces and balconies providing stupendous views over the mountains to the east, the hotel's best feature. Rooms are old-fashioned and aging a bit, but comfy enough.

The *Niaian Guest House* (⊕787/857-1240; ❷) is a cheaper, perfectly adequate alternative, with doubles equipped with air-conditioning, TV, and microwave at PR-143 km 57 in the *barrio* of Helechar, near the junction with PR-162.

The Town

The center of Barranquitas lies clustered around the main square, the modest but grandly titled **Plaza Bicentenaria Monseñor Miguel A. Mendoza**, adorned with an ornate iron bandstand (or *gazebo*) and delicate fountain. Locals claim it's the prettiest plaza in Puerto Rico, and while that's debatable, it is ringed by an attractive blend of Art Deco, Spanish, and contemporary architecture. Chief among the latest is the glass-faced **Moderna Biblioteca Municipal** (Mon–Thurs 8am–8.30pm, Fri 8am–4.30pm; ⊕787/857-6661), the new town library, a stylish cube that wouldn't look out of place in any modern Spanish city. You can access the **Internet** here for free. It's also worth a quick peek inside the church of **San Antonio de Padua**, which has a fine Spanish colonial facade, its gleaming white walls and modern interior dating from the restoration of 1988. Note the simple, modernist stained-glass windows and marble floors inside. The first church was built here in 1804 but was destroyed by hurricanes in 1825 and 1928 – the current building dates from 1933. The simple town hall or **Alcaldía** was completed in 1928, and is being restored.

Casa Natal Luis Muñoz Rivera and around

The town's chief attractions lie west of the plaza. One block away on Calle Muñoz Rivera is the **Casa Natal Luis Muñoz Rivera** (Tues–Sun 8.30am–4.20pm; $2), the birthplace and childhood home of **Luis Muñoz Rivera** (1859-1916), the poet turned politician who fought for Puerto Rican autonomy and later US citizenship (see p.362). Widely respected throughout the island, he was part of the greatest political dynasty in Puerto Rico: his father, Luis Muñoz Barrios, was mayor of Barranquitas between 1856 and 1874, while his equally celebrated son, Luis Muñoz Marín, became the first elected governor of Puerto Rico (see p.362). Muñoz Marín's daughter, Victoria Muñoz, also served in the legislature and ran unsuccessfully for governor in 1992.

The simple clapboard house was constructed in 1850, a wonderfully preserved example of *criollo* architecture, with honey-gold walls, corrugated roof, and shuttered doors, and windows opening up to a narrow, cream-colored porch. The interior is embellished with period furniture and portraits of the great man, and you can take a peek at a replica of his office and his actual car, a rare 1912 Pierce Arrow kept in the attached garage. Note that the informative exhibition outlining his life and work is in Spanish only.

Muñoz Rivera was buried at the **Mausoleo Familia Muñoz Rivera** (Tues–Sun 8.30am–4.20pm; free), where the body of Luis Muñoz Marín joined him in 1980. The stately tomb is surrounded by a small garden on Calle Padre Berríos, while inside murals depict key events in both men's lives. To get here from the *casa natal*, keep walking up Calle Muñoz Rivera and turn left. Opposite the tomb is the cozy-looking wooden house known as **Casa Pueblerina**, once the home of Mercedes Negron Muñoz. Better known as **Clara Lair** (1895-1973), Negron Muñoz is regarded as one of the island's greatest poets. Also nearby is the **Museo de las Artes y Antropología**, a tiny museum of Taíno artifacts closed at the time of writing – volunteers are expected to open it only during the *Feria Artesanías* in July.

Eating

Eating options in central Barranquitas are disappointingly poor, with *Cafeteria Plaza* (Mon–Sat 6.30am–4pm) at Calle Muñoz Rivera 21 on the plaza, next to the town hall, one of the few places to grab an inexpensive meal or sandwich. Most locals will direct you to restaurants outside town, the most popular being 犬 *El Coquí Here* (closed Mon-Wed; ☎787/857-3828), a rustic, shack-like restaurant serving tasty Puerto Rican classics and a few unusual specialties: home-made smoked pork sausages, smoked chicken, and goat and rabbit meat platters with *mofongo*. You'll find it north of Barranquitas, along the narrow but surprisingly frenetic PR-152, at km 3.6 (Sear's even has a department store here, tucked in among the car dealerships) – look for the sign on the right.

Bosque Estatal de Toro Negro

West of Aibonito the Ruta Panorámica climbs ever higher, eventually skirting the loftiest mountains in the Central Cordillera and slicing through the heart of the **Bosque Estatal de Toro Negro** (also known as the Reserva Forestal Toro Negro), one of the largest forest reserves on the island. This is the longest continuous stretch of the highway and the most rewarding, an emptier road that traverses the roof of the island along a series of misty ridges draped in thick sierra palm and pine forest. The route affords almost endless vistas of the north and south coast, glittering on the horizon, but a relatively well-maintained 18km network of **hiking trails** provides the opportunity to explore the forest's cool interior. As usual, other than the ubiquitous *coquí* and assorted lizards, the most prolific wildlife you are likely to encounter are **birds**, with thirty species reported in the forest, including some rare birds of prey: the Puerto Rico sharp-shinned hawk (*falcón de sierra*) and the broad-winged hawk (*guaraguao de bosque*).

Accommodation

The only way to **stay the night** within the forest is to **camp**. The *Los Viveros* campground (☎787/724-3724; $4 per person) in the Área Recreativa Doña Juana (see p.336) has a small parking lot, barbecue pavilions, showers, washbasins, and toilets. It's one of the most tranquil campgrounds on the island, close to the gurgling waters of the Quebrada Doña Juana and several trails, but as usual you'll need to obtain a permit from the DRNA in advance (see p.28).

Tours

Ecoquest Adventures and Tours (☎787/616-7543; ⓦwww.ecoquestpr.com) organizes energetic tours of the forest ($149 for a full day), which are pricey, but a good way to experience the area if you're staying in San Juan and have limited time. They'll take you to a private *finca* next to the reserve where you'll hike to the Quebrada Rosa, a tributary of the Río Toro Negro, and zip-line across the river.

Exploring the forest

The Ruta Panorámica passes through the Toro Negro on PR-143, and all points of interest are accessible off this road. The forest covers around 6700 acres and is divided into seven segments: the most convenient for visitors contains the **Área Recreativa Doña Juana** and peak of the same name, while after a small gap, a larger and higher section incorporates the watershed of the Río Toro Negro,

Cerro Maravillas, and Puerto Rico's tallest mountain **Cerro de Punta**. Although the latter peaks are easy to climb, it's frustratingly difficult to explore this potentially more dramatic section without a specialist map and preferably a local guide, as trails are unmarked and hardly ever maintained – casual hikers should stick to the Area Recreativa Doña Juana for a taste of the forest. Note that locations along PR-143 are given in kilometers starting at PR-10, just outside Adjuntas (see p.344), not Aibonito.

Mirador Villalba Orocovis

Soaking up the vast panorama unfolding from the **Mirador Villalba Orocovis** (Wed–Sun 9am–6pm; free), it's easy to feel you've reached the very top of Puerto Rico. To the south, Ponce and the Caribbean seem remarkably close, and on the other side of the road you can just make out the north coast. The *mirador* is a series of landscaped platforms atop a 2000ft ridge in the Montañas de Corozal, just before the Toro Negro proper and around 28km west of Aibonito, at PR-143 km 39.8. Parking spaces are plentiful inside the gates, but even if you pass by when it's locked up on Monday or Tuesday, just pull over on the road to catch the views. The *Restaurante Villa Oro* on site is really just a small shack serving up fritters and other snacks when the *mirador* is open.

Area Recreativa Doña Juana

Laced with easy walks through virtually untouched expanses of forest, the **Area Recreativa Doña Juana** is the best place to abandon your car and get **hiking**. Around 6km beyond the *mirador*, this is the first and most enjoyable section of the Toro Negro, set along the banks of the Quebrada Doña Juana, a bubbling tributary of the Río Toro Negro.

The forest **information office** (daily 7am–4pm) is at km 32.4, 600m beyond the small **parking area** for the swimming pool. Pick up basic maps here and ask about the latest conditions of the trails (rangers usually speak Spanish only), though serious hikers should order topographical maps from the US Geological Survey before they arrive (see Basics, p.50). The most rewarding trail starts opposite the office, the 4.4km **Camino El Bolo**, which climbs gradually to the **Torre Observación**, a wooden lookout tower. When you reach the sealed road at the top of the ridge, turn left – the final section to the tower branches off this road to the right, five minutes beyond here. The climb to the top should take 45 minutes to one hour, an enchanting hike through a staggering variety of vivid tropical flowers and *palo colorado* trees, and usually deserted – reach the summit and it really feels like being lost in the wilderness, with little more than the breeze and chirping frogs for company. To get back, return to the sealed road and turn right to continue down to PR-143, or turn left to find the **Vereda La Torre** (tower trail), another path which leads back to the parking lot. This is a grass and gravel track that makes a slightly faster alternative to the Camino El Bolo. Hiking down this way, the Vereda La Torre ends at the **Piscina de Agua**, an aging and wholly unattractive concrete swimming pool fed by a stream, usually open in July and August only (daily 9am–5pm; $1). From here, take the **Vereda La Piscina** (pool trail), a 500m sealed path that follows the Quebrada Doña Juana down to the parking lot.

Los Viveros

In between the parking lot and the information office is the small turning to the campground, **Los Viveros**, a short 200m walk or drive along a steep, narrow road (heading west, it's on the right). You can continue along the road on foot from the campground, turning right at the bridge and following the muddy clay path another 1km down the river to the **Charco La Confesora**, a large pond, and a couple of other trails: the Camino Doña Petra (1.5km) connects with PR-564 to the east, while further downstream the Camino Ortolaza (2km) leads west to PR-143. You can make a loop by returning to the campground on the main roads, as traffic is light, especially during the week, but take extra care on the corners. Some trails are poorly marked so take a map with you.

Cerro Maravillas

Known as *El Cerro de los Mártires* ("Mountain of the Martyrs"), **Cerro Maravillas** (3960ft) is the most infamous peak on the island and accorded shrine-like reverence by Puerto Rico's independence movement. On July 25, 1978, two independence activists were ambushed here while preparing to destroy the communication antennas on top, and the subsequent cover-up of their execution-style murder resulted in a massive public outcry (see p.365).

A few kilometers beyond the Area Recreativa Doña Juana, PR-149 branches north off the Ruta Panorámica to Jayuya (see p.338), but if you continue on PR-143 for another 6.5km you'll reach the junction with PR-577. Signposts to Cerro Maravillas are nonexistent, and the road is easy to miss: turn right up PR-577, a gravel road that leads to the summit (the fifth-tallest peak in Puerto Rico), and about 500m along you'll see two stone crosses (and sometimes Puerto Rican flags and flowers) marking the spot where **Arnaldo Darío Rosado** and **Carlos Soto Arriví** died. A memorial is held here every July 25, attended by hundreds of people. In between the radio masts on top you'll get magnificent vistas of the south coast, the Lago El Guineo (a small reservoir) to the east, and the summit of Cerro de Punta to the west.

Climbing Cerro de Punta

The **tallest peak in Puerto Rico** and a relatively straightforward climb, **Cerro de Punta** (4390ft) is a few feet shorter than Ben Nevis (the UK's highest point), a lofty mound of cloud forest often draped in bewitching threads of mist. As you'd expect, the views are mind-blowing, and best appreciated in the mornings before the clouds move in. Few tourists make it to the summit, adding to the sense of isolation, though you may see workers tending to the communication towers on top. Don't hesitate; it's perfectly legal to scale the mountain.

From the large parking lot at its base, just under 5km from the turning to Cerro Maravillas, a weathered and severely potholed cement road leads 1.5km to the antennas on top: it's only advisable to take your car if you have a four-wheel drive, though plenty of time-pressed travelers manage to grind their rental vehicles to the summit. Note that the parking lot and road are unmarked: heading west, it's on your right at around km 17 on PR-143. The route up is fairly steep, but shouldn't take more than an hour if you decide to hike it. Beyond the communication towers, the actual grassy peak (the *punta* itself) can be reached via an overgrown stairway – a concrete block marks the summit. On a clear day you can see up to 100km, with a hazy San Juan in the distance.

For more of a challenge, tackle the peak from the northern side – the trail starts at *Hacienda Gripiñas* (see p.341) and can be hard to follow, so ask at the hotel for directions first. Assuming you don't get lost, experienced hikers should be able to get up and down in one day.

Eating

You're better off bringing a picnic to the Toro Negro, as **eating** options are scarce, but on weekends you can grab some wood fire-roasted barbeque at *Las Cabañas Doña Juana* (Sat, Sun & holidays 9am–6pm) on PR-143, 2km beyond the Area Recreativa Doña Juana and just before the junction with PR-149. Buy a whole roast chicken for $6, or half for $3, with other snacks including *yuca* (white manioc), *arroz can Gandules*, *guineos*, and *alcapurrias*, all between $0.50–2.

From the Toro Negro to Jayuya

From the Toro Negro and the Ruta Panorámica the best way to **Jayuya** is to head north on PR-149 then PR-144, cutting through the thickly wooded hills and mountains that separate the valleys of the Río Toro Negro and Río Grande de Jayuya. En route are some of the most absorbing sights in the region: poignant museums, ancient Taíno petroglyphs, and an elegant waterfall.

Salto de Doña Juana

Just 2.3km north of the Ruta Panorámica, PR-149 passes right in front of the **Salto de Doña Juana**, a graceful 200-foot waterfall framed by rocky cliffs, where the chilly waters of the Quebrada Doña Juana tumble into the Río Toro Negro. The falls are at around km 41.6, but the road here is very narrow and the only place to stop is a small space just beyond the bridge over the river. Failing that, you can make a brief stop on the bridge itself, as the road is not particularly busy. The junction with PR-144 is another 1.4km from the falls.

Hacienda San Pedro and Café Tres Picachos

Coffee aficionados should check out the family-owned plantations in the hills off PR-144, producers of some addictively aromatic gourmet brews. **Hacienda San Pedro** (☎787/823-2083, ⓦwww.cafehaciendasanpedro.com), just off the main road at PR-144 km 8.4, established in 1894 by Tomás Rivera, has the most character. It's been operated by three generations of the Atienza family since 1931, producing a rich, spicy coffee with a bitter chocolate aftertaste (it also contributes to the famous Yauco Selecto brand). You can buy ten-ounce bags for $9, and much larger quantities in the store on site, try an espresso or a cappuccino, and visit their small museum, which has exhibits about the farm and the coffee-making process. Legends of Puerto Rico (☎787/605-9060, ⓦwww .legendsofpr.com) runs specialist tours of the plantation from San Juan (Oct to early Dec, Mon–Fri).

Meanwhile, the Martínez Rivera family produces the highly rated **Café Tres Picachos** (Mon–Sat 8am–6pm; ☎787/828-2121, ⓦwww.cafetrespicachos.com) at PR-539 km 2.7, off PR-144 in the *barrio* of Saliente. The brand was established in 1960 by the Torres Díaz family and acquired by the current enthusiastic owners in 1999. You can visit the plantation to buy freshly roasted coffee, and if you call in advance, take a peek at their small **Museo de Antiguedades** (Mon–Sat 9am–4pm), a dusty but oddly compelling collection of Taíno artifacts and coffee-related paraphernalia. The coffee is named after **Los Tres Picachos** (3894ft), the nearby mountain whose three peaks are said to represent the three camels of the Biblical Holy Kings (or Three Wise Men).

Museo El Cemí

After twisting through jungle-coated mountains for around 8km, PR-144 drops into the Jayuya valley and the barrio of **Coabey** (km 9.3), home to a couple of striking museums. Both are clearly visible from the road, with plenty of parking nearby.

The **Museo El Cemí** (Mon–Fri 9.30am–4pm, Sat & Sun 9am–3pm; $1) is one of the most distinctive buildings on the island, a dappled white and grey dome set in a grassy park, with a mouth-like entrance that resembles a giant fish. Architect

▲ Museo El Cemi

Efrén Badia Cabrera won the competition to design the museum, which opened in 1989 in the form of a giant *cemí*, a representation of the Taíno gods and one of the most common artifacts dug up on the island. Inside you'll find an upper gallery of vivid Taíno **petroglyphs**, marked in white and depicting various symbols and anthropomorphic images, while the frist-floor archeological collection comprises stone tools, axes, necklaces, pottery, stone collars, and examples of the *cemí* itself, the "spirit of god," all with English labels. The back room contains little of interest, and overall the collection is rather modest, but given the setting, certainly more evocative than city museums. Don't miss the plaque denoting a small **Taíno burial site** outside: thanks to pressure from the United Confederation of Taíno People (see p.341), the remains of a 1500-year-old indigenous woman and other human bones found here are no longer on display inside the museum. Note that the museum usually closes for lunch around noon to 1pm, but if locked at other times, wander over to CEDETRA (see below) across the parking lot to find someone with the keys.

Museo Casa Canales and CEDETRA

The old wooden house opposite the Museo El Cemí is the **Museo Casa Canales** (Mon–Fri 9.30am–4pm, Sat & Sun 9am–3pm; $1), a typical rural *criollo* home of the late nineteenth century, but also an emotive memorial to the failed aspirations of the island's *independentistas*. The original was built by **Don Rosario Canales Quintero** (1854–1924), one of the founders of Jayuya in 1883 and its first mayor in 1911. However, what you see today was meticulously built from scratch as a replica in the 1990s, as the original collapsed in the 1970s. With a backdrop of towering, forest-covered mountains and creaky timbered floors, this is about as evocative of old Puerto Rico as it gets, each room faithfully stocked with period furniture. The house also serves as a simple local history museum: the Sala Jayuya contains documents and other bits and pieces relating to the town, while the Sala Paliques is a study dedicated to the son of Rosario Canales, the writer and humorist **Nemesio Canales Rivera** (1878–1923), who wrote under the pseudonym Paliques. The Sala Revolución commemorates the **1950 uprising**, when the rebels stored weapons and met here before marching on the town. One of the leaders, **Blanca Canales Torresola** (1906–1996), was the daughter of Rosario Canales.

The collection of modern buildings near the museum forms the **Centro de Desarrollo y Trabajo** (CEDETRA), an artist collective that includes the **Tienda Artesanal** (Tues 11am–4.30pm, Wed–Sun noon–5.30pm), a shop selling local Taíno-inspired carvings, instruments, books on the area (in Spanish), ointments made from the seeds of native trees, and elegant, locally carved *santos*. CEDETRA also includes two very small museums, both worth a quick peek: the **Museo del Café** ($1) has exhibits on the local coffee industry, while the **Museo El Zapatero** (free) displays bits and pieces on the tradition of local shoe-making. Both are nominally open daily 8am to 4pm, but you might need to ask at the shop to get someone to unlock the doors.

La Piedra Escrita

Another 2km along PR-144 from Coabey, just beyond the 7.5km mark, **La Piedra Escrita** is one of the most accessible **Taíno petroglyph** sites on the island. From the parking lot, a wooden boardwalk switchbacks down to the Río Saliente and an enormous 30-foot high granite boulder that almost blocks the river. The rock forms a natural pool of cool, peat-colored water that attracts plenty of swimmers, but far more impressive are the 52 curly petroglyphs clearly marked in white on the side of the stone. The abstract carvings date from around 600 to 1200 AD and comprise mystical spiral shapes, simplistic stick figures that seem to represent people, and the heads of unidentified creatures with big round eyes. Research into Taíno petroglyphs is relatively new, and while it's not known what any of these symbols mean, an increasingly vocal Taíno movement is demanding that La Piedra Escrita is better protected and treated with respect (daredevils tend to use the rock as a diving board). You can clamber back to the parking lot straight up the river bank via the stone stairway opposite the rock, from where it's just over 1.5km into central Jayuya.

Jayuya

Nestling on the banks of the Río Grande de Jayuya, deep in the Central Cordillera, the mountain town of **JAYUYA** might seem unremarkable, but it's come to occupy a central role in the mythology of modern Puerto Rican identity. Littered with low-key but enigmatic reminders of the island's past, the town is the closest thing Puerto Rico has to a Taíno spiritual center, most vividly expressed during the annual **Festival Nacional Indígena**. Traditionally regarded as the stereotype of hicktown by sophisticated *sanjuaneros*, Jayuya's symbolic importance was recognized in 1950, when *independentistas* briefly occupied the town and proclaimed the Republic of Puerto Rico (see p.365). Like Barranquitas, Jayuya also has a reputation as an arts and crafts center, and more recently, the area has been rebuilding its reputation as one of Puerto Rico's top **coffee-producing** regions. Other festivals worth attending are the **Fiestas Patronales de Jayuya**, held over the week leading up to September 9 to celebrate La Virgen de La Monserrate, and the **Festival del Pueblo del Tomate** at the end of April, with stalls and events honoring the humble tomato, another local crop. For information on festivals and sights in the area, contact the Oficina de Cultura y Turismo Municipal at ℡787/828-4618.

Accommodation

Hotel Posada Jayuya (c/Guillermo Estévez 49, ℡787/828-7250; ❸) is the most central **place to stay**, with its main entrance and parking lot on Calle Libertad overlooking the river. It's not bad value and popular with locals, though its numerous rooms are a bit worn.

The 🏃 *Parador Hacienda Gripiñas* (℡787/828-1717, 🌐www.haciendagripinas .com; ❺) is hard to beat for historic charm, a former coffee plantation established in 1853 and a hotel since 1975. Rooms are fairly compact and simply decorated, with air-conditioning and cable TV, but set within a series of inviting white-timbered buildings with rusty red roofs on the hillside, all with wonderful views across the mountains. Coffee bushes surround the property and the two pools are fed by mountain streams. Breakfast is included at the excellent restaurant (see p.344) and you can pick up good-value all-inclusive deals on the website – singles can get rooms for under $100. The hotel sits in an isolated valley at the end of PR-527 at km 2.5, around 4km south of Jayuya.

The *Hacienda Casa Taina* (℡787/828-2270, 🌐www.haciendacasataina.com) at PR-528 km 1.8, south of the town, is a large, modern alternative that looks a bit like a Mediterranean villa, its simple, comfortable rooms are embellished with Taíno artwork.

The Taíno nation: "We are still here"

Jayuya's **Festival Nacional Indígena** takes place at the end of November each year (usually on the weekend closest to Nov 19), an enthusiastic celebration of Taíno dances and rituals enhanced with craft stalls, live folk music, piles of deep-fried *criollo* food, and the very Puerto Rican tradition of selecting a Taíno beauty queen. The whole town takes part, regardless of their racial origins: indeed, until recently much of what was termed "Taíno" in the festival was based on flimsy Spanish sources from the sixteenth century, and it was generally assumed that the Taíno or *indios* were either wiped out or fully assimilated by the Spanish centuries ago.

Yet many Puerto Ricans claim this is simply not true. Forced to hide their roots for fear of prejudice and mockery, many families have maintained ancient Taíno customs in private, some even worshiping **Yukiyú** (the Taíno supreme deity). Aided by regional organizations such as the United Confederation of Taíno People (🌐www.uctp.org) in New York, Puerto Rico's Taíno groups are attempting to be recognized in the US as an official tribe, though this is unlikely unless the island becomes a state. One of the most prominent is the **Jatibonicu Taíno Tribal Nation of Boriken** (🌐www.taino-tribe.org), led by a descendant of *cacique* Orocobix, leader of the central mountain nation of Jatibonicu, while Carmen Yuisa Baguanamey Colón Delgado is the heir of *cacique* Caguax and hereditary chief of the **Taíno Turabo Tribe** (🌐www.indio.net/aymaco), once based around the modern city of Caguas.

Other than attending the festival, the easiest way for travelers with limited time to experience Taíno culture is to stay at *La Paloma Guest House* near El Yunque (see p.118). You can also contact the **Consejo General de Taínos Borincanos** (✉brendalugo@hotmail.com, ℡787/568-1547), based in Trujillo Alto, which acts as a coordinating body on the island, or activists at **El Caney del Quinto Mundo** (Taíno Longhouse Learning Center; ℡787/847-5039; 🌐www.prtc.net/~caney/caney.htm) on the borders of the Toro Negro, who hope to eventually run workshops, volunteer programs, and a visitor center in the mountains.

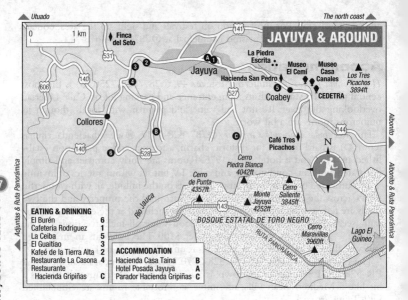

EATING & DRINKING

El Burén	6
Cafeteria Rodriguez	1
La Ceiba	5
El Guaitiao	3
Kafeé de la Tierra Alta	2
Restaurante La Casona	4
Restaurante Hacienda Gripiñas	C

ACCOMMODATION

Hacienda Casa Taina	B
Hotel Posada Jayuya	A
Parador Hacienda Gripiñas	C

(Map labels: Finca del Seto, La Piedra Escrita, Museo El Cemí, Museo Casa Canales, Los Tres Picachos 3894ft, Jayuya, Hacienda San Pedro, Coabey, CEDETRA, Collores, Café Tres Picachos, Cerro Piedra Blanca 4042ft, Cerro de Punta 4357ft, Monte Jayuya 4252ft, Cerro Saliente 3845ft, Río Jauca, BOSQUE ESTATAL DE TORO NEGRO, RUTA PANORÁMICA, Cerro Maravillas 3960ft, Lago El Guineo, Aibonito, Adjuntas & Ruta Panorámica, Aibonito & Ruta Panorámica)

The Town

Jayuya is a laid-back mountain community proud of its indigenous heritage, with Taíno symbols and tribal markings daubed onto fences and curb sides all over town. Though a farm was established here in 1533, Spanish settlers in the valley did not prosper, and the settlement wasn't officially founded until 1883, when it was named after the last Taíno *cacique* of the area, Hayuya.

Start at the central **Plaza de Recreo Nemesio R. Canales**, named in honor of the eminent local writer, his bronze statue gracing the square along with an enormous representation of **El Sol de Jayuya**, one of the most vivid of all Taíno petroglyphs found in Puerto Rico. Discovered in the *barrio* of Zamas, it's become one of the symbols of the town. The simple church, **Nuestra Señora de la Monserrate** is usually locked, but features a classic Spanish Colonial facade in pale yellow, crowned with three bells. The bird's-eye view over the town and mountains beyond are enough to justify the short climb up the stone steps to the cultural center from here, but just before the top, standing guard over the town, is Tomás Batista's **sculpture of Cacique Hayuya**. The image was created in 1969 to commemorate the Taíno ruler – his village was destroyed by the Spanish in 1513 during the aftermath of the Taíno rebellion (see p.357). Behind the bust is **La Tumba del Indio Puertorriqueño**, a tomb containing a human skeleton symbolizing the island's native population, interred here in 1974 and framed by reproductions of two petroglyphs, *La mujer de Caguana* and *La Danzante del Otoa*. You'll have to peek through the rails at the actual tomb, as it's usually locked up – as with other indigenous sacred sites, it's attracted its share of criticism in recent years from Taíno activists who believe it's grossly disrespectful to display the remains of their ancestors. The words inscribed on the walls loosely translate to "An Indian of Borinquen, a primitive man of the island, whose blood and culture live on in our race."

Above the tomb, the **Centro Cultural de Jayuya** (Mon–Fri 8am–noon & 1–4pm; free) on Calle San Felipe is a fine Neoclassical building constructed in

1920, which serves as the municipal hospital until 1966. The center has two rooms of permanent exhibitions (a small collection of Taíno artifacts and wooden *santos*), and some space for temporary local art displays.

With no official **parking lots** in town, leave your car where you can find a space near the plaza, or aim for the unofficial parking areas near the bridges over the river.

Finca del Seto

To get a taste of the area's rich **coffee-growing** traditions, arrange a visit to **Finca del Seto** (ⓔfincadelseto@aol.com), a small plantation nestling in the shadow of Cerro Morales on PR-531, north of Jayuya in the *barrio* of Caonillas La Ceiba. Owned by a couple of well-traveled US expats, the farm is a flourishing example of Puerto Rico's independent coffee producers, with fine Arabica berries handpicked, washed in spring water, and dried in the sun. Their fresh, open-kettle roasted coffee, *Finca del Seto Café*, is sold in one-pound ($11.60) or eight-ounce bags ($6.25) – try this rich, potent brew and you'll understand why Puerto Rico was once the coffee capital of the world. They also sell raw beans ($8 per pound), fabulous home-made *salsa picante* sauce made with honey, rum, and homegrown peppers ($4 per 7oz bottle), crystallized ginger from the farm ($6 for 6oz), sea salt from Cabo Rojo ($5), and a variety of delicious banana and mango jams and chutneys ($6–7 for 8oz). To visit and get directions, the owners prefer you **email** in advance.

Eating and drinking

As usual, many of the best **restaurants** in the area are in the hills surrounding Jayuya town center, though there are a couple of cheap places near the plaza: to grab a cake, bread, or drink, try the *Panadería Repostería El Rey* on the southwest corner. **Nightlife** is virtually non-existent, but some locals tend to congregate in the shack-like *Colmado El Indio* for a few beers after work, which hangs over the hillside on Calle San Felipe near the cultural center – the views over the town are magical at night.

El Burén PR-528, km 5.4 ☎787/828-2589. If you're not in a hurry, make time for this rustic country diner, tucked away in the hills southwest of town and offering a vast panorama of mist-drenched mountains. The menu features all the usual Puerto Rican classics, but this is one place you really ought to try them: the ubiquitous *mofongo* is made with freshly mashed plantains here and filled out with rich seafood, while the home-made *sorrullitos* (corn fritters) make an addictive side. Closed Mon-Wed.

Cafeteria Rodriguez c/Guillermo Esteves (near *Posada Jayuya*). No-frills place serving up standard *comida criolla* and lip-smacking roast chicken, in the old Jayuya market building on the main street. Inside you'll find a few tables, locals sipping potent cups of coffee, and the smell of roast meats wafting out the door.

La Ceiba PR-144 km 8.9 ☎787/828-301. This popular local café, run by the Oliveras González family, is the best place to grab a bite on the Coabey side of Jayuya (it's near the *Museo el Cemí*). It's a casual affair, usually open all day, with a small seating area inside and shack on the road serving cheap *tostones*, rice and beans, *pechuga* (all under $7), and various cocktails, beer, and rums, especially popular on the weekends.

El Guaitiao PR-144 (near the Shell garage and the junction with PR-531). Anyone craving sumptuous barbecue *lechón* and roast chicken (from $4) should make a stop at this roadside grill on weekends, though it also usually opens for drinks Thurs–Sun evenings. *Guaitiao* is a Taíno word for a peaceful meeting between strangers.

Kafeé de la Tierra Alta PR-144 km 2.8 (just west of the town center). This is a modern canteen-type place where you order first at the counter before taking out or eating indoors. It serves fast food like fried chicken, but also sandwiches, and local staples such as *arroz blanco guisado* from $1.50. You can also get basic *comidas Chinas* here, with dishes such as pepper chicken from $5, but don't expect authentic Chinese. It's on the right, with some space for parking.

Restaurante La Casona PR-144 km 1.3
☎787/828-3347. On the main road beyond
Guaitiao, this restaurant is a wooden house with
veranda, timbered interior, and lots of parking,
usually open for lunch Mon–Fri 10am–3pm. It's
the most convenient place for a sit down meal
of Puerto Rican food near town, with pool tables
and live music livening things up in the evenings
Wed–Sun, when it stays open till late. Mains
from $7.

Restaurante Hacienda Gripiñas PR-527 km 2.5,
☎787/828-1818. Inside the *parador* (see p.341),
the best feature of this popular *mesón gastronómico's* (formerly known as *Don Pedro*) is its location,
a handsome building on the old coffee plantation,
the main room graced by a palm-like tree soaring
up through the floor. The Puerto Rican dishes are
much better than the generic seafood, steaks, and
soups, with the chicken and shrimp *asopao* one of
the standouts. Mains from $8.

Adjuntas and around

Cradled between some of the highest peaks on the island, **ADJUNTAS** is a
remarkably traditional rural community, a million miles from urban Puerto Rico.
It sits on one of the island's primary north–south arteries, PR-10, 50km south
of Arecibo and 30km north of Ponce, but with the highway now bypassing the
town, its torpid center seems frozen in the 1950s, with none of the strip malls
and fast-food outlets that grace most Puerto Rican towns – for now. It's also
known as *La Ciudad del Gigante Dormido* ("city of the sleeping giant") after the
ridge of mountains on its western side (which vaguely resemble the outline
of a giant, lying face up) and, more optimistically, the Switzerland of Puerto
Rico – the highly tenuous connection being its low temperatures (an average
of 72° Fahrenheit) and surrounding high country. The town is no longer a
major producer of citron (*cidra*), though it remains an agricultural community at
heart, and is perhaps best known in Puerto Rico today as the home of one of
the island's most successful conservation movements, **Casa Pueblo**. This local
organization waged a long but eventually successful campaign against local open-
mining of copper and gold deposits, and is today at the forefront of the Puerto
Rican environmental movement. The town's biggest festival is the **Fiestas
Patronales de Adjuntas** at the end of July, held in the main plaza commemorat
its patron San Joaquín. Adjuntas lies just off the Ruta Panorámica, around 32km
from the heart of the Toro Negro.

Accommodation

The most comfortable place to stay is the *Parador Villas Sotomayor* (☎787/829-
1717, ⓦwww.paradorvillassotomayor.com; ❸), a mini-resort around 2km
north of town at PR-522 km 0.2 (just off PR-123 at km 36.6), in a quiet
valley surrounded by jungle. Its 35 modern bungalow villas have basic doubles
with air-conditioning and satellite TV, though it also has larger rooms for four
to six people with kitchenettes. Extras include a swimming pool, tennis and
basketball courts, pool table, bikes for rent, and horseback riding – the activities,
family focus, and all-inclusive offers are extremely popular with Puerto Ricans
on weekends.

Cheaper and more convenient for the town center is the *Hotel Monte Río*
(c/César González 18; ☎787/829-3705; ❶), a budget option with simple but
adequate doubles and friendly staff. All come with rackety air-conditioning,
clean bathrooms, and local TV, but furnishings are bit frayed around the edges.
Get a room on the third floor, where the balconies provide pleasant views
of the town, the large pool, and surrounding hills (check out the "sleeping
giant" from the back). The near-legendary **buffet** in the restaurant began as a

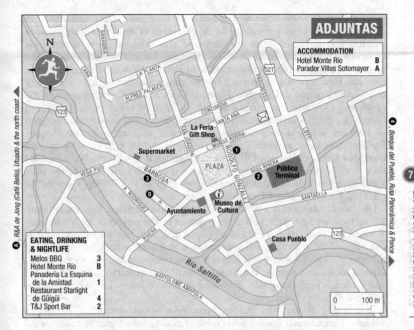

◀ R&A de Jong (Café Bello), Utuado & the north coast

ADJUNTAS

N

ACCOMMODATION
Hotel Monte Río   **B**
Parador Villas Sotomayor   **A**

La Feria
Gift Shop

Supermarket

PLAZA

Público
Terminal

Ayuntamiento

Museo de
Cultura

Casa Pueblo

Río Saltillo

**EATING, DRINKING
& NIGHTLIFE**
Melos BBQ   3
Hotel Monte Río   B
Panadería La Esquina
   de la Amistad   1
Restaurant Starlight
   de Güigüi   4
T&J Sport Bar   2

0   100 m

◀ Bosque del Pueblo, Ruta Panorámica & Ponce

stop-gap in the aftermath of Hurricane Georges in 1998 and is one of the best deals on the island (see p.347), but it can be a little tricky to find the hotel: coming into Adjuntas, keep following signs for PR-123 past the plaza, and when you turn right onto Calle Barbosa, look immediately for a small lane through the buildings on the left, next to Popular Finance. Hard to spot, but you should see a tiny sign to the hotel here.

The Town

Adjuntas was formally established in 1815 on the banks of the Río Saltillo (which eventually becomes the Río Grande de Arecibo), though a settlement has stood here since the early eighteenth century. Its modern center lies up from the river around the impressively manicured **Plaza Arístides Moll Boscana**, named after local hero, physician and writer Dr. Arístides Moll (1880-1965). The plaza has been completely remodeled, with a modern church at each end, and the Ayuntamiento (town hall) at the southwest corner, a striking building with a green facade sporting some fancy Mudéjar tiling. Next door is the town's cultural and tourism department (Mon–Fri 8am–4.30pm; ☎787/829-5039), another historic structure doubling as the **Museo de Cultura**, a mildly interesting collection of documents and artifacts. On the north side of the plaza, **La Feria Gift Shop**, c/Muñoz Rivera 21, sells touristy Puerto Rican gifts and crafts.

Casa Pueblo

The most compelling reason to stop in Adjuntas lies 200m south of the plaza on PR-123 (at c/Rodolfo González 30), an innovative cultural and environmental center known as **Casa Pueblo** (Mon 8am–1pm, Tues–Sun 8am–3.30pm; suggested donation $2; ☎787/829-4842, ⊛www.casapueblo.org). The arresting pink *criollo*-style house was purchased in 1985 by a group of environmentalists that had already been protesting the development of local **open-air copper mining** for five years – the mining posed a catastrophic threat to the local ecosystem. It took fifteen years of campaigning, but in 1995 the government passed a bill prohibiting open-air mining in Puerto Rico, and by the following year the land formerly threatened by the mine was turned into a 748-acre reserve, the **Bosque del Pueblo**. Founder Alexis Massol-González received the prestigious Goldman Environmental Prize in 2002 on behalf of the group, and today Casa Pueblo supports sustainable development and conservation projects all over the island, also conducting a number of toxicity studies on Vieques. Perhaps their most ambitious scheme so far is the creation of a **biological corridor** linking seventeen DRNA forest reserves across Puerto Rico: in 2004 they received government approval to proceed with the first stage of the plan, a conservation program that covers 29,398 acres of the Pueblo, Guilarte, La Olimpia, Toro Negro, and Tres Picachos forests.

The main house acts as a performance center and art space, with a small shop selling local arts and crafts, coffee beans grown by the project (Café Madre Isla), T-shirts, and books. It also has a small display area with some desultory exhibits of *santos* and Taíno artifacts, while most of the wall space is dedicated to charting the group's history and environmental campaigns through photographs and various media coverage. At the back is a small **Mariposario** (butterfly house) and garden, where caterpillars are reared on lettuce leaves. The whole place is powered by solar energy.

To visit the Bosque del Pueblo, make reservations with Casa Pueblo in advance. Enlightening guided tours of the fauna and flora usually take around two hours and cost $3. To get there head back along the Ruta Panorámica (PR-143) to PR-140 and go north till you reach PR-605. The reserve is a few winding kilometers up this road.

Eating and drinking

Adjuntas is an excellent place to try home-style **Puerto Rican food**, and though your choices are fairly limited, everything is superb value. On the north side of the plaza at Calle Rodolfo González 56, the *Panadería La Esquina de la Amistad* sells basic cakes, bread, and snacks in a grand 1922 building, as well as popular *pan de hogaza* (rustic loaves with a touch of *anise*, originating in northern Spain) in the mornings ($1–2). The *Supermercado* at Calle Barbosa 7, not far from *Melos BBQ*, holds enough staples to put together a **picnic**.

Adjuntas coffee

Once the largest exporter of citron in the world, R&A de Jong (☎787/829-2610, ⓦwww.cafebellopr.com), founded by Dutchman Andries de Jong in the 1960s, is now dedicated solely to the production of **Café Bello**, a high-quality **coffee**. Their plant is just north of town at PR-123 km 36.6 – you can stop to buy coffee but it's best to email or call in advance if you can. You can also buy gourmet coffee at **Hacienda Patricia** (☎787/259-2152, ⓦwww.patriciasqualitycoffee.com), home of the Segarra family's sun-dried and woodfire-roasted Arabica beans. You can usually try their product in a small café on site, a plantation that was established in 1900, right on the Ruta Panorámica, about 11km before Adjuntas (on the left just after the junction with PR-140).

Restaurants

🏃 **Hotel Monte Río.** Famed throughout the region for its filling home-cooked and unfeasibly cheap lunch buffet of *criollo* classics: you'll get a choice of two types of rice with beans, four meats, two salads, two desserts, sides such as plantains, and as much juice and soda as you can drink. Sun you get eight meats and a truly delectable *flan*. Eat as much as you like any day for just $5.89 – one of the best bargains on the island. Mon–Fri 11am–3.30pm, Sat & Sun 11am–2pm.

Melos BBQ c/Barbosa 18. This no-nonsense diner with self-service counter and plastic tables serves some of the cheapest food on the island, and is the best place for breakfast. Egg, toast, and ham plates start at $1.50, while the big lunch and dinner menus feature home-made burgers, BBQ chicken ($2.89), and a similar *criollo* buffet to the hotel ($5.89), which is just behind it – it's run by the same chef. The buffet here usually extends to dinner, but the hotel is a far nicer place to sit down.

🏃 **Restaurant Starlight de Güigüi** PR-123 km 32.7 ☎787/829-1823. This restaurant attracts diners from across the island, mainly for its huge plates of *chuletón a la starlight*, luscious pork chops served with a giant pile of plantains ($7). The wooden veranda is packed out on weekends, so get here early. It's right on the *ruta*, a few minutes' drive south of town on PR-123. Don't confuse this restaurant with the far inferior "original" *Restaurant Star Light* down the road: established in 1967, the owner later leased this place to chef Güigüi, but seeing the latter's success, kicked him out, forcing Güigüi to start his own restaurant.

Nightlife

Almost everything shuts down in Adjuntas after 6pm, and other than slumping in quiet hotel bars, nights comprise of little more than listening to the cacophony of *coquís* and watching twinkling lights from your hotel balcony – you might also be serenaded by the explicitly unromantic thumping of *reggaetón* tunes from car radio as bored youths cruise up and down the main streets. If you want to mingle with locals on weekends, try the bar at *Hotel Monte Río* or *T&J Sport Bar*, which occupies an old clapboard house on Ríos Rivera near the plaza, open till 11.45pm on Thursdays, and till 1.45am on Fridays and Saturdays.

Around Adjuntas: Bosque Estatal de Monte Guilarte

Covering around 3460 acres of dense sierra palm forest, the **Bosque Estatal de Monte Guilarte** covers the mountains west of Adjuntas, at an altitude of between 2600 and 4000ft. The most accessible sections lie on the Ruta Panorámica (PR-518), close to **Lago Garzas**, a storage reservoir built for a hydroelectric power station, and around **Monte Guilarte** itself, the reserve's highest peak.

Accommodation

Camping at Guilarte is not allowed, but the DRNA manages five rustic **cabañas** ($20 per night) close to the information office (see p.348). Each cabin has four berths with mattresses, and room for six people (you must provide your own bedding), but as always, you'll need to contact the DRNA in advance to stay here (see p.28).

Lago Garzas

From Adjuntas, PR-518 rises swiftly into the mountains, passing the placid waters of **Lago Garzas** after around 9km (note that PR-518 and the *ruta* are both unmarked at the junction with PR-123 in Adjuntas – you need to turn left at the small bridge over the Río Saltillo). This reservoir was built between 1936 and 1943 on the edge of the Guilarte forest (it's not actually part of the reserve), and only a small portion of its 91 acres is visible from the road. Fed by three mountain streams, it's reputed to be the cleanest lake in Puerto Rico, and you can get out on the water by calling the **Gigante Fishing Club** (☎787/829-5768) on the weekends. The club charges a fee of $350 for groups using their own kayaks and boats on the lake, but will usually allow you to join for a small fee (or for free) if you call in advance – friendly local manager Willy (☎787/829-5919) will also let you use the kayaks on weekdays from around 10am. You can fish (for largemouth bass, sunfish, and even white catfish) and swim in the lake, though it's usually quite cold.

You'll pass the road to the clubhouse just before the lake, at around km 7.5. There are toilets here but not much else. Once you've passed the lake on PR-518, look out for the "morning glory" spillway on the left, which looks like a giant plughole.

Monte Guilarte
Just under 5km from Lago Garzas (at km 12.2), PR-518 meets PR-131 in the heart of the forest: turn left here for **Monte Guilarte** (3934ft), the sixth highest peak on the island and one of the few that isn't sprinkled with antennas. The road ends a few meters ahead at a small parking lot and trail that leads to the peak – the hike to the top normally takes 45 minutes to an hour, and you'll probably have it to yourself, especially on a weekday. The path can be slippery but it's a relatively easy climb, rewarded by stellar views over the whole of western Puerto Rico.

On weekends a *kiosco* opens near the parking lot, serving all the *criollo* favorites, and back at the junction you'll find the forest **information office** (Mon–Fri 7am–3.30pm, Sat & Sun 9am–5.30pm), where you can check current conditions, but little else (no maps).

From Monte Guilarte it's another 50km to **Maricao**, one of the longest, most spine-jarring sections of the Ruta Panorámica along narrow, often potholed roads through some of the most rural and isolated districts of Puerto Rico. You won't see much traffic, and the only village en route is **Castañer**, which has a gas station and basic café. Take your time: this bucolic landscape of close-knit communities and family farms, lush palm plantations, and sprawling mango trees, is a window into the lost world of the *jíbaro*, rapidly disappearing in ever-modernizing Puerto Rico.

Maricao and around

Justly regarded as **La Ciudad del Café** ("coffee city"), the languid mountain settlement of **MARICAO** is one of the most traditional on the island, the haunt of Taíno rebels, *jíbaros*, and some of the world's best **coffee** for over two hundred years. At harvest time the town is bathed in the aroma of roasting coffee beans, blazing red berries plucked from bushes that carpet the slopes nearby. Other than enjoying the pleasures associated with its premier crop, Maricao makes an enchanting last or first stop on the Ruta Panorámica, with its celebrated **coffee festival**, a small but engaging **fish hatchery**, and the vast **forest reserve** just out of town.

Some history
The name of the town is said to derive from a local tree with bright yellow flowers that the Taíno called *maricao*, though the more fanciful explanation involves a legend that dates back to the Spanish conquest. The story goes that a local Taíno girl, conveniently given the Spanish name María, fell in love with one of the Spanish conquistadors and tipped him off about an imminent Taíno attack.

Coffee to keep the devil awake

"Con café de Maricao, hasta el diablo se desveló"

The words of eminent Puerto Rican poet **Luis Lloréns Torres** (who attended school here) eloquently capture the powerful quality of Maricao's **Arabica coffee beans**: "after drinking coffee from Maricao, even the devil couldn't sleep."

Maricao's rainforest environment, volcanic soils, and proximity to cooling sea breezes make it perfect for coffee growing, while its location on the western side of the island protects it from hurricanes. To fully appreciate its rich coffee legacy, attend the three-day **Festival del Acabe del Café** in February (usually around President's Day), an annual celebration that marks the end of the coffee harvest (Sept–Jan). It's one of the island's most popular festivals, so be prepared for crowds. In addition to special exhibitions and live music concerts, the central plaza is packed with stalls selling arts and crafts, *criollo* food, and of course, locally produced coffee.

Disappointingly, it can be hard to buy real Maricao coffee at other times, as local shops tend to stock mass-marketed brands. Try *Colmado Ericob*, on Calle 1 de Abril in town, which will grind local coffee beans to order (Mon–Sat). Failing that, it's always worth visiting the plantations in person: **Café Hacienda Juanita** is still produced at the Hacienda Juanita (see below), a direct descendant of the legendary coffees that once graced the tables of the Vatican, and can be purchased at the hotel shop for $8.50 for eight ounce. **Hacienda Adelphia** (☎787-473-9512; ⓦwww .cafedemaricao.com) at PR-105 km 37.5, in Sector Union, produces the much-sought-after **Offeecay** brand. Its gourmet Gold series coffees (ranging $8–9 for eight-ounce bags) are for serious connoisseurs. You can buy them at the festival or directly from the plantation, but you must call ahead. **Café Real de Puerto Rico** (PR-105 km 23.6; ☎787/833-1698) is produced by a local collective in the Maricao and Jayuya areas, but is primarily sold via ⓦwww.cafedepr.com. An eight-ounce bag is $6.50 while a pound is $9.75. **Hacienda Caracolillo** (PR-105 km 42.8; ☎787/838-2811) in the *barrio* of Indiera Baja; is part of the Grupo Jiménez stable and produces **Café Concierto** ($12.95 for eight ounces), an exquisite roast, as well as contributing to the respected export brand, **Yauco Selecto**. Call in advance to ask about buying fresh from the plantation.

Incensed at her betrayal, the locals promptly tied María to a tree and killed her. Maricao is said to come from a combination of *mari* (for María) and *cao* meaning sacrifice. The early Spanish settlement of Villa Sotomayor (near today's Aguada) was similarly warned by the love-struck sister of Taíno *cacique* Guaybana about the rebellion of 1511 (see p.357), perhaps a precursor of the Maricao story.

Whatever the truth, hundreds of Taíno refugees did find sanctuary here during the Spanish conquest, and the town's other sobriquet, *El Pueblo de las Indieras* ("town of Indian settlements"), acknowledges these indigenous roots, which by the nineteenth century had resulted in a thoroughly mixed *criollo* population. The modern settlement grew up around a parish established in 1864 as part of San Germán, but by 1874 it had been granted independent status. Today Maricao is 60km from Adjuntas and 28km from Mayagüez, and undergoing a major renovation which should be complete by 2009: roads are being resurfaced, public buildings constructed, and a new hotel is slated for the town center.

Accommodation

Until the new hotel is up and running, it's not possible **to stay** in Maricao itself (though you can spend the night in the Bosque Estatal de Maricao, see p.351), but it's only 2km to the ⚞ *Hacienda Juanita* (PR-105 km 23.5; ☎787/838-2550, ⓦwww.haciendajuanita.com; ❸), one of the island's most enchanting hotels. At an altitude of 1600ft and surrounded by incredibly tranquil, forest-coated hills and gardens, some of its white timbered buildings date back to 1834, when the 24-acre coffee plantation was established by Corsican immigrants (a small amount of coffee is still produced here, though it's been primarily a hotel since 1976). Rooms are tastefully furnished with wooden pillar beds and chairs, antiques, and satellite TV; it also has a pool, tennis courts, and nature trails. Add around $40 for breakfast and dinner packages.

The Town

Maricao has a small, compact center of ramshackle wooden *criollo* houses with verandas, and a smattering of cheap cafés and shops, though it's rarely busy – on Sundays the place seems totally abandoned. While sights may be lacking around central **Plaza de Recreo Luis Muñoz Rivera**, the town does have a certain lazy charm, and its narrow streets are perfect for aimless wandering. The main church, dedicated to **San Juan Bautista de Maricao**, was completed in around 1898 on the site of an earlier wooden chapel, and features an elegant square tower, and a simple arched main entrance. As was typical for the time, the church incorporates a blend of classical styles, with its Gothic portals and arcades, Romanesque roof, and Baroque base and brickwork. Unless it's in use, the church is usually locked. You can normally park around the plaza, but if it's busy aim for the **parking lot** near the swimming pool and sports center on the edge of town.

Just outside the center, on PR-410 a few meters from PR-105 (the Ruta Panorámica), a cleft in the hillside hides the **Gruta San Juan Bautista**, a small grotto and waterfall dedicated to San Juan (St John). A short pathway and steps lead up both sides of the statues above the waterfall, an image of Jesus being baptized by the saint, though vandals had snapped off the Baptist's hands at the time of writing. It's a shady, peaceful spot and easy to park nearby.

Vivero de Peces de Maricao

Tucked away in a meandering valley at the end of PR-410, 2km from town, the **Vivero de Peces de Maricao** (Thurs–Sun 8.30–11.30am & 1–3.30pm; free) is a sleepy fish hatchery, raising around 200,000 largemouth bass, sunfish, and catfish annually to stock the island's reservoirs. It's not very large or busy and other than strolling past the handful of pools here, observing the hordes of fish in various stages of development, there is not much to do, but the landscaped ponds and gardens on the banks of the Río Maricao (fish are also kept in the river) are extremely tranquil, lost deep in the forest. You'll find plenty of parking at the gates.

Salto de Curet

Around 6km east of Maricao, the **Salto de Curet** is a minor but forceful waterfall that feeds a large natural swimming pool at the end of PR-425, 2km off PR-150. The water makes for a pleasant place to cool down, and the surrounding country is smothered in wild coffee bushes. The last section of road to the parking area is very rough and impassable for non-SUVs, so you might want to leave your car on the verge and walk down – the river is about five minutes away.

Eating and drinking

Like Adjuntas, Maricao has only a handful of **places to eat**, but most have heaps of character and fabulous home-cooked Puerto Rican food. **Nightlife**, unsurprisingly, is limited. In town itself, there are several cheap, no-frills canteens knocking out *criollo* staples, but none is especially good.

El Batey de Guariken c/José de Diego, near the plaza. One of the most intriguing bars/*colmados* on the island, littered with *independentista* paraphernalia and quirky farm artifacts – locals come here to gossip, buy snacks, and sip beers in the evenings. It's usually open Sat & Sun from around 11am till the last customer leaves, and some weekdays.

Cafeteria y Restaurant El Buen Café c/Corchado 8. This hole-in-the-wall facing the plaza knocks out reasonable Puerto Rican staples, one of the better places in town for a quick snack or meal.

La Casa de Los Tostones Gigantes PR-120 km 22.7 ☎787/838-5572. This inviting outdoor restaurant is just off the *ruta* on the edge of town, set under a grove of giant bamboo in what looks like a lush tropical garden. But the food is the real star: try the *palitos de plátano* ($3), bananas cut and fried like chips with special mayonnaise-like sauce; *rellenas con bacalao guisado* ($4.50), bananas with stewed codfish; and a host of other local specialties such as the shrimp *mofongo*

(mains $8–12), all served with giant house *tostones* and rounded off with a mouthwatering home-made vanilla *flan*. Fri–Sun 11am–8pm.

La Casona de Juanita, *Hacienda Juanita* (see p.349), ☎787/838-2550. Even if you're not staying at the hotel, it's worth eating at its charming restaurant, set in a timbered plantation building with a terrace overlooking the valley below. It's open for breakfast 8am–10.30am, then noon–9pm for lunch and dinner (last orders 8pm). Specialties include *Serenata de Viandes con Bacalao* (cod with local vegetables), *salcocho criollo* (creole soup), *arroz con gandules* (rice with pigeon peas), and the sensational *pastelon de guineos niños La Juanita* ($11.75), corned beef and sweet banana pie. End the meal with guava and cheese ($2.25).

Lee Mary's Pizza c/José de Diego 6. This is another canteen-type place that serves basic pizza ($5), cakes, and *frituras*, along with Café Rico and Yaucono brand coffee. It's on PR-105 on the way heading out of town and open most days.

Around Maricao: Bosque Estatal de Maricao

Created in 1919, the **Bosque Estatal de Maricao** covers around 10,000 acre making it one of the largest forest reserves on the island, home to 26 bird species (eleven endemic) and hundreds of different trees, plants, and flowers. The problem is that only a fraction is easily accessible to visitors and most people end up simply breezing through on the Ruta Panorámica. The forest **information center** (Mon–Fri 7am–3.30pm, Sat & Sun 8am–3.30pm; ☎787/838-1040) is signposted off the main road (PR-120) at around the 16.2km mark, 2km beyond La Torre de Piedra and around 6km before Maricao. They don't have any maps, but if you can speak Spanish the rangers can tell you about a couple of trails in the area, and the road to the office leads up to a **picnic area** with fine views of the west coast.

Accommodation

The Compañía de Parques Nacionales runs the functional *Centro Vacacional Monte del Estado* (☎787/873-5632; cabins ❷, villas ❸) at km 13.2 on PR-120, a rustic holiday camp with 24 large *cabañas* and villas equipped with water heater and fireplace, primarily targeted at local families. It does have a pool, playground, and table tennis tables, among the activities on offer, and can be fun for kids. It's $3 to park your car. See p.28 for booking information.

Nearby, the *Parque Ecológico Monte del Estado* is a good spot for **camping**: small *casetas* (for three people) are $15, while larger ones for six are $30. There are toilets, barbecue pits, baths, and showers on site, but not much else. Check-in at the *Centro Vacacional* (same phone number). The site is located near a spectacular *mirador* overlooking the west coast, and will eventually include a new eco-resort of cabins based on the Maho Bay Camps in the Virgin Islands. The whole site uses solar power and has recycling stations for garbage.

▲ La Torre de Piedra

La Torre de Piedra

Coming from Adjuntas, the forest starts around 45km from Monte Guilarte, at the junction of PR-366 with PR-120, but stopping is pointless until you've passed the *centro vacacional* and reach **La Torre de Piedra**, a few meters further on (km 14). This 40-foot stone observation tower looks a bit like a square medieval castle turret, a whimsical product of the Civil Construction Corp in the 1930s. This is the last major viewpoint on the *ruta*, a 2600-foot perch offering a vast panorama of the entire west coast, from Cabo Rojo to Mayagüez and beyond, but also the bizarre symmetry of karst country to the northeast (see p.210). You can park here but note that the tower is likely to be closed until 2009 for restoration, and sadly the view from the ground is mostly obscured by vegetation. A decent alternative is the *mirador* within the *Parque Ecológico* (see p.351).

Montoso Gardens

Before you reach Maricao it's worth arranging a stop at the beautifully maintained **Montoso Gardens** (daily; $5 suggested donation; Ⓦ www.montosogardens.com, Ⓔ montoso.gardensatyahoo.com) at PR-120 km 18.9, a 90-acre botanical garden, tropical flower and fruit farm stretching from the Río Prieto to the summit of Pico Montoso. This is a working farm, but with over six hundred species of tropical flowers, nuts, spices, and palms on display, it's also an absorbing place to explore. Visitors are allowed to take photos and sample the fresh fruits, and can also order plants and seeds, but you must make reservations by email in advance.

Founded in 1987 by US horticulturist Bryan Brunner, limited commercial production was started in 1999. Future projects include the restoration of the original coffee hacienda house and the construction of cottages for overnight stays – check the website for the latest details. You'll find the gardens beyond *Monte del Estado* and the Torre de Piedra, on a small sealed road off PR-120 at km 18.9 (on the left coming from Adjuntas). Pass three houses on the left, and the next black gate is Montoso Gardens.

Contexts

Contexts

History

The fate of Puerto Rico has been tied to foreign powers since Juan Ponce de León waded ashore in 1508. Yet Puerto Ricans remain proud of their *criollo* heritage, a mix of Taíno, African, and European cultures, and maintain a fierce identity despite their gradual absorption into the American melting pot – the island also has a strong tradition of struggle and rebellion, beginning with desperate Taíno resistance against the Spanish and ending, most recently, with the successful campaign to eject the US Navy from Vieques.

Prehistory

Like much of the Caribbean, little is known of the history of Puerto Rico before the arrival of the Spanish – its flourishing civilizations used no form of writing and were comprehensively wiped out in the early years of colonization. The **oldest human remains** were found on Vieques (El Hombre de Puerto Ferro, see p.163) and date from four thousand years ago, evidence of the **Archaic** (*Arcaico*) or Ortoiroid culture of simple hunter-gatherers that migrated across the Caribbean between 2500 and 200 BC. After 200 BC, communities on the island became more sophisticated, developing farming and ornate pottery. Traditionally divided into three separate peoples, anthropologists now believe that cultures developed through a more complex blend of migration and integration. The first phase is known as the **Igneri** (or Saladoid), when yucca, corn, sweet potato, and tobacco were introduced from the mainland. Between 600 and 1200 AD the Igneri evolved into autonomous groups or tribes and life became increasingly ritualistic, religious, and more organized (*bateyes* or ball-courts became important) – this period is known as the Ostionoid or **Pre-Taíno**. By the thirteenth century the island was dominated by the **Taíno**, the people encountered by the early Spanish explorers.

The Taíno

When Christopher Columbus sailed into the Caribbean in 1492, the people he met described themselves as *taíno*, but rather than the name of a tribe, the word simply meant "good" or "noble." On Puerto Rico, the tribes actually called themselves **Boriken** (Borinquen or Boriquén in Spanish), their name for the island. The Taíno label has stuck, however, applied as an umbrella term for various peoples sharing similar culture from Cuba to the Bahamas.

The Taíno lived in small communities scattered across the island, their cultivation of cassava, corn, and tobacco supplemented by hunting and fishing. By 1508, Spanish sources indicate that the island was divided into at least twenty major Taíno kingdoms, each ruled by a chief or **cacique** but under the nominal control of an overlord, **Agüeybaná I**. Agüeybaná (meaning "great sun,") held court at Guainía, on the south side of the island. However, it seems more probable that the power of *caciques* was measured in terms of people not territory, and the existence of kingdoms with actual boundaries is unlikely. Of more importance was the **spiritual life** of the Taíno, a pantheist system of animist belief marked by the creation of numerous **cemís**, stone idols, and the worship of **Yukiyú**, their

Most Puerto Ricans (around 80 percent) are classified as White, predominantly of Spanish origin, with 8 percent Black, 0.4 percent Amerindian (Taíno), and 0.2 percent Asian (mostly Chinese). However, so many Taíno women were taken as wives by the early Spanish colonists, it's likely that the real genetic picture is far more complex: some DNA tests suggest that up to 60 percent of the population has Taíno genes. In Puerto Rico, the word **criollo** has come to refer to the mixing of all these racial and cultural elements, and is applied generally to anything native to the island, while **Boricua** represents the island itself: deriving from the Taíno word **Boriken** (meaning "brave lord"), Puerto Ricans often use the phrase *Yo soy Boricua* ("I am Boricua") to identify themselves.

chief deity, and **Atabey**, his mother. **Juracán** was a malevolent god, associated with the vicious storms that batter the Caribbean and from whose name the word "hurricane" derives (the Taíno also gave us the hammock, from *hamaca*).

The Spanish conquest

Without question, the period of **Spanish rule** – which lasted almost four hundred years – has had the most influence on Puerto Rican culture. In addition to the Spanish language, Catholic Church, and the social and culinary traditions that dominate the island today, mangos, coconuts, bananas, yams, goats, pigs, cattle, sugar cane, and coffee were all introduced after 1493.

Columbus

We'll never know for certain where **Christopher Columbus** (Cristóbal Colón in Spanish) first landed on Puerto Rico – records indicate that the island was sighted on his second voyage to the New World on November 19, 1493, and that his seventeen ships took on fresh water somewhere on the west coast. Though Aguada celebrates the event every year, new research suggests the fleet anchored closer to the modern towns of Añasco or Rincón. Portentous as this first contact was, it had little immediate impact: **Hispaniola** (modern Haiti and the Dominican Republic) remained Spain's primary base in the region, and it was another fifteen years before colonization was attempted in an organized way. Columbus is credited with naming the island, however: **Isla de San Juan Bautista**, after St John the Baptist.

Juan Ponce de León

Sailing with Columbus on that second voyage was **Juan Ponce de León** (1460–1521) a steely conquistador who had earned his military stripes fighting the Moors in Granada. After arriving in Hispaniola he quickly defeated any Taíno resistance on the island, and was rewarded with the governorship of Higüey province. Ever restless, he landed on the south coast of Puerto Rico on **August 12, 1508**, intent on fresh conquest.

After a friendly exchange with *cacique* Agüeybaná I, he sailed along the north coast of the island and ended up at today's San Juan Bay, which he named "**Puerto Rico**." Ponce de León was appointed **the first governor** of the island by the king of Spain, his initial settlement established inland and named

Caparra (see p.104), but thanks to an ongoing dispute between the Spanish Crown and Diego Columbus (heir to Christopher's rights in the New World), was replaced by Juan Cerón twice in subsequent years.

Almost immediately, the Spanish began to strip the island of its modest **gold** reserves. The Taíno were set to work digging in open-cast mines and panning for gold in rivers, a system of effective enslavement dubbed the *encomienda*. Caparra was proving wholly unsuitable as a base, though Ponce de León was adamant that it should remain near the gold mines and farms in the Toa valley. After lobbying by the city treasurer, Pedro Cárdenas, friars of the Hieronymite order (who had the authority to mediate the dispute) ordered settlers to move to today's **Old San Juan** in 1516, and the new city was formally recognized in 1521. Ponce de León sailed for Florida the same year on his quixotic quest for the **Fountain of Youth**, and after being injured by a poison arrow in a skirmish with Native Americans in Florida, died in Havana, Cuba.

Taíno rebellion

The harshness of the *encomienda* system soon alienated the Taíno. **Cristóbal de Sotomayor**, who had established **Villa Sotomayor** in 1510, Spain's second colony on the island, was particularly hated. In November 1510, a *cacique* known as Urayoán had a Spanish captain drowned in the Río Añasco, proving that the Spanish were not immortal beings as the Taíno had feared. In January 1511 a war council brought several *caciques* together under the leadership of "*El Bravo*," **Agüeybaná II** (Agüeybaná I, his uncle, had died in 1510), and the **Taíno Rebellion** began soon after, Villa Sotomayor duly razed to the ground and its leader slain. The Spanish recovered quickly, dispatching forces from Caparra and killing Agüeybaná II in the Battle of Yagüecas. The rebellion rapidly disintegrated thereafter, thousands of Taíno scattered, killed, or sold into slavery: though small groups fought on in the mountains until the 1580s, the Taíno were annihilated – by 1530 fewer than two thousand lived on the island.

The Spanish colony: early challenges

By the 1530s Puerto Rico had become a relative backwater, a bulwark protecting Spain's burgeoning South American empire rather than an economic asset in its own right. With the exhaustion of the gold mines, modest trades in sugar, ginger, and cattle-raising kept some cash flowing in, though **smuggling** flourished well

Rich harbor

Puerto Rico means "rich harbor," originally applied by Ponce de León to today's San Juan Bay (San Juan was the name of the whole island), and though they're often attributed to a map-reading error, no one really knows how the current conventions arose. In the sixteenth century it seems likely that officials did not distinguish between the new capital city and the sparsely populated island: the colony was simply known as **San Juan Bautista de Puerto Rico**. In 1514 the island was divided into two *partidos* (regions), Puerto Rico and San Germán, and by the 1600s the former had become applied to the whole island, while the city name was shortened to San Juan.

into the eighteenth century. Spanish settlers totaled just over four hundred in 1530, outnumbered by the ever-dwindling Taíno and over two thousand **African slaves**, increasingly crucial as a labor force. For much of the subsequent two hundred years the island remained sparsely populated and generally neglected by its colonial master; by 1699 the population of Puerto Rico was barely six thousand.

English and French attacks

It wasn't long before Spain's gold-drenched American empire attracted the attention of other European powers. A motley fleet of **French privateers** (known as "corsairs") sacked San Germán for the first time in 1528, attacking subsequent incarnations of the town into the 1570s, and San Juan became increasingly fortified, with **El Morro** the focus of defensive efforts (see p.71). The first **English** attacks on Puerto Rico took place in 1585, when **Sir Richard Grenville**'s fleet, bound for the nascent colony of Roanoke, Virginia, holed up for a month in Guayanilla Bay on the south coast. In 1595 it was the turn of **Sir Francis Drake**, the feared sea captain the Spanish called "El Draque" (the dragon). Warned in advance, the Spanish were waiting for him: Drake's 27 ships were bombarded as they entered San Juan Bay, and he was forced to retreat. In 1598, George Clifford, **Earl of Cumberland**, was far more successful, remaining the only invader to ever capture El Morro in battle. Learning from Drake's mistakes, he landed his troops on Escambrón Beach, east of Old San Juan, occupied the by-then deserted city, and forced the surrender of El Morro fifteen days later. Holding the city proved far more challenging, however, and with his troops virtually wiped out by dysentery, he was forced to abandon Puerto Rico in less than two months.

The Dutch

In 1625, Puerto Rico was sucked into Spain's long struggle with **the Dutch**. Eager to establish a base in the Caribbean, General **Boudewijn Hendricksz** surprised Governor Juan de Haro with a frontal assault on San Juan Bay, taking the city and laying siege to El Morro. After a bitter campaign which saw savage battles, looting, and the burning of much of San Juan, the Dutch were forced to retreat within five weeks. The devastation of the city prompted the construction of massive stone walls in the 1630s, but though San Juan was spared further attacks for another one hundred and fifty years, the rest of Puerto Rico continued to be raided by privateers and pirates.

The eighteenth century: growth and reform

In the eighteenth century Puerto Rico's **population** increased dramatically, rising to nearly 130,000 by 1795, in part bolstered by immigrants from the Canary Islands and Ireland, and French settlers fleeing the wars in Haiti. **Smuggling** remained the foundation of the economy throughout the period, despite Spanish attempts to reform trade, reduce tariffs, and allow concessions to foreign importers. **Military restructuring** instituted by Alejandro O'Reilly in the 1760s proved crucial, as the island remained a target for foreign powers: without a strong fleet, the imposing fortifications of San Juan, though impressive, emphasized Puerto Rico's continued vulnerability.

The great plague

When the Europeans (and African slaves) came to the New World they brought with them something deadlier than guns and steel: **germs**. Most experts today agree that smallpox, influenza, and measles virtually destroyed Pre-Columbian America, killing as many as 95 percent of the population in just 130 years. By November 1518 **smallpox** had reached Hispaniola: it wiped out a third of the native population before moving on to Cuba and Puerto Rico, where it had equally devastating consequences. In fact, many historians believe that this epidemic was the same strain that eventually killed the Inca emperor Wayna Qhapaq in 1525, along with 200,000 of his people.

The English mounted several minor assaults on the island in the eighteenth century, but the most serious challenge took place in 1797, when Admiral Henry Harvey and seven thousand troops under **Lieutenant-General Sir Ralph Abercromby** attacked San Juan. Having just seized the island of Trinidad the English were confident of success, but after landing his troops safely east of the city, Abercromby failed to dent San Juan's formidable defenses or the spirit of the rapidly swelling local militias, reinforced from all over the island. Calculating that a prolonged siege was pointless, he abandoned the attack after a few weeks – the withdrawal has since been portrayed as an epic Puerto Rican victory.

The birth of nationalism

By the early **nineteenth century** Spain's vast American empire was beginning to crack, and **Simón Bolívar** led one South American province after another to independence. Despite a growing sense of **nationalism**, Puerto Rico's ultra-conservative landowners insured that by 1826, the island, along with Cuba, remained the last of the Spanish colonies in the region.

The Cádiz Cortes

In 1810 the Spanish government called for a parliament that included the colonies for the first time, the **Cádiz Cortes**. Puerto Rico's delegate was **Ramón Power y Giralt**, sometimes regarded as "the first Puerto Rican" in his role as explicitly representing the island and its people. The Cortes duly delivered **Spain's first constitution**, guaranteeing limited representation in local government, which was enthusiastically adopted in Puerto Rico in 1812. However, fearing a loss of power, the Spanish king abolished the constitution two years later, and instead offered the **Cédula de Gracias**, a royal charter pledging free trade and tax breaks and perks for foreigners emigrating to Puerto Rico. Exiles from Haiti, South America, and Europe (including thousands of Corsicans) flooded to the island and the **economy**, largely on the back of the slave-driven **coffee and sugar industries**, boomed for the next sixty years.

Rebellion and repression

Puerto Rico remained part of the Spanish Empire but small groups of activists did consider **rebellion**. It's also true that the repressive regime of **Governor Miguel de la Torre** (1823–1837) successfully cracked down all on forms of dissent with a network of spies, heavily enforced laws, and swift punishment.

Liberals kept a low profile and political progress remained stymied well into the 1860s. De la Torre's regime was successful in convincing most Puerto Ricans that independence would lead to social and economic disaster, but it was the threat of **slave rebellion** that really insured loyalty to Spain. Alleged conspiracies in Bayamón in 1821 and Naguabo in 1823 (both crushed before anything happened) led to the imposition of a harsh **slave code** in 1826, but despite this, a further fourteen plots were exposed by 1843. In that year slaves briefly captured the town of **Toa Baja**, before being brutally suppressed.

The Grito de Lares

By the 1860s, reformers such as **Eugenio María de Hostos** and **Ramón Emeterio Betances** were becoming increasingly disillusioned with the lack of political progress in San Juan. Often considered the "**father of the nation**," Betances (1827–98) was the son of a wealthy landowner, and had been educated in France. Returning to Puerto Rico in 1856 to practice medicine, he immediately became involved in underground **abolitionist societies**. Along with his friend **Segundo Ruíz Belvis** (1829–67), a landowner from Hormigueros, he gradually came to believe that independence from Spain was the only way to solve the island's problems. Both men were exiled by the authorities in 1867: written that year, Betances' "**Ten Commandments of Free Man**" included the abolition of slavery, the right to elect leaders, and freedom of speech.

Betances and his co-conspirators planned to strike in 1868. The rebellion began on September 23 in **Lares**, when six hundred rebels led by Manuel Rojas captured the mountain town, arrested local officials and set up a provisional government. The next day they marched on San Sebastián, but their attack was repulsed by local militia, and in the days that followed the insurrection fell apart: by December over five hundred rebels had been arrested. Betances, on the run himself in St Thomas, was unable to help. Though a total failure, the **Grito de Lares** ("Cry of Lares") was the first serious attempt to overthrow the colonial government and declare independence, a symbolic watershed that led to the formation of real political parties and a government that was far more sensitive to the mood of the people.

Puerto Rico's own pirate

Travel anywhere along the coast of Puerto Rico and you'll eventually hear about **Roberto Cofresí**, the homegrown pirate with Robin Hood-like status and a seemingly inexhaustible supply of buried treasure – his birthplace of Cabo Rojo proudly sponsors the "only statue to a pirate" in the Caribbean. Born in 1791 to a wealthy family, Cofresí started out as a legitimate trader, becoming a pirate around 1818: no one knows why, though legend blames ill-treatment at the hands of a foreign sea captain. Ranging from the Dominican Republic to Vieques and St Thomas in the west, his colorful exploits involved plundering and capturing foreign ships (generally from Spain or the US), but also protecting helpless children, and aiding the poor, cementing his patriotic reputation. Following a bruising encounter with a US Navy ship, Cofresí was captured, tried, and executed in Old San Juan in 1825. Numerous biographies, ballads, short stories, and articles have idolized him ever since.

The abolition of slavery

With the conclusion of the US Civil War in 1865, Brazil, Cuba, and Puerto Rico were the only remaining slave societies in the Americas. However, pressure from the US and Great Britain, combined with grassroots sympathy for the slaves among the population, meant that abolition seemed finally possible. Puerto Rican delegations were now regular participants in the Spanish Cortes, and with the Liberal faction in power in Spain in 1873, abolitionists led by **Baldorioty de Castro** (1822–1889) were able to achieve the **emancipation of all slaves** on the island on March 22. Slaves still had to work for their masters for three years (on contract), and the latter were also to be compensated for their loss of "property." The **abolition of slavery** was one of the main factors in the decline of the sugar industry in subsequent decades, and **coffee** instead, became the premier export crop.

The fight for autonomy

Baldorioty de Castro started fighting for **autonomy** – self-government within the Spanish Empire – in the 1870s, and in 1887 he joined with like-minded activists such as poet **José de Diego** (1866–1918) to create an **autonomist party**. The authorities reacted with the usual wave of repression, jailing the leaders and employing brutal tactics and torture known as *compotes* – Baldorioty de Castro died in 1889 after a period in prison. Things changed when the Liberals again took power in Spain, finally granting **Puerto Rico full autonomy** in 1897. Now led by **Luis Muñoz Rivera** (1859–1916), the autonomist party **won the first elections** in March 1898, just in time for the Spanish-American War.

The Spanish-American War

Puerto Rico became American because of Cuba. When the **Cuban War of Independence** resumed in 1895, José Martí and other Cuban leaders were openly fighting not just for Cuban but for Puerto Rican independence from Spain, and Betances kept in contact with all parties from his exile in Paris. In the 1890s the two groups worked closely together, and at first even courted US help in dislodging the Spanish.

Spurred on by a jingoistic press and businesses with sugar investments in Cuba, pressure for US involvement grew intense – the final pretext for war was the mysterious sinking of the battleship *USS Maine* in Havana harbor in February 1898, blamed on Spanish forces. The **Spanish-American War** began in April, and although Cuba remained the main theater of operations, Puerto Rico was affected almost immediately by a crippling navy blockade. After San Juan was bombarded by the US Navy in May, **General Nelson Miles** landed 3400 troops virtually unopposed in Guánica on the south coast on July 25. After a small skirmish outside Yauco, he marched into **Ponce** on July 28 without a fight and was greeted with cheering crowds. From here the US army was able to spread out across the island, though by the time an **armistice** was declared on August 13, Spanish resistance was starting to become far more effective.

Betances was horrified that the island seemed to have replaced one colonial ruler with another, writing "what's wrong with Puerto Ricans that they haven't yet rebelled?"

Eugenio María de Hostos tried to rally the *independentista* cause, but while the Treaty of Paris signed in December 1898 granted Cuban independence, Puerto Rico (along with Guam and the Philippines) was simply handed over to the US. General John Brooke was sworn in as the first US governor, and after 390 years, the Spanish were gone.

Early US rule

After a short period of harsh **US military rule**, the **Foraker Act** of 1900 granted Puerto Rico an elected House of Delegates, chosen every two years, to act as the island's legislature in tandem with an Executive Council. The members of the council, along with the island's governor, were all nominated by the US President. De Diego was appointed to the council, but soon resigned after becoming disillusioned with US rule, which remained decidedly colonial until 1917.

José Celso Barbosa (1857–1921) established the **Partido Republicano** (Republican Party) in 1899 to fight for **US statehood**, and won the first two elections, but in 1904 De Diego and Luis Muñoz Rivera created the **Unión de Puerto Rico** (UPR) to fight for greater self-government: the Union Party won every election from 1904 to 1928.

The Jones Act and US citizenship

In 1910 Luis Muñoz Rivera was elected Resident Commissioner of Puerto Rico to the US Congress, lobbying tirelessly until his death in 1916 for **US citizenship** but also greater **autonomy**, "on the sly" as Rosario Ferré put it. With President Wilson eager to consolidate US ties in the Caribbean as a bulwark against German expansion, the **Jones Act** was finally signed in March 1917, granting US citizenship to all Puerto Ricans and replacing the Executive Council with an elected senate. The governor was still appointed by the US President.

The 1920s to World War II

Puerto Rico experienced a cataclysmic **earthquake** and **tsunami** in 1918, killing 116 people and virtually leveling Mayagüez, yet the island's greatest natural catastrophe of the twentieth century was still to come, striking on St Philip's Day, September 1928. Known as **Hurricane San Felipe**, it killed over three hundred people and destroyed thousands of acres of property, effectively wiping out the island's burgeoning **sugar** and **tobacco** industries. With the **Great Depression** that began in 1929 and **Hurricane San Ciprián** in 1932 adding to the island's woes, the economy was crippled in the 1930s.

From the 1920s Puerto Rico's political parties became increasingly fragmented. Despite **women achieving the vote** in 1929, progress towards greater autonomy remained snail-paced and calls for independence became increasingly violent (see opposite). Frustrated by the lack of progress, **Luis Muñoz Marín** (1898–1980), respected lawyer and charismatic son of Luis Muñoz Rivera, established the **Partido Popular Democrático** (Popular Democratic Party, PPD) in 1938 to fight for the immediate freedom of the island – the party won elections in 1940 and 1944.

Around 65,000 Puerto Ricans fought in **World War II**, and though returning veterans had a modernizing influence on the nation, the island was otherwise unaffected by the conflict.

The independence movement

When the Union Party dropped the independence of Puerto Rico from its platform in 1922, disgruntled supporters created the **Partido Nacionalista** (the Nationalist Party) to continue the fight for self-determination. **Pedro Albizu Campos** (1893–1965) a Ponce lawyer, became leader of the party in 1930, determined to get results, and the Nationalists vigorously contested the 1932 elections. Failure convinced Albizu that increased **militancy**, not electoral campaigns, was the only way to advance his agenda, and relations with the police rapidly deteriorated in the 1930s.

After a confrontation between students and police in 1935, four Nationalists were killed in what became known as the **Massacre de Río Piedras**, and in 1936 activists Hiram Rosado and Elías Beauchamp **assassinated** Police Chief Francis Riggs – they were both executed by police on capture. Albizu was imprisoned in the US for the next ten years, while his followers were targeted in the **Ponce Massacre** of 1937 (see p.288), a shameful episode that resulted in the deaths of five Nationalists, twelve civilians, and two policemen. Despite widespread outrage at these events, the Nationalists failed to win lasting political support. Campos didn't help by portraying Puerto Rican culture as entirely Hispanic: in 1936 he made the dubious claims that Spain "had every intention of giving Puerto Rico its liberty" and that Spain was the "founder of North and South American culture."

The Commonwealth of Puerto Rico

After World War II, the administration of US President Harry Truman moved quickly to dismantle the last vestiges of colonial rule in Puerto Rico. In 1946 **Jesús Piñero** was the first Puerto Rican to be appointed governor, and 1947 the Jones Act was amended to allow Puerto Ricans to vote **for the position of governor** for the first time. By now Muñoz Marín had come to believe that the **economic development** of Puerto Rico was more important than political independence. Dissenters formed yet another political party in 1946, the **Partido Independentista Puertorriqueño** (Puerto Rican Independence Party, PIP) led by Gilberto Concepción de Gracia. The PIP differed from Albizu's Nationalists in one crucial aspect: they were committed to achieving the independence of Puerto Rico by peaceful, electoral means. In 1948 Luis Muñoz Marín became the **first elected governor** of Puerto Rico, with his *populares* (PPD members) sweeping the legislative elections and the PIP coming in second – Muñoz Marín remained governor of a largely unified nation until 1964.

On July 25, 1952, the **Constitution of Puerto Rico** was approved by voters in a referendum, and the island became the **Estado Libre Asociado** (Commonwealth), the system that remains in place today. This allows self-government in internal affairs as well as fiscal independence, although islanders cannot vote in US presidential elections. Furthermore, the US Congress retains full authority to determine the status of the territory and apply federal law as appropriate. The US also handles defense and foreign relations (such as drafting Puerto Ricans into the military).

Operation Bootstrap

In the 1940s Muñoz Marín and **Teodoro Moscoso** (who became head of the Puerto Rico Industrial Development Company or **Fomento** in 1950) helped conceive a program of radical industrialization known as **Operation Bootstrap**. The aim was to boost Puerto Rico's economy by attracting external investment through a system of tax breaks and capital loans, a policy that resulted in hundreds of US factories being established on the island between 1948 and 1968. By the 1960s textile factories had given way to larger petrochemical plants, and from the 1970s US pharmaceutical companies made Puerto Rico their base. The economy boomed, vehicle ownership exploded, and living standards rose. Since the gradual unraveling of Bootstrap in the 1980s, Puerto Rico has remained relatively wealthy compared to other parts of the Caribbean, but unemployment remains high, and poverty is far more widespread than in any state on the mainland – and the island also remains heavily dependent on financial assistance from the US government.

Nuyorican soul

Puerto Ricans started **emigrating to the US** in the 1920s, but the real surge came in the 1950s and 1960s, when thousands arrived in **New York**, flooding the enclave known as **El Barrio**, or Spanish Harlem, in uptown Manhattan, and expanding into the Bronx and Brooklyn. Thanks to a thriving **cultural movement** (p.358), these migrants gradually became known as **Nuyoricans**. The community is celebrated by the **Puerto Rican Day Parade** (ⓦwww.nationalpuertoricandayparade.org), which first took place in 1958 and now regularly attracts 100,000 participants and an audience of three million. Depending on how you count them, at least four million Puerto Ricans live in the mainland US today, with around half in New York, though in reality movement back and forth makes this number hard to quantify. You'll rarely hear the redundant term "**Puerto Rican American:**" unlike most immigrants, who must make a symbolic break with their mother country by becoming US citizens, Puerto Ricans are born Americans and face no such dilemma. Nevertheless, although the US community retains passionate cultural links with the island, and has made a huge impact on Puerto Rican culture, art, and literature as whole, there are obvious differences, and many "Nuyoricans" have received a frosty reception on returning to their ancestral home.

The postwar Nationalist movement

Not everyone was happy with the PPD and Muñoz Marín. Albizu was released in 1947, but was **jailed again** four years later and had little further impact on the island's politics. His arrest was prompted by the events of 1950, when Nationalists attempted uprisings all over the island: armed attacks were made on La Fortaleza (the Governor's mansion), the police headquarters in San Juan, and in fourteen other towns, resulting in 28 deaths. The most serious was the **Jayuya Uprising**, when Nationalists led by Blanca Canales effectively captured the town of Jayuya, and the military took three days to restore order – much of the town was destroyed by fire. Albizu was also blamed for the failed attempt of Griselio Torresola and Oscar Collazo to **assassinate President Truman** in Washington, DC, a few days later. Torresola and a policeman were killed, and in the aftermath over three thousand *independentistas* were arrested. Muñoz Marín called them an "insignificant" group of "mad, grotesque, and futile violence-makers ... inspired by communism" – and most Puerto Ricans seemed to agree with him.

Finally, in 1954 four Nationalists led by Lolita Lebrón opened fire from the gallery of the Capitol Building in Washington, injuring six Congressmen, hardening opinion in the US still further and effectively silencing the independence movement for two decades. Albizu was pardoned by Muñoz Marín in 1964 and died the following year, having claimed to have been the subject of human radiation experiments in prison.

Terrorism

In the **1970s** a new generation of radicals became committed to Albizu's aim of independence through revolution. In 1978, activists Carlos Soto Arriví and Arnaldo Darío Rosado were killed, execution-style, by police whilst attempting to blow up communication towers on **Cerro Maravillas**. The subsequent cover-up became a major scandal and decisively impacted gubernatorial elections in the 1980s. In the late 1980s it also emerged that the FBI had been keeping secret files, known as **Las Carpetas**, on anyone suspected of harboring independence sympathies, an issue that remains controversial today.

The **Fuerzas Armadas de Liberación Nacional** (FALN), set up to further the cause of Puerto Rican independence, was responsible for more than 120 bomb attacks in the US between 1974 and 1983, mainly in New York City. Leader **Filiberto Ojeda Ríos** also helped create the Ejército Popular Boricua (Boricua Popular Army) or **Los Macheteros** in 1976, responsible for numerous attacks since 1978. In 2005, Ojeda Ríos was finally located by the FBI (he had been a fugitive for almost fifteen years), and was killed after an exchange of gunfire.

Culebra and Vieques

Though the majority of Puerto Ricans rejected violence as a means for achieving greater autonomy, opposition to the numerous **US military bases** scattered across the island was far more widespread. The US Navy had occupied parts of **Culebra** in 1903, but in the early 1970s a diverse coalition of local organizations began to protest against the navy presence there, resulting in the departure of the military in 1975. Vast swathes of **Vieques** had also been occupied and used as target practice by the US Navy since 1941. The accidental death of civilian **David Sanes** in 1999, killed by bombs dropped during target practice, re-energized the **Navy-Vieques protests** and initiated popular civil disobedience that united the country. Protestors camped on Navy land, supported by Independence Party leader **Rubén Berríos** and a host of Puerto Rican and American celebrities – many were jailed. Protests continued until the US agreed to leave the island in 2003, and in 2004 the **Roosevelt Roads Naval Station** on mainland Puerto Rico was also closed.

Stalemate

The first **plebiscite** on the political status of Puerto Rico was held in 1967, with 60.4 percent of voters **supporting the Commonwealth**, 39 percent opting for statehood, and only 0.6 percent voting for independence (though with the PIP refusing to participate, their supporters tended to abstain). In the aftermath **Luis Ferré** created the pro-statehood **Partido Nuevo Progresista** (New Progressive Party, PNP), going on to win the governorship in 1968 and setting the pattern that continues today, of power switching alternately between the PNP and PPD.

The 1980s and 1990s

By the 1980s it was becoming clear that Puerto Rico was **bitterly polarized** about its political future. PPD governor Hernández Colón's second term (1985–1993) focused efforts on boosting the economy after the recession of the early 1980s and the devastation wreaked by **Hurricane Hugo** in 1989, which destroyed farms and left 28,000 people homeless. The election of PNP candidate **Pedro Rosselló González** in 1993 raised the hopes of statehood supporters, but another **referendum** that year showed support for the Commonwealth at 48.9 percent versus 46.6 percent for statehood, and the following plebiscite, held in 1998, was boycotted by the PPD: 50.5 percent of voters opted for "**none of the above**," and only 46.7 percent for statehood. Rosselló focused instead on anti-crime campaigns, infrastructure projects, and an aggressive privatization program (including the sale of public health facilities). Embroiled with scandal, the PNP were defeated in 2001 by **Sila Calderón**, Puerto Rico's first female governor, best known for presiding over the closure of US military bases on the island.

Puerto Rico today

Rosselló returned in 2004 to challenge PPD candidate **Aníbal Acevedo Vilá** in a bitterly contested election: Vilá won by just 3000 votes (48.4 percent), sparking a lengthy legal challenge by Rosselló, who never really accepted the result. Vilá's administration tried to focus on bread-and-butter issues to avoid the debate on political status, and the status quo seems unlikely to change in the near future. Many Puerto Ricans fear that statehood would result in a dilution of Hispanic culture and the eventual replacement of the Spanish language (not to mention imposition of Federal income taxes), while most seem to believe that independence would lead to economic catastrophe and political chaos (Rubén Berríos' Independence Party received just 2.74 percent of the vote in 2004). Conventional wisdom suggests that the current situation, though not ideal, delivers the most economic benefit to the island whilst retaining a degree of healthy separation from what is perceived as the Anglocentric mainland.

Catholic saints

Puerto Rico has been a **Roman Catholic** country since the Spanish Conquest, with 85 percent of the current population members of the Catholic Church and just 8 percent of Protestant faiths. While attendance has been falling since the 1970s, you'll still see churches overflowing with worshipers on Sundays, and the island's pilgrimage sites attract loyal crowds of believers. Like all Christians, Catholics believe the central tenets of the Bible's New Testament, but one of the most unique aspects of Catholicism is the **worship of saints**. In the Middle Ages, saints were regarded as powerful sources of material and spiritual favors, thanks to their proximity to God in heaven: not only did saints make the mysteries of the Church seem more human, it was believed that they were far more likely to take pity on wretched sinners than God himself. Only the **Pope** in Rome (head of the Catholic Church) can confer sainthood: the process is known as **canonization** and cannot begin until at least five years after a person's death. At least one miracle is required for **beatification**, the first stage, while a second miracle is required before sainthood is declared – both must be certified by a series of meticulous Church investigations. Miracles can be anything from an apparition after death to curing terminally ill patients. **Charlie Rodríguez** is so far the first Puerto Rican to be beatified (see p.148).

In Puerto Rico, every church you visit will be dedicated to a saint. In addition, all of the island's 78 municipalities have patron saints, each with an annual feast day, usually celebrated by a boisterous *fiesta*. The following guide describes a few of the principal figures, though there are hundreds of others.

The Virgin Mary

Mary is the most important saint in the Catholic Church, the "mother of God," chosen for the Immaculate Conception of Jesus at the heart of the New Testament. In Catholic churches, you'll tend to see more people praying to Mary than at the main altar, the idea being that she is more compassionate than even Christ and, as his mother, is in the best position to intercede on your behalf. As Catholic scholar Richard McBrien says, "Christ locks the front door of heaven to keep out unworthy sinners, while Mary lets them in through a side window."

Santería

Puerto Rican Catholicism is in theory identical to that practiced by the Pope, but a folk religion known as **Santería** developed in parallel with the official church, a syncretism of African (particularly Yoruba) and Catholic beliefs that also flourished in Cuba. Slaves forced to adopt Christianity on arrival in Puerto Rico began to identify their traditional African gods or *orishas* with Christian saints, often to avoid persecution: the Yoruba deity of thunder, Chango, became the equivalent of St Barbara, while Ogun (god of fire, iron, and war) was linked with St Peter and St James. Today thousands of Puerto Ricans happily practice elements of Santería whilst remaining devout Catholics, buying candles, potions, and charms in **botánicas**, herbal medicine stores catering specifically to the former – many are owned by a priest or priestess of Santería (*santero* or *santera*), who can provide consultations and advice on everyday problems.

C

In practice, the worship of Mary can seem quite confusing. Churches and shrines tend to honor specific **apparitions** of Mary that have appeared over the years, each with their own special name and set of accompanying miracles and powers. In Spanish, any dedication that begins with **Nuestra Señora** ("Our Lady") or **La Virgen** refers to an incarnation of Mary.

Nuestra Señora de Guadalupe

The most revered apparition of Mary in the New World is known as **Nuestra Señora de Guadalupe**, appearing on Tepeyac hill near Mexico City in December 1531. What makes this incarnation of Mary so special was that she spoke Nahuatl, the language of the Aztecs, and appeared to an Amerindian convert named Juan Diego (who was canonized in 2002). But most importantly, she left physical evidence of her presence: a life-size image of Mary as a dark-skinned Aztec woman was miraculously impressed onto the cloth carried by Diego. She went on to become **patron saint of Mexico**, and **Ponce** in Puerto Rico, celebrated with Mexican flair on December 12.

La Virgen de la Candelaria

This tradition of Mary originated in the **Canary Islands** and was brought to Puerto Rico by immigrants in the eighteenth century, becoming patron saint of Manatí, Mayagüez, and Lajas. The apparition is said to have appeared to shepherds around 1400 in Tenerife, and became associated with the Feast of the Purification of Mary or **Candlemas** held on February 2.

La Virgen del Carmen

One of the most popular incarnations of Mary during the Spanish Conquest, **La Virgen del Carmen** is patron saint of Arroyo, Barceloneta, Cataño, Cidra, Culebra, Hatillo, Morovis, Río Grande, and Villalba. In her role as patron of fishermen and the sea, she is also celebrated in Aguadilla each year. Her origins lie within the **Carmelite Order**, originally a community of monks based on Mount Carmel in Israel, established in the twelfth century – their dedication to Mary gradually led to the association of the name, though it became popularized thanks to the cult of English saint Simon Stock who died in the thirteenth century. Simon (who was a Carmelite) is said to have been given a **scapular** (two pieces of material joined together by two ribbons over the shoulders, worn as a symbol of salvation) when Mary appeared to him in 1251. Though the modern order considers this story pure legend, scapulars are still worn by the faithful. Her feast day is July 16.

Nuestra Señora de la Monserrate

One of the most popular saints in Puerto Rico, this version of Mary stems from a sacred statue, said to have been carved by St Luke around 50 AD and brought to Spain. Lost until 880, it was discovered on **Montserrat** north of modern Barcelona, which has since become a major pilgrimage site: in the Middle Ages the statue was said to have miraculous powers, its face remaining **black** despite constant cleaning. During the Spanish Conquest numerous churches in the New World were named in honor of **Nuestra Señora de la Monserrate** (the Spanish rendering of the Catalan original) and today she is the patron saint of Aguas Buenas, Hormigueros, Jayuya, Moca, and Salinas, with her feast day on September 8 (also the birthday of Mary).

Nuestra Señora del Rosario

Our Lady of the Rosary or **Nuestra Señora del Rosario** is associated with the Catholic devotion known as the **Rosary**, referring to both a set of prayer beads and the prayer itself, which comprises 150 Hail Marys. The story that an apparition of Mary gave the first Rosary to St Dominic in 1208 is now viewed as myth by the Church, and the first Feast of the Rosary was established by the Pope in 1573 to celebrate the victory over the Turks at Lepanto (attributed to diligent recital of the Rosary). Today she is patron saint of Naguabo, Vega Baja, and Yauco, and her feast is still celebrated on October 7.

San Juan Bautista (St John the Baptist)

John the Baptist is a seminal figure in the New Testament, a mystical prophet that predicts the rise of Jesus and later baptizes him – infamously beheaded by Herod Antipas on the behest of Salome, he was later venerated as one of the most important saints. Christopher Columbus was particularly fond of St John, and **San Juan Bautista** became the first name of Puerto Rico, later applied to the capital city, and the **patron saint of the island**. John is also patron saint of Orocovis and Maricao, and his feast day is June 24.

Santiago Apóstol (St James the Apostle)

One of the original twelve disciples of Jesus, St James or **Santiago Apóstol** was one of Christ's closest followers and the first apostle to be martyred. Despite being buried in Jerusalem, a tradition emerged that he had either visited or was reburied in Spain, at the town of **Compostela**. As his cult grew, the town became one of the most important pilgrimage sites in the Catholic world, James honored as the **patron saint of Spain**. Invoking his name in battle was so efficacious he became known as Matamoros ("Moor-slayer") in the Middle Ages for his supposed help in defeating the Moors, and in the sixteenth century Spanish colonists brought his cult to Puerto Rico. Today he is patron saint of Chile, Guatemala, Nicaragua, pilgrims, pharmacists, laborers, and sufferers of arthritis. In Puerto Rico he's patron of Aibonito, Fajardo, Guánica, and Santa Isabel, but the most exuberant celebration of his feast day (July 25) takes place in Loíza (see p.107).

San Antonio de Padua (St Anthony of Padua)

Regarded as one of the greatest ever Church teachers, **San Antonio de Padua** (1195–1231) was born in Lisbon, became a Franciscan friar and later preached all over northern Italy. Buried in Padua, he became patron saint of Brazil,

Portugal, travelers, and the poor, but is best known for being the **finder of lost articles**. In Puerto Rico, Anthony is a popular *santos* (usually depicted with the infant Jesus seated on a book), and patron saint of Barranquitas, Ceiba, Dorado, Guayama, and Isabela. His feast day is June 13.

San José (St Joseph)

San José, the husband of the Virgin Mary and the adoptive father of Jesus, is another immensely popular saint, patron of workers, fathers of families and a "happy death." His main role in the Bible is to take in Mary after the Immaculate Conception, and he rarely appears in later sections of the New Testament, suggesting he died before the public ministry of Jesus began. He is the patron saint of Ciales, Gurabo, Lares, Luquillo, and Peñuelas, as well as numerous places all over the world including Canada, Mexico, Peru, and the Mission to China. His primary feast day is March 19.

San Miguel Arcángel (Michael the Archangel)

In Catholic tradition **San Miguel Arcángel** is the leader of the angels and protector of the people of Israel, a powerful figure who appears primarily in the Old Testament and Revelations. Patron saint of Cabo Rojo, Naranjito, and Utuado in Puerto Rico, he is also traditionally considered the patron of soldiers, Germany, England, the sick, grocers, and police officers. His feast day is September 29, also known as **Michaelmas**.

Art and culture

P uerto Rican culture is remarkably dynamic, though outside the US it has a surprisingly low profile, and in Europe tends to be completely overshadowed by that of Cuba, especially when it comes to music. Like Cuba and the Dominican Republic, Puerto Rican art has deep roots in the Spanish colonial period, as well as taking inspiration from the island's diverse cultural elements. But what really sets Puerto Rican popular culture apart from its neighbors is the **US connection**, which since World War II has dramatically influenced the path of numerous artists, singers, and writers from the island. Indeed, since the 1920s much of what is considered Puerto Rican art or literature has been created by Puerto Ricans born or living in the US, particularly **New York** (see box p.364). US-based Puerto Rican artists are included here because although their central focus tends to be (quite naturally), the experience of Puerto Ricans living in the US, this reflects the greater debate over the cultural and political future of the island itself. But while New York has been important, the domestic art and music scene has also remained vibrant, a proudly independent, Spanish-speaking community that sees itself as more *Latino* than *Americano*.

Fine art

Puerto Rican art in the early Spanish colonial period was generally restricted to **religious** works, usually commissioned for churches, and so-called **caste paintings** made for rich Spanish officials, formal portraits depicting the various races on the island. The first major Puerto Rican painter was **José Campeche** (1752–1809), a masterful exponent of what tends to be called **viceregal art**, the application of European techniques and styles to the colonies of Latin America. Campeche created over four hundred works, most of them for churches and executed in a formal Baroque style that was becoming outmoded in Europe. In the 1700s, Rococo was in vogue, and learning from an exiled Spanish court painter, Campeche mastered this more florid style, exhibited in his numerous **portrait paintings**: his studies of governors, military men, and the upper crust of San Juan society offer a comprehensive snapshot of colonial society at the time. Little is known about his private life, other than that he was the son of a freed slave and an immigrant from the Canary Islands.

The second Puerto Rican master was **Francisco Oller** (1833–1917). He received his first major commission at the age of fifteen (a church painting), but unlike Campeche, Oller left the island for Europe in the 1850s, studying in Madrid and ending up in Paris in 1858. Here Oller joined the **Impressionists** and hung out with Paul Cézanne in the 1860s. Though he spent many years in Europe, Oller tended to paint scenes from Puerto Rico, utilizing not just Impressionist techniques on landscapes, but also a bold Realism to portray slavery, poverty, and other social injustices. His most celebrated painting in Puerto Rico, *El Velorio*, is on display at the University of Puerto Rico's history museum (p.85).

The most acclaimed Puerto Rican artists to follow Oller were **Ramón Fradé** (1875–1954) and **Miguel Pou** (1880–1968). Often considered part of the romantic **Costumbrismo** school, with its idealized view of rural Puerto Rico, Fradé's *El Pan Nuestro* (Our Bread) pays homage to the *jíbaro* (Puerto Rican peasant farmer) and is on display in San Juan's national gallery (p.73).

Pou had a similar focus, painting Puerto Rico landscapes and earthy *jíbaro* types from his base in Ponce, still home to many of his works.

Modern art has blossomed in Puerto Rico since the 1950s, though many artists have chosen to live in the US. New York-born **Rafael Tufiño** is known for his somber paintings of the island, while Francisco Rodón and sculptor Tomás Batista came to prominence in the 1960s – much of the latter's statuary is on display in plazas around the island. Carlos Irizarry and Myrna Báez are best-known for their abstract paintings, often with a socio-political theme, while San Juan-based Jorge Zeno dabbles in surrealism. The **contemporary art scene** is particularly dynamic, with galleries all over the island showing the latest work.

Dance and music

Puerto Rico has an incredibly rich musical legacy, ranging from folk music inspired by Spanish and African traditions to salsa, modern Latino pop, and the ever-fashionable beats of *reggaetón*.

Folk music

Throughout the Spanish colonial period, **folk music** flourished in rural Puerto Rico, a rich tradition that started with *décimas* (ten-stanza couplets), *coplas* (ballads), *villancicos* and *aguinaldos* (Christmas carols), all of which derived from Andalusian music that came to Puerto Rico in the late seventeenth century. The **seis** evolved from the *décimas*, a fast-paced music and line dance that became emblematic of the Puerto Rican countryside. Ballads would often be accompanied by simple maracas (*güiro*), or a more refined ten-string instrument known as the **cuatro**, and sung by usually male *trovadores* (troubadours).

One of the most popular folk singers today is **Andrés Jiménez**, known as *El Jíbaro* for his proudly Puerto Rican themes. An enthusiastic activist, Jiménez produced an album of protest songs entitled *Son de Vieques* in 2001 at the height of the US Navy-Vieques protests. He is also considered part of the **Nueva Trova** movement, the "New Ballad" style that originated in Cuba and is characterized by folk songs with a political protest theme. In fact **Cuban styles** have continuously blended with Puerto Rican folk traditions over the years. **Bolero** spread quickly to Puerto Rico in the early twentieth century, with **Rafael Hernández** and **Pedro Flores** becoming two of the most successful band leaders: Hernández's *Lamento Borincano* is still loved not just in Puerto Rico but also in Mexico. **Trío Vegabajeño**, led by Fernandito Alvarez and one of the most beloved Puerto Rican *bolero* groups, was formed in 1943 and dominated Puerto Rican music into the 1960s.

Danza

Considered Puerto Rico's national dance and the most formal of its musical traditions, the **danza** was introduced to the island's fad-conscious high society in 1842. The genre is thought to have derived from the *habanera*, brought to the island by Cuban immigrants and resembling a less rigid version of the waltz and classical music of Europe. Puerto Ricans soon made it their own, and the first *danza* composer was **Manuel Gregorio Tavarez** (1843–1883), followed by his student, **Juan Morel Campos** (1857–1896), whose melodies continue to be played across the island. The most famous *danza* is "La Borinqueña", its lyrics transformed into a nationalist anthem by Lola Rodríguez de Tió.

Bomba and Plena

The African communities in Puerto Rico developed their own styles of dance and music based on traditions carried across the Atlantic. The **bomba** involves singers accompanied by drums, maracas, and *palillos* or sticks. Usually in pairs (but without touching), dancers move in ever more complicated or vigorous ways, challenging the drummer to respond with similarly more intense rhythms. By far the most celebrated exponent of *bomba*, **Rafael Cepeda** and his family maintain the tradition with the Ballet Folklórico de La familia Cepeda.

Since the 1960s *bomba* has been promoted as a national dance, usually paired with **la plena**. *Plena* is a type of rural narrative song, a sort of Puerto Rican country music, developing along the south coast of the island in the late nineteenth century from similar drum-driven African traditions, and also using improvised call-and-response vocals. In the 1930s the style was popularized by **Manuel Jiménez**, or El Canario, and further expanded by artists such as **César Concepción**, but by the late 1960s the genre had almost disappeared. Like *la bomba*, *plena* has been revamped since the 1980s, in part thanks to increased tourism and the efforts of artists like Willie Colón and **Plena Libre**.

Salsa

Perhaps the best known of all Latin sounds, the origins of **salsa** are extremely complex and much debated, with Puerto Rico, Cuba, New York, and even Colombia all claiming to be the "home" of the genre. The truth is that salsa is a fusion of several different styles – cha-cha-cha, mambo, *guaguancó, son montuno* – all predominantly Cuban, but brought together with the jazz of Harlem and cooked up in **New York** by primarily Puerto Rican musicians. Nevertheless, in modern salsa's formative years in the late 1960s and 1970s, it's true that the role of Cuba was underplayed for political reasons. The real roots of salsa lie with Cuban band leader **Arsenio Rodríguez**, who expanded Cuban *son* to create *son montuno* in the 1930s, a style which formed the basis of the **mambo** craze of the 1940s. Latin big bands blossomed in New York after World War II, the three most popular led by Cuban trumpeter Mario Bauza, and Puerto Ricans **Tito Puente** and **Tito Rodríguez**, all incorporating various up-tempo styles ranging from mambo to early salsa – the term, however, was popularized in the late 1960s by **Fania Records**, the New York label that essentially created the modern sound with its stable of predominantly Puerto Rican musicians, the **Fania All-Stars**: Johnny Pacheco (who started Fania in 1963), Willie Colón, Pete "El Conde" Rodríguez, and **Héctor Lavoe** (see p.287) among them. In the 1970s salsa became a harder, edgier sound than its predecessors, increasingly urban and political than light and tropical, taking its inspiration from the impoverished *barrios* of the US as much as the Caribbean. Lavoe in particular often performed deeply melancholic songs, with his signature "El Cantante" describing the pain that often lies behind the apparently easy life of the entertainer. He went on to have a successful solo career, his tragic life and premature death in 1993 only serving to confirm his superstar status.

Meanwhile, **El Gran Combo** formed in 1962, soon becoming Puerto Rico's most popular salsa band and now regarded as a national treasure – they still perform on the island and are well worth checking out. Since the 1980s **Giberto Santa Rosa** and **Marc Anthony** have also been popular, with protégé **Victor Manuelle** rising to prominence in the last few years as a crooning proponent of *salsa romantica*.

Latino pop

Some of the world's biggest Latino pop stars are Puerto Rican, chief among them **Ricky Martin**. It's been a while now since he made a splash in the English-speaking pop world (his hit "Livin' la Vida Loca" was in 1999), but in Latin America he remains one of the greatest superstars of all time, idolized by fans from Miami to Argentina. Born in San Juan in 1971, Martin started his career with **Menudo** in 1984, and continues to perform, make records, and act on stage and TV. He still owns a home in the city, and in 2000 founded the **Ricky Martin Foundation** (Ⓦwww.rickymartinfoundation.org) to fight child trafficking. Five-member Menudo was put together in Puerto Rico in 1977, one of the first ever boy bands and incredibly popular worldwide in the 1980s – they re-formed in 2007.

Puerto Rico has produced numerous other pop stars, from Chucho Avellanet in the 1960s and 1970s to Carlos Ponce in the late 1990s, but one of the most consistently successful, selling over ten million records worldwide, is **Chayanne**, currently based in Miami. Of the US-born Puerto Rican stars, **Jennifer Lopez** has regularly topped the Billboard charts since her first hit in 1999.

Reggaetón and hip-hop

The bass-thumping, car-rattling rhythms of **reggaetón** have become the defining sounds of Puerto Rican youth since the late 1990s, with a global appeal that has long since outgrown the island. Though rapping is a crucial element, *reggaetón* is more than just Spanish hip-hop, with a distinctive back-beat known as "dem bow" that is part Jamaican dance-hall, part salsa: the "reggae" part of the name is a bit deceptive, and the genre owes more to Shabba Ranks than Bob Marley. The roots of Puerto Rican *reggaetón* are often attributed to Panama, where Spanish rappers collaborated with Jamaican ragamuffin DJs in the early 1990s, but Puerto Rican hip-hop was also well established at that time, with rappers such as **Vito C** and producer **DJ Playero** laying the ground work for later *reggaetón* artists.

Today, the top *reggaetón* artists all hail from Greater San Juan: **Daddy Yankee** was one of the first to make it big, his 2004 mega-hit "Gasolina" still one of the best-selling *reggaetón* tracks; Grammy-winner **Don Omar**, involved in an ongoing feud with Yankee about who is *El Rey del Reggaetón*; Don Omar's mentor and producer **Héctor El Father**; **Tego Calderón**; and Grammy-winning duo **Calle 13**. One of the newest sensations and certainly the youngest is nine-year-old **Miguelito**, a miniature *reggaetonero* who has spawned a whole sub-genre of kiddie rappers, including Mimi, the "the pretty girl of *reggaetón*" and the Reggaeton Niños.

Rock en Español: Puerto Rico

Pop may get all the attention, but Puerto Rico also has a small but thriving **rock scene**, despite losing ground since the 1990s. **La Secta Allstar** released their debut album in 1997, going on to become the most successful Puerto Rican rock band (the band was formed in Florida, but its members were all born in Puerto Rico), and the first to be nominated for a Grammy in 2005. Other bands from the 1990s retain faithful audiences: **Fiel a la Vega** continues to tour and make records, while up-and-coming **Black Guayaba** won the Grammy in 2008 for best Latin Rock album.

Film

Movies arrived in Puerto Rico with the Americans in 1898, but it wasn't until the 1950s that a small-scale **domestic film industry** really took off, and Puerto Rican actors made an impact in **Hollywood**. The first locally made Puerto Rican film was *Un Drama en Puerto Rico*, shot in 1912 by Rafael Colorado D'Assoy, but subsequent efforts to establish local production companies were short-lived.

The Golden Age

Everything changed in 1953 with the release of **Los Peloteros** (The baseball players), the story of a penniless children's baseball team inspired to victory by an enigmatic coach, played by Ramón Ortiz del Rivero. Directed by US photographer Jack Delano and still regarded as a classic, the film was part of a government initiative to use movies as a way to boost education and modernize the island. The División de Educación de la Comunidad went on to produce or fund around 117 short and feature-length films with some of Puerto Rico's most gifted actors and directors, a process accelerated by the introduction of television in 1954. Films of note include the musical *El Otro Camino* (1955) and romantic drama *Maruja* (1958), both starring Axel Anderson, a German expat, as well as a host of local actors who became big stars on local TV.

This Golden Age of *cine Puertorriqueño* didn't last, however: in the 1960s Mexican films dominated the Spanish-language market and by the 1970s Puerto Rican film production had virtually collapsed.

Hollywood and West Side Story

Just as the domestic movie industry was beginning to take off, Puerto Ricans were finally making their mark in **Hollywood**. **José Ferrer** (1909–1992) made his debut with Ingrid Bergman in *Joan of Arc* in 1948, receiving an Academy nomination for best supporting actor. Ferrer won the **Oscar for best actor** for the 1950 film version of *Cyrano de Bergerac*, becoming the first Puerto Rican to win the award. A long and successful career in Broadway and movies followed, including a memorable pserformance in *Lawrence of Arabia* (1962).

Despite the success of Ferrer and a thriving domestic film industry, perceptions of Puerto Rican culture were ultimately shaped by the movie adaptation of the Broadway hit, **West Side Story** (1961) much to the frustration of Puerto Ricans ever since. Loosely adapted from *Romeo and Juliet*, the story of love amidst the rivalry between white and Puerto Rican gangs in New York's Upper West Side has been criticised for its stereotypes of *machismo* violence and gossipy, subservient women. It nevertheless garnered a best supporting actress award for **Rita Moreno**, the first Puerto Rican woman to win an Oscar. Born in 1931 in Humacao, Moreno moved to New York as a child and went on to star in numerous movies and TV shows.

The 1980s and beyond

Since the late 1980s Puerto Rico has experienced a mini-boom in locally produced movies, and though many have been highly acclaimed, audiences tend to view them as strictly art-house material. Output and revenues remain light years behind the Hollywood blockbusters.

In the 1980s the revival was led by the work of **Jacobo Morales**, whose *Dios los Cría* (1979), a critical examination of Puerto Rican society through a series of five stories, led to several other lauded movies including *Lo que le Pasó a Santiago* (1989), the first Puerto Rican film to be nominated for an Oscar (for foreign film), and most recently *Ángel* (2007). Marcos Zurinaga's *La Gran Fiesta* (1986) is an accurate portrayal of life in San Juan the 1940s, while Luis Molina Casanova's comedy *La Guagua Aérea* (1993), set in 1960 and following a group of Puerto Ricans as they prepare to fly to New York, was the most financially successful Puerto Rican film of the decade.

Recent hits have included *Cayo* (2005), a poignant story of a cancer-ridden Vietnam War vet who returns to Culebra to make peace with his past; *Casi Casi* (2006), a high school comedy; and *Maldeamores* (2007) starring Luis Guzmán, comprising three separate love stories. Today, the **Comisión de Cine de Puerto Rico** (ⓦwww.puertoricofilm.com) is responsible for the local film industry, though much of its efforts have been spent attracting US film-makers to shoot on the island.

Puerto Ricans in Hollywood

Puerto Ricans have continued to excel in Hollywood, with **Raúl Juliá** (1940–1994) best known in the US for his role in the *Addams Family* movies. **Benicio del Toro** won an Oscar for his work in *Traffic* (2000), alongside **Luis Guzmán**, who has appeared in numerous movies. **Roselyn Sánchez** came to international prominence in kitschy *Rush Hour 2* (2001), despite remaining committed to the domestic film industry – she starred in *Cayo* (see above) and *Yellow* (2007), about a Puerto Rican dancer who moves to New York.

The now well-established Puerto Rican community in the US has also produced several major stars, notably **Jennifer Lopez**, born in the Bronx to Puerto Rican parents from Ponce. In 2007 she starred in *El Cantante* with husband **Marc Anthony**, about the life of salsa superstar Héctor Lavoe. Though the film upset some Lavoe fans with its focus on Puchi (Lavoe's forceful wife and Lopez's character) and the tragic star's drug addiction, both key performances are excellent and the live salsa sets are fabulous. Brooklyn native **Rosie Perez** has been the star of several movies (*White Men Can't Jump*, *Fight the Power*) and remains a strong campaigner for Puerto Rican rights in the US, highlighted by her thought-provoking movie *Yo Soy Boricua! Pa' Que Tu Lo Sepas!* (I am a Boricua, just so you know!) in 2006. The film primarily explores the identity of New York-based Puerto Ricans, and offers a rather romanticized version of Puerto Rican history, eulogizing Albizu Campos; the Spanish colonization is unequivocally described as "genocide."

Literature

Puerto Rico has a rich **literary heritage**, though due to high illiteracy rates and repressive publishing laws, little fiction was produced on the island until the 1820s.

The Spanish period

Modern Puerto Rican literature has its roots in the **nineteenth century**, when the introduction of the printing press in 1806 made it possible for budding poets to publish, work in a growing number of publications and pamphlets. One of the first was **Miguel Cabrera**, the Arecibo-born poet whose *Coplas del Jíbaro* (1820) depicted uniquely *criollo* themes. **Manuel A. Alonso** (1822–1889) caused a sensation with *El Gíbaro* in 1849, a collection of verses that praised the simple virtues of the Puerto Rican *jíbaro*, helping to create a more romantic image of the hard-working peasant class (see p.328). Influenced by the European Romantics, Puerto Rican writers began to produce highly nostalgic portraits of the island's past, often to mask their nationalist sympathies. The most admired poets of this period were **José Gautier Benítez** (1851–1880), who penned the highly senti-mental *A Puerto Rico* in 1879, and **Lola Rodríguez de Tió** (1843–1924), who was exiled in the 1870s.

Considered the father of Puerto Rican theater, **Alejandro Tapia y Rivera** (1826–1882) started writing plays in the 1840s and was also the island's first novelist. Though heavily influenced by Romanticism, his play *La Cuarterona* (1847) was the first work of fiction to tackle the issues of slavery and racial discrimination.

Spanning the transition from Spanish to US rule, **Manuel Zeno Gandía** (1855–1930) published four novels between the 1890s and 1920s, known as the *Chronicles of a Sick World*. His more realistic portrayals of gritty Puerto Rican rural life, inspired in part by the work of Émile Zola, effectively ended the Romantic period. His masterpiece is *La Charca* (The Pond, 1894), a tragic story that ends with the heroine committing suicide: the pond is a metaphor for the endless cycle of poverty and sickness experienced by the island's peasantry.

The US occupation

The **US occupation** that began in 1898 dramatically changed the literary scene on the island. Leader of what was termed the **Generation of '98**, politician **José de Diego** (1866–1918) was also an accomplished **poet**. His *Final Act*, in which the poet imagines his own funeral and subsequent redemption, of the most powerful Puerto Rican poems ever written, a trope for the way freedom cannot be denied a human being, even in death. Popular poets like **Luis Llorens Torres** (1876–1944), who wrote *El Patito Feo* (The Ugly Duckling), and novelist **Nemesio Canales** (1897–1923) adopted much of De Diego's independence agenda, while **Luis Palés Matos** (1898–1959) was a pioneer of revolutionary Afro-Antillano poetry in the 1920s, blending Spanish with words from Afro-Caribbean culture.

The 1930s

In the 1930s, **Enrique A. Laguerre** (1905–2005) created some of the most memorable fiction exploring the island's struggle for identity, beginning with his first major novel, *La Llamarada* (The Flare-up) in 1935 – the heartbreaking tale of a young plantation owner torn between ambition and sympathy for the very laborers he exploited, it vividly represented life in rural Puerto Rico at the time. Much admired in Puerto Rico, he kept writing well into the 1990s, and produced over thirty books and was nominated for the Nobel Prize for Literature in 1999.

Nationalist **Juan Antonio Corretjer** (1908–1985) became one of the most popular **poets** in the 1930s, while 1937 saw the publication of *A ras del Cristal* (Cracked Glass) by Mercedes Negron Muñoz, better known as **Clara Lair**, another poet who continued to publish to great acclaim in the postwar period. Yet the greatest poet of the period, and often considered one of the greatest poets in Latin America, was **Julia de Burgos** (1914-1953), a brilliant but troubled poetic genius who spent much of her adult life struggling for recogni-tion – beset by depression and alcoholism, she died a pauper in East Harlem, New York, at the age of 39. Her most famous poem is *El Rio Grande de Loíza*, a powerful and lyrical evocation of Puerto Rico, and a lament for its continued colonial status.

Postwar and contemporary writers

Since World War II much Puerto Rican literature has focused on charting the experience of **migrants** to the US mainland, exploring the conflict between *acá* (here) and *allá* (there). **René Marqués** (1919–1979), one of the most lauded modern Puerto Rican playwrights, tackled these themes in *La Carreta* (The Oxcart), first performed in 1951. The drama follows a rural family as it moves first to the slums of San Juan and then to New York in search of a better life, only to end in tragedy. **Pedro Juan Soto** (1928–2002) lived in New York and Puerto Rico, and was one of the first true bilingual writers, his best-seller *Spiks* published in 1956, while fellow New York émigré **Jesús Colón** (1901–1974) firmly established the Puerto Rican migrant theme with his landmark *A Puerto Rican in New York* (1961). Colón inspired writers such as **Piri Thomas** (author of hard-hitting *Down These Mean Streets*), **Esmeralda Santiago** (best-known for her moving autobiography *When I was Puerto Rican*), **Nicholasa Mohr** (whose *El Bronx* collection earned her a finalist position for the National Book Award), **Pedro Pietri**, and **Giannina Braschi** (writer of the first "Spanglish" novel, *Yo-Yo Boing!* in 1998), part of what became known as the **Nuyorican Movement** (New York-based Puerto Rican artists). **Miguel Algarín** founded the Nuyorican Poets Café in New York's East Village in 1973, where other Puerto Rican poets such as Miguel Piñero, Ed Morales, and Marita Morales flourished. Back in Puerto Rico itself, **Rosario Ferré** is probably the island's leading woman of letters today, author of the highly acclaimed *House on the Lagoon* and many others (see p.384 for more on contemporary fiction).

Wildlife and the environment

Considering its small size and rugged topography (60 percent of the island is covered in mountains), Puerto Rico boasts remarkably diverse ecosystems, ranging from the bone-dry forests of Guánica and balmy coastal plains to the sopping-wet slopes of El Yunque and pockmarked landscape of karst country. Puerto Rican **wildlife** is equally varied, and typically for an island, endemic species are numerous. The range of **bird species** is especially impressive, while Puerto Rico's extraordinary **marine life** remains one of its biggest attractions, nourished by the rich reefs, mangrove swamps, and coral-rimmed cays along its coast. Exploited by intensive agriculture and the industries of Operation Bootstrap (p.364), the island's **environment** has certainly taken a beating over the years, but grassroots ecological movements have been gaining strength since the 1970s, and the government has stepped up efforts to maintain forest reserves and delicate coastal areas. The fierce struggle between development and conservation continues, however, with **overpopulation** and the **tourism industry** placing the heaviest pressures on the island's limited natural resources.

Fauna

Puerto Rican wildlife is dominated by small, often unique species, and unless you're an avid ornithologist, the crystalline waters off the coast provide the richest and most accessible slice of activity. Most of the animals you'll see on land were brought by the Spanish, though the practice of introducing alien species into the wild goes on today.

Mammals

Puerto Rico has no large land animals native to the island, and **bats** are the only **mammals**, with thirteen species documented so far. Ten of these, including the red fig-eating bat, are cave-dwellers in El Yunque National Forest, playing an important role in island ecology, particularly by limiting the growth of mosquito populations.

Almost all the other mammals you're likely to come across in Puerto Rico are non-native, most arriving with the Spanish. If you spot a sleek, ferret-like creature darting across the road ahead of you, it's probably a **mongoose** – there are thousands on Vieques and all over rural Puerto Rico, sobering examples of what happens when man's interference with nature goes disastrously wrong. The small Indian mongoose was introduced to the island in 1877 to control **rats** that were gnawing away at sugar cane, but the two populations basically ignored each other and the mongoose instead set to work gobbling down eggs and generally causing mayhem within the island's delicate ecosystems. Vicious and hard to catch, mongooses also carry rabies and should be studiously avoided. Feral **dogs** can also be a problem on the edge of towns, and even **cats** have multiplied to plague proportions in some places – the colony outside the walls of Old San Juan is successfully being controlled. One of the main causes of both phenomena is the tendency for Puerto Ricans to release unwanted pets into the wild, a practice that has had some bizarre consequences (see below). **Rhesus monkeys** have also gradually colonized areas of the island, often escapees from experimental colonies on Cayo Santiago (see p.137), Isla Desecheo (p.243), and La Parguera, where they have become especially troublesome. Cattle remain the most productive of the Spanish imports, while **Paso Fino** horses (p.140) are the most celebrated and certainly most valuable animals on the island. The best place to see them wandering around is on Vieques.

Reptiles and amphibians

Though the island sports 25 amphibian and 61 reptile species, many endemic, it's the much-loved national symbol, the **coquí**, which gets the most attention. This tiny **frog** is actually extremely hard to see, and its real claim to fame is the rhythmic and surprisingly powerful "co-QUI" call it makes, often seeming to blanket the whole island at night. The common coquí is the most prolific of the seventeen species identified on Puerto Rico, though many of the others are extremely rare, hidden in the thick forests of El Yunque. Lengths range between 0.5 and 3 inches and colors vary among shades of green, brown, and yellow, though you're more likely to see an image of one in a tourist store than the real thing in the wild.

What you will see are **anolis lizards**: Puerto Rico is literally swarming with them, the sharp-mouthed lizard being the most common and measuring under 2 inches. Typically yellowish-brown, it makes a real contrast to the bright green **emerald anole**, a larger species that measures 2.7 inches in length. The largest Puerto Rican land lizard is the **Mona ground iguana**, giants that can grow to be 3.9ft long and found solely on the Isla de Mona. However, **green iguanas**, another introduced species, have become a real problem all over Puerto Rico, feeding off garbage to grow to equally monstrous proportions – machete-wielding park-keepers scour golf courses, airport runways, and gardens to chase them away.

Puerto Rico's eleven **snake** species are generally considered non-lethal, with the Puerto Rican Boa the largest (maximum length of 12ft) followed by the Puerto Rican Racer, which does have a venomous bite that is mildly poisonous. Again, far more deadly **boa constrictors** have been released into the wild in the past, and most bizarrely, the **spectacled caiman**, a type of alligator, now thrives in Lago Tortuguero after being introduced by bored pet-owners.

Birds

Puerto Rico is a **bird-watching** cornucopia, with many tours catering solely to ornithologists. Of the 349 bird species recorded on the island, about 120 breed here regularly. Undoubtedly the most famous, but one of the hardest to spot, the rare **Puerto Rican parrot** (*cotorra puertorriqueña*) has been the focus of an intense conservation program since the 1960s, centered on a small wild population in El Yunque National Forest. El Yunque is rich in bird life, home to numerous hawks, hummingbirds, bananaquits, warblers, and the endemic Puerto Rican Tody. Elsewhere, the forest reserves in karst country are inhabited by flycatchers, pigeons, vireos, the Puerto Rican lizard cuckoo, and the green mango (the hummingbird, not the fruit). Other bird-watching favorites include the dry forest at Guánica, laced with todies, troupials, bullfinches, thrashers, and the rarer Puerto Rican nightjar; and the Bosque Estatal de Maricao, noted for its elfin-woods warbler, Puerto Rican pewee, and Puerto Rican screech-owl. For more on Puerto Rican birds, go to the bird-watching section of ⊛www.adventourspr.com or check out the book listed on p.387.

Marine life

With a coastline fringed by mangroves, dense seagrass beds, and swathes of coral reef, Puerto Rico offers a rich stew of **marine life**, despite serious problems with pollution and reef degradation over the years. **Reef fish** are the most kaleidoscopic and easiest to spot when diving or snorkeling, with over two hundred species recorded off the island, including several types of **shark**. The most prolific species tend to be neon blue angelfish, white and blue-striped grunts, parrotfish, porcupine fish, spiky scorpion fish, red snapper, triggerfish, delicate wrasses, and the odd ray, with giant crabs, lobsters, and moray eels peering out of the coral. Schools of mullet and Spanish mackerel gather further out, tailed by prowling barracuda.

Puerto Rico also attracts deep-sea sports fishermen for its plentiful supply of **blue marlin**, but also dolphinfish (mahi-mahi or *dorado*), wahoo, yellowfin tuna, sawfish, and sailfish. **Tarpon** and **snook** flourish in the island's lagoons and bays.

Some native **freshwater fish** inhabit Puerto Rico's reservoirs and rivers, but most species have been introduced. Since 1936, the hatchery at Maricao (see p.350) has been raising 25,000 fish annually to stock the island's lakes, predominantly largemouth and peacock bass, but also catfish.

One of the most popular marine mammals, found mostly on the south coast of Puerto Rico, is the hippo-like **manatee** or sea cow, often seen lazily grazing over seagrass beds or near the mangroves surrounding La Parguera. Generally 9ft long, the manatee is an endangered species, frequently involved in collisions with small boats and numbering an estimated three to four hundred. In 1991, a battered baby manatee was rescued by the Caribbean Stranding Network, and after being nursed back to health was released into the wild in 1994. Dubbed **Moisés** and something of a national icon, the hapless manatee took a long time to adapt and was struck by a boat in 1996, but he remains healthy and continues to hang out on the east coast of Puerto Rico (see ⓦwww.manatipr.org).

Humpback whales are commonly seen off Rincón and Aguadilla, where they congregate for breeding and calving between January and March, while small groups of **dolphins** frolic off the coast of Culebra and Vieques. **Sea turtles** are perhaps the most remarkable but endangered of all the sea creatures that visit Puerto Rico. The two most common species are hawksbill and leatherback, with Culebra the most important and generally best-protected nesting site (see p.183). Turtles also lay eggs all along the east and west coasts, though these sites are harder to protect: the biggest threat to turtles is not poachers, but the destruction of habitat by tourism and residential projects. For more information check ⓦwww.seaturtle.org.

Flora

When the Spanish hacked their way into the mountainous interior of Puerto Rico in the sixteenth century, they discovered a flourishing tropical jungle, most of the trees and plants skillfully utilized by the native Taíno for food, materials, and medicines. Thanks to comprehensive reforestation, Puerto Rico's great forests and trees are much recovered and a system of state reserves guarantees preservation. The leafy **ceiba** (kapok or silk-cotton tree) is the national tree of Puerto Rico, the oldest examples serving as tourist attractions in places like Ponce and Vieques. By far the most memorable tree on the island is the flaming royal poinciana, known locally as the **flamboyant** (pronounced with the "t" silent), splashed with brilliant orange and yellow flowers that bloom between May and August – many areas are carpeted with them, creating some of the most enchanting scenes on the island. The **Puerto Rican hibiscus** is a large dark pink or crimson bloom and the national flower of the island, growing on trees primarily around the northeast of the island. Other flowering trees include the **robles** (whitewood or white cedar), which sports white and purplish blooms in the spring, and the fragrant **mamey tree**, which blossoms in spring or summer and also produces edible fruit. **Breadfruit** and especially **mango** trees are also widespread in the foothills of Puerto Rico, the latter exploding with juicy fruit in the summer. **Tropical fruits** such as avocado, *quenepa* (Spanish lime), papaya, *parcha* (passion fruit), and pineapple are abundant all over the island.

Puerto Rico's tropical **rainforests** are dominated by sierra palm, *tabonuco*, and *palo colorado* trees, with cloud forest clinging to the highest peaks – tiny orchids often litter the forest floor (see El Yunque p.112). The coast is rimmed with forests of gnarly mangroves, and beaches lined with scrubby patches of seagrape, and scattered coconut palms, less prolific than they once were, while the dry forests of Guánica feature their own unique vegetation (see p.306). **Mangroves** play a particularly important role in coastal ecosystems, providing protection from erosion and recycling nutrients, crucial in the formation of Puerto Rico's celebrated **bioluminescent bays**. The key to the unique micro-environments created by large mangrove forests is their vast root systems, which prevent sediment brought in by the tides from flowing back out to sea.

Threats to the environment

When the Spanish arrived in Puerto Rico, the island was not an idyllic paradise. The Taíno worked hard and died young, burning parts of the forest in order to cultivate vast plots of cassava, corn, and tobacco. Much of the island remained smothered in virgin forest, however, and the Spanish conquerors almost immediately set to work hacking this down – progress was slow outside the San Juan area, and it wasn't until the nineteenth century that **deforestation** reached its zenith. Vast tracts of woodland were stripped to make way for sugar cane and coffee plantations, a process that continued under the US occupation. Though early attempts at **forest conservation** had started in the 1870s, it wasn't until these industries had collapsed in the 1930s that lasting changes were made. Large areas of the island, now abandoned, were reclaimed by **reforestation** programs, most noticeable in El Yunque National Forest and throughout the Cordillera Central. Ironically, just as the interior was beginning to recover from years of intensive agricultural exploitation, migration to the cities fed a population boom, and **Operation Bootstrap** (see p.364) led to rapid **industrialization**. Today, thanks to stricter enforcement of laws and a move away from manufacturing, Puerto Rico is greener than many of its neighbors, but the island is still grappling with a glut of gas-guzzling SUVs, as well as the long-term effects of industrial and chemical pollution. The destruction of offshore reefs by over-fishing has been exacerbated in recent years by global warming, with large banks of coral destroyed by bleaching in 2005. The coast is further threatened by tourism projects and the boom in property development, often providing holiday homes for wealthy *sanjuaneros*.

Environmental movements

Though the Puerto Rican and US governments operate agencies on the island dedicated to conservation, much of the impetus for change in the past has come from grassroots movements. On the government side the **US Fish and Wildlife Service** (®www.fws.gov) is especially active, and in 1968, in tandem with the DRNA (Department of Natural and Environmental Resources), and other local agencies, it launched the **Puerto Rican Parrot Recovery Plan**. Threatened with almost certain extinction at the time, the parrot population has since expanded, and though numbers remain low the program is the island's most successful so far: the World Conservation Union (®www.iucn .org) considers 26 animal species (including eleven species of coquí) in Puerto Rico endangered (fourteen critically), and at least six bird species have become **extinct** since 1500. The Puerto Rico Breeding Bird Survey was established in 1997 to help monitor the status of bird populations, while the Sociedad Ornitológica Puertorriqueña (®www.avesdepuertorico.org) also supports bird conservation. Meanwhile, in 1970 the government created the **Conservation Trust of Puerto Rico** (®www.fideicomiso.org) as a private, non-profit organization, to protect the island's natural resources, primarily through the acquisition and donation of lands of great ecological or historic value. It now manages 18,000 acres, including Las Cabezas de San Juan and the Cañón de San Cristóbal.

Novelist turned environmental activist **Enrique Laguerre** was the first Puerto Rican public figure to link nationalism and a commitment to ecological conservation, arguing that Puerto Rico's intense pursuit of socioeconomic development had led to unfettered urban sprawl and destructive consumerism. **Dr Neftalí García**, often regarded as the founder of the environmental movement in Puerto Rico, has taken this thesis further since the 1960s, making a connection between the island's subsidiary status within the US and the abuse of its environment. Chemist by training, García works with the **Misión Industrial de Puerto Rico** (☎787/765-4303), a church-sponsored environmental group founded in 1969 and based in San Juan. The group has fought for the creation of recycling facilities on the island (recycling schemes are slowly being implemented across Puerto Rico), and against unwanted housing developments, proposals to build seventeen mega-landfills, and the spread of chain stores and mega-malls. Founded in 1960, the **Sociedad de Historia Natural** (Natural History Society, ®www.naturalhistorypr.org) took a different approach, lobbying to influence government policy on such issues as the conservation of the Cañón de San Cristóbal, the mangroves at Jobos Bay, and the protection of the Isla de Mona.

In **Vieques** and **Culebra**, ecological awareness grew out of the struggle to rid both islands of the US military from the 1970s onwards, with the latter in particular home to a passionate band of activists fighting for various causes: the continued clean-up of toxic military waste, conservation of coastal reefs and endangered turtles, unlimited beach access, and the prevention of unbridled condo development. Another watershed was reached in the 1980s, when the **Casa Pueblo** movement (see p.345) mounted its campaign against strip mining, ultimately successful in 1995 and spawning an internationally respected conservation group. Founded in 1987, the **Fundación Puertorriqueña de Conservación** (®www.fundacionpr.org) is another non-profit organization working for conservation on the island, and in recent years **Rincón** (p.234) has become one of the most ecologically active towns, led in part by the Surfrider Foundation (®www.surfrider.org).

Books

espite its glittering literary history you'll find translations of many of the most famous Puerto Rican books in short supply – New York-based authors are the easiest to get hold of. In contrast, there are plenty of books on the history, music, and cuisine of Puerto Rico, though outside of North America you'll rarely find these in bookstores; stores order online or visit shops like Borders in San Juan.

Fiction also autobiography and poem

Julia de Burgos *Song of the Simple Truth: The Complete Poems of Julia De Burgos* (Curbstone Press). The poems of arguably Puerto Rico's greatest poet are brought together in this bilingual edition for the first time, including her powerful eulogy to the island, *Río Grande de Loíza* – the translation retains much of the original magic.

Rosario Ferré *The House on the Lagoon* (Plume). Beautifully crafted historical saga in the mold of Gabriel García Márquez, following the fortunes of the wealthy Mendizabal family and their house on the shores of Condado lagoon. Sprinkled with references to Ponce, San Juan, actual events, and *criollo* culture, this makes for ideal holiday reading.

Manuel Zeno Gandia *The Pond* (Markus Wiener). Gandia's 1890s classic gets a decent airing in this 1999 translation, though be prepared: his "pond" is a dark, grim world of doomed love, incest, rape, starving kids, and soul-destroying poverty. Gandia's descriptions of the lush rural landscapes of nineteenth-century Puerto Rico are just as vivid, however, and the story has plenty of twists and turns before the inevitable denouement.

Piri Thomas *Down These Mean Streets* (Vintage). Published in 1967, this is a raw evocation of life in Spanish Harlem and the racist suburbs of Long Island for a Puerto Rican migrant in the 1940s and 1950s. Thomas spits out his autobiographical prose, a snappy and sometimes bitter invective against the prejudice of the time.

Luis Rafael Sánchez *Macho Camacho's Beat* (Dalkey Archive Press). This comic novel follows the lives of several *sanjuaneros* in a poetic, sometimes whimsical second-person style, littered with advertising slogans, jokes, and pop culture references. The story explores the effects of Americanization on the island, a powerful theme that has lost none of its relevance.

Esmeralda Santiago *When I Was Puerto Rican* (Da Capo Press). Santiago's simple but moving prose tells the story of her early years in rural Puerto Rico, the struggles of her parents, and her eventual migration to New York – she paints an unforgettable portrait of the island, and beautifully describes the contrast with the US culture she encounters. Part of an absorbing trilogy that includes *Almost a Woman* and *The Turkish Lover*.

Roberto Santiago (editor) *Boricuas: Influential Puerto Rican Writings – An Anthology* (One World). Collection of essays, poems, and short stories from a wide range of Puerto Rican authors, many of whom are hard to find in translation elsewhere, notably José de Diego and René Marqués.

Pedro Juan Soto *Usmaíl* (Sombrero Publishing Company). The author of *Spiks* wrote this classic about the US Navy occupation of Vieques in 1959, when there seemed little hope of anything changing. Following the life of *Usmaíl*, a *viequense* boy abandoned by his parents, it vividly depicts island life, with a palpably pro-independence bias.

Luisita López Torregrosa *The Noise of Infinite Longing: A Memoir of a Family – and an Island* (Rayo). Another autobiographical work, about growing

up in Puerto Rico in the 1950s. Each chapter begins in 1994, at the funeral of the author's mother – the resulting reminiscences create a complex portrait of Puerto Rican rural life, cultural roots, and the pain of exile.

Hunter S. Thompson *The Rum Diary* (Bloomsbury). Written in 1959 before Thompson had perfected his crazy, hallucinatory style, and not published until 1998, this story centers on a journalist who moves from New York to work on a small newspaper in San Juan in the late 1950s: a world of drunken, sex-starved US expats, laced with hefty doses of jealousy, treachery, and violence.

History and politics

Eliza Dooley *Old San Juan* (Puerto Rico Almanacs). This little gem, first published in 1955, is packed with all sorts of engaging facts and stories about Puerto Rico's oldest settlement. You can pick it up in El Morro and some San Juan bookshops. Dooley also wrote the *Puerto Rican Cook Book* (1950); the one-time resident of the island later disappeared and is "presumed deceased."

Ronald Fernández *The Disen- chanted Island* (Praeger). Crisp modern history of Puerto Rico from a Nationalist perspective, focusing on the island's struggle for independence and its relationship with the US since 1898. Fernández also wrote *Los Macheteros*, an eye-opening account of the home-grown terrorist organization.

Luis A. Figueroa *Sugar, Slavery, and Freedom in Nineteenth-Century Puerto Rico* (University of North Carolina Press). Academic but absorbing account of the black contribution to the history of Puerto Rico. The book traces the progress of freed slaves after abolition in 1873.

Robert H. Fuson *Juan Ponce de León and the Spanish Discovery of Puerto Rico and Florida* (McDonald and Woodward). Other than easy-to-read books for kids, little has been written on conquistador Ponce de León, but this is a great read for history buffs, providing a balanced portrait of Puerto Rico's first governor.

Elizabeth Langhorne *Vieques, History of a Small Island* (Vieques Conservation & Historical Trust). This slim locally produced book is the only real history of Vieques, though it concludes in the mid-1980s, just before things got inter- esting. Can usually be purchased in Esperanza for $1–2.

A.W. Maldonado *Luis Muñoz Marín, Puerto Rico's Democratic Revolution* (Universidad de Puerto Rico). This relatively new biography of Luis Muñoz Marín is also a fasci- nating political history of the island, beginning with Luis Muñoz Rivera and ending with Marín's death in 1980.

Fernando Picó *History of Puerto Rico* (Markus Wiener). The standard history of the island, written by one of Puerto Rico's pre-eminent scholars. The English translation is a bit dry in places, though to be fair this is aimed primarily at an academic audience – Picó concentrates on themes and tendencies, rather than dates and personalities.

G.J.A. O'Toole *The Spanish War: An American Epic 1898* (W W Norton & Co). This detailed, colorful tome remains the standard work on the war that proved so fateful for Puerto Rico. O'Toole covers the Puerto Rican campaign in detail, and it's his treatment of events in the US and Cuba that provide a fascinating context.

Irving Rouse *The Taínos: Rise and Decline of the People Who Greeted Columbus* (Yale University Press). Using Spanish accounts, archeological evidence, linguistic, and biological clues, the author has pieced together a remarkable history of the Taínos, beginning with their initial colonization of the Antilles five thousand years ago.

Olga Jiménez de Waggenheim *Puerto Rico* (Markus Wiener). This self-styled interpretive history charts the island's progress from Pre-Columbian times to 1900, with a slightly fresher approach than that of Picó. The author has also written an excellent book on the *Grito de Lares* (same publisher).

Hildreth N. Waltzer *Eugenio María de Hostos: A New Interpretation* (Centro Pro Hostos de Nueva York). This rare overview of Hostos and his work makes fascinating reading – an energetic and peripatetic man, but also frail and fallible, the book reveals a mass of contradictions between his personal and public life.

Music

Patricia J. Duncan *Ricky Martin: La Vida Loca* (Grand Central Publishing). Puerto Rican law requires that every guide to the island includes at least one book on the Latin pop sensation – this is the fans' favorite, tracing Martin's career from eight-year-old child actor to pop sainthood. Serious fanatics only.

Juan Flores *From Bomba to Hip-Hop* (Columbia University Press). Follows the development of Puerto Rican music in the US since World War II, covering *bomba* to Latin *boogaloo* and hip-hop. The chapter entitled "Lite Colonial" is a blunt discussion about the island's status.

Josephine Powell *Tito Puente: When the Drums Are Dreaming* (AuthorHouse). This revealing biography of one of the greatest Latin musicians was written by Puente's former dance partner, and is littered with evocative accounts of clubs, concerts, and jam sessions, as well as crucial details about Puente's early life in Spanish Harlem.

César Miguel Rondón *The Book of Salsa: A Chronicle of Urban Music from the Caribbean to New York City* (University of North Carolina Press). Books on salsa are surprisingly thin on the ground, but this is one of the best, thanks to a sparkling translation of Rondón's original Spanish volume.

Marc Shapiro *Passion and Pain: The Life of Héctor Lavoe* (St. Martin's Griffin). Fans of *El Cantante* should enjoy this book, though it's not a typical biography, more a series of intriguing anecdotes and stories about the legendary salsa singer. Some might find the book concentrates too much on Héctor's drug problems and not enough on his struggles with Fania Records.

Food and drink

Charles Coulombe *Rum: The Epic Story of the Drink That Conquered the World* (Citadel). Serious connoisseurs of Puerto Rico's national drink should grab a copy of this comprehensive history, tracing the development of the "kill devil" of Barbados to the rum empire of Bacardi.

Yvonne Ortiz *A Taste of Puerto Rico: Traditional and New Dishes from the Puerto Rican Community* (Plume). This sophisticated take on Puerto Rican cuisine was written by a French-trained former chef, and includes personal recipes as well as traditional dishes. Purists will prefer Valldejuli (below), but this is a solid choice for those looking for a modern, well-presented Puerto Rican cookbook.

Carmen Aboy Valldejuli *Puerto Rican Cookery* (Pelican). This is the acknowledged bible of Puerto Rican cooking, translated from the original Spanish (*Cocina Criolla*) volume, which has remained a bestseller since the 1960s. Written by the matriarch of a wealthy Puerto Rican family (with a chapter on rums from her husband), the instructions for hundreds of dishes are simple and easy-to-follow, including all the classics.

Miscellaneous

David Maraniss *Clemente: The Passion and Grace of Baseball's Last Hero* (Simon & Schuster). Baseball fans should check out this enjoyable biography of Puerto Rico's greatest player, covering Clemente's impoverished early life, his sporting success, and experiences of racism over his long career.

Herbert Raffaele *A Guide to the Birds of Puerto Rico and the Virgin Islands* (Princeton University Press). Comprehensive guide describing and illustrating all bird species on the island – serious bird-watchers consistently praise this as the best field guide, with detailed color plates included along with useful background on the ecology of the region.

Language

Language

Spanish

nglish and Spanish are the official languages in Puerto Rico, but the vast majority of Puerto Ricans only speak **Spanish** fluently. In the major tourist areas, particularly San Juan, most of the people you're likely to deal with will speak or understand English, but learning a few phrases in Spanish will prove invaluable for traveling around the island, especially if you plan to use taxis or *públicos*. Puerto Ricans learn modern Spanish in school, based on Castilian (*castellano*), but the language you'll hear on the streets is likely to be quite different. **Puerto Rican Spanish** (*español puertorriqueño*) evolved from the Spanish spoken by immigrants from Andalucía and the Canary Islands, but incorporates Taíno words, pronunciation habits from African dialects, and even English words or phrases in a blend known as "Spanglish."

Pronunciation

Though the rules of **pronunciation** for all forms of Spanish are straightforward and basically the same, there are some noticeable differences between Puerto Rican and Castilian Spanish. For example, the word endings -ado, -ido, or -edo are frequently replaced with -ao, -ío, and -eo respectively. Pronouncing "r" as "l" is also a trait of Puerto Rican Spanish that has its origin in southern Spain, and like the rest of Latin America, Puerto Ricans follow the Andalucían convention (known as *seseo*) of pronouncing "c" before e and i as an "s" instead of the lisped "th" common in Castilian Spanish (*cerca* is "sairca" instead of "thairka.") Finally, there is a tendency to drop the s and d from the end of words, so you'll often hear *muchas gracias* (thank you) spoken *mucha gracia*. Normally you stress any vowel with an **accent**, otherwise all words ending in a vowel, n, or s are stressed on the second to last syllable, while all words ending in other consonants (usually d, l, r, and z) are stressed on the last syllable. All vowels and most consonants tend to follow the same rules as their English counterparts, and combinations have predictable results.

a as in "father."

e as in "get."

i as in "police."

o as in "hot."

u as in "rule."

c soft as in "celery" before e and i; hard otherwise, as in "catch."

g like the ch in "loch" before e or i; hard otherwise, as in "go."

h is always silent.

j also like the ch in "loch"

ll as in the y in "yes."

n as in English, unless it has a tilde (accent) over it, when it become ny: *mañana* sounds like "manyana."

qu pronounced like the English k.

r as in "right," but usually rolled.

rr very strongly rolled.

v sounds like b: *vino* becomes "beano."

z is the same as a soft c: *cerveza* is thus "servesa."

Idiom and slang

Puerto Rican Spanish is rich in idiom and slang, a result of the influence of Taíno, African, and even English words and conventions. Though much of it is unique, some slang is common to other Latin American countries, particularly Cuba and the Dominican Republic.

Basic Puerto Rican vocabulary

Several everyday Puerto Rican words, especially when it comes to eating and drinking, differ completely from their Castilian equivalents. These are not slang words but established conventions, more akin to the differences between North American and British English.

el carro	car	la guagua	bus, *público*, van, or pick-up truck
el chavo	a penny, or money in general	el guineo	banana
la china	sweet orange	el jueye	crab
el colmado	grocery store or neighborhood corner shop	lunchiar	to go to lunch
		los mahones	jeans
los espares	spark plugs	el peso	dollar
las gomas	tires (literally "rubbers")	los tennis	trainers/sneakers
		el zafacón	trash can/waste basket

Popular expressions and slang

The following list is just a sample of the vast range of Puerto Rican expressions and slang words. Most of the idiosyncratic phrases and terms used on the island reflect various aspects of Puerto Rican culture, though the most dynamic source of slang these days is *reggaetón* – it's sometimes hard for even Puerto Ricans living overseas to keep up.

A calzón quitao Literally "without pants on," but sometimes translated as "the naked truth" or "honestly."

Ahí va, a las millas del chaflán! Used to dismiss someone driving too fast or running their mouth, roughly equating to "there they go, at the speed of light."

Algarete "Wayward" in Spanish, used to describe something messy or out of control; also *revolú*.

Ay, Bendito! Roughly "good grief" or "oh dear." Often used to express surprise, pity, or dismay, but can also be sarcastic.

Babilla Street slang for "guts" or courage (and the latest album from rapper Vito C). Other terms frequently used on *reggaetón* tracks are *sacale todo el sudor* ("make her sweat"), *sueltate* ("get loose"), *vamos pa encima* ("lets get to it"), and *pegate* ("get close").

Bochinche Light-hearted gossip or noise at a party or office.

Caco Pejorative term reserved for young and generally tasteless *reggaetón* fans, roughly equating to the British "chav" or American "wanksta" (fake gangster): think Ali G, lots of bling, and bright designer labels.

Chévere Means "excellent."

Chonkear From the English "to chunk," meaning "to throw-up."

Como alma que lleva el Diablo! Comical phrase used to describe someone leaving in a hurry (usually in a mood), literally running off as if their "soul was possessed by the devil."

Coño Equivalent in usage and vulgarity to "shit."

Está brutal "You're brutal," used as an insult or more usually a compliment ("you're the best").

Jangueo Means "hanging around," from *janguear*.

Maceta Literally "flower pot," but used to mean tight-fisted or cheap.

Mano Short for *hermano*, meaning brother.

Ñoña es! No way!

Pana A close friend, good mate; also *broki* (meaning "brother").

Pegao From the Spanish *pegar* meaning "to stick," traditionally used to describe the crunchy rice that sticks to the bottom of the pan (the best bit), but often used in *reggaetón* to mean dancing close together, or just "hip" or "popular."

Se lució el chayote Sarcastic phrase used to dismiss annoying, speeding, or showy drivers. *Chayote* is a gourd-like vegctable, so the phrase equates to something like, "that vegetable was really brilliant."

Tumbao Afro-Caribbean word used to describe female sexiness, or a confident, sexy attitude.

Volando bajito Another term used to describe speeding drivers, roughly "flying low," but also sneaky people that try to do things without anyone else finding out.

¿Y qué? So what?

Spanish language basics

Essentials

Sí, No, Vale	Yes, No, OK	Buen(o)/a, Mal(o)/a	Good, Bad
Por favor, Gracias	Please, Thank you	Gran(de), Pequeño/a or Chico/a	Big, Small
Disculpe	Sorry		
Permiso or Perdón	Excuse me	Caliente, Frío	Hot, Cold
Dónde, Cuando	Where, When	Más, Menos	More, Less
Qué, Cuánto	What, How much	Hoy, Mañana	Today, Tomorrow
Aquí/Acá, Allí	Here, There	Ayer	Yesterday
Esto, Eso	This, That	Los servicios or baños	Toilets
Ahora, Más tarde	Now, Later		
Abierto/a, Cerrado/a	Open, Closed	No entiendo	I don't understand
Con, Sin	With, Without	Quiero, Quisiera	I want, I'd like

Greetings and responses

Hola	Hello	Me llamo...	My name is...
Hasta luego or Adiós	Goodbye	Soy inglés(a)	I am English
Buenos días	Good morning	...Americano(a)	...American
Buenos tardes/noches	Good afternoon/night	...Australiano(a)	...Australian
¿Cómo está? or ¿Qué tal?	How are you?	...Canadiense(a)	...Canadian
		...Irlandés(a)	...Irish
		...Neozelandés(a)	...a New Zealander
Mucho gusto	Pleased to meet you	...Escosés(a)	...Scottish
De nada	You're welcome	...Galés(a)	...Welsh
¿Cómo se llama usted?	What's your name?		

Numbers

Un/uno/una	1		Veinte	20
Dos	2		Veintiuno	21
Tres	3		Treinta	30
Cuatro	4		Cuarenta	40
Cinco	5		Cincuenta	50
Seis	6		Sesenta	60
Siete	7		Setenta	70
Ocho	8		Ochenta	80
Nueve	9		Noventa	90
Diez	10		Cien	100
Once	11		Ciento uno	101
Doce	12		Doscientos	200
Trece	13		Doscientos uno	201
Catorce	14		Quinientos	500
Quince	15		Mil	1000
Dieciséis	16			

Time and days

¿Qué hora es?	What time is it?		Un día	A day
Es la una	It's one o'clock		Una semana	A week
Son las dos	It's two o'clock		Un mes	A month
Dos y media	Two thirty		Lunes	Monday
Mediodía	Noon		Martes	Tuesday
Medianoche	Midnight		Miércoles	Wednesday
La mañana	The morning		Jueves	Thursday
La tarde	The afternoon		Viernes	Friday
La noche	The night		Sábado	Saturday
Está noche	Tonight		Domingo	Sunday

Asking directions and getting around

¿Cómo puedo llegar a…?	How do I get to…?		… el aeropuerto	…the airport
¿Es está la carretera para…?	Is this the right road to?		…la gasolinera más cercana	…the nearest petrol/ gas station
¿Está cerca/lejos?	Is it near/far?		… el banco	…the bank
Voltée a la izquierda/ derecha	Turn left/right		… el cajero automático	…the ATM
Siga derecho	Go straight ahead		… la librería	…the bookstore
Frente	Opposite		… la lavandería	…the laundry
Al lado de	Next to		… el mercado	…the market
Dónde está…?	Where is…?		… la farmacia	…the pharmacy
… el terminal de guaguas/públicos	…the bus station		… los correos	…the post office
… la parada de guaguas	…bus stop		… el supermercado	…the supermarket
			… la oficina de turismo	…the tourist office

¿A qué hora abre/ cierra?	What time does it close/open?	Gasolina	Petrol/gas
De dónde sale la guagua/público para…?	Where does the bus to…leave from?	Llénelo por favor	Fill it up please
		Autopista	Motorway/highway
¿Cuánto cuesta hasta…?	What is the fare to…?	Carretera	Road/route
		Mapa	Map
¿Es está la parada para…?	Is this the stop for…?	Calle	Street
		Avenida	Avenue
¿Dónde puedo coger un taxi?	Where can I get a taxi?	la bicicleta	Bicycle
		la moto	Motorbike
Llévenos a está dirección	Take us to this address		

Road signs

Adelante	Means "Ahead" or "advance:" it's your right of way at the upcoming junction	Luz/luces	Traffic light/s
		Norte	North
		Oeste	West
		Pare	Stop
Alto	Stop	Paseo solo para parados de emergencia	Lane for emergencies only
Autos con cambio exacto	Cars with exact change only		
Bosque Nacional	National forest	Peligroso	Danger
Carretera en construcción	Road under construction	Peso maximo	Maximum weight
		Salida	Exit
Cruce	Crossroads	Sur	South
Derecho	Straight ahead	Termina autopista	End of highway/ motorway
Entrada	Entrance		
Entrada y salida de camiones	Entrance and exit for trucks	Termina Zona 60	End of the 60mph zone
		Transito	Indicates direction of traffic, usually on arrow sign
Esquina	Corner		
Estacionamiento	Parking		
Este	East	Vehiculos lentos o pesados usen carril derecho	Heavy or slow vehicles use right lane
Hacia	To (towards/in the direction of, usually accompanied by road number)		
		Vehiculos Pesados 50	Heavy vehicles 50mph
INT/Interseccion	intersectión	Velocidad maxima 60	Maximum speed 60mph
Lomo	Speed bump		

Accommodation

hotel	Hotel	en el primer piso	…on the first floor
¿Tiene una habitación?	Do you have a room?	Doble/cama matrimonial	Double bed
con dos camas	…with two beds		
con vista al mar	…facing the sea	Individual	Single

Es para una persona/dos personas	It's for one person/two people	¿Puedo ver la habitación?	May I see the room?
para una noche	…for one night	No me gusta	I don't like it
¿Incluye el desayuno?	Does it include breakfast?	Llave	Key
		Piscina	Swimming pool
		Baño	Toilet/bathroom
		Balcón	Balcony

Puerto Rican menu reader

Basics

Aceite	Oil	Huevos	Eggs
Ají	Chili	Huevos fritos	Fried eggs
Ajo	Garlic	Huevos revoltillos	Scrambled eggs
Almuerzo	Lunch	Mesa	Table
Antojito	Snacks	Miel	Honey
Arroz	Rice	Pan	Bread
Azúcar	Sugar	Queso	Cheese
Botella	Bottle	Sal	Salt
Carta	Menu	Salsa de Tomate	Tomato sauce
Cena	Dinner	Servieta	Napkin
Cuchara	Spoon	Sopa	Soup
Cuchillo	Knife	Tenedor	Fork
Cuenta	Check	Tostada	Toast
Desayuno	Breakfast	Vaso	Glass
Ensalada	Salad	Vinagre	Vinegar
Frituras	Fried snacks, fritters		

Cooking styles

A la brasa	Braised	Frito/a	Fried
A la parrilla	Grilled	Guisado/a	Stewed
A la plancha	Grilled	Lonjas	Slices/strips
Ahumado/a	Smoked	Revoltillo	Scrambled
Al horno	Baked	Tostado/a	Toasted
Asado/a	Roast		

Puerto Rican dishes

Alcapurria	Taro fritter stuffed with meat	Arroz y Habichuelas	Rice and beans
Amarillo	Baked plantain	Asopao (Sopon)	Thick soup/broth
Arroz con Gandules	Yellow rice with green pigeon peas	Bacalaíto	Codfish fritter
		Carne guisada puertorriqueña	Puerto Rican beef stew
Arroz con Pollo	Yellow rice with chicken	Chicharrón	Pork crackling
		Chillo entero	Fried whole red snapper

Croquetas de pescados	Fish croquettes	Pastelón de carne	Meat pie
Cuchifrito	Deep-fried pork pieces	Patas de Cerdo	Pigs' trotters
Empanada	Turnover/puff pastry, usually fried	Pionono	Plantain fritter
		Queso Blanco, Queso de Hoja, Queso del País	Puerto Rican white cheese
Empanadilla	Small turnover		
Galleta por Soda	Soda cracker	Relleno	Ground beef and mashed potato fritters
Mofongo	Fried and mashed green plantain, usually stuffed with meat		
		Serenata de Bacalao	Codfish salad
		Sorullo de maíz, Sorullito	Cornmeal fritter shaped like a cigar and stuffed with cheese
Mondongo	Thick beef and vegetable soup		
Pasteles	Shredded root vegetable dumplings/ tamales		
		Tacos	Deep-fried rolls
		Tostones	Fried green plantains
Pastelón de Platano	Plantain pie		

Fish (pescados) and seafood (mariscos)

Albacora	Swordfish	Jueyes	Crabs
Anchoas	Anchovies	Langosta	Lobster
Atún	Tuna	Lobina	Largemouth bass
Bacalao	Cod	Merluza	Hake
Barbudo	Catfish	Mero	Red grouper
Calamares	Squid	Pulpo	Octopus
Camarones	Prawns, shrimp	Robalo	Snook
Carrucho	Conch	Sardinas	Sardines
Chapín	Trunkfish	Salmón	Salmon
Chillo	Red snapper	Trucha	Trout
Chopa	Sunfish	Tucunaré	Peacock bass
Dorado	Mahi-mahi/dolphin-fish		

Meat (carne) and poultry (aves)

Albóndigas	Meatballs	Domplin	Dumpling
Bacon	Bacon	Filete	Beef tenderloin
Bistec	Steak	Gallina	Hen
Buey	Beef	Guinea	Guinea hen
Butifarra	Pork sausage	Gandinza	Pork liver
Cabrito	Baby goat	Jamón	Ham
Carne Vieja	Dry salted beef	Lechón asado	Roast suckling pig
Cerdo	Pork	Pavo	Turkey
Chorizo	Spicy sausage	Pato	Duck
Chuleta	Pork chop	Pechuga	Breast (usually chicken)
Chuletón	T-bone steak		
Churrasco	Skirt steak	Pernil de Cerdo	Pork shoulder
Conejo	Rabbit	Picadillo	Minced beef
Cordero	Lamb	Pinchos	Kebab (skewered meat)

Pollo	Chicken	Solomillo	Sirloin
Ropa vieja	Shredded beef	Ternera	Veal
Salchichón	Salami		

Fruits (frutas)

Aguacate	Avocado	Mamey	Mamey (thick red fruit, mostly eaten in preserves)
Caimito	Starfruit		
Cereza	Cherry		
China	Orange	Melón	Melon
Coco	Coconut	Pana, Panapen	Breadfruit
Fresa	Strawberry	Parcha	Passion fruit
Granada	Pomegranate	Piña	Pineapple
Guanábana	Soursop	Plátano	Plantain
Guayaba	Guava	Quenepa	Mamoncillo or Spanish lime
Guineo	Sweet banana		
Lechosa	Papaya	Tamarindo	Tamarind
Limón	Lemon	Toronja	Grapefruit
Limón Verde	Key lime	Uvas	Grapes
Lima	Lime		

Vegetables (verduras/vegetables)

Apio	Celery	Maíz	Corn
Berenjena	Eggplant/aubergine	Malanga	Starchy, tubular root vegetable
Calabaza	Pumpkin		
Cebolla	Onion	Name	Yam
Chayote	Squash family (vegetable pear/christophine)	Papa	Potato
		Papas fritas	French fries
		Pimiento	Bell pepper
Cilantro	coriander	Repollo	Cabbage
Gandul	Green pigeon pea	Tomate	Tomato
Garbanzo	Chickpea	Yautía	Taro root
Habichuela	Bean	Yuca	Cassava

Sweets (dulces) and desserts (postres)

Arroz con dulce	Rice pudding	Galleta	Biscuit/cookie
Boudin de pasas con coco	Coconut bread pudding	Helado	Ice cream
		Hojaldre	Puff pastry
Dulce de papaya	Candied papaya	Limber	Frozen fruit juice
Dulce de plátano	Ripe yellow plantains cooked in red wine, sugar, and spices	Nisperos de batata	Sweet-potato balls with coconut
		Tembleque	Custard made from coconut milk and sugar
Flan	Custard/crème caramel		

Drinks (bebidas)

Agua	Water	Horchata de ajonjolí	Drink made of ground sesame seeds, water, and sugar
Agua de coco	Coconut juice		
Agua mineral	Mineral water		
...con gas	...sparkling	Jugo	Juice
...sin gas	...still	Leche	Milk
Batidas	Fruit shakes	Leche de coco	Coconut milk
Café	coffee	Maví	Fermented drink made from the bark of the *maví* tree
Café con leche	strong black coffee with steamed milk		
		Piragua	Shaved ice drizzled with syrup
Café negro	black coffee		
Café puya	unsweetened black coffee	Refrescos	Sodas/fizzy drinks
		Ron	Rum
Café tinta	espresso	Té	Tea
Cerveza	Beer	Vino tinto	Red wine
Coquito	Rum eggnog (Christmas drink)	Vino blanco	White wine
		Vino rosado	Rosé wine
Guarapo de caña	Sugar cane juice		

Glossary

Bahía Bay.

Balneario Beach with facilities such as showers and toilets, often translated as "public beach," though all beaches on the island are technically public.

Barrio Neighborhood or city district.

Biblioteca Library.

Bohío Thatched Taíno hut, also applied to simple *jíbaro* dwellings.

Bosque Estatal State forest.

Cañón Canyon.

Capilla Chapel.

Casa House.

Cascada Waterfall.

Cayo Cay, small island.

Cementerio Cemetery.

Embalse Reservoir.

Ermita Chapel.

Estadio Stadium.

Faro Lighthouse.

Finca Farm.

Fuerte Fort.

Iglesia Church.

Malecón Waterfront promenade.

Mirador Viewpoint.

Parque Park.

Playa Beach.

Plazuela Small plaza.

Puerta Gate, door.

Puerto Port.

Punta Headland, point.

Quebrada Stream; small river.

Retablo Altarpiece.

Río River.

Salto Waterfall (from "to jump" or "leap.")

Santos Figurines of popular saints, carved from wood.

Travel store

D: Rough Guide
DIRECTIONS for
short breaks

Available from all good bookstores

Visit us online
www.roughguides.com

Information on over 25,000 destinations around the world

- **Read** Rough Guides' trusted travel info
- **Access** exclusive articles from Rough Guides authors
- **Update** yourself on new books, maps, CDs and other products
- **Enter** our competitions and win travel prizes
- **Share** ideas, journals, photos & travel advice with other users
- **Earn** points every time you contribute to the Rough Guide
  community and get rewards

BROADEN YOUR HORIZONS

Small print and
Index

A Rough Guide to Rough Guides

Published in 1982, the first Rough Guide – to Greece – was a student scheme that became a publishing phenomenon. Mark Ellingham, a recent graduate in English from Bristol University, had been traveling in Greece the previous summer and couldn't find the right guidebook. With a small group of friends he wrote his own guide, combining a highly contemporary, journalistic style with a thoroughly practical approach to travelers' needs.

The immediate success of the book spawned a series that rapidly covered dozens of destinations. And, in addition to impecunious backpackers, Rough Guides soon acquired a much broader and older readership that relished the guides' wit and inquisitiveness as much as their enthusiastic, critical approach and value-for-money ethos.

These days, Rough Guides include recommendations from shoestring to luxury and cover more than 200 destinations around the globe, including almost every country in the Americas and Europe, more than half of Africa and most of Asia and Australasia. Our ever-growing team of authors and photographers is spread all over the world, particularly in Europe, the USA, and Australia.

In the early 1990s, Rough Guides branched out of travel, with the publication of Rough Guides to World Music, Classical Music and the Internet. All three have become benchmark titles in their fields, spearheading the publication of a wide range of books under the Rough Guide name.

Including the travel series, Rough Guides now number more than 350 titles, covering: phrasebooks, waterproof maps, music guides from Opera to Heavy Metal, reference works as diverse as Conspiracy Theories and Shakespeare, and popular culture books from iPods to Poker. Rough Guides also produce a series of more than 120 World Music CDs in partnership with World Music Network.

Visit www.roughguides.com to see our latest publications.

Rough Guide travel images are available for commercial licensing at www.roughguidespictures.com

SMALL PRINT

Rough Guide credits

Text editor: Anna Owens
Layout: Nikhil Agarwal
Cartography: Ed Wright
Picture editor: Emily Taylor
Production: Rebecca Short
Proofreader: Kate Berens
Cover design: Chloë Roberts
Photographer: Tim Draper
Editorial: **London** Ruth Blackmore, Alison
Murchie, Andy Turner, Keith Drew, Edward
Aves, Alice Park, Lucy White, Jo Kirby, James
Smart, Natasha Foges, Róisín Cameron, Emma
Traynor, James Rice, Emma Gibbs, Kathryn
Lane, Christina Valhouli, Monica Woods, Mani
Ramaswamy, Joe Staines, Peter Buckley,
Matthew Milton, Tracy Hopkins, Ruth Tidball;
New York Andrew Rosenberg, Steven Horak,
AnneLise Sorensen, April Isaacs, Ella Steim, Anna
Owens, Amanda Tomlin; **Delhi** Madhavi Singh, Karen D'Souza
Design & Pictures: **London** Scott Stickland,
Dan May, Diana Jarvis, Mark Thomas, Nicole
Newman, Sarah Cummins; **Delhi** Umesh
Aggarwal, Ajay Verma, Jessica Subramanian,
Ankur Guha, Pradeep Thapliyal, Sachin Tanwar,
Anita Singh

Production: Vicky Baldwin
Cartography: **London** Maxine Repath, Katie
Lloyd-Jones; **Delhi** Jai Prakash Mishra, Rajesh
Chhibber, Ashutosh Bharti, Rajesh Mishra,
Animesh Pathak, Jasbir Sandhu, Karobi Gogoi,
Amod Singh, Alakananda Bhattacharya, Swati
Handoo, Deshpal Dabas
Online: **London** George Atwell, Faye Hellon,
Jeanette Angell, Fergus Day, Justine Bright,
Clare Bryson, Aine Fearon, Adrian Low, Ezgi
Celebi, Amber Bloomfield; **Delhi** Amit Verma,
Rahul Kumar, Narender Kumar, Ravi Yadav,
Debojit Borah, Rakesh Kumar, Ganesh Sharma
Marketing & Publicity: **London** Liz Statham,
Niki Hanmer, Louise Maher, Jess Carter, Vanessa
Godden, Vivienne Watton, Anna Paynton, Rachel
Sprackett, Libby Jellie; **New York** Geoff Colquitt,
Nancy Lambert; **Katy Ball**; **Delhi** Ragini Govind
Manager India: Punita Singh
Reference Director: Andrew Lockett
Operations Manager: Helen Phillips
PA to Publishing Director: Nicola Henderson
Publishing Director: Martin Dunford
Commercial Manager: Gino Magnotta
Managing Director: John Duhigg

Publishing information

This first edition published November 2008 by
Rough Guides Ltd,
80 Strand, London WC2R 0RL
345 Hudson St, 4th Floor,
New York, NY 10014, USA
14 Local Shopping Centre, Panchsheel Park,
New Delhi 110017, India
Distributed by the Penguin Group
Penguin Books Ltd,
80 Strand, London WC2R 0RL
Penguin Group (USA)
375 Hudson Street, NY 10014, USA
Penguin Group (Australia)
250 Camberwell Road, Camberwell,
Victoria 3124, Australia
Penguin Group (Canada)
195 Harry Walker Parkway N, Newmarket, ON,
L3Y 7B3 Canada
Penguin Group (NZ)
67 Apollo Drive, Mairangi Bay, Auckland 1310,
New Zealand

Cover concept by Peter Dyer.

Typeset in Bembo and Helvetica to an original
design by Henry Iles.

Printed and bound in China

© Stephen Keeling 2008

416pp includes index

A catalogue record for this book is available from
the British Library

ISBN: 978-1-85828-354-8

1 3 5 7 9 8 6 4 2

Help us update

We've gone to a lot of effort to ensure that the
first edition of **The Rough Guide to Puerto Rico**
is accurate and up to date. However, things
change – places get "discovered", opening hours
are notoriously fickle, restaurants and rooms raise
prices or lower standards. If you feel we've got it
wrong or left something out, we'd like to know,
and if you can remember the address, the price,
the hours, the phone number, so much the better.

Please send your comments with the
subject line "**Rough Guide Puerto Rico Update**"
to ® mail@roughguides.com. We'll credit all
contributions and send a copy of the next edition
(or any other Rough Guide if you prefer) for the
very best emails.

Have your questions answered and tell others
about your trip at
® community.roughguides.com

Acknowledgments

Stephen Keeling: Thanks to Madeline Santiago Figueroa at the Puerto Rico Tourism Company; Ahmed Naveiras at Rums of Puerto Rico; the gracious Edmundo Fernández; Jessica Almy Pagán and Miguel Ortiz at La Caleta; Fermín Candelario in Ponce; Clara Morciglio for all her help in Yauco; Matthew Kavanaugh; Jen Gold and Lauren Hatfield for their generosity and advice in Vieques; the indomitable Jim Petersen and Elias Robinson in Culebra; Mary Lee and daughter Suzie in Guánica; Carlos Valentine and Nicolas Mejias at the Ermita del Espinar; Gary and Jeanette Pollard; Susanne Jorgensen at the Finca del Seto; and all the kind Puerto Ricans that helped make researching this book a real pleasure. Lastly, thanks to Anna Owens and Amy Hegarty in the New York office, and to Tiffany Wu, whose support, as always, made this book possible.

The editor thanks Stephen for his wonderful writing, research, and dedication to the project. Huge thanks also go to Emily Taylor, Ed Wright, Nikhil Agarwal, Scott Stickland, Steve Horak, Andrew Rosenberg, Róisín Cameron, April Isaacs, and Courtney Miller.

Photo credits

All photos are © Rough Guides except the following:

Cover
Front picture: El Morro fortress, Old San Juan © Mark Lewis/Alamy
Back picture: Street parade at the Ponce festival © Tim Draper/Rough Guides
Inside back picture: Le Lo Lai performance in Old San Juan © Tim Draper/Rough Guides

Introduction
Puerto Rican Coqui frog © Florida Images/Alamy
Vendor on beach © Greg Roden

Things not to miss
02 Paso Fino horses on pasture © Photolibrary
09 Scuba Diving © Courtesy of Puerto Rican Tourist Board
14 Bioluminescent Bay © Frank Llosa

Festivals of Puerto Rico color section
Danza Week © Roberto Adrian/istock
Puerto Rican man during the Festival of Santiago Apostol © Tony Arruza/Corbis

Puerto Rican food and drink color section
Worker with ripe coffee cherries © Benjamin Lowy/Corbis

Black and whites
p.291 Caja de Muertos © Frank Arzola

SMALL PRINT

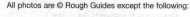
Selected images from our guidebooks are available for licensing from:

ROUGHGUIDESPICTURES.COM

Index

Map entries are in color.

INDEX

I

413

Map symbols

maps are listed in the full index using colored text

Highway	Museum
Major paved road	Cave
Minor paved road	Hacienda/manor house
Pedestrianized road	Lighthouse
Ruta Panorámica	Viewpoint
Unpaved road	Ruins
Steps	Tower
Footpath/trail	Observatory
Minor trail	Church (regional map)
San Juan Tren Urbano & station	Golf course
Ferry route	Gardens
Waterway	Gateway
Wall	Fuel station
Chapter boundary	Information office
Place of interest	Post office
International airport	Internet access
Domestic airport/airfield	Hospital
Mountain range	Transport stop
Peak	Parking
Waterfall	Building
Spring	Church (town map)
Recreation area	Market
Campsite	Stadium
Ranger station	Cemetery
Tree	Park/National park
Bunker	Beach